ALSO BY SAMUEL HAWLEY

NONFICTION

I Just Ran:
Percy Williams, World's Fastest Human

Speed Duel:
The Inside Story of the Land Speed Record in the Sixties

America's Man in Korea:
The Private Letters of George C. Foulk, 1884-1887

Inside the Hermit Kingdom:
The 1884 Korea Travel Diary of George Clayton Foulk

FICTION

Bad Elephant Far Stream

Homeowner With a Gun

THE

IMJIN WAR

JAPAN'S SIXTEENTH-CENTURY INVASION OF KOREA AND ATTEMPT TO CONQUER CHINA

SAMUEL HAWLEY

CONQUISTADOR

THE IMJIN WAR: JAPAN'S SIXTEENTH-CENTURY INVASION
OF KOREA AND ATTEMPT TO CONQUER CHINA
Second Edition

Copyright © 2014 by Samuel Hawley
Published by Conquistador Press, 2014

Library of Congress Cataloging-in-Publication Data

Hawley, Samuel Jay, 1960-
The Imjin War : Japan's sixteenth-century invasion of Korea and attempt to
conquer China / Samuel Hawley.
p. cm.
Previously co-published by the Royal Asiatic Society, Korea Branch, Seoul and the
Institute of East Asian Studies, University of California, Berkeley, 2005; reprinted
by the RASKB, Seoul, 2008.
Includes bibliographical references and index.
ISBN 978-0-9920786-2-1
1. Korea—History—Japanese Invasions, 1592-1598. 2. Japan—History, Military—
To 1868. 3. Korea—Foreign relations—Japan. 4. Japan—Foreign relations—Korea.
5. China—Foreign relations—Korea. 6. Korea—Foreign relations—China.
7. Japan—Foreign relations—China. 8. China—Foreign relations—Japan.
I. Title
DS913.4 .H38 2014
951.9/02

Conquistador Press
www.conquistadorpress.com

Visit the author at:
www.samuelhawley.com

Warfare is the greatest affair of the state,
the Tao of survival or extinction.

T'ai Kung's Six Secret Teachings
4th century B.C.

CONTENTS

MAPS AND TABLES

PREFACE TO THE NEW EDITION

IT WILL SOON BE TEN YEARS since *The Imjin War* was co-published in October 2005 by the Royal Asiatic Society in Korea and the Institute of East Asian Studies at UC Berkeley. My foremost thanks then, and now, is to Kim Kyong-mee for the many hours she spent with me, twice a week over the course of two years, translating the various Korean-language sources that were used in the preparation of this book. I would also like to renew my thanks to Kim Young-duk and Bae Sue-ja, respectively the president and general manager of the RASKB at the time *The Imjin War* was originally published; to IEAS managing editor Joanne Sandstrom for her copyediting skills; and to the So-ae Memorial Foundation and Poong-san Corporation, without whose support this book would never have been published in the first place.

The Imjin War book received virtually no marketing when it was first released and distribution was confined to just a few sources. Normally such lack of publicity and availability would doom a book to wither and die, unknown and unsold. But for some reason *The Imjin War* didn't wither. Readers found it, word got around and the initial print run of 2,000 copies eventually sold out. In 2008 a second printing was made.

As an older and wiser author today, more aware of the harsh realities of the book business, I look back on this modest success with a measure of wonder. When I set out to find a publisher in 2003, after four years of solitary research and writing, I contacted a number of literary agents and publishing houses, pitching it as a popular history for general readers, and I sat back expecting to receive at least a few favorable replies. Fifty-seven rejection letters followed, each assuring me that a book on a presumably obscure sixteenth-century war in Korea wouldn't sell. To all the people who bought *The Imjin War* anyway when it finally came out, despite this conventional wisdom that they weren't supposed to; to everyone who devoted the hours required to read through its many pages; to everyone who has said or written kind things about it over the years and encouraged me to write more—to all these people I would like to say: *Thank you.*

This new edition of *The Imjin War* is largely identical to the original version. The main difference is that I have eliminated the center section of pictures, replaced the Acknowledgements with this new Preface and designed a new cover. Everything else, including the text, is the same. I remain very proud of this book. It was a labor of love that required more time and drive and energy than I could ever muster again, and so I have decided to let it stand as I originally wrote it.

It has grieved me over the years to receive emails from people saying that they wanted a copy of *The Imjin War* but couldn't find one to buy, or that the only copy they could locate was being sold for an outrageously high price. It is my hope that this more reasonably priced paperback edition, coupled with easier availability and more widespread distribution, will overcome these problems.

Samuel Hawley
Kingston, Ontario, Canada
September 2014

INTRODUCTION

ON DECEMBER 8, 1941—December 7 on the American side of the international date line—army and navy forces of Japan launched a surprise attack on Western colonial possessions in Asia and the Pacific, initiating what would come to be known in Tokyo as the Great Pacific War. It was the final, ultimately disastrous step in an expansionist phase in Japanese history that had already led that nation into three other wars of increasing ambition: the Sino-Japanese War of 1894–95, the Russo-Japanese War of 1904–05, and the campaign to conquer China begun in 1931. By the summer of 1942, eight months into the Great Pacific War, the empire of Japan extended from Manchuria to Burma on the Asian mainland and south across the Pacific as far as the islands of Java and New Guinea. Then, in the face of overwhelming American power, it began to fall apart.

Today, this fifty-year period of international aggression tends to be regarded as an aberration in Japan's long history, the only time most people are aware of when the Land of the Rising Sun dispatched armies overseas to conquer foreign lands. This, however, is not the case. The Sino-Japanese War, the Russo-Japanese War, the invasion of China, the Great Pacific War—they all had an important antecedent that is little known in the West. In May of 1592, some 350 years before the attack on Pearl Harbor, the state of Japan, recently unified under a dictator named Toyotomi Hideyoshi, sent a huge army across the strait from Kyushu to Pusan on Korea's southern tip. Its objective was first to invade that neighboring kingdom, then to press on to Beijing and conquer China. Once China was securely in Hideyoshi's grasp, he planned to extend his hegemony even farther: south into Vietnam, Cambodia,

Thailand, and Burma; offshore to Sumatra, Java, Taiwan, the Ryukyu Islands, and the Spanish colony of the Philippines; west to India—perhaps even all the way to that distant place where the strange bearded men came from who had first appeared in Japan fifty years before, the southwestern barbarians who claimed to be from a country called *Porutu-gal.*

Hideyoshi, in short, was intent on conquering the whole world as it was then known to him, an ambitious goal for what was in fact the first centrally directed war of overseas aggression in the history of Japan.

The resulting conflict immersed Japan, Korea, and China, plus token forces from as far away as Thailand, in nearly seven years of bloody war. It came to be known to the Japanese under a variety of appellations, from the prosaic "Korean War" to the more poetic "Pottery War" and "War of Celadon and Metal Type," references to the spoils that Hideyoshi's armies took back with them to Japan. The Chinese would refer to it simply as "the Korean Campaign," a designation lumping it together with two other military campaigns that occupied the armies of China in the 1590s, despite the fact that it dwarfed the other two in size. To the Koreans, who suffered by far the greatest devastation and loss, it would come to be known as *Imjin waeran*, "the bandit invasion of the year *imjin* (water dragon)," commonly rendered in English as "the Imjin War."

Since this book relies most heavily on Korean sources and a Korean perspective, this is the title that I have chosen: *Imjin waeran*, "the Imjin War."

The scale of the Imjin War was immense. It far exceeded any conflict that had occurred in Renaissance Europe up to that time. The army of invasion that Toyotomi Hideyoshi sent to Korea in 1592 totaled 158,800 men, three times the size of the largest army that any European nation in the late sixteenth century could muster and put into the field. Add to this the nearly 100,000 Ming Chinese troops ultimately dispatched by Beijing to Korea to counter the approaching threat, plus the many tens of thousands of Korean soldiers and guerrilla fighters who participated in the war, and the total number of combatants rises to something in excess of 300,000 men. The most contemporary European comparison, the "invincible armada" that was sent by Philip II of Spain to invade England in 1588, by contrast involved 30,500 Spaniards against an Elizabethan military that in its entirety amounted to not much more than 20,000 men.

The Imjin War did not result in a redrawing of the boundaries of the nations involved. When the fighting finally ended in December of 1598, China, Japan, and Korea were each left with exactly the same territory they had started with seven years before. The impact of the war was nevertheless profound. For Japan it marked the end of its military age, or at least the beginning of the end, an international crescendo of conflict capping more than a century of civil war. After the death in 1598 of the war's architect, Toyotomi Hideyoshi, and the subsequent rise to power of Tokugawa Ieyasu, Japan would enter the longest unbroken period of peace in its history, the Tokugawa era of 1601 to 1867. In China, the strain of responding to Japanese aggression in Korea would greatly weaken the already declining Ming dynasty, undermining its ability to resist the Manchu forces that would ultimately overwhelm it to establish a dynasty of their own, the Qing. And in Korea, while no corresponding dynastic change took place, the war weakened the country so severely that it would not fully recover for centuries to come.

What follows is the most comprehensive account in the English language of this important conflict, the Imjin War, still so little known in the West. It lays a framework for understanding Japan, Korea, and China as they existed four hundred years ago. It recounts the five years of diplomatic maneuvering and misunderstanding that preceded the outbreak of hostilities. It gives a detailed account of the entire six-and-a-half-year conflict, from the first day of the Japanese invasion in 1592 to the final bloody clashes of 1598. It introduces the pageant of characters involved: the warlords and kings, the officials and envoys, the commanders and soldiers, and the common people who suffered and died. And it conveys, I hope, something of the drama, the tragedy, and the emotion of this fascinating episode in the history of the East, for it is nothing less than an epic tale and deserves to be told as such.

A NOTE ON DATES

THE LUNAR CALENDAR was used in China, Korea, and Japan until the late nineteenth century, after which it came gradually to be replaced by the Gregorian calendar favored in the West. In some older English-language histories of the Far East, no attempt is made to distinguish between these two systems; the thirteenth day of the fourth month, for example, is written simply as April 13. The Western solar and Eastern lunar calendars, however, come nowhere near converging in this neat fashion, rendering such conversions highly inaccurate. The day the Imjin War began, for example, the thirteenth day of the fourth month in 1592, was in fact May 23. To avoid confusion, all Korean and Chinese lunar dates in the main text of this volume have been converted to the Western calendar using Keith Hazelton's *Synchronic Chinese-Western Daily Calendar, 1341–1661 A.D.* (Minneapolis: University of Minnesota Press, 1985); Japanese lunar dates, which often vary by a day, were converted using Paul Y. Tsuchihashi's *Japanese Chronological Tables from 601 to 1872* (Tokyo: Sophia University, 1952). In notes referring to primary sources dated using the lunar calendar, the original lunar date is given in day/month/year format, followed in parentheses by the corresponding solar date.

The situation is more complex in the matter of naming years. In Korea alone three separate year designations were used during the Choson dynasty: the reign year of the emperor of China, the reign year of the Korean king, and the year designation according to the combined zodiacal- and element-based cycle of sixty. The year 1592, for example, was known alternately as Wanli 20, Sonjo 25, and the year Imjin. When one adds to this the different pronunciations employed by the Chinese and the altogether different emperor reign year designations used in Japan, the picture becomes even more confusing. For the sake of clarity, all years in the text of this volume will be given in Western terms and Eastern year designations will be confined to the notes.

PART 1

THE
THREE KINGDOMS

Enraptured by the evening sunset
the boys tending cattle
on the grassy bank of the clear river
trill on their flutes
while the dragon dozing beneath the water
seems to wake and rise.[1]

Chong Chol (1536–94)
Songsan pyolgok (Song of Star Mountain), c. 1578

CHAPTER 1

Japan: From Civil War to World Power

ON SEPTEMBER 23, 1543, a large Chinese junk appeared off the coast of Tanegashima, a small, finger-shaped island forty kilometers to the south of Kyushu. It carried a crew of more than a hundred men, apparently Chinese, plus a few extremely odd-looking creatures with bearded faces and long noses, the likes of which the people of Tanegashima had never seen before.

The leader of this strange assembly was a Chinese man by the name of Wu-feng—in fact the notorious pirate Wang Chih traveling under one of his many aliases. To the Tanegashima islanders this Wu-feng seemed a scholar, for although they could not understand his language, nor he theirs, he showed them that he could write Chinese characters and indicated that they could thus communicate in writing. None of the islanders clustered along the beach could understand these complicated ideographs, but they knew of a man on the island who could, a village chief on the west coast by the name of Oribe. He was therefore summoned to communicate with this scholar-sailor Wu-feng, a.k.a. Chinese pirate Wang Chih.

Oribe conversed with Wu-feng by tracing characters in the sand with his cane. He began by asking, "Those men on your ship—where are they from? Why do they look so different from us?"

"They are traders from among the south-western barbarians," wrote Wu-feng in reply, meaning that they were Portuguese. "These traders visit the same places in the hope of exchanging what they have for what they do not have. There is nothing suspicious about them."

Oribe then wrote that the island's capital, Akaogi, was a better place to go in search of trade. It was the seat of Lord Tokitaka, master of Tanegashima, and the largest town on the island. This was arranged, and the foreign ship bearing the Portuguese strangers arrived at Akaogi on the twenty-seventh of the month.

During their stay at Akaogi, the Portuguese introduced Lord Toki-taka and his retinue to a curious and wonderful device. It was "two or three feet long," went one contemporary description, "straight on the outside with a passage inside, and made of a heavy substance. The inner passage runs through it although it is closed at the end. At its side there is an aperture which is the passageway for fire. Its shape defies comparison with anything I know. To use it, fill it with powder and small lead pellets. Set up a small white target on a bank. Grip the object in your hand, compose your body, and closing one eye, apply fire to the aperture. Then the pellet hits the target squarely. The explosion is like lightning and the report like thunder. Bystanders must cover their ears."

It was of course a gun, in particular an arquebus, a lightweight form of matchlock musket that could be fired from the shoulder without need of the supporting rest that heavier muskets required. It consisted of an iron barrel set in a wooden stock, with an S-shaped brass serpentine affixed to the right side. Several feet of saltpeter-soaked wick, or "match," were needed for the weapon to remain useable for any appre-ciable length of time, for example throughout the course of a battle. The arquebusier would thread one end of this match through the serpentine, light it, and keep it constantly smoldering; the rest he would wind around the stock of the weapon, or around his arm. When he wished to fire he raised the weapon to his shoulder, slid back the brass cover to expose the gunpowder, then took aim and pulled the trigger, sending the serpentine down into the firing pan like a bird pecking the ground. After a moment's pause, the match glowing at the end of the serpentine would ignite the gunpowder, sending a lead bullet exploding out the end of the barrel with a tremendous kick and a cloud of black smoke.

Lord Tokiaki was immensely impressed by this simple but highly effective instrument. Still communicating through the Chinese pirate

Wu-feng by means of written characters, he asked the Portuguese traders to tell him its secret. "The secret," came the reply, "is to put your mind aright and close one eye."

Tokiaki found this somewhat confusing. "The ancient sages have often taught how to set one's mind aright," he said. "If the mind is not set aright, there is no logic for what we say or do. . . . However, will it not impair our vision for objects at a distance if we close an eye? Why should we close an eye?"

To this the foreigner replied, "That is because concentration is important in everything. When one concentrates, a broad vision is not necessary. To close an eye is not to dim one's eyesight but rather to project one's concentration farther."

"That corresponds to what Lao Tzu has said," replied the delighted Tokiaki. " 'Good sight means seeing what is very small.' "

Disregarding the high price the Portuguese were asking for these wonderful weapons, Lord Tokiaki purchased two specimens and devoted his every waking hour to mastering their use. Soon he was able to hit the target almost every time. He also had one of his retainers learn from the barbarians how to prepare the powder mixture that was clearly so essential.

Following the departure of the traders, Lord Tokiaki ordered his craftsmen to make copies of his two prized firearms. What they produced resembled the foreign weapons outwardly, but would not fire, for they did not know how to close the barrel at the weapon's shoulder end. This problem was solved in the following year, 1544, when a second foreign ship arrived at Tanegashima. There was among the crew this time an ironworker whom Lord Tokiaki's craftsmen sought out for advice; one story has it that a blacksmith even offered his daughter in exchange for lessons. In any event the problem of closing the end of the barrel was soon solved, and within little more than a year the Tanegashima craftsmen had produced twenty or more working copies of the original barbarian gun. Lord Tokiaki then set his retainers to work learning how to use them, until they too could to hit the target almost every time.[1]

These lightweight muskets introduced into Japan by Portuguese traders in 1543 were not the first firearms to arrive on those shores. A variety of gunpowder-based weapons had already been imported from China, the birthplace of gunpowder, over the previous two centuries, first bombs and flame-spewing tubes, then cannons, and finally handheld guns. None of these Chinese imports, however, were ever widely used by the Japanese in warfare, for they were too crude and clumsy and ineffective to rival the bow and arrow, sword, and spear. The amazement that Lord Tokiaki and the people of Tanegashima evinced at their first sight of a Portuguese musket was therefore probably more a reflection of the isolation of their small island than of the actual state of knowledge then prevailing in Japan. To the more worldly leaders on the main islands, the musket would have seemed a more familiar weapon, an improvement on existing technology that transformed the handheld gun from an interesting but impractical oddity into an effective killing machine.[2]

Within a few years of its arrival on Lord Tokiaki's remote southern island, the technology to manufacture Portuguese muskets, referred to at first as *tanegashima*, spread to the main island of Kyushu, where a number of gunsmiths who had gained reputations for themselves opened "schools" and began training apprentices. These apprentices then moved elsewhere to open businesses of their own, crafting muskets in the distinctive style of their master—the same design, the same weight, the same caliber. In this way gunsmithing shops and factories spread all across Kyushu and then onto Honshu, where Sakai, near Osaka, and Kunitomo, just south of present-day Tokyo, became major production centers.[3]

By the 1560s muskets were being turned out throughout most of Japan at a rate of at least several thousand per year. These weapons were as good as those being manufactured in Europe at that time and had the important advantage of greater standardization. In Europe there was virtually no standardization in the caliber of firearms; each gun needed its own bullet mold. This meant that if a soldier ran out of bullets in the heat of battle or if his little bag of lead slugs slipped from his belt and was lost, his weapon was rendered useless. He could not borrow bullets from a fellow soldier, for they would not fit his barrel. Nor could he run to a nearby supply wagon and grab a handful. In Japan the existence of gunsmithing schools did much to alleviate this problem.

The different schools produced guns of widely varying caliber,[4] so it was not possible to equip an entire army with one standard weapon. But it *was* possible to equip a smaller corps of men with guns of a standard caliber simply by purchasing weapons from the same factory, and thus from the same school. This increased the utility of the Japanese musket and made the men who wielded them that much more effective.[5]

The first Portuguese muskets arrived in Japan during a time that Japanese familiar with Chinese history called *sengoku*, "the age of warring states," after the period of civil war preceding China's own emergence as a single, unified state some seventeen hundred years before. It was a 130-year period, from the 1460s until 1590, when the entire country was in constant upheaval.

Sengoku was caused fundamentally by a lack of central authority. It was a problem with roots extending back into the twelfth century, when the emperor in Kyoto began to slip from his position of undisputed power. A line of military dictators known as *shogun* arose to fill the resulting power vacuum. At first they governed the country under the ostensible authority of the emperor. By the early thirteenth century, however, the imperial throne had become so powerless that even this pretense was dropped, and the shogun's capital in Kamakura became the real seat of government.

In 1333 the Kamakura shogunate, weakened by its fight against the invading Mongol armies of Kublai Khan, fell to a new line of military dictators known collectively as the Ashikaga shoguns. The Ashikaga, never very strong to begin with, would undergo a slow decline over the next hundred years. This probably explains why the third shogun in the line, Ashikaga Yoshimitsu, resumed Japanese relations with China after a long period of quiescence by sending a tribute mission to the court in Beijing in 1401. The title "King of Japan" that the Ming emperor bestowed upon him lent authority to the Ashikaga's shaky rule, and the substantial income derived from the de facto trade that occurred during tribute missions provided much-needed wealth for maintaining armies, supporting regal lifestyles, and running the country.

But even this was not enough for the Ashikaga shoguns. Their decline was inexorable. By the early sixteenth century they no longer had the military power or financial clout to effectively control the country. And so there arose yet another power vacuum in Japan. But this time there was no one to fill it.

The inevitable result was civil war. With neither the shogun nor the emperor able to guarantee property rights or the rule of law, ambitious men began to take charge. The sixteenth century opened with hundreds of regional lords and small groups all vying for each other's territory and all arming to protect their own. Slowly, through conquest and the formation of alliances, these factions began to coalesce. By the middle of the sixteenth century the entire nation was in the hands of feuding war lords called *daimyo*, each holding his own private domain, none beholden to any central authority.

It was at this time that the musket first appeared in Japan. Prior to this, warfare not just in Japan but in the Western world as well had remained substantially unchanged for nearly two thousand years, each generation going to battle with essentially the same bows and swords and arrows and spears. Indeed, as military historian Gwynne Dyer has observed, "competent professional armies chosen at random from any-where between 500 B.C. and A.D. 1500 would stand a roughly equal chance in battle against each other—and that span of years could probably be pushed all the way back to around 1500 B.C. (the time of Megiddo) if the earlier armies were allowed to exchange their bronze weapons for iron ones."[6] The introduction of the musket into sengoku Japan challenged and ultimately shattered this longstanding equilib-rium. To survive the Darwinian rigors of the age required absolute pragmatism on the part of every daimyo intent upon survival, a deter-mination to use any and every means at his disposal to crush the enemy and take his land before being similarly crushed in return. The musket's value as a killing machine was therefore quickly recognized. Muskets were not expensive to produce; the more affluent daimyo could afford to have them turned out by the thousands. They did not require care-fully crafted arrows, only simple lead balls. Their range and striking power was also superior to those of any traditional weapon. A musket, for example, could lob a slug nearly half a kilometer, compared to a maximum range of 380 meters for the heaviest—and most difficult to use—Japanese composite bow; at the closer distances at which most battles were fought, it could pierce iron armor that an arrow could only scratch. Finally, and most important, a musket was easy to use. This more than made up for its major weakness, its slow rate of fire. Even with practice it took nearly a minute to load and fire a musket, a period of time that would be only marginally reduced by the later introduction of pre-measured powder charges. A skilled archer, in contrast, could fire at least six well-aimed arrows in a minute. Skilled archers, however, took many years to train, they needed great muscular strength to wield the heaviest and in turn most dangerous bows, and they were therefore rare and expensive in sengoku Japan. The skills necessary to handle a musket, on the other hand, could be taught to anyone in just a few weeks. Adding a corps of musketeers to one's army was thus considerably more cost- and time-effective than adding a corps of archers. All one needed was the cash to buy the weapons and a supply of able-bodied men.[7]

These various practical advantages would make the musket a key weapon in the latter part of the sengoku era, when it would have a significant effect on the course of the history of Japan. Had the nation's daimyo been confined to the traditional weapons of sword and spear and bow, the sengoku period would very likely have dragged on for much longer than it did. The introduction of the musket into Japanese warfare ensured that this did not occur. It gave a significant advantage to those daimyo who embraced it, doomed their less foresighted rivals, and ultimately hastened the advent of national unification.

One such daimyo who recognized the importance of the musket early on was Oda Nobunaga. He was a violent individual reportedly from the day he was born in 1534, biting the nipples of every wet nurse employed to suckle him. Upon his father's death in 1551, Nobunaga inherited a small, ill-defined domain in Owari Province on central Honshu, near the present-day city of Nagoya, plus a few tenuous alliances with neighboring daimyo that soon fell apart. Almost from the start the twenty-year-old warlord found his diminutive domain under attack. For the next several years Nobunaga managed to keep the predators at bay while he moved against rival factions of his own Oda house to bring all of Owari Province under his sway. Then he turned his attention outward.

His first great victory came in 1560. Imagawa Yoshimoto, a much more powerful daimyo than Nobunaga with territory stretching across three provinces to the east, had long had his eye on Oda land. In 1554 and again in 1558 he sent small forces into Owari that Nobunaga managed to beat back. In 1560 Imagawa returned to finish the job, this time at the head of a forty thousand-man army. Nobunaga, with just two thousand men under his command, wisely chose not to meet this superior force in the traditional way. Instead he ambushed the invaders during a blinding downpour, when they were totally off guard and unable to see how small his army was. The strategy succeeded. The Imagawa army was put to flight, and Imagawa Yoshimoto himself was killed.

The tide was now turning for Oda Nobunaga. In 1564 he took complete control of former Imagawa holdings in the provinces of Mikawa, Totomi, and Suruga after Imagawa Yoshimoto's heir fled to a monastery. The Saito family fell in 1567, and with it the province of Mino to the north. Then came parts of Omi, Ise, and Iga. In 1568 Nobunaga entered Kyoto, deposed the puppet Ashikaga shogun supported by his rivals, and installed his own, Ashikaga Yoshiaki. When Yoshiaki rebelled against his benefactor's heavy hand and tried to form an alliance against him, Nobunaga drove him into exile and brought the Ashikaga shogunate to an end. In the 1570s Kawachi Province fell to him, then the rest of Omi. Then Setsu. Kai. Echizen. Noto. Hida. Etchu. Shinano. Wakasa. By 1582, when he was assassinated by one of his own vassals, Oda Nobunaga controlled all or portions of thirty-one of Japan's sixty-six provinces and roughly one-third of its land mass.

Why was Oda Nobunaga such a successful conqueror? Because he was unconventional. To begin with, he did not rely on traditional samurai armies, mounted on costly horses, wielding expensive swords and wearing fancy lacquered armor. Instead he based his army upon the lowly *ashigaru*, the foot soldier. They could be easily recruited from the peasantry, they were cheap to arm, and they were easy to train. Second, Nobunaga's forces were highly mobile. By improving roads, building bridges, and installing troop-ferrying ships on Lake Biwa, Nobunaga was able to move his armies around central Honshu with a speed that confounded his enemies. He also embraced the new technology of the musket. He started with an arsenal of five hundred weapons in the early 1550s. By 1575 he had ten thousand, enough to rival any daimyo. He gained this technological upper hand by capturing the two main centers of firearms production on Honshu, Sakai in 1569 and Kunitomo in 1570. After that most of the muskets produced outside Kyushu and its offshore island of Tanegashima came to him, along with the lion's share of the gunpowder. The advantage of possessing all these muskets would become glaringly apparent in the celebrated Battle of Nagashino in 1575, when three thousand of Nobunaga's musketeers effectively destroyed the army of Takeda Katsuyori with withering volley fire from behind the protection of a wooden palisade. When the battle was over, ten thousand of Takeda's men—sixty-seven percent of his entire army—lay dead in the field, and with them many of the traditional notions of warfare in Japan.

One final factor contributed to Oda Nobunga's success: he was ruthless. In his private life he was a man of refined tastes. He was, for example, an avid practitioner of the art of tea, and considered the right to hold a private tea ceremony the greatest honor he could bestow upon a vassal. In his battles and political machinations, however, Nobunaga cast aside all niceties. Conquest was his goal, and he was prepared to do whatever was necessary to achieve it. His early campaigns to unite the Oda house and win control of his home province of Owari resulted in the deaths of a number of his own family members. In 1565 he confirmed an alliance with the Asai family by offering his sister in marriage. When this alliance crumbled six years later, family ties did not prevent Nobunaga from slaughtering his in-laws. In his 1571 campaign against the heavily armed Buddhist stronghold on Mount Hiei, countless monks were slain and the entire monastery complex, including shrines, was burnt to the ground. After his campaign in Echizen Province he wrote, "There are so many corpses in Fuchu that there is no room for more."[8] It would be wrong to depict Nobunaga's brutality as differing in kind from that of rival daimyo. He was just better at it.

Oda Nobunaga's ultimate goal was to bring all of Japan under his power. This was the case from at least 1567, when he began using a personal seal bearing the maxim *tenka fuchu,* "the realm subjected to military power." His method of national unification, however, was slow and painful, for it ensured resistance at almost every step. For most of

Nobunaga's enemies, to capitulate without a fight meant losing every-thing, except perhaps their lives. Most chose to fight. Had Nobunaga lived, therefore, it was by no means certain that he would have succeeded in unifying the country, for a number of very formidable daimyo still stood in his way. Even if he had gone on to win ultimate hegemony over all Japan, it would likely have taken him many more years. That the task was accomplished in only nine years was due to the very different unification strategy pursued by his successor, Toyotomi Hideyoshi.

The rise of Hideyoshi exemplifies a fundamental aspect of this "nation at war" period called *gekokuji*: "the subjugation of the high by the low." He was the son of a farmer who rose to become the most powerful man in Japan, the unifier of the nation, and the commander of the mightiest army in Asia.

Hideyoshi was born in the village of Nakamura in the Owari domain of the Oda family in 1536 or 1537. He was named after the god Hiyoshi-maru, to whom his mother prayed prior to his birth. According to one account, he came into the world with all his teeth, and with such a wizened little simian face that he was nicknamed Sarunosuke, "Little Monkey."[9] Little is known of his family background and early life. Biographies penned during his lifetime, even under his own guidance, are sketchy and often wildly fanciful; Hideyoshi in his later years was clearly more interested in acquiring noble antecedents than in preserv-ing the facts of his humble origins. What is known with some degree of certainty is this: his father was a peasant with the single name of Yaemon—being a member of the lowest stratum of society, he did not possess a family name. Yaemon may have served for a time in Oda Nobuhide's small army, until a battle injury forced him back to the fields. He then married and had two children: Hideyoshi and a daughter named Tomo. He died soon after, in 1543, and Hideyoshi's mother, whose name is unknown, married a man called Chikuami who, like Yaemon, was affiliated in some minor way with the Oda house, prob-ably as an occasional foot solider in the small Oda army. By this second marriage Hideyoshi's mother had two more children, a daughter and a son. This son, Hidenaga, would figure prominently in Hideyoshi's life in years to come, as would one of his sister Tomo's sons, Hidetsugu.

In 1558 Hideyoshi, like his father and his stepfather before him, entered the service of the Oda house, then under the control of Oda Nobunaga. The young Hideyoshi could not have cut a very impressive figure. He was probably not much more than five feet tall and 110 pounds,[10] a scrawny version, perhaps, of his diminutive European counterpart, five-foot-one-inch-tall Napoleon. He would have had the wiry strength typical of a peasant in a pre-industrial society or of a laborer in the third world today. And he was most definitely homely; two nicknames Nobunaga liked to use for the farmer's son were "Monkey" and "Bald Rat."[11] Still, there must have been something remarkable about him, a useful cunning, a surprising intelligence, an unshakeable valor, a talent for organization and leadership, for within twelve years he had risen from the lowest menial position to become a general commanding three thousand men, and one of Nobunaga's ten principal vassals.

Serving under Nobunaga could not have been easy. He was quick-tempered and rude and offensive to his vassals, and bullied them unmercifully. There must have been countless occasions when the "Monkey" Hideyoshi had to placidly smile at his master's rough jokes and insults, and then march off through blinding rain or summer heat to carry out his every wish. Hideyoshi endured it, never uttering a word of resentment. He patiently served, bided his time, and waited for his chance.

Other Oda vassals were not so stoic. Akechi Mitsuhide found Nobunaga particularly offensive, and over the years stored up a burden of resentments that would eventually drive him to rebel. Some incidents were trivial, such as when Nobunaga got drunk, seized Akechi in a headlock, and thumped his bald head like a drum. Others left lasting scars. While besieging a castle in Tamba Province, Akechi promised that two brothers would be spared if the castle surrendered, and sent his own mother in as a hostage to guarantee his word. The castle duly surrendered. Then Nobunaga arrived and ordered the brothers burnt regardless, shattering the agreement Akechi had made. The relatives of the two men, still holding Akechi's mother hostage, burnt her to death in revenge. Akechi received Tamba Castle as his reward. But he never forgave Nobunaga, and he never forgot.[12]

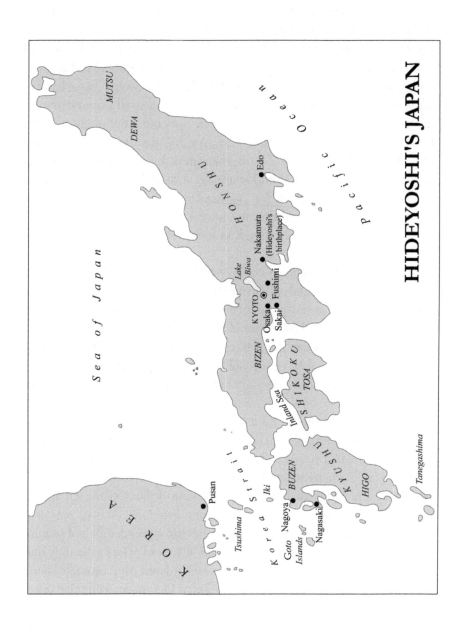

HIDEYOSHI'S JAPAN

Hideyoshi learned a great deal during his twenty-four years within the Oda house. In his private life he strove to acquire his master's same refined tastes in noh theater, cherry-blossom viewing, poetry writing, and the art of tea. In later years he would speak with emotion of the great honor he had felt when Nobunaga had granted him the privilege of holding his own tea ceremony. In combat, Hideyoshi learned the value of foot soldiers over mounted samurai and of muskets over bows; musket-bearing ashigaru would play a part in all of his campaigns. He learned to be every bit as imaginative in battle as Nobunaga. In 1582, for example, he constructed a three-kilometer-long dike to divert a nearby river into the Mori clan's impregnable Takamatsu Castle and succeeded quite literally in flushing them out.

Hideyoshi also learned the value of a mobile army and decisive action—a lesson that would serve him well when Nobunaga was finally killed.

It came in the summer of 1582. Some weeks earlier Nobunaga had invited rival daimyo Tokugawa Ieyasu to a banquet at his Azuchi Castle to cement an alliance. He asked Akechi Mitsuhide, whose bald head he had once drummed, to make the necessary arrangements. Akechi threw himself into the work, ordering the very best dishes and organizing all sorts of lavish entertainments to please his master. Then, just as the feast was about to begin, Nobunaga ordered him to leave at once and join Hideyoshi in the siege of Takamatsu Castle. Barred from a banquet he himself had prepared at great personal expense, Akechi left in a rage and returned to his Tamba Castle, ostensibly to gather an army to help Hideyoshi. But instead of marching on to Takamatsu, he set off for Kyoto—and Nobunaga.

Akechi arrived with his men at dawn on June 21 and forced his way into Honnoji Temple, where Nobunaga was staying. Nobunaga fought back desperately, but it was apparent the situation was hopeless. As fire began to spread through the temple, he retreated to a back room, opened his robe, and slit open his stomach. He died twitching on the floor at the age of forty-nine. The flames soon reduced his body to ashes. Akechi then marched his force against the mansion where Nobunaga's son and heir, Nobutada, was residing. A similar scene unfolded there, with Nobutada too committing suicide.

Hideyoshi learned of Nobunaga's death the following day. It threw him into almost manic action. This was his golden opportunity, and he meant to seize it. He quickly wound up the siege of Takamatsu Castle—his systematic flooding of the edifice had already brought the Mori to the brink of surrender—and on June 23 began the march to Kyoto. In less than a week the battle lines were drawn. On the one side was Akechi with an army of ten thousand. On the other was Hideyoshi, backed by several barons from the vicinity of Kyoto, with twenty thousand men. They met on the plains of Yamazaki, at the foot of a mountain called Tennozan, on July 2, just eleven days after Nobunaga's death. Akechi arrived early, under the cover of darkness and in a heavy downpour, encamping his troops on the plain and sending musketeers and archers up the slopes of the mountain so that he could command the heights. But Hideyoshi was already there; he possessed Tennozan. With the light of dawn the two armies met; Akechi's soon fell apart, and Hideyoshi's slaughtered. The fighting lasted two hours. Akechi attempted to retreat, but was apprehended and cut to pieces by a group of villagers and his body delivered to Hideyoshi. It was then taken to the burned-out Honnoji Temple in Kyoto to placate Nobunaga's spirit.

The Battle of Yamazaki was a watershed. It marked the passing of the reins of power from Oda Nobunaga to Hideyoshi, who would then go on to drive Japan so very much farther. It would change the course of the history of that country and in turn affect all of East Asia. In the centuries to come a new word recognizing the seminal influence of those two hours in 1582 would be added to the modern Japanese lexicon: *tennozan*, a decisive victory, military or political, that settles an important issue once and for all.

While impeccably loyal to Nobunaga during his master's lifetime, Hideyoshi always remained his own man. He was never as eager as Nobunaga to throw his soldiers into battle if an easier victory could be had in some other way—through guile, through patience, through appeasement. It was a difference that would become more apparent following Nobunaga's violent demise. After consolidating his hold on the former Oda domain in 1583, Hideyoshi cast aside Nobunaga's strategy of national unification through annihilation, of crushing rivals one by one and dividing up their land among his own loyal retainers. He was willing to forget past rivalries and leave daimyo in place as long as they recognized his overriding authority. As he wrote to Date Masamune prior to that daimyo's capitulation, "I do not enquire closely into the past of those who surrender to me. That is the law of heaven and I follow the same rule."[13] It was a fundamental change that would greatly shorten the unification process. Rival daimyo now had a choice. They could fight Hideyoshi's increasingly formidable armies and risk losing everything, including their lives. Or they could swear allegiance to him and in exchange keep most if not all of their lands and their positions as regional daimyo. There were other obligations, of course. Taxes had to be paid. Surveys had to be conducted to determine the exact value of fiefs in terms of the number of koku of rice they could annually produce.[14] Troops had to be contributed to the ongoing unification campaign. Family members had to be sent as hostages to Kyoto as an added assurance of loyalty, a common practice during this period. But these were not onerous burdens, certainly not when compared with the financial and human cost of continued war. Nor were they extracted without compensation; Hideyoshi was a generous hegemon. Daimyo joining him in his ongoing campaign of national unification were rewarded for their service with bigger fiefdoms, bigger incomes, and even occasional gifts of gold and silver and costly presents.

Hideyoshi, then, was promising the daimyo of Japan security, stability, peace, and wealth, and all at the relatively modest price of acknowledging him as the nation's ultimate lord and master. For many it was an offer they could not refuse. Certainly not every daimyo bowed before Hideyoshi without a fight. But those who did resist did not hold out for long or with nearly the ferocity that Nobunaga would have encountered, for the attractions of capitulation were now so much greater.

The year 1584 saw Hideyoshi in a standoff with Tokugawa Ieyasu, the short, pudgy, wily daimyo of Mikawa and Totomi Provinces to the east of Kyoto. They engaged in two limited engagements early that year, but there seems to have been a feeling of mutual respect between the two men, for neither would launch a full-scale assault against the other. Instead they waited. Eventually the pragmatic Tokugawa gave in to the clearly more powerful Hideyoshi. He swore allegiance to him in 1586 and was allowed in return to keep all of his holdings. To seal the

alliance, Ieyasu gave Hideyoshi his second son for adoption, and
Hideyoshi gave Ieyasu his mother as a hostage and his half-sister in
marriage. (She was already married but Hideyoshi had her divorced.)

Chosokabe Motochika proved a more stubborn foe. He had recently
made himself lord of all four provinces on Shikoku, the smallest of the
three main islands comprising the Japanese archipelago (after Kyushu
and Honshu; Hokkaido would not enter the Japanese polity for another
three hundred years). As was becoming his practice, Hideyoshi sent a
letter to Shikoku calling for its submission, but Chosokabe treated it
with contempt. Hideyoshi therefore prepared to invade. With his stepbrother Hidenaga and nephew Hidetsugu leading the way, Hideyoshi's
growing army of 150,000 men crossed the Inland Sea in 1585 and bull-
dozed the stubborn daimyo into submission within a month. Chosokabe
wisely chose to surrender before his situation became completely
hopeless and was allowed a fief of one province as a reward. The rest of
the island Hideyoshi divided among his followers. He was now greater
than his predecessor Oda Nobunaga, possessing fully one-half of
Japan—and the richest and most populous half at that.

Next it was Kyushu's turn. Shimazu Yoshihisa was the dominant
lord here. He possessed most of the territory on the island, and he had a
formidable army and plenty of muskets manufactured in Kyushu's own
burgeoning arms-production centers. He consequently saw no reason to
answer a peremptory call to surrender from an upstart daimyo on faraway Honshu. The Shimazu family, after all, had been a power on Kyushu
for fourteen generations, while this Hideyoshi by all accounts was nothing
more than a peasant. Hideyoshi responded with unprecedented force.
Hidenaga led the way at the beginning of 1587 with an advance army of
sixty thousand. Within two weeks two more generals arrived, bringing
the number to ninety thousand. Then Hideyoshi himself landed with his
main army, swelling the total force facing the Shimazu to an astounding
quarter million men. Shimazu Yoshihisa surrendered four months later,
shaving his head and adopting a monk's name to show that the fight
had left him. Like Chosokabe on Shikoku, he chose to sue for peace
rather than fight to the end and was duly rewarded with territory on the
southern end of the island valued at half a million koku.

The provinces of eastern Honshu were the next to fall to Hideyoshi.

The major campaign here was against Hojo Ujimasa, who held nine provinces centering on the present-day city of Tokyo, then a fishing village known as Edo. Once again the might of Hideyoshi's new Japan was mobilized to bring this recalcitrant daimyo to heel. The onslaught quickly drove Hojo into siege in his castle at Odawara, a formidable structure of wide moats and thick stone ramparts and soaring keeps. Hideyoshi did not need to employ any labor-intensive siege-breaking strategies this time; no earthen dikes and diverted rivers were required now. He simply encircled the castle with his own line of moats and walls—placing the enemy "in a birdcage" as Hideyoshi called it[15]—and then settled his army down to wait in as much comfort as he could arrange. Merchants were invited to the camp, concubines were sent for, entertainers were brought in, buskers performed, tea ceremonies were held, and on the whole boredom and discontent were kept successfully at bay. The castle fell after four months, in September of 1590. The northern hinterland provinces of Dewa and Mutsu were easily subdued the following year, and with that the unification of Japan was complete.

Unlike Chosokabe and Shimazu on the islands of Shikoku and Kyushu to the south, Hojo Ujimasa held out too long against Hideyoshi to merit any sort of clemency or concession. He was ordered to kill himself upon the fall of Odawara Castle. Eight of his nine provinces were given to Tokugawa Ieyasu as a reward for his help in the campaign. This greatly increased the value of Tokugawa's fiefdom, making him the richest of Hideyoshi's vassals. It also brought him more firmly under control, removing him from his traditional base in Mikawa and Totomi, where he commanded deep loyalties. This was a strategy Hideyoshi had come to rely upon heavily and one that he would use again and again in the years to come. By shifting his vassals from one fiefdom to another, he severed any bonds they had forged with the local population, particularly their ties with their own circle of vassals. By moving them to richer fiefdoms, he ensured that they went willingly. In this way Hideyoshi himself remained the only constant before the eyes of the Japanese people, the only target for their undivided loyalty.

Throughout his rise to power Hideyoshi made great efforts to cast off his peasant origins and acquire higher social status. His first and most pressing task had been to acquire a suitable family name to add to the single one he had been allotted at birth. He started in the 1560s by borrowing the surname Kinoshita, "Under the Shade of the Tree," from his wife's side of the family. In 1573 he discarded this in favor of Hashiba, a combination of syllables from the names of two admired lieutenants in Nobunaga's service. After succeeding Nobunaga in 1582, he looked about for something more regal, and eventually laid claim to the exalted Fujiwara name by being formally adopted by one of his socially eminent vassals. Finally, with national hegemony in his grasp, even this was not enough. He needed a new surname of his own, one to legitimize his house and his heirs for what he hoped would be decades of unchallenged family rule. He became Toyotomi Hideyoshi, Hideyoshi "The Bountiful Minister."

Hideyoshi also needed a title. He initially entertained the thought of becoming shogun, and applied to the former shogun Yoshiaki in 1585 to adopt him so that he could claim this appellation. Yoshiaki refused, stating that Hideyoshi's lowly birth disqualified him from such a position. Yoshiaki was then residing under the protection of the Mori clan on the island of Kyushu, which had not yet been conquered, so there was little Hideyoshi could do about the rebuff. Instead he settled for *kampaku*, "imperial regent," a formerly lofty court position that had lost much of its importance over the preceding three centuries. He had the emperor remove the existing kampaku from office and assumed the role himself in 1585. Hideyoshi retained the title for six years, then passed it on to his nephew and just-named heir, Hidetsugu, in January of 1592. After that, and until his death, he was known as *taiko*, "retired imperial regent."

As Hideyoshi strove to acquire an impressive family name and lofty title, he also worked hard to develop the refined tastes of the upper class. From his lord Oda Nobunaga he acquired a taste for the tea ceremony. He would in time become a skilled practitioner of the art, with an unsurpassed collection of fine serving bowls and utensils and two portable tearooms that he carried with him in his travels around the country. He became reasonably adept at composing poems in *renga*, "linked verse," sessions, a popular leisure-time activity in which participants improvised short poems in turn, responding to or continuing the thought in the previous verse until one hundred or more "links" had been created. Hideyoshi also became involved in noh theater, first as a benefactor and later as the star in specially commissioned plays dramatizing his many exploits, for example *The Conquest of Akechi* and *The Conquest of Hojo.*[16]

By 1591, then, Hideyoshi, son of the peasant Yaemon from the village of Nakamura, was the supreme ruler of all Japan. His word was law from the balmy southern tip of Kyushu to Honshu's snowy northern forests, from the lowest beggar to Emperor Go-Yozei himself. He had become progenitor of the powerful and illustrious house of Toyotomi, a noh artist, a dab hand at renga, and something of a national patriarch for the art of tea. It was, in short, the most astonishing political and social rise in the nation's history, the ultimate expression of gekokuji.

And yet it was not enough. Hideyoshi wanted more. From as early as 1585 he began to express a desire to conquer China after he had finished unifying Japan. In a letter to one of his vassal daimyo in the ninth month of that year he stated, "I am going to not only unify Japan but also enter Ming China."[17] In 1586 the Jesuit priest Luis Frois recorded a conversation held at Osaka Castle in which Hideyoshi stated "that he had reached the point of subjugating all Japan . . . and, this done, [he would] entrust [the affairs of the country] to his brother Minodono [Hidenaga], while he himself should pass to the conquest of Korea and China."[18] In the following year, when embarking on his Kyushu campaign, Hideyoshi spoke of "slashing his way" into Korea, China, and even India beyond after he had all of Japan securely in his grasp.[19] In a letter to his wife O-Ne, written soon after the invasion of Kyushu, he wrote, "By fast ships I have dispatched [orders] to Korea to serve the throne of Japan. Should [Korea] fail to serve [our throne], I have dispatched [the message] that I will punish [that country] next year. Even China will enter my grip; I will command it during my lifetime."[20]

*   *   *

In general the reasons troops are raised are five: to contend for fame; to contend for profit; from accumulated hatreds; from internal disorder; and from famine.[21]

Wu Tzu Ping Fa (Master Wu's Art of War)
4th century B.C.

Why was Toyotomi Hideyoshi intent on conquering Asia—or more to the point, most of the world as it was known to him? The desire to prevent internal disorder was likely one of his motives: he needed continued conquest to maintain and strengthen his control over Japan.

By 1591 Hideyoshi's campaign of national unification had pacified the country in three ways. First, it had brought all the formerly feuding daimyo under his control, by force if necessary. Second, it had engaged the entire country in one national goal, that of reunification. Recently subdued daimyo were in fact often put to work contributing to this very unification campaign that had just subdued them, marshaling the people and resources in their disparate domains to serve Hideyoshi's purpose rather than their own. Third, it had kept Hideyoshi's vassals, old and new alike, content and obedient with the promise of larger fiefs obtained through new conquests.

But what would happen when there were no more daimyo to subdue and no more territory left to be carved up and disbursed to reward allegiance? What would happen when reunification was achieved and Japan was once more at peace with itself? Would peace and unity remain? Or would the now idle daimyo begin to plot, forge secret alliances, and then struggle anew for a greater share of power? If such concerns were in Hideyoshi's mind—and it is hard to believe they were not—then to extend his conquests overseas might have been seen as a logical response. By replacing the goal of national unification with Asian domination, Hideyoshi could keep his daimyo busy serving his will rather than their own (with the promise, of course, of huge new territories to be divided up) and the people and resources in their domains working hard to achieve his new national purpose. In this way internal stability could be maintained and time purchased for Hideyoshi and his heirs to solidify their grip on the country.

There was more behind Hideyoshi's invasion of the mainland, however, than a clear-eyed desire to forestall internal disorder. It is evident from the diplomatic correspondence he dispatched to various Asian nations before the war that he viewed himself as destined to conquer the world. "After my birth," he wrote to the Koreans in 1589, "a fortune-teller said that all the lands the sun shone on would be mine when I became a man, and that my fame would spread beyond the four seas. . . . Man cannot outlive his hundred years, so why should I sit chafing on this island? I will make a leap and land in China and lay my laws upon her."[22]

As Master Wu put it in the fourth century B.C., then, Hideyoshi's second motivation was "to contend for fame."

If Hideyoshi was intent on building an empire, why did he set his sights on such a lofty prize as China rather than on the more realistic goal of neighboring Korea alone? Hideyoshi's boundless confidence and ambition certainly had a good deal to do with the decision. But there was also a measure of strategic reasoning involved. To seize Korea was merely to chip a piece off the periphery of the Chinese empire, a piece that would likely cost him a good deal in men and wealth. After the task was complete, he would then have to rebuild his army before setting out to chip off another piece elsewhere. On the other hand, if he sent his forces in a rapid thrust through Korea to take Beijing, the entire world that the Ming Chinese presided over would fall to him. By seizing the center, in other words, the periphery would follow.

Hideyoshi's plan to "slash his way" to China, while ambitious in the extreme, was not as misguided as might at first appear. When he referred to the Chinese as "long sleeves," a reference to effeminate court officials in flowing robes unsuitable for combat, his disparaging imagery contained a kernel of truth: in the late sixteenth century China *was* weak; it *was* in a sense waiting to be toppled by a conqueror possessing superior force. Its standing armies were huge only on paper. In reality it would be hard pressed to scrape together an army of a hundred thousand often poorly armed and poorly led men. In the Battle of Sarhu in 1619, which marked the beginning of the final decline of the Ming, it took only sixty thousand Jurchen warriors to defeat the largest army Beijing could put in the field. This did not come close to what Hideyoshi possessed. He could muster a quarter million men. He could arm them with well-made muskets in the tens of thousands. He could place at their head generals who were battle hardened and highly skilled.

In 1591 Hideyoshi in fact possessed the most powerful military machine the world had ever seen. In Europe at that time even the best armies would probably not have been a match for the disciplined forces of Alexander the Great (356–323 B.C.); that degree of military power would not be acquired for another twenty or thirty years.[23] Against Hideyoshi, however, neither Alexander's hoplites nor any sixteenth-century "push of pike" European army would have stood a chance. When the taiko was sending 250,000 men armed with many thousands of muskets to Kyushu in 1587, and 158,800 men to Korea in 1592, the largest single-state armies in Europe rarely topped 50,000.[24]

Hideyoshi could not have known anything of the details of China's weakness, such as the number of soldiers Beijing could actually muster. The Ming emperor and his court scarcely knew such things themselves. Telling circumstantial evidence nevertheless did exist, evidence that Hideyoshi clearly knew about. Foremost was Ming China's longstanding inability to protect its coastline from wako pirates. From the late fifteenth century onward these pirates, a mix of Chinese and Japanese outlaws operating from bases in southern Japan and offshore Chinese islands, combined smuggling operations with smash-and-grab marauding along the rich coastal regions of southern and central China, operating with such impunity as to make it obvious that China had nowhere near the military might it customarily claimed. Until the 1550s and 1560s, when effective solutions were finally devised and the wako ceased to be a major problem, the best response Beijing could come up with was to move people and resources inland, away from the threatened coasts.

A second piece of evidence that might have added to Hideyoshi's perception of Ming China as weak was Beijing's seeming inability to control its vassal states. In the national tumult of the sengoku era, Japan had forgotten its tributary relationship to China, reestablished at the beginning of the fifteenth century by the third Ashikaga shogun, who had duly received investiture as the king of Japan, and had ceased sending tribute missions to the Chinese court. China subsequently did not issue a reprimand or make a response of any kind. In reality it did not care that much about its relationship with Japan and scarcely gave it a second thought after its tribute missions ceased. Hideyoshi, however, would not have seen it that way. As a military dictator used to controlling his vassals with a firm hand, he would have seen China's lack of response as a sign of weakness, an indication that it lacked the power to keep its tributary states in line.

Evidence such as this, when viewed from the perspective of late sixteenth-century Japan, led Hideyoshi to believe that the Ming dynasty was ready to fall to the power he possessed. He therefore set out, as conquerors have done since the beginning of recorded history, to extend his control into neighboring lands. He would take China because he believed he had the power to take it. Korea would come with the bargain, for it was the highway to the prize. The adventure would serve to aggrandize Hideyoshi's name and in turn the house of Toyotomi. It would prevent internal disorder by keeping potential rivals busy on the mainland, conquering territory to enrich themselves. And it would provide the country with a new, unifying national purpose: the quest for empire.

CHAPTER 2

China: The Ming Dynasty in Decline

IN THE LATE SIXTEENTH CENTURY China was by most outward appearances the mightiest nation on the face of the earth. Its territory was vast, stretching from the Pacific Ocean in the east to the edge of the Tibetan plateau in the west; from Burma and Vietnam in the south all the way north to Manchuria and the Mongolian steppes. It commanded the allegiance and received tribute from kingdoms as far-flung as Korea, Vietnam, Thailand, Java, Sumatra, the Philippines, Borneo, and, until the middle of the century, Japan. Its population was immense, somewhere in the vicinity of one hundred and fifty million, a staggering figure at that time. Its economy was huge, producing ever-increasing quantities of grain, cotton, silk, porcelain, tobacco, paper, peanuts, lacquer, ink, and indigo. It was the birthplace of history, the font of religious wisdom, the inspiration for philosophical insights, the source of technological innovation. It was the Middle Kingdom. The Celestial Empire. The Center of the World.

So much for outward appearances. In the late sixteenth century the Ming dynasty, which had ruled China for over two hundred years, was in fact beginning to totter.

There were a number of reasons for this, all with roots extending back to the very beginning of the dynasty and its first emperor, Zhu Yuanzhang. Zhu was born to the lowest peasant stock in 1328, during the middle years of the Yuan dynasty, when the formerly nomadic

Mongols of the north dominated China. As the Mongols' grip on the country loosened, uncoordinated peasant uprisings began to flare up, eventually coalescing into a groundswell that pushed the former nomads back onto the steppes. Zhu, a fiercely ugly man with great spots on his face, rose from obscurity in one of these fighting peasant bands to command the newly liberated country. The dynasty he went on to establish in 1368 returned the empire to native Chinese rule after a century of foreign domination and led to the restoration of many of the traditions of the former "real" Chinese dynasties of Tang (618–907) and Song (960–1279) that the Yuan had eclipsed. The renaissance spirit of the times would be reflected in the name selected for the new state: Great Ming, or "Bright." Zhu Yuanzhang himself would henceforth be known by his reign name Hongwu, "Vast Military Power."

One of the traditions restored under the Hongwu emperor was a return to government based on the philosophy originating with the sage Kong Fu Zi (551–479 B.C.), "Master Kong," known in the West as Confucius. In the centuries after Confucius's death, his ideas of virtuous conduct and the perfectibility of man through learning came to have a great influence on China before being eclipsed by Buddhism as the nation's dominant intellectual force. Then, in the eleventh century A.D., a group of scholars known as the Five Masters reinterpreted and revitalized the ancient wisdom of Confucius and his successors and brought it again to the fore, giving it a more rational theoretical base and identifying specific "principles" to which the "superior person" should adhere. This reinterpretation—what is today call Neo-Confucianism—would be most succinctly stated by Chu Xi in his 1175 work *Reflections on Things at Hand*. According to Chu Xi, every person should strive to advance as far along the road to sage-hood as his ability and destiny would allow. This could be done by cultivating oneself intellectually through study of the Confucian classics, by "reflecting on things at hand" in one's own life, and by practicing the virtues of filial piety, loyalty, sincerity, frugality, and "humaneness." "Study extensively, inquire accurately, think carefully, sift clearly, and practice earnestly," Chu wrote, quoting from the ancient *Doctrine of the Mean*. "Learning which neglects one of these is not learning."[1]

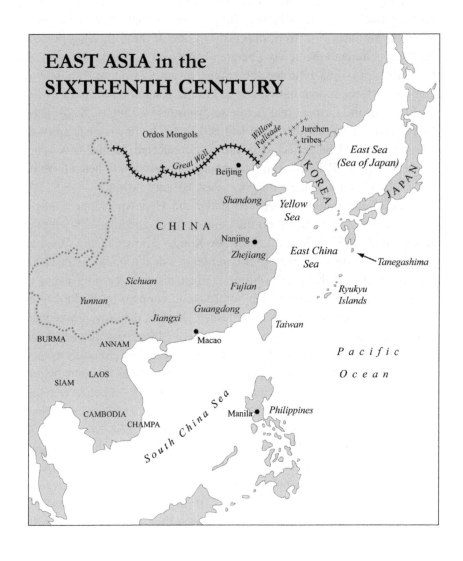

EAST ASIA in the
SIXTEENTH CENTURY

Ordos Mongols

Willow Palisade

Jurchen tribes

Great Wall

Beijing

KOREA

East Sea (Sea of Japan)

JAPAN

Shandong

Yellow Sea

CHINA

Nanjing

Zhejiang

East China Sea

Tanegashima

Sichuan

Fujian

Ryukyu Islands

Yunnan

Guangdong

Jiangxi

Taiwan

BURMA

ANNAM

Macao

Pacific

Ocean

LAOS

SIAM

South China Sea

CAMBODIA

CHAMPA

Manila

Philippines

With the start of the Ming dynasty, all government officials were recruited from among the sons of China whose families could afford to have them raised up and educated as Confucian gentlemen. There was no shortage of applicants, for according to Confucius it was only when private self-cultivation was combined with the holding of public office that one could achieve one's full potential. As is written in the *Analects*, "When a man in office finds that he can more than cope with his duties, then he studies; when a student finds that he can more than cope with his studies, then he takes office."[2] With the number of aspirants to office far exceeding the number of government posts, Ming China revived the civil service examination—a Tang-dynasty innovation refined in the Song—to winnow out those candidates with the greatest literary ability, the deepest knowledge of the classics, and the firmest grasp of the essential virtues. Those who passed and received a post in government usually possessed a profound understanding of what they were supposed to know. Many, for example, had committed the Confucian classics entirely to memory in their years of quiet study, together with reams of other texts, and could quote from them at length off the tops of their heads. They generally were not so well equipped with technical knowledge, leadership ability, and organizational skills, but that did not matter, as the civil service examination did not test such things. Being an accomplished Confucian scholar and gentleman was what counted. That was what prepared a man for the great work of leading the state.

While the Hongwu emperor found Neo-Confucianism useful for ordering his new Ming empire, he does not seem to have taken much personal interest in its doctrines and striving to become like a sage. Like the founders of most dynasties, he was despotic, temperamental, violent, suspicious to the point of paranoia, and had no compunction about putting to death officials who crossed him. This antipathy reached its zenith in 1380, when he found his prime minister to be plotting against him. The Hongwu emperor had the man beheaded, then had his family killed, then slaughtered his friends and relations, then moved on to his casual acquaintances, until the death toll reached forty thousand. He abolished the office of prime minister after that, along with the entire central secretariat, in effect cutting off the head of the bureaucracy, and conducted much of the nation's day-to-day business himself or through his inner circle of court eunuchs. His ability to plow through the resulting mounds of paperwork that accumulated before the throne was at times astounding: in one eight-day period he is said to have worked his way through 1,600 dispatches dealing with a total of 3,391 issues.[3] Future emperors would be energetic in this regard, but the bottleneck at the top would always remain.

In addition to placing China under strictly centralized control, the Hongwu emperor also insisted upon frugality—no more bloated governments living well and squandering resources on the backs of suffering peasants. This was in line with the Neo-Confucian principles of his bureaucracy, but an equally important factor may have been the Hongwu emperor's own peasant background, in particular his personal experience of hunger and even starvation. Land and income taxes under the Ming were therefore kept low, and the watchword throughout the land became self-sufficiency. Local communities were to police themselves, collect their own taxes, and deliver them to whatever destination the government specified. Government officials were paid only nominal salaries, almost nothing at all, in the expectation that they would provide for themselves. Military garrisons were ordered to support themselves through agriculture, thereby saving the nation the financial burden of paying for a standing army. Labor and tools for much-needed public works projects were supplied by local communities rather than from the public purse.

The many reforms and innovations that the Hongwu emperor forced upon China got the Ming dynasty off to an impressive start. In the coming decades agricultural production increased. Trade flourished. Government treasuries filled. The silted-up Grand Canal was dredged and put back into service. The Great Wall was repaired and strengthened. Four-hundred-foot-long "treasure ships" were sent out to the farthest reaches of the known world and came back laden with the riches of Java, Sumatra, Ceylon, India, Arabia, and even Africa. Indeed, in the early fifteenth century China was the preeminent naval power in the world.[4]

But then things changed. Following the autocratic reigns of the Hongwu emperor and his immediate successors, China's Neo-Confucian bureaucracy began to assert itself. Subsequent monarchs were gradually isolated within the Forbidden City in Beijing, confined to the role of tradition-bound figureheads, kept eternally busy with tedious court rituals and audiences and lectures. Trade, which had been given relatively free reign under the Yuan and early Ming emperors, was discouraged, for the quest for profit was regarded with distrust by Confucianists; in the Neo-Confucian world order, agriculture was the only real source of prosperity. The great treasure-ship expeditions were consequently halted, records of the journeys destroyed, and the very technology for building the massive vessels purposefully forgotten. In future, shipbuilding would be limited to small, coastal vessels, and all officially sanctioned international trade confined to tribute missions from vassal states. China, like the contemplative scholar-officials who controlled its destiny, turned inward and grew conservative. Stability, not development, became the national goal.

During the middle years of the Ming dynasty China did enjoy a prolonged period of stability. But it did not last. There were inherent weaknesses in the system, as established by the Hongwu emperor and altered by subsequent generations of bureaucrats, that made the empire increasingly difficult to govern and increasingly vulnerable to external threats.

First there was the problem of money, or more precisely the lack of it. The Hongwu emperor's insistence on frugality, low taxes, and self-sufficiency had worked well enough during his own reign, for he kept his palace expenses low and ensured that his nascent empire was managed with minimum expense by taking a personal—and if necessary heavy-handed—interest in the affairs of government. Unfortunately, the notion of imperial frugality did not long outlive him. Palace expenditure steadily increased with each subsequent monarch and became a serious drain on the national purse. The collection of taxes also became a haphazard affair. Tax quotas became hopelessly out of date; units of measure varied from region to region, causing endless confusion; most taxpayers were illiterate and did not fully understand what was expected of them; others simply did not pay, their debts eventually being written off for want of a means to collect them. The taxes actually received by the government, therefore, never came close to even the modest levels established by the Hongwu emperor.

The Hongwu emperor's vision of a self-sufficient government bureaucracy also proved problematic. He pegged government salaries so low that officials could scarcely afford to feed themselves and their families, let alone run government offices and regional administrations. Most had no recourse but to charge "fees" for the services they provided, a practice that further ate into government revenues and inevitably led to abuses.

Lack of money was not the only of the Ming dynasty's troubles. Equally serious were the inefficiency and at times incompetence of its leaders. Since a man's ability to enter government service depended entirely on his command of the classics, and his success in rising to power depended entirely upon his personal virtue, government officials not surprisingly possessed little of what would be regarded today as administrative ability or technical expertise. To China's sixteenth-century Neo-Confucian elite, personal virtue *was* administrative ability, for a man so equipped could accomplish anything. This sense of confidence not infrequently moved public-spirited officials to take on tasks for which they were singularly unsuited, including the planning of military campaigns and even the direct command of armies, secure in the belief that their lack of practical experience was more than made up for by their knowledge of the classics. In many situations it was a recipe for mismanagement, even disaster.

This emphasis on personal virtue not only left China's leadership ill-equipped to deal with situations requiring technical solutions or specialized knowledge, it also led it into all sorts of divisive wranglings that rendered it all the more ineffective. The fundamental reason for this was that there was no one standard for what constituted "personal virtue." A case in point is the collection of "fees" that most government bureaucrats had to engage in to survive. Strictly speaking this was corruption, but it was such a necessary part of the system that most preferred not to examine the issue too closely. A few rare officials were scrupulous in refusing any sort of additional payment for their services, and lived in abject poverty; others took full advantage of their positions, and amassed incredible fortunes, while the vast majority fell somewhere in between. So where should the line be drawn? As Ray

Huang has aptly described it, "Should a county magistrate, who by official order was entitled to an annual compensation of less than thirty ounces of silver, still be considered honest if he helped himself to 300 ounces, but not if he took 3,000? If he appropriated 5 percent of the district's gross tax proceeds, or 10 percent? At what point was honesty defined?"[5]

Of course it could not be defined. But that did not prevent Ming government officials from trying to do so. There was in fact a branch of government, the censorate, whose sole purpose was to monitor the conduct of government officials, from the lowest ninth-grade newcomer all the way up to the emperor himself. These censors were a fierce and at times dangerous lot. They wore badges on their chests featuring a *hsieh-chih*, a legendary beast that reputedly sniffed out men of immoral character and tore them to pieces—exactly what a censor could do to a government official's career if his virtue was found wanting. Every Ming official was subjected to the regular scrutiny of these morality police—every three years for regional officials and every six for those posted in the capital—and faced immediate demotion or discharge if even the slightest hint of misconduct was unearthed. During the first part of the dynasty these evaluations were particularly brutal, for the number of individuals passing the civil service exam and entering government service exceeded the number of retirees, necessitating large-scale dismissals to avoid overstaffing. It was only natural in the face of such a threat that civil servants began to band together into cliques, junior officials aligning with influential seniors for protection, senior officials in turn gathering a loyal following of juniors to help fend off or launch any political attack.

By the middle of the sixteenth century this process of alignment had resulted in clearly defined factions. Attempting to remain above the fray simply left one without any support, an easy target to be run out of office by one of the competing camps so that your post could be handed to one of their own. It was therefore expedient to choose sides. Government officials still spoke in the same pious terms of virtue and impropriety. The high-minded accusations of profiteering and indiscretion continued: charges that this man was getting rich from the public purse, that that man had not observed the correct mourning period for his

deceased parent, and that another had had an indiscreet liaison with
someone else's wife. But the words now concealed a deeper and more
damaging struggle—a struggle for power.

In addition to having an incurable case of financial anemia and a
government divided by factional strife, Ming China was also faced with
the increasingly worrisome fact of its own declining military strength. It
was once again a problem with roots reaching back to the dynasty's
beginning. To extend his ideal of self-sufficiency to this traditional
drain on the imperial purse, the Hongwu emperor had established garrisons (wei) at strategic points throughout the empire, allotting each a
tract of government land upon which the soldiers were to grow their
own food and provide for their own maintenance. These wei garrisons,
with a nominal strength of 5,600 men, were subdivided into 1,120-man
companies called so; hence this Ming military organization is often
termed the "wei-so army."[6] This notion of a self-sufficient military that
could switch as needed from peacetime pursuits to a wartime footing
had worked well for the Mongols in the preceding Yuan dynasty, the
transition from nomadic horseman to warrior having come naturally to
those foreign invaders. It did not work, however, for the Ming. Its
domesticated army became just that, domesticated—farming communities where military discipline was forgotten and the arts of war seldom
practiced. They were never fully self-sufficient either, but came over
the years to require more and more government support, first in the
form of grain shipments, for the soldiers were unable to grow enough
for themselves, and later, when grain became scarce, in silver.[7] Eventually even this was not enough to keep the soldiers from starving. They
rarely received the entire sum they were due, and corrupt officers
frequently withheld the rest. It therefore became common for men to
bribe their officers to allow them to leave the garrison to engage in outside work, often never to return. This practice, coupled with unrecorded
deaths and desertions, had drastically reduced the actual size of China's
wei-so army by the mid sixteenth century, even as the cost of its upkeep
was spiraling ever higher. It has been estimated that in some extreme
cases garrisons were reduced to only two or three percent of their
nominal strength.[8]

There was no official record kept in Beijing of these dwindling numbers. Garrison commanders were not in the habit of submitting accurate figures; many did not even know how many men were under their command. Most were happy to leave inflated figures on the books, for this ensured that inflated amounts of financial support continued to flow into the garrison's coffers, of which the commanders themselves often claimed the lion's share. Throughout the Ming dynasty the Board of War therefore simply copied the names of soldiers and commanders from old lists to new and sent these on to the emperor, leading him to believe that he still had a force of two million men under his command.

All but the most obtuse officials must have known, however, that the true figure was much lower, for there was ample secondary evidence of the military's drastic decline. In the 1550s, for example, Mongol raiders under Altan Khan were easily able to penetrate China's supposedly well-guarded northern frontier to haul off whatever prisoners and loot that they wanted. When they began pillaging in the vicinity of Beijing itself, the Board of War had great difficulty mustering just 50,000 men from garrisons near and far to repulse them, this despite the fact that there were supposed to be more than 107,000 soldiers stationed right there in the city. By the early 1570s there were in fact so few soldiers left cultivating garrison farms along the northern border that vast stretches of territory had reportedly turned to desert, even though the military rosters in Beijing still listed tens of thousands of troops stationed in the region.

As the number of soldiers in China's standing army dwindled, so too did their quality. Relying increasingly on local conscripts, press-ganged vagabonds, and hired mercenaries to fill the gaping holes in the wei-so ranks, the Ming army by the mid sixteenth century had become, in the words of the Minister of War, "an undisciplined mob."[9] In the face of battle it was often only the threat of instant death at the hands of their own officers that kept Chinese soldiers from fleeing; sometimes even this was not enough. They were a terror to friendly populations, stealing and looting with such abandon that locals at times regarded them with greater fear than any "enemy" they had been sent to quell. "This is their nature," wrote the Minister of War in 1562, "swinish greed and wolf-like brutality. They practice extortion and robbery in broad daylight; by night they pollute the women. Should anyone resist, then out comes the sword and that person's dead; they don't give murder another thought! Hence the proverb says, 'Cross, if you must, a Japanese bandit's path, but never a garrison soldier's.' Run into a Japanese, and there's still a chance you'll get away. But meet a soldier, and you're done for."[10] Another official, who generously placed the army's total strength in the 1550s at around 900,000 men, cautioned that fully two-thirds of them were of no use whatsoever, but rather "burden the country and are the source of many troubles. They start riots and try to revolt whenever the authorities are slow in paying them. They have even dared to kill government officials and rob and burn the houses of the people.... Nowadays much of our revenue is spent on the maintenance of these soldiers who are not only useless but are a cause of endless anxiety to the country."[11]

This breakdown in discipline reached a climax in March of 1592, when troops along the northwestern frontier mutinied over pay arrearages. They murdered the provincial governor, forced their commander in chief to commit suicide, and installed one of their own as leader. It took the shaken Ming court seven months to put down this mutiny, which they subsequently dressed up as a campaign against Mongol rebels rather than an internal insurrection by their own army.

As bad as the soldiers in China's armies could be, the officers could be worse. In Neo-Confucian Ming China, military leadership was a low-prestige career, which was commonly passed down from father to son. Officers were regarded by government officials as mere technical support staff and were treated accordingly. Even the highest-ranking and most experienced commanders were allowed no say in larger strategic matters, and could expect every decision they made in the field to be scrutinized and questioned by officials in Beijing, men who had never held a sword, witnessed a battle, or spent a night in a tent. To the Ming there was nothing odd about this, for by their reckoning no amount of practical experience could equal the wisdom of an official with a classical Confucian education. In the face of such disdain, military leaders themselves tended to treat their profession with a similar disregard. Hereditary ranks became family sinecures, a source of financial support to be worked like a business. Others simply bought commissions and got rich by misreporting garrison numbers to keep the

grain and silver shipments coming and by expropriating salary payments from their men. Many officers were illiterate or semi-literate, had
little knowledge of military tactics or leadership, and made little effort
to learn. They neglected the training and discipline of the men under
their command, putting them to work instead as laborers and personal
servants and allowing many to slip away entirely in return for a bribe.
When ordered against a foe, their primary concern often was not to win
a legitimate victory, but rather to concoct the appearance of a victory to
garner honors and rewards and to further their careers.

It was in the practice of taking heads that this degradation of both
soldiers and officers reached its lowest point. In Ming China fighting
prowess came to be quantified by the number of enemy heads taken in
battle, with rewards and honors distributed accordingly. This practice
led to horrendous abuses. In quelling the many border incursions and
internal revolts that came increasingly to plague China in the sixteenth
century, soldiers killed innocent civilians and beheaded them for the
reward—even the women, whose sex could be disguised by beating the
head with a wet sandal. In campaigns against the broad-faced, small-
mouthed Manchus, the heads of friendly Chinese noncombatants were
lopped off and steamed to make them swell up to an appropriate size.
Commanders were known to cut off the heads of their own fallen
soldiers in order to turn a defeat into a victory. Some officers who came
away from an engagement short of the 160 heads required for the award
of first-class merit would kill civilians to make up the number. Rebel
forces, meanwhile, picked up on this Chinese lust for heads and turned
it to their advantage, driving local villagers in front of them at the
scenes of battle, knowing this would satisfy the Ming forces and spare
their own ranks. In this manner victory upon victory was reported to the
government in Beijing as internal rebellions and border incursions continued unabated.[12]

The general weakness of China's military was brought into sharp
focus by the pirate raids that devastated the nation's rich east and south
coast regions for a period of twenty years beginning in the 1540s. These
pirates, an on-again, off-again problem in both Korea and China since
the fourteenth century, were traditionally regarded in both countries as
being from Japan, and thus were called *wokou*, "Japanese raiders"—

waegu to the Koreans, *wako* to the Japanese. The marauders active in the mid sixteenth century were in fact mainly Chinese with some Japanese and a few Portuguese adventurers mixed in, many of them operating out of bases on the Japanese island of Kyushu. They had turned to a life of brigandage in response to the strict prohibition on foreign trade that the Ming government had imposed after the relatively relaxed policies favored in the dynasty's earlier years. This naturally led to smuggling, an initially benign activity pursued by otherwise law-abiding citizens who became increasingly defiant as government attempts to clamp down on the problem drove the more determined smugglers to band together and take up arms. Branded now as outlaws and with nothing left to lose, such men started to live the outlaw's life, raiding and pillaging coastal towns and taking whatever they liked. It was easy work. Finding the coastal regions of the supposedly invincible Middle Kingdom almost entirely unprotected by either army garrisons or naval ships, the wokou fearlessly began to pick vast stretches of territory clean, sometimes in raids so large they resembled invasions. It was in the small raids, however, that piratical brazenness reached its peak. In one extraordinary episode that occurred in the autumn of 1555, a small band of renegades landed on the southeast coast aboard one or two ships and embarked on an inland rampage all around the former capital city of Nanjing, looting every town along the way without encountering any opposition from the 120,000 soldiers that the Board of War's outdated troop rosters still claimed were garrisoned nearby. "Finally," concludes the official account of the affair in the Ming dynasty annals *Ming shih*, "they were caught up at Yang-lin-ch'aio and exterminated. Throughout this episode there were only sixty to seventy persons, yet a distance of several thousand *li* was covered, the casualties totaled almost four thousand killed and wounded, and the raiding lasted more than eighty days."[13]

The Ming government initially tried to bring the wokou under control by military means, launching a campaign of "extermination" against them rather than a campaign of "pacification" through appeasement, the method it commonly employed on its northern frontier to co-opt external threats like the Mongols under Altan Khan. The pirates, after all, were operating in the heartland of China, not on the vulnerable northern border, where potential enemies had to be handled with care. They thus did not require pacifying; they required wiping out. The army commander and civilian governor in charge of the most badly affected areas were accordingly arrested and executed for dereliction of duty, inefficient regional administrations were bullied into shape, defunct military garrisons were roused to life, and eventually some telling blows were delivered against the pirates. It was not this, however, that ultimately solved the wokou problem. That would come later, in the late 1560s, when Beijing eased the restrictions on foreign trade that had given rise to the problem in the first place. It was an effective solution; by the end of the decade pirate raids had for the most part ceased. But it was also a sign of weakness, an instance where Beijing was forced to employ a policy of pacification through appeasement after finding itself unable to overcome the pirate problem solely by military means.[14]

This, then, was Ming China in the late sixteenth century. It was huge and rich and awesome, and commanded the nominal allegiance of many far-flung lands. Beneath this veneer of omnipotence, however, lay a host of weaknesses—political, economic, and military—that in turn gave rise to a never-ending succession of crises. For officials in Beijing, the act of governing entailed keeping the empire functioning and in one piece, putting out a fire here, papering over a problem there, then racing on to the next crisis that had in the meantime arisen. If it was not wokou pirate depredations in the southeast, it was Mongol raids in the north, an army mutiny on the Manchurian frontier, clashes on the Burmese border, a famine in the west—a crisis almost every year from the 1570s until the 1610s.[15] Beset by this cavalcade of threats, the Ming government became like the man in the circus who spins plates atop rods, immersed in the task of simply keeping the whole precarious setup from tumbling to the floor. Given the state of China in the late sixteenth century and the resources available to it, this was the best that it could possibly do.

It was in part glimpses of this weakness that led Toyotomi Hideyoshi, the unifier and self-appointed lord of Japan, to believe starting in the late 1580s that he could topple the Ming dynasty, conquer all of China, and then lay claim to its tributary states. Nor was he the only one entertaining such grand ideas. Spaniards and Portuguese residing in the Far East at this time, in Macao, the Philippines, Japan, and China itself, were eyeing the Middle Kingdom greedily as an incredibly rich but weak prize that was ripe for the picking. In 1576, for example, Francisco de Sande, the governor of Spain's recently acquired colony in the Philippines, sent a report home to Madrid from Manila recommending that King Philip II dispatch a military expedition to conquer China. The job could be accomplished, de Sande suggested, by four to six thousand well-armed Spaniards plus some Japanese and Chinese pirates who would gladly join the enterprise. They would sail to the southern Chinese coast from northern Luzon aboard a fleet of galleys built locally using the trees that grew so plentifully on the island. Once there a force of two or three thousand men would storm ashore and seize one Chinese province. "This will be very easy," de Sande assured the king, for the people "generally have no weapons, nor do they use any. A corsair with two hundred men could rob a large town of thirty thousand inhabitants. They are very poor marksmen, and their arquebuses are worthless." After that all the other provinces would naturally fall to the invaders, for the Chinese were a downtrodden people and would take the opportunity of the Spanish conquest to revolt against the Ming. "[F]inally," de Sande concluded, "the kind treatment, the evidences of power, and the religion which we shall show to them will hold them firmly to us."[16]

Approval of de Sande's scheme was not forthcoming from Madrid, so nothing more was done for the next ten years. Then, in April 1586, a second plan for the conquest of China, this one much more detailed and larger in scope, was presented at a meeting of colonial authorities and leading citizens in Manila and then sent to Madrid for the approval of King Philip II. This time the envisioned expeditionary force would be composed of several hundred Spaniards currently residing in the Philippines, 10,000 or 12,000 reinforcements sent out from Spain, and if possible 5,000 or 6,000 local Indians and an equal number of Japanese recruited by Jesuit missionaries in Japan—between 20,000 and 25,000 men all told. It was additionally suggested that the Portuguese be invited into the enterprise to make the invasion force even more overwhelming, so that its "mere presence and a demonstration will suffice to cause the Chinese to submit, with no great bloodshed." Great care should be taken in selecting the men to lead the expedition, "for it is very probable—nay, almost certain—that if this be not done, things will fare just as they did in the island of Cuba, and in other countries [i.e., the Aztec and Inca empires] that were once thickly peopled and are now deserted. If the Spaniards go into China in their usual fashion, they will desolate and ravage the most populous and richest country that ever was seen." The invasion plan called for Spanish forces to sail north to the Chinese coast from a staging area on northern Luzon aboard a fleet of ships built locally by natives working under the direction of Spanish shipwrights. They would land at Fujian Province while the Portuguese thrust simultaneously into Guangdong Province from their colony at Macao. The two armies, accompanied by China-based Jesuit priests serving as guides, would then independently slash their way north to Beijing and there establish themselves in ulti- mate authority, being careful to leave the existing Ming government apparatus in place because it was so effective at maintaining order among such a huge population. As for timing, the memorandum strongly advised that the invasion be launched as soon as possible or not at all, for the Chinese were becoming increasingly wary. A few years before, presumably when de Sande submitted his proposal, their vast country could have been snatched "with no labor, cost, or loss of life; today it cannot be done without some loss, and in a short time it will be impossible to do at any cost." It was therefore essential that the king give his immediate approval to the plan, for it "offered to his Majesty the greatest occasion and the grandest beginning that ever in the world was offered to a Monarch. Here lies before him all that the human mind can desire or comprehend of riches and eternal fame."[17]

Philip II never did approve the planned conquest of China. Had he done so and sent the requested reinforcements, the conquistadors of Manila would almost certainly have set sail, for they were completely serious in their intent and possessed the same extraordinary bravado that had already seen fellow Spaniards seize vast chunks of the New World with astonishingly small armies. Francisco Pizarro, for example, began the conquest of the Inca empire in the 1530s with as many men as would fill two highway buses. Who knows how far such boundless confidence and 25,000 men would have taken the Spanish in China? Considering the amount of time that China's ponderous military administration typically needed to rouse itself and respond to a threat, it is conceivable that a Spanish army, equipped with modern arquebuses and acting with decision, could have marched to the very gates of Beijing before being finally bogged down and overwhelmed by the sheer immensity of the land.

In 1573 a ten-year-old boy named Zhu Yijun ascended the Celestial Throne in Beijing and took the reign name Wanli. He was the four-teenth Ming emperor in a line extending back two hundred years to the dynasty's despotic founder, Zhu Yuanzhang, the Hongwu emperor. Zhu Yijun would go on to become the longest-reigning of these fourteen, occupying the throne until his death in 1620 and thus presiding over China during the years marking the Ming dynasty's final slide into morbidity, where its ultimate demise—in 1644 as it would turn out—was only a matter of time.

The young emperor's court officials must at first have regarded him with a certain measure of foreboding, for his recent progenitors were less than perfect monarchs. His granduncle, the fox-faced Zhengde emperor (reigned 1506–1521), had been much too energetic and inde-pendent for what by then had become a highly stylized and tradition-bound monarchy. He played games, drank, galloped about on horse-back, refused sedan chairs and walked, left the confines of the Forbidden City, ignored protocol, and in general kept his officials in a constant state of apprehension. The Wanli emperor's grandfather, the Jiajing emperor, became intolerant of criticism and increasingly dis-tracted from his royal duties during his long reign (1522–1566), surrounding himself with toadies and yes-men as he searched for an elixir to prolong his life. The Wanli emperor's father, the Longqing emperor (1567–1572), would not or could not even make the prescribed utterances during court audiences. For the first year of his reign he just sat on the throne like a statue while his secretaries spoke for him. After that even these appearances were cancelled.

It was thus with great joy and relief that the young Wanli emperor's courtiers came to perceive in him the makings of a great monarch. He took to his lessons in calligraphy, history, and the classics with delightful precocity and obediently tried to embody all the virtues as they were explained to him. In one particularly promising episode the eleven-year-old boy-emperor composed and wrote in a remarkably steady hand "Present Me to Goodness and Purify Me."[18] Yes, here was the makings of a virtuous and benevolent sovereign, just the sort of sage-king Ming China needed to restore its flagging fortunes.

During his childhood years the Wanli emperor was allowed to perform only a few simple royal functions. Until he came of age, Senior Grand Secretary Zhang Juzheng—"Tutor Zhang" to the young emperor—held the actual reigns of power. Zhang ran a tight ship. He did not countenance the overspending and ponderous inefficiency that had become the accepted norm in China. He cut palace expenditures on food and clothing and decorations, cancelled extravagant court functions, and took great pains to teach the young Wanli emperor to be frugal. He insisted that *all* taxes be collected, with no excuses, and with the resulting proceeds refilled government granaries and coffers. He dismissed officials suspected of profiteering, replaced inefficient governors and ministers with innovative newcomers, and expected every member of the government to lead the sort of austere lifestyle that their Confucian ideals demanded.

Zhang also tried to do something about the woeful state of the military. Knowing that the army's decline was due in part to the low caliber of its officer corps, he promoted capable, well-educated men to high command, and gave them the autonomy they needed to achieve results.

One such man was Qi Jiguang, probably the most successful general in the entire Ming dynasty. Qi was born into a hereditary military family in 1528. He was given a well-rounded education for the times, covering both the classics and the military arts, and inherited the rank of assistant commander upon his father's death in 1544. Qi was an intelligent and able officer and was soon given important commands, most notably in the eastern and southern coastal regions then being devastated by wokou pirate raids.

It was in his campaigns against these marauders that Qi Jiguang began to form his ideas on how to mold an untrained, undisciplined rabble into an effective fighting force. His reforms would never affect the entire Ming military; only top officials wielded that sort of overriding influence. What Qi was allowed to do was to recruit and train essentially his own personal army, a crack expeditionary force that the court could dispatch to wherever it was needed. To build this force Qi relied first upon discipline—iron discipline. He made numerous offenses punishable by having one's ears cut off, while disobedience or cowardice in battle were met with instant death. Training was equally essential, for as Qi astutely observed, even experienced soldiers rarely are able to put more than twenty percent of their fighting skill to use in the confusion of battle, while those who could utilize fifty percent "would have no rival."[19]

Qi also devised battle tactics that were cautious, heavy on defense, and ultimately very effective. In the 1550s he came up with something he called the "mandarin duck formation," a twelve-man unit consisting of a leader, shield men, lancers, fork men, a cook, and four men wielding a crude weapon of Qi's own devising: a length of bamboo with its leafy branches left intact to ensnare enemy swords and spears. The unit trained and fought as a team, protecting each other and above all the leader, all the while advancing slowly but inexorably against the enemy. Qi later improved upon this formation by devising a "battle wagon," a huge, two-wheeled cart, protected on all sides by wooden screens, which operated in some ways like a crude tank. Each was manned by twenty soldiers. Ten formed an assault party, four armed with muskets and the rest with swords, spears, and shields. As they advanced, the ten men remaining in the wagon would push it along, so that the assault team was never more than ten meters from safety. When the enemy attacked, all the men would fall back inside the wagon, where they would fight with their personal weapons and their *fo-lang-chi* guns, a crude, small-bore cannon so named because it had been introduced into China by the *farangi*, the Portuguese, a century before. For large-scale engagements, these wagons could be drawn into an impenetrable fighting square, with cavalry units sheltered within.[20]

With his emphasis on discipline, training, and cautious, well-thought-out tactics, General Qi Jiguang was instrumental in the 1550s and 1560s in quelling pirate raids along the coast. He was then reassigned to the northern frontier, where he reorganized defenses, repaired the Great Wall, built observation towers and training centers, and generally helped keep the Mongols in check. Finally, in 1574, having never lost an engagement in thirty years of service, he was promoted under Zhang Juzheng's tutelage to senior commissioner in chief, the highest military rank the Ming court had to give. For the next several years Qi was regarded as a hero, a general who knew how to train men, win battles, and get results. His manuals on tactics and training were widely read, and his collected works published and republished.

Then, in 1582, Senior Grand Secretary Zhang Juzheng died at the age of fifty-seven. During his tenure in office he had stepped on toes, threatened vested interests, and made many enemies in his drive to force efficiency upon the ponderous bulk of China. This enormous anti-Zhang faction now rose up to tear his reputation apart and undo everything he had done. From a modern perspective this might appear a disappointing and counterproductive backlash, for surely Zhang was the sort of man China needed to whip it into shape. Many of Zhang's contemporaries, however, did not see it that way. They regarded his reforms as upsetting the balance of things in the Celestial Empire, where inefficiency was the imperfect but unavoidable state where equilibrium lay. In demanding that *everything* work properly, Zhang was asking for more than the country could reasonably give. When he died, therefore, and the iron grip of his "hard policies" was loosened, China slipped inevitably and inexorably back into the comfortable inefficiency that had existed in the past. Tax collection once again became haphazard. Palace spending rose. Government coffers ran dry. Morally upstanding but administratively inept officials dismissed by Zhang were recalled, while those he had favored were demoted or purged.

Among them was General Qi Jiguang. His victories, his books, his success in building a formidable fighting force from the ground up all counted for nothing with his protector now dead and gone. He was a Zhang man, and so he had to go. The ailing general was turned out of office in 1583. His wife left him soon after and, with no income or personal wealth, he spent his declining years in poverty and unhappiness. Qi finally died on January 17, 1588, reportedly so poor he could not afford even medical care. By 1590 his mandarin duck formation was a forgotten curiosity and his formidable battle wagons an idle dream buried in unread books.

And what of the Wanli emperor, that promising young monarch who was now an obese, full-grown man with a deep, authoritative voice? The death of Grand Secretary Zhang Juzheng, his tutor, his mentor, and in many ways his father, changed him entirely. Anti-Zhang officials wasted no time in running to the throne with stories of Zhang's perfidy and succeeded in deflating the emperor's high regard for the man— perhaps too well. Zhang, he learned, was a hypocrite. He had insisted that everyone, including the emperor, live frugally while he himself resided in a grand mansion heaped with wealth. Zhang was a tyrant. He had dismissed virtuous men from office who should now be reinstated. Zhang was a fornicator. He had brought on his own demise through excessive sexual activity, bucking up his flagging libido with exotic aphrodisiacs.[21]

For the Wanli emperor it was devastating. That this man who had filled his head with so much talk of virtue was himself so clearly not virtuous led the emperor first to question the moral lessons of his youth and then cynically to reject them. After his austere childhood he now became greedy and grasping, building a personal fortune with the aid of his inner coterie of corrupt court eunuchs. He would no longer countenance the remonstrances of civil officials. When they criticized him in proper Confucian fashion for his overspending and inattention to duty, he had them beaten. When he perceived that some ambitious officials actually courted such beatings for the career-enhancing moral stripes it earned them, he simply ignored everything they said and wrote and sat in the Forbidden City doing nothing. He would not attend audiences. He would not approve appointments. He shirked his royal responsibilities and whiled away the days. It is hard to fully appreciate just how much frustration and anguish this caused for the men trying to keep the government running without the emperor's participation, but there are some telling glimpses in the historical record. On one occasion a grand secretary, after being repeatedly denied an audience with the emperor to discuss some important issue, became so agitated upon finally being admitted into the imperial presence that he lost control of his bladder and fell into a coma for several days.[22]

The Wanli emperor's contrariness reached its zenith in the late 1580s, when he refused to allow his firstborn son by his unloved empress to be installed as heir, insisting instead that a younger son by a favored concubine succeed him on the throne. At first he simply put off the succession ceremony year after year. Eventually, however, the issue was forced into the open and a deadlock occurred, one that the Ming government had neither the legal means to break nor the classical precedents to understand. This crisis of succession was the overriding concern of the Chinese court and civil service at the beginning of the 1590s. It was more serious than famines and droughts, economic woes and factional strife. It was more threatening than minority rebellions in the west, mutinies in the army, and renewed border incursions by the Mongols to the north.

As for developments in a faraway island nation called Japan, inhabited by a people referred to disparagingly in the Chinese dynastic histories as "dwarfs," they were scarcely given a thought in Beijing. As far as it was concerned, Japan was a tributary state of long standing—but not a very important one, since its territory was not contiguous to China's—with an on-again, off-again record of tribute missions dating back to at least the early seventh century. At the moment relations seemed to be off. No Japanese mission had arrived since 1549, bringing to a close a century and a half of friendly intercourse.[23] The Japanese currently seemed to be caught up in some sort of internal struggle, and the shogun, who the Ming emperor had invested with the title King of Japan back in 1401, was no longer in control. When they eventually managed to put their house in order, they would undoubtedly return to their proper place in the Chinese-centered world and resume the noble task of trying to emulate Sino-civilization.

In the meantime they hardly bore thinking about.

CHAPTER 3

A Son Called *Sute:*
"Thrown Away"

TOYOTOMI HIDEYOSHI, the indomitable conqueror, the irresistible unifier, the supreme despot of all Japan, was at heart a family man, a tenderhearted, affectionate, and sentimental provider who often fretted about the health and safety of his loved ones. Indeed, attending to his family circle seems to have fulfilled a longing in the man that went at least as deep as his desire to rule Japan and in turn the world.

Hideyoshi clearly idolized his mother, known to us only by her courtly title O-Mandokoro, and in his private correspondence constantly advised on and fussed over her health and happiness. In a letter to his wife in 1589 he observed that "if O-Mandokoro is kept in a small place, she may begin to feel depressed, and so please take care of her for the time being. But if [she is in a large place and] there are draughts, she will catch a chill in such surroundings and so you must not do that."[1] And in 1590, writing directly to his mother: "Go to some place and thus amuse yourself—and, please, become young once more. I beg you to do this."[2]

Hideyoshi exhibited such tender concern for many in his family circle. In a 1589 letter to his wife, the Lady Kita-no-Mandokoro, otherwise known as O-Ne, he wrote, "Take care of your health and have your usual meals in order not to make me feel anxious about you. Don't be careless."[3] And again, "I am always longing to have good news of you. . . . And I think that it would be better if you were less constipated, so why don't you take an enema? . . . I shall wait for a better report concerning your health and telling me how long it takes the enema to have its effect."[4] In an undated letter addressed to his adopted daughter Go-Hime he wrote, "I would like to know if you are in good spirits and if you have been taking more *kuko* [boxthorn] medicine. As I am so very fond of you, I invite you to come and live in Himeji soon. I want to supply you with everything you need, especially a palanquin if you want one."[5] And to his concubine Tomoji, "We were recently together for two or three days and enjoyed ourselves. I expect you were annoyed because we just stayed at home. Be of good cheer and take care of yourself so that you don't fall ill."[6] Hideyoshi clearly enjoyed the role of protector, patriarch, and benevolent provider. It was the inner world behind the castles, the armies, and the trappings of power that made his life complete.

And yet there was something missing. Hideyoshi had no son.

In 1589 Hideyoshi was in his early fifties and was becoming by his own reckoning something of a senior citizen, complaining often in his letters of failing eyesight, poor appetite, fatigue, and the white hairs on his head that were too numerous to pluck out. He was at an age where a great man might begin to think of resting on his laurels, assuming the comfortable role of patriarch while his sons carried on the more strenuous work of securing the power of his house and the greatness of the name of Toyotomi for centuries to come. But Hideyoshi did not have any sons. He had been married to O-Ne for twenty-eight years, but the union had produced no children. He had taken several concubines over the preceding two decades, but they too had failed him. One might indeed speculate that this lack of an heir may have been one of his motivations for wanting to conquer China. Without a son to carry on his name and inherit his greatness, he perhaps felt a driving need to do all the work himself, within his own lifetime, to make himself and his house so great that it would carry on irresistibly even after his death, even without an heir.

And then a miracle happened. One of his concubines, Yodogimi, announced that she was pregnant. In June of 1589 she bore a child, a son named Tsurumatsu. Hideyoshi was beside himself with joy, but pretended not to show it. To have done so would have tempted the gods to take away from him what he cherished most. The baby was therefore publicly referred to as *Sute*, meaning "abandoned" or "thrown away," and Hideyoshi struggled to hide the happiness he felt.

By all accounts he did not succeed. When he was with the boy he could not resist showering him with kisses, cradling him in his arms, and dandling him on his knee. And when his campaigns of unification took him away from his "young prince," he worried incessantly about the child's health and safety and longed to return, as seen in this letter written to Yodogimi from the siege at Odawara in 1590:

> You have sent me no word by letter and I find myself very anxious. Is the young prince getting bigger and bigger? It is very important to give strict orders to your men that they should keep your place safe from fire, and that they and their subordinates should not lapse into disorder. Around the 20th I shall certainly see you and embrace the young prince, and on that night I'll let you sleep at my side: so wait for me.
>
>   Sincerely,
>   Denka
>
> I repeat: you must tell them to keep the young prince from catching a chill; you must not be careless about anything. [7]

But little Tsurumatsu was a sickly boy. He had been weak from birth, and finally died in September of 1591. It was a terrible blow to Hideyoshi—to have tasted the joys of fatherhood and then to have his young prince snatched away at the age of only two. He could bring down castles and force powerful daimyo like the Hojo of Odawara to bow before him. But to protect this one little boy, the jewel in his family circle, was beyond even his great power.

Four months after Tsurumatsu's death Hideyoshi accepted the inevitable that he would never have a son of his own and named his twenty-three-year-old nephew Hidetsugu his adopted son and heir. He passed the title of kampaku, imperial regent, on to the young man, and became himself the taiko, the retired imperial regent.

It was perhaps not a coincidence that Hideyoshi now entered into a frenzy of activity for the coming invasion of Korea. With no biological son to carry on his name and ensure his greatness, he would have to accomplish it all himself in the few years he had left. He ordered work to begin on a castle at Nagoya on the coast of Kyushu, the point of embarkation from the country's southern tip. Requisitions were issued to all the daimyo to raise and arm troops. Stores and weapons were stockpiled. Maps were prepared. Ships were built and manned.

Finally, just eight months after the death of his beloved Tsurumatsu, the gargantuan task was done. Hideyoshi's army of invasion was ready to sail.

CHAPTER 4

Korea: Highway to the Prize

FROM AT LEAST THE SEVENTH CENTURY A.D. the Japanese have
referred to their island nation as Nippon, "Rising Sun," a reference, of
course, to the east. It is not the sort of name that would occur to a
people residing in Japan itself, for from their perspective "the east" is
nothing but the vast expanse of the Pacific Ocean. Where, then, did
Nippon come from? It almost certainly came from the Asian mainland,
from where Japan does indeed lie to the east, in the direction of the
rising sun. Specifically, it came from Korea.[1]

By the time the Chinese started recording history around the fourth
century B.C., a handful of small states are found to be occupying the
Korean Peninsula, foremost among them Old Choson, a kingdom with
roots extending back to a legendary founder named Tangun, who
established his royal residence near present-day Pyongyang some time
before 2,000 B.C.[2] By the fourth century A.D. these various rival states
had coalesced into three large kingdoms: Koguryo in the north, Silla in
the center and southeast, and Paekche in the southwest. During the next
two and a half centuries, a span known as the Three Kingdoms period,
these three states would combine Chinese statecraft, writing, science,
and thought with indigenous elements to create a unique Korean
culture—a process that was occurring to one degree or another in all
those states directly bordering what was then the emerging Middle
Kingdom. By the early eighth century, Silla had eclipsed Koguryo and
Paekche to gain control of most of the peninsula, uniting Korea for the
first time into a single political and cultural entity allied to Tang-dynasty

China. Silla was by all accounts a wealthy, refined, and outward-looking state, praised by travelers from as far away as India and the Middle East as a land of wonders and regarded by Koreans today as a cultural high point in their history. It was reportedly such an attractive place that many Arabs who visited there settled down and never returned home. As one Arab historian explained in 947, "Seldom has a stranger who has come there from Iraq or another country left it afterwards. So healthy is the air there, so pure the water, so fertile the soil and so plentiful all good things."[3]

By this time a unique culture was also emerging in Japan from a similar interplay of indigenous tastes and elements with foreign influences passing from Korea and China, particularly between the fourth and eighth centuries, when a significant influx of immigrants arrived on the islands from the kingdoms of Koguryo, Silla, and Paekche. The resulting native culture would evince a greater degree of selectivity in its borrowings from China than was the case in Korea, a luxury afforded the Japanese by their relative isolation offshore. They borrowed those aspects of mainland civilization that they considered useful or aesthetically pleasing, adapted others, and disregarded the rest (much as would be done with Western civilization starting in the late nineteenth century). This process of selective borrowing and adaptation would lead Japan and Korea to develop fundamentally different attitudes toward their giant neighbor to the west. While the Koreans believed themselves to be culturally equal to the Chinese because they shared in the greatness of Chinese civilization, the Japanese would come to regard the natural beauty and subtle shading of their own culture as surpassing China's with all its gaudy colors and its tedious emphasis on maintaining a high moral tone. It is difficult to put a date on when this sense of superiority emerged, but by the advent of the Imjin War it was definitely in place.[4]

This process of cultural identities diverging in Korea and Japan was mirrored in the political sphere. In Japan, political institutions initially developed along lines similar to Korea with the establishment in the seventh century of a centralized government based on the Chinese model—although unlike Korea, Japan's government only managed to extend its control over the nation's heartland, leaving much of the periphery to regional lords. Then in the early tenth century a feudal warrior class came to dominate the country and its emperor, giving rise to a line of shoguns and then sengoku civil war and lasting until the fall of the Tokugawa shogunate in 1867. During this long period of military rule the Japanese would come to reject the idea that China was the ruler of all it surveyed and eventually to believe that their own island nation, the "Land of the Gods," was just as important in the grand scheme of things. The Japanese were thus not nearly as accommodating as the Koreans when messages arrived from China at the start of the Ming dynasty inviting their submission. "Heaven and earth are vast," came the Japanese reply. "[T]hey are not monopolized by one ruler." Such defiance left the Ming incensed. "You stupid eastern barbarians!" wrote the Hongwu emperor in 1380. "Your king and courtiers are not acting correctly . . . ; you are haughty and disloyal; you permit your subjects to do evil. Will this not inevitably bring disaster upon you?"[5] The Ashikaga shoguns would eventually enter into a tenuous relationship with the Ming for whatever trading rights and legitimacy they could squeeze out of the deal, but their expressions of loyalty would never be very heartfelt.

In Korea, Chinese-style government continued to evolve as the Silla dynasty gave way to the Koryo (918–1392), a government eventually controlled by a civilian aristocracy of scholar-bureaucrats picked from the *yangban* upper class. Korea's location on the continent meanwhile continued to expose it to strong gravitational forces from China, drawing the peninsula into a subordinate relationship with its giant neighbor that would attain its most mature form in the Choson dynasty (1392–1910), which succeeded the Koryo. Throughout the fifteenth and sixteenth centuries Choson Korea was Ming China's most loyal vassal state, and was in turn regarded by the Chinese as their most civilized neighbor. It was a status in which the Koreans took great pride. They did not consider themselves to be fully equal to China. What country could presume to be equal to the Celestial Empire? But they did share in China's greatness by virtue of the fact that they had accepted its civilizing influences. The Koreans based their culture on Chinese culture. They studied Chinese history and the writings of Chinese sages. They modeled their court after the Chinese court, shaped their government administration along Chinese lines, and clothed their officials in Chinese robes. Their kings received legitimacy from the Chinese emperor in the form of the Mandate of Heaven. They followed the Chinese calendar, thereby recognizing the emperor's role as mediator between heaven and earth. They made Chinese morals their morals, Chinese laws their laws, and considered the Chinese mode of conduct superior to anything else. "[We made] our customs like that of the Flowery Land," stated the *Tong-mong-sun-seup*, a cornerstone text of a classical Korean education, "so that Chinese themselves praise us saying 'Korea is little China.'"[6]

Korea did not regard its cultural proximity to China as placing it above other nations—at least not diplomatically. Officially the Chinese emperor stood at the top of the heap as the ultimate power in the universe; the kings of Korea, Japan, Java, the Ryukyu Islands, Cambodia, Thailand, and all other tributary states were accorded positions of equal status below him, and non-tributary states scarcely entered the picture. Unofficially, however, Korea's worldview was more finely graded. China, the "civilized center," of course came first. Korea, the "small civilized center," came second, and all other nations fell further down the ladder according to their perceived level of Chinese cultural attainment.[7]

The Japanese did not fare well in this culturally determined Korean worldview. They were referred to deprecatingly by both the Chinese and the Koreans in their dynastic histories as "dwarfs" and were considered to be beyond the pale of civilization. This fact was confirmed for the Koreans time and again over the centuries during diplomatic exchanges with these uncouth neighbors across the sea. Korean envoys to the shogun's court would be subjected to what the Koreans considered inappropriate and even insulting seating arrangements and would observe a general ignorance of Chinese-style protocol. Japanese envoys to Seoul would conduct themselves in ways the Koreans found rude and at times arrogant. Japanese written communications would often not follow correct Sinocentric forms of address and date. The Japanese emperor, for example, would be referred to as "emperor"—the title reserved solely for the Son of Heaven in Beijing—rather than "king," an amazing presumption in the eyes of the Koreans for a ruler who could not even assert control over his own domain. The Koreans also took note of the often splintered state of Japan. There seemed never to be a single figure in overall control of the islands, raising the question of whether it was a nation at all. They were always fighting among themselves, acting as pirates toward their neighbors, and generally favoring violence and warfare over good conduct and peace. All in all they were an uncivilized, dangerous, arrogant people whom the Koreans, even more than the Chinese, regarded with particular disdain.[8]

While Korea looked down upon Japan from its lofty perch as "little China," it did not in turn kowtow slavishly to China from a corresponding position of abject servitude. Its secondary role in the Chinese universe was more about respect—the respect of a younger brother for his admired elder sibling. Korea expressed this respect by regularly sending tribute missions to the Chinese court beginning in the Unified Silla dynasty (681–935). The envoys presented their tribute, swore Korea's loyalty and devotion to China, observed all the necessary protocol, and made all the required gestures of submission. The Chinese for their part treated these envoys as honored guests, assured them of Korea's special relationship with China, and sent them on their way laden with "gifts" to take back to their king—turning the political exercise into a significant form of trade.[9] And for the most part that was it until the next Korean mission was dispatched. It was a cheap price to pay for the benefits each side derived. By paying tribute and expressing their loyal submission, the kings of Korea received the Mandate of Heaven from the Chinese emperor and thus legitimacy for themselves, and ensured that China would otherwise leave their kingdom alone. As for the Chinese, maintaining a tributary system with Korea and other neighboring kingdoms served to demonstrate the legitimacy of their own rule and made their empire more secure by turning potential enemy nations into a protective ring of buffer states.[10] It was a strategy that called for a light touch, for if the tributary relationship was made too onerous, no border state would want to enter into it, and if China was too heavy-handed, friendly buffers would soon rebel. From the Tang dynasty onward China for the most part maintained that light touch. Indeed, except in times of uncertainty or crisis it typically had no desire to meddle in the affairs of its tributary states so long as it was satisfied that they remained loyal.

By the late sixteenth century Korea had been a tributary state of China throughout most of the preceding one thousand years. It was a relationship that was not without its ups and downs. Things tended to be good when the Middle Kingdom was united under a native Chinese dynasty, for example the Tang (618–907), Song (960–1279) and Ming (1368–1644). Envoy missions were regularly exchanged, cordial relations maintained, and beyond that they left each other to their own affairs. During times of upheaval, however, relations often soured, especially when non-Chinese invaded China and established dynasties of their own.

Such was the case with the Mongol invasion of China beginning in the early 1200s and the subsequent rise of the Yuan dynasty (1271–1368). Between 1231 and 1258 the successors of Genghis Khan sent their mounted hordes six times against Korea, then under the Koryo dynasty, and eventually forced it to turn away from the declining Song dynasty and enter into a much more servile relationship with themselves. They then set their sights on Japan. The Koreans were required to build and man three hundred ships for the Mongols' first, unsuccessful, invasion attempt of 1274. For the second invasion in 1281 the Koreans were compelled to contribute nine hundred ships of double the capacity, and fifteen thousand men. But this too failed. As the gargantuan Mongol-Korean armada approached the Japanese coast, a typhoon blew in from the west, grinding vessel against vessel until the roiling sea was a mass of wreckage and floating bodies. For the Japanese it was a miracle, a heaven-sent intervention they would remember as the *kamikaze*, the divine wind. For the Mongols, it was the beginning of the end of their dream of world conquest.

After the failure of the invasion of Japan, the Mongol empire, and with it the recently established Yuan dynasty, began a slow and inexorable decline. The Yuan nevertheless maintained a tight grip on Korea for the next several decades. They exacted heavy tribute payments, exercised direct dominion over Korean territory, interfered in Korean politics, and in general conducted themselves in ways that ran counter to what Korea expected from the "Flowery Land." When the Yuan dynasty began to crumble in the 1350s, therefore, the Koreans cut off tribute relations, ceased using the Yuan calendar, stopped wearing Yuan court dress and hairstyles, and moved to reclaim formerly Yuan-dominated territory, for in the words of one Korean commentator, "Heaven dislikes the virtue of the barbarians." The new Ming dynasty, officially inaugurated in 1368, was then hailed as coming "from mid-heaven, in communication with sages and spirits of the past."[11] The Koreans readily entered into a tributary relationship with it, hopeful of a return to the sort of autonomy their kingdom had enjoyed during the enlightened Song dynasty that had preceded the Yuan.

Ming–Korean relations got off to a rocky start. The newly enthroned Hongwu emperor, anxious to establish his dynasty on a secure footing and consequently distrustful of all around, harbored suspicions about the Koreans throughout his thirty-year reign. Did they secretly remain loyal to the Mongols? Were they forging anti-Ming alliances with the Jurchen tribes of the east? These fears were not entirely unfounded. While it had no alliance with the Jurchen—Korea wanted only to drive them out of the northern territory they had seized during the declining years of Mongol power—there was indeed a significant pro-Yuan faction in Korea made up of those who had prospered under Mongol rule. Political affairs in Koryo, moreover, had become rather compli-cated by this point, for with the succession of the eleven-year-old King U in 1375, real power in Korea fell to the military men behind the throne, men whose loyalties the Ming court had no way of knowing. All this uncertainty placed a good deal of strain on relations between Ming China and Koryo Korea. Korean envoys were not always welcomed by the imperial court; some were even turned away at the border. The Chinese even went so far as to establish a garrison in northern Korea in 1388 on the grounds that the Koreans were failing to keep the Jurchen under control, an unpardonable breach of conduct in the eyes of many in the Koryo court.

It was this border incursion that proved the flash point that would bring the already weakened Koryo dynasty to an end. The power behind the throne, General Choe Yong, angrily ordered the Korean army north to rout the Chinese garrison and send it back across the Yalu River. The general heading this army, a fifth-generation officer and fellow power behind the throne named Yi Song-gye, opposed this anti-Ming expedition and revolted. Turning his forces back against the Koryo capital of Kaesong, he ousted General Choe and King U and seized control. Yi ruled the country for the next four years through a series of puppet kings, then ascended the throne himself in 1392 and established a new dynasty, with a new capital in Hanyang, later known as Seoul.

The first concern of Yi Song-gye, known to posterity as King Taejo, was to gain legitimacy for his dynasty. For this he turned to China. He dispatched an envoy to the Chinese capital to proclaim his succession and to swear loyalty to the Ming emperor. He solicited the emperor's advice before selecting the ancient name of Choson, "morning calm," for his new dynasty, a reference to the kingdom that had existed on the peninsula at the dawn of recorded history. He also began sending tribute missions west as evidence of his respect for the Celestial Empire and of his desire to resume *sadae* (serving the great) relations. Finally, in 1403, Choson Korea received formal investiture from the Hongwu emperor's successor, and with that, friendly relations between the two nations were restored. Korea once again acknowledged China as the center of the universe, and China in turn acknowledged its loyal and civilized vassal as "different from all other states."[12] As the relationship matured, Korea would send three or four embassies to China each year, while the Chinese reciprocated with an annual average of less than one.[13]

While Korea cultivated its sadae relationship with China into the fifteenth century, toward other countries it pursued a policy of *kyorin*, "neighborly relations." This was an outgrowth of the longstanding Chinese policy of *wai i chi mi*, which originally meant "to control and restrain wild horses and cows."[14] To both the Chinese and the Koreans, barbarian peoples, like wild animals, did not respond best to brute force. They needed to be eased into the Chinese-centered universe through appeasement and conciliation, where they might then be tamed through exposure to civilizing influences. For the Koreans this approach was also highly expedient during the early years of the Choson dynasty. Until the dynasty was firmly established and its armed forces built up to some semblance of strength, King Taejo and his immediate successors had little choice but to buy peace with appeasement.

There were two neighboring groups that put Korea's kyorin policy to the test during the early years of the Choson dynasty: the Jurchen to the north and the wako pirates to the south. The Jurchen were a tribal people from Manchuria who had taken the opportunity of declining Mongol power to push their way down into the northern reaches of the Korea. They relied on Korean grain and cloth and tools for their existence and were equally prepared to obtain them through raids or through trade, whichever proved most convenient. During much of the latter Koryo dynasty the Koreans had attempted to drive these people back into Manchuria, mostly with little success. King Taejo chose a different course. He would not risk weakening his own recently established dynasty by continuing to fight them. He opted instead for appeasement. Since the Jurchen needed Korean food and goods to survive, he set up frontier markets and allowed them to trade for them peacefully. Jurchen who had settled in northern Korea were not driven out. A line a garrison forts was instead established along the Yalu and Tumen Rivers, fixing Korea's northern boundaries as they remain to this day, and the Jurchen south of this border were accepted and naturalized as citizens of Choson and were in time integrated into Korean society. Jurchen leaders, meanwhile, were bought off with court rank and government positions. They were invited to Seoul to pay their respects to the king and engage in civilizing tributary relations, and not incidentally to profit from the de facto trade that such tribute missions entailed. They were, in short, given a stake in maintaining Korea's security, in return for which they used their influence to keep their people peaceful and under control.

King Taejo's policy of appeasement toward the Jurchen was largely successful. It secured Choson's northern border and bought his dynasty the peace it needed to gain legitimacy and establish itself. The Jurchen never entirely gave up their raiding ways, however, and would eventually reemerge as a significant annoyance in the latter half of the sixteenth century.

The wako pirates—waegu to the Koreans—were a much bigger problem. They arose from the Matsuura region of Kyushu and the offshore islands of Tsushima, Iki, and Goto, areas of marginal farmland and limited options. As a Korean envoy to these regions would later observe, "[T]he people's dwellings [here] are miserable; land is tight and, moreover, utterly barren, so that they do not pursue agriculture and can scarcely escape starvation; thus they engage in banditry, being of a wicked and violent cast."[15] The influence of these Japanese brigands eventually spread all along Kyushu's northern coasts and east to the Inland Sea. Then, in 1222, they turned their attention to Korea. From hidden lairs on Tsushima, less than thirty nautical miles off the Korean coast, they enjoyed several years of unopposed pillaging, until the Mongol invasion rendered the peninsula a more dangerous and thus less attractive target. A second surge in wako activity, this time not just in Korea but all along the Chinese coast and involving an increasing number of Chinese renegades, occurred with the decline of the Yuan and Koryo dynasties in the late fourteenth century. The Koreans were particularly hard-pressed this time to deal with the raiders, for they had not yet rebuilt their navy following the departure of the Mongols, who had forbidden them from possessing fighting ships. The wako pirates consequently owned the seas between Korea and Japan. Their dominance was so complete that they were able to seize entire fleets of cargo ships carrying tax rice from Korea's southern agricultural provinces to the capital of Kaesong in the north. When the Koreans began transporting grain overland, the wako simply moved inland to loot government granaries. Except for one setback in 1350, when Korean ground forces confronted the invaders and lopped off three hundred heads, the wako raided and pillaged at will. On occasion they arrived in fleets of more than three hundred ships, launching what amounted to small invasions of the seemingly defenseless Korean Peninsula. Indeed, its inability to deal with these depredations was a contributing factor in the Koryo dynasty's eventual demise.

As he had with the Jurchen, King Taejo sought to gain control over the wako by using a carrot rather than a stick. It was his only real option. Koryo Korea had already proven itself incapable of resisting them by force of arms. They would therefore have to be quelled through appeasement. "[I]f we attend on them with courtesy and nourish them with generosity," explained the aforementioned Korean envoy, ". . . then the pirates will all submit." Pirates were accordingly encouraged to settle down and become farmers in Korea's fertile southern provinces, where they could in time be absorbed into Korean society. Influential wako leaders were granted court titles, land, incomes, and the promise of a stable, comfortable life, with the understanding that they would guide their followers away from raiding and into more peaceful pursuits.

They were also offered the opportunity of free trade. This was a tremendous incentive to the wako to give up their raiding ways, the chance to reap substantial profits without risk to life and limb. Prior to this time the Neo-Confucian courts of both China and Korea had taken a dim view of commerce and profit, limiting officially sanctioned international trade in East Asia to the exchange of goods that took place within the context of tribute missions. China would adhere to this policy with regard to Japan for the next century and a half while relations between the two countries lasted, receiving only three ships on each of the sporadic tribute missions sent by the Ashikaga shoguns. Beyond this all trade that passed between China and Japan—and there was a fair bit of it—was handled illegally by smugglers and pirates. For King Taejo to throw Korea's doors open to international trade was therefore a remarkable change in policy, a significant break with Chinese precedent, and an indication of just how deep his concern was for the survival of his dynasty during its first tenuous years.

And for the most part it worked. Aside from one or two relatively minor setbacks—for example a resurgence of wako activity in 1419 sparked by a famine on Tsushima—early Choson's appeasement policy successfully quelled the pirates of western Japan, buying the dynasty the time and the peace it needed to establish itself and ensure its survival.

By the late 1410s, however, the Koreans had had enough of open doors. The number of Japanese flooding into their country had reached alarming proportions. The cost of free trade had become insupportable, for as the host nation Korea was obligated to cover all the expenses for each and every Japanese "envoy." Now that the Choson dynasty was established and its legitimacy confirmed, moreover, the need for free trade as a guarantor of stability had diminished, and Korea's Neo-Confucian government became anxious to once again bring this necessary evil under control. After all, trade was clearly something the Japanese needed more than the Koreans. They were sending more ships to Korea than Korea was sending to Japan. They were more eager to acquire Korean cotton, ceramics, scriptures, and bells than the Koreans were to acquire things Japanese. In the course of the fifteenth century, therefore, Korea's wako policy, and consequently its Japan policy, shifted away from free trade and wholesale appeasement and increasingly toward limited access and firm control.

To achieve this the Koreans needed allies at the source of the problem: Japan. They knew that both the Japanese emperor and the shogun could be of little help in controlling pirate and trade activity originating from Kyushu and its offshore islands; their power did not extend much beyond central Honshu. The Koreans turned instead directly to the regional lords of western Japan, in particular of Tsushima. This rocky, mountainous island situated halfway between Korea and Japan had long served as a stepping-stone for traffic between the two countries and had long relied upon trade with Korea for its survival. Its inhabitants were therefore well acquainted with Korean customs and language and had cultural and diplomatic ties to the peninsula that were nearly as strong as its ties to Japan. The Koreans for their part considered the island to have originally belonged to them, a valueless offshore possession known as Daema-do, which had subsequently been inhabited "by Japanese who were rejected by Japan and by people with nowhere to go."[16] Beginning in the early fifteenth century the Korean court began to move Tsushima further into its orbit by co-opting the island's dominant family, the So, with the grant of official court rank, a regular income, and the right to send fifty ships a year to Korea for trade. In return the So used their authority to control all Korea-bound traffic and to suppress the wako. Henceforth any ship seeking access to Korea had to obtain appropriate documentation from the So, for which the family was free to charge whatever levy they saw fit. The Koreans, meanwhile, restricted trade access to just the three ports of Ungchon, Tongnae, and Ulsan on the peninsula's southeastern tip. Any ship attempting to land elsewhere would be considered a pirate vessel and subject to attack. Any ship caught without appropriate documents from the So would be similarly suspect. Three routes north from the coast to the capital of Seoul were also designated specifically for Japanese use. In this manner the Koreans managed during the course of the fifteenth century to funnel all trade through Tsushima, the "Three Ports" (*sampo*), and the three designated routes, where it could be more easily monitored, limited, and controlled.

Trade relations with Japan were not broken off entirely, however. That would have abrogated Korea's kyorin policy toward the Japanese, still regarded by Seoul as essential for appeasing these uncivilized, violent, and potentially dangerous people. The flow of goods between the two countries therefore remained significant, albeit controlled. But the Koreans remained uncomfortable with all this seaborne traffic and economic penetration, and were constantly looking for reasons to reduce the flow of commerce as the Japanese sought ways to open it up. The growing presence of Japanese traders in Korea, for example, would become an issue in Seoul, restrictions would be imposed, the So family on Tsushima would petition to win back lost concessions, and Seoul would eventually relent for the sake of maintaining friendly relations. A gang of pirates returning from China with room in their holds for a bit more loot would strike the Korean coast, angering Seoul into another clampdown on trade, and the So into another round of petition writing. The burgeoning number of unruly Japanese residents in the Three Ports would next become worrisome, and the process would begin again. It became a familiar tug-of-war that would last throughout the sixteenth century, until the start of the Imjin War.

By the middle of the sixteenth century Choson Korea had moved far beyond its anxiety-ridden early years, when its continued existence was by no means assured. It was still plagued occasionally by Jurchen raids in the north and by the odd pirate attack along its southern coast. But these were now aggravating annoyances, not fundamental threats. A navy existed to strike back at the pirates, army garrisons stood in readiness along the northern frontier, and behind them all stood the might of the Ming. Sixteenth-century Choson Korea, at least by its own reckoning, was established, secure, and safe.

It was also different. Choson Korea was the only nation in the history of the world to adopt Neo-Confucianism as its official state ideology. Nowhere else were the writings of Chu Xi and his predecessors studied so deeply, debated so heatedly, and followed so exclusively. By the mid sixteenth century this fact had served to mold thinking and affect developments on the Korean Peninsula to a more profound degree than was the case even in China.

The first observable result of this was an ongoing attempt on the part of the country's officialdom to suppress Buddhism. One of the distinguishing features of Chu Xi Neo-Confucianism, as opposed to the original wisdom of Confucius himself, was that it went beyond expositions on self-cultivation and virtuous conduct and into fundamental metaphysical and spiritual discussions. It was thus regarded by Korea's scholarly elite as encompassing all the wisdom that a human being required, rendering Buddhism obsolete. Beginning early in the dynasty, extraordinary attacks were launched against this competing ideology, pointing out its defects to highlight Neo-Confucianism's strengths. "Those Buddhists," ran one memorial to King Sejong in 1424,

> what kind of people are they? As eldest sons they turn against their fathers; as husbands they oppose the Son of Heaven. They break off the relationship between father and son and destroy the obligation between ruler and subject. They regard the living together of man and woman as immoral and a man's plowing and a woman's weaving as useless. They abrogate the basis of reproduction and stop the sources of dress and food.

In the same memorial another writer observed that "beasts and birds that damage grain are certainly chased away because they harm the people. Yet even though beasts and birds eat the people's food, they are nevertheless useful to the people. The Buddhists, however, sit around and eat, and there has not yet been a visible profit."[17] The kings of Choson got the message. Over the coming decades they instituted increasingly harsh measures to "chase the Buddhists away," measures that went far beyond anything attempted in Ming China. Buddhist temples were ordered closed. The number of sects was severely limited. Religious buildings and images were destroyed. Property was appropriated. Monks were forced to grow their hair and lead "productive" lives. It was mainly thanks to the efforts of a handful of devotees hidden away in remote mountain monasteries that Buddhism was able to survive at all in Korea into the modern age.

As Choson Korea's suppression of Buddhism went beyond anything seen in China, so too did its emphasis on moralistic righteousness. To enter and rise in government service, ambitious Korean males, like their Ming counterparts, had to acquire a Neo-Confucian education with a solid grounding in the classics, pass the government's triennial examination, and remain highly virtuous and moral. Of these three steps the third was the trickiest. A single charge of impropriety could ruin a man's career or derail it at the very start. Particular care had to be taken not to run afoul of the censorate, an overseeing body charged with criticizing public policy and scrutinizing the conduct of government officials, the yangban upper class, and even the king himself. One negative word from it and an official might find himself tossed out of office or up on charges for which the penalty could be death.

In the latter part of the fifteenth century this censorate came to be manned by a large number of young scholars of an extremely moralistic, intolerant, and uncompromising bent. They were virulent in their criticisms of what they perceived as the shortcomings of others, particularly of the senior officials then dominating the reins of power. In 1498 these embattled officials struck back. Using as their weapon an obscure countercharge of slander against a long-dead king, they succeeded in having five of the censorate's most prominent members put to death and two dozen others exiled or dismissed. This bloody backlash, however, did not have the intended effect. It lent the survivors within the censorate even greater moral authority, which they subsequently used to mount a counterattack. Other purges followed in 1504, 1519, and 1545, but they were of no real use. The censorate, originally intended as an instrument of moral oversight, emerged as a branch of government wielding a power all its own, while talk of morality and virtue became the language of politics, a sword of words used by ambitious men to strike out at their opponents.[18]

By the middle of the sixteenth century these developments, coupled with the increasing competition for a fixed number of government posts, had made the political arena a dangerous place. Even genuinely virtuous men had to watch their backs and count their friends. Newcomers to government office consequently sought to align themselves with influential senior men for protection, usually someone from their own county or clan. Senior officials maintained followings of faithful juniors to back them in times of trouble and to lend a hand in attacks.

The result, of course, was factions. The year of their appearance is usually given as 1575, when two clearly defined camps arose known as the "Easterners" and the "Westerners," after the locations of the homes of their respective leaders, one in Seoul's east end and the other in the west. Neither side promoted any particular ideology or point of view. Their struggle was of a more personal nature, each side striving to advance its own members in government service by discrediting its opponents or driving them out, typically in a war of words centered on some obscure point of ritual observance or moral nicety.

The career of Chong Chol, author of the poem "Song of Star Mountain" quoted at the beginning of Part One in this book, is a good example of what life was like for a government official in these politically tumultuous times. Born into the higher reaches of the upper class, Chong saw his elder brother killed and his father exiled in the purges of 1545—all before he was ten years old. He went on to achieve the top place in the civil service exam in 1561 and rose to high government office over the course of the next fifteen years. Then, in 1575, his career entered a permanently rocky stretch. As one of the more outspoken and intransigent leaders of the emerging Western faction, Chong became the target for many of the attacks launched by the competing Easterners and found it necessary to resign and retire to the countryside in 1578. He returned to office in 1580, but after just one year was impeached again for being too uncompromising. He came back for a three-year stretch in 1581, then was run out of office again, this time on charges of being too fond of wine. He managed to get reinstated yet again in 1589 during a period of supremacy of the Western faction and rose all the way to Minister of the Left in the State Council before being once again unseated in 1591. The bone of contention this time was which of the king's sons should be named crown prince and heir. In a sly bit of backroom intrigue, Eastern faction head Yi San-hae encouraged Chong to recommend a son that they considered more worthy, but who was not the king's first choice. Yi then dropped his support at the last minute and took a conciliatory stand, leaving Chong all alone in opposing the king. He was sent into exile again for that, this time into the desolate far north, leaving the Easterners behind in Seoul to reestablish themselves in power.[19]

KOREA, 1592

LIAODONG, CHINA

Willow Palisade

Tumen R.

Hoeryong

Kanggye

Kilchu

HAMGYONG

Yalu R.

Uiju

PYONGAN

Hamhung

East Sea

Taedong R.

Pyongyang

HWANGHAE

Imjin R.

KANGWON

Kaesong

Kanghwa-do

SEOUL

Han R.

KYONGGI

Yellow Sea

Chongju

Chungju

CHUNGCHONG

Sangju

KYONGSANG

Chonju

Taegu

Kyongju

Ulsan

CHOLLA

Namwon

Kwangju

Chinju

Pusan

Sachon

Sunchon

Koje-do

Tsushima

Chin-do

It was during his various stints in the political wilderness that Chong Chol found the time to write the many poems for which he is now most famous. One theme he frequently returned to was the anguish and disillusionment he felt from his experience in government service:

> Pine-tree rising beside the road,
> what is it makes you stand there?
> Relax for a little while
> and stand down into the ditch:
> Every rope-gird peasant that carries an axe
> will want to cut you down. [20]

The year was now 1589. In Europe the Elizabethan navy under Lord Howard and Sir Francis Drake had just defeated the armada of Spain, signaling the decline of Spanish power and the beginning of the rise of England. Cervantes was in the prime of life. Peter Paul Rubens was learning to paint. John Donne was a teenager. Shakespeare and Galileo were twenty-five years old. John Calvin and Michelangelo were twenty-five years dead. The potato, introduced from South America, was becoming a staple. The smoking of tobacco was catching on. The spring-driven clock had just been invented, allowing for more accurate navigation at sea. The life insurance policy was five. Shorthand was four. The microscope was still being developed for its debut in the following year. And a fellow by the name of Bernard Palissy was condemned to the Bastille for suggesting that fossils were the remains of living things. He would die there.

On the other side of the world it was the year Wanli 11 in China—the eleventh year of the reign of the Wanli emperor. Senior Grand Secretary Zhang Juzheng had been dead for seven years and most of his reforms undone, returning the Celestial Empire to its former inefficient ways. Qi Jiguang, the Ming dynasty's most successful general, the man who had quelled the wokou pirates on China's eastern seaboard and kept the Mongols in check along her northern frontier, had died the year before, penniless and forgotten. The twenty-six-year-old Wanli emperor was into his recalcitrant stage, ignoring criticisms, shirking his duties, and amassing a personal fortune while his ministers fretted and fumed.

Japan was just emerging from the throes of sengoku civil war under

Toyotomi Hideyoshi. The "Bald Rat" had issued his "sword hunt" edict the year before, removing all weapons from the hands of farmers in preparation for the coming peace. His impressive castle at Osaka was newly completed after five years of labor involving thirty thousand men. Plans were being drawn up for a second castle far to the south at a place called Nagoya (modern-day Karatsu) on the island of Kyushu. Hideyoshi soon would be spending a great deal of time there.

And in Korea a fox sat on the throne in Seoul's Kyongbok Palace. The furry little creature had somehow found its way into the place and was discovered by horrified retainers actually sprawled on the royal seat. This was a very bad omen, for in Korea the fox was considered a sinister apparition, worse than a black cat in the West. Nor was this portent the only worrisome sign. Reports of strange occurrences throughout the kingdom had been accumulating for years, each laden with hidden meaning that seemed to point to some lurking evil or looming disaster. The Chongchon River had suddenly dried up and ceased to flow for many months. The planet Mars glowed blood-red in the night sky. Meteor showers blanketed Onsong in the far northeast. A flock of sparrows on Chiri Mountain in the south reportedly divided into two groups that fought each other until every bird was dead.[21]

What evil thing did these signs foretell? Some thought they warned of the rise of factions in Korean politics. King Sonjo's dying prime minister had in fact warned him at the beginning of his reign in 1569 that "opposing factions will arise and that in their train great evils will follow." In 1579, four years after the appearance of the Eastern and Western camps, Sonjo was again warned that "All the people have taken sides in this senseless war and even a man be a criminal there are plenty who will defend him. This means the ultimate destruction of the kingdom, and the King should act as a peacemaker between the factions."[22]

King Sonjo agreed. He understood, apparently better than most of his ministers, that when men allowed factional interests to guide their actions, the kingdom as a whole was poorly served. Unfortunately, there was not a great deal he could do. Unlike the emperors of Ming China and Japan, he did not claim any sort of divine authority. This had been the case with the kings of Korea for centuries past, resulting in a particularly turbulent history in which the throne was fought over, manipulated, attacked, and usurped. Korean kings, in short, sat on a tenuous perch, and Sonjo was no exception. He did not wield enough real power or instill enough fear to command an end to factional strife; such an order might well have led to his being usurped and exiled to some remote place. No, the best he could do was to suggest and cajole, and to lead by good example.

Such was the case in the early 1580s when Sonjo spearheaded a drive to renew interest in the study of the classics. If he could only refocus the attention of his officials on the wisdom of the past, he thought, they would see the error of their ways and end their petty feuds. The initiative failed. The problem was that Sonjo's officials already knew the classics too well. They were experts at molding the musings of Confucius and Mencius and Chu Xi into clever moral arguments to support or condemn almost anything they chose. As the eminent Neo-Confucian scholar Cho Kwang-jo observed in his treatise "On the Superior Man and the Inferior Man":

> when an inferior man attacks a superior man, he may point at him and call him an inferior man. Or someone may say that a man's words and actions are incongruous, or that he is fishing for fame.... Even when a superior man who fears that an inferior man might attain his purpose argues back and forth about the inferior man's motives, perhaps during a royal lecture, if the ruler does not like goodness with a sincere mind, he will not listen and make use of the superior man's words. On the contrary, he will be misled by the inferior man and doubt the superior man.[23]

King Sonjo undoubtedly liked goodness with a sincere mind. But that was not enough. Factionalism was too pervasive in his government to allow him to consistently separate superior men and their wise council from inferior men and their faction-driven lies. Instead he was misled. Time and time again.

And so the battle between the Easterners and the Westerners continued unabated into 1589, the one hundred ninety-eighth year of the Choson dynasty and the twenty-second year of King Sonjo's own reign. Feud lines deepened, resentments grew, and the two camps expanded to involve virtually every member of the government and much of the yangban upper class. For the moment the Westerners had the upper hand and were doing everything in their power to consolidate their gains and settle old scores. The Easterners were striking back where they could and were searching, always searching, for ways to turn the tables on their foes. And through it all the affairs of the kingdom were left to drift.

It was into this tumultuous political arena that an envoy appeared at the southern port of Pusan bearing a message from a largely unknown Japanese warlord named Toyotomi Hideyoshi.

PART 2

PRELUDE
TO WAR

To take by force this virgin of a country, Ming,
will be [as easy] as for a mountain to crush an egg.[1]

Toyotomi Hideyoshi, Japan, 1592

A small Japan that attacks the Great Ming Empire
resembles a little snail that climbs a big rock.
It is like a bee that stings the back of a turtle.[2]

King Sonjo, Korea, 1592

CHAPTER 5

"By fast ships I have dispatched orders to Korea..."

BY 1587 TOYOTOMI HIDEYOSHI'S DREAM of a unified Japan with himself as its undisputed lord and master was almost a reality. He had claimed much of the main island of Honshu soon after succeeding his usurped master Oda Nobunaga in 1582. The island of Shikoku had been subdued in 1585. Earlier in 1587 the southern island of Kyushu, stronghold of the Shimazu family, had fallen to him, the offshore island of Tsushima thrown in almost as an afterthought. The only work that remained to be done was to break the resistance of the Hojo family in the vicinity of present-day Tokyo and to bring the northern hinterland provinces of Dewa and Mutsu into line. Neither posed a particularly great obstacle; their subjugation was assured. It was simply a question of how long it would take Hideyoshi to bring his overwhelming power to bear upon them.

In 1587, therefore, the reunification of Japan was nearly complete and a new era of peace about to begin. The thought must have been somewhat unsettling for Hideyoshi. He had known nothing but war for his entire adult life. He excelled at war. He prospered in war. War had made him the unparalleled success he was. But how would he fare in peacetime?

Hideyoshi had no intention of finding out—at least not yet. Like Oda Nobunaga, he viewed the unification of Japan as only the first step in a much grander scheme: the conquest of Asia. Hideyoshi's ambition was that vast, his self-assurance that complete. He thought it only right that his power should extend beyond the confines of his small island nation to encompass the entire world as it was known to him. In his correspondence with foreign nations he would refer frequently to this as being his destiny; that it was preordained at his birth that he would conquer nations.

Political considerations at home may also have served to turn Hideyoshi's attention overseas, considerations that made a campaign of foreign conquest seem unavoidable following the completion of the unification of Japan. Unlike Nobunaga, Hideyoshi did not conquer Japan simply by crushing his opponents. He relied just as much upon appeasement and generosity as military strength. Rival daimyo who swore allegiance to him were usually allowed to keep much or even all of their lands and could then "earn" even more by helping Hideyoshi build greater armies to send against other daimyo. It was a compelling combination of stick and carrot that made many eager to serve him, allowing Hideyoshi to extend his authority throughout all sixty-six provinces in a remarkably short time. But this strategy had its draw- backs. Hideyoshi's vassals became accustomed to his generosity; they came to regard ever greater land holdings and incomes as their just reward for serving him. This was fine so long as there were areas of Japan left to conquer and spoils to divide. By the late 1580s, however, these were dwindling and would soon be gone. The next step would almost certainly be dissention among the daimyo. With no further battles to fight, no further riches to claim, and time on their hands, these idle veterans would begin to plot and scheme and form secret alliances in a bid for more power and more land. Hideyoshi did not intend to give them the chance. If they needed war to keep them busy and additional lands to keep them happy, then he could give it to them. As soon as he possessed all of Japan, he would send them to Korea, and after Korea, China. These far-flung lands would give his pyramid scheme of con- quest an almost unlimited base, with Hideyoshi and the house of Toyotomi secure at the top.

In 1587 Hideyoshi began to act. Neighboring Korea was his first target. His initial weapon was the pen rather than the sword. As Adrian Forsyth has observed with regard to the animal kingdom in *A Natural*

History of Sex, "It pays to advertise your strength to your rivals, otherwise you will waste much in the process of affirming it."[1] Hideyoshi accordingly drafted a letter to the Koreans calling upon them to submit to him or be invaded. "By fast ships I have dispatched [orders] to Korea," he wrote to his wife and confidant O-Ne, "to serve the throne of Japan. Should [Korea] fail to serve [our throne], I have dispatched [the message] that I will punish [that country] next year."[2]

The "fast ships" had in fact been sent by Hideyoshi's newest vassal, So Yoshishige, daimyo of the island of Tsushima. So had sworn allegiance to Hideyoshi earlier that year together with Kyushu's Shimazu Yoshihisa and was now responsible for Japan's relations with Korea. Tsushima's proximity to and long relations with Korea made the So family the logical choice for this diplomatic role. But it put them in a difficult position. The So themselves were eager to restore good relations with Korea, for these ties had been the source of considerable wealth for them over the past century and a half. Indeed, the So would have liked nothing better than for trade relations between Korea and a unified Japan to once again flourish, with themselves levying handsome fees on every cargo passing through their "Tsushima gate." Hideyoshi, however, was not concerned at this point with trade with the Koreans. He wanted to possess that country. He preferred to bully the kingdom into submission with threatening letters and thereby avoid a costly war, a technique that had worked well in the past in bringing many Japanese daimyo to heel. But if they did not submit his armies would sail.

What were the So to do? They would have been far better informed than Hideyoshi of the nature of things in Korea, namely that it was a fiercely loyal tributary state of Ming China and looked down upon Japan. The So consequently would have known that their master's blunt demand for surrender would not have the desired effect. At this early date, moreover, there may have been some question in their minds whether Hideyoshi actually meant what he said. Was he really prepared to send his armies across the strait if the Koreans failed to heed his warnings? Or was his message just a lot of bluster, a cheap attempt to subjugate the Koreans with empty threats? If that was the case then he would succeed only in alienating them further, and in the process damage the So's longstanding relationship with the Choson court.

It was considerations such as these that prompted So Yoshishige to alter Hideyoshi's first message to the Koreans in 1587. Hideyoshi's letter demanded that Korea submit to him and that it send a "tribute mission" to Japan as a sign of its obeisance. So softened this into a more palatable request for a "goodwill mission." He also decided not to deliver the message in person, probably in an attempt to distance his family as much as possible from Hideyoshi's still inflammatory demands. He sent a family retainer instead, a man by the name of Yutani Yasuhiro.

Sending Yutani was a mistake. He was a big man of about fifty with graying hair and beard, rough and hardened from years of civil war. He could command armies, lead assaults on enemy castles, and hack a man in two with his sword. But he knew little of diplomacy and next to nothing of how to win over the Koreans.

The trouble began soon after his arrival on the peninsula. On his way north to Seoul he made a habit of loudly demanding the best room in every inn. To the Koreans that was very bad form. When the men of Indong gathered along the road with spears in hand to demonstrate Korea's military power—a long-established custom—he laughingly observed, "The staffs of your spears are short indeed!" This was a simple statement of fact; Korean spears *were* short compared to the five-meter-long pikes favored in Japan.[3] The comment nevertheless had the ring of an insult. At Sangju, as the aging local prefect wined and dined him at considerable expense, Yutani commented on his host's gray hair, wondering why a man who had never seen battle, but whiled away the hours with music and dancing girls, would ever turn gray.[4]

The insults and boorish behavior continued in Seoul, confirming all the deep-seated prejudices that the Koreans had about the Japanese: they were ignorant; they were arrogant; they did not know the ways of civilized men. But, like this warrior Yutani, they were also dangerous. They had to be tamed with the greatest of care. Yutani therefore was not run out of Seoul as many a Choson official would have dearly loved to do. He was comfortably housed and well fed, but kept firmly at arm's length while the Koreans debated how best to proceed.

At this point the Choson government knew almost nothing of Toyotomi Hideyoshi, the unseen power on whose behalf the uncouth

Yutani had been sent. According to Yu Song-nyong, then a high-ranking official in the Board of Rites, the government office responsible for hosting foreign envoys, some were of the opinion that Hideyoshi was a Chinese man who had somehow found his way to Japan, where he lived in obscurity earning a living hauling firewood. Then "one day the king, while on an outing, met him on the roadway, and as he was an unusual man, received him into his company of soldiers. Courageous and expert at fighting, he accumulated meritorious deeds and became a great officer. As a result, he became powerful. At last he drove out Minamoto and took over his position." It was an interesting tale, but wholly untrue. Others within the Korean government asserted that "Minamoto" had in fact been assassinated by someone else and that Hideyoshi had killed the assassin and seized control of his fallen lord's domain. After that he went on to unify all sixty-six provinces of Japan into one country. This account was closer to the mark, but only marginally. It was not "Minamoto," for example—an apparent reference to the Ashikaga shogun who had long since sunk into obscurity—who had been assassinated, but rather Oda Nobunaga who had been usurped. In any case both versions added up to a very limited understanding of Hideyoshi and recent developments in Japan.

The contents of Hideyoshi's letter left them with little inclination to find out more. Even after the So's attempt to soften its message, the Koreans found it arrogant, rude, and completely lacking in diplomatic protocol and appropriate humility. Hideyoshi referred to himself throughout the document by the Chinese character *chin*, a highly honorific form of "me" reserved solely for the Son of Heaven in Beijing. He boasted in an unseemly fashion of how all of Japan "has come wholly into the grasp of me [*chin*] alone." He expressed dissatisfaction that Korea had been so remiss in sending missions to Japan, as if Korea were some sort of wayward tributary state to those islands. And he now called on them to mend their ways and send an envoy to Kyoto.[5]

It was on the whole such an utterly unacceptable document that the Koreans had difficulty deciding how or even if they should respond. King Sonjo himself, who was clearly still confused as to the actual course of events in Hideyoshi's rise to power, was of the opinion that they should send the envoy away empty-handed, for he came from a

country "where they had killed their own king."[6] Others agreed, adding
that the Japanese were beyond any hope of ever becoming civilized,
and there was consequently nothing to be gained by extending a
friendly hand to them. Finally, after keeping Yutani waiting for several
months, the Koreans sent him back to Hideyoshi with a note explaining
that Korea would be unable to dispatch the requested goodwill mission
to Japan because of the length of the journey and their uncertainty of
the way—an extremely transparent excuse.[7]

Hideyoshi was furious at the failure of this first mission. He charged
Yutani Yasuhiro with being in league with the Koreans and had him
and his entire family killed. So Yoshishige was also punished, although
less severely. He was deposed as daimyo of Tsushima and replaced by
his adopted son, twenty-year-old So Yoshitoshi, who, being also the
son-in-law of one of Hideyoshi's most trusted generals, Konishi Yukinaga, was considered more trustworthy.

In late 1588 Hideyoshi ordered Tsushima's newly appointed daimyo
to dispatch a second mission to Korea to arrange that kingdom's
submission. So Yoshitoshi personally took the lead this time. Accompanying him was an entourage of twenty-five men, including
Yanagawa Shigenobu, a leading retainer in the So household, and
Genso Keitetsu, a fifty-two-year-old Buddhist monk whose scholarly
presence, it was hoped, would help the mission find common ground
with the tetchy Koreans. The mission arrived in Seoul in February of
1589. They conducted themselves with more decorum than their predecessor, the unfortunate Yutani, and gave the Koreans less cause for
offense, although So Yoshitoshi himself was negatively perceived as
"young and fierce. The other Japanese all feared him. Prostrating themselves, they crawled before him, not daring to gaze upward."[8]

So delivered another letter from Hideyoshi to the Koreans:

> When my mother conceived me it was by a beam of sunlight that
> entered her bosom in a dream. After my birth a fortune-teller said
> that all the land the sun shone on would be mine when I became a
> man, and that my fame would spread beyond the four seas. I have
> never fought without conquering and when I strike I always win.
> Man cannot outlive his hundred years, so why should I sit chafing on
> this island? I will make a leap and land in China and lay my laws

upon her. I shall go by way of Korea and if your soldiers will join me in this invasion you will have shown your neighborly spirit. I am determined that my name shall pervade the three kingdoms.[9]

The Koreans found this second letter from Hideyoshi to be no better than his first: it was arrogant, rude, and almost beyond reason. It merely confirmed to King Sonjo that this warlord was too uncivilized to merit the court's attention and that his haughty epistles should be ignored. But many of Sonjo's officials were no longer so sure. After long discussion they came to the conclusion that Hideyoshi posed a real threat to the security of the kingdom and that friendly relations should therefore be established with him, to tame him by drawing him into the Sinocentric fold, and to take the measure of the man and gather firsthand intelligence on the situation in Japan.

The Koreans accordingly approached So Yoshitoshi with a proposal: they would send a goodwill mission to Japan to congratulate Hideyoshi on his unification of the country, but first Japan had to bring to justice a group of renegade Koreans who had aided Japanese pirates in raids along the nation's southern coast the previous year, killing a general and carrying off a number of prisoners. These outlaws were now hiding somewhere in western Japan, and the Choson court wanted them repatriated for punishment. Yoshitoshi, who by this time surely knew that the Koreans would never agree to send a tribute mission to Kyoto as Hideyoshi wanted, readily agreed. A goodwill mission would have to do. Yanagawa Shigenobu was sent back to Japan to take care of the matter and soon reappeared with ten of the wanted men bound in ropes, together with many of the Koreans who had been taken prisoner. The renegades were questioned before King Sonjo in Seoul's Hall of Humane Government, then were decapitated outside the city's West Gate.

The Koreans were satisfied. As a sign that cordial relations between the two countries could now begin, So Yoshitoshi was at last granted an audience with King Sonjo, where gifts were exchanged and all the niceties observed. Yoshitoshi received a fine horse, and in turn presented the king with a peacock and some arquebuses. Although the Koreans had long been acquainted with gunpowder and cannon, these were the first lightweight muskets they had ever seen. They found them to resemble dog legs.[10]

After a prolonged period of waiting on the weather and debating over who would be sent, the Koreans finally dispatched their promised goodwill mission to Japan in April of 1590, the first Korean mission to Kyoto in nearly one hundred fifty years. It was led by Ambassador Hwang Yun-gil, Vice-Ambassador Kim Song-il, and Recording Secretary Ho Song, an unavoidable choice mirroring the factionalism that had split the government in two. Ambassador Hwang, a soft-spoken and conciliatory man, was a member of the then-ascendant Western faction, while the mercurial Kim and secretary Ho were from the Eastern camp. Kim in particular resented Hwang's presence, and considered him much too timid to deal with the militaristic Japanese. Between them they would find little to agree about.[11]

The mission was accompanied south from Seoul and across the strait to Kyushu by So Yoshitoshi, Yanagawa Shigenobu, and the monk Genso; there would be no question this time of the Koreans not knowing the way. It was not a happy party on that long and arduous trip. During a stop on Tsushima en route to Kyushu, So Yoshitoshi invited the Koreans to a banquet in a temple, then promptly insulted them by entering the grounds in a sedan chair rather than alighting outside the gate and walking in.[12] Ambassador Hwang, the West man, was prepared to overlook this breech in decorum. Vice-Ambassador Kim, the East man, was not. "Tsushima is our vassal state," he stormed. "We came here on the imperial command of our majesty. How dare you insult us like this. I refuse to attend this banquet." Yoshitoshi apologized, blaming the sedan chair bearers for the oversight, and had the men killed and their heads presented before the Koreans. The Japanese treated Kim and his colleagues with more care after that but were not entirely able to avoid the slights and faux pas that Kim above all would continue to find so offensive in the coming months, leaving him with an entirely unfavorable opinion of the Japanese and their ways.[13]

The Korean embassy arrived in Kyoto in August of 1590 after four months on the road. They found it to be an urban center of considerable size, the political, commercial, and religious hub of the nation, with a population in the vicinity of 150,000.[14] It must have had something of the appearance of a construction site, though, for Hideyoshi was in the process of rebuilding, expanding, and glorifying the capital—and in turn himself. The work then under way would in fact so transform the face of the city over the next several years that, in the words of Hideyoshi biographer Mary Elizabeth Berry, "the Kyoto we know today is Hideyoshi's town."[15]

At its center was Hideyoshi's recently completed residence, the Jurakudai, a sprawling complex of moats surrounding walls encircling residential compounds and whitewashed castle keeps that had taken a hundred thousand laborers two years to build. It was as much pleasure palace as fortress stronghold, with pine-tree-lined promenades, decorative stone gardens, and a delicate pavilion atop the central keep for tea parties, moon gazing, and poetry composing. Elsewhere in the city ground was being broken, stones laid, and plans drawn up for myriad other projects, all funded by Hideyoshi's largess. Nanzenji temple was being refurbished. Work was under way or would soon begin on the Tofukuji, the Shokokuji, the Kenninji, the Toji, and the Honganji. Shrines were being constructed. A new bridge was being erected across the Kamo River. A stone and earthen wall was in the works that by the end of the following year would encircle the entire city.

Just a bit to the east of the city a truly major project was under way: the Hokoji. This structure, impressive in its own right, was intended to house a stupendous Daibutsu, an image of the Buddha forty-eight meters high that Hideyoshi had ordered cast from all the swords and metal weapons then being collected throughout the country in fulfillment of his sword edict of the previous year, a measure designed to demilitarize the nation's peasantry. It was an act, said Hideyoshi, "by which the farmers will be saved in this life, needless to say, and in the life to come." The project, however, had more to do with inspiring awe than saving souls, for Hideyoshi was no great Buddhist. His Hokoji would be the biggest building ever constructed in Japan. His Daibutsu would be the biggest cast image of the Buddha ever made, larger even than the Daibutsu in Nara, which had taken twenty-seven years to complete. And he would do it all in just five years.

The Korean mission was quartered in the Daitokuji, a large Buddhist temple complex in the northern end of the city. And then they waited. The summer heat gave way to monsoon rains and then to the coolness of fall, and still they waited, for Hideyoshi was not in town. He was away to the northeast at Odawara, presiding over the siege that was grinding down Hojo Ujimasa, the embattled daimyo of Honshu's central Kanto region. The taiko eventually returned to Kyoto in October, with the Kanto his and Hojo dead, but still the Koreans were kept waiting. Hideyoshi apparently wanted to receive them in an audience where he would preside alongside the emperor, presumably to overawe them with his power, but Emperor Go-Yozei rejected his petition to do so. It was not until December that the Korean mission was at last invited to appear before Hideyoshi at his gilded residence, the Jurakudai.

When foreign ambassadors visited Seoul, it was customary for the Choson king to host a costly banquet where a succession of succulent dishes soon had the tables groaning under the weight of food. Meat, fish, fruit, wine, and delicacies of every description—nothing was spared when the Koreans entertained honored guests.[16] Hideyoshi's reception of the Korean ambassadors was decidedly different. Ambassador Hwang, Vice-Ambassador Kim, and their entourage arrived at the Jurakudai by sedan chair and were allowed to proceed into the palace without alighting—a suitable sign of respect and a good start to the proceedings. They were then led into a reception hall where they laid eyes on Hideyoshi for the first time. He was seated at the head of the hall, clad in a black robe and gauze hat. He looked "short and common looking," with the dark skin of a peasant, but "his eyeballs gleamed and a ray of light shone upon people." Finally, after four months of waiting, the Koreans were able to deliver their letter, addressed from the "King of Korea" to the "King of Japan," congratulating Hideyoshi on his successful unification of Japan, and expressing a desire "to cultivate friendly relations with your nation."[17]

With this diplomatic task out of the way, a banquet would now have been appropriate as per the Korean and Chinese view of protocol. There were no tables of food in evidence, however, nor any other sign that a feast was about to begin. The Koreans and the Japanese in attendance were simply seated in rows before Hideyoshi, and a plate of glutinous rice cakes passed round. Then came a bowl of rice wine from which everyone took a sip. And that was all.

As the Koreans sat there in bemused silence, Hideyoshi suddenly rose and left the hall. No one moved. After a time he reappeared, now wearing everyday clothes and carrying a baby, presumably his son Tsurumatsu, his first and only child, born the previous year. He strolled around the hall, cooing to the child as if no one else was there, then stepped over to the musicians and ordered music to be played.

Next the baby peed on his clothes. This set Hideyoshi to laughing, calling for an attendant to come and take his dripping heir off his hands. With a wet stain running down the front of his robe, he then left the hall again as the Japanese all bowed their heads to the tatami mats, and this time he did not reappear. The audience was over.[18]

It was probably not Hideyoshi's intention to be rude to the Koreans. He understood and appreciated display better than anyone: display of power and wealth and generosity. Had he chosen to do so, he could have laid on a feast that would have left Hwang and Kim thoroughly content. His decision not to do so was more likely intended to demonstrate the absolute nature of his power. The emperor might be required to host a banquet on certain occasions or preside over ceremonies when the heavens dictated. But Hideyoshi was not. He hosted banquets when he *chose* to do so, not when they were required or expected. Today he favored something simple, then a walk with his son and a bit of music. He was Hideyoshi. He was above conventions. It was his place to chose.[19]

The Korean mission, still in the company of So Yoshitoshi and the monk Genso, left Kyoto almost immediately after this and traveled south to the port of Sakai, near Osaka, to await Hideyoshi's reply to the letter they had delivered from King Sonjo. Their mission on the whole must be deemed a failure. To begin with, they had done little to gather intelligence that would be useful to the government in Seoul—above all, of Hideyoshi's true intentions, and of the military strength he had at his command. The mission instead became caught up in recording everything that was "wrong" with Japan, and all the ways in which it diverged from the Chinese-oriented model of correct political and social order.

Their assessment of Hideyoshi—or more particularly Vice-Ambassador Kim's assessment, for his would hold sway—was perhaps the mission's greatest failure. They did not fully appreciate the power he possessed, and in turn the danger he posed. They focused instead on his lack of decorum, taking this to mean that he was contemptible and uncivilized, an unworthy recipient of a goodwill mission from the Dragon Throne in Seoul. In fact, Vice-Ambassador Kim chaffed under the very obligation of having to appear before him at all. Hideyoshi was not an emperor. Japan already had one of those, a false emperor by the name of Go-Yozei. (To the Koreans there was of course only one "true" emperor, the Ming emperor of China.) Hideyoshi was not a king either, although the letter from Seoul honored him with this undeserved title. The only title he claimed for himself was kampaku, or regent, up to the end of 1591, and taiko, or retired regent, thereafter, making him little more than a senior court official, an advisor to the throne. For a mission from the Choson court to appear before him was therefore not only inappropriate, it was humiliating.

A second shortcoming of the Korean mission was that it was unable to impress upon Hideyoshi and his inner circle exactly where Korea stood—namely that it was prepared to welcome Japan into its Chinese-centered world as a fellow tributary state but that it never for a moment entertained the thought of submitting to Hideyoshi or Japan. In fairness, it would have been difficult if not impossible for Hwang and Kim and their compatriots to convey such a message. In addition to the communication difficulties they faced—much of their "talk" with their Japanese hosts would have been conducted in writing using Chinese characters—they were allowed no direct contact with Hideyoshi himself, and anything they conveyed to his underlings probably never made it back to his ear for the simple reason that it was unhealthy to tell Hideyoshi what he did not want to hear. He had commanded that the Koreans send a tribute mission to him and submit. So Yoshitoshi subsequently appeared with a mission in tow, Hideyoshi drew his own conclusions, and no one around him dared tell him the truth.

Hideyoshi therefore never understood that the party of Koreans that came to Kyoto was merely a goodwill mission. To him it was a tribute mission, a sign that the Koreans had acceded to his demand for submission and that his conquest of Asia was proceeding as planned. He was in fact so pleased with the "tribute mission" that he bestowed a court promotion on So Yoshitoshi, the man who had brought the Koreans to heel, together with the honor of using the family name Hashiba, the name Hideyoshi himself had used for a time back in the early 1580s.

With so much misunderstanding in the air, it was not surprising that the reply from Hideyoshi to King Sonjo that was eventually handed to the Koreans at Sakai proved highly unsatisfactory. After reiterating his greatness, Hideyoshi thanked King Sonjo for sending a "tribute mission" and "surrendering to the Japanese court" and now ordered him to prepare to join Hideyoshi in his conquest of China. The Korean envoys protested vigorously, and eventually the Japanese relented by removing the reference to Korea's "surrendering to the Japanese court." But everything else remained.[20]

Back in Seoul, Ambassador Hwang and Vice-Ambassador Kim appeared before King Sonjo and his ministers in March of 1591 to give their respective assessments of Hideyoshi. Hwang, the Western faction member, described Hideyoshi as having the piercing eyes of a man of resourcefulness and daring. He seemed fully prepared to start a war, the ambassador said, and posed a great danger to Korea. Easterner Kim Song-il strongly disagreed. Hideyoshi had the eyes of a rat, he countered, and was not to be overly feared. He did not pose a danger, and would not start a war. There was, in short, no pressing need to take defensive measures.[21] With the balance of power in Seoul now swinging back in the Easterners' favor, this assessment of Kim's was accorded the most weight. During the following months, as additional evidence accumulated of Hideyoshi's warlike intentions, the realization gradually spread on both sides of the factional divide that Japan did indeed pose a legitimate threat and that Ambassador Hwang might have been right after all. By then, however, the issue had become politicized, making it difficult for anything to be accomplished in the way of defense preparations. Any call for the strengthening of forts and the raising of armies, regardless of how well-intentioned, was in effect a call to support the Western faction and consequently drove the now-dominant Easterners to argue against such measures. As will be seen in the next chapter, a few determined individuals did manage to get some defensive work done despite this political deadlock. But it would be too little, too late, to meet the maelstrom to come.

The monk Genso and Yanagawa Shigenobu had in the meantime

followed the Korean embassy back to Seoul and were doing all they could to get the government to accept Hideyoshi's unacceptable demands. Hideyoshi wanted a fight with China, Genso lied in a meeting with Kim Song-il and others, because China had for so long refused to accept Japan as a vassal. He thus had every right to proceed with his armies to Beijing to demand its recognition. All the Koreans had to do was clear the way and escape all harm. When the Koreans vigorously protested, Genso pointed out that Korea had actively participated in China's attempt to invade Japan in the late 1200s, and so it was only reasonable for Hideyoshi to expect them to allow him merely to pass now that he was setting out to exact his justifiable revenge. Again the Koreans refused.[22]

If there was one thing both factions could agree upon, it was that Hideyoshi's wild talk and grand schemes should not go unchallenged. A letter of response in which Seoul finally made its position clear was accordingly drawn up and handed to Genso and Yanagawa for delivery to Kyoto. Hideyoshi's plan to invade China, the letter began, was beyond comprehension, and his demand that Korea join him in the undertaking an indication of just how little he understood of the world. For Korea and China were like one family, "maintaining the relationship of father and son as well as that of ruler and subject. This inseparable and amiable relationship between Chung-Chao [China] and our kingdom is well known throughout the world. Your kingdom should be acquainted with this fact."

> We shall certainly not desert 'our lord and father nation' [China] and join with a neighboring nation in her unjust and unwise military undertaking. Moreover, to invade another nation is an act of which men of culture and intellectual attainments should feel ashamed. We shall certainly not take up arms against the supreme nation. As all the members of our nation are just and righteous persons, as well as cultured and intellectual in their attainments, [they] know how to revere 'our lord and father nation'.... We urgently hope that you will reflect on these things and will come to understand your own situation as well as ours. We would conclude this letter by saying that your proposed undertaking is the most reckless, imprudent, and daring of any of which we have ever heard.[23]

This was not what Hideyoshi wanted to hear. The Koreans had just sent to his palace what he had chosen to believe was a tribute mission offering their submission, and now they were scolding him like a schoolboy who had failed to learn his lessons. He immediately sent So Yoshitoshi back to Korea with one final warning: submit to me peacefully and open the way to China or face my armies and be destroyed. Yoshitoshi, appreciating the escalating danger of the situation, did not venture all the way to Seoul to deliver this message but handed it to the authorities in Pusan and remained aboard his ship in the harbor. When a reply was not forthcoming, he returned to Tsushima to prepare for war. Over the next several months the few remaining occupants of Pusan's "Japan House" packed up their things and quietly followed suit. By the spring of 1592 the compound was deserted.[24]

Korea was not the only target of Hideyoshi's "conquest through diplomacy" campaign of 1588 to 1592. He sent similar messages to the Ryukyu Islands, Taiwan, the Philippines, and India, informing the people there of his greatness and demanding that they submit.

King Shonei of the Ryukyus was the first of these to be approached. His was a small kingdom spread across a chain of islands between Japan and Taiwan that regarded itself as a vassal of Ming China but which for the sake of expedience also sent tribute to Japan. The Japanese consequently considered the islands a vassal of their own, falling within the jurisdiction of the Shimazu family of Kyushu, and assumed without question that King Shonei would submit. With the receipt of Hideyoshi's first letter demanding submission, King Shonei thus began walking a tightrope between actual loyalty to China and the appearance of loyalty to Japan. In June of 1589 he wrote apologetically to Hideyoshi that "our small and humble island kingdom, because of its great distance and because of lack of funds, has not rendered due reverence to you. However, now, in compliance with the instructions that our great lord, Shimazu Yoshihisa, has sent us, ... we have caused [an envoy] to proceed to your country, carrying with him a humble gift."[25]

Hideyoshi was pleased. "Of all the nations yours is the first to send an envoy," he magnanimously replied, "together with rare and unusual things. This has pleased us greatly.... From this time on, although our countries are separated by thousands of miles, we may nevertheless maintain friendly relations with the feeling that your country, together with the other nations that are within the four seas, constitute but a single family."[26]

Hideyoshi expected to win the submission of the Philippines in a similarly effortless manner, through written threats rather than actual invasion, for he had been informed by a Portuguese visitor to Japan that the islands were weak and largely undefended.[27] He therefore sent a letter to the Spanish governor in Manila, Gomez Perez Dasmarinas, stating that he was about to conquer China, "for heaven... has promised it to me," and intended to snatch up the Philippines as well for its failure to submit and send tribute to him. One of Hideyoshi's vassals, however, had recently assured him that Spain was a friend to Japan and that its colony in the Philippines would send an ambassador if asked. Hideyoshi therefore ordered his vassal, Harada Magoshichiro, to Manila to demand that an envoy be sent at once to his invasion head-quarters at Nagoya.[28]

This vassal Harada was a rather shifty character, a Japanese trader and adventurer intent on working the situation to his own advantage, much as the So family were attempting to do with their manipulation of relations between Korea and Japan. Upon arriving in Manila he did everything he could to soften the belligerent tone of Hideyoshi's mes-sage so that a favorable response could be coaxed out of the Spaniards, including presenting them with gifts that he purported to be from Hideyoshi but that he very likely purchased himself. Despite his efforts, the Spaniards remained suspicious. Harada seemed just a common trader, not the sort of man to be entrusted with a diplomatic mission of such importance. The supposedly official document he carried was also written entirely in indecipherable Japanese, limiting the Spaniards' understanding of it to Harada's own suspect translation. After ordering coastal defenses strengthened, supplies laid by, and forts built in the hills surrounding Manila for the women and children to take refuge in should the Japanese invade, Governor Perez Dasmarinas accordingly drafted a cautious reply to Hideyoshi's letter and placed it in the hands of a Spanish envoy to deliver personally to Japan. In it he observed that he had not been able to read or comprehend all that Hideyoshi had written, and that his reply was thus only "to the small portion of your letter that I understand, which had been no more than Faranda [Harada] has chosen to interpret for me." The governor also expressed concern that Harada might be some sort of charlatan and requested that Hideyoshi confirm to the Spanish envoys being sent to him that the man was a legitimate ambassador and the message he had delivered genuine. "If it is such," Dasmarinas stated, "then I shall respond to the friendship due so great a prince," and King Philip II of Spain would in turn be glad to extend his hand "in true friendship and alliance." Then: "Inasmuch as certain presents have been sent me but lately from Japon, which are of great value, I would wish to have some rare and valuable products of our España to send in return; but, since weapons are the articles most esteemed among soldiers, I am sending you with this a dozen swords and daggers."[29]

The Spanish envoy, a priest named Juan Cobo, arrived at Nagoya in the summer of 1592 to deliver Governor Dasmarinas' letter to Toyotomi Hideyoshi. Hideyoshi was intrigued by the opening lines of the document listing the far-flung lands that King Philip II possessed and asked the Dominican to point them out on a map. Father Cobo obligingly made a present to him of a globe with each Spanish possession labeled in Chinese and the distances listed between them.[30] How would Hideyoshi have viewed this representation of a world ringed with Spanish colonies while little Japan lay nestled off to one side? Did it occur to him that the Spanish Empire, the greatest in the history of Europe, was as great in its western hemisphere as China was in the East? Did it give him pause to consider that in challenging Spain as well as China he was contending for supremacy with both of the world's two great powers? Probably not. More likely he came away from his meeting with Father Cobo thinking that if the Spaniards could grab so much of the world, then surely he could grab even more. After all, he had sent a message to Manila demanding that an envoy be sent to him as a sign of the Philippines' submission, and here the envoy was. The envoy came bearing a letter that, after being translated into the sort of Japanese Hideyoshi's scribes knew he wanted to hear, contained a submissive tone absent in the original document. The letter was accompanied, moreover, by gifts looking very much like tribute, for whereas Governor Dasmarinas had written in Spanish that they were sent in thanks for the gifts he believed Hideyoshi had sent him, what Hideyoshi read in Japanese was that they were intended "to show due recognition to you." In Hideyoshi's mind, therefore, the Philippines had been won.

The same process of diplomatic misunderstanding on Hideyoshi's part bolstered by skewed translations and misrepresentations by retainers eager to please led him to believe that India was prepared to bow to him as well. The letter Hideyoshi dispatched to this distant land was delivered by Portuguese traders into the hands of the viceroy at Goa. Madrid was duly informed—Portugal had been annexed by Spain in 1580 and its colonial possessions subsequently claimed—and a Jesuit from Italy named Alessandro Valignano was ordered to Japan as a representative of India and in turn of Philip II. Valignano appeared before Hideyoshi in February of 1591, thereby adding India to the growing list of nations that Hideyoshi seems to have thought were being cowed into obeisance by his assertions of power and threats to invade. In his reply to the viceroy he stated, "Our authority has now been extended near and far to many nations in the outside world. These nations have manifested a sincere desire to maintain their existence under our benevolent rule. Rulers in the east, west, south, and north have made ready obeisance to us. The imperial commands of our sage Emperor may soon be transmitted to all corners of the world."[31]

Everything thus seemed to be going well for Hideyoshi in his campaign to conquer Asia through diplomatic correspondence. The nations of the world were all falling into line, preparing to greet his advancing armies and welcome his benevolent rule.

Then he received the letter from the Koreans in the spring of 1591. This was the first open and unequivocal rebuff he had encountered so far to his demands for submission, and it must have angered him greatly. After dispatching his final warning to Seoul, he turned to the Ryukyu Islands' apparently compliant King Shonei, demanding that he come to Japan with a large army to participate in the coming invasion of Korea. If he failed to do so, Hideyoshi warned, the Ryukyus themselves would be invaded.

There was no way King Shonei could accede to Hideyoshi's demands. Even if he wanted to aid Hideyoshi—and he did not—his kingdom was too small and his resources too limited to send any sort of force to Japan. He wrote back beseeching Hideyoshi to reconsider the matter. Hideyoshi eventually relented, requiring the Ryukyus instead to make annual payments of gold and silver and food, a reprieve of sorts, but one that would greatly burden the little kingdom in the years to come.

By this time King Shonei had set in motion a chain of events that would have an impact on faraway Korea. Hideyoshi's demands had driven him to write to his real sovereign, the emperor of Ming China, to ask for help, including with his letter copies of all of Hideyoshi's correspondence. This was the first word the Ming court received of the Japanese warlord's planned Asian conquest. They did not send the requested assistance to the Ryukyu Islands. They had enough to worry about at home, with a mutiny of troops along the northern border, a rebellion in the west, and above all the Wanli emperor refusing to allow his first son to be installed as heir. But King Shonei's letter started the Chinese thinking: why had they not been warned of this by their most loyal vassal, Korea? Surely the Choson court knew more about this potential threat than King Shonei, far out at sea on his remote islands. Did Korea's silence perhaps mean that it was in league with this barbarian Hideyoshi, and intended to turn against them?

Was "Little China" to be trusted?

CHAPTER 6

Preparations for War

THE WHEELS OF HIDEYOSHI'S WAR MACHINE began to turn in the summer of 1591. The first step was to establish a headquarters for his invasion force. Kyoto was out of the question; it was much too far from Korea to allow Hideyoshi any sort of direction of his invading armies. He would need to be on Kyushu, close to the action. The settlement of Nagoya[1]—present-day Karatsu—on the northern coast of Hizen Province was selected and work begun there on an enormous castle in November of that year. Tens of thousands of laborers were requisitioned from local daimyo, and under the guidance of Hideyoshi's trusted general Kato Kiyomasa a tremendous fortified complex began to take shape, surrounded by a double ring of defensive moats and walls.[2] From here it would be just eight hours with a fair wind to the halfway island of Tsushima, then another six hours to Pusan on Korea's southern tip.

To raise his invasion army, Hideyoshi turned to the daimyo. Each would be required to supply a predetermined number of troops in proportion to size of his fiefdom through a system termed *gunyaku*, or required military service. This was how Hideyoshi had completed the conquest of Japan, by ordering vassal daimyo to contribute divisions to swell the ranks of his army. It was how he raised laborers for his great construction projects in and around Kyoto, the palaces, the temples, and the Great Buddha that was slowly taking shape. It was how he built his sprawling invasion headquarters at Nagoya in the space of a few months. And it would be how he would muster a quarter-million-man army for the invasion of Korea.

When imposing military or labor levies, Hideyoshi made allowances for the distance over which daimyo had to transport their contributions. Daimyo nearest to the scene of an upcoming campaign or construction project were required to contribute relatively more, and those farther away relatively less. This system of sliding levies brought a degree of fairness to Hideyoshi's requisitions, recognizing the fact that the farther a daimyo had to transport a contribution, the more it cost him. In raising his army for the invasion of Korea, Hideyoshi seems to have followed such a plan. It worked like this: the daimyo of Kyushu, being nearest to Nagoya and in turn Korea, were required to provide six men for every hundred koku of rice that their respective domains were estimated to produce annually; daimyo farther away in the western provinces of Honshu were required to send five men per hundred koku; daimyo even further away on central Honshu were burdened to a correspondingly lesser degree, down to as few as two men per hundred koku. A navy was assembled in a similar manner, with a sliding levy for ships being imposed on Kyushu, Shikoku, and western Honshu daimyo with coastal domains. Sailors to man these ships were rounded up from fishing villages along the coast of Kyushu and the Inland Sea, at a rate of ten men for every hundred households.

Those are the broad strokes of how Hideyoshi raised his army. Upon closer examination, however, the picture is not so simple, and in fact is still not fully understood. To begin with there was the issue of tax exemptions. Daimyo who had rendered a particular service to Hideyoshi or who he otherwise favored were frequently rewarded with such exemptions in the form of having a portion of their domain declared tax free. In calculating troop requisitions for the coming invasion of Korea, Hideyoshi's sliding levy scale was therefore applied only to the taxable portion of each daimyo's domain. It seems fairly clear, moreover, that Hideyoshi's relationship with each daimyo often entered into the equation as well. Those he could trust and over whom he exercised firm control could be handed levy requirements with little worry that they would resist or rebel. Those over whom his control was weak, conversely, had to be treated more circumspectly. There were quite a few such daimyo in Hideyoshi's New Japan, men he had won over through negotiated settlement rather than decisive victory in battle. They tended to receive bigger tax exemptions and lighter military service demands, prompting some of their contemporaries to complain of the seeming arbitrariness of Hideyoshi's troop levies.[3]

The makeup of the invasion army assembling at Nagoya was therefore more complex than it might at first appear. The contributions sent by some daimyo, particularly long-time Hideyoshi allies, fit the sliding scale fairly well, while the contributions of others, particularly former enemies, did not. Kato Kiyomasa, for example, a native of Hideyoshi's own hometown of Nakamura and one of his most trusted generals, sent a contingent of 10,000 men from his 200,000-koku fief in Higo Province on Kyushu, a relatively heavy contribution from a domain that apparently had almost no tax exemption. Shimazu Yoshihiro, on the other hand, provided a force of equal size from his much larger 559,530-koku domain in nearby Osumi Province, suggesting a tax exemption rate of roughly seventy percent for this former enemy of Hideyoshi's, coaxed into the fold only after the latter's Kyushu campaign of 1587. From the island of Shikoku, long-time Hideyoshi loyalist Fukushima Masanori sent a force of 4,800 men from his 200,000-koku domain in Iyo Province, a reasonable contribution considering the distance he had to transport it. Yet Chosokabe Motochika, the former lord of Shikoku who had prudently bowed to Hideyoshi upon the latter's invasion of that island in 1585, sent just 3,000 men from his 220,000-koku fief in neighboring Tosa Province. Such discrepancies in contributions to the coming invasion reveal just how uncertain Hideyoshi's grip was on the newly unified Japan. The coalition of daimyo he had assembled still needed careful tending to keep them subservient. They had to be pushed to serve Hideyoshi, but not pushed too far, and kept happy with promises of more land and more wealth. There was no longer any more land to be conquered in Japan. In 1591 he had it all. With his planned invasion, however, he expected to grab untold millions of continental koku, enough to keep his vassals happy and under his control for decades to come.[4]

A staggering total of 335,000 men were mobilized nationwide in the spring of 1592 for the invasion of Korea. Of this number 235,000 were sent to invasion headquarters at Nagoya, and 100,000 were shifted about the country to strengthen areas left under-defended by the massive mobilizations. Of the 235,000 encamped in and around Nagoya Castle, 158,800 were earmarked to actually cross over to Korea. It was logistically impossible for Hideyoshi to send this entire force to Korea in one huge mass. Had he done so they would have starved. Instead he grouped the various daimyo-led units into nine separate contingents varying in size from 10,000 up to 30,000 men, the natural limit in the late sixteenth century to the size of a body of troops that could be kept fed and functioning in the field.[5] The daimyo commander of each of these units was provided with a map of the Korean Peninsula depicting its eight provinces and the three routes north. These maps were copies of one that So Yoshitoshi had acquired during his mission to Korea and presented to Hideyoshi. The taiko had taken it and painted each of Korea's eight provinces a different color to distinguish them. Henceforth each province would be identified among the Japanese by its corresponding hue on this map of operations: Cholla-do was the "Red Country," Chungchong-do the "Blue Country," Kyongsang-do the "Green Country," and so on.[6]

At first glance this invasion army seems to have been composed of the variety of Japanese troops that one would expect Hideyoshi's system of sliding levies to have yielded: 82,200 men, fifty-two percent of the total force, were from Kyushu; 57,000 (thity-six percent) were from Honshu; and 19,600 (twelve percent) were from Shikoku. It was a distribution that made sense: Kyushu bordered Korea, so Kyushu should contribute most; Honshu and Shikoku were farther away, so their contributions should be proportionally less. It would be wrong to infer, however, that Hideyoshi intended Kyushu troops to do fifty-two percent of the fighting, Honshu troops thirty-six percent, and Shikoku troops twelve percent. In examining the order of battle he drew up on April 24, 1592, a pattern emerges that reveals something of his domino strategy for the conquest of Asia.

Konishi Yukinaga's first contingent, Kato Kiyomasa's second, and Kuroda Nagamasa's third were charged with spearheading the invasion of Korea. This force consisted entirely of men from Kyushu and its offshore islands. They would sail first from Nagoya to Tsushima, reassemble on that island, then push on to Pusan. Once on Korean soil their mission was to drive north to Seoul as fast as they could. Contingents four through seven would then follow to reinforce the advance armies for the continued push to the Chinese border. These four contingents were also composed mainly of units from western Japan: the fourth and sixth were made up entirely of Kyushu men, the fifth came from the island of Shikoku, and the seventh from western Honshu. Contingents eight and nine, consisting of men from western and central Honshu, would in the meantime remain in reserve on their respective island bases at Tsushima and Iki, crossing to Korea as conditions warranted. A further force of 75,000 provided by Tokugawa Ieyasu, Date Masamune, Uesugi Kagekatsu, and other Honshu daimyo, would remain stationed at invasion headquarters at Nagoya. Hideyoshi did not plan to send this reserve into action; their job was to protect Nagoya in the event of a Chinese counterattack. Finally, a force of some 100,000 men was moved down from the Tokai and Kinai regions of eastern Honshu to protect the capital of Kyoto, which the Nagoya mobilizations had left inadequately defended.

Kyushu men, therefore, while comprising slightly more than half of Hideyoshi's invasion force, would do most of the actual fighting; Honshu divisions would back them up or remain at Nagoya as a "home guard." This troop utilization represented a new approach to conquest for Hideyoshi, a domino strategy designed to extend his rule overseas.

During his unification of Japan in the 1580s, Hideyoshi used the armies of subject daimyo to swell the ranks of his own personal force, intimidating foes with the immensity of his power by amassing armies in excess of one hundred thousand men. There comes a point, however, when an army is big enough—indeed, where it can become no bigger for want of resources to supply it. With all Japan now his, Hideyoshi had reached that point. There was no need to dispatch an even bigger and even more costly force to take the kingdom of Korea; one hundred and fifty thousand men would do. Now he would use his long left arm, Kyushu, to reach across the sea and take Korea. While Kyushu troops were doing the heavy work on the peninsula, forces from Honshu would back them up. Once the Koreans were subdued, they would be drawn into Hideyoshi's planned Asian conquest, supplying manpower and

JAPANESE INVASION FORCES, MAY 1592 [7]

	COMMANDER *(Domain Location)*	MEN	TOTAL
1.	Konishi Yukinaga *(Higo, Kyushu)* So Yoshitoshi *(Tsushima)* Matsuura Shigenobu *(Hizen, Kyushu)* Arima Harunobu *(Hizen, Kyushu)* Omura Yoshiaki *(Hizen, Kyushu)* Goto Sumiharu *(Goto Islands)*	7,000 5,000 3,000 2,000 1,000 700	18,700
2.	Kato Kiyomasa *(Higo, Kyushu)* Nabeshima Naoshige *(Hizen, Kyushu)* Sagara Nagatsune *(Higo, Kyushu)*	10,000 12,000 800	22,800
3.	Kuroda Nagamasa *(Buzen, Kyushu)* Otomo Yoshimune *(Bungo, Kyushu)*	5,000 6,000	11,000
4.	Shimazu Yoshihiro *(Osumi, Kyushu)* Mori Yoshinari *(Buzen, Kyushu)* Takahashi Mototane *(Hyuga, Kyushu)* Akizuki Tanenaga *(Hyuga, Kyushu)* Ito Yuhei *(Hyuga, Kyushu)* Shimazu Tadatoyo *(Hyuga, Kyushu)*	10,000 2,000 2,000	14,000
5.	Fukushima Masanori *(Iyo, Shikoku)* Toda Katsutaka *(Iyo, Shikoku)* Chosokabe Motochika *(Tosa, Shikoku)* Ikoma Chikamasa *(Sanuki, Shikoku)* Hachisuka Iemasa *(Awa, Shikoku)* Kurushima Michiyuki *(Iyo, Shikoku)* Kurushima Michifusa *(Iyo, Shikoku)*	4,800 3,900 3,000 5,500 7,200 700	25,100
6.	Kobayakawa Takakage *(Chikuzen, Kyushu)* Kobayakawa Hidekane *(Chikugo, Kyushu)* Tachibana Munetora *(Chikugo, Kyushu)* Takahashi Saburo *(Chikugo, Kyushu)* Tsukushi Jonosuke *(Chikugo, Kyushu)*	10,000 1,500 2,500 800 900	15,700
7.	Mori Terumoto *(Aki, Western Honshu)*	30,000	30,000
8.	Ukita Hideie *(Bizen, Western Honshu)*	10,000	10,000
9.	Hashiba Hidekatsu *(Mino, Central Honshu)* Hosokawa Tadaoki *(Tango, Central Honshu)*	8,000 3,500	11,500
			158,800

materiel for the continued push into China. When the region around Beijing was under Hideyoshi's control, he would require the Chinese to raise the forces necessary to extend his reach into the southern provinces of that vast Middle Kingdom. The southerners would then be used to subdue the west; the westerners would be sent against the Thais, Burmese, and Cambodians; and presumably the far westerners would then be commissioned to make the final push into India.

Hideyoshi, then, did not envision a vast Japanese army fanning out across China, down into Indochina, over the Himalayas, and onto the sweltering plains of the subcontinent. Only his rule would spread in this manner, carried farther and farther by locally levied native armies serving an inner core of Japanese troops. A purely Japanese army, or more precisely a Kyushu army, would only begin the process. It would act as the first domino in the cascade, a cascade that would extend Hideyoshi's rule to the farthest reaches of Asia.

The Japanese army of invasion that had assembled at Nagoya by April of 1592 was a formidable force, the Darwinian end product of more than a century of civil war that saw traditional military thought give way to more practical methods of killing. The way of the samurai was still considered glorious, quality horseflesh was still appreciated, and the finely crafted katana sword was still a highly valued thing. But they were no longer the mainstay in Japanese warfare. The lightweight arquebus had changed all that. It was relatively cheap to manufacture. It shot farther than a bow, and more important, packed a greater armor-piercing punch at the closer distances preferred in battle, usually one hundred meters or less. It was easy to use; an uneducated farmer could be taught to handle one effectively in just a few weeks. It did not demand the same degree of intestinal fortitude to wield in battle as did "short weapons" such as the sword and spear; Japanese arquebusiers commonly did their work from behind protective cover. And it gave a soldier an overwhelming, even shocking, advantage. As Oda Nobunaga's stunning victory in the Battle of Nagashino demonstrated, no amount of samurai skill or courage could prevail against a curtain of flying lead balls. In that seminal 1575 engagement, three thousand Oda foot soldiers stood behind a wooden paling with muskets in hand and patiently mowed down charge after charge of traditionally armed adversaries. After that Japanese warfare was never the same.

Samurai therefore did not constitute a very large portion of Hideyoshi's invasion army in 1592, nor were traditional cavalry units much in evidence. The use of horses was largely confined to daimyo commanders and their officers, custodians of the samurai tradition with their superbly crafted armor, fierce war masks, and exquisite swords. The bulk of the army was now the ashigaru, the foot soldier. These were mainly farmers and fishermen recruited and trained by daimyo from their respective domains, men like Hideyoshi's own father Yaemon. They would have been a rough lot, poorly educated and for the most part unable to read. They would not have traveled much; the march to Nagoya alone was likely the greatest journey many had ever taken. In looking ahead to the crossing to Korea, fear was probably the dominant emotion—fear of dying in a strange and distant place. Most probably wanted nothing more than to get the job done and return to their families. But on the other hand all the talk circulating through the camps of Korean and Chinese wealth must have been alluring, conjuring up visions of cities overflowing with booty, just sitting there for conquering Japanese soldiers to haul away home.

The ashigaru were equipped with swords and spears and bows in addition to lightweight muskets. A portion of these traditional weapons came from the various sword hunts Hideyoshi had conducted over the previous few years to disarm the peasantry of Japan. His edict of 1589 had declared that all weapons turned in would be used in the construction of the Great Buddha in Kyoto, but the stipulation that swords be collected together with their scabbards indicates that they were to be stored for future use, not melted down to make nails and bolts. One source states that a total of 5,000 battle axes, 100,000 long swords, 100,000 short swords, 100,000 spears, and 500,000 daggers were collected through sword hunts and daimyo requisitions and transported to Nagoya. This figure is undoubtedly inflated, but it is safe to say that Hideyoshi's army was generously supplied with traditional weapons.

Such was not the case with muskets. Subsequent letters sent home from Korea by Japanese commanders would repeatedly state that they had more than enough swords and spears and arrows and did not want any more. What they needed were more muskets. To the Koreans the invading Japanese seemed well equipped with these feared weapons; one source opined they had 300,000 of them.[8] This is a very unlikely figure. The exact number is not known, but inferences can be made from correspondence of the period. In his 1591 letter of requisition to the Kyushu daimyo Shimazu Yoshihiro, for example, Hideyoshi ordered that he arm 1,500 of his men with muskets, 1,500 with bows, and 500 with spears.[9] Considering that Shimazu contributed about 10,000 men to the invasion, and that no more than half this number were full-time fighting men (the rest would have been engaged primarily in logistical support work),[10] this would suggest that fifteen percent of his total force, or thirty percent of his fighting strength, was equipped with personal firearms. Applying this percentage to the total number of 158,800 Japanese soldiers sent to Korea, a more realistic total of roughly 24,000 muskets is obtained—still a crushing advantage over the Koreans, who had seen their first "dog leg" only the year before.

The various companies in Hideyoshi's army were highly self-contained. Each was led by a daimyo, thirty-eight in all. In every instance musket-bearing ashigaru formed the vanguard. It was their job to decimate enemy lines and, it was hoped, send them into retreat so that spear and sword units could then rush forward and finish them off with a minimum of resistance. Cavalry units no longer existed as such. Daimyo and their top men rode horses; the ashigaru foot soldiers, as their name implied, walked. Bringing up the rear, finally, were the porters and support staff, that long logistical train that comprised at least half of every unit. These were the nameless men who built fortifications, set up camp, hauled food and gear, cooked meals, and did the hundred and one other jobs that were indispensable to the operation of any army in the field. In the coming invasion of Korea, however, even the lowliest porters and laborers in the Japanese army would prove themselves quite capable of handling a sword or musket and joining in the fight, and so they must be factored into the fighting strength of each unit as quasi-soldiers rather than noncombatants.

These various companies were grouped into nine contingents. In the upcoming invasion the nine would occasionally work in coordination like divisions in a modern army to achieve some particular objective, but more often they would operate independently of one another. Indeed, the individual companies comprising each contingent would at times split up and go their own way. They were able to do so because Hideyoshi's invasion force, unlike the armies of China and Korea, was not a centrally controlled national army commanded by a government-appointed hierarchy of officers, but rather a loose confederation of regional armies that were in effect "owned" by the wealthy daimyo lords who raised, armed, and led them. Each of these daimyo had sworn allegiance to Hideyoshi and was committed to using his army to achieve Hideyoshi's goals, but beyond that he expected and was accorded a good deal of independence in how he organized and employed his men. It was a system that generally worked well for the Japanese. It meant, however, that Hideyoshi himself was the only one capable of effective supreme command; the only one with the clout to override the independent spirits of the daimyo and exercise control over the entire invasion force. The taiko knew this. It was therefore his intention to cross over to Korea in the wake of his advancing armies, reestablish his headquarters in Seoul once that city had been taken, and from there orchestrate the subsequent move on Beijing.

The Japanese army gathering at Nagoya in the spring of 1592 was the largest army ever assembled in Japan up to that time, and the most professional; a well-organized, well-supplied, and well-equipped war machine designed to project massive killing power. There was not an army anywhere in the world at that time that was superior to it, or probably even its equal. Contemporary armies in Europe were well equipped with muskets and artillery, but they came nowhere near to equaling the immensity of Hideyoshi's. By way of comparison, the Spanish armada that sailed for England in 1588 consisted of 30,000 men aboard 130 ships—one-fifth the size of the taiko's 158,800-man expeditionary force. There was in fact only one other country in the world that could raise an army of even 100,000 men, and that was Ming China. But the Ming, for all their manpower, did not have state-of-the-art arquebuses, only old-fashioned fo-lang-chi guns and a scattering of poorly made muskets that tended to blow up in your face.

There was, however, one chink in Hideyoshi's armor, one weakness that would prove telling if not fatal later on: his navy. Navies had not played much of a role in Japan's wars of unification, and consequently Japan's naval development lagged behind Korea's. Ships were used during the sengoku period mainly to transport troops, or on rare occasions as floating platforms upon which land battles could be extended offshore. In such engagements the usual objective was to decimate the men aboard enemy vessels with arrow and musket fire and then, when their ranks had been sufficiently weakened, to move in close for boarding to finish off survivors. Naval warfare, in other words, was conducted much like warfare on land: the idea was to kill enemy soldiers, not sink enemy ships.[11]

There were exceptions. In 1576 Oda Nobunaga approached Osaka with his army aboard a flotilla of three hundred small craft with the intention of storming the Mori stronghold. The Mori's own fleet met him in the harbor and in the ensuing battle seriously mauled Oda's floating army. To break the Mori's naval superiority, Nobunaga ordered one of his vassals, a co-opted pirate leader named Kuki Yoshitaka, to construct seven heavy ships, armored in part if not wholly in iron, that would be impervious to the Mori's arrow and musket fire. He returned to Osaka with a squadron of these vessels in 1578 and succeeded in annihilating the Mori's conventional fleet of light, wooden ships—the first recorded use of "iron ships" in the history of naval warfare.[12]

This amazing victory seems to have had little impact on Hideyoshi, who was a top Oda general at that time and undoubtedly acquainted with the battle and the shipbuilding activities of his fellow vassal Kuki. Instead of attempting to develop the idea of an armored ship impervious to enemy fire, he seems to have remained mired in 1592 in the old notion of the ship as a floating platform for land troops.

To transport his invasion force across to Korea, Hideyoshi ordered the maritime daimyo of Kyushu, Shikoku, and Chugoku (the western end of Honshu) to supply ships at a rate of two large vessels for every 100,000 koku of annual revenue. This core of large ships would have been augmented by several hundred existing smaller craft, fishing boats, and Inland Sea cargo ships. The resulting motley armada totaled approximately seven hundred vessels of various sizes, capable of carrying anywhere from just a few tens of men up to several hundred. To man them, fishing villages were required to provide ten sailors for every hundred households.

These seven hundred vessels were not warships. They were transports that were intended to ferry soldiers across to Tsushima Island and then on to Pusan. They were lightly built, they afforded the men on board little or no protection, and they had no onboard artillery other than the few cannon that were being transported to Korea, which in all likelihood were stowed as cargo and not mounted for use at sea. They were, in short, vulnerable to attack by the Korean navy. To provide this flotilla some measure of protection, Hideyoshi ordered Kuki Yoshitaka—the same man who had commanded Nobunaga's iron ships back in 1578—to oversee the construction of several hundred warships in the Bay of Ise on central Honshu's Pacific coast. The largest of these, of the atakebune class, were thirty-three meters long and carried a crew of one hundred and eighty. Smaller were the sekibune and the kohaya classes. Although heavier than the transport ships they would be convoying, all three of these classes were still significantly lighter than the warships of the Korean navy, and not as maneuverable. They also carried fewer cannon: the atakebune, the largest and presumably the most heavily armed, had only three guns, whereas the most lightly armed Korean battleship carried at least twelve.

Hideyoshi also attempted to augment his navy with European ships. The idea had been in his mind from at least as early as May 1586, when he expressed a desire to the Jesuit Gaspar Coelho to charter two Portuguese men-of-war for his planned conquest of China. He was prepared, he said, to pay handsomely for the vessels, and would additionally have churches built all across China and order the entire population converted to Christianity. Father Coelho, thinking Hideyoshi was merely daydreaming, agreed offhandedly to provide the ships (despite standing orders from his superior not to interfere in local politics). Hideyoshi reportedly was delighted. This intriguing twist never materialized, however, despite Hideyoshi's repeated requests to the Portuguese in the months leading up the war.[13]

To man the warships of his navy, Hideyoshi ordered a number of maritime daimyo on Honshu and Shikoku to raise a total of 9,450 men, a rather light force considering the gargantuan army they would be expected to protect. The daimyo at the head of these men would be his

"admirals." They included Kuki Yoshitaka with 1,500 men, Todo
Takatora (2,000), Wakizaka Yasuharu (1,500), Kato Yoshiaki (1,000),
the Kuwayama brothers, Ichiharu and Masaharu with 2,000, and the
Kurushima brothers, Michiyuki and Michifusa, with 700.[14] Some of
these daimyo admirals were the heirs of the wako pirates who had
terrorized the coasts of Korea and China up until the mid-1550s. Kuki
Yoshitaka, for example, was of the same Kuki family that had launched
raids from its lair on the Kii peninsula, while the Kurushima brothers
descended from an Inland Sea wako chief. Such men were to be found
elsewhere in the invasion force as well: Matsuura Shigenobu was a
descendent of the same Matsuura clan that had given rise to the wako
back in the thirteenth century; Goto Sumiharu was daimyo of the once
notorious Goto Islands. While lawless wako pirates may no longer have
existed in Hideyoshi's Japan, the tradition thus was in a sense being
kept alive as their now respectable descendants prepared to return to
Korea in the biggest wako raid East Asia had ever seen.

This, then, was Hideyoshi's navy. It consisted of a large number of
vessels, probably in the neighborhood of one thousand all told, but
many were small, light transport ships with little or no fighting capability.[15] Even the warships were not particularly strong or well armed, and
were commanded by daimyo with little or no naval experience, men
who regarded naval warfare as land warfare afloat. Whether any of this
concerned Hideyoshi is not known. We may surmise from his
unsuccessful attempt to secure Portuguese ships that he considered his
homegrown fleet less than invincible. On the other hand, he had not
encountered significant naval resistance during his unification of Japan
and probably did not expect to encounter any now, at least none that his
ships could not handle.

When the Kuki completed construction at Ise of the warships they
had been required to build, Hideyoshi ordered them to move the fleet
forward to his invasion headquarters at Nagoya, a journey of six hundred
kilometers. From there it would accompany the taiko's troop-laden
transports across the strait to Pusan, lashing any Korean warship that
ventured too close with a withering barrage of musket fire. That, anyway,
was the plan.

*   *   *

Some sort of Japanese aggression was by this time widely anticipated in Korea. Ambassador Hwang Yun-gil, who had led the "goodwill mission" to Kyoto in 1590, had warned the court in Seoul that Hideyoshi posed a real threat, and many believed him. Even Vice-Ambassador Kim Song-il, who officially contradicted everything Hwang said and sparked the dispute between the Eastern and Western factions over whether or not there would be a war, confided to fellow Easterner Yu Song-nyong, now Minister of the Left,[16] that he had not really meant what he said. "I also feel that there is no alternative, as in the end the Japanese will unleash war," he said. "But Hwang's words were too pessimistic, and those inside and outside the court will become bewildered and lose their self-control. That is the reason why I said what I did."[17]

A fight was clearly coming with Japan. Hwang and the Westerners knew it. Kim and the Easterners knew it. A full-blown invasion that would devastate the country and permanently cripple the dynasty was not expected. But something resembling a large wako pirate raid was. The Koreans had faced Japanese pirates on many occasions before, most recently in the 1550s. The official histories of the Choson dynasty and preceding Koryo dynasty made it clear that when Korea was unprepared, these marauders were capable of doing tremendous harm, but that with preparation they could be dealt with. So clearly preparation was required. But what sort of preparation? And how much? And where to start?

And what, in the meantime, should they tell Ming China?

The China issue arose upon the return of the Korean mission from Kyoto in the spring of 1591, bearing the letter from Hideyoshi that left no doubt as to his intentions: he wanted to invade the Middle Kingdom and usurp the Celestial Throne. To the Koreans, Hideyoshi's conceit was not only shocking, it was distasteful and obscene, and they were sorry they had ever exchanged envoys with him. Some members of the government now began to worry that China might think Korea had stepped beyond the bounds of the vassal–sovereign relationship by establishing relations with this Japanese barbarian without prior Ming approval, and feared that Beijing would be angry if it found out. "I am afraid," said Prime Minister Yi San-hae, "that unless we conceal the fact, the Imperial Court will consider it was a criminal act for us to have carried out an exchange of envoys with Japan on our own volition."

Minister of the Left Yu Song-nyong did not agree. He argued that, as a loyal vassal of China, Korea was duty-bound to inform the Ming court of these latest developments and to warn it of the looming threat posed by Japan. "Indeed," he added, "if those robbers really plan to invade China, others may inform the Emperor. Then the Celestial Court will unjustly suspect that we have concealed this business because we are in accord with the Japanese."

That was in fact exactly what was going on. By early 1591 word had already reached Beijing from elsewhere of Hideyoshi's plans for conquest, first from envoys dispatched by King Shonei of the Ryukyu Islands, then from separate messages sent by two Chinese men residing in Japan. Beijing awaited corroborative reports from Seoul, but the months passed and no word arrived, leading some to question the loyalty of Little China, and even to suspect that it might be somehow in league with Japan. Only Prime Minister Xu Guo, a former ambassador to the Choson court, stood up for Korea. "Korea has remained loyal to *sadae* [serving the great]," he said. "It cannot be in agreement with the rebellious spirit of the Japanese. Just wait awhile."[18]

Beijing waited. And the Koreans continued to talk. In the meantime, Inspector-General Yun Tu-su, who agreed with Yu Song-nyong about the need to inform the Ming of the threat posed by Japan, privately wrote a report of his own and gave it to Kim Ung-nam, the ambassador of a tribute mission then about to depart for Beijing, with orders to deliver it as soon as he arrived, a breach of protocol that would subsequently earn Yun a stint in exile in the countryside. This vague document, which made no mention of the envoys that had been exchanged between Korea and Japan but only of "rumors" the Koreans had heard, reached the Ming capital not long after the Ryukyuan envoy sent by King Shonei and thus eased some of the suspicion the Chinese were starting to feel. Mistrust would linger, however, for it would not be until early 1592 that an official embassy finally arrived from Korea with what was purported to be a full account of Hideyoshi's threats and demands and the events that had transpired over the past four years. And even then the Koreans felt it necessary to gloss over many of the details, particularly concerning the envoy exchanges, for they continued to fear that these would be misinterpreted as evidence of their truckling with Japan.[19]

While the question of whether to inform China was being debated in the halls of power in Seoul, attention was also being directed to the state of the nation's defenses. They were not in good shape. Something had to be done to shake up the military if an invasion was to be met.

Korea's military in 1592 was based upon an organizational framework that had existed since the beginning of the Choson dynasty two centuries before. It had been modeled to a great extent upon the defense structure of the preceding Koryo dynasty, which in turn had followed the general pattern of the military of Tang-dynasty China.[20] The nation's army consisted of five "guards": a Forward Guard for Cholla Province in the southwest; a Rear Guard for Hamgyong Province in the northeast; Left Guard for Kyongsang Province in the southeast; Right Guard for Pyongan Province in the northwest; and Middle Guard for the central provinces of Hwanghae, Kyonggi, Kangwon, and Chungchong. Each of these five guards maintained army garrisons and naval bases in their respective regions of the peninsula, plus an auxiliary force in Seoul to defend the capital and to serve as a national army in time of crisis.[21]

Overall command of Korea's armed forces was in the hands of the General Headquarters of the Five Guards in Seoul. Beneath this body were the nation's top generals. These generals did not actually command armies. It was the practice in Choson Korea to keep them all based in Seoul, under the controlling hand of the government and well removed from the armies they were ostensibly responsible for. This was done to protect the nation from the threat of insurrection. The Koryo dynasty had fallen in this very manner back in 1388, when General Yi Song-gye marched his army on the capital, usurped the king, and subsequently founded the Choson dynasty with himself as monarch. Once he was secure in power, Yi initiated the practice of separating generals from their armies to ensure that no one henceforth would be able to do what he had done and overthrow his own dynasty. Generals would be placed at the head of armies only when national security was threatened and a military response required. Otherwise they would be kept in Seoul.

The measure had its intended effect. Throughout its six hundred years of existence the Choson dynasty would never be seriously threatened by its own armed forces. But such internal security came at a price: it deprived the nation's top military leaders of hands-on command experience and left them to a great extent in the dark as to the state of the armies they would be expected to lead if and when war came. How many men did they have? Were they well armed? Were they being trained on a regular basis? Were they prepared to go to war at a moment's notice? For the generals of Choson Korea these were questions that would remain unanswered until a crisis was upon them and the time to prepare long past.

In terms of actual leadership in the field, the highest military rank in Korea was the commander. Each of Korea's eight provinces was assigned between one and three army commanders and navy commanders, with one of these posts being held concurrently by the province's civilian governor. No real distinction was made between army and navy; commanders and officers serving below them could be assigned to one as well as the other. Provinces of greater strategic importance, namely those in the south nearest the wako pirates of Japan and in the north bordering Manchuria, were assigned more commanders, while provinces of lesser importance were assigned fewer. The provinces of Kyongsang-do in the far southeast and Hamgyong-do in the far northeast, for example, were regarded as the first line of defense against foreign aggression and consequently were assigned a total of six commanders. This meant that, aside from the largely meaningless concurrent postings held by the provincial governor, a civil official with no military background, each province consisted of four tangible commands led by four professional commanders: a Right Army, a Left Army, a Right Navy, and a Left Navy. The southwestern province of Cholla-do was also regarded as key, primarily against seaborne invasion, and consequently it had three commands in addition to the governor's insubstantial posts: a Right Navy, a Left Navy, and one Army.[22] Chungchong Province bordering the Yellow Sea had two: an Army and a Navy. The provinces of Hwanghae-do and Kangwon-do, on the other hand, had little military command structure of any substance. These central regions were far removed from Korea's vulnerable southern coast and northern frontier, and consequently had only one army and one navy command post each, with both falling to the provincial governor. [23]

The officer corps for Korea's military was recruited by means of a periodic examination. It examined men on their knowledge of military science through the classical works of Sun Tsu and others, and tested their skill in the military arts of horseback riding and firing a bow, the quintessential weapon in Korean warfare. The quality of officers this system produced was often quite low. To begin with, it promoted the concept of "officer as prima donna." The ideal Korean commander was expected to be an expert horseman, a skilled archer, and a fearless warrior, the sort of man who could ride straight into an enemy line, firing arrows and slashing with sword, with the men under his command following close behind. He was not expected to be well versed in the more mundane arts of training men to fight as a unit. According to Minister of the Left Yu Song-nyong, who was greatly concerned about the state of the military, "not one in a hundred [officers] knew the methods of drilling soldiers."[24]

A second reason for the low quality of Korea's officer corps was lack of prestige: in Korea, as in China, a career in the military was not highly regarded. It was a distant second choice for those unable to pass the civil service exam and scale the lofty heights of government service; a suitable calling for the sweaty and not-too-bright, perhaps, but certainly not for a man of real intelligence. Once in the military, moreover, officers were constantly reminded of their inferior status by their haughty civil service counterparts, who freely second-guessed their military decisions and even took over their commands, secure in the belief that a civilian official's education in the classics qualified him for any task, including the command of troops. During the century preceding the Imjin War it had in fact become increasingly common for civil officials to be appointed provincial army and navy commanders. Such appointments were regarded as appropriate. For a province's civilian governor to hold the concurrent posts of army and navy commander was also considered a valid and useful assignment. Such men would have had absolutely no military experience to bring to the job. But they possessed the wisdom of the classics, and that was enough.[25]

The Korean army and navy were manned through conscription. All able-bodied males were subject to military service with the exception of the sons of the yangban upper class. This system was supposed to maintain a standing army and navy totaling 200,000 men, with an additional 400,000 reservists who could be called up in an emergency. These numbers may have been accurate early on in the dynasty, when military rosters were updated every six years. By the sixteenth century, however, the entire system was in disarray. Military rosters were no longer kept up to date, and all sorts of methods had arisen whereby families managed to keep their men out of the military, for example by hiring someone else to serve in their place, or by paying a fee in lieu of service. This latter method became especially prevalent, and led to rampant corruption in the armed forces, with officers bypassing the military examination and buying their commissions so they could then get rich by selling service exemptions. On the eve of Hideyoshi's invasion, therefore, the actual size of Korea's military was anybody's guess.[26]

The first steps were taken to prepare for the coming war with Japan in the months following the return to Seoul of the goodwill mission to Kyoto in 1591. Minister of the Left Yu Song-nyong would take a leading part in pushing for these defensive measures, breaking with the "there-will-be-no-war" line that was still being stubbornly adhered to by many of his fellow members of the Eastern faction when he realized the extent of the Japanese threat. At about this same time the Eastern faction itself split into two separate camps, the Northerners and the Southerners, over a difference of opinion regarding which of King Sonjo's sons by his various concubines—he had none by his queen—should become his heir. As the leader of the Southerners, Yu Song-nyong won the trust of the king with his conciliatory approach to the matter of succession, and with his willingness to step beyond factional lines for the sake of the defense of the nation.

Among the measures taken to beef up Korea's defenses was the appointment of new governors to the southern provinces of Kyongsang-do, Cholla-do, and Chungchong-do, with orders to prepare their commands for war. This entailed in part restocking local arsenals and tightening up conscription. In Kyongsang, for example, the province where any

Japanese attack was likely to occur, a drive was launched to put local farmers through six months of military training. Most able-bodied men found ways to avoid this service, however, likely by paying an exemption fee to corrupt military officials, leaving only teenagers, old men, and vagabonds in search of a meal to take the "required" training.

A building program was also launched to construct or extend fortifications at ten key southern towns, again in Kyongsang Province: Yongchon, Chongdo, Samga, Taegu, Songju, Pusan, Tongnae, Chinju, Andong, and Sangju. The program was misguided, for it was based on the entirely wrong assumption that the Japanese were skilled in naval warfare but weak on land. It also focused on building large enclosures to accommodate as many people as possible, rather than the small, easily defendable mountain fortresses that had proven effective in the past. At Chinju on the southern coast, for example, the town's small hilltop citadel was abandoned in favor of a sprawling fort on the river, encircled by walls so long that they would require a multitude of soldiers to defend them. While Kyongsang-do had become highly fortified by the start of 1592, therefore, and appeared ready for war, the question remained: could all those kilometers of walls be held?[27]

All these defensive preparations were met with stiff resistance from local populations and government officials. The additional burden of having to make weapons, build forts, and take military training—or more often pay a "fee" to get out of doing so—seemed to many like just another form of taxation, and an unjustifiable one too considering that the nation was currently at peace and that harvests had been poor throughout the previous several years. A good deal of the work that was planned was therefore never completed, and what was done was sometimes shoddy. One fort that was built is said to have been only ten feet long, with a defensive trench around it so shallow that even a child could scramble across.[28]

The Koreans at this point were acquainted with the fo-lang-chi, the heavy, long-outdated muskets that had been used in China for more than a hundred years. These were cumbersome and unreliable weapons, however, and consequently few were ever produced in Korea and they never saw much use. The altogether more serviceable arquebus, meanwhile, the lightweight musket then in common use in Japan, remained largely unknown. The only specimens in the country, those presented to the court by Tsushima daimyo So Yoshitoshi in 1590, were now packed away in a government warehouse in Seoul. Efforts to copy them would not be made until after the Japanese invasion began. In 1592 Korean soldiers were thus armed with essentially the same personal weapons that had been used by their ancestors for more than a thousand years: the double-edged sword, the bow, the spear, plus a handful of more exotic instruments such as maces, flails, tridents, and the distinctive half-moon spear, an enormous knife blade affixed to a long shaft. Of these the bow stands out as the quintessential Korean weapon. At less than one and a half meters long it was much shorter than a Japanese bow, but is said to have been capable of firing an arrow even farther, reportedly as much as 450 meters as opposed to 320. (The effective range in battle was of course much less.) This impressive range may have been due partly to its sturdy composite construction, but more likely to the use of the firing tube, a Korean innovation that allowed for the firing of a much shorter and hence lighter arrow that could travel greater distances. The Korean bow was difficult to string and fire, however, and like all bows required long years of training to master in addition to a good deal of muscular strength to use. Unlike the Japanese arquebus, therefore, it was of little use in the hands of untrained peasants, the sort of men then being conscripted into the Korean army in preparation for the coming war.[29]

While the Koreans may not have known much about the arquebus, they knew a great deal about cannons—more, in fact, than the Japanese did. They had learned how to make gunpowder from the Chinese in the fourteenth century,[30] and subsequently combined this knowledge with their skill at casting temple bells to manufacture cannons that fired stone and iron balls and enormous arrows weighing up to thirty kilograms and as thick as a man's arm. These weapons did not much resemble the smooth-barreled cannons on wheeled mounts later developed in Europe, the handsome weapons that in modern times are typically seen on display outside museums and in public parks. Korean cannons in the late sixteenth century were ugly, crude cylinders of metal, reinforced all along the exterior by a series of thick iron bands, with one or two handles or rings welded to the top to facilitate transportation. Few came affixed to any sort of permanent mount. The barrel itself was generally manhandled into position where needed and set atop some sort of firing platform or wheeled carriage. Four major types of barrels were manufactured: the *chonja* (heaven), the *chija* (earth), the *hyonja* (black), and the *hwangja* (yellow). They were named after the first four characters in the traditional student's primer for learning Chinese characters, much as a series of items in the West might be identified as A, B, C, and D. The chonja was the largest cannon in the series. It was made of copper, weighed from 300 to 420 kilograms, had a caliber of twelve to seventeen centimeters, and a barrel approaching two meters in length. The bronze hwangja, the smallest gun in the series, weighed between sixty and eighty kilograms, had a caliber of six to seven centimeters, and was slightly over one meter long. The bronze chija and the iron hyonja fell somewhere in between. All four of these guns could lob stone or iron balls and giant arrows over a distance of 600 to 1,000 meters, although the useful aimed range was undoubtedly much less. They could also be packed with small stones or lead slugs and fired into enemy ranks as a crude form of grapeshot.[31]

Also in the Korean arsenal was a bell-shaped mortar called the *daewangu* (big mortar), a 300-kilogram bronze bowl from which a heavy stone ball could be blasted with considerable inaccuracy over a distance of 300 to 400 meters, or more usefully at point blank range to knock down walls. There was a smaller version as well known as the *chungwangu* (medium mortar). The *hwacha*, or fire wagon, resembled a rectangular rack of pigeon holes mounted on a two-wheeled cart. Each hole held one gunpowder-propelled arrow, up to one hundred in all. When the contraption was ignited, it sent its entire load of arrows hurtling toward the enemy on one deadly fusillade. Finally, there was the recently developed *pigyok chinchollae* (flying-striking-earthquake-heaven-thunder), sometimes rendered as "the flying thunderbolt," a hollow iron ball packed with gunpowder and equipped with a fuse. This ingenious device was fired from a cannon over the walls of enemy fortifications and into the midst of the defenders clustered within, where, if all went well, it exploded.[32]

On the eve of the Japanese invasion the Koreans therefore knew little about muskets, but possessed a great deal of knowledge about other types of weapons employing gunpowder, particularly cannons. These weapons would do them little good on land in the coming conflict. At sea, however, it would be a different story.

One aspect of Korea's defenses that seems to have been given no attention on the eve of the Imjin War was its beacon-fire system, first built during the Koryo dynasty to provide a fast means of communication between the frontier and the capital. It consisted of 696 hilltop fire beacons laid out in lines stretching from Seoul to the northeastern and northwestern frontier with Manchuria, and down to the southeastern and southwestern coast. Each was manned around the clock, ready to relay any signal from hilltop to hilltop, using smoke by day and fire by night. Exposing the light of the fire once in the direction of the next beacon in the chain conveyed the message that all was quiet, two flashes meant that enemy forces had been sighted, three that they were approaching, four that they had crossed into the country, and five that fighting had commenced. Removing the cover entirely from the beacon to send a continuous light meant that reinforcements should be sent at once. It is said that a signal could be relayed in this manner from the most distant region in Hamgyong Province in the far northeast all the way to Nam Mountain in Seoul, a distant of more than 600 kilometers over rugged mountain terrain, in less than four hours. While this phenomenal time was admittedly achieved in a prearranged test, it was certainly true that, by using beacon fires, an early warning could be flashed from the northern frontier or southern provinces to Seoul in something under a day.

This was assuming, of course, that every beacon was manned all along the route. In fact they rarely were. An inspection of the northwestern fire line in the fifteenth century revealed numerous interruptions, with many beacons neglected and others totally unmanned. The reason was that no one wanted to do the work; tending the beacons atop lonely, windswept mountains was understandably a despised duty, which locals did their utmost to avoid. So difficult was it to coax locals into service that the task frequently was assigned to political exiles, whose desire to serve the government that had exiled them must have been less than ardent. Little seems to have changed by the start of the

1590s. With Korea's ingenious early warning system effectively useless for want of manpower, the fastest means of communication between the provinces and Seoul remained the horse and rider.[33]

Recognizing the need for strong leadership in the field, particularly in the vulnerable southern provinces of Kyongsang and Cholla, the Korean government appointed a number of new commanders beginning in 1591. The initiative began with King Sonjo soliciting recommendations of promising officers worthy of promotion to the rank of commander. A few of the resulting appointments were fortuitous and served to strengthen the nation's defenses. Many others did not.

A good example of an ill-conceived appointment is what occurred with regard to the Kyongsang Right Army. The army's present commander, Cho Tae-gon, was regarded in Seoul as too old and sick to be of any use in the event of war. Yu Song-nyong suggested that one of the nation's top generals, Yi Il, be sent south immediately to replace this man, so that he would have time to acquaint himself with his new command and prepare for the coming conflict. The Minister of War responded with the usual line that Yi Il, being a general, had to remain in Seoul. He would be sent south only if and when a war broke out. "If this were an incident of one morning," argued the exasperated Yu, "in the final analysis it would be unsuitable to send Il. Others would be sent. But when morning becomes a whole day, it perhaps would be advantageous to make proper preparations in anticipation of the event. But on the contrary, visiting generals gallop down to the provinces on the spur of the moment. They are acquainted neither with conditions in the provinces where they are sent nor the valor or timidity of the soldiers there. They shun the arts of war. We will certainly regret this later."[34] The Minister of War would not relent. The post of Kyongsang Right Army commander instead went to none other than Kim Song-il, the former vice-ambassador of the Korean mission to Kyoto, the man who had said there would be no war and that there was nothing at all to worry about. During the previous months he had continued to insist that fortress construction in Kyongsang-do be halted and had written a series of reports outlining how the province could be better administered to ease local dissatisfaction. In the end King Sonjo personally ordered the outspoken official south to that province, perhaps as something of a rebuke. The Border Defense Council expressed misgivings about the appointment, but it went ahead regardless. Kim, a civil official with no military experience, thus took command of one of the nation's key military posts just one month before the start of the war that he said would never come. As the subsequent course of events would show, he had the necessary courage to die for his country. But he lacked the skills to defend it.[35]

On a more positive note, a forty-six-year-old career soldier was promoted on Yu Song-nyong's recommendation from relative obscurity to the command of the Left Navy of Cholla Province. His name was Yi Sun-sin. His unexpected advancement to high command would prove to be one of the more fortuitous appointments made in the months leading up to the Imjin War.

Yi Sun-sin was born in Seoul in 1545 into a yangban family of modest means. His father, Yi Chong, possibly had been among that majority of upper-class aspirants to government office who had failed to pass the civil service exam and consequently had to settle for a quiet life in obscurity at the Yi family's country home at Asan in Chungchong Province. He was blessed with four sons whom he named after four of the sage kings of ancient China, with the addition of the character *sin*, meaning "vassal." The name of his third son, Yi Sun-sin, meant "Yi, Vassal of Shun," implying loyal service to a wise king.

Little is known of Yi Sun-sin's early life. Traditional Korean accounts describe him as a brilliant young man, well built and some-what taller than average, who passed up the opportunity for a distin-guished career in government and instead set his sights on the military, much to his parents' chagrin. It is equally possible, however, that the family simply could not afford to prepare all four sons for the civil service exam and that Sun-sin was consequently steered toward a more modest and more accessible military career. Whatever the case, after six years of arduous training at the family home in Asan, Yi Sun-sin went up to Seoul in 1572 to attempt the triennial military service examina-tion. He failed. A fall from his mount during the test of horsemanship shattered his leg and cost him the exam, and sent him back home to Asan. Finally, in early 1576, he passed the exam on his second try and, at the relatively advanced age of thirty-one, was commissioned as an officer at the lowest rank of grade nine.

The first fifteen years of Yi's career might be charitably described as checkered. He was an intelligent and competent officer with more ability than most, and was not without influential friends in the government to advance his career, notably Yu Song-nyong, a childhood playmate from Yi's early years in Seoul. What seems to have held him back was his refusal to engage in the cronyism and corruption that was then such an essential part of getting ahead in the military. He would not "play the game." Yi's ability and strong moral fiber in fact would make him a number of enemies over the years, particularly among corrupt and incompetent senior officers and peers who found his honesty threatening.

Yi's first assignment was to a remote hardship post on Korea's northern frontier, then being increasingly infiltrated by the Jurchen tribes of Manchuria. His competence was quickly recognized by the provincial governor and led to a promotion and transfer to a military training center in Seoul. He did not last long in this new billet, quickly alienating his superior officers by refusing to reserve special treatment for their friends and relations. A move to the army of Chungchong Province followed, and then, in 1580, into the Left Navy of the southern province of Cholla-do, where he had his first taste of naval service.

As captain of the Cholla port of Balpo, Yi Sun-sin once again ran into trouble. For some reason both the commander of the Cholla Left Navy and the provincial governor had it in for him and saw to it that he was relieved of his command. The inquiry that followed revealed the nebulous allegations against Yi to be groundless and resulted in a full exoneration and apology. But Yi was not returned to his former post. To save face for the commander and governor who had attempted to bring him down, he was demoted to grade eight and sent to the northern frontier where he had begun his career.

Yi seems to have taken this reversal in stride, doggedly setting out to distinguish himself and climb back into the middle ranks. To strike a blow against the Jurchen, who continued to cause trouble along the border with their incessant raiding, Yi prepared an ambush and then sent out a small party of soldiers to lure the tribesmen in. The Jurchen obligingly chased the party into the trap, where the bulk of Yi's waiting garrison proceeded to cut them to pieces. It was an impressive victory that attracted the attention of the government in Seoul and would have done wonders for Yi's career had he accorded some undeserved credit to his jealous commanding officer. He did not. His superior consequently made sure that Yi received no recognition for his initiative and valor by accusing him of acting without proper authorization. And so Yi was left to languish on the frontier for the next several years.[36]

In 1591 Yi Sun-sin appeared to be permanently mired in the middle ranks, a resourceful, courageous, and upstanding officer who, in the corrupt world of the Korean military, would forever be blocked from high command by more cunning but less able rivals. The emergence of the Japanese threat changed all that. When King Sonjo solicited recommendations for officers deserving of promotion to the rank of commander, Left Minister Yu Song-nyong saw the chance to rescue his childhood friend from obscurity and give him the sort of command his talents deserved. Thanks to Yu's recommendation, on March 8 Yi was promoted to the lofty post of Left Navy commander of Cholla Province. Some, including Kim Song-il, criticized this rapid promotion as being politically motivated, a case of Yu Song-nyong looking out for his cronies and pals, but the challenges were not vigorous and the appointment held.[37]

In 1591 Yi Sun-sin thus found himself once again in the navy, but this time in a position of great responsibility. In the coming war the Japanese would obviously arrive by sea from the south, on the coast of Kyongsang-do or Cholla-do; to land anywhere else would have entailed too great a sea voyage. The navies of these two provinces thus formed Korea's first line of defense. Yi understood this. He knew that the enemy had to be met at sea and beaten before they could land. During the following year he therefore threw himself into making his Cholla Left Navy as prepared as it could be. One of his first tasks was to learn as much as he could about naval command, something he would have known little about after fifteen years spent almost entirely in the army, commanding landlocked garrisons along the northern frontier. Yi's government friend in Seoul, Yu Song-nyong, helped him in this by sending Yi a book on military tactics that he himself had written "entitled *Defensive Strategy of Increasing Loss to the Enemy*, giving explanations on the land and sea battles with 'fire' attacks for sure victory."[38] After just one year of diligent study, this former army officer would be the foremost naval tactician in Korea.

Yi also did a great deal to prepare Yosu and the five outlying ports under his command for war. This was no easy task, for support from the government in men, money, and material was not very forthcoming. In many instances Yi had to conscript his own sailors and laborers, scrounge his own building supplies, and manufacture his own weapons. He had submerged cables laid across the harbor mouths of all his ports to protect them from seaborne attack. Port fortifications, crumbling after decades of neglect, were rebuilt. Cannons were cast and tested. Gunpowder was stockpiled. Armories were restocked.

And men were literally whipped into shape. Like many great commanders before him such as Ming general Qi Jiguang, Yi Sun-sin was a stern disciplinarian who administered floggings for minor infractions and executions for major ones. It was a time-honored tradition going all the way back to the earliest of the Chinese military classics, the fourth-century-B.C. *Book of Lord Shang*: "In applying punishments, light offences should be punished heavily; if light offences do not appear, heavy offences will not come. This is said to be abolishing penalties by means of penalties.... If crimes are serious and penalties light, penalties will appear and trouble will arise. This is said to be bringing about penalties by means of penalties."[39] It was a brutal way to ensure discipline. But it worked. Yi's ragtag assembly of conscripted peasants, vagabonds, and career soldiers did what he ordered them to do. They trained when he ordered them to train. And they would fight when he ordered them to fight.

The heart of Yi's command, of course, were his ships. He had fewer than fifty of them: twenty-four large battleships known as *panokson*, fifteen smaller warships, and a scattering of fishing boats. The panokson, or board-roofed ship, was the mainstay of his fleet. It was a heavily built vessel, about twenty-five meters long, powered mainly by oars, with an additional deck to separate the oarsmen below from the fighting men above. This upper deck was enclosed by high walls to afford the fighting men some protection and had a castle-like structure built in the

center from which the captain could issue commands. With a full complement of cannons and a well-trained crew, a seaworthy panokson was
superior to anything in the Japanese navy, a floating fortress that
Hideyoshi's lightly built and lightly armed vessels would be unable to
combat. Unfortunately for Yi, however, many of the panokson he took
command of in 1591 were not seaworthy. They were old and decrepit
and in desperate need of repair, and would keep his shipwrights
occupied into the early days of the war.

In addition to refurbishing his fleet of worm-eaten vessels, Yi, in
cooperation with his master shipwright Na Tae-yong, set out to build a
new type of battleship that would pack even more punch than the
panokson and be even more indestructible. They would call it the
kobukson, the "turtle ship." It would be a startling innovation in naval
warfare, a heavy, armored vessel, bristling with cannons pointing in
every direction, its top deck completely enclosed under an impenetrable
spiked roof resembling a turtle's shell. Only a few of these turtle ships
would be built and see service in the Imjin War. But they would be the
scourge of the Japanese navy.

CHAPTER 7

The Final Days

HIDEYOSHI WAS OFF ON A HUNTING EXCURSION at the start of 1592. It was a prolonged affair, perhaps intended to take him away from Kyoto and the bitter memory of his only child, Tsurumatsu, who had died at the age of two in the fall of the previous year. During the five-week sojourn, thousands of birds and animals were shot. Finally, on January 30, the great hunter returned to the capital "as though in triumph," arriving in a European-style carriage before a gathering of nobility and then displaying his bountiful catch.[1]

For his next adventure Hideyoshi planned to invade Korea and conquer China. He had initially intended for his armies to set sail on the first day of the third month—April 12 by the Western calendar—possibly because he considered the day lucky. He had begun his Kyushu campaign on this day in 1587, and his offensive against Hojo Ujimasa, lord of Odawara, on this day in 1590. But the first soon proved out of the question. Mustering his huge invasion force and getting it positioned at Nagoya and on the forward staging areas of Iki and Tsushima Islands was more time consuming than Hideyoshi and his planners had calculated upon. "D-Day" was thus pushed ahead to the twenty-first of April.

Hideyoshi was also waiting to hear from Tsushima daimyo So Yoshitoshi whether the Koreans had softened their stance and would "lead the way to Ming," thus sparing him the trouble of having to conquer their peninsula by force. So knew perfectly well that the Koreans had not. He had never been forthcoming with Hideyoshi, however, about the Choson court's adamant opposition to any talk of conquering China; like all the taiko's underlings, So told him what he wanted to hear and portrayed negative developments in ways that Hideyoshi would find pleasing. In the spring of 1592, therefore, Hideyoshi still harbored hopes that he could take Korea without a fight, and still believed that his vassal So Yoshitoshi was working hard to bring the Koreans to heel. But of course So was not; he knew that war was inevitable. He therefore remained on Tsushima, waiting for Hideyoshi's patience to run out and for orders to arrive for the invasion to begin.

A final factor contributing to the delay in launching the Korean expedition was Hideyoshi's own health. During March and April his eyes were causing him particular trouble and prevented him from giving the requisite farewell report to the emperor before departing south for Nagoya. This problem evidently eased at least partially some time in the middle of April, and Hideyoshi finally managed to deliver his report. Then, having received no word from So Yoshitoshi of a change in the Koreans' stance, he dispatched orders south on the twenty-fourth to proceed with the invasion.

Hideyoshi himself remained in Kyoto for another two weeks, enjoying the company of his wife and concubines. It was not until May 7, roughly the time his orders would have arrived at Nagoya, that he set out from the capital for the long journey south. His departure, like his return from the hunt three months before, was a magnificent and festive occasion. Hideyoshi, now the conquering general, rode out of the city on a fine horse, clad in brocade armor, a sword in one hand and a bow in the other. In his train came a bodyguard of seventy-seven warriors astride horses encased in armor, bearing gold gilt swords and spears. Sixty-six banners were borne aloft, symbolizing his unification of all sixty-six provinces of Japan.[2]

The baggage train must have been enormous. As at the siege of Odawara two years before, Hideyoshi did not intend for himself and his retinue to suffer during their time in the field. Entertainments of every variety would be provided, from music and dancing to noh theater and tea. For his tea ceremonies alone, Hideyoshi carried two portable tea-rooms: the quintessentially rustic Yamazato, a tiny mountain hut built from weathered beams and papered inside with old calendars, and the magnificent Kigane no zashiki, a finely crafted, three-mat chamber gilded entirely with gold, right down to the fire tongs. The two rooms perfectly represented the taiko's two sides. The golden Kigane was for the showman, the rags-to-riches parvenu who could not resist displays of extravagance. The Yamazato was for the cultured man of refined tastes: the poet, the patron of the arts, and the skilled practitioner of *chado*, the way of tea.[3]

Poetry and theater. Music and tea. Hideyoshi would always find time for these, even as he set out to conquer the world.

As Hideyoshi made his leisurely way south from Kyoto to Nagoya, the Koreans were still struggling with their defensive preparations. Work had been done to fortify towns, restock arsenals, and conscript men. But not that much. Certainly not enough.

To get some idea of how this defensive work was progressing, the government dispatched Generals Sin Ip and Yi Il on separate inspection tours in the spring of 1592. Sin went north, and Yi south. They returned to the capital a month later and delivered their reports. Both proved highly uninformative, describing only the condition of the swords, spears, bows and arrows in the armories that had been visited, while saying nothing of the state of the nation's standing armies, the existence of reservist lists, the condition of fortifications, and the general capability of each province to mount an effective defense. It might be inferred that Sin Ip was unimpressed with the defense preparations he observed, for he had people flogged and executed for negligence everywhere he went. But once back in Seoul he had little to say about it.

Following his return to the capital, General Sin visited Yu Songnyong at the latter's residence where they discussed defense issues, in particular the military capabilities of the Japanese.

"Sooner or later there will be a war," said Yu. "Since you are responsible for military affairs, what do you think about the power of the enemy today? Is he strong or weak?"

Sin replied that he was entirely unconcerned.

This annoyed Yu. "That is not the right attitude," he said. "Formerly the Japanese depended on short weapons alone, but now they are joined with muskets which are effective at a distance. We can't treat the affair lightly."

"Even if they have muskets," Sin replied, "they can't hit anyone with them."[4]

It was the same sort of empty bravado that Kim Song-il had indulged in after his return from Kyoto the previous year, assuring the Korean king and government that Hideyoshi was a paper tiger and that war would never come.

It was now May 11. The invasion was less than two weeks away.

On Korea's southern coast, Cholla Left Navy Commander Yi Sun-sin was continuing to work energetically to prepare his command for war. The task required constant vigilance. Earlier in the year, for example, he had received a report from the Traveling High Commissioner stating that the port of Sado was in fine condition and recommending rewards for the officers there. When Yi visited the port to inspect it personally, he found it to be in dreadful shape and was obliged to order floggings for its officers and men. Staff at the port of Pangtap had to be similarly punished for neglect. "Judging from their selfishness for personal gain without paying attention to public duties," Yi confided in his diary, "I can guess at their future." Corruption was clearly still a problem.[5]

May twenty-second. The day dawned clear at Yi's home port at Yosu. The commander had breakfast, then went down to the water's edge to test fire the "earth" and "black" cannons that had just been installed aboard his recently completed turtle ship. A staff officer of the Traveling High Commissioner was on hand for the demonstration. In the afternoon Yi engaged in some archery practice, as he tried to do most days; like any good Korean officer, he firmly believed in maintaining his skill with a bow. The rest of the day passed uneventfully.[6]

Twenty-four hours to go.

Hideyoshi was now nearing the southern tip of Honshu on his journey south from Kyoto, still two weeks away from his headquarters at Nagoya. His orders to proceed with the invasion had preceded him, and final preparations had already been made. Contingents one, two, and three, the spearhead of the invasion, were now in place at the forward staging area of Tsushima, the island in the strait between Japan and Korea. The remaining six contingents were encamped at Nagoya, ready to follow. Everything was set for the conquest of Korea. It was now just a question of waiting for the wind, which was blowing strongly from the wrong direction and whipping up the sea.[7]

The first three contingents poised to strike on Tsushima were led respectively by Konishi Yukinaga, Kato Kiyomasa, and Kuroda Nagamasa. Konishi, in his mid thirties, was the oldest of the three. He hailed from a wealthy merchant family in Sakai and had served Hideyoshi from the very beginning, when the latter had assumed the mantel of national unifier following the death of Oda Nobunaga in 1582. Hideyoshi first rewarded Konishi with a fiefdom in Harima Province on the Inland Sea, then moved him south to a more generous holding in Higo Province on Kyushu in the shake-up following that island's conquest in 1587.

Like many of his neighboring Kyushu daimyo, Konishi Yukinaga was a Christian. He had been baptized in 1583 and taken the Christian name Augustin, and was very friendly—some would say subservient—to the Jesuits who were then having so much success on the island. Most of the other daimyo in his first contingent were Christians as well. Tsushima lord So Yoshitoshi, Konishi's son-in-law, had been baptized in Kyoto in 1590 with the name Dario; his wife Marie was particularly supportive of the Portuguese fathers and did much to make Tsushima fertile ground for their proselytizing. Arima Harunobu of Hizen had been a Christian since 1579 and went by the name Protasio; Omura Yoshiaki, also from Hizen, was known as Sancho. Most of the soldiers in the armies commanded by these men were Christian converts as well. Matsuura Shigenobu was in fact the only daimyo in the entire contingent who was not a Christian, but many of the men he commanded were.

Second contingent leader Kato Kiyomasa was somewhat younger than Konishi: he was thirty in 1592. He had not been born to wealth, but was the son of a peasant from Hideyoshi's own village of Nakamura in Owari Province. His childhood nickname had been "Tiger," a prescient choice for a man who would become a warrior through and through. As one of Hideyoshi's fiercest and most austere commanders, Kato would have nothing to do with the refinements and diversions enjoyed by other daimyo, including Konishi Yukinaga and indeed, Hideyoshi himself. There was no room in his life for poetry, dancing, and tea. When he sat down in later life to pen his *kakun*, or "House Code," a list of guidelines for his samurai followers and heirs, Kato described such pastimes as shameful and ordered anyone who engaged in dancing to commit suicide. "Having been born into the house of a warrior," he advised, "one's intention should be to grasp the long and short swords and die."[8]

Like Konishi, Kato had served Hideyoshi from the beginning and was rewarded first with a fief on central Honshu, then with a new holding in Higo Province abutting Konishi's following the conquest of Kyushu. The two men thus followed similar career paths and by 1592 had come to be regarded by Hideyoshi as trusted members of his inner circle of more or less equal standing. The competition for the taiko's ear that must have taken place within this select group may indeed have been a cause of some of the tension that would soon arise between these two men. A second source was religion. Kato was a staunch adherent of the Buddhist Nichiren sect and distrusted the influence that the "southern barbarian" Jesuits were having on the likes of Konishi, Arima, Omura, and So. Not surprisingly, all the soldiers in Kato's second contingent ostensibly were Buddhists as well.[9]

The third contingent, finally, was led by a twenty-four-year-old commander named Kuroda Nagamasa. Although the youngest of the three, Kuroda was no stranger to battle. The son of longstanding Hideyoshi loyalist Kuroda Yoshitaka, young Nagamasa had first donned armor at the tender age of nine and had begun fighting along-side his father in the wars of unification not long thereafter. He inherited the Kuroda domain in 1589 when Hideyoshi, increasingly jealous of Yoshitaka's capabilities, forced the samurai scholar to retire. Like Konishi, Kuroda Nagamasa was a Christian, and supported the work of the Jesuit fathers. He went by the Christian name Damiao. In character he was closer to Konishi than to Kato: half warrior, half gentleman, a skilled commander and fearsome opponent when on the field of battle, but also capable of composing an apt renga couplet when relaxing with family and friends. In his own "House Code" Kuroda would later write, "The arts of peace and the arts of war are like two wheels of a cart which, lacking one, will have difficulty in standing."[10] Konishi would have approved.

There was little love lost between Konishi, Kato, and Kuroda on the eve of the Imjin War. Each was independent-minded, ambitious, and eager for glory in the coming campaign. Konishi and his first contingent would have a slight edge in the competition, for to them went the honor of leading the way across to Korea and establishing a beachhead at Pusan. Once that was accomplished, however, he was expected to wait for the other two contingents to arrive before beginning the concerted push north to Seoul, each contingent by a different route. So there would be glory enough for all.

May 23, 1592. The day dawned clear. The sea had calmed and the wind was right. At eight o'clock in the morning the 18,700 men under Konishi's command began boarding their transport ships massed off the beach at Owura on Tsushima's northern tip. By noon the last anchor had been raised and the fleet was under way. The battleships Hideyoshi had ordered built to protect the vulnerable transports from the Korean navy were nowhere in sight. They were still making their way to Nagoya from the Inland Sea and would not arrive at Tsushima for another two weeks. But Konishi wasn't worried. Korea lay just there to the north, unknowing and unprepared. He and his men perhaps could just make it out, a slightly darker hint of blue floating on the horizon like a distant mirage. Seven hours with a fair wind and they would be there.

PART 3

IMJIN

*The onrush of a conquering force
is like the bursting of pent-up waters
into a chasm a thousand fathoms deep.
So much for tactical dispositions.*[1]

Sun Tzu Ping Fa (Master Sun's Art of War)
4th century B.C.

CHAPTER 8

North to Seoul

OFFICIAL KOREAN DOCUMENTS in the sixteenth century were dated according to the reign year of the Chinese emperor or the Korean king. Fifteen ninety-two, being the twentieth year of the reign of China's Wanli emperor and the twenty-fifth year of the reign of Korean king Sonjo, was therefore referred to either as Wanli 20 or Sonjo 25. In everyday usage, however, a different and very ancient counting system was used to keep track of the passage of both the days and the years: the traditional cycle of sixty. Each increment in the cycle was given a name consisting of one of ten "heavenly stems" derived from the elements of wood, fire, earth, metal, and water,[1] and an "earthly branch" of one of the twelve zodiacal symbols: the rat, ox, tiger, rabbit, dragon, snake, horse, ram, monkey, rooster, dog, and pig.

Fifteen ninety-two was the twenty-ninth year in this cycle, the year called *imjin*, a name combining the ninth heavenly stem, seawater, with the sign of the dragon. The Koreans did not regard the year with any particular sense of foreboding. On the contrary, the advent of imjin may even have been considered fortuitous, for the year of the dragon was traditionally viewed as a time of opportunity and prosperity, tinged with just a hint of unpredictability.

Fifteen ninety-two changed all that. The events that would unfold on the peninsula beginning in May would sear the word imjin on the Korean consciousness as a synonym for death and destruction, the apocalypse, the end of the world. To this day *imjin waeran*, "the Japanese bandit invasion of the water dragon year," remains the closest that Korea has ever come to the abyss. There have been other times in her history that have brought destruction and tragedy on a terrible scale, most notably the Korean War of 1950 to 1953. But nothing can ever surpass the utter desolation of imjin waeran—the burned-out cities, the scorched earth, the broken families and snuffed-out lives. Among a people as homogeneous as the Koreans, the memory of this catastrophe not surprisingly is still very much alive today, more than four hundred years after the event. Indeed, it might even be said that they have not entirely forgiven Japan for it. Imjin waeran remains to this day a sub-text to the resentment and at times animosity that Koreans still feel toward the Japanese for their occupation of the peninsula from 1910 to 1945.

It began on May 23, 1592. A dense mist hung over the sea off Pusan early that morning, obscuring any sign of activity offshore. Chong Pal, the sixty-year-old commander of the Pusan garrison, left the port early for a day of hunting on Cholyong-do, a forested island at the mouth of the harbor so named for its population of deer. Emerging from the trees some time in the afternoon, he was one of the first to spy the armada, "covering all of the sea," approaching from the direction of Daema-do, as Tsushima was known to the Koreans. Suspecting that this could be the Japanese invasion that everyone was expecting and yet did not expect, Chong rushed back to Pusan to raise the alarm and prepare for the worst. Any doubts as to what he had seen were soon dispelled by corroborative reports from a lighthouse keeper farther along the coast and from a beacon-fire tender on a hill behind Pusan: a long battle line of ships, ninety in number, approaching from the south.[2]

The lead ships of the Japanese armada soon reached the waters off Pusan harbor and dropped anchor. Kyongsang Left Navy Commander Pak Hong observed their arrival from his nearby base at Kijang and began to tally the numbers for himself. There were easily ninety, as reported. Then one hundred. Then one hundred and fifty. The afternoon waned, and the ships kept coming. Two hundred. Two hundred and fifty. Three hundred. The sun eased below the horizon, and still the number continued to climb. And Pak's nerves began to fray.

Word of the Japanese arrival reached Kyongsang Right Navy Commander Won Kyun at his base on Koje Island to the west of Pusan that same afternoon. He could not at first bring himself to believe what was happening. In a dispatch to his colleague Yi Sun-sin, commander of the Cholla Left Navy based at Yosu farther to the west, Won reported that the approaching mass of ships was perhaps some sort of exceptionally large trade mission from Tsushima. As the afternoon progressed, however, and the number of ships crowding the bay off Pusan climbed to one hundred and fifty and beyond, Won was forced to the conclusion that an invasion was indeed under way and a disaster about to befall them.

Neither he nor Pak Hong, however, made any attempt that day or the next to attack the Japanese armada with the approximately one hundred and fifty heavy panokson battleships under their command, representing the bulk of the entire Korean navy. The two men simply watched and waited and sent off frantic dispatches, while the ships under their command, the most formidable weapons in the Korean arsenal and the first and most effective line in the nation's defenses, sat idle in their ports.

For the Koreans, this frozen inaction on the part of Won and Pak was the first of many strategic errors that would be made in the early days of the Imjin War. For although the two naval commanders did not know it, the gathering armada, while numerically daunting, was in fact vulnerable to seaborne attack and could have been dealt a heavy blow before it ever had a chance to send a single man ashore.

In the order of battle he had signed two months before, Hideyoshi urged his daimyo to be particularly careful to get their troops safely across the sea to Pusan, warning them that "the loss of one man or one horse through bad judgment will be regarded as a grave offense."[3] To ensure their safety, the invasion plan had called for a force of battleships to travel in convoy with the transports to protect them from the very ships that now sat idle in the Korean naval bases of Kyongsang Province. But such convoying had not occurred. When the first contingents of the invasion force were leaving Nagoya for their forward staging areas on Tsushima, the navy was still assembling on the Inland Sea. When the transports were at sea between Tsushima and Pusan, the navy was only just arriving at Nagoya. In fact, it would be more than a week before Hideyoshi's battleships would arrive at Pusan. Konishi had gambled that he could land his forces without their protection and was now in Korean waters with a fleet of light and largely unprotected transports—fishing boats really—that would have been no match for Korea's panokson if the challenge had been made. Had a different admiral been in command of either Kyongsang fleet, one willing to put his ships to sea and strike at the enemy, the outcome of these first few days might have been very different indeed.[4]

By nightfall on May 23 some four hundred ships bearing Konishi Yukinaga's first contingent had successfully traversed the seventy kilometers from Tsushima's northern tip and were crowding the waters off Pusan.[5] At seven thirty in the evening a single vessel separated from this force and advanced into the harbor. Aboard was So Yoshitoshi, the Christian daimyo of Tsushima, also known as Dario, who had served as Hideyoshi's emissary to the Koreans since 1589. Accompanying him was the scholar monk Genso, a member of the Tsushima mission to Seoul in 1589. The two men sent a letter to the commander of Pusan, Chong Pal, asking one last time that the way be cleared to China for the armies of Japan. They received no answer, and eventually returned in their ship and rejoined the armada.[6]

The die was now cast for a war with Korea. So Yoshitoshi and his father-in-law Konishi Yukinaga may have come to Pusan hoping that a show of force would cow the Koreans into acceding to Hideyoshi's demands, thereby avoiding the necessity of a fight. Chong Pal's rebuff ensured that this was not to be. With a huge invasion army waiting behind them on Tsushima, there was tremendous pressure on these two daimyo commanders not to spend time trying to arrange a settlement with the Koreans. It was, thought Konishi, "the will of Christ" that they now go ahead and use armed force.[7]

For the next several hours the Japanese armada sat motionless off-shore as the Koreans watched anxiously from behind the walls of Pusan Castle. Then, at four o'clock the next morning, May 24, the landings began. First ashore were the five thousand men under So Yoshitoshi. He was the logical choice to lead the way, for having visited Pusan several times in the past he knew the lay of the land and the nature of the defenses better than any of Hideyoshi's commanders. The arrival of this familiar and formerly friendly face may also have been intended to cause the Koreans at least momentary confusion. If so, it could not have lasted long. So and his men clearly had not come this time to conduct diplomacy or trade; they had come for war. They came ashore clad in armor of iron plates and leather shingles tied together to form a flexible yet nearly impenetrable shell. It covered their torsos and arms and formed an apron in the front. They wore flaring iron helmets, some with stylized buffalo horns and antlers screwed to the front, all with a jointed cowling affixed to the sides and back to protect the neck. High-ranking samurai rode horses. They wore grotesque war masks with fierce, grimacing faces, and were armed with two swords: a long katana and a shorter wakizashi, finely crafted, very expensive, and highly valued by their owner. Some may have carried bows as well, and a lesser number spears. They did not carry muskets. These effective but fundamentally dishonorable weapons went to the ashigaru foot soldiers, along with one "loan sword."

Next ashore was So Yoshitoshi's father-in-law, Konishi Yukinaga, at the head of seven thousand men. They followed an unusual banner featuring a huge, stuffed rendering of the white paper bags used by Japanese druggists to dispense medicine, a reference to the Konishi family's traditional involvement in that trade.[8] There were very likely crucifixes in evidence as well, for Konishi and his men, like So's company, were all Christians. Konishi himself rode a fine horse that Hideyoshi had presented to him at Nagoya before his departure, with the exhortation that he use it to "gallop over the heads of the bearded savages."[9]

After Konishi came Matsuura, lord of Hirado, the sole nonbeliever in the group. Then Arima. Omura. Goto. A total of 18,700 men in all, dressed for combat, ready to kill. The predominant colors were black and red: black armor and helmets, red banners and brocade. The multitude formed up in ranks, then split in two. Konishi led a portion of the men a few kilometers southwest along the harbor front to the fort at Tadaepo at the mouth of the Naktong River. The fort's defenders, under garrison commander Yun Hung-sin, managed to repel the first assault but were overwhelmed by the second and all put to the sword. So Yoshitoshi meanwhile led the advance on Pusan Castle itself. He formally called upon garrison commander Chong Pal one last time to surrender, asserting yet again that they were on their way to China and would not harm the Koreans if they would only step aside. Chong refused. Until he received orders to the contrary, he replied, he was duty bound to resist the Japanese advance.[10]

The aging officer then turned to his men and made his orders clear. "I expect you all," he cried out, "to fight and die like brave men! If any man attempts to turn and flee, I will personally cut off his head!"

The day was just dawning when the Japanese sounded their conch-shell trumpets to signal the attack. The ensuing battle was fierce but short, providing the beleaguered Koreans with their first taste of the stunning power of the arquebus. Their arrows and spears were no match for them. The defenders of Pusan Castle were felled by the hundreds by the flying slugs of lead that these strange "dog legs" spit out, a deluge of death that "fell like rain." The garrison fought until all their arrows were gone. Then Chong Pal himself was killed, and with that, at around nine o'clock in the morning, all resistance ceased.[11]

Once over the walls, "We found people running all over the place and trying to hide in the gaps between the houses," samurai chronicler Yoshino Jingozaemon would later record. "Those who could not conceal themselves went off toward the East Gate, where they clasped their hands together, and there came to our ears the Chinese expression, 'Manō! Manō!' which was probably them asking for mercy. Taking no notice of what they heard our troops rushed forward and cut them down, slaughtering them as a blood sacrifice to the god of war. Both men, women, and even dogs and cats were beheaded."[12] That it was assumed the Koreans spoke Chinese is an indication of how little the Japanese knew of their foe.

According to Japanese records, 8,500 Koreans were killed in the fall of Pusan and 200 prisoners were taken. Among the dead was Chong Pal's eighteen-year-old concubine, Ae-hyang. Her body was found lying beside the fallen commander. She had taken her own life.

Kyongsang Left Navy Commander Pak Hong, based at Kijang a short distance to the east, witnessed this battle from the top of a nearby hill. His nerve had been badly shaken the previous day, watching the arrival of the hundreds of ships comprising the Japanese armada. Now, as he witnessed the seemingly indomitable enemy take Pusan Castle and slaughter the defenders within, it broke entirely. He did not rush to his ships to fight the Japanese, whose intentions now were clear. Nor did he attempt to move his vessels to safer waters. Instead he ordered his entire fleet scuttled, a total of one hundred vessels, including fifty or more panokson battleships. He also had all his weapons destroyed and provisions burned so they would not fall into enemy hands. He then deserted his post and fled north all the way to Seoul, leaving behind thousands of bewildered soldiers and sailors who naturally followed his example and drifted away. [13]

So it was that the Kyongsang Left Navy, the strong left arm of the Korean navy and the first line of defense on the nation's south coast, self-destructed on the second day of the war. Pak Hong's ships did not sail a mile or fire a shot. They simply disappeared quietly beneath the waves. It was a tremendous gift to the Japanese, particularly to first contingent leader Konishi Yukinaga, who had taken a considerable gamble in coming to Pusan without the protection of warships. The sight of all those Korean ships wrecked in the harbor must have been heartwarming indeed for the ambitious Christian daimyo, visual confirmation that bold, swift action was what was needed to quell the Koreans, who were clearly unprepared for war.

The day after taking Pusan Castle and the garrison fort at Tadaepo, Konishi recombined his forces and marched on the fortress at Tongnae ten kilometers to the northeast on the main road to Seoul. This was the strongest fortification in the area, a stoutly walled citadel on a hilltop in front of Mt. Kumjong. It was by this time bursting with twenty thousand Koreans, a crush of ill-equipped soldiers, untrained conscripts, and a mass of panicked civilians. In overall command was Tongnae prefect Song Sang-hyon, a forty-one-year-old government official who in the coming hours would provide the Japanese with another lesson in just how badly Hideyoshi had miscalculated in thinking that the Koreans would ever willingly give passage to his armies and "lead the way to Ming."

As they had at Pusan, the Japanese gave Song Sang-hyon and the defenders of Tongnae one last chance to surrender before launching their attack, erecting a large sign outside the castle's south gate that read, "Fight if you want to fight. Or lay down your arms and let us pass." Song Sang-hyon wrote an unequivocal reply on a piece of wood and threw it over the wall: "Fighting and dying are easy," it read. "But letting you pass I cannot do."

Song knew the situation was hopeless, that the Japanese would inevitably breech the wall and take the fort just as they had at Pusan. His servant told him of a gap he had spied in the Japanese lines and urged him to flee before it was too late. Song refused. He would do his duty and die at Tongnae. His only regret was the pain this would cause his parents, so in the lull before the attack he sat down to write a final note to his father; one account adds the dramatic flourish that he bit the end of his finger and wrote the message in blood. "Our fortress is now under siege," it said, "surrounded by a multitude of enemy soldiers. There is no chance of rescue. The other garrisons are sleeping peacefully, oblivious to the danger we face. It grieves me to leave you, but a subject's duty to his king must come before a son's devotion to his father."

Song then turned to his servant. "When the fighting is over the bodies will be piled high. I have a mole the size of a small bean on my lower back. Remember that when you're looking for my corpse."

The Battle of Tongnae began at eight o'clock in the morning. According to Korean accounts it lasted twelve hours; the Japanese say it was over in four. The besieged Koreans, women included, fought with desperate ferocity, flinging arrows and spears and then stones at the attacking Japanese as Song Sang-hyon beat the great drum from an upper pavilion of the castle to urge his soldiers on. But once again the backward weapons the Koreans possessed proved no match for Japanese muskets. One by one the defenders were picked off by the deadly fire of the ashigaru. When resistance began to falter, the Japanese threw bamboo ladders against the fort's high walls and swarmed over the top, Konishi at the fore, sword in hand. A final crescendo of hand-to-hand fighting followed. And then it was over. Song himself was captured alive by a group of soldiers who tried to force him to bow before them. When he resisted they hacked him to death.

The Japanese suffered one hundred killed and four hundred wounded in the Battle of Tongnae. Korean deaths totaled five thousand. Upon hearing that Song Sang-hyon was among the fallen, So Yoshitoshi, who had been hospitably treated by the prefect during his prewar missions to Korea and was thus anxious to see him spared, ordered a funeral held and wrote a epitaph for his grave mound: "A Loyal Subject." Song was buried on the mountain behind Tongnae, in a grove of chestnut trees. His final letter eventually found its way north to his parents. Two years later, in 1594, a family member went to Tongnae to claim his body and carry it home.[14]

Kyongsang Right Navy Commander Won Kyun was approaching a state of panic at his base on Koje Island. The initial reports he had received of the appearance of the Japanese armada at Pusan to the east were followed in quick succession by news of the fall of Pusan Castle, then word of the events at Tongnae. Finally, in what was undoubtedly a confusing welter of facts and rumors, Won learned of the desertion of his colleague Pak Hong and the self-destruction of the Kyongsang Left Navy. With that any thoughts he may have had of resisting the invaders disappeared entirely. His only concern now was to flee. His retreat appears to have begun in an orderly fashion, with Won attempting to lead his fleet west to safety. But he soon panicked at the sight of a group of fishing boats in the distance that he mistook for the Japanese navy and, just like Pak Hong, ordered his ships scuttled and his weapons destroyed. He was himself preparing to abandon his flagship and run into the hills when two of his more stalwart subordinates reminded him of the consequences of flight. How would he be able to justify his actions, they asked, if he were to be accused of deserting his post? It would be better to stand his ground and send for reinforcements from Cholla Left Navy Commander Yi Sun-Sin. In the end a chastened Won decided to stay and fight. But there was little good he could do now. Of his original fleet of more than one hundred vessels, he had only four ships left.[15]

The fleets of both the Kyongsang Left and Right Navies were now gone, a total of some two hundred ships, two-thirds of the entire Korean navy, destroyed by their own commanders. All that remained in the south to resist the Japanese at sea were the fewer than one hundred ships of the Left and Right Navies of Cholla Province to the west. Fortunately for Korea, the commanders of these two navies, Yi Sun-sin and Yi Ok-ki, were made of sterner stuff than their Kyongsang counterparts.

*   *   *

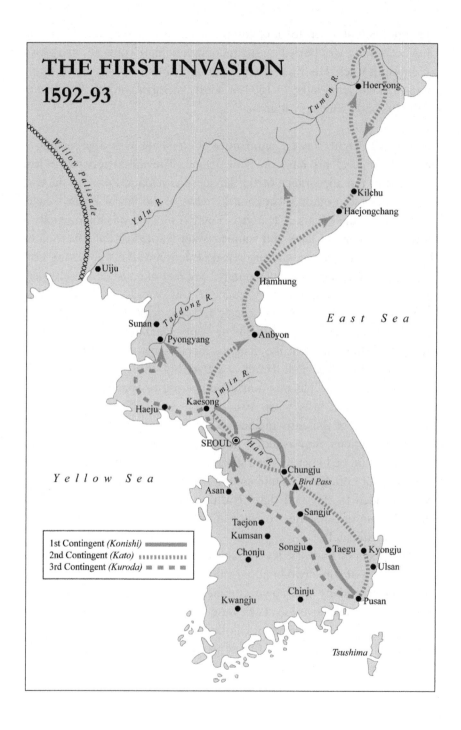

After taking Pusan and nearby Tongnae and establishing a beachhead for the invasion, Konishi Yukinaga did not wait for the arrival of Kato's second contingent and Kuroda's third before beginning the march to Seoul. This was a change in the invasion plan. Konishi may have secretly intended all along to push ahead of his rivals and claim the glory of seizing the capital solely for himself. Or perhaps the idea came to him with the surge of confidence he surely felt after taking Pusan, Tadaepo, and Tongnae in the space of just two days. Or perhaps he was anxious to break out of the Pusan beachhead and be on his way before the Koreans could mount a counterattack.[16] Whichever the case, on May 26, the third day of the invasion, Konishi, So Yoshitoshi, and the bulk of the first contingent set out on the long march to the Choson capital, 450 kilometers north over mountainous terrain. They traveled by the central route, up the middle of the peninsula, at an average speed of more than twenty kilometers per day, a blistering pace considering the skirmishes and battles they would fight on the way.

The first town they came to was Yangsan, which they found deserted. The magistrate and most of the population had fled into the hills. The route then took them up to the Chakwon Pass, where they were momentarily slowed by a hastily organized force of defenders. Their muskets soon swept this obstacle aside and they passed down to the town of Miryang, leaving three hundred dead Koreans in the mountains behind.

Taegu was next. General Yi Kak, the Left Army Commander for Kyongsang Province who had retreated from Tongnae soon after the Japanese landing, attempted to regroup his scattered forces at this fortress town in the center of the province. Reinforcements were also summoned from the town of Sangju farther north. But it was all too late. The Japanese were upon the city before any sort of defense could be mounted. Taegu fell on May 28.

The Koreans were now beginning to feel the full might of the Japanese onslaught. The enemy seemed invincible. Unstoppable. Indeed, was there any point in trying to stand against their muskets with mere arrows and swords and spears? The governor of Kyongsang Province, Kim Su, had issued a call to arms immediately after the start of the invasion and attempted to lead a force south to meet it near

Pusan. He had not gotten very far on his march, however, when he learned that Tongnae had fallen as well. With that he gave up any further thought of resistance and effectively rescinded his previous call to arms with a proclamation urging the people of the province to flee for their lives.

By May 29, one week after their landing at Pusan, it was beginning to look as if the Japanese army would cover the entire length of Kyongsang Province, fully half the distance from Pusan to Seoul, without encountering any serious resistance. They simply could not be stopped. As royal emissary Yi Ik reported to Seoul on May 31 from Mungyong on the province's northern border, "We face today an enemy equipped with divine power and skill. We have nobody to cope with them. I myself have no alternative but to meet death."[17]

For the Koreans there was perhaps a sense of déjà vu in all of this. In the twelfth century their armies had encountered a similar sort of enemy that had left them equally baffled and incapable of mounting any sort of effective defense. Then it had been the Jurchen tribesmen of Manchuria, who were expert horsemen. Their lightning-fast cavalry units galloped rings around the inexperienced foot soldiers of the Koryo army, dashing in to strike and then flying away again before the Koreans could respond. As one contemporary succinctly observed, "The enemy rode. We walked. We were no match for them."[18]

In 1592 the name of the game was no longer horses. It was guns. And the Koreans were shaking their heads over the new but somehow familiar refrain: "The enemy has muskets. We have arrows. We are no match for them."

News of the Japanese invasion began to filter west to Yosu, home port of Cholla Left Navy Commander Yi Sun-sin, at sunset on May 25. First to arrive were confusing reports from Kyongsang naval commanders Pak Hong and Won Kyun of an armada of Japanese ships that had arrived in Pusan harbor. Although it was still not clear what was happening, Yi sent dispatches to the five ports under his command ordering them to full alert and had his own warships form a battle line at the mouth of Yosu harbor to defend it against possible attack. He also sent dispatches west to Usuyong, home port of Cholla Right Navy

Commander Yi Ok-ki, inland to provincial governor Yi Kwang, and north to the court in Seoul.

The gravity of the situation became clear the next day, with the arrival of further reports that the Japanese had landed and taken Pusan Castle. Then, on the twenty-eighth, came word of the fate of Tongnae.[19]

And then the bombshell: both the Kyongsang Left and Right Navies were gone, scuttled by their own commanders, Pak Hong and Won Kyun. Pak had fled his post and was now far inland. Won was hiding somewhere along the coast to the west of Koje Island, with just four ships remaining from his hundred-ship fleet, pleading for Yi to send reinforcements.

Yi Sun-sin did not now rush headlong into battle. Two and a half weeks would pass before he would finally lead his fleet eastward from Yosu to meet the Japanese. One reason for the delay was a lack of orders. Prior to the outbreak of war the government in Seoul had not given its commanders in the south the authority to act as they saw fit in the event of an emergency. Each commander was charged simply with defending his assigned territory. For Yi this was the eastern coast of Cholla Province. To sally forth to Kyongsang Province and Won Kyun's aid would thus have been tantamount to abandoning his post.

It would also have been foolhardy, and Yi Sun-sin most certainly was not that. As he would later urge his captains before going into battle, "Don't act rashly! Be deliberate and calm, like a mountain!" In the coming months of the war these words would prove to be Yi Sun-sin's genius. He was coming to understand the power of the Japanese. But he remained confident that, with careful planning and judicious action, they could still be beaten at sea. The sea, after all, was where Korea's strength lay with regard to the Japanese. It was where it had beaten the wako pirates in the fifteenth century. And it was where it could beat them again, if cooler heads prevailed.

The two and a half weeks that elapsed before Yi Sun-sin sailed into the war were thus a time of calm and deliberate preparation. First, he decided that the most effective way to counter the Japanese would be to combine his modest force (he had twenty-four panokson board-roofed battleships, fifteen mid-sized vessels, and forty-six commandeered fishing boats that he would later discard as useless) with the vessels in

Yi Ok-ki's Cholla Right Navy to create a united fleet. It is clear from his diaries and dispatches to Seoul that he had begun organizing this soon after the start of the invasion. Second, Yi needed information on the waterways of Kyongsang Province before he could act—no small consideration, for Korea's southern coast is a maze of rocks and reefs and dangerous tides, any one of which can doom a vessel. He thus sent a request for charts to Kyongsang governor Kim Su and to Won Kyun in his refuge to the east, and when they arrived he studied them carefully.

Finally, Yi needed time to prepare his men mentally for the battles ahead. The news of the fall of Pusan and Tongnae, the destruction of both Kyongsang fleets, and the seeming invincibility of the Japanese had had an understandably demoralizing effect on virtually every man in the fleet. To have rushed them into battle in such a frame of mind would have been disastrous, for as the fourth-century-B.C. Chinese military classic *Ssu-Ma Fa* observed, "When men have minds set on victory, all they see is the enemy. When men have minds filled with fear, all they see is their fear."[20] Yi had to be confident that his men, particularly his captains, would not lose their nerve and in turn their heads at the first sight of the enemy. He needed to build up their anger and their confidence to the point where they were fully prepared to fight and win. In his diary entries for this period we thus find him holding numerous conferences with his captains, testing their resolve and leading them in solemn pledges to fight to the death. We find him questioning the magistrates of the towns under his jurisdiction to gauge their commitment to man the walls and fight. We find him offering encouragement to his men, stirring up their martial spirit, quelling their fears and imbuing in them his own grim determination to strike a telling blow against the Japanese.[21]

This is why Yi Sun-sin waited two and a half weeks before leading his ships into battle. This is why, when Won Kyun and Kyongsang governor Kim Su urged him to come to their aid, he replied with a request for charts. He refused to act rashly. He would proceed only with calm deliberation, "like a mountain."

All this was lost on Kyongsang naval commander Won Kyun, holed up in a cove to the east with his remaining four ships. In his view he had sent out a call for help that Yi Sun-sin had failed to answer. It was the first of numerous complaints that an increasingly resentful Won would make against Yi. Soon the two men would thoroughly despise each other.

With Korea's beacon-fire system in disrepair, it took four days for news of the Japanese invasion to travel the 450 kilometers north to Seoul. The first dispatch came by horse and rider, sent by Kyongsang Left Navy Commander Pak Hong. Pak himself was not far behind.

After more than a year of foot-dragging over defensive preparations, it was only now that the government appointed the generals needed to lead the nation's armies. In 1591 Minister of the Left Yu Song-nyong had urged that these appointments be made well in advance of the out-break of hostilities so that the generals would have time to acquaint themselves with their commands and mount an effective defense. But this went against the Choson practice of keeping generals in Seoul until the moment they were needed to lead troops into battle, and so Yu's suggestion was ignored. Now, just as Yu had predicted, "visiting generals" would have to "gallop down to the provinces on the spur of the moment" to defend the routes north to Seoul. For the top post of *dowonsu*, commander in chief of the armed forces in all of Korea's eight provinces, a fifty-eight-year-old civil servant named Kim Myong-won was selected—yet another example of the Korean idea that a classically trained government official with no military experience was capable of leading armies. Sin Ip, a bona fide army officer, was appointed to the secondary post of *samdo sunbyonsa*, "commander of the three provinces" of Kyongsang, Cholla, and Chungchong. Beneath Sin came Yi Il as *sunbyonsa*, "provincial commander," with responsibility for Kyongsang-do, and then a handful of *pangosa*, "county commanders," charged with defending specific strategic points.

With these crucial appointments out of the way, it was time to apportion blame for the crisis. The brunt of it fell upon Kim Song-il, the envoy who had returned from Japan in 1591 with assurances that war would never come. Kim, now serving as Kyongsang Right Army commander, was arrested for making a false report to the throne, a charge that carried an almost certain sentence of death. He was being transported to Seoul, bound as a prisoner, when his close friend Yu Song-nyong petitioned the king for a pardon and secured his release. Kim would be sent back to Kyongsang Province as a recruiting officer to raise civilian troops. He would fall sick and die there the following year.[22]

The Koreans had a good idea how the Japanese would march north. Because their kingdom was so mountainous (a local joke has it that if Korea were ironed flat it would be as big as China), long-distance traffic was necessarily confined to prepared routes that snaked through the labyrinthine valleys and cut across the otherwise impenetrable mountain ranges that crisscrossed the peninsula. There were three such routes linking Pusan and Seoul of which the Japanese were known to be aware: the eastern road through Kyongsang Province, the western road through Chungchong Province, and the central road, the most direct route to the capital, running up the middle of the peninsula. With these three routes in mind, the following defensive plan was accordingly drawn up. General Yi Il would head south along the crucially important central road to meet the Japanese advance while it was still in the southern province of Kyongsang. General Sin Ip would position his forces farther north along the central road in the town of Chungju, there to meet the Japanese if they managed to get by Yi Il. The county commanders, meanwhile, would fan out across the south to hold various strategic points: General Pyon Ki was charged with defending Choryong, "Bird Pass," a narrow defile in the Sobaek mountain range on the central road between the towns of Sangju and Chungju. General Yu Kuk-ryang would make a stand farther north at Chuknyong, "Bamboo Pass," a short distance south of Seoul. General Cho Kyong was sent south to meet any Japanese force that ventured up the western road through Cholla Province near the Yellow Sea coast, and General Song Ung-gil down the eastern road along the peninsula's opposite side. Commander in Chief Kim Myong-won, finally, would remain in Seoul for the time being to oversee defensive preparations there.[23]

All these generals had difficulty mustering armies to lead to the south. The military lists of soldiers stationed in and around the capital proved useless, for the vast majority of these men were absent, many excused due to sickness or for the prescribed two-year mourning period for a deceased parent. The company of three hundred supposedly crack troops assigned to Yi Il, for example—a miserably small force to begin with—turned out to consist in large part of hastily recruited students and clerks pulled out of government offices. Ordered to depart immediately for the south, General Yi decided to leave this useless rabble behind and set out with a guard of just sixty mounted men he knew he could rely upon. With this small "army," plus others he hoped to pick up along the way, General Yi was expected to halt the Japanese advance.[24]

The situation was only marginally better for Yi's superior, Sin Ip, who headed south from Seoul the following day. King Sonjo was on hand to see him off, together with a large portion of the capital's anxious population. In a brief ceremony the king presented Sin with an old and valuable sword symbolizing the military authority that was now being bestowed upon him. You have my personal permission, Sonjo said, to call up men in the provinces to form an army, to requisition whatever weapons you need from government armories, and to execute anyone who fails to obey your commands.[25]

King Sonjo and the people of Seoul expected great things from General Sin as they watched him depart, for he was one of the most highly regarded generals in the nation, with a distinguished career leading his vaunted cavalry against the Jurchen tribes of the north. He had expressed a great deal of confidence prior to the outbreak of the war of Korea's ability to resist the Japanese, assuring Yu Song-nyong that even if Hideyoshi's soldiers had muskets, "they can't hit anyone with them." Now that war was upon them Sin continued to talk along the same lines. The Japanese were rapidly outrunning their supply lines, he claimed, and were growing daily more vulnerable to the devastating cavalry charges he intended to unleash upon them. He vowed to stop them in their tracks, or to not come back alive. It was all brave talk, probably designed, like his earlier pronouncement on muskets, to buck up quavering government officials and nervous military men. Sin himself certainly was not foolish enough to believe it. He would have known that they were now facing something much more serious than a simple border raid.

As General Sin was setting out on his journey south to halt the enemy advance, the second contingent of the Japanese invasion force was arriving at Pusan. After a maddening delay waiting for favorable winds, it finally managed to make the crossing from Tsushima Island on May 28, five days behind the vanguard of Konishi Yukinaga. The second contingent consisted of 22,800 men, like Konishi's first contingent exclusively from the southern island of Kyushu, and was under the overall command of Kato Kiyomasa, the thirty-year-old lord of Kumamoto Castle in Higo Province.

Kato's second contingent, composed entirely of Buddhists of the Nichiren sect, came ashore near Pusan under a banner emblazoned in red with the mantra *namu myoho renge kyo*: "Glory to the Holy Lotus." The sect had been founded by the evangelical monk Nichiren, who had inspired the Japanese to stand firm against the Mongol invasions two hundred years before. Nichiren's adherents were now returning to the launching point of those invasions, Korea, to exact their long-awaited revenge.

Kato and his men would have cut a striking appearance as they waded and were ferried ashore. Kato himself was easily identifiable by the high-crowned helmets he favored. Painted in silver or gold, they were intended to look like the headgear worn by courtiers in the imperial court; to the modern Western eye they resemble an elongated shark's fin or stylized dunce cap. Unlike most other daimyo commanders and samurai warriors, he also sported a full beard, reportedly to ease the discomfort of his helmet cord, and carried a three-bladed lance, his favorite weapon for running down and skewering his enemies. Kato's higher-ranking subordinates sat astride horses in exquisitely made suits of armor, wide-brimmed, horned helmets, and snarling war masks. His foot soldiers wore plainer armor and simple iron-bowl helmets, and had identifying sashimono banners affixed to their backs bearing the image of a ring, Kato's family crest. They carried spears and swords and arquebuses, the dog-leg weapon the Koreans were coming to fear.[26]

Kato would have been in an impatient mood that day. There was no more ambitious commander in Hideyoshi's army, and the fact that his rival Konishi had had the honor of being the first into battle must have chagrined him greatly. But now they were both in the field, and their chances for glory henceforth would be equal. Konishi may have been first to Pusan. But Kato intended to be first to Seoul.

But where were Konishi and his army? Where was the prima donna daimyo now? His first contingent was supposed to wait at Pusan for the arrival of Kato's second contingent and Kuroda's third, after which they would race north simultaneously along the central, eastern, and western routes. Where was the Christian "Augustin" that Hideyoshi had such an inexplicable affection for?

The answer was a shock. Konishi, he was told, was gone. He had not waited for the arrival of the second and third contingents as per the plan, but had forged ahead for Seoul as soon as Pusan and Tongnae had been taken and was already several days' march to the north.

Kato was furious. For Konishi to steal a march on him and capture Pusan was one thing. For him to then race ahead and take Seoul as well was quite another. That was a degree of glory hogging that Kato would not allow. Mustering his forces for an immediate pullout, he struck north at a punishing pace along his pre-assigned eastern route. He stormed through Ulsan first, encountering no resistance. At Kyongju, capital of the ancient Silla dynasty, he easily smashed through the hastily assembled defenses, torched the city's thousand-year-old buildings and temples, and put three thousand people to the sword. Next it was Yongchon's turn, then Sinnyong's and Kumi's. His men must have been tired by now, but Kato did not relent. He pushed them on, marching day and night, determined to catch up to and pass his rival Konishi before he reached the gates of Seoul.

Kuroda Nagamasa's third contingent was the next army in the Japanese invasion force to arrive from Tsushima, very likely aboard some of the same ships that had ferried Konishi Yukinaga's first contingent across the strait to Pusan. They landed at the port of Angolpo, twenty kilometers west of Pusan, on May 29, one day behind Kato and six behind Konishi. Kuroda's troops were recognizable by the black disk on their sashimono banners, a visual representation of their commander's family name, which means "black field."[27] At twenty-three Kuroda was somewhat younger than both Konishi and Kato, and as such did not participate fully in the rivalry that so shaped the prickly relationship between those two. He came to Korea fully expecting glory, but not necessarily the largest portion of it.

After completing his landing and taking the nearby fort at Kimhae (his men cut off a thousand heads), Kuroda struck north by his pre-assigned route up the western side of the Korean Peninsula. It would take him through Changnyong, Songju, Chongju, and Suwon, and then on to the Han River and Seoul beyond.

There were now three Japanese armies en route to the Korean capital.

On June 2 Korean General Yi Il and his force of sixty cavalrymen from Seoul passed through Choryong Pass and descended to the town of Sangju in northern Kyongsang Province. He found no soldiers there to reinforce him; they had all been called away to defend the provincial capital of Taegu, eighty kilometers farther south. In a desperate bid to increase his force, Yi used grain from the local government storehouse to hire peasants to serve in his army, bringing his total strength to about eight or nine hundred men. It was an unruly and untrained mob, but Yi figured he would have a week, maybe longer, to whip them into shape before the enemy arrived.

He had scarcely a day. Konishi Yukinaga's first contingent had already taken Taegu by this point and was nearing Sosan, a few kilometers to the southeast. When a locally recruited peasant soldier brought this news to Yi, the general refused to believe it, and had the unfortunate man beheaded for spreading malicious rumors. It was simply too fantastic that an army could fight its way all the way from Pusan to Sosan, half the distance to Seoul, in just ten days. The man's report must have been corroborated, however, for on the following morning, June 3, Yi deployed his force on the slopes behind Sangju and prepared to do battle with the Japanese. He sat on his horse at the front of the army, resplendent in fine armor, his general's flag raised high. In front of him to the south was a small river and a heavy cover of forest. Beyond that lay Sangju.

Konishi's first contingent, meanwhile, had split into two groups five kilometers southeast of Sangju. Ten thousand men under Konishi and Matsuura Shigenobu headed straight for the town and took it without a fight. The remaining force of 6,700 under So, Omura, and Goto swung north and then west, bypassing Sangju to strike directly at General Yi's small force, which they had learned was awaiting them on the hill behind the town.

The Japanese approached the Korean army through the forest. Their scouts led the way, emerging from the trees in full view of the waiting Koreans, but well beyond the range of their bows—which in the hands of untrained farmers would not have been very far. Yi's officers observed the movement, but remembering the beheading of the man the day before, they held their tongues. They did not want to be accused of spreading malicious rumors.

Then smoke was seen rising from beyond the forest in the direction of Sangju. General Yi did not yet know it, but the town had already fallen. He ordered one of his officers south to investigate. The man apparently was reluctant to go, for as Yu Song-nyong relates in his *Chingbirok*, "The officer mounted his horse, two foot soldiers took the bit, and they went off very slowly." As they neared the bridge to cross the river, a shot rang out, the officer toppled off his horse, and a Japanese soldier ran out from beneath the bridge and hacked off his head.

Suddenly a mass of enemy soldiers appeared from the forest and proceeded to form up into three groups, a vanguard unit in the center backed by units on the left and the right. It was a standard Japanese battle array, the most effective way for organizing troops to have emerged from a century of civil war. The three units then began to advance in a wide and imposing arc, musketeers to the front, swordsmen and spearmen to the rear. When the distance between the two armies had closed to less than a hundred meters the musketeers began to fire into the crowd of Koreans waiting to meet them on the slopes ahead. A few more paces and the volleys began to tell, felling scores of General Yi's untrained men as they struggled to return fire with bows they scarcely knew how to use. At fifty meters they were staring straight into the muzzles of the Japanese guns, the air was filled with cries of pain and death was all around. For most of the Koreans, simple farmers and tradesmen who had never seen a battle, it was too much. They cast down their weapons and began a panicked retreat—the signal for the swordsmen and spearmen at the rear of the Japanese formations to rush forward and finish them off. Within minutes Yi Il's hastily organized army was reduced to heaps of headless corpses and blood-streaked peasants fleeing in terror through the trees.[28]

General Yi for his part made good his escape, discarding first his horse and then his armor in his scramble up the mountain behind the killing field. His retreat soon brought him to Choryong Pass. The county commander sent south from Seoul to defend the pass had either never arrived or had already fled—a monumental error, for Choryong presented all sorts of strategic advantages, a narrow gap in the mountains that even a small band of men could have held if they were determined and well equipped. Nor did General Yi attempt to mount any sort of defense. He raced over the crest of the mountain and down the other side, continuing his flight north to Chungju to join his superior, General Sin Ip, and leaving Choryong behind him entirely unguarded.

General Sin had assembled a sizable force at Chungju, a total of eight thousand men, mainly officers and soldiers who had fled the south in the face of the Japanese advance, augmented by units he had led down from Seoul. Sin's original intention had been to march this force up to Choryong Pass to make a stand, where the rocky terrain and the narrowness of the pass would work to their advantage. The unexpected appearance of a bedraggled Yi Il, shorn of his horse, his armor, and his army, caused him to change his mind. With Sangju fallen, Yi's army annihilated, and the Japanese already marching on Choryong Pass, General Sin decided to remain at Chungju. He would do battle with the Japanese here, in an open field, not in the mountains above the town. One of his lieutenants urged him to abandon this plan and take up a position in the surrounding hills. Sin brushed the advice aside. "Our cavalry is useless in the rough terrain of the hills," he replied. "So we must make our stand here, in the field."[29]

At midday on June 6, as the Japanese were descending the mountain road from Choryong and drawing near Chungju, General Sin Ip accordingly arrayed his forces outside the town on a stretch of flat ground beside a hill called Tangumdae. In hindsight it seems a dreadful choice, a deathtrap offering no chance of retreat, hemmed in by the South Han River behind and Tangumdae to the right. Sin has been often criticized ever since for choosing to make his stand here. His decision is regarded as a fatal symptom of his overconfidence, and of his misguided determination to use his much-vaunted cavalry units. Perhaps so. There is, however, another dimension to the coming battle that needs to be understood before Sin Ip's measure can be fairly taken.

Tangumdae was indeed a death trap, affording the Korean army no possibility of retreat. This fact has been clear to every historian who has subsequently written about the battle. It would have been even clearer to General Sin himself. Indeed, this is possibly why he chose it. Placing troops in a hopeless situation with no avenue of escape was a long-established Chinese military strategy that had over the millennia resulted in a number of remarkable victories against seemingly insurmountable odds. It worked on the principle that a man with no hope of escape will instinctively fight for his life with the desperate ferocity of a cornered animal, and in so doing would become an almost unbeatable warrior. As one of Korea's few seasoned generals and as a literate man, Sin would have known of this tradition from a reading of the Chinese military classics of Shang Yang, Sun Tzu, and others, and from the histories of the ancient dynasties of Han and Qin and Tang that educated Koreans studied so diligently. He would have known that in certain desperate situations, the Chinese strategy called "fighting with a river to one's back" was sometimes the only option a general had.

One of the earliest recorded examples of "fighting with a river to one's back" occurred in the second century B.C., when the Han Chinese commander Han Hsin positioned his troops in the bottom of a gorge with their backs to a river to meet the opposing army of the Chao. With no possibility of retreat, his men were forced to fight for their lives and in the end won a great victory. After the battle, Han's officers asked him to explain his unusual strategy, observing that in *The Art of War* Sun Tzu clearly stated that battles should be fought with hills behind and water in front.

> "This is in *The Art of War* too," replied Han Hsin. "It is just that you have failed to notice it! Does it not say in *The Art of War*: 'Drive them into a fatal position and they will come out alive; place them in a hopeless spot and they will survive? Moreover, I did not have at my disposal troops that I had trained and led from past times, but was forced, as the saying goes, to round up men from the market place and use them to fight with. Under such circumstances, if I had not placed them in a desperate situation where each man was obliged to fight for his own life, but had allowed them to remain in a safe place, they would have all run away. Then what good would they have been to me?"[30]

General Sin Ip's situation was similar to Han Hsin's. His force consisted for the most part of green troops and drafted peasants, poorly
armed and terrified and apt to run as soon as the fighting began. And
yet a victory had to be won. The alternative was unthinkable, for
beyond Chungju nothing stood between the Japanese and Seoul. The
coming battle would therefore have to be a do-or-die struggle, and
General Sin positioned his forces to achieve that end. At Tangumdae.
With a river to their backs and no avenue of retreat, they would not be
able to break and run as General Yi Il had reported his own men had
done from the hills behind Sangju. With the cavalry leading the way
and the mass of untrained recruits forced to fight for their lives, Sin's
rabble might possibly be able to stop the Japanese advance. If not they
would do the proper thing by their king and die in the attempt.

After eight days and nights of forced marches along the eastern
route to Seoul, Kato Kiyomasa's first contingent caught up to Konishi
Yukinaga's second at Mungyong, north of Sangju, where the eastern
route to Seoul merges with the central route to cross the Sobaek mountain range. Kato, greatly angered at what he viewed as Konishi's
duplicity in racing ahead from Pusan, insisted that his second contingent now take the lead for the final push to Seoul. Konishi refused. The
two contingents, a total of something less than forty thousand men
(both Konishi and Kato would have left garrisons at the principal towns
they had taken), thus began the stiff climb into the mountains toward
Choryong Pass in a spirit of mutual hostility. They traversed the pass
without encountering any resistance and were down the other side late
in the evening of June 5. The city of Chungju lay straight ahead, and
with it, according to a captured Korean, a substantial army consisting of
"many generals of valour, six or seven thousand troops, and many
archery experts."[31]

It was at Chungju that Kato intended to exact his revenge. If Konishi
insisted on leading the way to Seoul, so be it, let him lead. Kato
accordingly halted his forces and camped well south of the town, letting
his rival forge ahead alone to meet the waiting Koreans. He fully
expected that Konishi would get himself into trouble by trying to take
on Sin Ip's army single-handed and would require rescuing, making
himself look foolish and incompetent while at the same time handing

Kato the chance to earn glory by rushing to his aid. That, anyway, was the plan.[32]

Konishi was very obliging. He took the opportunity Kato handed him and rushed ahead toward Chungju. His forces approached the city along a valley from the southeast. As at Sangju, they separated into two groups a few kilometers short of the town, So and Konishi breaking left and the others to the right. As they neared Tangumdae they fanned out farther, until they were arrayed in a vast arc facing General Sin and his force of eight thousand.

It was two o'clock in the afternoon of June 6. Konishi divided his force into three main units, 10,000 men under himself and Matsuura forming the vanguard in the center, So Yoshitoshi's 5,000-man contingent swinging around to the left, and 3,700 men under Arima, Omura, and Goto branching to the right. Then, with musketeers at the front and swordsmen and spearmen bringing up the rear, they advanced on the Koreans crowded in a mass at Tangumdae. General Sin's forces were soon being torn to pieces by flying lead, men falling everywhere in extraordinary numbers. The Japanese attack was so unexpectedly ferocious that a wave of panic spread through the jostling ranks of the Koreans, driving men to turn and run and leading to a general rout. General Sin managed to lead his cavalry forward in a single desperate charge, but musket fire stopped his mounted warriors before they could break the enemy lines. Soon the ground of Tangumdae was littered with bloodied Koreans, writhing horses, and discarded spears and flails and swords, and the future of warfare was made clear to Sin Ip. Like Yi Il at Sangju, he and several of his commanders spurred their horses away from the scene of the disaster and escaped with their lives. The rest of the Korean army scattered in every direction, thrashing through the waters at the back of Tangumdae, floundering through the rice paddies on either side in a desperate bid to get away. Most did not get far. They were methodically run down and cut to pieces by the Japanese sword and spear corps, which had moved to the fore as soon as the enemy was in full retreat and reduced to an easy target.[33]

When the day was done General Sin Ip and his army of eight thousand had ceased to exist, and the strategy of "fighting with a river to one's back" had been proven invalid in the face of technological change. Had the battle been fought at close quarters with traditional weapons, like Han Hsin's second-century B.C. stand against the Chao, Sin and his men might have had a chance with their swords and flails and arrows and spears. But against muskets they had no chance.[34] According to Japanese accounts, more than three thousand of Sin's men were beheaded that day and several hundred taken prisoner. The severed heads were lined up for the customary post-battle viewing, and then the noses were cut off and packed in salt for shipment back to Japan. Under normal circumstances the heads themselves would have been kept, but in the Korean campaign there were simply too many. Henceforth noses would become the generally accepted trophies of war. They were much more portable.

General Sin Ip himself did not long survive the battle. Prior to his departure from Seoul he had pledged to stop the enemy advance in the south or die in the attempt, and he intended to remain true to his word. Halting at a spring a short distance from Chungju, he gathered his commanders about him and explained that after suffering such a terrible defeat he would be unable to face the king. He then threw himself into the water and let his heavy armor drag him down. Two of his officers followed suit.[35]

The first and second contingents of the Japanese invasion force camped that night at Chungju. Some time in the evening second contingent leaders Kato Kiyomasa and Nabeshima Naoshige arrived at Konishi Yukinaga's camp to discuss the final advance to Seoul. Kato, chagrined at Konishi's success that day, came spoiling for a fight. The meeting opened with So Yoshitoshi spreading out two large maps before the assembled daimyo, one depicting the routes to Seoul and the other a detailed map of the capital itself. After examining the Seoul map, Kato pointed to one of the labeled streets. "Why don't you attack this road?" he suggested to Konishi. The street he was indicating was noted for its many drugstores and was labeled as such on the map with a Chinese character for "pharmacy."

It was a not-too-subtle jibe against Konishi, whose family had long been engaged in the business of selling medicines. "For warriors," he replied to Kato coldly, "family background is of little importance."

Kato then complained that Konishi had so far been hogging the lead in the advance to Seoul and that henceforth they should take turns at the fore. This was only proper, he added, for according to the rules of conduct laid down by Hideyoshi, advancing contingents should take turns in the lead. (This was true, but only when contingents were advancing along the same road, which Kato and Konishi were not.)

"We are already very close to Seoul," said Konishi, "so there is no point in talking about who should take the lead. It would make more sense for us to split up again and advance along separate roads, and see who reaches Seoul first."

"How shall we decide who takes which road?"

"We could draw lots."

"Ah, yes," replied Kato. "That's how things are decided among tradesmen, isn't it?"

For Konishi this was too much. "You deliberately try to insult me!" he roared, reaching for his sword. It was only thanks to the timely intervention of Nabeshima Naoshige and Konishi's colleague Matsuura Shigenobu that the two men were kept from fighting. Once a degree of calm had been restored, Konishi offered Kato his choice of routes north. There were two. One proceeded to the capital in a direct north-west line, but crossed the Han River just south of Seoul, where it was at its widest. The other followed a more roundabout course, first north and then west, but crossed the Han at its headwaters, where it was narrow and not as much of an obstacle. Kato immediately choose the direct route. They would leave, it was decided, first thing in the morning. The two daimyo commanders then parted company, outwardly calm but burning with anger inside.

Kato Kiyomasa did not wait until morning to depart. He left that same night. When Konishi heard of this he immediately set out too.[36]

The Korean court and government were in the meantime anxiously waiting for the good news to arrive that General Sin Ip had halted the Japanese at Chungju. As everyone in the capital knew, from King Sonjo down to the beggars in the streets, Sin's army was the last force of any size that stood between them and the approaching hordes of "robbers." Anything less than victory was therefore unthinkable.

The news finally came on June 7, not long after Kato and Konishi

had parted ways at Chungju. According to one account it came in the
form of an exhausted soldier, bloodied and half naked, arriving at a run
at Seoul's South Gate. General Sin's army, he said, had been destroyed;
he himself was one of the few to escape. The Japanese were at that
moment marching on Seoul. "Flight is your only hope!"[37]

Panic spread through the city like wildfire. Throughout the day
masses of people gathered up their possessions and pressed through the
gates and into the countryside beyond, fleeing in every direction in
search of safety. Sunset came, the time when the gates were normally
closed and locked for the night. But still the crush continued. The
guards had fled, leaving the ironclad doors unattended. Night fell, but
the great bell at Chongno did not sound the end of the day. The bell
ringer too was gone.

During the evening an emotional meeting between King Sonjo and
a number of his top ministers was held at Kyongbok Palace to decide
what to do. Most of the officials present spoke out strongly in favor of
remaining in Seoul. "The royal tombs are here," they said. "The tablets
of your ancestors are here. Where could you go? We have to remain in
the capital and hold out until relief arrives." Prime Minister Yi San-hae
alone ventured to point out that there were precedents for the king
evacuating the capital when danger threatened, but he was quickly
silenced by the others. They would not countenance any talk of flight,
and urged King Sonjo to dismiss Yi for having even made the
suggestion.

But of course Yi San-hae was right: staying and fighting were out
of the question. Only seven thousand ill-trained, ill-equipped soldiers
were stationed in Seoul, not nearly enough to defend the twenty-seven
kilometers of wall that encircled the city, a visually impressive string of
stone that had been constructed in the 1440s more to express the king's
power with its vastness than as an actual line of defense. The capital
was certain to fall to the superior power of the Japanese, and the king, if
he insisted on remaining behind, would be captured when it did. King
Sonjo saw this clearly, even if his ministers other than Yi San-hae did
not. And so he was left to make the painful but necessary decision
largely on his own: he would evacuate Seoul and move farther north,
across the Imjin River to the walled city of Pyongyang, former capital

of the ancient kingdom of Koguryo.[38]

It was at this same time that the question of royal succession was settled once and for all. This had been a point of contention since the previous year, when the Eastern faction had employed it with some skill to end the Westerners' two years of political ascendancy and reestablish themselves in power. It was such a contested issue, however, that it had resulted in the Easterners splitting into two sub-cliques, the Southerners and the Northerners, one side supporting the king's temperamental and lazy eldest son, eighteen-year-old Prince Imhae, as the rightful heir, and the other Prince Kwanghae, one year Imhae's junior but generally perceived as more studious and upstanding. On June 8, with no time left for discussion or debate, the matter was hastily decided: Imhae was passed over and Kwanghae officially installed as crown prince.[39]

Throughout the night between June 8 and 9 frantic preparations were made by the royal household for the evacuation of Seoul. Piles of straw sandals were collected to shod the tender feet of the king and court for the long journey ahead. Horses were secured and saddled. The king's ancestral tablets were ordered packed up and shipped north. But that was all. Everything else was left behind: ancient books, paintings, treasure chests, silk gowns, porcelain, gold, silver, buildings filled with centuries of government documents. Even food for the trip.

The sky was just beginning to lighten the next morning when King Sonjo and newly installed Crown Prince Kwanghae (Bright Sea) mounted their horses and led a procession of family members, courtiers, and government officials out of the capital's New Gate, bound for the Imjin River and the safety of the north beyond. Princes Imhae and Sunhwa departed separately with an entourage of their own. They were to head into the remote mountain fastness of the north-eastern province of Hamgyong, where they could hopefully rouse the local people into resisting the Japanese. Wails of despair and shouts of anger went up from those citizens still remaining in Seoul at the sight of their departing king. There could no longer be any hope; the capital, the heart and soul of the kingdom, was being abandoned to the invaders.

Seoul now descended into anarchy. Frantic citizens continued to flee for their lives through the city's gates, carrying bundles and babies, clutching family treasures, pushing carts, shepherding frightened children, crying in anguish at the ending of their world. Others began to loot. There were hundreds of empty homes, palaces, and government buildings left wide open across the capital, full of abandoned riches just waiting to be claimed.

Then the fires started. Citizens angry at what they felt was the desertion of their king torched Kyongbok-gung (Palace of Shining Happiness), Changdok-gung (Palace of Illustrious Virtue), and Changgyong-gung (Palace of Glorious Blessings). The king's private treasure house went up in flames, then the royal granary. Government buildings housing the deeds of ownership for the capital's slaves were also set ablaze, very likely by the slaves themselves. It was an orgy of rage and greed and terror that continued unabated throughout the morning hours, consuming the city before the Japanese had even arrived at the gates.

The king and court, meanwhile, were pressing on northward, the men on horses, the queen and concubines in palanquins. They had not gone far when it started to rain, so heavily that some of the unwieldy palanquins had to be abandoned and the lower-ranking concubines mounted on horses. Soon individuals started to lag behind, then drop out. Still the royal party pressed on, for everyone feared that the Japanese might be hot on their heels, about to appear at any moment over the crest of the last hill. A stop was made in the afternoon at the Pyokje way station to give the tired travelers a chance to eat and rest. *Sonjo sillok*, the annals of King Sonjo, makes a point of mentioning here that the side dishes served to the king and queen had to be thrown together to haste and that there were no side dishes at all to serve to the crown prince. He had to settle for rice and soup alone. After this additional indignity the royals were on their way again, wallowing through the mud in a torrential downpour, tired and miserable in their sodden silk robes.

It was well after dark when the royal party arrived at the ferry crossing on the south bank of the Imjin River. They had covered fifty kilometers in fourteen hours, and were wet and hungry and utterly exhausted. For many, accustomed as they were to a life of luxury and ease, the day's journey would have been the hardest physical exertion they had ever had to endure, leaving them distraught and in tears. In the pitch darkness the ferryman was summoned, and King Sonjo together with half his entourage crowded into his small craft. The rest were left behind. It was now, seated in the ferry at mid stream, that Sonjo himself at last broke down. The sight of their king sobbing uncontrollably on the deck was so upsetting that soon everyone present was reduced to tears as well.

When they reached the north bank, the ferry was sunk and the rope spanning the river cut to slow any Japanese who might be close behind. The weary travelers then continued on a little farther to the Tongpa way station, where food and shelter could be had. They arrived some time after midnight, tired and famished, only to find that the food was all gone: the porters who had preceded them with the royal household's few possessions had wolfed everything down, leaving the king and his party to go to bed hungry. In the morning the porters themselves were gone. The situation was looking grim, when the governor of Hwanghae Province arrived with an escort of several hundred soldiers and fresh horses. He led the royal entourage north to the next way station and sat them down to their first proper meal in two days. They then pushed on to Kaesong, capital of the Koryo dynasty (918–1392), arriving inside the stout city walls sometime after nightfall.

Once again inside the safety of the walled city and with lookouts posted to give warning of an enemy approach, it was decided to have a day of rest before pushing on to Pyongyang.[40]

The vanguard of the Japanese army left Chungju in a downpour in the early hours of June 8 to continue its advance on Seoul. Konishi Yukinaga led his first contingent due north and crossed the south branch of the Han River, swollen now from the heavy rains, then started looping west toward the capital's East Gate, staying close to the river's north bank. Kato Kiyomasa's second contingent was meanwhile racing in a straight northeast line toward Seoul's southern side. It was a more direct route, but would necessitate crossing the Han within sight of Seoul, where it was very wide and more apt to be heavily defended.

The Han was no mere stream. In its passage just south of Seoul it was a kilometer and more across. It was spanned by no bridges, and seemingly would have presented a formidable obstacle to even the best-trained and best-equipped armies. Some accounts state that the Koreans now took the judicious step of destroying all craft along the river's south bank to impede Kato's advance.[41] Others claim that Konishi himself sent men ahead in disguise to destroy the boats and thus slow his rival.[42] It is possible that both accounts are true, with the Koreans destroying boats at one point along the river and Konishi's men at another. In any case Kato arrived at the Han within sight of Seoul to find no boats available with which to effect a crossing.

It was Korean commander in chief Kim Myong-won's intention to make a stand against the Japanese as they attempted to cross the Han. It was a good position to mount a defense. Kato's men would not be able to cross such a wide expanse of water in force without a large number of boats. At best they would be able to straggle across in small groups, which could be cut down by a relatively small body of defenders as they attempted to wade ashore. Unfortunately for Kim, he had only about fifty officers and a thousand men with which to do the job. He had been ordered by the king to defend the capital, however, so he led his small force out Seoul's South Gate and on to the north bank of the river. They would not remain there for long.

Kato's forces arrived at the Han opposite what is now Seoul's Yongsan district on June 11. The absence of boats does not seem to have fazed the determined daimyo at all. He had his musketeers lob fusillades across the water at the Koreans on the other side—they were too far away to hit, but the noise seems to have shaken them badly—then set his troops to work cutting down trees from the surrounding hillsides and lashing them together to make rafts. The sight of this force, so much larger than his own, so fiercely attired, so well armed, and so clearly determined to get across the river, unnerved Kim Myong-won entirely. Ignoring the protests of one of his officers, he stripped off his armor and donned civilian clothes, then mounted his horse and sped away, leaving the men in his command to scatter to the four winds. When the Japanese finished their construction work later that day, they were thus able to begin ferrying troops across the river unopposed. The operation continued on into the night. Finally the entire second contingent was on the north bank of the Han with not a single

Korean soldier in sight. The walls of Seoul now lay only an hour's march ahead.[43]

Kato Kiyomasa arrived outside Seoul's South Gate sometime before dawn on June 12. The city was quiet. Yi Yang-won, who had been charged with defending the walls while Commander in Chief Kim Myong-won went forward to meet the Japanese at the Han, had sensibly chosen to evacuate with his handful of men upon hearing of Kim's own hasty retreat. Any mounting elation Kato may have felt, however, was instantly snuffed out by his first clear view of the walls. For there were the banners of first contingent leader Konishi Yukinaga, and raised high among them his family symbol of the pharmacist's bag. The reviled tradesman had beaten him to the prize. The first contingent in fact had reached Seoul's East Gate just a few hours before. They had found the entrance closed and barred. After scouting about for a time in the darkness, a floodgate through the wall was discovered and pried open by a samurai named Kido Sakuemon, using a number of musket barrels tied together as a lever.[44] It was a small victory for Konishi, a besting by moments in a long and arduous race. The capture of Seoul, moreover, was only the first step in Hideyoshi's grand scheme; there would be more enemies to defeat and more glory to win before the conquest of Asia was complete. Still, Kato must have felt a good deal of resentment at being beaten again, and at being initially denied entry to the city by the men Konishi had assigned to guard the South Gate. In the coming months these two commanders would go their separate ways in the campaign to take the north. But the animosity between them would continue to simmer, and would resurface later.

It had taken Konishi and his first contingent just twenty days to cover the 450 kilometers from Pusan to Seoul, traveling at an average speed of nearly twenty-three kilometers per day. Kato's second contingent, starting five days after Konishi's, had done it in fifteen days, maintaining an average pace of over thirty kilometers per day. Three hundred and fifty years later, at the start of World War II, the Germans would marginally improve on this blistering pace during their blitzkriegs into Poland, Belgium, and France. But they did so with trucks and tanks and trains and had the advantage of reasonably smooth roads. That the Japanese in 1592 nearly equaled them on foot, over rough, circuitous dirt tracks and rocky mountain passes, is a testament to the power of Hideyoshi's expeditionary force. Against such a juggernaut it seemed the Koreans could do nothing at all.

The Japanese arrived at Seoul to find it largely deserted and a number of its buildings and palaces already reduced to smoldering ruins. Even the king's own Kyongbok Palace was gone, the only sign of its existence the blackened stone foundation pillars of its Kyonghoe-ru banquet hall, the Hall of Happy Meetings. Later Korean writers have dated this destruction to coincide with the arrival of the Japanese.[45] But this is not so. The work had been done by the Koreans themselves three days earlier, in the anarchy that followed the fleeing of their king. The Japanese had certainly burned other towns and cities on their drive north. They had done so to punish any resistance to their advance. Kyongju had resisted, and had been burned. Sangju and Chungju had resisted, and had been burned. But Seoul had not resisted. Konishi and Kato found its walls undefended, its gates open, and its few remaining inhabitants quiet and compliant. There was thus no reason to mete out punishment here. The capital of Japan's newest province could be left intact.

Kuroda Nagamasa and his third contingent arrived in Seoul four days later, on June 16. With him came Ukita Hideie's eighth contingent, a force of ten thousand men from Bizen Province on western Honshu; the two groups had met at Kumsan during the advance to the north and had proceeded on together. The remaining five contingents of Hideyoshi's 158,800-man invasion force, contingents four and six from Kysuhu, contingent five from Shikoku, and contingents seven and nine from Honshu, were by this time all on Korean soil, mostly in the vicinity of Pusan. The Japanese navy, meanwhile, had completed its ferrying operations—some of Hideyoshi's ships likely had to make two or three crossings of the strait before the task was done—and was free to begin probing west along Korea's southern coast.

The first order of business for the Japanese army in Korea was to finish the job of subduing the country. Once the peninsula was firmly in hand, its people, its rice, and its wealth could then be marshaled for the coming push to Beijing. Japanese soldiers and supplies could also be moved north more easily in preparation for the China campaign, by ship up the west coast from Pusan to the Han River and Seoul, then to the Taedong River and Pyongyang, and finally to the Yalu River in the far north that marked the Chinese border. Establishing this seaborne supply line was in fact essential. Without it, every soldier would have to walk the one thousand kilometers from Pusan to the Yalu, and every bag of gunpowder and sack of grain would have to be carried overland.

The subjugation of Korea was to proceed as follows. After a couple of weeks of rest in Seoul, Kuroda was to march north and take the west coast province of Hwanghae; Konishi would proceed beyond that into the far northeastern province of Pyongan, up to the Yalu River and the Chinese frontier; Kato would subdue the far northwestern province of Hamgyong, which extended to the Tumen River marking Korea's border with Manchuria. The other daimyo generals would in the meantime fan out across the peninsula and secure Japan's hold on the remaining provinces: Mori Terumoto and his thirty thousand-man seventh contingent would hold the southeastern province of Kyongsang; the sixth contingent under Kobayakawa Takakage would take the southwestern province of Cholla, which had been bypassed during the push to take Seoul; Fukushima Masanori's fifth contingent, the Shikoku division, would take the central west coast province of Chungchong; the fourth contingent under Shimazu Yoshihiro and Mori Yoshinari would quell the remote east-coast province of Kangwon; and Ukita Hideie's eighth contingent would hold Seoul itself and the neighboring province of Kyonggi. Ukita, one of Hideyoshi's adopted sons and the husband of his adopted daughter Go-Hime, was to serve as interim commander in chief of Japanese forces in Korea until Hideyoshi himself arrived to take charge. It would thus fall to him to keep the other daimyo in line and on task, a daunting responsibility for a young man of nineteen.

The arrival of the Japanese in Seoul proved much more peaceable than the Koreans had feared. They announced disingenuously that they had come to Korea to save the people from their oppressive king, and had no intention of harming anyone so long as they were compliant and obeyed the rules. Those who did not, those deemed to be criminals and looters and agitators, were dealt with harshly, burned at the stake in front of the Great Bell at Chongno that remains on the spot to this day. Law-abiding Koreans, however, were according to Hideyoshi's orders not to be harmed in any way and were encouraged to go about their business. Over the coming weeks the citizens who had fled into the hills, particularly the shopkeepers and trades people, thus drifted back into the city, reopened their businesses, and tentatively resumed their lives, seeking to accommodate themselves to life under the Japanese. Some even managed to prosper, for the invaders were willing to pay for the things they needed, giving rise to a lucrative trade supplying the enemy.[46]

Commander in Chief Ukita Hideie took up residence at Chongmyo, the only palatial compound in Seoul that had survived the fires set in the wake of King Sonjo's flight. The surrounding area was turned into a military camp. To the Koreans this was a terrible insult, for Chongmyo was to them a sacred place, the ancestral temple where the royal lineage tablets of the Choson dynasty had been stored up until their removal just a few days before. Ukita's occupancy, however, did not last long. Soon after his arrival, strange things started happening in the middle of the night that left him spooked. Then his soldiers began dying for no apparent reason, struck down, it was said, by the spirits of the ancestors that resided in the place. According to the Korean annals, it was these supernatural goings-on that drove Ukita to burn Chongmyo and move his headquarters to the Nambyol-gung, the mansion where emissaries from China were traditionally housed, on the site of what is today the Westin Choson Hotel in the heart of downtown.[47]

The burning of Chongmyo was but one of many examples of a ham-fisted approach to empire building guaranteed to alienate the Koreans. The Japanese would act in much the same way three hundred years later when they returned to colonize Korea, and again in the early 1940s when they tried to forge an Asia-wide "Co-Prosperity Sphere." They arrived to occupy Seoul in 1592 with a clear understanding of the mechanics of how to reorganize the country to fit into Hideyoshi's grand scheme; of the administrators that would have to be appointed, the regulations imposed, and the vast land surveys that would need to be conducted to parcel up the peninsula for redistribution to worthy daimyo lords. What they did not understand was how to win over the Korean people to accept this new system of rule. Hideyoshi's generals had vague notions of prodding them into accepting their new role as subjects of the taiko, into following Japanese customs, and even in time into speaking Japanese. But how did they propose to achieve this end? The burning of Chongmyo demonstrates that Ukita and his fellow daimyo really did not know. For every step they took to win over the Koreans, they took two missteps such as the burning of Chongmyo that served only to alienate them further.

This lack of finesse does not change the fact, however, that it was Hideyoshi's intention in the summer of 1592 to co-opt Korea, not lay waste to it, an intention he made clear in an order issued prior to the invasion prohibiting disorderly conduct and harsh treatment of Koreans.[48] This was how the taiko liked to conquer new lands: subdue your enemy with an overwhelming show of force, take his oath of loyalty, then co-opt him quickly and get him onto your team. In 1585 he had cowed the Chosokabe clan of Shikoku into submission with a mighty invasion army and had then rewarded them for their submission with a sizable domain and handsome income. The Chosokabe were then incorporated into the next step of national unification, the conquest of Kyushu. Events on Kyushu in the period 1587–92 unfolded in much the same way. An enormous invasion army forced the dominant Shimazu family on that island to swear allegiance to Hideyoshi. They were treated well after that, and set to work preparing for the taiko's invasion of Korea.

Now it was Korea's turn to join the fold. Hideyoshi's armies had already demonstrated his overwhelming power with their twenty-day march on Seoul. If everything continued according to plan, the kingdom would soon cease its resistance to Hideyoshi's benevolent rule, accepting its role as the first acquisition of the Japanese empire and the staging area for the conquest of Ming.

CHAPTER 9

Hideyoshi Jubilant

NEWS OF THE STUPENDOUS SUCCESS of his armies in Korea filtered back to Toyotomi Hideyoshi at his Nagoya headquarters just days after the start of the invasion. First came word of the fall of Pusan and Tongnae and the rapid advance north. Next to arrive were reports of the taking of Taegu and Kyongju and of the rout of the Koreans at Sangju. Then came the heartening news of the decisive battle at Chungju, where Konishi's first contingent wiped out the only sizable force the Koreans had been able to muster. The campaign was progressing more favorably than even Hideyoshi had hoped. If he had embarked on the enterprise with any secret doubts, they must have fallen away now. It no longer seemed a question of if he would succeed in conquering Korea and then China, but only a matter of when.

"By now we have taken various castles in Korea," Hideyoshi wrote to his mother in the middle of June, "and I have sent my men to besiege the capital there. I shall take even China around the 9th month [October 1592], so I shall receive [from you] the costumes for the [next] festival of the 9th month in the capital of China.... When I capture China, I'll send someone to you in order to welcome you there."[1] And to his wife, "We have already captured a great number of castles in Korea. I have heard that it takes about twenty days to reach the capital of Korea from the harbor that we have taken, and I have sent my men toward that capital. I expect to besiege the capital in a short time. When I have assembled the ships, I shall have my men cross over. As I expect to take China, too, I look forward to sending men [from there] to welcome you."[2]

On June 25 came the greatest news so far: Seoul had fallen, and without a fight. This must have left even the taiko himself astonished. During the wars of unification it had taken his armies months to subdue the island of Shikoku. It had taken months to conquer Kyushu. It had taken months to crush the recalcitrant Hojo at Odawara. But now it appeared that the entire kingdom of Korea, a land nearly as large as the whole of Japan, would be his in a matter of days. His generals were rolling up that country just as fast as they could march. Claiming China would take longer, of course, but only because it was so vast. Hideyoshi did not expect to encounter any more resistance there than he was meeting in Korea, for the Chinese in his opinion were effeminate "long sleeves" who did not know how to fight. To his military mind history clearly demonstrated this. From the fourteenth century right up into Hideyoshi's own lifetime, wako pirates had raided China at will from their bases in southern Japan, pillaging all along the coast and at times far inland despite their often remarkably small numbers. The lesson to be learned here was obvious. If China's supposedly great armies could not stop even small bands of audacious raiders, how could it possibly stand up to Hideyoshi's incomparably more powerful expeditionary force?

The victory of his armies was therefore assured, at least in Hideyoshi's own mind. As he wrote triumphantly to Kato Kiyomasa and Nabeshima Naoshige in July of 1592, the subjugation of Korea was being "carried out as easily as dust is swept up with a broom," and would very shortly be complete. "There is no reason why Tai-Min [China] should not meet the same fate.... [Y]ou and your men of tested military experience and courage will be able to overcome the army of Tai-Min as easily as great mountain rocks roll upon and crush eggs." After that "India, the Philippines, and many islands in the South Sea will share a like fate. We are now occupying the most conspicuous and enviable position in the world."[3]

On June 27, two days after learning of the fall of Seoul, Hideyoshi dictated a letter to his wife O-Ne, formally known as Lady Kita-no-Mandokoro, stating that he would be leaving for Korea shortly to take personal command of his forces there and that he would take with him all remaining reserve units currently encamped at Nagoya. To prepare for this sea crossing "[a]ll the transports and other vessels that are now in Korean waters have been called back to Japan." Assuming that the weather would not delay him—typhoon season was just beginning—Hideyoshi hoped to be in Seoul by the middle of July and in Beijing before the end of the year. After that "Her Excellency Kita-no-Mandokoro will be requested by our Lord to join him in due time. Further detail concerning this matter will be entered into at the time when our Lord sails for Korea."[4]

In a second letter written the same day to his nephew and adopted son and heir Hidetsugu, the kampaku of Japan then residing in Kyoto, Hideyoshi outlined in twenty-four articles how he planned to organize the overseas empire that he now saw taking shape:

1.   Your Lordship [Hidetsugu] must not relax preparations for the campaign. The departure should be made by the First or Second Month of the coming year [1593].

2.   The Capital of Korea fell on the second day of this month. Thus, the time has come to make the sea crossing and to bring the length and breadth of the Great Ming under our control. My desire is that Your Lordship make the crossing to become the Civil Dictator [i.e., kampaku] of Great China.

3.   Thirty thousand men should accompany you. The departure should be by boat from Hyogo. Horses should be sent by land.

4.   Although no hostility is expected in the Three Kingdoms [Korea], armed preparedness is of the utmost importance, not only for the maintenance of our reputation but also in the event of an emergency. All subordinates shall be so instructed. . . .

[In articles 5 through 15 Hideyoshi gives Hidetsugu detailed instructions for how he should organize his crossing to Korea, including what provisions, arms, and armor to take, the amount of silver he should withdraw from the treasury, and how many porters he should employ on his march.[5]]

16.   After our military campaign in China is begun, we shall request Miyabe Keijun to take entire charge of the national capital of Korea. He will be summoned to Korea in due time. Your Excellency is hereby instructed to advise Miyabe to prepare for this important post.

17.   Since His Majesty [Emperor Go-Yozei] is to be transferred to

the Chinese capital, due preparation is necessary. The imperial visit will take place the year after next [1594]. On that occasion, ten provinces adjacent to the Capital shall be presented to him. In time instructions will be issued for the enfeoffment of all courtiers. Subordinates will receive ten times as much (as their present holdings). . . .

18. The post of Civil Dictator [kampaku] of China shall be assigned as aforementioned to Hidetsugu, who will be given 100 provinces adjacent to the Capital. The post of Civil Dictator of Japan will go either to the Middle Counsellor Yamato [Hideyoshi's half-brother, Hidenaga], or to the Bizen Minister [Hideyoshi's adopted son, Ukita Hideie], upon declaration of his readiness.

19. As for the position of the Sovereign of Japan, the young Prince or Prince Hachijo shall be the choice.

20. As for Korea, the Gifu Minister [Hashiba Hidekatsu, allied to Hideyoshi by marriage] or Bizen Minister [Ukita Hideie] shall be assigned. In that event the Middle Counselor Tamba [Kobayakawa Hideaki] shall be assigned to Kyushu.

21. As for His Majesty's [Emperor Go-Yozei's] visit to China, arrangements shall be made according to established practices for Imperial tours of inspection. His Majesty's itinerary shall follow the route of the present campaign. Men and horses necessary for the occasion shall be requisitioned from each country involved.

22. Korea and China are within easy reach, and no inconvenience is anticipated for any concerned, high or low. It is not expected that anyone in those countries will attempt to flee. Therefore, recall all commissioners in the provinces to assist in preparations for the expedition. . . .

23. As for the persons who are to take charge of Heian-Jo [Kyoto] and of the Juraku palace in our absence, their names will be announced later.

24. Miyabe Keijun, Ishikawa Sadamasa, and other persons should begin immediately to prepare for the work to be assigned them. I hereby request Your Excellency to advise them to present themselves at our military headquarters [at Nagoya] as soon as they can.[6]

In sum, then, Hideyoshi foresaw the Korean campaign soon drawing to a close. In the coming weeks he hoped to cross over to that country to take personal command of his armies for the big push on to Beijing. Then would begin the task of organizing his nascent empire and putting a new administration in place. Korea would become in effect a fourth island in the Japanese archipelago, with either Hashiba Hidekatsu or Ukita Hideie at the helm in Seoul. (Hashiba was currently leading the ninth contingent in Korea and Ukita the eighth.) Hidetsugu, presently kampaku of Japan and thus second only to Hideyoshi, would assume the loftier position of kampaku of China, with a new kampaku being appointed to take command solely of Japan. Emperor Go-Yozei would be installed in Beijing's Forbidden City as emperor of China, and his son and heir would assume the now-subsidiary role of emperor of Japan. Finally, with Japan, Korea, and China all firmly in his grasp, Hideyoshi envisioned extending his reach even further, into India, presumably sometime after 1594. He did not intend doing this himself, but rather would leave it to those worthy daimyo who rendered him good service in the coming China campaign. They "will be liberally rewarded with grants of extensive states near India, with the privilege of conquering India and extending their domains in that vast empire."[7]

So there it was. Hideyoshi's empire would extend from the northern tip of Honshu to the southern tip of India. It would stretch north into Manchuria and Mongolia, and eastwards through China to the Tibetan plateau. It would branch south into Vietnam, Thailand, Burma and Cambodia. It would reach offshore to the Philippine Islands, Taiwan, and Hainan. It would, in short, embrace what Hideyoshi would have regarded as virtually the entire known world.

And what of Hideyoshi himself? What would his role be in this huge empire, the largest the world had ever seen? First he would remain for a time in Beijing. Then he would appoint a deputy to stay there in his place, while he himself would settle in a permanent residence at the southern port city of Ningpo, where the Chinese mainland comes closest to Japan.[8] In these comfortable semitropical surroundings he would simply exist as the taiko, the kingmaker and puppet master, the omnipotent being who sat quietly to the side, controlling everything, missing nothing, governing the governors with a firm but generally benign hand.

Not everyone agreed with Hideyoshi's plans. Some felt he was reaching too far in trying to conquer China, and that he should satisfy himself with just a piece of southern Korea. By far the biggest worry in that summer of 1592, however, was not that Hideyoshi wanted to rule the world, but rather that he planned to leave Japan and sail to Korea to take personal command of his armies. A number of his inner coterie of daimyo, members of the imperial court, his wife, even his eighty-year-old mother, all expressed grave reservations about this. To them the idea seemed uncharacteristically reckless, particularly for a man who had during the course of his career displayed such patience, astuteness, and plain common sense.

One of their concerns was the taiko's health. Indeed, it is evident in his private correspondence that Hideyoshi himself was worried about this; it was probably a main reason why he was not already in Korea, commanding his armies in person. He was no longer the youthful "Bald Rat" who had caught Oda Nobunaga's eye, nor the steely-eyed warrior who had emerged victorious at Tennozan. Hideyoshi was now an old man. Although only in his mid fifties, he looked and apparently felt much older, a small, wizened wraith, worn out and used up after thirty years of war. Loss of appetite, first reported in 1585, had become a serious problem, leaving him thin and weak, his face gaunt, his cheekbones sharp. His eyesight was troubling him as well, to the point where he was having difficulty writing letters.[9] Hideyoshi had high hopes of returning to health, and during the summer of 1592 sent a glowing report to his mother of the progress he was making. But even by his own reckoning he was scarcely fit for war. "Do not worry," he wrote on June 15, "as I find myself more and more in good health and have a good appetite.... I am feeling better and better, and I am happy to say that yesterday, after a tea ceremony in Rikyu's style, I enjoyed eating a meal. How is your appetite?... It is not necessary to worry about me. I am so well that I can go outside for a walk and have meals more and more often."[10]

Eating a meal. Going for a walk outside. These are prerequisites for a happy retirement, not for leading armies in the field and enduring the hardships that that entails. If Hideyoshi was serious about going to Korea, it was thus imperative that the trip be postponed until he had at least recovered a greater portion of his strength. Otherwise he would only succeed in destroying his health for good.

An even greater worry than Hideyoshi's health was the prospect of Hideyoshi's absence. He had completed the unification of Japan barely two years before. He had done so by co-opting a number of powerful rivals, allowing them to retain sizable land holdings, large armies, and positions of power in exchange for oaths of loyalty to him. Japan was at peace now, domestic affairs were in order, and every peg was in its hole. But would all this remain so if Hideyoshi withdrew his commanding presence? If he were now to leave Japan and set off on some distant adventure, what were the chances that conflict would break out anew? If that happened and Hideyoshi was many weeks away in Korea or worse yet China, might not Japan slip back into anarchy before the news reached him and drew him home?

These concerns must have been weighing heavily on the mind of Emperor Go-Yozei in Kyoto, for that summer he took the unusual step of writing to Hideyoshi to urge him to abandon his plan:

> Your plan to proceed to Korea, braving great storms and dangerous seas, is both too serious and too desperate to be considered. You should realize how precious is your life and how necessary you are to the national welfare. A man of your genius and attainments may direct an army thousands of miles distant and be able to win a brilliant victory, as great military leaders of yore have done. Moreover, the military men whom you have already sent to the continent, together with those whom you are about to send, will be capable of conducting the military work satisfactorily. For the sake of the throne and for the sake of the empire, we urgently request that you abandon your plan to go in person.[11]

This personal appeal from the emperor did little to sway Hideyoshi. He remained adamant about crossing to Korea as soon as his health allowed. But the emperor was not alone in his concern. The inner circle of daimyo attending Hideyoshi with their reserve forces at Nagoya were equally adamant that he abandon his plan. They warned him of the dangers of the sea crossing to Pusan during typhoon season, particularly for the large number of men and ships that Hideyoshi was proposing to take, and they urged him to postpone his trip for at least a few months.

The danger certainly was real. It was a typhoon, after all, that had wrecked the Mongol armada of Kublai Khan in the thirteenth century when he attempted to invade Japan.

According to Hideyoshi it was these entreaties that eventually caused him to change his mind and postpone his crossing. In a letter of explanation sent to his daimyo commanders in Korea later in the fall, he announced that he would be joining them at a later date than had been originally planned, on account, he said, of the weather:

> All preparations for crossing the waters having been completed, I made ready to sail. However, Iyeyasu, Toshiiye, and several other prominent military men came forward and begged that I change the plans, saying that the hurricane season was approaching, and that the transportation of our troops to Korea would require several months, extending to even August and September, after which water traffic would be closed because of the stormy weather. The transportation of troops in these seasons would cause great loss of life and possibly end in disaster. Therefore, we decided to postpone sailing to Korea until next March when the sea should be open and the sailing safe.
>
> Taking the God of War and other deities as witnesses, we pledge that this decision to delay is wholly contrary to our desire, but was necessary because of conditions. As it is a settled national question that Tai-Min [China] is to be conquered, my plan of sailing to the continent and assuming personal charge of our entire army in the coming spring will certainly be carried out.[12]

Was weather the only concern that prompted Hideyoshi to postpone his trip to Korea? Possibly not. There may also have been political considerations behind his decision. At some point during July, Hideyoshi held a council meeting with the principal daimyo attending him at Nagoya: Maeda Toshiie, Gamo Ujisato, Asano Nagamasa, and Tokugawa Ieyasu. (Maeda, Gamo, and Asano were all *fudai* daimyo, meaning that they had voluntarily entered Hideyoshi's service early in his career, and had risen to prominence on his coattails. Tokugawa Ieyasu was a *tozama* daimyo who risen to prominence independently and allied himself with Hideyoshi in the later stages of national unification.) At this meeting Hideyoshi proposed that he, Maeda, and Gamo lead their forces to Korea to help finish off that country and add their weight to the upcoming push to Beijing. Tokugawa Ieyasu, he said, would stay behind to oversee affairs in Japan. No one present openly questioned this idea. After the meeting, however, Asano Nagamasa muttered that "Hideyoshi is out of his mind." The taiko, overhearing this comment or having it reported to him, flew into a rage and confronted Asano. "What do you mean insulting me in this way?" he roared. "If you have a reason for making such a rude speech I will hear it; otherwise I will cut off your head!"

"You can cut my head off whenever you please," replied Asano coolly. "But as to what I have said, of course I have a reason for it.... You say that it is your intention to go in person to Korea...and that you will leave the whole of these sixty-odd provinces in the hands of Tokugawa Ieyasu. Now, you are perfectly well aware that by dint of years and years of hard fighting you have only just succeeded in bringing the whole of Japan under your control. At present there is peace. But why? Only because you are feared. Your departure to another country would be a signal for a general uprising. The great lords who have been humiliated would take this opportunity of avenging themselves on you. At such a crisis what could Tokugawa do? It is because you do not see this, because your usual sharpness in forecasting what is likely to happen under given circumstances seems to have left you, that I say you are out of your mind...."

Asano's explanation had little effect. Hideyoshi drew his sword and rushed at his retainer, but was restrained by Maeda and Gamo. "If Nagamasa is to be beheaded," they said, desperately trying to calm him, "let it be done by someone else. It is beneath the dignity of a man of your rank to slay a subordinate." Asano in the meantime was quietly hustled out of the room, and returned to his home to wait for what he expected would be an inevitable sentence of death.[13]

A few days after this episode, an event occurred that changed Hideyoshi's mind and saved Asano's life. A message arrived at Nagoya from the nearby Kyushu province of Higo that a minor vassal of the Shimazu, one Umekita Kunikane, had refused to join the expedition to Korea and was intending to march his force instead against Nagoya Castle. According to the Shimazu family history, Umekita acted as he did because he feared he would be punished by Hideyoshi for being so tardy in raising the force required of him and leading it to Korea.[14] But this was not the whole story. Umekita in fact had the sympathy of at least one member of the Shimazu, the clan Hideyoshi had subdued during his conquest of Kyushu in 1587, and he undoubtedly hoped that his small action would draw large support from this daimyo family and lead to a general uprising. But in this Umekita made a fatal miscalculation. The Shimazu were not willing to openly resist Hideyoshi, certainly not with him at Nagoya, less than two hundred kilometers away. Umekita's rebellion thus remained an isolated occurrence, involving no more than one hundred and fifty samurai. It was quickly crushed by the Shimazu themselves, most of the participants were killed, and the leading Umekita sympathizer in the family, Shimazu Toshihisa, was forced to commit suicide.[15] The threat to national peace and unity therefore subsided almost as soon as it arose. But the affair nevertheless awoke Hideyoshi to the truth of what Asano had said just days before. If he had been away in Korea when Umekita made his move, what might the Shimazu have done? Would they have acted promptly to control the situation? Or would they have joined this rebel, thinking they could reclaim their lost island before Hideyoshi could respond? The nation clearly required the taiko's own commanding presence if peace and unity were to be maintained.

Hideyoshi therefore summoned Asano back to Nagoya Castle to apologize and to thank him for his candor. As a sign of his renewed favor he offered Asano's son the honor of putting down the rebellion, but shortly thereafter word arrived that the Shimazu themselves had already completed the task.[16]

If Hideyoshi was concerned that Japan might fall apart in his absence, he certainly could not admit it, for that would have been an admission that he was not in full control. Nor could he cite his own ill health, for that would have made him look feeble. In the end the only reason he could openly give for postponing his trip to Korea was the weather. Which consideration was foremost in his mind we do not know. All that is certain is that the decision was made and that it was made some time prior to July 28, as revealed in a letter he penned to his wife on that date: "As I said the other day," he wrote, "since I have been told that the sea will be calm in the 3rd month [April of the following year, 1593], I have decided to postpone my visit to Korea until spring and to greet the New Year in Nagoya. . . . [P]lease do not worry."[17]

Hideyoshi was now caught on the horns of a dilemma. To safeguard the fragile unity he had imposed on the nation over the past ten years, he had to remain in Japan. In this regard his decision to postpone his trip to Korea was the right one. By putting off the journey, however, he was placing his great dream of empire in jeopardy. The Korean campaign was proceeding very nicely at the moment, even without his personal leadership. The news from the front was excellent, better than even he could have hoped. But Hideyoshi was no fool. His success in unifying Japan is evidence of just how well he could manipulate powerful men, and by inference of how well he understood them. He knew he could not crush every rival from Satsuma Province in the south to Mutsu in the north and make everyone his groveling servant. That approach would have greatly prolonged the process of national unification. Instead he cut deals, allowing rivals to keep large land holdings and positions of power in exchange for oaths of loyalty to him. It was this approach that so speeded up the drive toward national unification after Hideyoshi seized the domain of his fallen master, Oda Nobunaga. But it meant that Hideyoshi's Japan was governed at the provincial level by a number of powerful and strong-willed men, daimyo who had outwardly sworn loyalty to Hideyoshi, but inwardly remained quite independent.

These were the generals who were now fighting in Korea. They were doing Hideyoshi's bidding. But their loyalty and fear of him would take them only so far. They were all still more or less on track in these early days of the war, reveling in the glory of the thing as they slashed their way to Seoul. But in time their individualism was bound to assert itself, leading them to question Hideyoshi's orders, to resent their hardships, and to compete among themselves for honors they felt they deserved. The first signs of this were already appearing in reports Hideyoshi was receiving of the rivalry between Kato Kiyomasa and Konishi Yukinaga. This must have worried him. He must have understood that, sooner or later, his unquestioned leadership would be needed in the field to hold his enterprise together and keep it moving forward. When this critical point would be reached one could only guess. Did

Konishi, Kato, Kuroda and their colleagues have the determination to carry on all the way to Beijing without Hideyoshi at the lead, urging them on? Would they only go as far as the Yalu River before their enthusiasm petered out? Or would they stop at Seoul?

CHAPTER 10

The Korean Navy Strikes Back

NOW THAT HIDEYOSHI'S ARMIES had advanced halfway up the Korean Peninsula to Seoul, it was becoming essential that a seaborne supply line be established so that reinforcements, weapons, and food stores could be brought forward in preparation for the coming push into China. The entire enterprise hinged on the opening of this sea route. Without it, everything would have to be carried all the way from the Pusan beachhead to the advancing front, and every soldier would have to walk, a distance already of hundreds of kilometers over mountainous terrain. After completing their task of ferrying the first eight contingents of the Japanese army from Nagoya to Pusan, therefore, squadrons from Hideyoshi's seven-hundred-ship fleet began probing westward along Korea's southern coast, feeling their way through treacherous channels, around rocky headlands, and into potentially hostile territory, reaching out for the Yellow Sea and the way north.

They made it about eighty kilometers. Then the Korean navy stopped them in their tracks.

The Korean navy by this time was in very bad shape, both the Kyongsang Left and Right Navies, fully two-thirds of its entire force, having been scuttled by their own commanders, Pak Hong and Won Kyun, soon after the arrival of Hideyoshi's armada at Pusan. Pak, based at the nearby port of Kijang, panicked upon witnessing the Battle of Tongnae and fled inland to safety after ordering his fleet sunk and all his weapons destroyed. Won Kyun, upon receiving this astonishing news at his base on Koje Island forty kilometers to the west, tried to lead his own fleet farther west to safety before the Japanese arrived to destroy him, but soon mistook distant fishing boats for approaching enemy battleships, and in a panic he too ordered his vessels scuttled and prepared to flee north. Entreaties and threats from two of his lieutenants finally brought him to his senses. But by then it was too late; only a handful of vessels from his hundred-ship fleet were still afloat. With this remnant of the Kyongsang fleet, Won Kyun went into hiding in the coves along Korea's southern coast, from where he began sending desperate requests for reinforcements westward to Yosu, home port of Cholla Left Navy Commander Yi Sun-sin.

Yi Sun-sin did not charge into battle upon hearing of the Japanese invasion, nor upon receiving requests for reinforcements from his colleague Won Kyun. He waited for two and a half weeks. He had a number of reasons for this. First, there was the matter of orders. Yi was charged first and foremost with protecting his own command, the eastern coast of Cholla Province. Until he received orders from Seoul freeing him to act on his own recognizance, he was thus duty bound to remain at his post. Second, Yi needed time to prepare for action. He needed to strengthen the defenses of the ports under his command. He needed to acquire maps of the treacherous coastal waters of Kyongsang Province, and intelligence on the intentions and movements of the Japanese. He hoped to organize a united fleet of some ninety ships with his colleague Yi Ok-ki, commander of the Cholla Right Navy, for separately their respective forces were rather skimpy for taking on the Japanese.

Finally, Yi needed to be sure of his men. This meant whipping up their confidence and fighting spirit so that they would not lose their nerve in the face of the enemy as their Kyongsang counterparts had done. It also meant punishing deserters. When several men tried to escape in the night in early June, Yi sent out troops to round them up, then ordered them executed and their heads displayed, "to calm down the agitation and confused minds within the camp."[1]

June 12, 1592. The day Seoul fell to the Japanese. In Yi Sun-sin's camp another sailor attempted to desert. Yi had the man arrested and his head cut off and hung on a pole.[2] Then he made ready to sail. He had intended to await the arrival of Cholla Right Navy Commander Yi Ok-ki so that they could combine their fleets, but in the end orders from Seoul drove him into battle alone. The Choson court, perhaps responding to complaints from Won Kyun that Yi was slow in sending rein-forcements, ordered him to form a united front with Won's Kyongsang Right Navy. The order showed a lack of understanding of the situation, for Won's "fleet" now consisted of only four battleships and a few fishing boats; Yi Sun-sin's original intention to link up with Yi Ok-ki's intact fleet made much more sense. But orders were orders. And so he sailed east alone.

Yi led his fleet out of Yosu harbor at two o'clock in the morning of June 13. He had thirty-nine fighting ships under his command (twenty-four large panokson and fifteen smaller decked vessels called *hyeupson*), plus forty-six "sea ears," small, open boats that would serve as couriers and scouts. They enjoyed a following wind as they headed east, saving the sailors from having to row. They continued on throughout the next day, then passed the night at Sobipo.

The Cholla Left fleet arrived at Tangpo the next day for the planned rendezvous with Won Kyun. The appointed hour came and went, but Won failed to arrive. Scouting craft were sent out to locate him. He finally appeared on the following morning aboard a single warship, bringing with him news of Japanese ships off Kadok-do, "Lonely Island," fifty kilometers to the northeast, on the far side of Koje-do. Over that and the following day the other remnants of Won's beaten fleet trickled into the harbor, raising his total contribution to the com-bined Cholla-Kyongsang fleet to four warships and two small craft. With Won at his side as ordered, Yi now continued sailing east, toward Koje Island and the Japanese.

June sixteenth. As the Korean fleet rounded the southern end of Koje Island and began working its way north along the coast, a scouting vessel approached Yi's flagship with a message: "Japanese ships at anchor in Ok-po port." Okpo lay inside a large bay only a little farther along the Koje coast. So it would be there, not Kadok Island, where the first naval battle of the war would be fought.

The fleet took up battle positions at the mouth of Okpo harbor at noon the following day, the smaller craft branching to the left and right while the heavier battleships, including Yi's flagship, formed a line in the center. Won Kyun lingered some distance to the rear. Yi sent a message down the line to each of his captains, warning them not to give way, but to "stand like mountain castles." Then he ordered the advance.

As the Koreans proceeded through the harbor mouth they could make out more than fifty enemy transports riding at anchor in front of Okpo village, most flying red ensigns that Yi assumed indicated the unit to which they belonged. The vessels were largely unmanned; the invaders were all ashore, ransacking the village in search of loot and setting fire to the houses. This was in violation of the orders Hideyoshi had issued in February and reiterated on June 6 not to engage in "arson or massacre" or any "act of outrage"; his objective in Korea, after all, was not to alienate the Koreans, but to win them over and make them cooperative, useful pawns in his drive to build an empire.[3] Hideyoshi was not on the scene to enforce his orders, however, or to witness the general lack of cooperation among the Koreans that was giving his subordinates an excuse to act as they did.

The air around Okpo was so full of smoke that the Japanese did not see the approaching Korean fleet until it was almost upon them. When the alarm was finally raised, panic swept through their ranks. Some sprinted back to their ships and attempted to escape. Others ran in the opposite direction, up into the hills. Of those ships that managed to get under way, none ventured into the bay to meet the Korean fleet, but cut off to the left and right, hugging the shoreline in a race for safety. The Koreans, rowing strongly to the beat of Yi Sun-sin's war drum, soon had them hemmed into the port, "like fish on a skewer." The Japanese fought back with their muskets, but these weapons, so effective in land battles, had little effect against the thick wooden hulls and bulwarks of the Korean warships. Yi's twenty-eight large battleships were able to close with the Japanese vessels with little fear of damage, blasting cannonballs and iron-tipped arrows at point-blank range through their hulls and showering fire arrows upon the unprotected decks. The Japanese, fighting for their lives now and pulling desperately at the oars, began throwing stores overboard to lighten the load and distract the Koreans, but they were unable to get away. With comrades falling all around them, many finally gave up the fight, leaping into the sea and swimming to shore, leaving their abandoned vessels for the Koreans to burn.

When the battle was over, twenty-six Japanese ships had been foundered by cannon fire or reduced to smoldering hulks by fire arrows. The floating debris of battle covered the bay: bloody clothing, boxes of supplies, broken oars, splinters of wood—and corpses, many bristling with arrows, two with jagged stumps where their heads had been. "The flames and smoke on the sea covered the skies," Yi later reported in his dispatch to court, "while the fleeing Japanese hordes scurried into the forests with shrieks of fear."[4]

On the Korean side only three men had been wounded. Not a single man was killed, nor a single ship lost. Elation swept through the combined fleet, and calls went up to pursue the thrashed "dwarfs" into the hills and cut down every one of them. Commander Yi was sorely tempted; he as much as anyone craved the total annihilation of the enemy. But he knew the risk outweighed the potential reward. To send his marksmen into the thick forests ashore to hunt for the escaping Japanese would yield a few heads at best and would meanwhile leave his fleet under-defended inside the confines of Okpo harbor, vulnerable to a counterattack from other squadrons of Japanese ships. Yi also realized the fundamental wisdom of avoiding a land fight, for that was where the enemy's strength lay. His own strength lay at sea, so on the sea he would remain. He therefore led the fleet into open water to pass the night.

His men had only just begun to prepare a much-needed meal when a patrol boat drew near and raised the alarm: "Five large enemy ships sailing nearby!" Yi immediately set off in pursuit. The Japanese made a dash northward to the mainland port of Happo, where they leapt ashore and fled before the Korean warships were upon them. This time Yi gave no thought at all to pursuit inland, for it was now nearing midnight, and they were well within Masan harbor, in the heart of enemy-held territory. He satisfied himself with ordering the five ships burned.

The fleet spent the remaining hours of the night off the northern tip of Koje Island, arrayed in battle formation, resting but alert. They did not rest long. Soon after sunrise on June 17, news was received from a group of refugees that thirteen Japanese vessels had recently been at anchor farther along the coast to the west. The Koreans set sail in search of this new group and came upon them later that day at Chokjinpo. As in the Okpo engagement, the Japanese were caught completely by surprise, too busy ransacking and torching the village to notice the approaching Korean fleet until it was too late. This time they made no pretense of fighting, but fled en masse into the hills. So for a second time in twenty-four hours the Koreans set about looting and then burning Japanese vessels, unopposed.

As the Koreans stood on their decks, watching with satisfaction as flames consumed the enemy ships, a refugee hailed them from shore. He was carrying a baby on his back, wailing loudly and begging for help. He was brought out to Yi's flagship, where the commander and his officers questioned him as to the movements and actions of the Japanese. The man replied with a pitiful tale of how the "robbers" had thoroughly looted the port and carted off everything of value, even the horses and cows. He himself had been separated from his wife and aged mother in the panic, and was desperate to find them. Could they help him? Yi was moved by the refugee's plight, and offered to take the man with him to escape the Japanese. But the man would not go. With his baby on his back he returned to shore and wandered off through the smoke in search of his family.

With the man gone, Yi's pity turned to wrath. He and Kyongsang Right Navy Commander Won Kyun began to plot further attacks at Chonsongpo and Kadok Island, where more enemy vessels had been sighted, and of even sailing right into the enemy's stronghold at Pusan harbor and burning every ship.

Suddenly a messenger burst in with the dreadful news, now eight days old, of the fall of Seoul and King Sonjo's flight to the north. For Yi and Won, Confucian men born and breed to filial piety, this indignity to their king was too much. They burst into tears and fell into each other's arms. What was left, with the capital now fallen and the king chased off his throne? Was their country finished? Was the war already lost? In light of the uncertainty of the situation, the two commanders decided to dissolve their combined fleet and return to their respective home ports to rest their men, repair and rearm their vessels, and await additional news from the north.[5]

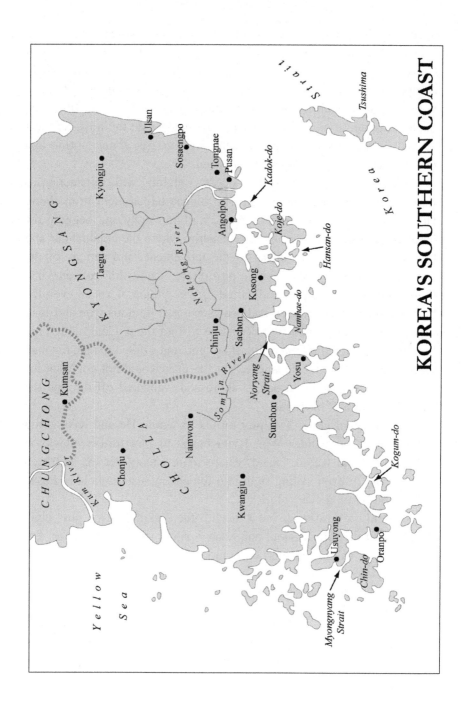

Arriving back at Yosu on June 18, Yi wrote a long dispatch to the Korean court reporting the momentous happenings of the previous week, notably the destruction of over forty enemy ships. He also mentioned the capture of a large amount of stores and booty from the Japanese, including sacks of rice, suits of armor, helmets, masks, shell trumpets, "and many other curious things in strange shapes with rich ornaments [which] strike onlookers with awe, like weird ghosts or strange beasts." Yi ordered a sampling of the more curious items, including a musket and "one left ear cut from a Japanese," to be boxed up and shipped north to the Korean court.

In his dispatch Yi reported the taking of only two enemy heads. This was due, he explained, to the fact that whenever the enemy vessels were "driven into a corner, the sailors jumped ashore and ran away, so we could not catch them."[6] Of his own casualties, Yi listed just three men wounded, all at the engagement at Okpo, adding that two of these injuries had been caused by friendly fire. As he went on to explain, a group of his men who had seized a Japanese vessel during the battle were fired upon by Kyongsang Right Naval Commander Won Kyun's ships. Reading between the lines, it would seem that Won had stayed to the rear while the real fighting was taking place and therefore had not seen the ship fall to Yi's men. In any case it was the sort of carelessness that the normally restrained Yi could not let pass. "Nothing is more shameful than a commander's loose discipline over his subordinates like this," he wrote in his dispatch, adding, "I hope [such conduct] will be corrected by the Court." This was the first of many negative references to Won Kyun that would enter Commander Yi's dispatches in the coming months, fueling the feud that was developing between these two men.

Yi Sun-sin was now a hero. He had delivered the first telling blow to the Japanese invaders and had given his countrymen a reason to hope that maybe, just maybe, they could drive them back across the sea. But he made it difficult for the government to honor him, for he spoke his mind too freely and questioned his superiors when he thought they were wrong. It had been his conviction since being appointed commander of the Cholla Left Navy in 1591 that the coming Japanese invasion should be met at sea, where Korea's strength lay, and not on land as the government in Seoul intended. The government did not agree. Rather than beefing up the southern fleets as Yi urged them to do, they focused instead on building walls and fortifying southern towns. The overwhelming success of the Japanese invasion when it finally came was thus seen by Yi as all too predictable, and he could not help but point this out. "It may be a foolish thought," he wrote in his dispatch of June 9, prior to sailing into battle, "but in my opinion the enemy attacks fiercely, trampling our fair land under iron feet, because we allowed him to set foot on our shores instead of fighting him at sea."[7] Now, on June 19, having amply demonstrated that the Japanese could indeed be beaten at sea, Yi voiced his dissatisfaction one more time:

> It seems to me that because national defense against enemy attack depended solely upon the army, defending weakly fortified city walls, instead of upon the navy fighting at sea, our fair land of many hundred years has become the enemy's stamping-ground overnight. When I think of this tragedy I am choked with sadness and I cannot utter any more words. Should the enemy invade this province by sea, I shall go out to sea and defend it at the risk of my own life, but in the event of the enemy coming by land the generals without horses have no way to fight.[8]

King Sonjo and his ministers rejoiced at Yi Sun-sin's success in resisting the Japanese. But not everyone appreciated his candor. In pointing out the deficiencies in the government's prewar defense policies, Yi was questioning the actions of powerful and influential men, men who could do him a great deal of harm.

It is not clear which Japanese units Yi Sun-sin met and annihilated in the Battles of Okpo, Happo, and Chokjinpo between June 15 and 17, 1592. Some sources assert that they belonged to Todo Takatora,[9] but it is also possible that they were under the command of Mori Terumoto or Kobayakawa Takakage.[10] One thing is certain, however: these enemy forces did not constitute the full might of the Japanese navy, such as it was. They were mainly transport vessels that were no match for the heavy Korean warships and their batteries of guns.

Hideyoshi had planned to provide his invasion force with strong naval protection. But his confident daimyo generals had not felt much need for it. They crossed over to Korea while the Japanese navy was still organizing itself at Nagoya and landed at Pusan without encountering any resistance at sea, thus confirming their assumption that the Korean navy could be disregarded. By the time Hideyoshi's navy finally arrived at Pusan two weeks later, the vanguard contingents under Konishi, Kato, and Kuroda were already two-thirds of the way to Seoul, the entire southern half of Korea lay wide open for the taking, and the Korean navy, if indeed there was one, remained totally silent.

All of this heady success led the Japanese to become even more careless with regard to naval matters during the first few weeks of the war. When the main force of their navy finally reached Pusan on June 6, two weeks behind Konishi's first contingent, it gave little thought to defending its beachheads and securing command of the sea to the west. It was largely taken for granted that Japanese ships would be able to sail unmolested along the southern coast and into the Yellow Sea, the route to advance bases to the north. Indeed, what was the point of keeping men on ships in harbors to the south, guarding against a nonexistent seaborne threat, when there was so much work to be done inland? Several commanders of the Japanese navy thus left their ships and joined their army counterparts in the race up the peninsula. Wakizaka Yasuharu, for example, naval commander for the Tsushima theater, marched his crews north to defend a position near Yongin before eventually returning to his ships at Pusan. Naval commander Kurushima Michiyuki was ordered to prepare residences for Hideyoshi to use during his coming trip to Seoul, and so he too spent his first days in Korea somewhere inland, far from the ships he was supposed to command.[11]

The squadrons that Yi Sun-sin had met and annihilated in June of 1592 were thus not the cream of the Japanese navy, if such can be said to have existed. They were disorganized bands of mainly transport ships that were probing westward with the intention of securing the Korean coastline between Pusan and the Yellow Sea, and doing a little looting along the way. They did not expect to encounter much resistance from the Koreans, certainly not in the form of formidable armored warships, and when they did they beat a hasty retreat.

The loss of more than forty of their ships awoke the Japanese to the fact that the Korean navy was not yet beaten. It was still not seen as posing a very great threat, however, for according to the reports brought back to Pusan the Koreans had fewer than fifty large and medium-sized ships. Still, the problem had to be dealt with. The southern coastline had to be secured so that Japanese ships could begin ferrying reinforcements and supplies north via the Yellow Sea to the advancing front. A second operation to stamp out resistance along the southern coast was therefore launched in early July. This time it would comprise not just transports. There would be warships under the command of such maritime daimyo as Kurushima Michiyuki, Kamei Korenori, and Wakizaka Yasuharu.

Cholla Left Navy Commander Yi Sun-sin spent nearly three weeks at his home port of Yosu following the Okpo campaign, resting his men, repairing his ships, and planning a second operation against the Japanese. The hiatus was finally broken when word arrived from Won Kyun, based farther east in Kyongsang Province, that Japanese naval forces were beginning to advance in earnest along the southern coast. They were already as far as Sachon, dangerously close to Commander Yi's home port. Yi knew that Yosu could not stand against a land attack and that the only way to forestall the Japanese was to attack them at sea before they advanced any farther. Not waiting for the arrival of Yi Ok-ki's Cholla Right fleet, Yi Sun-sin immediately sailed east on July 8 with just twenty-three warships. This time he discarded the small sea ear fishing boats—he had found them of minimal use during the previous campaign—but added something altogether more formidable: the *kobukson*, or turtle ship.

Yi and his master shipbuilder Na Tae-yong did not invent the kobukson as is often assumed. It had been developed some two centuries before, to combat the wako pirates then causing havoc along Korea's coasts. Its first appears in the historical record in 1413, in a brief report in the annals of King Taejong of the monarch viewing a mock battle between a kobukson and a Japanese warship.[12] The vessel by all accounts proved highly effective. Over the course of the next century and a half, however, the value of the kobukson seems to have been forgotten as Korea's military preparedness waned, until it finally became just a dim memory preserved in history books.

It was this dim memory that Yi Sun-sin resurrected and refined. No contemporary account exists of exactly what the vessel he built looked like. Yi himself has left us only this vague description:

> Previously, foreseeing the Japanese invasion, I had had a Turtle Ship specially built with a dragon's head, from whose mouth we could fire our cannons, and with iron spikes on its back to pierce the enemy's feet when they tried to board. Because it is in the shape of a turtle, our men can look out from inside, but the enemy cannot look in from outside. It moves so swiftly that it can plunge into the midst of even many hundreds of enemy vessels in any weather to attack them with cannon balls and fire-throwers.[13]

Yi's nephew, Yi Pun, who served under the commander during the latter part of the war, added a few more details in the biography of his uncle that he subsequently wrote:

> He invented a warship of the same size as a board-roofed vessel [panokson]. On its upper deck were driven iron spikes to pierce the feet of any enemy fighters jumping on it. The only opening was a narrow passage in the shape of a cross on the surface for its crew to traverse freely. At the bow was a Dragon-head in whose mouth were the muzzles of guns, and another gun was at the stern. There were six gun ports each, port and starboard, on the lower decks. Since it was built in the shape of a big sea turtle, it was called *Kobuk-son* (Turtle Ship). When engaging the enemy wooden vessels in a battle, the upper deck was covered with straw mats to conceal the spikes. It rode the waves swiftly in all winds and its cannon balls and fire arrows sent destruction to the enemy targets as it darted at the front, leading our fleet to victory in all battles.[14]

The description in *Sonjo sujong sillok*, the revised annals of King Sonjo compiled some fifty years after the war, is so similar to Yi Pun's that it was likely based upon it.[15]

These two passages contain virtually all the information we have of the turtle ship from individuals who actually saw one or heard of it firsthand. For more detail it is necessary to move forward to a description of the vessel written two hundred years later for inclusion in *The Collected Works of Yi Sun-sin*, compiled and published in 1795.

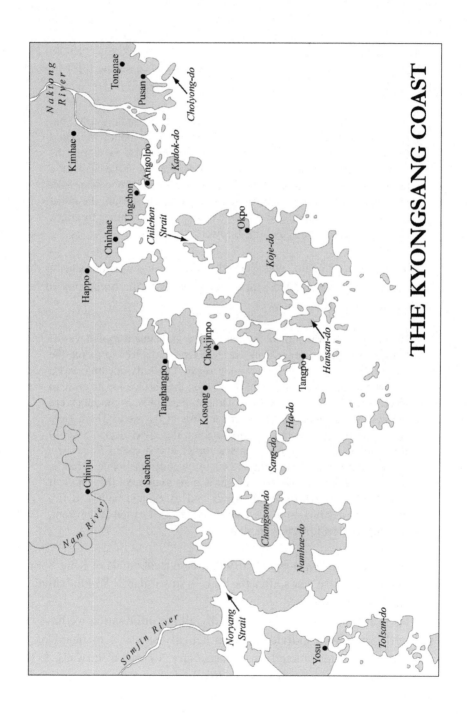

THE KYONGSANG COAST

The editors of this work listed the sizes of the kobukson's key timbers, the number of cabins, ports, and oars, and various other bits of information like the exact size of the dragon's head adorning the bow. Adding this information to Yi Sun-sin's and Yi Pun's descriptions, the following picture of the turtle ship emerges. It was roughly twenty-eight meters long, nine meters wide, and six meters high from its flat, keeled bottom to the top of its roof. It was, in other words, a fairly large ship for its day, but sat quite low in the water, allowing it to come in under the high "castles" of Japanese fighting ships and blast away at their hulls near the waterline. A sloping roof of stout planks was laid on top of the bulwarks, totally encasing the vessel like the shell of a turtle, with just a narrow slit at the apex to allow a mast and sail to be raised and lowered. The roof was covered with iron spikes to disable enemy attackers if they attempted to board. The primary means of propulsion, particularly in battle, when speed and maneuverability were of prime importance, were twenty sculling oars, ten per side, each oar handled by two or three men. Cannons pointed out from loopholes on port and starboard, bow and stern, about fifteen guns in all. The interior of the vessel, finally, consisted of two decks: a lower propulsion deck for the oarsmen, and an upper fighting deck for archers launching regular and fire arrows and for gun crews manning *chonja* (heaven), *chija* (earth), *hyonja* (black), and *hwangja* (yellow) cannons mounted on wooden carriages.[16]

Yi Pun's assertion that straw mats were laid upon the roof to disguise the spikes might seem at first unlikely as this would have turned the kobukson into a floating tinderbox, ready to be set alight by the many fire arrows used in sea battles at that time. Keeping the mats soaked with seawater, however, would not only have solved this problem, but additionally would have made the roof fire retardant.

By far the biggest point of contention regarding the turtle ship is whether or not its spiked roof was covered with iron plates. Early English-language accounts of the Imjin War usually described it as such, typically adding that it was the world's first ironclad ship. This latter claim is certainly not true. Fifteen years earlier in Japan, Oda Nobunaga had employed ships armored in some manner with iron against the fleet of the rival Mori clan in Osaka Bay, a technological innovation that the Japanese never capitalized on. Indeed, it is unlikely that Yi Sun-sin's turtle ship was iron plated at all. The evidence to support this claim does not exist. An ironclad ship would have been something new in Korea in the late sixteenth century and would certainly have excited comment somewhere in the many letters and diaries and reports that survive from this period. Yet Yi himself makes no mention in either his diary or his reports to court of any sort of iron plating covering the roof of his kobukson. Nor does his nephew Yi Pun in his biography of the admiral. Nor does Korean prime minister Yu Song-nyong in his own account of the war. (Yu describes the kobukson as "Covered by wooden planks on top."[17]) Nor do the annals of King Sonjo, that exhaustive compilation of dispatches, reports, conversations, and comments from this period running into the many thousands of pages. In fact, no mention exists in any contemporary Korean account of the war that the turtle ship was ironclad.[18]

Another factor weighing against iron plating is the difficulty that Yi Sun-sin would have faced in acquiring enough metal to cover even one large ship, let alone several. In his treatise in support of the iron plating theory, Bak Hae-ill, extrapolating from the iron cladding on the doors of Seoul's fifteenth-century Namdaemun Gate, estimates that six tons of metal would have been needed to cover the roof of one turtle ship with plates two to three millimeters thick.[19] That is a lot of iron, the equivalent of the vessel's entire complement of cannons. Considering that Yi Sun-sin received so little support from the government and had to scrounge most of the materials he needed to repair and outfit his fleet, the acquisition and use of such a load of iron would have been difficult, and probably would have been considered more usefully employed in the casting of additional cannons, enough to outfit an entire new ship. Yi himself considered it worth mentioning in his diary the relatively insignificant amount of fifty pounds of iron that he sent to Cholla Right Navy Commander Yi Ok-ki as a gift in early 1592.[20] And yet nowhere does he mention acquiring and using six tons of the metal—that's twelve thousand pounds—to cover his turtle ship.

Such a lack of evidence cannot rule out completely the possibility that the turtle ship had some sort of iron plating on its roof. But it does seem to weigh heavily against it. Until further information comes to light to the contrary, the likeliest conclusion is that Yi Sun-sin's turtle ship was armored only insofar as it was constructed of heavy timbers and covered with a thick plank roof studded with iron spikes—which against the light guns of the Japanese was armor enough.[21]

If there is no evidence in the historical record that the kobukson was ironclad, where did this idea come from? One hypothesis is that it may have come from the West. The first tales of Yi Sun-sin and his turtle ship to reach Europe and the United States were carried back by Westerners who visited Korea as it started to open to the world in the late 1870s. A British naval expedition to Korea in 1883, for example, included an account of the curious vessel in its official report, which subsequently appeared in a Chicago newspaper.[22] Ensign George Foulk of the U.S. Navy heard similar stories during his wide-ranging travels on the peninsula in 1884, and actually saw what locals claimed to be the ribs of a turtle ship lying in the sand at Kosong on the coast of Kyongsang Province.[23] To a Westerner of this period, these descriptions of an indestructible warship with a roof like a turtle's back would have conjured up an immediate association: the Confederate ironclad the *Virginia* (a.k.a. the *Merrimac*) and its Union counterpart the *Monitor* which had battled each other in the American Civil War some twenty years before. It is possible that the inevitable comparison of Yi's warship to these two ironclads of recent memory led to the assumption that it too was fitted with iron plates and not simply "armored" with a heavy timber shell. This progression from casual comparison to statement of fact can be roughly charted. In his 1892 account of Hideyoshi's invasion, George Heber Jones wrote that "aided by his famous 'Tortoise Boat,' a prototype of the 'Monitor' of the American Rebellion, [Yi Sun-sin] literally swept [the Japanese] off the coast waters of the peninsula."[24] William Griffis took this a step further in 1894 in *Corea. The Hermit Kingdom*, describing Yi's ship as "apparently covered with metal."[25] By 1905 the transformation to fact was complete. "Its greatest peculiarity," wrote Homer Hulbert of the turtle ship in his *History of Korea*, "was a curved deck of iron plates. . . . [I]t anticipated by nearly three hundred years the ironclad war ship."[26]

Yi Sun-sin's armored kobukson thus went from being regarded as "like" the ironclads of the American Civil War to being itself an ironclad, an assumption that gained weight the more often it appeared in print. It was an assumption that was readily accepted by the Koreans, who were then trying to deal with a flood of Western pressures and innovations that was making them appear to the world as a weak and backward people. In this atmosphere of vulnerability the idea that a Korean had invented the ironclad ship nearly three centuries before was immensely appealing, for it demonstrated that Korea was not a backward country, but in some things had actually preceded the West. The belief that Yi Sun-sin's kobukson was an ironclad ship thus resides firmly in the consciousness of Koreans today, despite the lack of evidence to support the claim, for it is more than just a historical artifact. It is a symbol of national pride.

One of the more distinctive features of the turtle ship was the impressive dragon's head that adorned its bow. This head is depicted in modern-day models and illustrations in an attractive upraised position like a cobra rearing to strike, together with the explanation that smoke from burning gunpowder and sulfur was emitted from the dragon's mouth to terrorize the enemy and obscure the vessel's movements. In his own description of the craft, however, Yi Sun-sin states that a cannon could be fired through the mouth, something that could not have been done if the head was upraised. It must have projected straight out from the bow in a less majestic manner.

The genesis of these two images is found in *The Collected Works of Yi Sun-sin* published in 1795, a compilation of Yi's war diary and official dispatches, additional accounts penned many years after his death, and commentary written by the editors themselves. Among this latter material are two illustrations of the turtle ship. The first, labeled *tongjeyong kobukson*, is an estimation of what the vessel originally looked like in the early fifteenth century, with a dragon's head projecting straight out from the bow. The second illustration, labeled *Cholla chwasuyong kobukson*, depicts a turtle ship that was still extant in 1795, anchored at Yosu, home port of the Cholla Left Navy, which was said to resemble the revised turtle ship Yi Sun-sin developed in 1592. It has two dragon heads: an upraised one above, and a downward-projecting one below that seems to emerge from the bow just beneath the fighting deck where the cannons would have been. If a vessel resembling the Cholla chwasuyong kobukson did see service in the Imjin War, then it may have been a later innovation, one of the several additional turtle ships Yi had constructed after 1592. The editors of Yi's *Collected Works* may also be wrong: the illustration may depict a vessel built long after the war. The only description that Yi himself has left us indicates that the dragon's head on his turtle ship projected straight out from the bow, as on the tongjeyong kobukson. If his ship had two heads like the Cholla chwasuyong kobukson, then the lower head must have projected forward and been positioned higher, at the gun deck.[27]

After leaving his home port of Yosu on July 8, Yi Sun-sin met Won Kyun at Noryang Bay and the two men once again formed a combined fleet. From there they headed toward Sachon, a port dangerously close to the Cholla border, where according to reports Japanese ships had already arrived.

By this point Yi evidently had little use for the Kyongsang Right Navy commander and his fleet of four ships, for he gave Won the job of "finding Japanese killed by arrows or bullets anywhere on the battle-ground, and [cutting] off their heads." Yi personally saw no value in this glory-seeking practice and instructed his own men not to waste their time with it. "Rather than cutting off the heads of a few dead enemies," he told them, "you are expected to shoot many of the living enemy. My eyes will judge who fights best."[28] But the job seems to have suited Won Kyun very well. It gave him the battle honors he craved while keeping him out of the actual fighting, where he was apt to do more harm than good.

Yi and Won arrived at Sachon later that same day to find more than four hundred enemy soldiers fortifying positions on the rocky hill above the port. Red and white banners had been raised in a line stretching three kilometers along the coast. A number of ships, all flying white ensigns, rode at anchor just offshore, including twelve large "pavilion vessels" with high castles built on their decks. Yi did not want to attack the ships where they lay. Such a close approach to shore would expose his force to enemy fire from the heights above and put his heavy ships at risk of running aground with the ebbing tide. He preferred to deal with the enemy in open water, where there would be ample room to maneuver. Suspecting that the Japanese might feel overconfident at the sight of his mere twenty-three ships, Yi made a tentative entrance into the bay, then turned to retreat. Sure enough, more than half the Japanese on shore rushed to their ships to pursue the fleeing Koreans. Soon they were just where Yi wanted them, in the middle of the bay.

And so the battle began. With the impregnable turtle ship captained by Na Tae-yong leading the way, the speedy Korean warships cut a swath through the lighter, slower, less maneuverable Japanese craft, ramming them, blasting away with cannon, setting them ablaze with fire arrows, and raining death upon their unprotected crews. The Japanese fought back as best they could, but their bullets and arrows were of little use against the heavy plank tops and sides of Yi's board-roofed ships and turtle ship. Seeing his men begin to hesitate, Japanese commander Wakizaka Yasuharu is said to have leapt onto the gunwale of his flagship and cried, "These vessels the enemy are using are only like our *mekura-bune* (blind ships).[29] What is there to worry about? Board them and show what you are made of!" According to this Japanese account of the battle, Wakizaka and several of his retainers then managed to draw in one of the Korean warships with a grappling hook and scramble onto its roof, but were beaten back by withering counter-fire.[30]

The Japanese remaining on shore, meanwhile, began to direct musket fire at the Koreans to aid their own fighting sailors. Looking up at the hill, Yi Sun-sin could make out a number of Koreans—identifiable presumably by their native clothing—standing alongside the "robbers." This caused him such rage that he threw his usual caution aside and ordered his oarsmen to dash toward shore, where he proceeded to hammer the enemy positions with his "heaven" and "earth" cannons. The fusillades eventually drove the enemy from the bluff, but exposed Yi's flagship to heavy musket fire. Yi himself was struck by a bullet in the left shoulder, and blood flowed profusely down his torso and leg. He concealed the wound until the fight was over so as not to alarm his men—an indication of the importance that the sheer force of his personality played in galvanizing his men into an effective fighting force. Several others were also wounded in this engagement, including Yi's turtle ship builder and captain, Na Tae-yong, but no one mortally. Later accounts claim that after the battle Yi dug the bullet out of his shoulder with a dagger,[31] but this would seem to be an apocryphal touch, designed to inflate the Yi legend; according to Yi's own account the bullet passed cleanly through his shoulder and exited out the back.[32] The wound must nevertheless have been serious and painful, and the fact that Yi would continue his campaigning for several more days and not mention it again in his diary is in itself remarkable.

With the daylight nearly done and all the larger Japanese vessels destroyed, Yi withdrew his force to the open sea to pass the night. Before departing he left a few of the smaller enemy ships intact and in place as a lure for the Japanese who had fled inland. Eager for total annihilation, he hoped that these scattered remnants would attempt to use the vessels to return to Pusan, thereby offering him a second chance to destroy them out on open water.

On the following morning, July 9, word arrived of a squadron of Japanese ships sighted a little farther to the east, at the harbor of Tangpo. The Korean fleet immediately made off in that direction, arriving before noon to find twenty-one enemy vessels at anchor along the beach, nine of them as large as the Koreans' own board-roofed ships. One of them appeared to be the flagship of the fleet. A pavilion ten meters high was erected on its deck, "surrounded by a red brocade curtain with a large Chinese character 'Yellow' embroidered on each of the four sides. Inside the pavilion was seen a Japanese commander with a red parasol in front. He showed no expression of fear, like a man resigned to death." This was Kurushima Michiyuki, one of the daimyo leading the advance party of the Japanese navy west to the Yellow Sea. With him was a force of seven hundred fighting men, plus crews. It would be the last day of his life.

Once again the turtle ship led the way into the fray, striking out at every vessel it passed. One of the panokson closed with Kurushima's flagship. An arrow struck the Japanese commander in the brow; then a second pierced his chest and sent him toppling off his pavilion, whereupon one of Yi's officers hacked off his head with a sword.[33] The sight so unnerved the rest of the Japanese force that they abandoned the fight and fled into the hills, leaving the Koreans once again to burn their ships unopposed.[34]

Aboard one of the Japanese ships that fell to the Koreans that day, a curious piece of booty was recovered and carried to Yi Sun-sin. It was a gold fan packed in a black lacquer case. Written on the center of the fan were the words, "sixth month, eighth day, Hideyoshi," to the right of this "Hashiba Chikuzen-no-kami," and to the left "Kamei Ryukyu-no-kami." Yi took these inscriptions to mean that "the Japanese commander, whose head was cut off, must be Chikuzen-[no-kami], the garrison commander of Chikuzen."[35] He was mistaken. "Hashiba, Lord of Chikuzen" was in fact the appellation used by Hideyoshi himself ten years before. In 1582, when he was still consolidating his hold over the territories of his recently deceased master, Oda Nobunaga, Hideyoshi secured the allegiance of Kamei Korenori, a fellow daimyo in Inaba Province, by promising to give him the Ryukyu Islands whenever they should be conquered. As proof of his word, Hideyoshi took his fan from his belt and inscribed it with his and Kamei's names, the date, and the words "Ryukyu-no-kami," "Lord of Ryukyu." This fan remained a prized possession of Kamei's for the next decade and was now evidence of his presence at the Battle of Tangpo, alongside Kurushima. Kamei lost all five ships under his command that day, but managed to escape with his life.[36]

After completing the destruction of the Japanese fleet at Tangpo, Yi and Won Kyun spent the next two days scouring northern Koje Island and then west along the mainland coast, searching for more enemy ships. Not a single Japanese vessel was sighted. On July 12 Cholla Right Navy Commander Yi Ok-ki at the head of twenty-five large warships finally caught up to Yi Sun-sin, bringing the combined strength of the Korean fleet to fifty-one large battleships plus many smaller craft. The arrival of these ships and reinforcements raised the spirits of Yi Sun-sin's tired men immeasurably.

Then came news: enemy ships at Tanghangpo.

Tanghangpo, at the head of a narrow inlet ten kilometers from the open sea, was a potentially dangerous place to take on the Japanese. Yi Sun-sin, Yi Ok-ki, and Won Kyun accordingly approached it with caution. A scout was first sent ashore to inquire whether the bay was wide enough for their ships to maneuver. It was. Then a small advance party of warships was sent through the narrow neck of the inlet to locate the enemy. This was soon done and signal arrows sent up, calling the rest of the fleet forward. Leaving four of their ships behind to pick off any Japanese ships that attempted to flee, the two Yis advanced into the bay at maximum speed.

They arrived at Tanghangpo to find twenty-six enemy ships anchored along the shore: thirteen small and four medium-sized vessels, plus nine large ships as big as a Korean panokson. All of them were painted black except for the largest one, the flagship. It had a three-story pavilion upon its deck that was painted in red, blue, and white and wrapped in a skirt of black cloth, and looked to Yi Sun-sin like a Buddhist shrine. Four of the vessels flew large banners painted with the characters *namu myoho renge kyo*: "Glory to the Holy Lotus," the incantation of the Buddhist Nichiren sect.

The Korean fleet, unable to form a straight battle line in the confines of the bay, arranged itself this time in a circle. With the turtle ship again leading the way, the battleships took turns sweeping in to loose their fusillades of cannonballs, iron bolts, and fire arrows upon the Japanese, then fell back to reload as the next ship in the circle moved in. The relentless pressure soon had the Japanese on the defensive, so much so that Yi Sun-sin realized they would likely abandon their ships and flee inland, depriving him yet again of the opportunity of destroying them completely, not just their ships but their crews as well. He therefore gave the order to fall back in a feigned retreat, coaxing the Japanese to counterattack, out into open water. The ploy worked perfectly. The Japanese, assuming that the battle was turning in their favor, left the relative safety of shore and advanced into the bay in pursuit. When they were just where he wanted them, Yi ordered his ships to come about and surround the Japanese, and blast their ships to splinters. The large flagship with the pavilion on top drew the heaviest fire. According to Lee Sun-sin,[37] a trusted captain in Yi Sun-sin's Cholla Left Navy, "The enemy Commander, aged about 24 or 25, of strong physique, wearing magnificent dress, stood alone holding a long sword in his hand and fought to the last without fear as he directed his eight remaining subordinate warriors. I shot an arrow at him with all my might, but it was not until he had been shot through and through with more than ten arrows that he shouted loudly and fell, after which his head was cut off. The remaining eight Japanese were also shot down and beheaded." Soon all the Japanese ships had been sunk or set ablaze. Only a few survivors managed to swim to shore and escape into the hills. All that remained was for Won Kyun to move forward to hack off the heads from the enemy dead.[38]

For the next four days the Korean fleet sailed from port to port along the coast of central Kyongsang Province, searching for additional enemy squadrons to attack. They spotted a few ships scurrying back toward the east and safety but were unable to run them down. It soon became apparent that the Japanese navy had retreated to Pusan and that the fighting was over until they decided to venture west again. On July 18, therefore, Yi Sun-sin, Yi Ok-ki, and Won Kyun dissolved their combined fleet and returned to their respective ports to rest and rearm for the next campaign.

At the time of their parting Won Kyun expressed a desire to get together with Yi Sun-sin immediately to write and submit a joint battle report. Yi stalled, saying that there was no need for haste, and presumably leaving Won to assume that they would prepare a joint report a little later on. Yi then went ahead and wrote a lengthy and detailed dispatch on his own without any input from Won. In it he once again had phenomenal numbers to report: seventy-two enemy vessels destroyed at the cost of not a single Korean ship; eighty-eight Japanese heads taken and countless others killed, against Korean losses of only eleven killed and twenty-six wounded. Yi was careful to explain that the low head count was due to standing orders he had issued to his officers not to waste time with this self-aggrandizing practice, the sole purpose of which was to win glory and rewards. Yi promised that he would recommend those who fought well, "even though they cut off no heads." And indeed, in this and every other battle report he sent to the Korean court, he included the names of all the officers he considered worthy of reward, with urgings that these rewards be issued as soon as possible to encourage their morale. This was in line with the teachings of the ancient Chinese military classics, as well as being plain common sense: "Beneath fragrant bait there will certainly be dead fish. Beneath generous rewards there will certainly be courageous officers."[39]

As for Won Kyun, Yi Sun-sin made no effort to cast him in a

favorable light or secure for him a reward. On the contrary, he pointed out that the Kyongsang commander had lost his entire fleet at the start of the invasion and so had nothing to command in the recent campaign, and by inference nothing to contribute. This upset Won when he heard of it, and resulted in the tensions that already existed between the two men giving way to open hostility. Henceforth they would submit separate battle reports.[40] Just as hurtful as Yi's words, however, was the fact that recognition was not forthcoming. As Yi Sun-sin was rewarded with letters of commendation and one promotion after another—to court rank Junior 2B in June, Junior 2A in July, and Senior 2A in September—Won Kyun received nothing. Won evidently made his dissatisfaction known to the government, for in early October it was recommended that he and Yi Ok-ki receive promotions and letters of commendation in recognition of their service alongside Yi Sun-sin.[41]

Why did the Korean navy under Yi Sun-sin enjoy such superiority over the Japanese? First, the Koreans had better ships. With their two banks of sculling oars, Yi's turtle ship and board-roofed ships were faster and more maneuverable than anything the Japanese possessed. They were more heavily built, with sides and roofs of thick wooden planks that were impervious to Japanese muskets. They were well equipped with large cannons that could blast a stone or iron ball clean through a Japanese hull. With these three strengths a Korean battleship could close to within just a few meters of an enemy vessel and smash it to splinters with little fear of counter-fire, for the Japanese navy at this point did not possess cannons in any appreciable number. It only had lightweight muskets, an effective weapon against the flesh of Korean soldiers and horses on land, but of little use against the thick wooden shell of a Korean battleship.

The Koreans also benefited from a more unified system of naval command. In these early sea battles of the war, Cholla Left Navy Commander Yi Sun-sin naturally took the de facto lead of the Korean navy in the south—he was fifteen years older than thirty-two-year-old Cholla Right Navy Commander Yi Ok-ki and correspondingly more experienced—a role that would be formally recognized by the court in the coming months with his promotion to the special rank of supreme naval commander. On the Japanese side there was no one in a comparable position of overall authority. The Japanese navy was composed of a loose assembly of squadrons, each belonging to and commanded by a separate daimyo, each looking out for his own interests, each deciding for himself what he would and would not do. No one, in other words, was bound very closely by orders. There was in fact only one man with enough authority to compel these naval commanders to work together to achieve a single objective, and that was Hideyoshi. But Hideyoshi was not on the scene. He was still at Nagoya, ostensibly waiting on the weather. In his absence the commanders of the Japanese navy thus had to work out among themselves ways for dealing with the Korean threat, with egos and rivalries and jealousies all coming into play, a fact that hampered their ability to face down Yi Sun-sin's united fleet.

All these advantages that the Koreans enjoyed at sea—better ships, better guns, and a more unified system of command—are evidence of a more sophisticated understanding of naval warfare than that possessed by the Japanese. In 1592 Hideyoshi and his commanders still had a medieval conception of warfare at sea. To them it was little more than an extension of warfare on land, with ships serving as fighting platforms from which opposing forces tried to pick one another off with arrow and musket fire, followed by grappling and boarding to finish off survivors. The goal, in short, was to kill enemy sailors, not sink enemy ships. They thus armed their vessels accordingly, with lightweight arquebuses, not heavy cannons.[42]

The Koreans saw things the other way around. For Yi Sun-sin, Yi Ok-ki, and Won Kyun the primary purpose of naval warfare was to destroy enemy ships. They thus armed their panokson and kobukson with cannons to sink them and fire arrows to burn them. Kill an enemy, after all, and you only kill one man. Destroy an enemy ship, however, and you destroy much of its crew as well, leaving the rest floundering in the water where they then could be hacked to death.

If the immediate purpose of war is killing and destruction, then the Japanese were better at it on land, while the Koreans excelled at sea.

CHAPTER 11

On to Pyongyang

AFTER ABANDONING THE HAN RIVER, Commander in Chief Kim Myong-won, the government official given the impossible task of defending Seoul with no more than a thousand troops, was ordered to gather as many men as he could and make a stand fifty kilometers north at the Imjin River, the next obstacle the Japanese would encounter on their march to China. The call was thus put out for Korea's scattered forces to assemble at the Imjin. Over the next two weeks a steady stream of soldiers and commanders, some retreating from the south, others coming down from the north, began arriving at the north bank of the river, swelling Kim's meager ranks to a total of ten thousand men. Among those present were Vice-Commanders Sin Kal and Han Ung-in, General Yi Il, who had been routed by Konishi Yukinaga's first contingent at Sangju, and General Yu Kuk-ryang, previously charged with defending Bamboo Pass on the road north to Seoul.

The king and his entourage of government ministers were in the meantime on a brief layover in the walled city of Kaesong a few hours farther north. It was here, on June 11, 1592, that King Sonjo caved in to mounting pressure to place the blame for the crisis on the shoulders of Yi San-hae, Prime Minister of the State Council and as such the highest-ranking official in the land. Yi was dismissed from office and sent into exile. Yu Song-nyong, previously second to Yi as Minister of the Left, was promoted to Prime Minister, Choi Hung-won became the new Minister of the Left, and Yun Tu-su, Minister of the Right.[1]

Later that same day King Sonjo held a public audience to "comfort the people" and allow them to voice their grievances. Paper was also distributed so that anyone who wished to do so could submit their thoughts in writing. It was something the king felt he needed to do, for he knew that his subjects were angry—angry at the government for failing to apprehend the Japanese threat, and angry at Sonjo himself for abandoning Seoul, a fact made painfully clear by the shouts and insults hurled at him as he left and by the fires and looting that started immediately thereafter. Reports were also coming in that some of the trades people of the capital were already reopening their shops and doing business with the enemy, evidently reassured by public proclamations that the Japanese had come to Korea merely to free the people from their oppressive king and had no wish to harm anyone. All this came as a shock to King Sonjo, an example as he saw it of his own people betraying their country and siding with an enemy force. But it was also a chastisement of his government and indeed himself that had to be addressed.[2]

In the course of this audience a man prostrated himself before Sonjo and asked that exiled government minister and Western faction leader Chong Chol be restored to office. Chong, formerly Minister of the Left, had been dismissed by King Sonjo in 1591 and his faction subsequently eclipsed by the Easterners as a result of a disagreement over which of the king's sons should become the crown prince. Sonjo had been angry at Chong at the time for opposing his own choice of heir. Now, however, the king was eager to satisfy the people, so he agreed to the petitioner's request, recalled Chong Chol from exile, and dismissed Eastern faction leader Yu Song-nyong as Prime Minister to atone for the "mistake." After less than a day the State Council was therefore shuffled again, with Choi Hung-won becoming Prime Minister, Yun Tu-su Left Minister, and Yu Hong Right Minister.[3] Yu Song-nyong's dismissal was evidently a face-saving measure. He would continue to play a leading role in the war effort, particularly in making preparations for the coming of the Ming army, and in January of the following year would become the top civilian overseer of the nation's armed forces with the specially created wartime position of *dochechalsa*, "National High Commissioner." Yu would eventually be reappointed Prime Minister following the dismissal of Choi Hung-won in December of

1593 for reasons of ill health, and this time would hold on to the post until the end of the war in 1598.[4]

King Sonjo, Crown Prince Kwanghae, and their retinue resumed their flight north on June 13, this time not stopping until they reached Pyongyang. They arrived on the sixteenth and were led through the gates to safety by an escort of three thousand troops. Finally, for the first time since abandoning Seoul a week earlier, the king and government in exile of Korea were able to settle down in a degree of comfort and take stock of the situation. It was, in a word, desperate. The Japanese had already taken the southern half of the peninsula including Seoul, and judging from the speed of their advance would be across the Imjin River in fairly short order and on their way to Pyongyang. It thus seemed inescapable that Korea would cease to exist, probably before the end of the year, unless China intervened.

During the first days of the invasion the Korean government debated long and hard over whether to request military aid from China. Those ministers opposed to doing so were primarily worried about the negative repercussions that this would have on Korea. First it would mean relinquishing control of the situation to Beijing, something that no government official was eager to do. Korea, after all, was a sovereign nation, albeit a vassal of China, and did not want to take a back seat in dealing with matters on its own territory. There was also the burden to consider of having to feed Ming soldiers once they arrived on Korean soil, a drain on government resources that would leave that much less for the maintenance of the nation's own troops, further hampering Korea's ability to defend itself and manage its own affairs. Newly appointed Minister of the Left Yun Tu-su additionally pointed out that any military aid that Beijing might send would probably be in the form of troops from the neighboring Ming province of Liaodong—rapacious, undisciplined louts who might conceivably do more harm than good to the Koreans they would be ostensibly coming to help. Such concerns were foremost in Seoul during the opening days of the war, and so the first dispatches sent to Beijing merely informed the Wanli emperor of the fact of the invasion without asking for assistance.

As the Japanese continued their advance on Seoul, however, the tide of opinion within the government began to turn in favor of requesting aid from China. The first and most obvious reason for this change was the awful realization that Korea might be swallowed up entirely if the Ming did not soon intervene. But it was not just fear of the Japanese that drove King Sonjo and his ministers to turn to China. They were also growing apprehensive of the Korean people themselves. Since the beginning of the war, long-simmering public resentment over excessive taxation, rampant factionalism, and incompetent, abusive officials had exploded into full-blown anger against the rulers of the nation. The public blamed the government for the present calamity and was now dangerously estranged. The decision to request military assistance from China was therefore made not only in the interests of protecting the kingdom from the invading Japanese, but also to prop up the now-disgraced ruling elite, for it was from the Ming that King Sonjo and in turn his ministers derived their own legitimacy.[5] After the fall of the capital and the retreat to Kaesong and then Pyongyang, the Korean government thus sent a second envoy to Beijing, this time carrying a plea for help. When this did not elicit an immediate response, a third message was sent. Then a fourth.[6]

In China, meanwhile, confusion abounded and suspicions brewed. To begin with, it was not immediately clear what was occurring in Korea. Had a large-scale invasion actually taken place as the Korean government was reporting? Or was Seoul merely overreacting to a somewhat larger than usual wako pirate raid, the sort that had intermittently plagued both countries for centuries past? This issue was eventually cleared up, and Beijing acknowledged that something very big and very serious was taking place in Korea. But then the question arose about Hideyoshi's true intentions. Did he really want to conquer China as the Koreans claimed? Or was he only after their tributary state Korea, with the Koreans inflating his intentions to attract Chinese aid? And if he really was aiming for China, were the Koreans in fact being swept aside? Or were they secretly helping him along?

Suspicions about Korea's playing a secret role in Hideyoshi's planned conquest began to appear in China upon receipt of the first reports of the war. These suspicions were sparked mainly by the incredible speed with which the Japanese were marching up the peninsula: from Pusan to Seoul, a distance of 450 kilometers, in just twenty days. Suspecting that the Japanese could not be advancing toward China as quickly as they were without active support from the Koreans, the governor of Liaodong, the Chinese province bordering Korea, sent an agent to Pyongyang to investigate. The equally suspicious central government in Beijing also dispatched an official of its own across the Willow Palisade.[7] These representatives eventually returned to report that the Koreans were fighting desperately to resist the Japanese advance, that tens of thousands of their soldiers had already been killed, and that they had done nothing that could be regarded as treasonous toward the Celestial Throne. Trust in Little China was thus restored, leading to a deeper commitment to help in Beijing and in turn throwing the ponderous wheels of the Chinese military machine fully into motion. By then, however, it was already well into August, three months after the first Japanese soldiers had stepped ashore at Pusan.

This initial confusion and suspicion over what was happening in Korea explains in part why the Ming government was slow in responding to King Sonjo's plea for help and why this response when it came was initially rather small. But it was not the whole story. Throughout the summer of 1592 Beijing had other concerns on its plate that were very preoccupying indeed. By far the biggest of these was the so-called Ordos Campaign. Earlier that year in March, two months before the start of the Japanese invasion of Korea, an officer assigned to a garrison along China's northwestern frontier led his troops in mutiny, forcing their commander in chief to commit suicide. Their grievance was a common one in the Chinese army: they weren't being paid. This was a problem that had arisen early in the Ming dynasty, as the self-supporting garrisons established by the Hongwu emperor slowly gave way to a reliance on paid mercenaries whose salaries the Ming treasury was increasingly unable to afford. It had led to dissention before, but this time the matter got completely out of hand. A local Mongol chieftain named Pubei, who had previously been co-opted by the Ming and rewarded with a high military rank, joined the rebellion and was then pushed to the fore as its leader. What had started as an isolated mutiny within the army thus flared into a full-blown Mongol uprising that soon had all of Shenxi Province in an uproar, and the Ordos Mongols on the steppes beyond the Great Wall poised to enter the fray.

The episode was embarrassing for local officials, for it could easily be said that the mutiny that had sparked it all was a symptom of their own mismanagement of regional affairs. In their reports to Beijing they therefore tried to downplay the role of the army, painting Pubei and his Ordos Mongols as the source of all the trouble. It was a believable fiction; border clashes with the Mongols were a common and genuinely worrisome occurrence. The Ming government of course were not fooled by it, but they nevertheless accepted it as the official version of what had happened; to have openly admitted the truth that its own army had mutinied and that one of its own provinces was in chaos would have revealed a dangerous weakness in the empire. Beijing then moved to restore order, dispatching troops to the northwest at the very time when the king of Korea was requesting that help be sent to the east. The Chinese, not nearly as strong as their outdated military rosters implied, did not have enough manpower in the summer of 1592 to deal simultaneously and in force with its own internal troubles as well as Hideyoshi. It could deal with only one emergency at a time, and the mutiny-cum-rebellion within its own borders seemed the most pressing. It would in fact not be until the Ordos Campaign had been concluded in October of 1592 that Beijing was finally able to turn its full attention to the threat posed by the Japanese and muster an army of respectable size.[8]

With the bulk of its armies tied up in the Ordos Campaign, and with the picture of what was happening in Korea still somewhat murky, China's initial response to King Sonjo's request for military aid was necessarily limited. The best it could do was raise an army of one thousand men to protect the retreating king. This expeditionary force, under the command of General Tai Zhaobian and "Attacking Commander" Shi Ru, began marching toward the beleaguered peninsula in July of 1592.

On the far side of the Yellow Sea, the vanguard of the Japanese invasion was nearing the end of two weeks' rest in Seoul. On June 25, two days before resuming their march toward China, first contingent leaders Konishi Yukinaga and So Yoshitoshi dispatched a letter north to King Sonjo, expressing a desire to restore peace between their two countries.

It is true that Toyotomi Hideyoshi wants to attack Great Ming by way of your country. However, we Japanese generals do not wish to travel thousands of leagues to go as far as China, although we have been ordered to come here. For this reason, we are desirous of making peace with your country first, so that we may be able to make peace with Great Ming also through the good offices of your country.

If your country advises China to accept our proposal for resumption of peace between China and Japan, the three countries would be able to enjoy peace. We cannot think of any more ideal measure than this. Moreover, we Japanese generals would be saved further trouble, and the people would be greatly relieved. This is the unanimous opinion of us Japanese generals.[9]

It was not the first such message that Konishi and So had attempted to send to the Korean court since the start of the war. At the outset of the invasion they had given a similar letter to the governor of Ulsan whom they had captured at Tongnae, instructing him to carry it north to the government in Seoul. The governor, afraid that his reputation would be tainted if it were known that he had been captured and then released, made up a tale of having escaped from Japanese custody and never delivered the letter. Upon reaching Sangju, roughly halfway to the capital, the two Japanese commanders tried again to send a message north to Seoul, entrusting it to a captured Korean in the same manner as before. This second letter read in part, "The Governor of Ulsan when made prisoner at Tongnae was released and entrusted with a letter to which no answer has been returned. If you wish for peace, then send Yi Dok-hyong to meet us at Chungju on the 28th [June 7th]." (Yi Dok-hyong had been the official in charge of entertaining Hideyoshi's envoy, So Yoshitoshi, during So's prewar mission to Seoul, and therefore was well known to the Japanese.) This letter did find its way to Seoul, undoubtedly to the great embarrassment of the governor of Ulsan. The situation was so desperate by then that the Koreans were prepared to try anything, and so Yi Dok-hyong was dispatched south to Chungju to see what the Japanese wanted. Before he got there, however, news reached him of the fall of that city and of the defeat of General Sin Ip's army, and so he turned around and returned to Seoul.[10]

This talk of peace appears at first glance unnecessary, considering that Konishi and So had already swept through half the country in less than a month and seemed set to take the rest before the summer was out. Nor did it accurately express their master Hideyoshi's true objective, namely the conquest of Korea and China and the creation of a pan-Asian empire. In expressing a desire for peace, what were these two daimyo commanders up to? To begin with, they were taking a page from Hideyoshi's own book. The taiko himself was a great believer in winning battles without a fight, in bending adversaries to his will by co-opting rather than crushing. With their talk of peace, Konishi and So were attempting to win over the Koreans in a similar manner. As Hideyoshi had conquered Kyushu by co-opting the Shimazu clan, and Shikoku the Chosokabe, so they hoped to conquer Korea by co-opting the dominant lord of the land, namely King Sonjo and his governing elite.

In attempting to win over the Koreans, however, Konishi and So were prepared to go beyond anything Hideyoshi would have sanctioned, for they knew better than he the resistance they had to overcome. Ever since his first visit to Seoul in 1589, So Yoshitoshi understood that bringing the Koreans to heel would be far more difficult than dealing with Chosokabe Motochika or the Shimazu. He saw that these foreign people lived in a different world from the Japanese, one that they regarded as superior, and that they would resist conquest far more bitterly than Hideyoshi seemed able to imagine. During his prewar negotiations with the Koreans So therefore found it necessary to take great liberties in his diplomatic dealings, on the one hand softening Hideyoshi's demands so as not to offend the Koreans, on the other blunting the Koreans' rebuffs so as not to enrage Hideyoshi, and ultimately confusing both sides as to the true intentions of the other.

The situation So and Konishi faced in the summer of 1592 was not so very different. Hideyoshi had assumed that cutting a swath up the peninsula and capturing Seoul would be tantamount to conquering Korea. But he was mistaken. His invasion forces had now cut their swath, and with amazing speed too, but all they had really taken was the swath itself, a long supply line that could be easily severed, leaving them stranded 450 kilometers inside enemy territory. A further advance to Pyongyang would take them 650 kilometers out on this limb and place them in even more danger. In this light Konishi's and So's talk of peace makes sense. They were anxious to achieve a quick settlement with the Koreans while the initiative was still theirs, something that would consolidate their gains and relieve the pressure on their flanks. Then they could turn their attention to selling the settlement to Hideyoshi.

*   *   *

When Wu Ch'i engaged Ch'in in battle, before the armies clashed one man—unable to overcome his courage—went forth to slay two of the enemy and return with their heads. Wu Ch'i immediately ordered his decapitation. An army commander remonstrated with him, saying: "This is a skilled warrior. You cannot execute him." Wu Ch'i said: "There is no question that he is a skilled warrior. But it is not what I ordered." He had him executed. [11]

Wei Liao-tzu (Master Wei Liao)
4th century B.C.

It was at this time that the Koreans won their first victory on land, a small but heartening exception in a seemingly endless stream of bad news. Following the abandonment of the Han River defenses and the subsequent fall of Seoul, Commander in Chief Kim Myong-won ordered the scattered units under his authority to regroup at the next line of defense, the Imjin River. This was not an easy task, for the respect that Kim commanded had suffered a blow with his precipitous retreat from the Han, an action that some took as a sign not just of a lack of military experience, but also of personal courage. It was possibly for this reason that one of Kim's deputy commanders, Sin Kak, did not obey his order to fall back and regroup at the Imjin. Instead he remained with his men in the vicinity of Seoul, sending word to Kim that he intended to join forces with another commander. Commander in Chief Kim was angered by this and immediately sent a dispatch north to the government in exile accusing Sin of refusing to obey orders and recommending that he be punished. The government agreed. An official was sent south to Sin Kak's camp with an order for his execution.

Soon after this official set out, the Korean government received word that Sin Kak's forces had achieved a victory over the Japanese at Yangju, a small town between Seoul and the Imjin River. They had evidently attacked a party of men from Ukita Hideie's eighth contingent who had ventured north from the capital and were pillaging the place, and had beaten them decisively and cut off sixty heads. This news caused the government to have a sudden change of heart about Sin, and a second official was hastily dispatched south to halt his execution. But it was too late. By the time the official arrived at Sin Kak's camp the commander had already been killed.[12]

The Battle of Yangju was a minor engagement as far as the Japanese were concerned. But for the Koreans it was an important victory, a sign that the hated "robbers" could be beaten after all. Sin Kak thus was raised up as a hero and Kim Myong-won painted as the villainous instigator of his death.[13] In fairness to Kim it should be pointed out that, for all his shortcomings, he was the commander in chief of Korea's armed forces and as such had to ensure that his orders were obeyed. Whatever the merits of Sin's victory at Yangju, the fact remained that he had disobeyed a direct order to fall back to the Imjin River and join the forces that were being gathered there. In the harsh system of military justice employed in pre-modern armies, the punishment for that was death.

The Japanese advance resumed on June 27, after two weeks' rest in Seoul. Leading the way was the first contingent under Konishi Yukinaga and Tsushima daimyo So Yoshitoshi; Kato Kiyomasa's second and Kuroda Nagamasa's third followed shortly thereafter. As they had done all the way from Pusan, these three contingents would continue to serve as the vanguard for the coming push into northern Korea, toward the Chinese border.

The going was easy until they reached the Imjin River, the point that today marks the western border between North and South Korea. Here they ran into trouble. The road to the north had led them onto a bluff that dropped down sharply to the river, with the only way to the water being a narrow and rather treacherous gully. This they could manage. But then there was the river to cross, no easy feat without boats. And on the opposite side, arrayed on a flat and easily defensible expanse of sand, were thousands of Korean soldiers and cavalry, armed with arrows and spears and swords and flails, waiting to cut them down as soon as they attempted to step ashore. It appeared that the hitherto helpless Koreans had finally managed to mount an effective defense. With the route to the north now blocked, the joint forces of Konishi, Kato, and Kuroda set up camp, sat down, and started to wait.

*   *   *

There are five dangerous faults which may affect a general:
1. *recklessness, which leads to destruction;*
2. *cowardice, which leads to capture;*
3. *a hasty temper, which can be proved by insults;*
4. *a delicacy of honor, which is sensitive to shame;*
5. *over-solicitude for his men, which exposes him to worry and trouble.* [14]

> *Sun Tsu Ping Fa* (Master Sun's Art of War)
> 4th century B.C.

The Koreans did indeed have the Japanese checked. Commander in Chief Kim Myong-won had succeeded in amassing a sizable force on the far bank of the Imjin River, together with all the boats for miles in either direction. He was soon joined by Han Ung-in, the government minister who had been sent to Beijing earlier that year to deliver the first full report on the Japanese threat. Upon his return Han was given command of three thousand experienced soldiers from the northern province of Pyongan and sent south to join Kim Myong-won in the defense of the Imjin, bringing the total Korean force assembled there to ten thousand men, the largest army so far to be placed in the way of the enemy advance. The Koreans' position was ideal, for there was no way for the Japanese to cross the river en masse to take them on. Even if they managed to acquire some boats, the best they could do would be to ferry across their soldiers in small groups, easy prey for the Koreans when they attempted to land. All the Koreans had to do to hold the Japanese at bay, therefore, was stand their ground and wait.

But it was not to be. While the Korean army holding the north bank was numerically and visually impressive, its effectiveness was greatly hampered by the lack of a clear chain of command. It was a situation inadvertently aggravated by the Korean government itself. When Han Ung-in was sent south to join the defense of the Imjin, the government,

chagrined by the recent Sin Kak affair, had informed him that he was
not subject to orders from Kim Myong-won. This was undoubtedly
intended to prevent another vice-commander from being accused of
disobeying orders and facing execution. But of course it also served to
further undercut Kim's authority and divide the Korean army. Against
the experienced and determined Japanese, this lack of unity would
prove fatal.

Konishi, Kuroda, and Kato waited for ten days on the Imjin's south
bank, until it became clear that the Koreans were not going to give way
without a fight as they had at the Han. Then they decided to try a ploy:
they pretended to retreat. The feigned retreat had already become a
favorite tactic of Korean sea hero Yi Sun-sin, an effective way to draw
inexperienced and overconfident Japanese naval commanders into open
water where he could then finish them off. But it had a much longer
pedigree than that. Among the seven military classics of ancient China,
the fourth-century B.C. work *Sun Tzu Ping Fa* (Master Sun's Art of
War) makes the general observation that "All warfare is based on
deception. . . . Hold out baits to entice the enemy. Feign disorder, and
crush him. . . . Pretend to be weak, that he may grow arrogant."[15] The
Ssu-ma Fa (The Marshal's Art of War), written a few decades later,
recommends specifically that "If you are contending for a strategic
position, abandon your flags [as if in flight, and when the enemy
attacks] turn around to mount a counterattack."[16]

This is precisely what the Japanese did. After ten days of sitting idly
on the south bank of the Imjin, Konishi, Kato, and Kuroda doused their
fires, packed up their gear, and made a show of beginning to march
dejectedly back toward Seoul. For many of the Koreans watching from
the river's north bank it was a beautiful sight. The tide was turning! The
enemy was retreating! One inexperienced young commander who had
just come down from the north, Sin Kil, immediately set up a call to
cross the river to pursue the routed robbers and cut off their heads. The
older and more experienced commander Yu Kuk-ryang stepped
forward and tried to calm him down, pointing out that the wisest course
would be to wait and see what developed before rushing to the attack.
This outraged Sin Kil. He called Yu a coward and drew his sword as if
to cut him down. Yu escaped physical injury, but the accusation of

cowardice dealt a serious blow to his honor, a soft spot for many Korean military leaders that, when touched, all too often drove them into ill-advised, knee-jerk displays of martial valor usually ending in defeat. Yu, unfortunately, was no exception. "Since I was a young man," he replied indignantly, "I have been a soldier, following the flag and fighting battles wherever duty has taken me. How can you now accuse me of being afraid to die? The only reason I have urged you to be cautious is that I fear your impetuosity and inexperience will lead us all to destruction." Then, to prove his courage beyond question, Yu abandoned his better judgment and insisted on leading the attack across the river himself. Sin Kil agreed.

Government official Han Ung-in was in the meantime whipping up his own three thousand men to join the attack. Some of these troops, seasoned veterans who had seen action against the Jurchen tribes of the north, were reluctant to cross the river and attempted to point out to Han that the Japanese withdrawal might be merely a ruse. Han instantly silenced them by having several executed. Commander in Chief Kim Myong-won, who thought the planned attack ill-advised, looked on with disapproval but could do nothing; the government had specifically exempted Han from obeying his commands.

With Yu Kuk-ryang leading the way, a portion of the Korean army crossed the Imjin River and scrambled up the bluff on the south bank. There was no sign of the enemy, only their abandoned camps. They then proceeded south toward the trees—and into a hail of withering musket fire, for the Japanese had not retreated after all, but were hiding in the woods beyond. The Koreans made a rush back to the river. The first to get there piled into the boats and tried to get away, capsizing some in their panic. Others leaped off the bluff and into the water, "like leaves blowing in the wind." The Japanese, in hot pursuit, descended upon them and finished them off. The aged commander Yu Kuk-ryang, intent to the last on proving his courage, reportedly dismounted from his horse and said, "This is the place where I will die." It was. And he did. So did Sin Kil.

All was not yet lost for the Koreans at the Imjin. Significant casualties had been sustained in the assault, but there was still a large body of men on the north bank of the river, and they had made a present to the Japanese of only a few boats. They were thus still in a position to keep the invaders pinned down if they would only stand their ground.

They did not. Upon witnessing the slaughter on the river's south bank, one of the commanders on the far shore, a civil official with no military experience, got on his horse and galloped away. Those who observed his flight mistook him for Kim Myong-won, and soon the cry went up, "The commander in chief is running away!" The false report spread like wildfire, the rank and file lost their nerve, and soon men began scattering in every direction. And so the supremely defensible north bank of the Imjin River was abandoned by the Koreans, served up on a platter to the undoubtedly delighted Japanese. By July 7 the entire Japanese force had crossed the river and was marching toward Kaesong, which they soon occupied without a fight.[17]

After taking Kaesong, the Japanese vanguard did not proceed in a body toward Pyongyang. Instead the three contingents separated and headed off in different directions. Konishi Yukinaga continued north into Pyongan, the northwestern province running from the city of Pyongyang to the Yalu River and China beyond, the territory through which the Korean king would be passing in his continuing flight to safety. Kuroda Nagamasa swung west into Hwanghae Province. This would entail a brief detour to subdue a string of midsize towns near the Yellow Sea coast, then a return to the main route north in the vicinity of Pyongyang, where he would rejoin Konishi. Kato Kiyomasa, finally, proceeded to the remote northeastern province of Hamgyong. This would be anything but a brief detour. Hamgyong was a wilderness of mountain peaks and forests running all the way to the Manchurian border and would keep the bearded daimyo occupied for months.

This division of forces at Kaesong was to have a potentially significant bearing on the course of the war. By sidetracking Kato in Hamgyong and leaving the task of opening a route to China in the hands of Konishi and Kuroda, the strength and in turn the forward momentum of the Japanese advance was effectively cut in half. As mentioned above, moreover, Konishi and his son-in-law So Yoshitoshi were trying to reach a settlement with the Koreans that would bring the fighting to an end. The task of "slashing a way to China" and capturing

Beijing had thus fallen to the two men least eager to do the job. Kato, on the other hand, *was* fully committed to Hideyoshi's plan to conquer China. Of all the daimyo serving in Korea, he would remain truest to his master's grand design. As he wrote to Hideyoshi from Kaesong on July 9, shortly before separating from the other contingents, "The expeditionary force under the command of this humble subject is going to conquer Hamgyong-do, a remote province in the northeastern part of Korea. The place is located far from the territory of Ming, more than ten days' journey. If your highness wishes to cross the sea to conquer Ming, please give me an order at the earliest possible date. In that case, I will speed by day and night to your place to take the lead in the conquest."[18]

If the assignments had been distributed differently, therefore, and Kato had proceeded into the crucial central province of Pyongan rather than to Hamgyong off to the side, who knows how far he might have gone? He probably would not have tried to advance all the way to Beijing; he still seemed to think that Hideyoshi soon would be arriving to oversee that final push. But he might have slashed his way farther north than Konishi eventually did, perhaps all the way to the Yalu River and into China beyond. It would have been a bold thrust, it would have exposed his men to extreme risks, and it might even have resulted in the annihilation of his force. But it would have been in keeping with the fierce and loyal Kato.

It was now July 10. In Pyongyang King Sonjo called a meeting of his ministers to discuss what should be done now that the Japanese had crossed the Imjin River and were approaching the city. Minister of Personnel Yi Won-ik began by expressing the widely held view that Pyongyang should be held even if it meant dying to the last man. If that was to be done, Minister of War Yi Hang-bok cautioned, then plans had to be immediately drawn up; waiting until the situation was desperate and then hastily throwing a defense together—as had been done at Seoul—was not the way to proceed.

King Sonjo then spoke up. He did not think it was safe for him to remain in Pyongyang, he said. He wished to move elsewhere. Two options were then discussed for the evacuation of the king: the town of Yongbyon on the road to Uiju and China beyond, and Kanggye in the far northeast. "I have been advised by my military men," Sonjo said, "that the terrain around Kanggye is advantageous."

"I have just returned from Kanggye," offered Chong Chol, the Western faction leader Sonjo had recently recalled from exile at the request of a petitioner at Kaesong. "It is cold and the ground is infertile, so it would be difficult to feed any soldiers stationed there."

Minister of the Left Yun Tu-su added that Kanggye was also too remote. "It has long been said," he observed, "that if you are at the center you can get things done, but if you go off to the side you cannot issue commands."

"Then I cannot go to Kanggye," replied King Sonjo.

In the end it was decided that when it became necessary for the royal household to evacuate Pyongyang, King Sonjo would go north to Yongbyon. The idea was also broached that Crown Prince Kwanghae should proceed separately to Kanggye or some other place in the northeast. The reason for this probably had to do with Sonjo's often repeated desire to "comfort the people," a euphemism for quelling public dissatisfaction with the government and in turn with himself. Making the royal presence more widely felt across the north, it was perhaps hoped, would mollify the people, calm their rebellious inclinations, and in turn remind them of their duty to support their king and resist the Japanese.[19]

The time for the royals to flee the city came very quickly. On July 16 Konishi Yukinaga with his vanguard first contingent arrived at the south bank of the Taedong River, within sight of the walls of Pyongyang. The Kyushu daimyo had now entered the vastness of Pyongan-do, the northwestern province of Korea that had been promised to him as a fief.[20] He was joined within a few days by Kuroda Nagamasa's third contingent, flush with success after its sweep through Hwanghae Province. There were no boats and no other way to cross the Taedong to continue their march on the city, so as at the Imjin River they set up camp and sat down to wait. Their presence soon had Pyongyang in an uproar. City and government officials tried to prevent the populace from fleeing, for everyone would be needed to defend the walls if they were to stand any chance of repelling the Japanese. There are thousands of troops to man the walls, the officials announced to the public. There are plenty of weapons, and abundant food and supplies, enough to withstand a siege for many months. Pyongyang is a strong fortress city; it will not fall like Seoul. But the people would not listen. As it is written in the *Ssu-ma fa*, "When men have minds filled with fear, all they see is their fear."[21]

On that same day King Sonjo and his entourage began making preparations to resume their northward flight. First the queen was sent northeast to Hamhung in Hamgyong Province, where she hopefully would be safe and able to spread the royal presence. Then the Tablet Guard, a select body of men responsible for transporting and safeguarding the nation's most precious possession, the ancestral tablets of the Choson dynasty, was dispatched. The sight of this august force marching solemnly toward the gate leading to the north road created an uproar among those citizens who still remained in the city, for the evacuation of the ancestral tablets, the embodiment of royal power, meant that King Sonjo himself would be soon leaving too. A crowd armed with clubs and stones gathered and blocked the guard's way, and angrily confronted the official at its head. "You called upon us to protect the city," they cried indignantly, "but now here you are running away yourself when danger threatens." After a prolonged shouting match the guard managed to shoulder its way through the gate and proceeded on its journey. The mob then marched on the palace where King Sonjo was staying and forced its way into the inner courtyard, shouting, "If the king leaves it will be the same as handing us over to slaughter!" Yu Song-nyong came out and reprimanded the people for their unruly conduct and rude behavior in front of their sovereign, and finally managed to cow them into submission and shoo them into the street. But any hope that the citizenry of Pyongyang would stay and defend the walls was now lost. With the knowledge that their king would soon be leaving, the exodus that had already bled the city of much of its population continued unabated, until the ancient Koguryo capital was entirely deserted.[22]

The day after reaching the Taedong River just south of the city, Konishi Yukinaga and So Yoshitoshi attempted for a fourth time since their arrival in Korea to contact the Korean government. A message was sent across the river requesting a meeting with Yi Dok-hyong, the same government official they had asked to meet at Chungju. Yi had never made it to that meeting; upon receiving word that Chungju had fallen, he had halted his journey and returned to Seoul. He was subsequently sent to Beijing to seek Chinese aid and had just arrived back in Pyongyang when the message arrived from the Japanese requesting that he attend a parley.

The meeting took place early the next day, July 17, in the middle of the Taedong, Yi Dok-hyong in one boat, Japanese representatives Yanagawa Shigenobu and the monk Genso in another. (Both men, it will be recalled, had been aides to So Yoshitoshi in his prewar negotiations with the Koreans.) Yi began by asking why the meeting had been requested. "Because we don't want this war with your country," replied Genso. "Previously, from Tongnae and Sangju and then Seoul, we sent messages to your king asking for a settlement, but the only answer we have received has been continued resistance all the way here. But we're still prepared to be reasonable. So we ask you again: clear the way to China and let us pass, and save yourselves from destruction."

Significantly, Genso did not speak of the Japanese armies as having been sent to conquer China. All they wanted was to have "friendly relations" with the Ming. It was therefore quite unreasonable for the Koreans to stand in their way—and pointless too, for the Koreans had already proven themselves incapable of resisting the Japanese advance. They now lay prostrate on the ground, bloody and broken, unable to fend off the blows being inflicted upon them, let alone strike back. So why wouldn't they just step aside and bring all the pain to an end? Why were they so stubbornly refusing to let the Japanese "make contact" with China? Was that asking so much?

From the Korean perspective, of course, it was asking for the world. It was patently obvious by now that the stated desire of the Japanese for "friendly relations" with Beijing was disingenuous. They wanted to conquer China and unseat the Ming, a sacrilege so foul to the Koreans that they recoiled from it in horror. Yi Dok-hyong's reply to Genso was thus unequivocal, and left no room for negotiation. "Ming is just like a father to our country," he said. "Even if we face destruction there is no way we can accede to your demands." Then he added, "If it is true that you want to negotiate a settlement with us and have friendly relations with China, turn your armies around and return to your country. If you do that, we will then consider the matter."

That was not what Yanagawa and Genso wanted to hear. "Our armies only go forward!" they said angrily. "We know nothing of retreat! If this is your answer then there can be no peace." With that the boats were untied and returned to their respective shores.[23]

On the following day the Japanese, in an effort to break the deadlock and shock the Koreans into doing something foolish, lashed together a handful of rafts and floated a unit of musketeers to the middle of the Taedong to fire upon Pyongyang. The Korean forces within the city did not precipitously abandon their defenses as the Japanese undoubtedly hoped they would. But the demonstration did prompt King Sonjo to flee. On July 19 he slipped out of the city and resumed his flight north to Yongbyon, a journey, he was told, that would take five days.

Commander in Chief Kim Myong-won was ordered to stay behind and oversee the defenses of the city, together with government ministers Yun Tu-su and Yi Won-ik. The three men had a large number of soldiers at their disposal, reportedly about ten thousand, certainly more than had been present in Seoul in the days before its fall. But holding an entire city required citizens as well, people fighting for their homes, bodies enough to protect every foot of the wall.[24] But of these very few remained. Kim, Yun, and Yi thus decided that rather than wait for the Japanese to attack and surely overwhelm them, they would instead go on the offensive and strike the enemy in their camps, sapping them of their strength and resolve and perhaps even driving them back.

The plan was to quietly transport a body of men across the river on boats in the middle of the night and then to rush into the Japanese camps under the cover of darkness, slaughtering as many as they could before the Japanese had a chance to react. It was a good plan. The defenders of Pyongyang had observed that the Japanese seemed relaxed and unwary in their string of camps along the banks of the Taedong and correctly surmised that they would be susceptible to a surprise night attack. When the designated night came, however, it took the Korean commanders longer than anticipated to get their men across the river in the darkness, and thus it was nearly sunup when they stormed into the first of the enemy camps. The raid began as intended, with several hundred of Konishi's men killed and many horses captured. But then the sun rose and the tables turned. Perceiving what was going on in the hazy light of dawn, the Japanese in the other camps, mainly Kuroda's men, rose up in a counterattack that soon put the Koreans in flight back to the river's edge.

When they got there, their boats were gone. The oarsmen, frightened by the turn the battle had taken, had sculled out to midstream, leaving their comrades stranded. Many of the Koreans ultimately managed to save themselves by retreating some distance upstream to a spot where, with the level of the river unseasonably low, they were able to wade across and race back to Pyongyang. But in doing so they gave away a vital piece of intelligence, something the Japanese had been looking for over the past ten days: a way to cross the Taedong. The ecstatic pursuers returned to their camps to report their discovery. After seeing to their dead and wounded, Konishi's and Kuroda's men began breaking camp and preparing to resume their march north. Next stop: Pyongyang.[25]

With the knowledge that the Japanese would soon be across the Taedong and outside the city walls, any lingering thoughts of defending Pyongyang were cast aside. As the day wore on the last remaining inhabitants streamed out of the gates and into the hills. By dusk Yun Tu-su and Kim Myong-won were frantically having their men sink cannons and arms into a nearby pond so they would not fall into enemy hands. Then they fled too. Kim Myong-won fell back north twenty kilometers to Sunan to regroup his forces, while Yun Tu-su rushed on ahead to report to the king. As the highest-ranking government official present at Pyongyang, he took full responsibility for its fall, and offered to accept whatever punishment was due. King Sonjo declined, and absolved him of any blame. "Our country is already ruined," he replied, evidently feeling that all hope was lost. "Any talk of punishment now is useless."[26]

The Japanese crossed the Taedong and approached Pyongyang to find the gates of the city wide open, beckoning them to enter. Sensing a trap, Konishi and Kuroda climbed a nearby hill from where they were able to look over the walls and see if there was an army waiting within.

There was not. The city was deserted; not a man, woman, or child remained. Reassured, the two daimyo led their men into Pyongyang. It was yet another prize on the road to the north, and a fat prize too, for within the city's warehouses they found more than seven thousand metric tons of rice, enough to feed their army for the next several months.[27]

As the Japanese were helping themselves to Korean rice in Pyongyang, Yu Song-nyong was rushing from town to town in the northwest, stockpiling grain to feed the Chinese troops that the Ming government had promised to send. It was no easy task, for the local people, desperate and unruly with the Japanese approaching and their king on the run, were in revolt in many places, breaking into government warehouses and looting all the grain and supplies. Despite these difficulties, Yu managed to amass a sufficient store of provisions and had it transported to the small town of Chongju, near the Yellow Sea coast some eighty kilometers south of the Chinese border (not to be confused with the larger town of Chongju farther to the south). Here again an armed mob of locals gathered with the intention of carting everything away. Yu had eight of the ringleaders seized and beheaded on the spot, and succeeded in frightening the crowd off and securing his supplies. He then proceeded to build similar stockpiles in other towns, ready to feed the Chinese whenever they should appear—and in turn giving them no excuse to pillage the countryside, as Yu rightly feared they might.[28]

Following their departure from Pyongyang on July 19, King Sonjo and his entourage of government officials made their way north to Yongbyon, within 150 kilometers of the Chinese border. It was here that the first confused reports caught up to them of fighting in the vicinity of Pyongyang, leaving everyone in low spirits and expecting the worst, and anxious to continue their retreat. The king in his despair now spoke of crossing the Yalu River and seeking asylum in the neighboring Chinese province of Liaodong. The idea had been suggested once before, at Tongpa, after the first day's flight north following the evacuation of Seoul, and had been opposed by Yu Song-nyong on the grounds that it amounted to abdication. Now other officials in Sonjo's entourage tried to dissuade him. The people of

Liaodong, they warned, were a savage lot; the Chinese might deny the
royal party entry; and what would the king's subjects, already alienated
by his abandonment of Seoul, think of him if he abandoned the very
kingdom of Choson itself? "Then tell me where I should go!" Sonjo
retorted, clearly upset. "I can accept dying in China, but I do not wish
to be killed by the Japanese." The meeting came to an end with the
issue unresolved. The royal retreat would continue, but its final destination remained unknown.[29]

From Yongbyon the road to China that King Sonjo and his retinue
were following turned west toward Uiju on the banks of the Yalu River.
They had not gone far when they ran into the first bit of good news in a
very long time: the Chinese had arrived! It was a small army, a token
advance force of a thousand men under the command of General Tai
Zhaobian and Attacking Commander Shi Ru. But it was a start. And
more important, it was evidence that Ming truly was a big brother and a
loyal friend to the Koreans and could be counted on to save them in
their hour of need. With a show of humble gratitude, Sonjo greeted
General Tai with these heartfelt words: "While I have failed to protect
my kingdom, the sight of you and your troops here today, having traveled so far from your esteemed land, fills us with confidence and awe,
and will surely strike boundless fear into the heart of our mutual foe."[30]

With General Tai's force leading the way as his personal bodyguard, King Sonjo resumed his journey toward the Yalu, arriving at
Uiju on the river's southern bank on July 30, 1592. He had now
retreated to the farthest reaches of his kingdom. Proceeding any further
would take him into China, a step that the king's officials, particularly
Yu Song-nyong, had strongly advised against. With the presence of
General Tai's soldiers providing a measure of safety, Sonjo was now
willing to follow this advice. He would remain in Uiju for his kingdom
to be restored to him.[31]

It was during his sojourn at Uiju that King Sonjo wrote a poem
expressing his anguish over the crisis that had befallen the nation, and
placing the blame for it squarely on the factional strife that had dominated Korean politics in the years leading up to the war. If only the
Easterners and the Westerners had attended to the nation's business
more conscientiously; if only they had not allowed their disagreements

to cloud their better judgment. Perhaps then the Japanese invasion could have been averted, and King Sonjo himself, the monarch forever caught in the middle, spared the unbearable shame of having to abandon his capital and flee north to the Yalu River.

> As I wail to the moon over the border mountain,
> The winds of the Amnok [Yalu] wave pierce my bowels for aye;
> O, my courtiers, do not say again
> East or West from today! [32]

CHAPTER 12

The Battle for the Yellow Sea

THE JAPANESE INVASION OF KOREA was now in its third month. The three vanguard contingents of Hideyoshi's army had advanced 685 kilometers up the peninsula from their Pusan beachhead, undeterred by mountainous terrain, swift rivers, walled towns, and hastily mustered local armies. They had taken the capital of Seoul on June 12 and were across the Imjin River by July 7. Konishi Yukinaga's first contingent and Kuroda's third were now three-quarters of the way up the peninsula in the city of Pyongyang, resting their men, repairing their gear, and preparing for the next stage in the invasion, the push to the Yalu River. All they needed before continuing their advance were supplies and reinforcements.

The need for supplies and reinforcements had in fact grown acute. A tremendous amount of rice had fallen to the Japanese upon their capture of Pyongyang on July 24. But rice was just one of many items needed to keep an army on the move. They needed new muskets and lances to replace those that had been damaged or lost. They needed lead bullets and gunpowder to replenish depleted stocks. They needed new shoes and clothing. They needed additional iron and leather plates to repair damaged armor.

The Japanese also needed men. While the first and third contingents under Konishi and Kuroda had disembarked at Pusan with a total of nearly thirty thousand, they had nowhere near that number by the time they reached Pyongyang, probably less than twenty thousand all told. What had happened to the rest? To begin with there had been attrition.

Minor losses suffered in battles and skirmishes with the Koreans from Tongnae Castle to the Taedong River were by now beginning to add up, putting a significant dent in the fixed number of men Konishi and Kuroda had started out with. Other troops had fallen sick along the way or were otherwise unable to make the long march north. Still others had been left behind to garrison strategic points along their line of march, which for the time being remained their only supply route.

The farther the Japanese had advanced, therefore, the weaker they had become. Their diminished strength was perhaps enough to sweep aside any lingering Korean resistance that still lay between Pyongyang and the Yalu River. But what about the Chinese? The closer Konishi and Kuroda advanced to the Chinese border—it was now only 250 kilometers away—the likelier it became that they would run up against an army from the Ming, an army that, if the Koreans were to be believed, would be huge. Hideyoshi's daimyo generals, having so far enjoyed nothing but success, had no reason to suddenly doubt their ability to challenge and beat the Chinese. But they knew it would take a great deal of manpower to do so, more than they currently possessed.

And here lay the problem. The only supply line Konishi and Kuroda had available to them was the 685-kilometer-long land route from Pusan, totally inadequate for the tens of thousands of men and the heaps of supplies that had to be moved north prior to taking on the Ming. The only practical method of transportation was by ship, around the southwestern tip of the Korean Peninsula, north through the Yellow Sea, then inland via the Taedong River to Pyongyang. This of course had been Hideyoshi's plan all along. He anticipated no complications in opening such a seaborne supply route. Nor did his naval commanders. It was a complaisance that if anything increased following the start of the invasion, for the only evidence the Japanese saw of a Korean navy in southern waters was the wreckage of the Kyongsang Left Navy, destroyed by its own commander, Pak Hong. After completing the task of ferrying Hideyoshi's 158,800-man invasion force to Pusan, therefore, top Japanese naval commanders like Wakizaka Yasuharu, Kuki Yoshitaka, and Kato Yoshiaki made no effort to secure a supply route around the southwestern end of Korea and into the Yellow Sea. As far as they were concerned the route was wide open. Instead they left their ships and journeyed inland to help with the land invasion, for they assumed they would not be needed until Konishi, Kuroda, and Kato advanced to Seoul and points beyond and called upon them to begin the work of ferrying men and materiel north.

Yi Sun-sin's "Slaughter Operation" in June awoke the Japanese to the fact that the Korean navy still posed a threat and that the essential supply route north via the Yellow Sea was not open after all. Upon receiving word at his headquarters in Nagoya of this setback, Hideyoshi sent a letter to Wakizaka Yasuharu, dated July 31, ordering him to form a united fleet with Kuki Yoshitaka and Kato Yoshiaki and neutralize the Korean navy once and for all.[1] By this time, however, Wakizaka, Kuki, and Kato had already swung into action. Initial reports of serious losses off the southern coast had sent the three commanders hurrying south from Seoul on July 15, back to Pusan to assemble their fleets.

Wakizaka was the first to be ready to sail. In the second week of August, not waiting for Kato and Kuki to finish getting their own fleets in order, he sailed west out of Pusan harbor, toward an enemy he was confident he could defeat on his own.

In Pyongyang, meanwhile, Konishi Yukinaga remained upbeat about the supply situation. Yes, they had underestimated the strength of the Korean navy and had lost a significant number of ships as a result. But the threat had now been perceived, and steps were being taken to deal with it. It was thus only a matter of time before the supply route through the Yellow Sea was secured and reinforcements started flowing north. With the knowledge that his force of less than twenty thousand would soon swell to titanic proportions, Konishi sent a taunting letter north after the retreating Korean king. "The Japanese navy will soon be arriving with reinforcements of one hundred thousand men," it said. "Where will your majesty flee to then?"[2]

Konishi's crowing was premature. While his message was still on its way north after the retreating Korean court, events were unfolding in the south that would ensure that he would never receive those much-anticipated reinforcements. Indeed, over the next few days the momentum of the entire Japanese invasion would be lost, thanks to the efforts of Cholla Left Navy Commander Yi Sun-sin.

It was the Korean navy under Yi's command, it will be recalled, that had foiled the casual first attempts of the Japanese navy to reach the Yellow Sea in the first half of July. In a string of victories at Sachon, Tangpo, Okpo, and Tanghangpo, he and his colleagues Yi Ok-ki and Won Kyun had destroyed more than one hundred ships while suffering few losses of their own. Seeing that they had driven the Japanese all the way back to their base at Pusan, the three commanders decided to separate and return to their respective bases to rest their men, repair and rearm their vessels, and wait for the enemy to make the next move.

This quiet interlude came to an end in the second week of August, when intelligence reached Yi Sun-sin at his home port of Yosu that small groups of Japanese ships were beginning once again to probe westward out of Pusan. This time the Korean commanders went immediately into action. On August 10 Yi Ok-ki, the thirty-two-year-old commander of the Cholla Right Navy, arrived at Yosu to form a combined fleet with the older Yi Sun-sin. They spent all the next day in a joint training exercise to practice a new battle array Yi Sun-sin wished to employ: the "crane-wing formation."

In their campaign of the previous month, the two Yis had either met the enemy in a straight battle line when conditions permitted, or when space was limited had adopted a circular method of attack, with their ships taking turns sweeping in upon the enemy to loose their fusillades of cannonballs and fire arrows. Such tactics served them well, leading them to victory in every engagement. But still Yi Sun-sin was not satisfied, for on several occasions a significant number of Japanese had managed to swim to shore and escape. The crane-wing formation was designed to prevent this from happening. It consisted of a large, forward-facing semicircle of vessels, heavy battleships in the center and lighter craft out on the "wings," with a smaller, wedge-shaped array of ships positioned directly behind the battleships in the center. Its purpose was simple: to surround the enemy with two enveloping wings, forcing their ships into the center of the semicircle toward the overwhelming firepower concentrated there. If Yi could draw the Japanese fleet into this vortex, no ship would escape destruction, and few if any men would remain alive to make that desperate swim to shore. His victories would then be just as he wanted them: the total annihilation of the Japanese at sea.

Following their day of joint maneuvers, the united Korean fleet under the overall command of Yi Sun-sin sailed east to Noryang to rendezvous with Won Kyun's Kyongsang Right Navy. The seven recently repaired vessels under Won's command brought the total strength of the combined Korean fleet to fifty-five warships. Two or possibly three of these were kobukson, the spiked-back, dragon-headed "turtle ships" that Yi Sun-sin and shipwright Na Tae-yong had recently constructed.[3] The rest were panokson, "board-roofed ships," a more traditional type of battleship with a protective fortress built upon the deck, and the mainstay of the Korean fleet. This force then continued on to the port of Tangpo, where they had scored such a decisive victory the month before. Here they received intelligence from a local farmer that a large Japanese fleet was making its way west from the direction of Pusan, and was at that moment riding at anchor just a few hour's sail to the north at Kyonnaeryang, a narrow strait between Koje Island and the mainland.

The Koreans set sail north early the next morning, August 14. They had covered only half the distance when they encountered two Japanese patrol boats, which immediately turned around upon spotting them and fled north into Kyonnaeryang Strait. Yi initially gave chase, but broke it off upon sighting a large body of enemy ships in the strait, waiting in battle formation. This was the fleet under the command of Wakizaka Yasuharu. It consisted of thirty-six large ships, twenty-four medium-sized vessels, and thirteen small boats: seventy-three ships all told.

Won Kyun, emboldened by their recent victories in June, was eager now to charge into Kyonnaeryang and deal the Japanese another heavy blow. Yi Sun-sin was not. He cautioned that the waters in the strait, averaging just four hundred meters across, were too narrow to allow their ships room to maneuver without fear of colliding with one another and contained numerous submerged rocks and jagged reefs that would be difficult to avoid in the confusion of battle. Yi also did not want to fight the Japanese so close to land, where they could easily swim to shore once the battle turned against them. He therefore ignored Won Kyun's urgings and held his fleet back in the open waters off Hansan

Island, where there was plenty of room to fight and where the only land within swimming distance were a few barren islets offering nothing but slow death by starvation. From here he sent a small detachment of ships forward into the strait to challenge the enemy and draw them out. The ruse, which he had previously used with great effect at the Battles of Sachon and Tanghangpo, once again worked perfectly. The Japanese, spotting the small Korean force, immediately moved to counterattack, whereupon the Koreans turned about and headed back to open water where the bulk of their fleet lay.

The two fleets met just north of Hansan Island, the Japanese ships strung out in a line, the fastest ships to the fore, the Koreans arrayed in the crane-wing formation they had practiced at Yosu just a few days before. The ensuing battle was a fiercely fought and desperate affair. The Japanese this time were not aboard transports. They had warships and were ready to fight. But the Koreans with their thoroughly protected and heavily gunned vessels were too much for them. Impervious to Japanese arrow and musket fire in their heavy panokson battleships and two or three turtle ships, the Koreans proceeded to blast gaping holes into the hulls of the enemy vessels, set their flimsy wooden pavilions ablaze with fire arrows, and "hailed down arrows and bullets like a thunderstorm." Yi Sun-sin's own account of the battle is a litany of death and destruction, the name of each avenging angel carefully inscribed:

> Kwangyang Magistrate O Yong-tam also dashed forward, breaking and capturing one large pavilion vessel. He hit the enemy Commander with an arrow, and brought him back to my ship, but before interrogation, he fell dead without speaking, so I ordered his head cut off.... Sado Commandant Kim Wan captured one large enemy vessel and cut off sixteen Japanese heads including a commanding officer; Hungyang Magistrate Pae Hung-nip captured one large enemy vessel, cut off eight Japanese heads, and forced many others to drown in the water; Pangtap Commandant Li Sun-sin captured one large enemy vessel but cut off only four Japanese heads, because he was more interested in shooting down the living than in cutting off the heads of the dead. Then he chased and destroyed two more enemy vessels, burning them completely; Left Flying Squadron Chief Yi Ki-nam captured one enemy vessel and cut off seven Japanese

heads; Left Special Guard Chief Yun Sa-kong and Ka An-ch'ack captured two enemy pavilion vessels and cut off six Japanese heads; Nagan Magistrate Sin Ho captured one large enemy vessel and cut off seven Japanese heads.[4]

The fighting lasted throughout the day, ranging across the water off Hansan Island and then back into Kyonnaeryang Strait as the battered remnants of the Japanese fleet attempted to get away. Finally, with the onset of darkness and sheer exhaustion, the Koreans broke off their pursuit and returned to the open sea to rest. Of the seventy-three Japanese ships they had encountered, they had captured, sunk, or otherwise destroyed fifty-nine. Most of the fourteen vessels that managed to escape had in fact never really entered the battle at all; they had lagged behind in the initial Japanese assault out of Kyonnaeryang Strait and had then fled the scene upon seeing that the battle was turning against their more enthusiastic comrades. They did not stop until they reached Kimhae, several kilometers up the Naktong River near their home base at Pusan.[5]

One of these fourteen vessels that got away was a small *hayabune* (fast ship), carrying fleet commander Wakizaka Yasuharu. According to the Wakizaka family chronicler, "Arrows struck against his armour but he was unafraid even though there were ten dead for every one living and the enemy ships were attacking all the more fiercely. As it was being repeatedly attacked by fire arrows, Yasuharu's fast ship was finally made to withdraw to Kimhae."[6] According to Korean accounts, Wakizaka lost his nerve and fled.[7]

As for the number of Japanese dead, the Koreans had their head count, but it in no way reflected the heavy losses they inflicted that day. For every man beheaded, there were twenty, thirty, even fifty others who must have drowned or otherwise sunk unnoticed to the bottom. Some four hundred men did manage to get clear of their foundering ships and swim to a nearby islet (Japanese records say two hundred), but it was not long after they dragged themselves exhausted onto the shore that they realized they were in a death trap, with no food and no means of escape. The ranking captain among this group, taking responsibility for their plight, sat down on the beach and committed suicide by slicing open his belly. The rest, as Yi Sun-sin had foreseen, were left like "hungry birds in a cage."[8]

The news of the Hansan-do disaster found its way back to the Japanese base at Pusan in just a matter of hours and stirred into action the other two naval commanders, Kuki Yoshitaka and Kato Yoshiaki. They immediately set sail with a combined fleet of forty-two ships, but only went as far as the port of Angolpo, twenty kilometers to the west. They hoped to meet the Korean navy close to home, at a place of their own choosing.

Yi Sun-sin's patrol boats brought him word of this new enemy movement on August 15, the day after the Battle of Hansan-do. He immediately advanced northeast along the coast of Koje Island, then west toward Angolpo. Sure enough, he found forty-two Japanese ships at anchor inside the port and along the shore, twenty-one of them very large vessels, some with three-story pavilions built upon the decks. The situation was unfavorable for a direct attack, for the harbor was small and the water there dangerously shallow at ebb tide. Yi thus resorted once again to his usual tactic for coaxing the enemy into open water: the tentative advance followed by the feigned retreat. He and Won Kyun proceeded into the harbor to challenge the enemy, leaving Yi Ok-ki with his twenty-three ships to wait in ambush on the open sea. This time the Japanese did not take the bait. Admirals Kuki and Kato, clearly intent on not repeating their comrade Wakizaka's mistake, held their fleet in place, daring the Koreans to attack them where they lay.

That is just what Yi Sun-sin did. Upon realizing that the Japanese could not be coaxed out of the confines of the bay, he divided his fleet into small assault teams and sent them in against the enemy fleet in turns, particularly against the ostentatious pavilion ships that were the flagships of the enemy commanders. The sound of battle soon drew Yi Ok-ki out from his place of ambush to join the fight, and together the two Yis proceeded to pound the Japanese to pieces. As at Hansan-do it was a hard-fought battle, for the Japanese did not quickly abandon their ships and flee onto the shore as they had done the month before; they fought the Koreans for hours, rowing their dead and wounded to shore in small boats and returning each time with reinforcements. The battle continued in this manner until sunset. Finally, with most of their ships burned or sunk or awash in the shallows, the remaining Japanese gave up the fight and escaped into the nearby mountains.

Yi Sun-sin did not finish off all the remaining Japanese ships following the retreat of the enemy inland. He left a few boats intact, for he reasoned that if the fleeing enemy had no means of escape they would turn against the defenseless local population. He then led the way out of the harbor to pass the night. When they returned to Angolpo the next morning they found that the boats that had been left intact were gone, and with them the Japanese who had run into the hills. Yi Sun-sin and his men found evidence in twelve blackened heaps on shore that the Japanese had cremated their dead before making good their escape. "There were charred bones and severed hands and legs scattered on the ground," Yi recorded, "and blood was spattered everywhere, turning the land and sea red, revealing the innumerable Japanese dead and wounded."[9]

Over the next two days Yi Sun-sin led his fleet east to the mouth of the Naktong River and then back toward the west, but found no trace of enemy ships. Nor was he able to track down the few boats that bore the survivors of the Battle of Angolpo. These had managed to slip away under cover of darkness, sheltering in the coves of Koje Island before finally returning to Pusan. Among the survivors who made it back to safety on these spared boats were Kuki Yoshitaka and Kato Yoshiaki, who now joined their colleague Wakizaka Yasuharu as the first daimyo commanders to have suffered a serious defeat at the hands of the Koreans. With no enemy fleets left to fight, and with their men exhausted and supplies running low, the three commanders of the united Korean fleet decided to call off their operations and return to their home ports. On the way west they passed the barren islet where the four hundred Japanese survivors of the Battle of Hansan-do had been marooned. These unfortunate men were now growing weak after having gone several days without food, and could be seen sitting dazed on the shore. Since Hansan-do fell under the jurisdiction of Kyongsang Right Naval Commander Won Kyun, Yi Sun-sin gave him the responsibility of finishing off these "hungry birds in a cage." It was a gift to the glory-seeking Won; all he had to do was lay offshore with his ships until the trapped Japanese were thoroughly weakened and defenseless, then land a party of soldiers to harvest their heads. As an indignant Yi Sun-sin subsequently reported to the Korean court, however, Won Kyun failed in even this simple task. He fled the area soon after being left behind by Yi Sun-sin and Yi Ok-ki, spooked by a false report of the approach of a large Japanese fleet. Left unguarded, the marooned Japanese lashed together rafts from the wreckage of their ships that had by this time drifted to shore, and managed to traverse the few kilometers to Koje Island, where they found food and safety. "In this way," Yi concluded, "the fish in the cooking pot jumped out, to our great indignation."[10]

This second offensive by the Korean navy, like its "Slaughter Operation" in early July, was an unmitigated disaster for the Japanese. Hideyoshi's navy had lost approximately a hundred ships, this time many of them their best battleships under the command of their most competent admirals, and had managed to sink not even a single Korean vessel in return. They had succeeded in inflicting a few casualties on the Koreans, but according to Yi Sun-sin's count these totaled only 19 dead and 114 wounded. No reliable figure exists as to Japanese casualties. The heads that Yi's men cut off and the box of salted ears they sent north to the court as evidence of their valor in no way reflected the full extent of the carnage they had inflicted. Following the war, however, a Korean named Che Mal, who had been captured in the early days of the invasion and taken to Hideyoshi's headquarters at Nagoya to work as a clerk, stated that he had seen reports sent from Tsushima at about this time that placed the total number of men killed in battles with the Korean navy at over 9,000. [11]

Whatever the true number, it is clear that Toyotomi Hideyoshi regarded these losses as unacceptable. It is also clear that he now doubted the ability of his navy to overcome Korean resistance in southern waters and establish the much-needed supply route around the southwestern tip of the peninsula and north through the Yellow Sea. On August 23 he ordered naval commander Todo Takatora forward from Iki Island to reinforce his colleagues in Korea, and dispatched orders to Pusan halting naval operations along the southern coast.[12]

Yi Sun-sin's victories in the Battles of Hansan-do and Angolpo have been described as one of the main factors leading to the ultimate failure of Hideyoshi's campaign to take Korea and conquer China. This assessment was first forwarded by Korean prime minister Yu Song-nyong in his *Chingbirok*, an account of the war that he wrote some time between 1604 and his death in 1607. Of Yi Sun-sin's Hansan-do and Angolpo campaign Yu had this to say:

> The Japanese had now taken Pyongyang, but they did not dare advance any farther without first receiving reinforcements via the Yellow Sea. Thanks to this one operation led by Yi Sun-sin, such reinforcements would never arrive. By denying their navy entrance to the Yellow Sea, Commander Yi effectively cut off one arm of the Japanese advance.
>
> Now that Cholla and Chungchong Provinces had been secured, moreover, it was possible for the government to maintain traffic and communications between this southern region and the coasts of Hwanghae and Pyongan Provinces to the north, thus paving the way for national rejuvenation. Chinese waters were also secured, particularly the coastline around Liaodong and Tianjin, thus giving the Ming government time to send troops overland to help Korea to beat back the invaders. All these accomplishments must be attributed to nothing but Yi Sun-sin's victory at Hansan-do. Indeed, it must have been an act of divine providence.[13]

Yu's assessment of the importance of these events has been generally accepted by modern historians. Some have seen Yi Sun-sin's naval success as the most important factor leading to the failure of Hideyoshi's campaign;[14] others have described it as one factor among several. But few have discounted it altogether.

And rightly so. There can be no doubting that Hideyoshi's armies in Korea needed reinforcements if they were to continue their advance with any degree of confidence. As things currently stood there were fewer than thirty thousand Japanese troops in the north, not nearly enough to slash their way to Beijing. Hideyoshi launched his invasion with the clear intention of sending these reinforcements north by ships via the Yellow Sea. The only alternative, to march everyone and carry everything over 650 kilometers of mountainous roads and trails, would be far too slow and laborious. In preventing the Japanese navy from entering the Yellow Sea, therefore, Yi Sun-sin was not merely making a nuisance of himself off to one side. In stopping the Japanese navy's westward advance he had thrust a wrench into the heart of Hideyoshi's war machine. In the coming weeks and months the Japanese would encounter other obstacles in Korea, principally the arrival of large numbers of Chinese troops and determined resistance from local guerrilla fighters. The rout at sea, however, would remain the first serious setback in their planned invasion of the mainland, and as such possibly the most important one, for in blocking the flow of reinforcements, it significantly weakened their land forces and in turn rendered them that much more vulnerable in the land battles to come.

CHAPTER 13

"To me the Japanese robber army will be but a swarm of ants and wasps"

If trouble arises within a hundred li, *do not spend more than a day mobilizing the forces. If trouble arises within a thousand* li, *do not spend more than a month mobilizing the forces. If the trouble lies within the Four Seas, do not spend more than a year mobilizing the forces.*[1]

Wei Liao-tzu (Master Wei Liao)
4th century B.C.

IT TOOK THE MING CHINESE nearly three months from the start of the Japanese invasion to recognize the gravity of the situation in Korea. The decision to mobilize the empire's armed forces was not made until August 8, 1592. One of the reasons for this slow response was a lack of understanding of what was actually taking place on the peninsula to the east. At first the Chinese assumed that the frantic appeals for help from the Koreans were merely an overreaction to an unusually large wako pirate raid, the kind that had plagued the Koreans and the Chinese for centuries past. Once they realized that Hideyoshi's invasion was in fact much more than this, the government in Beijing then began to suspect that the whole thing was a plot that the Japanese had cooked up with the Koreans. How else could the incredible speed be explained with which the Japanese were advancing toward China's eastern frontier? Could they fly? Or were the supposedly loyal Koreans actually helping them along?

The Chinese were also preoccupied with pressing matters closer to home during these opening months of the war, notably the army-mutiny-cum-Mongol-uprising that had its northwestern frontier in a tumult beginning in March of that year. At the very moment when the Koreans were clamoring for military assistance in the east, Beijing was busy dispatching reinforcements to the northwest to put down this serious threat to internal security. Throughout the summer and fall of 1592 this so-called Ordos Campaign took almost all the armed strength that China could muster, including the army in Liaodong, the province nearest to Korea.

Beijing was not totally without resources during these trying months. In July it dispatched a token force of a thousand men under Tai Zhaobian and Shi Ru to aid the Koreans. This small army met King Sonjo on July 26 at Kwaksan, fifty kilometers inside the Korean border, and accompanied him and his entourage to the border town of Uiju on the Yalu River, where it remained as his personal bodyguard. From there King Sonjo continued to send messages and envoys west to Beijing, imploring the Wanli emperor for more help in driving the invaders back. The Chinese eventually responded in August by raising a second army, this time of five thousand men, mostly cavalry and spearmen, under the command of General Zhao Chengxun, regional vice-commander of Liaodong. The decision by this time had been made to mobilize the empire's armed forces, but that would take months. For the time being this was as large an army as the Chinese could send.

General Zhao had recently returned to his home base in Liaodong Province from the northwestern frontier, where he had enjoyed great success in putting down the rebellious Mongol tribes in the ongoing Ordos Campaign. The uprising there had still not been completely stamped out, but the rebels were now under siege in the city of Ningxia, and it was only a matter of time before they were overrun, their ringleaders executed, and their heads placed on display. Zhao was thus the man of the hour in Beijing, and was brimming with confidence as he led his army east to Korea. Upon arriving at Uiju in mid August, he assured King Sonjo and members of the Korean government that now that he was on the scene the Japanese problem would soon be solved. Upon learning that the enemy was still holed up at Pyongyang, he even went so far as to raise a glass of wine and exclaim, "Heaven is indeed good to keep them there for me." The Korean generals cautioned Zhao not to take the Japanese so lightly, but he brushed their concerns aside. "To me," he replied, "[the general] who, at the head of three thousand fighting men, . . . annihilated a Mongol army of one hundred thousand, the Japanese robber army will be but a swarm of ants and wasps. They will soon be scattered to the four winds."[2]

In Pyongyang, meanwhile, the Japanese army under Konishi Yukinaga was still anxiously awaiting the appearance of the first ships along the Taedong River bearing reinforcements from Pusan. But the days passed and the ships never came. Konishi also requested that reinforcements be sent up from the capital of Seoul and regions farther south, but few were sent. Supreme Commander Ukita Hideie was duty-bound to remain with his force in Seoul until Hideyoshi himself arrived to assume overall authority, while daimyo garrisoning other cities found themselves increasingly embattled by local resistance and in need of every man. Upon receiving word of the approach of a sizable Chinese army from the north, therefore, Konishi had nothing but his own troops and his own cunning with which to hold the city.

Chinese general Zhao Chengxun joined forces at Uiju with Shi Ru, the "attacking commander" in charge of the thousand-man bodyguard that had preceded him to Korea, and together the two men led their army to Pyongyang. They arrived outside the north wall of the city in a pouring rain near dawn on August 23, everyone plastered with mud and uncomfortable in wet armor. The darkness and weather had masked their approach; the Japanese inside the city were caught completely off guard. Deciding to make the most of this, Zhao sent his men charging at the undefended Chilsongmun, "Seven Stars Gate," and got his army inside the city before the startled Japanese could grab their weapons and respond.

What followed began for Konishi's men as a fight for their lives. They soon realized, however, that the attacking Chinese army was in fact rather small. They thus started falling back and spreading out, encouraging the Ming troops to split up and chase them down the city's narrow streets. When Zhao's concentrated attack had been dispersed in this manner, the Japanese then turned and began to counterattack. The Chinese, outnumbered and facing increasingly effective arquebus fire, were soon turned about and sent fleeing back toward the Seven Stars Gate. Konishi's men followed, hacking down stragglers as they went. Just outside the city they came upon a number of Ming troops floundering in a muddy depression. These men were quickly dispatched. Others were cut down along the road to the north. By the end of the day three thousand Chinese lay dead or dying in the rain and the mud, including Attacking Commander Shi Ru, the second in command.[3]

Commanding General Zhao Chengxun was among those who managed to escape with their lives. He mounted his horse and rode hard for the north, not stopping until he was back at Uiju on the Chinese border. He remained here for two days, in company with King Sonjo and his government in exile. It rained incessantly, and Zhao's soldiers, huddled on the bare ground in soaking armor, spent the time complaining bitterly and blaming Zhao for their ignominious defeat. During this brief halt the general attempted to downplay to the understandably anxious Koreans the severity of the defeat, dressing it up as a tactical withdrawal forced upon him by the heavy rains and muddy roads. They were not to worry, he said; it was only a minor setback. He would soon return from China with more soldiers and attack the Japanese again. With that General Zhao left Uiju and returned to his home province of Liaodong where, evidently fearing punishment, he proceeded to draft a report to Beijing blaming the Koreans for the debacle at Pyongyang. Their lack of support, he claimed, had turned certain victory into defeat. An envoy subsequently sent to Korea to investigate this accusation found it to be groundless.[4]

Following their victory in the First Battle of Pyongyang, the Japanese sent a taunting message north to the Koreans saying that the Ming assault had been like "a herd of goats attacking a tiger."[5] Privately, however, their elation was tempered by a creeping sense of danger. The Chinese had been soundly defeated. But they would likely be back, and in much greater numbers. On September 12 Konishi

Yukinaga thus traveled south to Seoul for a conference with supreme commander Ukita Hideie and his three military advisers, Ishida Mitsunari, Otani Yoshitsugu, and Mashita Nagamori, plus Kuroda Nagamasa and Kobayakawa Takakage. What would be needed to guard against the return of the Chinese, it was decided, was a defense in depth: a line of forts between Pyongyang and Seoul that would allow Konishi's forward forces to effect a controlled withdrawal in the event of overwhelming attack. The forts would be garrisoned by Kuroda's third contingent, already on the scene in Hwanghae Province, and by Kobayakawa's sixth contingent, currently encamped on the northern border of Cholla Province. It would be redeployed to Kaesong in the following month.[6]

Konishi and his colleagues were right to be cautious, for China at last was beginning to stir. The defeat of Zhao Chengxun's army at Pyongyang had finally awakened Beijing to the fact that the Japanese invasion was no mere sideshow on the periphery of the empire, but a real danger to China itself. Hideyoshi's armies apparently were every bit as powerful as the Koreans had been saying all along, and it seemed certain that they would try to cross the Yalu River and enter the Middle Kingdom if left unchecked. This realization threw Beijing into a heated debate over national survival. Should they leave Korea to its fate and concentrate on amassing forces along their own border? Or should they throw all their strength against the invaders while they were still in Korea, and thus save their loyal tributary state? Minister of War Shi Xing eventually set the tone with his statement that China's fate was inextricably tied up with Korea's, and that the Ming therefore had little choice but to march to its aid:

> If Japan should complete the occupation of Korea, her next objects of conquest would be Liao-Tung [Liaodong] and other districts of Manchuria. Then the Shan-Hai-Kuan in the Great Wall would be under her control. Our imperial capital, Peking, would then be in danger. Therefore, Korea's present national suffering is a serious national event to us. Were the Emperor Tai-Tsu [the Hongwu emperor, founder of the Ming dynasty] on the throne today, he would give serious attention to this matter.[7]

And so the matter was decided: Korea had to be saved. On October 6, 1592, the Wanli emperor sent the following imperial edict to King Sonjo that left no doubt about Chinese support:

> We have now sent our two state ministers in charge of civil and military affairs to Manchuria with instructions to take with them experienced troops one hundred thousand strong selected from Liao-Yang and other military stations, and then to proceed to your country in order to destroy the robber troops. ... If the military force of Korea would cooperate with our imperial army and attack those atrocious creatures from both sides, we should be able to exterminate them. ... We have ascended the throne in accordance with the command of heaven and have come to rule both the Hua [Chinese] and the barbarian peoples. Peace has prevailed within the four seas and the myriad of nations therein are enjoying prosperity and happiness. Nevertheless, those insignificant and malignant brutes have dared to come forward and overrun your country. In addition to sending our troops to your land, we have issued imperial edicts to several military stations in the southeastern coast provinces as well as the Liu Chiu [the Ryukyu Islands], Siam, and other nations. We have instructed them to muster several hundreds of thousand fighting men and invade Japan. These troops will soon cross the sea to that island country and destroy their haunts. The day will soon come when that whale-like monster Hideyoshi must submit his head and be slain. Then the waves will again become quiet.[8]

(The poor Ryukyu Islands! Having first been called upon by Hideyoshi to raise a force to help invade Korea, they would now be ordered by China to help invade Japan. Such a counter-invasion would never take place. But the Ryukyus, Siam, and other Southeast Asian kingdoms would eventually respond to Beijing's call for help and send troops to Korea.[9] These never amounted to more than token units. But they nevertheless added an interesting touch of international solidarity to the conflict.)

In addition to his edict, the Wanli emperor placed a bounty on the heads of those "robbers" he deemed most responsible for Korea's present woes:

1. Any person who should either capture or kill the atrocious Hideyoshi, who [has] originated the trouble in Korea, [will] be elevated to

nobility with the rank of marquis and [will] receive the corresponding reward.

2. Any person who should either capture or kill Hidetsugu [will] be elevated to nobility with the rank of marquis.

3. Any person who should kill Konishi Yukinaga, Ukita Hideie, or other Japanese military leaders of similar rank in Korea [will] be rewarded with five thousand taels of silver.

4. Any person who should propose and successfully carry out a plan for the restoration of peace in Korea [will] be elevated to nobility with the rank of count, and [will] receive a reward of ten thousand taels of silver.[10]

These were strong and uncompromising words from the Chinese court and must have warmed the hearts of King Sonjo and his ministers, for they had an unshakeable belief in the limitless power of the Middle Kingdom. They had warned the Japanese, both during their prewar negotiations and later in the brief meeting with Konishi at the Taedong River, that to challenge the awesome might of China was to court certain defeat. Now, at last, they hoped to be proven correct. Hideyoshi and his islanders would be reminded in no uncertain terms of their relative insignificance in a Chinese-centered world, and would be punished severely for their temerity in thinking that they could invade a loyal and civilized kingdom like Korea and usurp the Celestial Throne in Beijing.

That, anyway, was the hope.

While King Sonjo and his government in exile clutched at the promise of salvation from China, events were unfolding in southern waters that would have a much more immediate impact on Hideyoshi's plans. Indeed, if the Japanese could be said to have been dealt with like a "swarm of ants and wasps" at any time during the Imjin War, it would be now, at the hands of naval commander Yi Sun-sin.

Following its drubbing by Yi in August, the Japanese navy under the command of Wakizaka Yasuharu, Kuki Yoshitaka, Kato Yoshiaki, and Todo Takatora, retreated to its Pusan stronghold and did not venture west again. Hideyoshi in fact issued orders to his naval commanders not to challenge the Koreans and to cease trying to open a sea route into the Yellow Sea. They were to restrict their activities to rebuilding their strength, defending their positions at Pusan and on Koje Island, and ferrying men and supplies across the strait from Nagoya.

At his base at Yosu, Cholla Left Naval Commander Yi Sun-sin had spent the month following his return from the extraordinarily successful Hansan-do and Angolpo campaign training his men and strengthening his fleet. A number of ships that had been hastily put into production upon the outbreak of the war four months earlier were just now being completed, swelling the combined strength of the Korean navy to a respectable 166 ships, 74 of them large battleships. With this tremendous increase in the size of his fleet, Yi Sun-sin began to consider seriously a plan that he and Won Kyun had dreamed up back in June "for washing away the national disgrace": a direct attack upon Pusan. Yi had discarded the scheme then as dangerous and even foolhardy. Now, flushed with the success of the previous months and possessing a navy that had tripled in size, it seemed like the right thing to do.

The operation began on September 29, when Yi Sun-sin and Cholla Right Navy Commander Yi Ok-ki led their ships east from Yosu. Kyongsang Right Navy Commander Won Kyun's small flotilla joined the group the following day, and together they continued on in the direction of Pusan. They reached the estuary of the Naktong River, a few kilometers west of the city, on October 4. Here a scouting craft brought word that some five hundred enemy vessels lay at anchor in Pusan harbor. The number was not unexpected, but it must nevertheless have sent a chill down the spines of even the most steely nerved of the Koreans. They had already proven themselves the most dangerous and the most confident warriors in the service of King Sonjo. They had met and defeated more than fifty enemy ships at Okpo, twenty-one ships at Tangpo, twenty-six at Tanghangpo, seventy-three off Hansan Island, and forty-two at Angolpo. They had unleashed a degree of blood-and-thunder destruction that had forced the Japanese to fall back all the way to Pusan and had left them unwilling to venture out again. But could the Koreans really take on an armada of five hundred ships? Could they challenge almost the entire bulk of the Japanese navy, concentrated in one place, at one time?

The answer came on October 5. The combined Korean fleet fought a strong east wind around the headland between the Naktong River and

Pusan, pitching and rolling heavily through the rough seas. In the waters off Pusan harbor they encountered several small groups of Japanese vessels, each of which they burned and destroyed, 24 ships in all. Then they proceeded into Pusan harbor itself, toward what Yi Sun-sin estimated to be 470 enemy ships, anchored close to shore in three sprawling masses. As the Koreans approached, they could see the crews of these ships jumping overboard and joining their comrades in the fortifications on the heights above the shore.

The fight that followed was a replay of the Battle of Sachon, but on a huge scale. The Koreans sculled their warships as close to shore as they dared, splintering the hulls of the unmanned Japanese ships with their cannons and setting them ablaze with fire arrows. The Japanese fought back from behind their fortifications on the heights above, unleashing a barrage of musket fire and a rain of arrows, and occasional stone cannonballs, "as big as rice bowls," fired from Korean cannons that had been captured at Pusan and Tongnae.[11] But, as usual, they were unable to inflict any serious damage upon the heavy Korean warships and the warriors ensconced within. They pockmarked the thick planking with lead balls; they festooned the hulls and roofs with arrows until they bristled like porcupines. But they could not stop the Koreans, nor save their own fleet.

Yi Sun-sin and his combined fleet destroyed 130 Japanese ships in Pusan harbor that day. They would have claimed more, but the light was nearly gone. Yi thus ordered his captains to withdraw to the open sea to pass the night. According to his subsequent dispatch to the throne, Yi initially intended to return to Pusan the following day to destroy more of the enemy fleet, but discarded this plan after realizing that to deprive the Japanese of all their vessels would leave them trapped in Korea with no avenue of retreat. "[S]o I changed my operational plan to repair and re-supply our ships before returning to annihilate the enemy when he is driven to sea by a major counter-offensive on land." It was an idea that Yi would mention frequently in the months and years to come: a coordinated, two-stage push against the Japanese that would ensure their complete annihilation, first a land attack to drive them south and back onto their ships, then a sea assault to finish them off when they were out in open water. "With this idea in mind,"

Yi concluded, "I disbanded the combined fleet and returned to my headquarters on the second of ninth moon [October 6]."[12]

The Korean navy's attack on Pusan had been astonishingly successful. It had destroyed fully a quarter of the Japanese fleet at a cost of just five men killed, twenty-five wounded, and no ships lost. It had also extinguished any lingering hopes the Japanese may have had of somehow gaining access to the Yellow Sea and ferrying reinforcements to their comrades in Pyongyang. From this point onward the prospect of amassing an army in the north large enough to march on Beijing was well and truly dead.

Despite the Wanli emperor's edict promising "experienced troops one hundred thousand strong," China was in no position in the fall of 1592 to dispatch a sizable army to Korea, nor did it possess anywhere near the wherewithal to launch a counter-invasion of the Japanese home islands. In October it received an offer of substantial military assistance from Nurhaci, chieftain of the united Jurchen tribes—later known as the Manchus—on China's northeastern border, an offer that, had it been accepted, might have changed the course of the war. Beijing, however, politely declined. Although Nurhaci had recently entered into tributary relations with China, he was seen as a serious and rising threat and acceptance of his offer to send his cavalry south into Korea tantamount to an invitation for him to further expand his power.[13] No, if China wanted to save Korea, it would have to send troops of its own. There was not a great deal it could do, however, until the Ordos Campaign against the Mongols was settled. This would not occur until October with the fall of the city of Ningxia, where the rebels had taken refuge. After that, troops would have to be shifted all the way from the Mongolian border in the northwest to Korea in the east, a journey of more than two thousand kilometers. All this would take many weeks if not months. Beijing thus started looking for ways to buy some time.

It was at this time that a tall, bearded stranger named Shen Weijing presented himself at Beijing with an offer to help. Shen was evidently some sort of adventurer who had been attracted to the capital from Jiaxing on the central coast, near present-day Shanghai, by the emperor's edict offering ten thousand taels of silver and noble rank to anyone who could restore peace in Korea. He was a complete unknown in government circles and was regarded by some as rather unsavory. But he had a persuasive way about him, and apparently knew a great deal about Japan through his friendship with a man who had lived in those faraway islands for several years, the captive of wako pirates. He could even speak some Japanese. He therefore seemed just the man to engage the Japanese in time-consuming but ultimately meaningless negotiations. Shen was thus granted the military title of commander and dispatched east to see what he could arrange with Konishi Yukinaga in Pyongyang.[14]

Shen Weijing reached the town of Uiji on Korea's northern border in September, and in an audience with King Sonjo announced that seven hundred thousand Ming troops would soon be on the way. Sonjo, who evidently recognized hyperbole when he heard it, said that even six or seven thousand soldiers might be able to stop the Japanese if they were sent immediately to Korea. If Beijing delayed much longer, however, even a much larger army would have a difficult time in driving the enemy back.

"Your's is a genteel country," replied Shen smoothly, "so you do not understand the ways of war. These things cannot be rushed. The Liaodong army has just completed a campaign elsewhere in the empire, and its strength is depleted. We need to build this force up before we send it here." When Sonjo continued to press for immediate aid, Shen tried a different tack. "The relief army needs to consider three things," he said, "the portents of heaven, the lay of the land, and the people. These were not considered prior to the first battle of Pyongyang, and that is why we lost."

The meeting ended with Shen presenting King Sonjo with a supply of silver coins, a gift from the emperor in Beijing. He offered to have the coins weighed to show that none had been pilfered en route. The king declined, indicating that he trusted the Ming envoy. But he did not. The day after this meeting, Sonjo is reported to have said, "It is hard to believe what Commander Shen says." This mistrust of Shen would remain with Sonjo and his ministers until the end of the war.[15]

From Uiju, Shen Weijing proceeded south to the headquarters of the Korean army at Sunan, a short distance north of Pyongyang. From here he sent a letter on into the city asking for a meeting with the Japanese commander. A parley was arranged for October 4. Shen left the Korean camp and proceeded to Pyongyang with just three aides and no military escort, displaying a degree of courage that impressed both the Koreans and the Japanese. "Not even a Japanese," Konishi Yukinaga would later compliment Shen, "could have borne himself more courageously in the midst of armed enemies."[16]

Upon arriving at the occupied city, Shen sat down in a cordial atmosphere with Konishi, Tsushima daimyo So Yoshitoshi, and the monk Genso, who could read and write Chinese. The Japanese took the same approach they had tried with the Koreans during their prewar negotiations, a request for seemingly small concessions that might serve as the thin edge of the wedge leading to eventual domination. All Japan wanted, wrote Genso, was friendly relations with China and Korea. They had attempted to establish a cordial connection with the Koreans and had gone to great trouble to send embassies to Seoul over the previous few years to achieve this end. But the Koreans had unreasonably refused to reciprocate these well-intentioned gestures and send embassies of their own to Japan. Hence the present invasion had come about. Similarly, Genso went on to explain, all Hideyoshi really wanted from China was friendly relations, honest trade, and an exchange of embassies, something Beijing would undoubtedly have granted before now had the Koreans not stubbornly stood in the way.

All this talk of friendly relations was completely disingenuous coming from the leaders of an army that had just slashed its way 650 kilometers up the Korean Peninsula, slaughtering thousands along the way. But it nevertheless struck a receptive cord with Shen. As he had explained to officials in Beijing prior to his departure, negotiations with the Japanese should be conducted with an understanding that what they really wanted was trade. Shen had previously come to this conclusion because what he knew of Japan came from a man who had been captured by Japanese wako pirates, for whom trade *was* the overriding concern. The evidence confronting Shen now of course told a very different story. From what the Koreans told him, and from what he could see with his own eyes, the Japanese were clearly intent on conquest, not on establishing trade relations. This uncomfortable fact, however, left no room for negotiation, and if there was one thing Shen wanted it was to return to Beijing with a settlement in hand—any sort of settlement, something to take him one step closer to the riches and noble title that the Wanli emperor had promised. So he readily accepted the benign intentions that the Japanese fed him and responded with assurances that he would encourage the Chinese government to extend a friendly hand. A fifty-day armistice was signed to give Shen time to bring this about. During this period he would convey the Japanese position back to his superiors in Beijing and return with a high-ranking envoy, plus hostages as a sign of goodwill. Then they would all sit down again in Seoul and draw up a lasting peace.[17]

The signing of the fifty-day armistice, which they had been allowed no say in, left the Koreans feeling angry and somewhat betrayed— particularly when work units of Japanese soldiers began filing out of Pyongyang to harvest crops in the neighboring fields, confident they would not be attacked. Some of the Korean commanders complained that they did not have enough provisions to keep their men idle for fifty days and that if they were going to attack they should to do so at once. But an attack now was out of the question. As untrustworthy as Shen Weijing seemed, the fact remained that he was an envoy of the imperial Ming court. The terms of the truce he had negotiated therefore had to be respected.[18]

Shen Weijing arrived back in Beijing to find that the government no longer seemed interested in negotiating with the Japanese. This change in attitude had been brought about by the recent conclusion of the Ordos Campaign on the Mongolian frontier. The campaign had ended in spectacular fashion, with the rebels besieged by Ming troops at their stronghold of Ningxia and with the Ordos Mongols to the north making repeated attempts to come to their aid. As roving Chinese divisions beat back these successive Mongol incursions, the besiegers at Ningxia set about constructing a dike eighteen kilometers long all around the city. When it was finished, water from a nearby river was diverted into the space between the dike and the city walls, and slowly began to eat away at the rebels' defenses. Finally, in the middle of October, the walls were breached and the city taken. Those rebel leaders who had not already committed suicide were rounded up and killed.[19]

With the Ordos Campaign over, Beijing was at last able to turn its full attention to the conflict in Korea. An army of thirty-five thousand men was drawn together, mainly from units returning from the fighting in the northwest. Overall command was given to Li Rusong, a forty-three-year-old army officer from the Korean border province of Liaodong, the eldest son in a family that had immigrated to the region from Korea six generations before, during the early years of the Ming dynasty. Li was not universally liked. A number of his contemporaries regarded him as arrogant, and his superiors had previously accused him of being a lone wolf who ignored orders and acted on his own. In October of 1592, however, Li's star was on the rise. Earlier that year he had led the first body of reinforcements in the Ordos Campaign in Shenxi Province, and had subsequently served with distinction in fending off Mongol attacks and crushing the Ningxia rebels. For this good service he was promoted to the lofty rank of chief military commissioner and given charge of the expeditionary force that was to be sent to Korea. He was also admonished by the Wanli emperor to henceforth obey all commands from his superior, who in the coming Korean campaign would be sixty-two-year-old Vice-Minister of War Song Yingchang, supreme civil administrator of all military affairs in the border regions threatened by the Japanese advance.[20]

With the northwestern frontier once again under control, the Ming government had grown less interested in tying up the Japanese with talk. Upon his return to Beijing from his meeting with Konishi Yukinaga, negotiator Shen Weijing was thus brushed off and referred to Song Yingchang for further instructions. Song in turn ordered Shen to return to Pyongyang and tell the Japanese that no further talks would take place until they had withdrawn their forces all the way back to Pusan. Shen, with absolutely nothing now to offer the Japanese, turned around and retraced his steps south, arriving at Pyongyang on December 23, 1592, a month past the expiration of the fifty-day armistice he had previously arranged. He met with Konishi a second time and relayed Vice-Minister of War Song's conditions, which were flatly refused. The Japanese nevertheless tried to keep the game alive. They would not retreat one inch, they told Shen, unless the Chinese first provided a guarantee that Japanese trade ships would be allowed to enter the harbors of Zhejiang Province on the central Chinese coast.[21]

This counter-offer surely would not have pleased Hideyoshi. He had sent one of the largest invasion forces in history to the continent to obtain more than trading rights. Nor did it hold any attraction to the Chinese. When Shen Weijing returned with it to China in January 1593, Li Rusong's army of thirty-five thousand was poised in Manchuria, ready to march.

CHAPTER 14

A Castle at Fushimi

THE SIGNIFICANCE OF RECENT SETBACKS in the Korean campaign, in particular the failure of his navy to enter the Yellow Sea and move reinforcements north, surely had not escaped the notice of Toyotomi Hideyoshi. He was, after all, one of the premier military strategists of the age, and had made the Yellow Sea supply route the lynchpin in his invasion plan. The growing realization that he was to be denied access to this route by an unexpectedly strong Korean navy must therefore have forced him for the first time to question his ability to take Beijing and conquer China. Hideyoshi did not openly acknowledge any such misgivings in his correspondence from this time; throughout the autumn of 1592 he continued to speak of crossing to Korea and taking personal command of his armies there for the next big push to the north. There is evidence, however, that he had privately begun to scale back his plans with regard to China.

In the late summer of 1592 the bad news from Korea was overshadowed for Hideyoshi by the death of his mother, known to us only by her noble title of Lady O-Mandokoro. Hideyoshi had been extremely close to his mother throughout his life, and in her declining years had taken to worrying and fussing incessantly about her—increasingly so after a serious illness laid her low in 1588. At that time the taiko is said to have begged the heavens to spare her "for three years, or two years, or if that is not to be then only for thirty days."[1] Lady O-Mandokoro was spared for four years. In Hideyoshi's private correspondence from this time one senses a melancholia at the inevitability of loss and at times an almost desperate desire to make his mother well again, or at least as comfortable as possible until the day came when she would have to leave him. In a typical letter from 1589 to a lady-in-waiting he wrote, "If O-Mandokoro is kept in a small place, she may begin to feel depressed, and so please take care of her for the time being. But if [she is in a large place and] there are draughts, she will catch a chill in such surroundings and so you must not do that."[2] And again, in a letter addressed directly to his mother in 1590, "Go to some place and thus amuse yourself—and, please, become young once more. I beg you to do this."[3]

It is clear that family was extremely important to Hideyoshi. The personal glimpses we get of him from his private correspondence reveal a man who delighted in being in the company of his wife, his concubines, and his adopted children, and who pined for them when the business of war took him away from home. Indeed, the greatest pleasure he seems to have derived from being a dictator did not come from wielding power, but from taking care of family and friends—a fact revealed in his choice of family name, Toyotomi, meaning "Bountiful Minister" or "Abundant Provider."

In August 1592 Hideyoshi became anxious about his mother's health, and on the thirtieth of the month he left his invasion headquarters at Nagoya to pay her a visit at her mansion in Osaka on central Honshu, a journey of many days to the northeast. He arrived only to find that Lady O-Mandokoro had passed away on the very day he had left Nagoya. The news is said to have caused him to faint with grief.[4] Hideyoshi remained in the vicinity of Osaka and Kyoto for several months after that, in mourning for his mother, close to the remnants of his shrinking family circle, particularly his first wife O-Ne (Lady Kita-no-Mandokoro) and his favorite concubine, twenty-five-year-old Yodogimi. It was not until near the end of the year that he finally returned to Nagoya and resumed active oversight of the Korean campaign.

By the time he returned to Nagoya, Hideyoshi viewed the conquest of China in a different light. It is unlikely that the death of his mother in itself caused this change; more immediate strategic concerns, in particular the failure of his navy to open a supply route to northern Korea via the Yellow Sea, must have been foremost in his mind.

O-Mandokoro's passing, however, and Hideyoshi's subsequent hiatus in Kyoto, proved to be a turning point in the Korean campaign, a period of transition from the heady early days of the invasion, when everything was going better than expected, to a grittier phase where the Japanese war machine began slowly to veer off course. Hideyoshi understood the significance of this change. We know this because he began construction of a castle at Fushimi.

On June 27, 1592, with his invasion still on track and the conquest of Korea and China seemingly certain, Hideyoshi revealed his long-term plans in a letter to the kampaku in Kyoto, his nephew and heir apparent Hidetsugu. This document listed the various appointments and shifting about of personnel that Hideyoshi planned to make once his conquests were complete. Emperor Go-Yozei, for example, would be transferred to Beijing to replace the Wanli emperor, with his son the crown prince replacing him on the throne in Japan. Hidetsugu himself was also to go to Beijing to serve as kampaku of China, with either Hideyoshi's half-brother Hidenaga or Ukita Hideie succeeding him as kampaku of Japan. Hideyoshi did not bother to mention in this letter what he himself would do—not surprising, for the document was a list of instructions for Hidetsugu. On the same day that this letter was written, however, Hideyoshi's private secretary sent a second letter to Hideyoshi's wife reiterating many of the appointments the taiko planned to make and adding that Hideyoshi himself would journey to Beijing "before the end of this year.... He will at first reside in Beijing, whence he will control the national affairs of China, Japan, and Korea. After the founding of the new empire is completed, he will appoint some man of worth as his deputy at Beijing, and will establish his own permanent residence at Ningpo."[5]

In the summer of 1592, then, Hideyoshi intended to live out his life at Ningpo, a seaport on the central Chinese coast offering access to Japan, a convenient place from which to oversee the overseers of his empire. By the end of the year this plan had been abandoned. Upon his return to Nagoya from his period of mourning for his mother, Hideyoshi began work on a permanent headquarters and retirement palace at Fushimi, in the vicinity of the capital. Kyoto governor Maeda Gen'i was entrusted with overseeing its construction. On January 13, 1593,

Hideyoshi wrote to Maeda, summoning him to Nagoya. "Because I have many orders to give before I go to Korea," he wrote, "please come over here...and...bring with you an expert carpenter who should bring a plan of Fushimi. Because the problem of *namazu* is so important for the construction of Fushimi, I would like to have the castle constructed in such a way that it will be hard to attack from the *namazu*.... I intend to have [Fushimi Castle] done very carefully, in accordance with Rikyu's preferences and discretion."[6]

Hideyoshi wanted a solid and secure retirement home, one that would not be vulnerable to earthquakes, which were popularly believed to result from the movements of the *namazu*, the mythical giant catfish that carried the Japanese islands on its back. It would be built in the style of Sen no Rikyu, the tea master whom Hideyoshi had ordered to commit suicide in 1591 for reasons unknown, a decision he now seemed to regret. Something of the essence of this "Rikyu style," which would come to have such a profound influence not only on the Way of Tea but on Japanese culture as a whole, can be seen in the following anecdote concerning the tea master and Hideyoshi. Rikyu one summer had cultivated a garden of morning glories, a flower that at the time was extremely rare in Japan and renowned for its beauty. Hideyoshi, eager to see these flowers for himself, asked Rikyu to invite him to a tea gathering for this purpose. Rikyu agreed. On the morning of the visit, Hideyoshi arrived at Rikyu's house expecting to find the garden bursting with morning glories. But there were no flowers anywhere. He passed through the gate and proceeded to Rikyu's tearoom, and still did not see any flowers. Finally he entered the tearoom and there, floating in a container of water, was a single, perfect blossom.[7]

Fushimi Castle, then, would be significantly less grand than the Jurakutai, which Hideyoshi had ordered built a few years before. It would encompass gardens, pine groves, artlessly placed rocks, natural wood beams—a place of harmony and tranquility of which Sen no Rikyu would approve. It would mark the final step in Hideyoshi's rise from peasant to gentleman, the step where he moved beyond the nouveau riche ostentation of his recent warlord past to ascend to the highest reaches of cultured grace.

As work began on Fushimi Castle in late 1592, Hideyoshi continued to speak of crossing to Korea and taking command of his armies there. His anticipated date of departure, weather permitting, would be the third month—April by the Western calendar—of 1593, eleven months after the embarkation of the vanguard units of his invasion force. He would "take charge of everything personally," he said, "and then make a triumphal return" to Japan.[8] What did Hideyoshi hope to accomplish during this victorious interlude on the mainland? How did he propose to advance the stalled front now that the Korean navy had the Yellow Sea supply route firmly blockaded, upsetting his plans for moving reinforcements north? One can only guess. His plan to retire at Fushimi rather than at Ningpo, however, would seem to suggest that he was no longer confident of being able to slash his way to Beijing.

CHAPTER 15

Suppression and Resistance

LONG BEFORE HIDEYOSHI STARTED GIVING OFF SIGNALS in late 1592 that he was wavering in his resolve to enter China and capture Beijing, his daimyo generals in Korea were expressing more open doubts. In early July, for example, seventh contingent leader Mori Terumoto wrote a letter to a family member back in Japan stating, "It is said that this country is larger than Japan. For this reason, our current strength is not sufficient to rule this country. Besides, the language barrier makes it even more difficult for us to deal with the people here. Although the Chinese are said to be weaker than the Koreans, I wonder if we will be able to provide enough men to enter and rule that country."[1] Mori had never been very enthusiastic about Hideyoshi's plans for mainland conquest. The doubts he expressed in this letter, however, written scarcely six weeks into the invasion, soon came to be shared by many of his colleagues as the reality of the situation in Korea forced them to abandon any hope of conquering China and adopt a more realistic goal: the subjugation of Korea.

Hideyoshi at this point assumed that with the fall of Seoul and the northward advance of his vanguard contingents to Pyongyang, the Korean Peninsula was already his. His commanders in the field knew otherwise. They knew that all that had really been captured was a strip of territory stretching from Pusan to Pyongyang, and a string of strategic cities and towns along the way. They knew, moreover, that the Koreans' determination to resist had not been broken with the capture of their capital and the flight of their king. On the contrary, it was building, threatening to sever supply lines and leave tens of thousands of Japanese soldiers cut off in the north. In light of these developments it seemed foolish to attempt to advance any further toward China— even if reinforcements could be transported north via the Yellow Sea, which of course they could not, due to the blockade being imposed by the Korean navy. To advance farther would stretch Japanese positions even more thinly and would leave them even more vulnerable to Korean counterattack.

It would also be greedy. Hideyoshi's generals had already grabbed an enormous chunk of Korean territory, enough nearly to double the size of his empire and reward everyone handsomely with a good deal to spare. Why, then, reach any further, and put everything at risk? Surely the wise thing to do would be to consolidate control over the lands through which the Japanese armies had already marched, and avoid an all-out confrontation with the Chinese, which would be difficult to win. In light of these circumstances it seemed best to adhere to the Japanese proverb *asu no hyaku yori, kyou no go-ju:* "Tomorrow's one hundred [is worth] fifty today."

As the summer heat of 1592 gave way to the coolness of autumn, the Japanese invasion force accordingly began to fan out across Korea in an effort to stamp out resistance and take possession of the land. Once this was done, they would organize and administer each region "according to Japanese rules,"[2] as Hideyoshi had ordered earlier in the year. This meant that all weapons would be confiscated and the populace pacified and returned to their fields. Tax assessment roles would be compiled, and co-opted or coerced officials put to work extracting the assessed sums from a compliant peasantry to finance the governance of their newly conquered province. Then fiefs would be parceled out to deserving daimyo, and Korea would become fully integrated into the taiko's empire, just as Shikoku had been after it had fallen to Hideyoshi in 1585, and Kyushu in 1587, and the northern Honshu provinces of Mutsu and Dewa in 1591.

The nine contingents of Hideyoshi's invasion force were each tasked with pacifying a different region of Korea. The southeastern province of Kyongsang, the first to fall to the Japanese at the start of the invasion, was to be held by the twenty-five thousand men of Fukushima

Masanori's fifth contingent, most of them from Shikoku; neighboring Cholla Province, the "Red Country" that had been largely bypassed in the initial thrust north, went to Kobayakawa Takakage and his sixth contingent from Kyushu, a total of fifteen thousand men. The mountainous central province of Kangwon on the east coast was to be subdued by Mori Yoshinari and Shimazu Yoshihiro of the fourth contingent, at the head of fourteen thousand men. Seoul and neighboring Kyonggi Province would be held by overall invasion leader Ukita Hideie and his eighth contingent. In the north, third contingent leader Kuroda Nagamasa was responsible for Hwanghae, the central province bulging into the Yellow Sea, while Konishi Yukinaga and So Yoshitoshi remained in Pyongyang and vicinity, waiting for reinforcements so they could begin the final push north into Pyongan Province. Kato Kiyomasa, finally, was to pacify Hamgyong, the remote hinterland province in the northeast.

Of all the daimyo commanders in Korea, second contingent leader Kato Kiyomasa, the "demon general" to the Koreans,[3] would remain the most committed to his master Hideyoshi's goal of pan-Asian conquest. While many of his colleagues grew cautious as the invasion ground to a halt and effectively abandoned the plan of entering China in favor of the more modest objective of the subjugation of Korea, Kato alone remained unchanged. He continued to believe that Hideyoshi would soon arrive on the peninsula and that Beijing would then be theirs; and he continued to act with the same daring that had characterized the first heady weeks of the war, thrusting deep into Hamgyong Province, leading his troops hundreds of kilometers into enemy territory, all the way to the Tumen River and Manchuria beyond.

Kato had crossed the Imjin River north of Seoul with Konishi Yukinaga and Kuroda Nagamasa in early July, and together they had marched into Kaesong. From this ancient walled town Kato dispatched a letter south to Hideyoshi, indicating that he was still committed to the idea of China conquest and was unhappy at the prospect of being diverted off the main line of march to Beijing. "The expeditionary force under the command of this humble subject," he wrote, "is going to conquer Hamgyong-do, a remote province in the northeastern part of Korea. The place is located far from the territory of Ming, more than ten days' march. If your highness wishes to cross the sea to conquer

Ming, please give me an order within the earliest possible date. In that case, I will speed by day and night to your place to take the lead in the conquest."[4]

The three vanguard contingents of the invasion force separated just north of Kaesong, with Konishi and Kuroda continuing due north and Kato veering northeast toward his assigned province of Hamgyong, in company with fellow Kyushu daimyo Nabeshima Naoshige and a force of twenty thousand men. They were now leaving the central road and striking into unknown and often trackless territory, and were thus in need of guides. Two locals were dragooned for this purpose. When they attempted to plead ignorance of the route, Kato ordered one of them hacked to pieces. The second man, terrified, agreed to show the way. A Korean who could speak some Japanese was also found and pressed into service as an interpreter.[5]

After a week's march over poorly marked trails, the second contingent entered Hamgyong proper. The province's Southern Army commander, Yi Hoon, who should have been the first to meet them, deserted his post and fled north toward the Manchurian border. He was later seized and killed by locals in the vicinity of Kapsan. The provincial governor, Yu Yong-rip, attempted to follow suit, but the soldiers he had been assigned to lead, enraged at his cowardice, ran him down and turned him over to the Japanese.

These astonishing actions on the part of the soldiers and citizens of Hamgyong were precipitated by a deep-seated loathing for the government in Seoul, a government they felt had abused them and overtaxed them for far too long. Since the early years of the Choson dynasty, officials in the capital seemed to regard this hinterland region as little more than the nation's beast of burden, to be worked in the fields and given nothing in return for the heavy taxes they paid. Now, with its army commanders and officials fleeing in all directions as the Japanese approached, it appeared that the unfortunate people of Hamgyong were to be abandoned as well. Why, then, should they resist the Japanese and risk almost certain death? Why not let the enemy clean out the venal officials and the cowardly commanders and rid the province of an administration that had mistreated them for so long?

Such thoughts were widespread in Hamgyong at the time of Kato's arrival in July of 1592, and thus his march toward Manchuria went largely unopposed. He led his second contingent northeast through the strip of populated territory that lay between the East Sea coast and the range of mountains that formed the spine of Hamgyong, through the towns of Wonsan, Hamhung, Pukchong, and Kimchaek. They traveled fast, justifying the tales already circulating throughout the province that Kato's army moved like the wind, covering a hundred *li* (fifty kilometers) and more in a day.

The Japanese traversed more than half of Hamgyong-do, coming within two hundred kilometers of Korea's northern border, before they encountered their first serious resistance. It occurred near the town of Kilchu, outside a grain warehouse called Haejongchang. Upon receiving news of Kato's advance, the province's Northern Army commander, Han Kuk-ham, evidently made of sterner stuff than his southern counterpart Commander Yi, had rounded up a body of troops from the "Six Forts," a string of army garrisons in Hamgyong's northeast corner, and marched them south to stop the invaders. He nearly succeeded. In the ensuing battle the Koreans under Han proved more courageous and skillful than any Kato had met so far, unleashing such a barrage of well-aimed arrows upon the Japanese that they were forced to take shelter inside the warehouse of Haejongchang itself. Then Commander Han made a tactical mistake. Rather than heed his subordinates' advice to rest his men and wait, he precipitously ordered an immediate mass attack on the building. The Japanese inside, having formed barricades from sacks of grain, were ready for them. The Koreans charged into a wall of concentrated, disciplined musket fire that decimated their closely packed ranks. Badly stung, Han retreated to his camp on a nearby mountain, planning to attack again the following day.

He would never get the chance. During the night Kato led his men out from the protection of the warehouse and quietly encircled the Korean position, being careful to leave a single opening on one side. At dawn, with the mountain slopes wreathed in fog, the Japanese raised their muskets and began to fire. The onslaught threw the unwary Han and his men into an instant panic; they had assumed that the Japanese were still holed up at Haejongchang. They turned to flee—straight through the gap that Kato had provided and into a nearby swamp. The

Japanese were soon upon them and proceeded to cut them to pieces. Commander Han managed to flee with his life. He would later be captured by a band of renegade Koreans and handed over to Kato, and remain in Japanese captivity for the next several months.[6]

After its victory over the Koreans at Haejongchang, Kato's second contingent broke in two. The second in command, Nabeshima Naoshige, made his headquarters in Kilchu and set to work imposing order on Hamgyong Province "according to Japanese rules." Garrisons were established at strategically important towns along their route of march, supplies were purchased or requisitioned, weapons were confiscated, land was registered, and a system of taxation set in place. The local population, terrified of the Japanese and in many cases resentful of their own leaders, proved for the most part submissive and compliant. Some of the tax assessment rolls that Nabeshima compiled during these months are still in existence, signed by local Korean officials who pledged to the accuracy of the information on pain of "having all our heads cut off."[7]

In the meantime Kato Kiyomasa led an expeditionary force north to the Tumen River, skirmishing and sowing terror all along the way. It was during this campaign that he stumbled on two very valuable prizes: the Korean princes Sunhwa and Imhae. They had been sent to the northeast following the evacuation of Seoul as part of the court's effort to spread the royal presence across the far north to rally the support of the people. The princes initially took up residence in Kangwon Province and the southern part of Hamgyong, but were driven farther north by the arrival of Kato and his men. This retreat eventually took them to the remote northeastern border town of Hoeryong, on the southern bank of the Tumen River. They could not have found themselves in a more inhospitable spot, for Hoeryong was a place of exile for political unde-sirables and was thus home to a good many men with strong anti-government sentiments. These feelings of resentment had burst forth soon after the arrival of the Japanese in the province, with a minor government official named Kuk Kyong-in overthrowing the tenuous local authority and proclaiming himself a general, with a following of five hundred men. When Princes Sunhwa and Imhae, together with their entourage of family members and government officials, miraculously appeared in their midst, Kuk and his cohorts lost no time in seizing them and trussing them up. Kuk then sent a message south to the advancing Japanese, saying that he wanted to side with them and hand over his prize.

It was this letter that brought Kato Kiyomasa to Hoeryong. When he arrived in the town on August 30 and saw the two princes tied up like common criminals and forced to kneel in the dirt, he angrily turned to Kuk and said, "These are the sons of your king! How can you keep them tied up like this?" He then had their ropes removed and took them to his camp for a meal. Sunhwa and Imhae would continue to be well treated throughout their period of captivity, as was the Japanese custom with important hostages. The officials accompanying them would not fare so well. They were kept locked up in a small, cold room for many months, were frequently bound, and suffered considerable privations. As for Kuk Kyong-in, he was rewarded with the position of governor in the new provincial administration.[8]

After sending the Korean princes south to Kyongsong, Kato led eight thousand of his men, reinforced by three thousand Koreans, across the Tumen River into Manchuria, ostensibly to see how well the vaunted Jurchen tribesmen could fight. They had not gone far when they came upon the first "Orangai" (barbarian) fortress. "As dawn was breaking," records Kato Kiyomasa's chronicler, "we arrived . . . and drew up our ranks. As is the usual way in this strange country . . . [Jurchen fortresses] are not only enclosed securely in front, but at the rear they have recourse to high stone walls in mountain recesses. When we saw that it did not appear to be very well defended, the [Korean] men of Hoeryong went forward, while the Japanese went round to the mountain at the rear, and with 50 men or 30 men working together prised out the stones using crowbars, and the wall collapsed." The Jurchen fortress was quickly seized, and many of its defenders undoubtedly slaughtered.

The next day the three thousand Koreans who had participated in the attack withdrew back across the Tumen River, leaving Kato's forces to deal with the nearly ten thousand agitated tribesmen from the surrounding region who had been assembled to counterattack. The battle that ensued was for the Japanese a very close thing—so close that Kato ordered that all the heads cut off be discarded after counting. There were reportedly eight thousand. The fighting eventually ceased, Kato's chronicler concludes, when "an exceptionally heavy rain fell on our behalf, and blew in the faces of the Orangai, so they withdrew."[9]

And so Kato forded back across the Tumen River and returned to Korea. He had now covered an extraordinary distance from Pusan, more than fifteen hundred kilometers, all on foot and horseback, through unknown and hostile territory. When measured from the actual starting point of the invasion, Hideyoshi's Nagoya headquarters on the island of Kyushu, his achievement becomes all the more astonishing, equivalent almost to Napoleon's march from Paris to Moscow in 1812. This incredible foray would earn Kato a reputation in Japan for courage and daring that has endured to this day. It would inspire numerous Tokugawa and Meiji period woodblock prints depicting him crossing to Korea, fighting Korean and Chinese troops, and, most popular of all, hunting tigers armed only with his trademark three-bladed spear. It would also solidify his reputation among the Koreans as the most fearsome of Hideyoshi's daimyo commanders, a ferocious, almost inhuman apparition, instantly recognizable by the strange, conical helmets he wore, and by the death and destruction he left in his path.

Following his campaign in the far north, Kato returned south and took up residence at Anbyon near the border between the provinces of Hamgyong and Kangwon. He took with him the two Korean princes and the officials he had captured. They would remain with him for the next several months. On October 25 he sent a letter to Hideyoshi boasting that he had now subdued the entire province of Hamgyong from north to south, and that he had done such a thorough job of it that there was not the slightest chance of further resistance. Things were going so well that he had been able to turn over the fortresses at Heoryong and Kyongsong to Korean allies who had sworn allegiance to him. Disturbances might occur elsewhere in Korea, he wrote, where control had not been firmly established, but there was no worry of that in Hamgyong. Not with him in charge.[10]

Kato's claims were premature. The people of Hamgyong, cowed by the Japanese and indifferent to the fate of their own leaders, had initially proved an easy conquest. But they soon came to chafe under the strictures of foreign occupation: the swaggering samurai, the summary executions, the lawless soldiers who took whatever they wanted. During the closing months of 1592 and into 1593, local resistance began to build and to coalesce into guerrilla bands that eventually would grow strong enough to place Nabeshima Naoshige's headquarters at Kilchu under siege. A campaign was also launched to strike back at those Koreans who had sided with the enemy. The most notable victim was Kuk Kyong-in, who had handed the princes over to the Japanese. For this he would be beaten to death.

As Kato swept with relative ease through Hamgyong-do, his colleagues in other parts of Korea were having a more difficult time. Not only were they being frustrated in their attempts to subdue the provinces assigned to them, they were in some areas actually being driven back. The Korean opposition that they faced was divided into three distinct groups: guerrilla bands of civilian volunteers, independent groups of monk-soldiers, and regrouped units of government troops.

By the early summer of 1592 the majority of the regular armed forces still remaining in Korea, a total of approximately 84,500 men,[11] had been driven far to the north by the Japanese advance. A large portion of these troops were now encamped at Sunan, a short distance beyond Pyongyang, waiting for assistance from China before they dared attempt a counteroffensive. Throughout the country, meanwhile, particularly in the south, private citizens were awakening from the initial shock of the invasion and were beginning to take up arms on their own accord to resist the Japanese. The guerrilla bands of civilian volunteers that subsequently came into being were called *uibyong*, "righteous armies." Their leaders were for the most part upper-class yangban scholars—literate, well-educated landowners who commanded the respect of the peasantry, and who in many cases possessed the wealth necessary to outfit private armies. A few had some military experience; most were just committed amateurs who learned as they went along. They were all driven by a deep sense of patriotism, a desire to protect their families, their land, and their king, and an all-consuming hatred of the Japanese. Beginning in June of 1592, one month after the start of the invasion, these civilian volunteers harassed the enemy throughout the south, threatened supply lines, massed together to attack strongholds, and gradually succeeded in turning the peninsula into an ungovernable headache for the Japanese.

Significant military activity among the civilian population first occurred in Kyongsang-do, the southeastern province through which the Japanese vanguard under Konishi Yukinaga and Kato Kiyomasa had marched during their twenty-day blitzkrieg north to Seoul in May and June. During this incredibly rapid advance a number of important cities in the province had been taken, including Pusan, Taegu, Kyongju, and Sangju. But the province as a whole had been by no means subdued. The Japanese had in fact taken only a strip of territory running up its center, with large regions on either side being left untouched. As news of this catastrophe spread, and with it the realization that government troops were unable to protect them, villagers and townspeople throughout the province formed guerrilla bands and leaders began to emerge, men like Kim Myon, Chong In-hong, and Kwak Jae-u.

Kwak Jae-u, one of the most flamboyant of these civilian commanders, remains particularly revered in Korea today. He was known as the "Heaven Descending Red Coat General," so named for the unique coat and trousers he wore, dyed red in the first menstrual blood of young girls. Kwak believed this turned the garments into a sort of armor by infusing them with yin energy, which would repel the yang energy of Japanese bullets.[12] Tales of Kwak's exploits have been told and retold by Koreans for the past four hundred years, with the usual embellishments being added along the way. He remains today a figure instantly recognized by young and old alike, a Korean folk hero of a stature similar to America's Sam Houston or Davy Crockett.

Kwak was from a respectable yangban family in Kyongsang Province. He was by all accounts well educated, intelligent, and a forceful and persuasive speaker. But he tended to be too outspoken and temperamental for his own good. Although he passed the civil service exam at the age of thirty-four, he submitted an essay that was so critical of the authorities that it sank any chance he had of securing a government post. With nothing else to do, Kwak spent the next several years in quiet retirement, apparently doomed to live out his days in obscurity.[13]

Then the Imjin War began, providing this prickly, outspoken "failure" a chance to prove his true worth to the nation. Immediately after the

start of the invasion, Kwak began raising a force of civilian volunteers
to protect those parts of Kyongsang that had not yet been overrun by
the Japanese, reportedly selling his patrimony to raise money to arm his
men. In a typically stirring recruitment speech at the village of Uiryang,
he roused the locals to action with the following words: "The enemy is
fast approaching! If you don't stand up and do something now, your
wives and your parents and your children will all be slain! Are you
going to just sit here and wait for the sword to fall? Or will you join
with me now, and go to Chong-am ford! I can see that there are
hundreds of strong young men among you. If you will make a stand
with me at Chong-am; if we can together prevent the Japanese from
crossing the river, you will teach the enemy something about the bravery
of the men in these parts! And you will keep your town safe!"[14]

By mid summer of 1592 Kwak Jae-u, the "Red Coat General," had
raised a force of one thousand men in this manner and was beginning
to prove a nuisance to the Japanese units assigned to hold the south.
According to popular lore he dashed about Kyongsang so quickly that
the Japanese came to believe that he possessed magical powers and
could transport himself and his men across vast distances in the twink-
ling of an eye. The mere sight of Kwak's fiery red coat was thus
supposedly enough to send the enemy into instant retreat. While such
tales are undoubtedly exaggerated, the "Red Coat General" does seem
to have been a skilled guerrilla leader. He wisely avoided meeting the
Japanese in open battle, where they had amply proved themselves to be
superior. Instead he concentrated on harassing them and wearing them
down. He ambushed small parties of Japanese when they were out foraging for food. He severed supply lines. He delivered rapid strikes
against enemy strongholds when their guard was down, then melted
back into the hills.

And he used trickery wherever he could. When the Japanese
attempted to enter a new district, Kwak is said to have sent men into the
hills surrounding their camp, each carrying a frame bearing five torches
so that the enemy, thinking they were surrounded by a large force,
would be unable to sleep for fear, and would flee the area the next
morning. According to another tale, probably apocryphal, he once dug
up an ancient tomb and placed a large lacquered box full of hornets

beside the excavation for the Japanese to find. Sure enough, when the Japanese stumbled upon the box they assumed that it was a treasure trove that had been plundered from the grave and greedily pulled it open—only to release the furious insects and be badly stung. The next day, the now wary Japanese came upon a similar treasure box, conveniently sitting beside a second excavated tomb. Thinking that the Koreans were trying to use the same trick a second time, they threw it into the fire to burn up the hornets that they supposed were inside. But this time the box did not contain hornets. The wily Kwak had instead filled it with gunpowder, resulting in an explosion that killed a hundred Japanese.[15]

As a heroic guerrilla leader, Kwak Jae-u remained just as critical and cantankerous as he had before the war. It was a trait that quickly made him enemies. One of the first was Kim Su, the governor of Kyongsang Province. During the first days of the war Kim had led a force of several thousand government troops south from the provincial capital of Kyongju to meet the Japanese. Upon hearing of the fall of Tongnae, however, he concluded that the invaders could not be stopped, so he retreated with his army and issued a public order for the people of Kyongsang to flee into the hills. Kwak Jae-u was furious when he learned of this and sent Kim a heated letter accusing him of cowardice and listing seven reasons why he should be put to death. It was the start of an ongoing feud. Kim, deeply offended, wrote back to Kwak, calling him a "robber," and sent a letter north to King Sonjo accusing the "Red Coat General" of disloyalty to the throne. Kwak then wrote a letter of his own to the king: "Governor Kim ran away from his post of duty, and when I upbraided him for it he called me a robber. I have killed many of the 'rats,' but as I have been called a robber I herewith lay down my arms and retire."[16]

After abandoning his life as a guerrilla leader, Kwak was drawn into the government in recognition of his contribution to the war effort, serving first as a section chief in the Ministry of Justice in late 1592, magistrate of the town of Songju in 1593, then magistrate of Chinju in 1595. As a government official Kwak remained just as prickly as ever and continued to alienate others with his criticisms and apparent arrogance, so much so that at one point he was dismissed and sent into exile. He finally withdrew from government service altogether, saying, "If I am not going to be listened to then I may as well leave." He lived out the rest of his life in the countryside, declining offers of other appointments, immersed in scholarship and literary work under the pen name Mangudang, "Hall of Forgotten Cares."[17]

The people of the neighboring southwestern province of Cholla-do, meanwhile, had not been inactive. It was from bases along this region's southern coast that Korean naval commander Yi Sun-sin delivered the first blows against the Japanese beginning in June, sinking nearly three hundred of their ships and preventing them from establishing the crucial supply route north via the Yellow Sea. It would now be from this region's fertile inland plains that some of the most eminent uibyong leaders—most notably the scholar-warriors Ko Kyong-myong, Kim Chon-il, and Cho Hon—would arise and begin organizing guerrilla bands to resist the Japanese.

Ko Kyong-myong was a yangban landowner from the town of Changhung on the far southwestern tip of the peninsula, a typical upper-class gentleman who had had to settle for a quiet life of scholarship after failing to pass the civil service exam in his youth and obtain a government career. Upon receiving the shocking news that the Japanese had occupied Seoul and forced King Sonjo to flee, Ko put up posters throughout the region calling for recruits, and soon organized an army of peasants, slaves, and scholars numbering between six and seven thousand. King Sonjo sent a letter of thanks south to Ko when he heard of this, along with General Kwak Yong to provide experienced military leadership, which Ko himself lacked. Kwak brought with him several hundred government troops.

Ko's initial intention had been to lead his force north to Seoul and attack the Japanese there. They had only just begun their march to the capital when they learned that enemy forces were being amassed on Cholla's northern border at Kumsan with the evident intention of over-running the province, which had been bypassed in the initial invasion. Ko and General Kwak Yong thus made a change of plans: they would attack Kumsan first and forestall the Japanese invasion of Cholla-do, then resume their march against Seoul.[18]

Ko Kyong-myong and General Kwak reached Kumsan with their

combined force of civilian volunteers and government troops on August 16, 1592. They arrived with a total of only eight hundred men; the bulk of their six to seven thousand-man force had either deserted along the way or the number of volunteers that Ko had raised had been much smaller than historical records show. Inside the walls of the town was a force of indeterminate size from Kyushu under fifty-nine-year-old Kobayakawa Takakage, the seasoned commander of the sixth contingent, the oldest daimyo to serve in Korea during Hideyoshi's war. On the first day of the battle General Kwak threw his troops against the walls of the town in a direct frontal attack, but their heart wasn't in the fight and they were easily driven back. Ko's patriotic followers enjoyed somewhat more success. With their leader beating a large drum to urge them on, the uibyong managed to breach the outer ramparts of the town's defenses and set a number of buildings inside the walls ablaze with their hwapo fire tubes. They were unable to advance any farther, however, and eventually withdrew for the night.

The Koreans went on the offensive again the next morning, General Kwak's soldiers against the north gate, Ko's volunteers at the gate to the west. By this time the Japanese within the walls had devised a plan. Having observed the previous day that the government troops were less motivated than Ko's fiery-eyed volunteers, Kobayakawa's men concentrated their fire against Kwak's soldiers at the north gate and soon put them to flight. The sight of their retreat, as the Japanese had undoubtedly hoped, broke the resolve of the uibyong to the west. A cry soon arose from Ko's ranks—"The government soldiers are running away!"—and their lines began to waver and then break. With that the Japanese threw open the gates and went on the offensive. In the confusion of the counterattack Ko Kyong-myong's horse threw him to the ground and ran off, leaving him bruised and on foot. Ko's lieutenants, seeing that the battle was lost, tried to get their leader onto another horse and away to safety. The graying scholar refused to budge. "Save yourselves," he told them. "But I will not retreat." Ko's eldest son Chong-hu pleaded with him to withdraw, but still the old man would not relent.

Several men stayed with Ko to the end. Two of them, An Yong and Yu Paeng-no, shielded him with their bodies when the hand-to-hand fighting commenced and were cut to pieces. Then Ko himself fell, and with him his second son, Ko In-hu.[19]

Ko Kyong-myong and his band of civilian volunteers, one of the first guerrilla armies to emerge after the start of the war, did not inflict much damage on the Japanese during their short-lived period of resistance. But the courageous way in which they met death must have left the Japanese defenders of Kumsan with a sense of foreboding of the tide of resistance that was rising against them. It also served as an example to and fueled the anger of thousands of other potential guerrilla fighters—including Ko's one surviving son, Ko Chong-hu. After the loss of his father and brother at Kumsan, Chong-hu organized his own force of guerrillas under the banner "The Band That Seeks Revenge." And so the fight passed from father to son, and Cholla remained a dangerous place for the Japanese to enter.[20]

Elsewhere in Cholla Province a fifty-five-year-old scholar-official named Kim Chon-il was raising an army of his own. Unlike other uibyong leaders like Ko Kyong-myong and Kwak Jae-u, who had failed to achieve their ambition of a government career, Kim had passed the civil service exam as a young man and had subsequently risen to the middle ranks of public office—although he never quite made it into the company of the *daesin*, that select group of top officials of rank 3A and above. At the outbreak of the war he mustered a force of three hundred men in his hometown of Naju in southwestern Cholla, with the intention of leading them north to Uiju to protect their endangered king. They all swore an oath prior to setting out that they would fight to the death and sealed the vow with a drink of blood after ancient Korean military custom. Kim and his followers then started marching north, picking up volunteers along the way until their numbers had swollen to several thousand. They never made it as far as Uiju. Kim instead made his base in an old mountain fortress south of Seoul, launching hit-and-run attacks on Japanese units in the area and dealing harshly with any locals suspected of truckling with the foe. In August of 1592 he then led them farther north to the royal fortress on Kanghwa-do, an island at the mouth of the Han River fifty kilometers west of the capital, which for centuries past had been maintained as a place of refuge for the king. Here they dug themselves in and became yet another knot of resistance that the Japanese could not dislodge.[21]

One final uibyong leader who demands introduction is Cho Hon, a talented forty-eight-year-old government official whose outspokenness during the prewar years had guaranteed him a rocky career in public office, punctuated with occasional dismissals and even a banishment or two. Cho was an untiring letter writer who penned hundreds of memorials to the throne over the years suggesting ways the country could be reformed. In the late 1580s one of his particular grievances was the government's willingness to receive emissaries from Japanese dictator Toyotomi Hideyoshi. Hideyoshi was unworthy of a relationship with Korea, Cho thundered, because he had "killed his king" prior to seizing power for himself. This misconception, universally held within the government, probably grew from the Koreans' misunderstanding of the final demise of the Ashikaga shogunate during the ascendancy of Oda Nobunaga in the 1570s. Oda did not actually "kill" the final Ashikaga shogun, Yoshiaki—who had by this time been reduced to a puppet—but rather sent him into exile. The Ashikagas, moreover, while they had indeed been granted the title "King of Japan" by the Ming court nearly two hundred years before, had never been the ultimate monarchial authority in Japan. The emperor was. But Cho understood none of this. To him Hideyoshi was a foul usurper who had upset the proper order of his society and as such should be ostracized. As for the emissaries he sent to Seoul, Tsushima daimyo So Yoshitoshi, the retainer Yanagawa Shigenobu, and the monk Genso, Cho wrote to King Sonjo suggesting that their heads be cut off and hung in the street.[22]

Pronouncements like this earned Cho Hon the reputation of a hothead and fanatic in the years prior to 1592. He proclaimed that war was coming, but no one would listen. He reportedly even sat outside the gates of Kyongbok Palace for three days, wailing and striking his head on the ground in an attempt to awaken the king to the danger facing the nation. But still he was ignored. Then, just as he had predicted, the Japanese attacked, providing Cho with vindication. During the first weeks of the invasion the now-prescient official raised a force of eleven hundred civilian volunteers in the central province of Chungchong. They would participate in two major engagements during the next few weeks: the retaking of Chongju and the second battle of Kumsan.

They would not fight alone. At the same time that leaders like Cho Hon were raising "righteous armies" of civilian volunteers, a second resistance movement was gathering momentum, one that, although numerically quite small, would play a significant role in the battles ahead. This was the rise of the monk-soldiers.

It was King Sonjo who first considered calling upon the nation's monks to rise up and fight the Japanese. Prior to the war the Korean government wanted nothing to do with this religious community, and in fact had done everything in their power to suppress it. But now they needed the manpower. They needed every able-bodied man they could get, even those who insisted on shaving their heads and wearing the robes of a monk. Sonjo knew that any call to arms from himself or his government would be ignored by this disaffected group; the call would have to come from someone who commanded the monks' respect. Early in the summer of 1592 the king accordingly summoned the aged Buddhist master Hyujong from his mountain retreat to ask him to organize the nation's monks into some sort of resistance movement to fight the Japanese.

Korea's monks had every reason to be disaffected and unwilling to help the government, for throughout the previous two centuries they had been mercilessly persecuted by the kingdom's Neo-Confucian elite. The founders of the Choson dynasty had adopted Neo-Confucianism as their official state ideology—making Choson Korea the only nation in history to do so—because they believed it contained a model for perfect government. To firmly establish Neo-Confucianism, it was thought necessary to suppress the competing ideology of Buddhism, which had served as the foundation of the preceding Koryo dynasty. From the beginning of the fifteenth century onward the pressure that was brought to bear on Korea's Buddhists was therefore unceasing. Temples were closed throughout the land. Buddhist property was appropriated. The law allowing the ordination of monks was rescinded. The number of sects was reduced, and then reduced again, until only two remained: the Meditation School (Sonjong) and the Doctrinal School (Kyojong). And through it all a steady stream of anti-Buddhist rhetoric poured out of Seoul, in many instances attacks of the most virulent nature.

By the start of the Imjin War, Korea's long-reviled and officially outcast Buddhist community thus had every reason to loathe the government and welcome its demise, even at the hands of a foreign invader. It would take seventy-two-year-old Buddhist Master Hyujong, also known as Sosan Taesa, "Great Master of the Western Mountain," to fire up their patriotism and draw them into the war. Hyujong was the most highly regarded Buddhist monk in Korea at that time, and indeed of the entire Choson dynasty. Orphaned at the age of nine and adopted by a local town magistrate, he was sent to a Confucian academy and given a classical education, but failed to pass the civil service examination and gain a government career. He subsequently became a monk and founded a movement to reconcile Neo-Confucianism and Buddhism, a necessary first step if the embattled, struggling religion was ever to recover any of its lost ground. In the 1550s Hyujong served successively as the director of the Doctrinal School and then of the Meditation School. Finally, in 1557, he retired to a mountain hermitage, venerated by Buddhists of both sects and grudgingly admired by many in government. If any man could get Korea's monks to set aside their anti-government feelings and take up arms against the Japanese, it was this great master, deep in meditation on his western mountain. King Sonjo accordingly sent out the call from Uiju, and Hyujong soon replied.

Why was Hyujong willing to help King Sonjo and a government that had done so much to suppress his religion? First, he would have welcomed the opportunity the war provided for his followers to prove their patriotism and worth, and by so doing hopefully win greater recognition and acceptance from the state. Second, on a personal level he owed a debt of gratitude to Sonjo himself. Three years earlier the instigator of a minor rebellion had falsely used Hyujong's name to try to win the nation's monks over to his misbegotten cause. The incident was quickly put down and Hyujong imprisoned on charges of treason, but he was subsequently released after Sonjo looked into the matter and found the monk innocent.[23]

When King Sonjo asked for Hyujong's help in rallying the nation's monks, he was therefore calling in a favor he expected to be repaid. Hyujong did not disappoint him. On July 16, 1592, the newly appointed "commander of the monk-soldiers of the eight provinces" issued a manifesto calling upon all able-bodied monks throughout the land to leave the solitude of their mountain retreats and rise up against the Japanese:

> Hold your banners high, and arise, all you monk-soldiers of the eight provinces! Who among you have not been given birth in this land? Who among you are not related by blood to the forefathers? Who among you are not subjects of the king? Confucius taught us to lay down our lives to achieve Benevolence. Sacrificing oneself for a just cause and suffering in the place of the myriad souls is the spirit of Bodhisattvas. . . .
>
> You monk-soldiers of all the monasteries! Abandoning a just cause and swerving from the right path in order merely to survive in hiding—how can this be the proper way? The cunning enemy, the monster, will never take pity on you. Once the land perishes how then do you propose to stay alive? Put on the armor of the mercy of Bodhisattvas, hold in hand the treasured sword to fell the devil, wield the lightning bolt of the Eight Deities, and come forward. Only then can you do your duty. Only then can you find the way to life. Let the aged and the weak pray in the monastery. Let the able-bodied come out with their weapons to destroy the enemy and save the land.
>
> Whether or not the people will survive, whether or not the land will remain, depends on this battle. It behooves everyone with the sacred blood of Tan'gun flowing in their veins to defend the country with their lives. When even the trees and grass rise as warriors, how much more should red-blooded people?[24]

More than eight thousand monk-soldiers *(sungbyong)* answered Hyujong's call to arms. They were rallied by regional Buddhist leaders like Choyong, abbot of Taehung Monastery in Cholla Province; Yujong, abbot of Kangwon's Naejang Monastery; Yonggyu, abbot of Chongyon Monastery in Chungchong; and Yongjong, abbot of Kyonggi Province's Chongyong Monastery. They did not amount to a large force, particularly when compared to the tens of thousands of government soldiers now sitting idle in camps to the north. In the coming months, however, they would more than prove their worth. They saw their first serious combat alongside Cho Hon's civilian volunteers at the Battle of Chongju. The date was September 6, 1592.

Chongju occupied a strategic location on the main north–south transportation artery running up the middle of the Korean Peninsula. It also served as the economic center for the entire central region and housed a large government granary. Its loss to the Japanese had thus been a heavy blow. The city had been taken on June 4 by the third contingent under Kuroda Nagamasa during their march north from Angolpo to Seoul. After securing this prize and its wealth of grain, Kuroda had continued on to the capital, leaving behind a small unit to hold the city until reinforcements arrived. These additional forces, contingents four through nine, crossed over to Korea during the next several weeks and subsequently fanned out across the southern half of the peninsula, extending Japanese control outward from the vanguard contingents' main line of march. A force of seventy-two hundred men under Hachisuka Iemasa of the fifth contingent eventually arrived at Chongju to relieve the garrison Kuroda had left behind and then settled down to an uneventful three months' wait.

It was essential to the Koreans that Chongju be retaken. With this strategically placed city back in their hands, guerrilla armies and monk-soldiers could work to sever the main Japanese supply line and in turn cut off the enemy forces that were now far to the north in Seoul and beyond. Chongju was also the key to protecting Cholla Province, for it would have to be taken before an advance could be made on the border town of Kumsan, where enemy forces were amassing for an intended thrust into the southwest.[25]

Government official turned guerrilla commander Cho Hon took the lead in the move to retake Chongju. He had already recruited eleven hundred civilian volunteers in Chungchong Province, but feeling this was not enough manpower, he solicited government troops from the provincial governor, Yun Son-gak, who still had a number of regular troops under his command. Yun had been responsible for the initial loss of Chongju and was thus eager to see it retaken. He was not interested in taking joint action, however, but rather sought to requisition Cho's own forces so that he could lead them himself in an attack on Chongju and thereby redeem his honor. Cho declined. He instead formed an alliance with the monk commander Yonggyu, who in answer to Buddhist master Hyujong's call to arms had raised a force of a thousand warrior-monks. Yonggyu had initially intended to lead his men only in independent actions, but came to see the wisdom of joining forces with Cho Hon's civilian volunteers for a concerted attack on Chongju.

The Koreans converged on Chongju on September 6. Cho's eleven hundred civilian volunteers approached from the north and east, while Yonggyu's warrior-monks, backed by five hundred regular troops grudgingly provided by Chungchong governor Yun, gathered outside the west gate. Many of the men did not have proper weapons, but carried axes and farm tools, anything that could be used to chop or hack or impale. The number of Japanese within the walls of the town is unknown, but was probably fairly small. Hachisuka Iemasa had not expected to encounter any strong resistance and thus earlier in the summer had sent a portion of his force northeast to garrison the nearby town of Chungju. When the Koreans arrived, moreover, some of his men were away foraging for food and the city's defenses were lax.

The battle began when a unit of Japanese musketeers, stripped to their loincloths in the heat of late summer, came out from the fortress to attack Cho's massed volunteers while they were still some distance from the town. The Koreans fell back to the cover of the trees, then fanned out to the left and right until they had the exposed enemy surrounded. The musketeers were then put on the defensive with a hail of arrows, and in a rush forward were finished off. Many of their muskets were captured, but the Koreans did not know how to fire them, and so for the time being could only use them as clubs. With this advance party of Japanese out of the way, the Koreans advanced on the walls of Chongju itself, intent on launching an attack. Before they could do so, however, the sky blackened and a heavy rain began to fall, drenching Cho Hon and his men. It was decided to fall back to a hill overlooking the town and resume the attack the next day.

Some hours later a Korean woman slipped out of Chongju and brought Cho Hon and his volunteers word that the Japanese within had given up and were preparing to leave. Cho, suspecting that she might be a spy sent to lure them into the city, sent a few men to peer over the walls and report what was going on. They discovered that the woman was right: the Japanese were indeed withdrawing. Before sunrise the next morning the jubilant Koreans broke through the gates and took the town without a fight.[26]

With Chongju back in Korean hands, the way was now clear to attack Kumsan farther to the south, where guerrilla leader Ko Kyong-myong had met his end the month before, and where Japanese forces were still poised for an intended move into Cholla Province. By this point more than twenty thousand regular troops had been mustered in Cholla-do to protect the province. Had these government soldiers been combined with Yonggyu's monk-soldiers and Cho Hon's civilian volunteers for a coordinated attack against Kumsan, the Japanese might very well have been routed. Unfortunately for the Koreans, mutual jealousies and feelings of ill will prevented this from happening. In his official report on the Battle of Chongju, Chungchong governor Yun Son-gak falsely gave all the credit for the victory to his government troops and praised Yonggyu and his monk-soldiers, but scarcely acknowledged the presence of Cho Hon and his civilian volunteers. This slight angered Cho, and he submitted his own report highlighting the cowardice of the government troops. By September relations between the civilian volunteers, monk-soldiers, and government troops had become strained, with each side distrustful of the other.

In that same month the government ordered its troops in Cholla Province to begin preparing for an attack on Kumsan in cooperation with the monk-soldiers and Cho Hon's volunteers. Cho, still smarting from the shabby treatment he had received in the wake of the retaking of Chongju, was reluctant to participate. He would attack Kumsan alone, he said. His unwillingness to cooperate with government troops and monk-soldiers was met with disapproval from all quarters, even by some within his own ranks. Cho, however, remained adamant, and when the planned joint attack on Kumsan was repeatedly delayed he insisted on proceeding alone. Monk commander Yonggyu tried to stop him, pointing out that the only way to take Kumsan would be through joint action with government troops. Cho would not listen. "When the king is humiliated," he replied with great emotion, "we subjects must not be afraid to die. The time for that is now!" With that he set out with his seven hundred men. They arrived at Kumsan on September 22 and set up camp three kilometers outside the town.

Many thousands of Japanese troops were by this time gathered within the town under sixth contingent leader Kobayakawa Takakage, plus reinforcements that had arrived during the previous month. Kobayakawa had received word that the enemy force encamped outside his stronghold was only a small one, and was unsupported by other units. He thus decided to take the offensive. During the night a body of troops slipped out of the town and swung around behind the Korean camp. Then the gates of Kumsan were thrown open, and the Japanese struck Cho's army simultaneously from the front and the rear. "You can only die once!" Cho reportedly shouted to his men. "So do it bravely!" They did. Cho Hon's volunteers fought and died to a man during the course of that night, all seven hundred of them. When Cho's brother visited the battlefield the next day to collect his remains, he found the commander lying under the unit's banner, surrounded by the bloody bodies of his many faithful men. Among the dead was Cho Hon's own son, Cho Wan-gi, clad in a general's uniform, it was said, because he had wanted the Japanese to direct their fire toward him and not at his father. All seven hundred bodies eventually would be interred in a grave mound that would come to be known as the Tomb of the Seven Hundred Martyrs.[27]

News of the disaster at Kumsan could not have come as much of a surprise to monk commander Yonggyu and his monk-soldiers; they had considered Cho Hon's intention to attack the Japanese stronghold alone foolhardy from the start. But they nevertheless did not condemn him. As they saw it, the real villain in the affair was Yun Son-gak, the self-serving governor of Chungchong Province who had hogged the glory for the earlier victory at Chongju, frustrating Cho and driving him to take the precipitous action he did. These considerations, coupled with the example Cho had set with his own courageous death, stirred Yong-gyu and his monks to do the same. Not waiting for the arrival of government troops, they marched on Kumsan and spent three days trying to storm its walls, until heavy losses, including the death of Yonggyu himself, forced them to retire.

The disaster at Kumsan illustrated once again how distrust and jeal-ousy often worked to sabotage Korean efforts to resist the Japanese. The Koreans had now attacked the walls of that town three times, under Ko Kyong-myong, Cho Hon, and the monk Yonggyu, but still the Japanese remained ensconced within. If anything can be said to have been accomplished by this terrible loss of life, it was that it made the Japanese reluctant to proceed with their plan to enter Cholla Province and bought the government time to organize its own troops and prepare some sort of defense.[28]

Elsewhere in the country civilian resistance was meeting with considerably more success. One such place was the ancient walled town of Yonan in Hwanghae Province near the Yellow Sea coast. It was here that third contingent leader Kuroda Nagamasa had encountered the only stubborn knot of resistance during his sweep through Hwanghae in July while en route to the north. Eager to catch up to his colleague Konishi for the taking of Pyongyang, Kuroda had not bothered to stop and clear out this relatively isolated and insignificant town, but resolved to return and deal with it later, after Pyongyang had been taken. This he did on October 3, 1592.

The defenders of Yonan, numbering no more than eight hundred, were under the command of Yi Chong-am, a former magistrate of the town and a man commanding deep respect. Yi had overseen preparations for the defense of the town during the preceding weeks and had kept with him his brother and his family, an indication to the townspeople that he was prepared to commit all to the coming fight and expected them to do the same. As it turned out they did.

The Japanese began their siege by constructing an attack tower from which they could fire muskets and fire arrows over the walls. This terrified the Koreans, for most of the buildings of Yonan had thatched roofs and would burn like kindling at the first touch of flame. But luck was with them: the wind shifted as the Japanese went on the attack, blowing the smoke and fire back into their faces and setting their own camp alight. Kuroda's troops then made a direct attack against the walls of the town. But each time they were driven back by a hail of arrows and showers of boiling water. After this first inconclusive contest Kuroda withdrew for a time, but only to get more troops. When he appeared again on October 6, this time with three thousand men, the defenders of Yonan realized the situation was probably hopeless. Inspired by Yi Chong-am, the leaders swore to die fighting, and sealed their vow with a drink of blood. Then they gathered their rocks and arrows and spears and prepared to meet their end as best they could.

The second battle of Yonan was fought with terrible ferocity. The Japanese threw everything they had against the walls, and the Koreans, men and women, the children and the aged, all raged back with desperate fury. Wood was thrown over the walls into piles along the base, then set alight to prevent the Japanese from approaching with their scaling ladders. This kept them at bay for a time, but they eventually found a way through the flames and were once again on the walls, swarming up "like ants." With the Korean defenses seemingly on the verge of collapse, Yi Chong-am climbed atop a pile of kindling and ordered his son to set it alight if the Japanese cleared the top of the wall, shouting that he would rather burn than be taken alive. His exhausted followers, stirred by this display of determination, held their ground and fought like cornered beasts with anything that came to hand: stones, sharpened sticks, handfuls of eye-scorching soap powder. Finally the Japanese fell back, and they did not attack again. With his losses reaching alarming proportions—certainly more than he could afford on one insignificant town—Kuroda was forced to withdraw and the town of Yonan was saved.[29]

The successful defense of Yonan illustrates a trait of the Koreans in warfare that would be demonstrated on numerous occasions during the war, and indeed throughout the Choson dynasty: a degree of courage and ferocity when defending a wall that went beyond anything they could muster when fighting on open ground. This would be remarked upon in the late nineteenth century by William Griffis, one of the first historians to attempt any sort of extensive chronicling of Korean history in the English language. "The Koreans are poor soldiers in the open field," Griffis observed in 1892,

> and exhibit slight proof of personal valor, . . . but put the same men behind walls . . . [and] they are more than brave, their courage is sublime, they fight to the last man and fling themselves on the bare steel when the foe clears the parapet. The Japanese of 1592 looked upon the Korean in the field as a kitten, but in the castle as a tiger. The French [who attempted to take Kanghwa Island] in 1866 never found a force that could face rifles, but behind walls the same men were invincible.[30]

* * *

One week after the successful defense of Yonan, a force of Korean government troops scored an important and interesting victory with the retaking of Kyongju far to the south. Kyongju, the capital of the Silla dynasty and during Choson times the administrative center of Kyongsang Province, had been captured by Kato Kiyomasa's second contingent during the early days of the war, when Kato, Konishi, and Kuroda were all racing to be the first to reach Seoul. A small force of Koreans had attempted to stave off the Japanese at that time, but their hastily assembled defenses had been easily smashed. Three thousand people were put to the sword in the reprisals that followed, and many of the city's historic buildings were burnt to the ground. In the consolidation of the south that subsequently occurred, the city was garrisoned by troops from the fifth contingent from Shikoku, under a commander named Tagawa Naiki. Tagawa's men enjoyed several weeks of uneventful occupation. Then, toward the end of September, a large force of Koreans appeared from the west.

This native army consisted of five thousand government troops under the command of recently appointed Kyongsang Left Army Commander Pak Jin. (His predecessor in the position, Yi Kak, who had proved so ineffectual in the face of the initial Japanese assault, had been reassigned elsewhere.) The first round went to the Japanese. Tagawa, taking the offensive early against the numerically superior Koreans, sent a body of men out of the city from a back gate to circle around and attack from the rear, a bold and entirely successful gambit that sent Pak and his men into a precipitous retreat.[31]

They soon returned—and this time they brought with them a secret weapon. It was called the *pigyok chincholloe* (flying striking earthquake heaven thunder), translated by one writer as the "flying thunderbolt."[32] In the early hours of October 12, under the cover of darkness, Pak sent a group of soldiers up to the base of the walls of Kyongju where they set up and fired the weapon, hurling a mysterious ball of iron into the midst of the enemy camp. "It fell to earth," a Japanese chronicler tells us, "and our soldiers gathered about it to look. Suddenly it exploded, emitting a noise that shook heaven and earth, and scattering bits of iron like pulverized stars. Those who were hit dropped dead on the spot. Others were knocked down as if by a powerful wind."[33] Only thirty-odd men were killed in the blast, but it so panicked Tagawa's garrison that it abandoned the city and fled to Sosaengpo, leaving Kyongju and a large store of rice to the Koreans.[34]

The pigyok chinchollae would be employed on other occasions in the Imjin War, notably at the First Battle of Chinju in November 1592, and at the Battle of Haengju in March of the following year. It was invented some time earlier in the reign of King Sonjo by Yi Chang-son, head of the government's firearms department, probably as an adaptation of the catapult-fired *pi li hu pao* (heaven-shaking thunder) bomb previously developed in China and used against the Japanese in the failed Mongol invasion in 1274. Unlike the pi li hu pao, however, the pigok chincholloe was shot with gunpowder from a mortar, making it the world's first mortar- or cannon-fired explosive shell. It was manufactured in various sizes, from a twenty-one-centimeter version fired from the Korean's largest mortar, the daewangu, down to ten-centimeter models shot from the medium-sized chungwangu. The projectile itself was a hollow cast-iron sphere packed with gunpowder and pieces of shrapnel, with a delayed action fuse inserted through an opening in the top, consisting of a length of cord wound around a screw-like wooden core in turn inserted in a sleeve of bamboo. After the mortar was charged with gunpowder, the sphere was placed in the mouth, the end of the fuse protruding from its top was lit, and then the mortar was fired, hurling the device over a distance of five to six hundred paces. After it landed its fuse would continue to burn, spiraling down through the center of the sphere until it reached the base of the bamboo sleeve, ignited the gunpowder, and exploded the shell.[35]

The last major battle of 1592 occurred at the city of Chinju on Korea's southern coast, west of the Japanese stronghold at Pusan. The fortress here was reputed to be one of the most unassailable in all of southern Korea, a claim that may have been true earlier in the Choson dynasty, when it was still a compact hilltop citadel, the sort of fortification that the Koreans excelled at building and defending. The government's prewar building program, however, had compromised Chinju's defenses. By greatly lengthening its walls to accommodate more of the local population, the cardinal rule of fortress-building, "keep it small," was forgotten, and Chinju rendered more difficult to defend.

Fortunately for the Koreans, the thirty-eight hundred defenders of Chinju were led by a courageous and able commander named Kim Si-min who had been appointed magistrate of the city the month before. About seventy of Kim's men were also equipped with muskets, the first batch of such Korean-manufactured weapons to see service in the war. The Japanese were thus in for a surprise. (The Koreans had known of muskets since at least 1589, when Japanese envoy So Yoshitoshi presented one to the court as a gift. Government minister Yu Song-nyong had urged at the time that it be adopted by the army as a standard weapon, but it was only after the start of the war that production was authorized.)[36]

The Japanese arrived outside the walls of Chinju on November 8, a body of 15,570 men from the seventh contingent from western Honshu under the leadership of Kato Mitsuyasu, Hasegawa Hidekazu, Nagaoka Tadaoki, and Kimura Shigeji. They advanced to within firing distance; then the ashigaru gunners leveled a thousand muskets at the walls and let loose with a thunderous volley. Their intention was probably to see if the defenders within could be frightened into retreat by a mere show of force, a gambit that had been successfully employed against the Koreans before. The ploy did not work at Chinju. Inside the city, Kim Si-min had his men under firm control. He had placed them at strategic points all along the walls of the fortress, with strict orders to keep their heads down and to hold their fire until the Japanese had advanced to the walls. The initial Japanese fusillade thus met with no response. The pall of gun smoke slowly cleared, but still nothing came flying over the parapets from the Koreans. All remained quiet, as if the city was deserted. Later that night Kim sent a musician up to the top of the fortress to play his flute, to impress upon the Japanese that he and his men were unafraid and calm.

Having failed to shake the defenders of Chinju with their initial display of musket fire, the Japanese set to work preparing for an all-out assault on the walls. Erecting an enclosure to hide their activities from the Koreans, the men of the seventh contingent lashed together a three-story-high siege tower, plus scaling ladders of pine and bamboo, high enough to reach the top of the walls and wide enough to accommodate half a dozen men on each rung. The Koreans within the fortress, meanwhile, were making preparations of their own. They added to their stock of arrows and melted lead into musket balls. They placed piles of rocks at convenient intervals around the walls and kept kettles of water on the boil. They bundled straw around packets of gunpowder to make crude incendiary devices. They drove spikes through heavy planks, then sharpened the iron points.

And so the First Battle of Chinju began. The Japanese opened fire from the top of their siege tower, using the height of the construction to lob shots over the wall and into the city, keeping the heads of the Koreans down while the scaling ladders were moved into place. The first wave of assault troops then ran forward and attempted to climb up the walls and storm over the top. There soon were so many warriors jostling to be *ichiban nori*, "first to climb in," that the ladders nearly collapsed under the weight. Samurai leader Hosokawa Sudaoki was among them, the *Taikoki* tells us, "accompanied by foot soldiers on ladders on his right and left. [He] strictly ordered 'Until I have person-ally climbed into the castle this ladder is for one person to climb. If anyone else climbs I will take his head!' [T]hen he climbed. Because of this the ladder did not break and he got up, and the men who saw him were loud in his praise. . . . [B]ut when he tried to make his entry from within the castle, spears and naginata were thrust at him to try to make him fall, and lamentably he fell to the bottom of the moat."[37]

Other warriors followed Hosokawa. Thousands of them. They were driven back by a hail of arrows and musket balls, stones and red-hot chunks of iron. Those who were not killed or knocked to the ground by these projectiles had their upturned faces scalded by showers of boiling water or were impaled with spears or by spiked boards dropped on their heads. Some ashigaru fell to the ground in pairs and small groups, all nailed together on the same heavy plank.

Then flaming bundles of straw came flying over the walls. They landed in the midst of the Japanese clustered at the base of the ladders, waiting to get a foot on the first rung. They seemed innocent enough, harmless little fires providing a bit of warmth on a chilly autumn day. But then the flames reached the packet of gunpowder nestled within and the flaming bundle exploded, killing or maiming anyone nearby.

The Japanese assaulted the walls of Chinju in wave after wave throughout that day—and the next day, and the next, and the next. The Koreans, under the steady hand of General Kim, held their ground. Eventually bands of civilian volunteers arrived to aid the defenders. One group, too small to attack the Japanese directly, climbed to the top of a nearby hill and beat drums and lit torches so that the enemy would think that they had been flanked by a large Korean force. They were soon joined by a second band of two hundred men, sent by the "Red Coat General," Kwak Jae-u. Kwak's men scrambled up the slopes above the Japanese camp and roared, "The Red Coat General is mustering soldiers from all over the south, and will soon be arriving with a huge army!" Then came news that a large group of civilian volunteers, numbering some two thousand, was on its way to relieve Chinju, obliging the Japanese to divert a portion of their force away from the walls to guard the approaches to the city.

The Battle of Chinju raged for five days. The final assault occurred in the early morning hours of November 13. On one side of the city the Japanese extravagantly illuminated their camp with torches and made a show of packing up their gear and preparing to leave, all within full view of the wary Koreans. Then, at a given signal, the torches were extinguished and an all-out attack was launched against the far side of the city, one group of ashigaru laying down a screen of covering fire, forcing the Koreans away from the parapets above, while a second group attempted one last time to storm over the top of the walls. The defenders within by this point were in desperate straits. There was scarcely a stone remaining inside the city to hurl at the attackers, and the wood and thatch roofs of all the buildings had been reduced to ash by Japanese fire arrows, leaving the city a patchwork of blackened and smoldering heaps. But the Koreans stuck to their walls and fought on. At one point in the battle Kim Si-min himself was mortally wounded in the forehead by a musket ball, but this was kept from his men so they would not lose heart. They did not, and the defenses of Chinju held. In the end Kato Mitsuyasu and his fellow commanders halted the attack, and did not venture another. With their losses growing alarmingly high (by some accounts nearly half their force), and increasingly anxious about counterattack from the rear, it was decided to lift the siege and withdraw. This was done under the cover of a sudden downpour. The Koreans did not attempt to pursue.[38]

The Japanese would return to Chinju the following summer, driven by a fury that would see it burned to the ground and all its inhabitants killed. For the time being, however, the city was saved.

It was native Korean resistance such as this, both on land and at sea, that brought Hideyoshi's drive to conquer Asia grinding to a halt. Because of Korean naval commander Yi Sun-sin, the taiko was denied the supply route through the Yellow Sea that he so desperately needed to transport reinforcements to northern Korea to continue the advance on Beijing. And now, because of a groundswell of native resistance from civilian volunteers, monk-soldiers, and reassembled government troops, simply hanging on to Korea itself was proving a troublesome task. Inevitably, the frustrations that this caused the Japanese in the field would lead them to ignore Hideyoshi's prewar imperative to treat the Koreans kindly in order to win them over, and to rely instead on violence and terror to beat them down. Fifteen ninety-three, the second year of the war, would thus come to be dominated by atrocities on the part of the Japanese, atrocities that would in turn serve only to deepen the hatred of the Koreans and steel their determination to resist. At any cost.

The commitment of large numbers of Ming troops to the war effort in early 1593 would add tremendously to the impetus that would ultimately drive Hideyoshi's forces back toward Pusan. It must be stressed, however, that China's coming contribution to the effort would not make the difference between victory and defeat, but would rather hasten what was already an inevitable outcome. By the end of 1592 the Koreans had overcome their initial shock at being invaded, and had pieced together a haphazard campaign of grassroots resistance that would ultimately make their country ungovernable for the Japanese. Hideyoshi's armies were by no means beaten by December of 1592. But attrition was starting to eat away at their strength. Of the initial force of 158,800 that had landed on Korean soil in the late spring and early summer of 1592, fully one-third would soon be gone, casualties of battle, victims of hunger and exhaustion and disease. Korean losses would be many times higher. But they were willing to bear the sacrifice. The Japanese were not. It would probably have taken several years of guerrilla warfare before the Koreans wore the Japanese down to the point where they were forced to leave the peninsula altogether. But this they would have done—with or without the help of the Ming Chinese.

CHAPTER 16

Saving History

IN AUGUST OF 1592 a unit of Japanese soldiers began advancing on the walled town of Chonju, the administrative center of the southwestern province of Cholla, with the intention of occupying the place and laying claim to the region. The provincial governor, Yi Kwang, was desperate to save the town, and joined with Yi Chong-nan, an elderly official formerly in charge of the city's repository of historical records, in mounting a defense. A force of civilian volunteers was first sent ahead to stop the Japanese at a mountain pass leading to the town. The defenders erected a wooden barrier across the pass and fought bravely to hold it, but the Japanese were too strong for them and they were pushed aside. In front of Chonju, meanwhile, Yi Kwang and Yi Chong-nan had organized the local citizenry in erecting banners by day and torches by night, so that when the Japanese approached they would be tricked into thinking that a formidable force was encamped there and determined to defend the town. The ruse worked. When the Japanese drew near Chonju and spied the torches and banners in the distance, they assumed that a large Korean army was waiting to meet them, and prudently decided to withdraw and leave Chonju for another day.[1]

The defense of Chonju was in itself a relatively insignificant affair involving few defenders and little loss of life, a minor episode lost amid the greater conflicts and conflagrations of the opening months of the Imjin War. For the Koreans, however, what happened outside the walls of that town in the summer of 1592 had a deep and enduring significance. For in turning back the Japanese, Yi Kwang, Yi Chong-nan, and the citizens of Chonju had not just saved their town, they had saved the very history of Korea.

There was not a people anywhere in the pre-modern world with a greater regard for history than the Koreans. From as early as the Silla dynasty virtually every event occurring during the reign of each king, no matter how small and seemingly insignificant, was painstakingly recorded and preserved so that future generations could benefit from the lessons learned. The Koreans were of course greatly influenced in this by the Chinese, who were themselves great historians. By the second century of the Choson dynasty, however, Korea's record keepers had come to surpass their Middle Kingdom counterparts. In terms of completeness, accuracy, and objectivity, the multi-volume *sillok* ("true record" or "annals") that was compiled for the reign of each Choson king marked a pinnacle in the recording of history in the world up to that time.

The sources used in the compilation of the true record of the Choson dynasty were many and varied. First and most important were the records kept by the court historians. These included the transcripts for every royal audience as written down by the two officials who sat to the left and right of the king, one charged with recording his words, the other his actions. The court historians also kept diaries of all the happenings in the capital and elsewhere that they deemed important. Other valuable sources included the records kept by the various ministries of government, the diaries and journals of key ministers, and the tens of thousands of dispatches that arrived in Seoul from officials posted throughout the land.

In keeping a record of the affairs of state, great emphasis was placed on objectivity. In this respect the Koreans seem to have been superior to the Ming Chinese. The court historians in particular were expected to write with impeccable honesty. Even the king was not to be exempt from their critical gaze. In 1456, for example, King Sejo himself enjoined his court historians to write about his reign warts and all. "What I do right and wrong," he said, "all people see. It is not right that anything should be hid. The historical officers should record in detail what actually happens." In 1508 King Chungjong similarly instructed the historians to record "exactly what the King did, whether it be right or wrong, without hesitation."[2] Indeed, the fact that Korean accounts of the Imjin War are so replete with tales of cowardly commanders and self-serving officials is not due to some sort of national weakness of character on the part of the Koreans. It is because the Koreans of the Choson dynasty kept such a candid record of their times, recording for posterity their weaknesses as well as their strengths.

It was only after the death of a monarch that all the historically significant documents produced during his reign were collected and compiled into the multi-volume set of books that have survived to the present day. After the requisite six months of mourning had elapsed, a board of editors was appointed, a group of some thirty men assisted by a small army of clerks, and the daunting work begun of plowing through stacks of court histories, private diaries, ministry journals, and government dispatches. It was a task that commonly took several years. When the true record was finally complete, no one was allowed to read it, for the unvarnished truth the document was supposed to contain would undoubtedly have angered some, which in turn would have intimidated the historians and editors involved and compromised their integrity. Once again even the king was not exempt from this injunction. In 1431 King Sejong asked to see the completed annals for his father's reign, but his request was denied. As the Minister of the Right explained, the purpose of the annals was to provide an unbiased account of the affairs of state for future generations. "Even though Your Majesty should read them," the minister cautioned, "you probably should not wish to alter them. And if you see them, other kings after you will wish to do likewise. The historical officers will thus be afraid to write accurately, thinking they might be dishonestly accused."[3]

After the collected annals were complete, the document was sent to the printer and four copies made. During the early years of the dynasty these were written by hand. Beginning in the late fifteen century the four copies were printed by means of recently invented movable type, still a laborious process involving the use of thousands of individual Chinese characters. The four copies were then placed in storage and the original manuscript destroyed by immersing it in water to wash away the ink.

With the four sets of the true record complete, the challenge was to ensure their safekeeping throughout the centuries to come. During the Choson dynasty the Koreans adopted the expedient of storing the four sets of books in four separate repositories scattered across the kingdom: one set was kept at the royal palace in Seoul; the other three were sent with great pomp and ceremony to storage facilities in the south-central cities of Chungju, Songju, and Chonju. In this way the survival of Korea's historical record was assured, for any given calamity could claim only one set of books. In 1538, for example, the caretakers of the repository at Songju burnt the wooden building to the ground, and with it all the books in their charge, while trying to smoke out pigeons that had nested under the eaves. The conflagration caused considerable inconvenience and expense, but no irreparable harm was done, for three other sets of the true record remained, the ones in Chungju, Chonju, and Seoul. Within five years the destroyed building had been rebuilt, a replacement set of the record printed, and the Songju repository restored.

This system of separate repositories worked very well over the centuries in safeguarding Korea's historical record. If a fire claimed one of the repositories, the other three would remain, and thus a new copy could be made to replace the one that had been lost. Only the most bizarre coincidence or act of God could claim two repositories, but even then two others would remain. As for losing three repositories, that was frankly inconceivable. How could disaster strike simultaneously in three separate parts of the country?

During the Japanese invasion it did. In June of 1592 Konishi Yukinaga's first contingent crushed the army of Sin Ip at Chungju and occupied the city. In the reprisals that followed, the first repository went up in smoke. Four days later, in the looting and arson that followed King Sonjo's evacuation of Seoul, Kyongbok Palace was burned to the ground by the local citizenry, and with it the attached second repository and its precious store of books. In their march north from Pusan to Seoul, Kuroda Nagamasa and the men of his third contingent captured and burned the city of Songju. And so the third repository was lost.

By July of 1592 the inconceivable had thus happened: three of the four sets of Korea's historical record had been destroyed. The Japanese move against Chonju in the southwestern province of Cholla, home of the fourth and final repository, consequently was regarded as a profound threat not just to the town itself, but to the nation as a whole. If Chonju fell and the books stored there were stolen or destroyed, the loss would be irreplaceable. The city therefore could not be allowed to fall. And in the end it did not, thanks to the successful defense organized by Cholla governor Yi Kwang and former guardian of the books Yi Chong-nan.

Following the withdrawal of the Japanese from the vicinity of Chonju, Yi Chong-nan and the officials responsible for the town's repository realized that the hundreds of volumes in their charge would have to be moved to a safer place, far from the possibility of enemy attack. A caravan of horses thus set out from the city, bearing 577 precious books. The first leg of the journey took them south to a remote hermitage in the nearby Naejang (Inner Sanctum) Mountains. The repository, together with its sacred portrait of King Taejo, the Choson dynasty's founder, remained here for the next ten months, carefully guarded, periodically aired and dried in the sun, and attended to with ceremony and reverence. Then in 1593 it was decided that even this remote mountain retreat was situated too far south for safety. And so the books and the sacred portrait were moved again, first overland to Asan on the Yellow Sea coast, then farther north by ship to Haeju, then to fortified Kanghwa Island at the mouth of the Han River. Finally, toward the end of the war, they were transferred yet again, this time to a temple on Mt. Myohyang, in a cliff-top aerie accessible only by ladder. Here, at last, the true record of the kings of Korea was deemed to be safe.[4]

PART 4

STALEMATE

Being victorious in battle is easy,
but preserving the results of victory is difficult.[1]

Wu Tzu Ping Fa (Master Wu's Art of War)
4th century B.C.

CHAPTER 17

The Retreat from Pyongyang to the "River of Hell"

BY THE BEGINNING OF 1593 the Japanese army in Korea was beginning to falter. In the southeastern province of Kyongsang, the city of Kyongju had been retaken by the Koreans, a full-scale assault on Chinju had been repelled with heavy losses, and attacks by guerrilla bands had rendered large parts of the region unsafe for Japanese troops. To the west, Kobayakawa Takakage's attempts to subdue Cholla had failed, and that province remained almost entirely in Korean hands. In the central-eastern province of Kangwon, Japanese troops had abandoned most of that region in order to protect the central road leading from Pusan to Seoul, which was coming under increasing attack. Kuroda Nagamasa's men in the central-northern province of Hwanghae were doing likewise, leaving most of the province to the guerrillas in order to safeguard the vital road leading north from Seoul, the only means of supply for the forward units occupying Pyongyang. Even in Hamgyong Province, which Kato Kiyomasa had by his own reckoning subdued so completely the previous fall, civilian resistance was becoming a serious threat. The Japanese headquarters at Kilchu came under attack, co-opted Korean administrators were assassinated or driven into the hills by guerrillas, and the province's nascent government of occupation was reduced to a shambles.

In addition to having to deal with growing local resistance, the Japanese invasion army was also having difficulty obtaining enough to eat. For the past seven months they had relied for their subsistence mainly on supplies purchased or seized from the Koreans, the previous year's harvest. By the beginning of 1593 these stores were nearly all used up and not much had been grown in the meantime, for throughout the country farmers had fled their homes and abandoned their fields. What little remained in the countryside that was edible was also becoming more difficult to get, for foraging parties were now prime targets for guerrilla attacks. Nor was much being sent across from Japan, due in large measure to the reticence of the Japanese navy to risk an encounter with the Korean battleships under Commander Yi Sun-sin. Of those meager supplies that did arrive from home, moreover, almost nothing could be transported north to the units needing them most. By the beginning of 1593 this lack of supplies had become so critical for the Japanese that some units were facing the prospect of starvation.

The Japanese now were caught in a dilemma. They did not have enough fighting men in Korea to beat down local resistance and secure their grasp on the peninsula. But they could not ship additional units over from Kyushu because they did not have enough food to support them. Indeed, they did not have enough to feed the men already there.

Of all the occupation forces scattered throughout Korea, none was in worse shape than Konishi Yukinaga and the men of the first contingent encamped at Pyongyang. They had been stalled in the city for the past five months and had given up any thought of advancing farther north. They had also given up hope of ever receiving reinforcements and supplies by ship up the Taedong River from the sea, for as long as the Korean navy blocked access to the Yellow Sea a seaborne supply route would remain nothing but a dream. Indeed, the arrival of reinforcements now would have been a mixed blessing, for it would have meant more mouths to feed. Konishi and his men had secured a large amount of grain when they captured the city in July of 1592, but with fifteen thousand men to support this was eventually exhausted, and the army of occupation in Pyongyang was forced to rely on what meager supplies could be foraged from the vicinity—an increasingly dangerous undertaking—or carried north from Seoul on the backs of horses and men. With the harsh Korean winter now upon them, the men of the first contingent hunkered down in their frozen billets, grimly watching their numbers being whittled away by hunger, cold, exhaustion and disease, pining for the warm and hospitable shores of Kyushu which many now feared they would never see again.[1]

By the beginning of 1593, therefore, the Japanese army was being constricted from one end of the country to the other by Korean resistance and lack of food, forced out of outlying areas and back onto the central line of march that they had followed during their initial advance up the peninsula the previous year. Their point of farthest northern advance remained unchanged. To the south of this, however, all they really held was a narrow corridor of territory running from Pusan to Pyongyang, and even this was becoming difficult to protect. The Japanese had not yet lost a major land battle and had in almost every engagement inflicted far greater losses than anything they themselves had sustained. Their initially large numbers were limited, however, and in the vastness of Korea were being steadily whittled away. In a head count conducted later in the spring, it was discovered that Konishi Yukinaga's spearhead first contingent, which had totaled 18,700 men at the start of the invasion, had only 6,626 able-bodied men left, a decline of sixty-five percent. Kato Kiyomasa's 22,800-man second contingent was down to 13,980 men, a loss of thirty-nine percent. After half a year of attrition, the Japanese in Korea had scarcely 100,000 men all told.[2]

With the campaign to conquer Korea on the verge of collapse, the Japanese commanders in Seoul charged with overseeing operations on the peninsula dispatched a message to Kato Kiyomasa recalling him from the northeastern province of Hamgyong, saying that his men were urgently needed in the south. It is important to note that this message was sent to Kato before the Chinese entered the war in force (the only experience of Ming troops so far had been at the First Battle of Pyongyang, a resounding victory for the Japanese), an indication that Korean resistance was playing a major role in turning the tide of the invasion.[3] This order undoubtedly caused Kato some anguish; of all the daimyo commanders serving in Korea, he would be most consistent in opposing retreat. By the time he received it, however, the situation in the north had taken a drastic turn for the worse.

* * *

On the far side of the Yellow Sea, China was ready for war. Seaports were now closed all along the east coast to guard against Japanese attack. Foreigners everywhere were eyed with suspicion. And troops, thousands of them, were now amassed in Liaodong, the province nearest to Korea, awaiting orders to cross the Yalu River and attack the Japanese.

As was the custom with the Chinese, this expeditionary force gathered in Liaodong was under the supreme command of a civil administrator, Vice-Minister of War Song Yingchang. Song would not immediately cross into Korea, however, or take part in any of the battles to come. This would be the job of Commander in Chief Li Rusong, an experienced general of distant Korean extraction who had served with distinction in the recently concluded Ordos Campaign on the empire's northwest frontier, the army-mutiny-cum-Mongol-uprising that had been Beijing's foremost concern throughout most of 1592.

Li's army consisted of 35,000 fighting men divided into left, center, and right divisions. One of these divisions was under the command of Li's younger brother, Li Rubo (a second of Li's brothers and a cousin served on his staff); the other two divisions were led by Zhang Shijue and Yang Yuan. The bulk of this force was composed of men from Liaodong Province, augmented by a contingent of three thousand from the east-coast province of Zhejiang. They were divided into cavalry and artillery units, and foot soldiers armed with spears and bows and arrows. Some wore coats of chain mail that were said to offer effective protection; many carried short, blunt swords that would be no match for the razor-sharp katana of the Japanese. They had few if any muskets, but did possess a large number of smallish cannon in the hands of the three thousand-man contingent from Zhejiang.[4] Most of these weapons were probably of the fo-lang-chi variety, a small-caliber gun copied from Portuguese samples captured by the Chinese some decades before (hence the name, derived from *farangi*, the Chinese term for Europeans). An average-sized fo-lang-chi was between one and two meters long and fired a lead ball of no more than five centimeters in diameter, the ball being shoved down the barrel and a gunpowder cartridge being slotted into an opening at the rear. The Chinese expeditionary force may also have had larger cannons, but if so only a very few. The "generalissimo," for example, which was commonly used to blast a mass of pebbles and iron scrap into the face of an attacking enemy, weighed up to six hundred kilograms and thus would have been a tremendous burden over the snowbound mountain passes between Liaodong and Korea.[5]

Like most Ming soldiers, Li Rusong's expeditionary army was made up mainly of paid mercenaries, recruited from the ranks of outcasts, bandits, and peasants who had fallen on hard times. They cared little for patriotism; they fought for food, money, and the chance to loot. The only discipline they responded to was the threat of death at the hands of their commanders. Otherwise they tended to be riotous, totally without scruples, and at times more dangerous to friend than foe. This fact was nowhere better illustrated than in the Ming practice of taking heads. Throughout the sixteenth century the Chinese determined the success of a fighting man, from the lowest soldier to the highest commander, by the number of enemy heads he took: the more heads one could produce at the end of a battle, the greater the honors and rewards one stood to gain. Not surprisingly, this incentive as applied to the generally undisciplined, amoral ranks of the Chinese army led to abuses, with civilians, sometimes even women, being killed by the very soldiers sent to protect them so that their heads could be submitted for reward. If a head was too obviously that of a civilian, a bit of steaming or beating with a wet sandal usually disguised it enough. Even unit commanders at times participated in this fraud to increase their "head count" to the one hundred and twenty needed to win first-class battle merit.[6]

This, then, for good or ill, was the Ming force that was gathered in Liaodong Province at the end of 1592, poised to march to Korea. It was ostensibly being sent in response to the Korean government's repeated entreaties for help in beating back the Japanese. China's main concern, however, did not lay with the survival of Korea, as much as it respected its loyal vassal to the east. Its number one objective was to safeguard its own borders. The two kingdoms would thus be at odds from the very start of their alliance against the Japanese, for the Chinese were not committed like the Koreans to annihilating the "robbers"; all Beijing really wanted was to push the invaders back toward the south. In the coming weeks and months, therefore, the Koreans were assured of receiving from China less than they bargained for in terms of military aid, and more in terms of trouble.

*   *   *

The Japanese forces occupying Pyongyang knew nothing of the large Ming army that was moving their way. By the beginning of 1593 Korean guerrilla activity had left them isolated within the walls of the city and had deprived them of the native spies who had previously provided so much useful information. As far as they knew, negotiations were still under way with the Chinese through Ming envoy Shen Weijing.

Shen, it will be remembered, had been dispatched by Beijing in September of 1592 to parley with the Japanese. The talks were intended to buy the Chinese time enough to bring the Ordos Campaign to a conclusion and shift troops eastward into Liaodong. Shen himself was not apprised of this; he set out for Pyongyang in the belief that Beijing really did want him to return with the makings for a lasting peace. The ensuing talks were a mutually satisfactory parade of lies, with the Japanese asserting that all they wanted was friendly relations with China, and the cagey Shen reciprocating with assurances that Beijing would welcome them with open arms.

After arranging a fifty-day armistice, Shen returned to China to find that no one was interested in a settlement. On the contrary, a large army had been amassed in Liaodong during his absence, and everyone seemed intent on war, not peace. After delivering his report, Shen was ordered to return south and tell the Japanese that there would be no more talking until they had withdrawn their forces all the way back to Pusan. Shen thus returned to Pyongyang with nothing whatsoever to offer the Japanese. He entered the city on December 29, 1592, more than a month past the expiration of the fifty-day armistice, and once again the two sides sat down to talk. Konishi began by questioning Shen about a rumor that he had returned to Korea with a great army in tow. Shen assured him that this was not true. There is no army, he said; I have come with an entourage of only fifteen men. With this matter out of the way, the two sides proceeded to see if they could find some common ground. And of course they could, for Konishi was eager for peace in almost any form, while Shen wanted to win the riches and royal title that Beijing had promised to whoever was able to restore peace in Korea. The settlement they reached was this: the Japanese would withdraw their forces from Pyongyang, but Beijing would first have to guarantee Japanese ships access to ports along China's eastern coast.[7]

The Koreans found Shen Weijing far more secretive during his second visit to their country. He did not let them know much of the nature of his mission, and he kept his distance from government interpreters, the only Koreans who understood the Chinese language he spoke. Board of Rites minister Yun Gun-su was one of the few officials who managed to extract any information from him of the talks that had taken place in Pyongyang. Yun was not happy with what he heard. When they had met previously, Yun reminded Shen, "I told you that if the Japanese returned the two princes and all other prisoners, together with all the land they have seized, then and only then can peace negotiations go ahead. If even one of these conditions is not met, however, there can be no peace." Shen replied that it had not been possible to negotiate with Konishi for the return of the captive princes, Imhae and Sunhwa, as they were not under his jurisdiction, but rather were being held by Kato Kiyomasa. Konishi was responsible only for Pyongyang, and so a Japanese withdrawal from Pyongyang was all he could arrange. Yun Gun-su was not satisfied with this, and began pressing Shen to have the Ming army sent south to drive the Japanese out of Pyongyang. Shen explained that dispatching troops was entirely up to the supreme civil administrator, Song Yingchang. He himself had no say in the matter. "But Song will listen to you," Yun continued to press. "Please urge him to send the army."

Finally Shen lost his temper. "If your country is so anxious to kill the Japanese, then go ahead and kill them yourselves!" he said, adding a disparaging comment about the Korean army that indicated he thought it was not up to the task. Then: "The Japanese vanguard forces holding Pyongyang are very strong, and would be difficult to beat. If we can trick them into withdrawing, however, even if there are 100,000 enemy soldiers in Seoul we can easily defeat them." In the meantime the Koreans were to set aside any suspicions they had that China was concerned only with protecting itself and did not plan to send an army to Korea. "If China only wanted to defend its own borders," he said, "we would be pursuing a different strategy. Why would we go to all this trouble if we did not wish to help Korea?"[8]

With that Shen Weijing resumed his journey north to Beijing. He was stopped in Liaodong Province by Ming commander in chief Li Rusong, who was by this time advancing toward Korea with his 35,000-man expeditionary force. Upon hearing of Shen's friendly talks with the Japanese at Pyongyang, Li became so outraged that he ordered the hapless envoy arrested and put to death. It was only thanks to the last-minute intercession of a member of Li's staff that Shen did not die that day. The livid commander was urged to spare Shen and leave the Japanese in Pyongyang with the impression that negotiations were still under way, for they would then not expect an attack. Li saw the wisdom of this, and placed Shen in custody in case he might prove useful later on in furthering the ruse.[9]

And so Li and his army resumed their march toward Korea with prisoner Shen Weijing in tow. They passed through the Willow Palisade, the wall of wooden stakes intended to keep the Jurchen tribes of Manchuria out of Liaodong, then struck into the mountain wilderness that lay between China and the kingdom of Choson. The going was difficult, for it was now January, the route was rough and covered with snow, and the weather deathly cold. Finally, on January 26, they reached the north bank of the frozen Yalu River. Commander in Chief Li mounted a crimson sedan chair as suited his position, and banners were unfurled. Then the great Ming army marched across the ice and entered the Imjin War.

King Sonjo was waiting to greet Li Rusong at the gate into Uiju on the Yalu's south bank. "We are here," announced the Ming commander, "to destroy the vicious enemy, so your majesty can put his heart at rest." Sonjo responded with words of gratitude and profound relief. The Japanese invasion, he said, had done great harm to the country and driven him to take refuge in this remote corner. "But now, thanks to the emperor's generosity, you have come with a great army, and will drive the Japanese out of our land and bring our government back to life."[10]

Sonjo's relief at the arrival of the Chinese army was completely sincere and unsullied by doubt, for it marked for him the end of many months of despair and rekindled hopes that the war could be won. But not everyone regarded this event in an equally positive light. Now that the Chinese had arrived on the scene in force the prosecution of the war would pass unquestionably into their hands, leaving Korea a bystander in many of the battles and events to come. This fact had already been amply demonstrated by the negotiations that had taken place in Pyongyang between Shen Weijing and Konishi Yukinaga. The Koreans were excluded from both rounds of talks and had had difficulty even obtaining information as to what had taken place. There was also the problem to consider of feeding these additional 35,000 Chinese mouths—and just as important, keeping them away from mischief, for the soldiers of Liaodong were known to be an unruly bunch, often little better than thugs. The question that hung in the air was: Did the arrival of the Ming army really spell Korea's salvation? Or would it be yet another burden for this troubled kingdom to bear?

Commander in Chief Li Rusong's expeditionary force was joined at Uiju by the Chinese troops that had been encamped there over the past several months as a bodyguard to King Sonjo. When he began the march south at the end of January, therefore, his command had grown to some 43,000 men.[11] They would be joined at Sunan, the Korean army headquarters thirty kilometers north of Pyongyang, by 10,000 native troops led by Yi Il, the Korean general who had been defeated by Konishi Yukinaga's first contingent at the Battle of Sangju in June the previous year, and by regional commander Kim Ung-so. At nearby Pophung monastery, meanwhile, 4,200 monk-soldiers led by the revered monk Hyujong, "Great Master of the Western Mountain," were assembled and ready to march.[12] The allied force of Chinese and Korean soldiers poised to attack Pyongyang thus totaled approximately 58,000 fighting men. They would be armed with arrows and swords and light cannons, but few muskets. In the coming battle they would face 15,000 highly experienced Japanese troops, well equipped with muskets but possessing few cannons.[13]

The Japanese defenders holed up in Pyongyang remained unaware of this gathering storm until it was almost upon them—which was exactly what Commander Li had planned. While en route south from Uiju, Li sent a message ahead to the Japanese stating that official Ming envoys were on their way to Pyongyang to continue with the next phase of peace negotiations. It was of course a ruse, but Konishi did not see through it. With Korean guerrilla activity having deprived him of virtually all his native spies, and in turn of any intelligence of what was going on beyond the walls of Pyongyang, he could only conclude that Shen Weijing's shuttle diplomacy had borne fruit. The news of the approaching envoys was greeted with delight by Konishi and his comrades, and prompted the monk Genso to write a poem heralding the coming peace:

> Japan has ceased fighting and China has surrendered.
> Kyushu and the four seas will now become one family.
> The spirit of happiness will melt the snows.
> In the coming spring, the flower of peace will bloom.[14]

Eager to reach a settlement so that they could all go home, Konishi sent a party of twenty men north to greet the Ming envoys and escort them into the city. Most of the men did not return. One version of events has it that they were welcomed by Shen Weijing at Sunan and the two sides sat down to a banquet. Then, when the conviviality was at its height, the Japanese were surrounded and attacked and all but three were killed.[15] According to a second version, the Japanese escort was simply ambushed on the road.[16] In any event a handful of survivors managed to race back to Pyongyang and raise the alarm, awakening Konishi at last to the fact that there would be no peace settlement with the Chinese, but only a bloody war. For the men of Kyushu under his command, cold and hungry, sick of battle and far from home, the dominant reaction was likely despair.

February 5, 1593. The great allied army of Chinese and Korean soldiers, a force of nearly sixty thousand men, arrived in the vicinity of Pyongyang, "the flat place," and proceeded to set up camp on the frozen ground north of the city. The spirits of the men were high; they were eager to rush the walls with their vastly superior numbers and teach the Japanese a lesson. The sight of this multitude and their tens of thousands of horses must have sent a wave of foreboding through the ranks of Konishi's men, a grim realization that for the first time in the Korean campaign the odds were stacked heavily against them. They nonetheless managed to make a good show of their defiance, lining the walls in their thousands, shouting, firing their guns, sounding horns and beating drums and generally making as much noise as they could. Inside the city behind them Konishi Yukinaga prepared for what he knew would be a hard-fought battle. Two thousand-man units were assigned to each of the four gates where attacks would probably come: the Chilsong Gate on the north, the Potong Gate on the west, and the two gates piercing the wall on the south. He would hold the rest of his force in the center of the city as a mobile reserve.[17]

There were not supposed to be any Korean civilians still residing in the area. Ten days earlier, in his meeting with King Sonjo at Uiju, Commander in Chief Li Rusong had recommended that a message be sent ahead calling for the evacuation of the city and its environs, for once the fighting started no distinction would be made between Korean and Japanese. Everyone would be killed. King Sonjo agreed to do so.[18] Now, encamped outside Pyongyang, Li Rusong gave any Koreans still in the vicinity one last chance to remove themselves to safety, erecting a white flag with the following words written upon it: "We will kill everyone except those Koreans who surrender now and come under this flag." The annals make no mention of anyone coming forward.[19]

The battle began the following day with an attack by Hyujong's monk-soldiers against the walled temple complex of Yongmyongsa on Moranbong hill commanding the northern approaches to the city. It was occupied by one thousand enemy troops under Matsuura Shigenobu. So long as Moranbong remained in Japanese hands, the allied Chinese-Korean force would be vulnerable to counterattack from the rear. It was thus essential that it be taken. Li Rusong assigned Hyujong's monk-soldiers to the task because they were more experienced in mountain warfare than his own men and the Korean regulars, and had the patriotism and determination necessary to succeed with an uphill attack against withering opposition. The monks did not let him down. The fight for Moranbong raged for two days and nights and claimed the lives of more than six hundred of Hyujong's men. Finally, with Chinese troops under Wu Weichong providing support from the west, Matsuura and his surviving men were forced to fall back to Pyongyang.[20]

With Moranbong taken, the main assault on the city could begin.

Early in the morning of February 8 Li Rusong held a ceremony with
burning incense to ensure that the omens were good. They evidently
were. After his men had eaten breakfast, he ordered them to fall into
line and led them south to attack Pyongyang. They advanced slowly out
of camp, their closely packed ranks "looking like the scales on a fish,"
the hooves of the horses pulverizing the ice on the road into a multitude
of tiny crystals that rose into the air like a haze and sparkled in the sun.
As they drew near the city they could see the Japanese lined up along
the walls to meet them. They had adorned the ramparts with colored
banners and sharpened spikes, and now exposed the blades of their
swords menacingly for the advancing Chinese and Korean soldiers to
see. The allies then fanned out around the city, the central Ming column
under Yang Yuan and Zhang Shijue taking the north and the west, the
left column under Li Rusong's younger brother Li Rubo the southeast,
and the Koreans under Yi Il and Kim Ung-so the southwest. (The city's
east wall bordered the Taedong River and thus was not approached.)

When all the units were in position a cannon was fired to signal the
attack. Chinese and Korean archers went to work setting the buildings
of the city ablaze with their fire arrows while the gunners began
pounding the gates with cannonballs. While this was going on scaling
ladders were brought forward and wave after wave of men surged up
the walls. It was hard going through a hail of musket balls and arrows
and stones, then over the sharpened spikes that bristled along the top of
the wall. During the course of the morning's fighting these defenses
proved too much for the allies, and their assault gradually petered out.
Commander in Chief Li Rusong, observing that his soldiers were losing
spirit, rode up near the wall, lopped off the head of a man who was
attempting to retreat and carried the object lesson from unit to unit for
everyone to see. Then he shouted, "Five thousand liang of silver to the
first man over the wall!"

Driven forward by the threat of execution and the promise of
reward, the allied troops roused themselves for a renewed assault. Ming
commander Wu Weichong, leading his men from the front, was
wounded in the chest, and another had his feet crushed by a large stone
dropped from above. But the attacking forces did not falter. Finally a
handful of men managed to claw their way up to the top of the wall

and, after fierce hand-to-hand fighting, cleared an opening on the parapets for their comrades to follow. At about the same time the Chilsong (Seven Star) Gate gave way to the incessant pounding of cannons, leaving a gaping hole through which the Chinese and Koreans could flood into Pyongyang.

The Japanese had already made preparations for this breach in their defenses. When it became clear that the city's outer perimeter could no longer be held, they pulled back from the walls and into their last line of defense, an earth and log fort previously constructed in the tight northern corner formed by Pyongyang's triangular wall. The Chinese and Koreans, seeing that resistance had ceased along the ramparts, poured into the city through the breached gate, thinking they had the battle nearly won. The Japanese, however, were not done yet. As the allied attackers pressed forward toward the rough inner fortress, a jostling mass of horses and soldiers and banners and flags, Konishi's men leveled their muskets through the hundreds of loopholes that pierced their barricades and began to fire. The result was a slaughter. Barrage after barrage of lead balls and arrows tore into the closely packed ranks of the Chinese and Koreans, leaving hundreds dead and dying and throwing the rest into a panicked retreat back through the smashed Seven Star Gate and out of the city.[21]

That was the end of the Battle of Pyongyang. Li Rusong sounded the gong signaling a withdrawal and returned with his men to their camp north of the city to pass the night, leaving a guard of mainly Korean troops behind to watch over the Japanese holed up in their fort. Li had breached the walls as planned, but had sustained heavy losses in doing so, and still had not defeated the enemy within. On the contrary, with the Japanese now cornered and their firepower concentrated, it would take the sacrifice of hundreds if not thousands more Chinese and Korean attackers to complete the job and snuff them out. Anxious to avoid such a costly second round, Li sent a message to his opponent Konishi Yukinaga, offering him the chance to evacuate the city without a fight. "My army is quite sufficient to annihilate you to the last man," he wrote. "But I do not wish to kill so many. I will therefore leave a way open for you to withdraw. Take it, and leave at once."

It was an offer the pragmatic Konishi could not refuse. The first day's fighting had cost him as many as twenty-three hundred casualties, a loss his already depleted numbers could not bear. A large portion of his supplies had also been captured. When the Chinese and the Koreans attacked again, he and his men might be able to hold out for a morning, a day, perhaps two or three. But no amount of courage could resist the onslaught of fifty thousand men. Ultimately the Japanese defenses would fall and, as Li had said, everyone would be killed. Konishi thus wrote back to the Ming commander, "We will withdraw. See that our way is not blocked." Li agreed, and issued orders to the Koreans to let the Japanese army leave the city unmolested. The evacuation took place later that night, Konishi's men silently filing out of Pyongyang through its southern gate, crossing the frozen Taedong River and marching south on the road to Seoul.[22] "Wounded men were abandoned," samurai chronicler Yoshino Jingozaemon writes, "while those who were not wounded but simply exhausted crawled almost prostrate along the road."[23]

The retaking of Pyongyang was bittersweet for the Koreans. They had reclaimed their city as intended, but the victory had not really been their own: with the arrival of Ming commander Li Rusong and his army, native troops under Yi Il and Kim Ung-so had been reduced to mere helpers. Li also was clearly not committed to destroying the Japanese invaders, but was intent only on driving them away from China and back toward the south. His decision to allow Konishi and his men to leave Pyongyang without a fight must have frustrated the Koreans immensely, for they were thirsting for revenge for what the Japanese had done. There was even talk that Li had accepted a bribe from Konishi in exchange for allowing him and his men to retreat.[24] The inevitably bad conduct of the Ming troops was also becoming an aggravation. In the Battle of Pyongyang the Chinese made little distinction between Japanese soldiers and Korean civilians when it came to killing "enemies" and claiming their heads—just as Li Rusong had warned King Sonjo would be the case. News of these abuses found its way to Beijing and resulted in the sending of an official to Korea to investigate. Nothing came of it, however, for in the end the outraged Koreans declined to press the matter for fear of offending Commander in Chief Li.[25]

This Ming official sent to Korea was also charged with looking into the suspiciously high enemy casualty figures that Li and his civilian superior, Song Yingchang, had reported to Beijing. According to Song's report, the Japanese lost 16,047 men in the fighting, plus 10,000 others who burned to death in the fires that scorched the city, plus numerous others who were taken captive. Enemy losses were so extreme, Song bragged, that scarcely a tenth of the troops defending the city were able to escape.[26] As with the accusations of civilian killings, nothing came of the charges of exaggeration leveled against Li, although had the Ming official bothered to check with the Koreans he would have found that there had been no more than 15,000 Japanese stationed at Pyongyang, and that their losses may have been as low as 1,285.[27] This episode is but one of many examples of how the Korean historical record of the Imjin War is decidedly more accurate and more reliable than the records kept by the Ming Chinese. The Chinese were prone to exaggeration in ways that the Koreans were not, primarily because they had so much to prove. Their country, after all, was the Middle Kingdom, the most important nation in the world as they saw it, and as such could not afford to be seen as weak in any way. So we read of the emperor threatening to send a million-man army against the Japanese, when in fact the empire had only forty thousand-odd troops to spare. And so we find Ming commanders inflating victories at times to staggering proportions, for it was an easy step from exaggeration for the good of the nation to exaggeration for personal honors and rewards.

It took Konishi Yukinaga and his first contingent nine terrible days to retreat from Pyongyang to Seoul. After an exhausting day's march they arrived at the first fort on the road to the south only to find it abandoned; the garrison commander had assumed they had been destroyed and had already withdrawn his force. And so Konishi's men were forced to keep moving, without food or rest or a fire for warmth. The Koreans urged Li Rusong to lead his army in an immediate pursuit to cut them down before they reached the safety of the capital. The Ming general demurred. If the Koreans were so eager to attack, he said, echoing Shen Weijing's earlier comment made to Yun Gun-su, they were welcome to do so on their own. In the end neither of the allies made a move to pursue and Konishi and his men were allowed to straggle back to Seoul unmolested, evacuating all remaining garrisons en route. They arrived on February 17, exhausted, starving, and suffering horribly from frostbite. According to Yoshino Jingozaemon, "The only clothes they had were the garments worn under their armour, and even men who were normally gallant resembled scarecrows on the mountains and fields because of their fatigue, and were indistinguishable from the dead."[28]

While it would seem that Li Rusong was not overly eager to do battle with the Japanese, this was not the only reason why he was slow to pursue them after their withdrawal from Pyongyang. A more important consideration was the matter of supplies: food for his tens of thousands of horses and more than forty thousand men. The supplies that the Chinese had brought with them, coupled with the stocks that the Koreans had provided them in the far north, had got the Ming army as far as Pyongyang. But these were now nearly exhausted; more would have to be arranged before any further advance could be made. Li Rusong thus held his army in place for five days after the Battle of Pyongyang, giving National High Commissioner Yu Song-nyong, the Korean official charged with overseeing military affairs, time to race ahead to arrange the necessary food stores and horse fodder along the main road to Seoul. During these frantic days Yu was at times just a few hours behind the retreating Japanese, slogging through muddy roads churned up by the passage of their horses and men. Once again the official secured all that was needed and the great Ming army was able to resume its advance.[29]

As Li Rusong led his army south from Pyongyang he was pleased to find that the Japanese had evacuated all their garrisons along the road to Seoul. When he reached Kaesong, the main city and strongest fortification on the way to the capital, and found it too abandoned, the Ming commander began to feel very confident indeed, for it seemed he now had the Japanese well and truly on the run. His army marched into the city on February 19, the division under his younger brother, Li Rubo, leading the way through the gates. A halt was made here for a few days to rest the men, with the Koreans once again raising a chorus of protests for them to press on. Then the march was resumed to the Imjin River. After crossing this obstacle, the Ming and Korean allies established their camp at Paju, forty-five kilometers north of Seoul.[30]

By this time the order to fall back to Seoul had reached second contingent leader Kato Kiyomasa at Anbyon on the border of the remote northeastern province of Hamgyong. Kato, in his own mind the most daring and successful of all the daimyo commanders in Korea, was not eager to comply, for it meant abandoning all he thought he had achieved in Hamgyong to support his less able comrades in the south. The local situation, however, was not as rosy as Kato claimed. By the beginning of 1593 the citizens of Hamgyong, who had been so compliant the previous year, had become unruly and ungovernable, with guerrilla attacks increasingly common. There was also the Chinese army to consider. The farther south it advanced, first to Pyongyang, then to Kaesong, and then across the Imjin River toward Seoul, the greater the danger became that Kato and his men would be cut off in the north.

News of this looming peril was brought to Kato by an envoy sent from Pyongyang by Ming commander Li Rusong, together with an order that he surrender with all his troops. But Kato was not the surrendering type. By way of an answer he had one of his Korean captives, a young woman reputed to be the most beautiful in the kingdom, tied to a tree, and then with the Ming envoy looking on he impaled her with a spear. With this demonstration of Kato's determination in hand, the Ming envoy turned about and headed west to make his report. Kato and Nabeshima Naoshige, meanwhile, began the long march to Seoul. They left Anbyon in a rainstorm on February 22, the Korean princes Sunhwa and Imhae in tow.

The journey must have been hard. The second contingent had more than two hundred kilometers of rugged mountain wilderness to cross in the freezing cold, and were harried along the way by bands of guerrillas. No major engagements took place, but the constant strain must have deprived Kato's men of sleep at night, and left them constantly fearful throughout the day of falling behind or being separated from the group. There were freezing streams to ford, and raging torrents that could only be traversed by cutting down trees and floating across, immersed in the ice-cold water. Despite these difficulties, Kato and Nabeshima managed to get their contingent south in good order, arriving at Seoul on the first of March to bring the total forces congregated there to fifty-three thousand.[31]

While this consolidation in Seoul of Japanese forces was taking place, one unit stubbornly remained encamped fifteen kilometers north of the capital, its leader refusing to fall back within the safety of the city walls. He was Kobayakawa Takakage, the feisty old commander of the sixth contingent. Kobayakawa, it will be recalled, had spearheaded the failed attempt the previous year to subdue the southwestern province of Cholla. After this, in October, he had been redeployed north to garrison the city of Kaesong, the main town on the road between Pyongyang and Seoul. With the tide of the invasion having turned by the beginning of 1593, Kobayakawa was ordered to evacuate Kaesong and pull his forces back to Seoul. He refused. He disagreed with the decision to retreat, viewing it as an indication of both lack of resolve and lack of experience among the leadership of the Korean campaign. During Konishi's retreat from Pyongyang, the remaining garrisons along the main road to the capital were evacuated. But still Kobayakawa would not move. It finally took a personal visit from Otani Yoshitsugu, one of the three commissioners assigned to oversee operations in Korea, to persuade the commander to withdraw his forces, and then only after Otani agreed to grant Kobayakawa the lead in what was regarded as the coming decisive battle with the Chinese.

By this point the Chinese and Korean allied army was on the verge of entering Kaesong. Kobayakawa managed to get his troops clear of the city only hours ahead of the advancing enemy and back across the Imjin River to the vicinity of Seoul. But even then he refused to enter the capital itself, choosing instead to camp alongside the main road fifteen kilometers to the north. As he explained to his annoyed colleagues who rode up to urge him to move his troops back, "You have always been under the great Taiko (Hideyoshi), who has been ever victorious. You know nothing of defeat, and consequently nothing of how to turn defeat into victory. But that's an old experience with me; so leave this matter in my hands. There is a vast difference between our numbers and the enemy's. Suppose we do win one or two battles; they will yet keep pestering us like so many swarms of flies. Unless it is a life-and-death fight, these fellows won't be cowed. We've gone back far enough; now is the time to seek life in the midst of death."[32]

And so Kobayakawa sat down to await the arrival of the Chinese, and with them what he believed would be the decisive battle, the *tenno-zan*, that would turn the course of the war back in their favor. The place he had chosen to camp was near the first rest station along the main road north from Seoul. It was called Pyokje.[33]

It was now February 27. At his camp at Paju just south of the Imjin River, Commander in Chief Li Rusong's confidence was running high. He had forced the Japanese out of Pyongyang, driven them back along the main road south, taken Kaesong without a fight—and now, he hoped, was on the verge of capturing Seoul. To begin the final phase of the advance on the capital, he sent a party of three thousand men on ahead under Ming commander Zha Dashou and Korean general Ko On-baek as the rest of his forces slowly geared up to follow. In the vicinity of the rest station at Pyokje, fifteen kilometers north of Seoul, Zha and Ko came upon a lightly armed unit of Japanese and gave them a severe mauling. Initial reports put the number of enemy heads taken at six hundred;[34] the actual figure was probably much lower. Upon receiving word of this, Commander Li raced ahead of his main army with just one thousand cavalrymen, evidently expecting to win an easy victory against what he assumed was a weak and demoralized foe.

The omens were against Li Rusong from the start. As he drew near Pyokje, where Zha and Ko had scored their victory, he was thrown from his horse and sustained a cut on his face. Things seemed to brighten shortly thereafter when his men spotted a small and apparently isolated party of Japanese soldiers watching them from the slopes of a nearby hill. Li divided his cavalry into two groups and charged to the attack, chasing the fleeing Japanese up the hill and down into a long, narrow valley beyond—and straight into the bulk of the Japanese army.

Kobayakawa Takakage himself stood at the fore. He commanded 20,000 men, drawn mostly from his sixth contingent, divided into four groups. They had recently been joined by four units of reinforcements sent north from Seoul under the overall direction of young Ukita

Hideie, bringing the total Japanese presence at Pyokje to 41,000 men.[35]
Li Rusong and his cavalry were at first hopelessly outnumbered and in
desperate peril. Li himself was very nearly killed when one of Kobayakawa's officers closed with him, but was spared at the last moment
when one of his commanders sacrificed his life to save him.

Before Commander Li's force could be totally annihilated, General
Yang Yuan hurried to the rescue with the main body of the Ming army,
bringing the Chinese forces to 20,000 men. The fighting now took on
epic proportions, a total of 61,000 combatants crowding the narrow
valley, the Japanese unable to put their muskets to good use in the great
push and shove, the Ming cavalry for their part bogged down by mud
and deprived of space, forced to dismount and fight on foot. The outcome of the battle was thus determined mainly by swords in hand-to-
hand combat, the short, straight, double-edged stabbing weapons of the
Chinese against the gently curving, single-edged Japanese katana, sharp
enough to cut through bone. The battle raged from ten o'clock in the
morning till noon, until the superior numbers and weapons of the
Japanese forced Li Rusong and his army to begin to fall back. The
fighting continued up the pass on the road north to Paju, the Japanese
making better use of their musket squads now, the Chinese leaving a
trail of dead bodies behind. Finally, with the onset of darkness,
Kobayakawa ceased his pursuit and led his men back to Seoul, reportedly returning with 6,000 Ming heads.[36]

Li Rusong downplayed the disaster at Pyokje in his subsequent
report to the Koreans, leaving them with the impression that only a few
hundred men had been lost. The true figure was much higher, although
perhaps not as high as the Japanese claimed. In any case the debacle
took all the fight out of Li and his generals. They had now had a good
taste of combat against the Japanese, fighting them behind walls at
Pyongyang and on open ground at Pyokje, and wanted nothing more to
do with them. The Koreans, led by High Commissioner Yu Song-
nyong, urged Li to press on with his southern advance and try again to
retake Seoul. Li refused. It was not that he was discouraged by recent
setbacks, he explained. The problem was the weather. With the rains
having left the ground too muddy for battle, it would be better to fall
back and rest his men and wait for conditions to improve before

attempting any further advance. He accordingly withdrew with his army first to the Imjin, then back across the river to Kaesong.

In his report to Beijing Li made it clear that he had no intention of attacking the Japanese in Seoul, no matter how dry the ground or how rested his men. There were more than 200,000 enemy troops in the capital, he claimed, far too many for his meager forces to defeat. (The actual figure was between fifty and sixty thousand.) The terrain in Korea would remain too wet for fighting throughout the summer season. An epidemic was sweeping through his ranks. There was dissension among his officers. And Li himself was sick and no longer fit to command, due perhaps to the fall he had taken from his horse. It would be best, he concluded, if someone were appointed to replace him.[37]

In the days that followed, additional reasons presented themselves to Li Rusong that served only to firm his resolve not to stay and fight. First, the Japanese had burned the grass off most of the fields in the vicinity of Seoul, leaving the Ming cavalry when they arrived with no fodder for their horses. The situation was so critical that ten thousand horses died within just a few days, worn out from the journey south and the fighting, and now with no pastures in which to graze and recover their strength. Then word arrived that Kato Kiyomasa was marching toward Pyongyang from his area of operations in the northeast. This was not true. Kato was making straight for Seoul. The false report nevertheless provided Li, whether he believed it or not, with an excuse to retreat all the way back to Pyongyang, ostensibly to protect the city from Japanese counterattack, and so prevent his army from being caught between Japanese forces to the north and the south.

The Koreans, having placed so much hope in China's "celestial army," must have been beside themselves with frustration as they watched Li and his men turn away from Seoul and fall back to the north.

Seoul by this point was a smoldering ghost town, with scores of corpses lying unattended in the streets. In the early hours of February 24 local citizens had started a number of fires in an attempt to assist with what they hoped was their imminent liberation. The Japanese garrisoning the city had responded with terrible ferocity. Prior to marching north to join Kobayakawa, they massacred every Korean man they could lay their hands on to preempt further uprisings occurring while they were away. The only men reported to have escaped the slaughter were those who disguised themselves in women's clothing. Large areas of the city were also burned, in part in retaliation, in part to deprive Chinese and Korean troops of cover when they eventually arrived and laid siege to the place. The city was therefore further depopulated as women and children, their homes destroyed, fled into the countryside in search of shelter.[38]

This was the city that the victors at Pyokje returned to, a once great capital of culture and refinement, now reduced to little more than a blackened walled enclosure. In such grim surroundings elation over the mauling they had given the Chinese could not have lasted long. The battle, after all, had cost them considerable casualties. It also promised to be only the first round in a long, drawn-out fight, for the Chinese would certainly be back. The question thus arose among the Japanese commanders: should they remain in the capital and await a second Chinese attack? Or should they retreat to the south? Kato Kiyomasa, just back from Hamgyong Province, joined Kobayakawa Takakage in opposing the idea of retreat on principle alone; now was the time to stand and fight, they argued, and show the Ming what Japanese warriors were really made of. The pragmatic Konishi Yukinaga and others were less eager to risk their lives to prove such a point. The option of retreat, however, was by no means without risk, for it meant abandoning the relative safety of the walls of the capital and taking to the open road, where they would be vulnerable to attack.

Indeed, although the Ming army had retired to Pyongyang, the Japanese in Seoul were now surrounded on all sides by native Korean troops, guerrillas, and monk-soldiers, and were thus unable to venture into the surrounding countryside in anything but large, well-armed groups. Several companies of Korean government soldiers still remained to the north, forces under Commander in Chief Kim Myong-won at the Imjin River, General Yi Bin at Paju, and Generals Ko On-baek and Yi Si-on at Haeyu Pass.[39] Twenty kilometers to the west at Chasong, a force of one thousand monk-soldiers attacked a Japanese unit and, at a cost of nearly half their number, succeeded in driving them back within the city walls. Two thousand monks under Yujong achieved similar results ten kilometers to the northeast at Surak-san, driving the Japanese garrison there back into Seoul and claiming the mountain for themselves. A third contingent of six hundred monks made an attack at Ichon in the southeast, again suffering heavy losses, but again driving the Japanese back into the capital.[40]

And at Haengju to the west lay the biggest thorn of all: twenty-three hundred Koreans under Cholla Province Army Commander Kwon Yul, holed up in a wooden stockade on a bluff overlooking the Han River.

Kwon Yul was a fifty-five-year-old civil servant of middling rank from a family of note in Kyongsang Province. Before the war he had served, on Yu Song-nyong's recommendation, as magistrate of Uiju on Korea's border with China, and later as magistrate of Kwangju in the southwestern province of Cholla. Immediately following Hideyoshi's invasion he raised troops in the Kwangju region and led them north in a failed attempt to halt the Japanese advance before it reached Seoul. He then returned south and participated in the defense of Cholla Province, which the sixth contingent of the Japanese army under Kobayakawa Takakage was threatening to overrun. Kwon distinguished himself by defeating Japanese units in two engagements, the Battles of Ungchi and Ichi, in the second week of August. Recognizing his ability, the government appointed him army commander of Cholla Province in the following month.

By this time Kwon had come to the conclusion that the Japanese were too skilled in warfare to be defeated on open ground, and that the Koreans should therefore fall back on their traditional strength of fighting from behind walls.[41] He would make his first attempt at this in October of 1592 from a base at Toksan, a mountain redoubt two days' march south of the capital, overlooking the main road from Pusan to Seoul. From an ancient Paekche dynasty fortress that they strengthened and enlarged, Kwon and his men attacked enemy foraging parties and small units passing along the road and generally proved troublesome enough that the Japanese high command in Seoul sent a company south to besiege the fortress. The effort, we are told, was soon abandoned. According to one report, Kwon fooled the Japanese into giving up and returning to Seoul by having a horse rubbed down with rice grains until its coat sparkled in the sun. To the Japanese watching in the distance it appeared that the animal had just been washed, a sign that the Koreans within had ample stores of water to withstand a lengthy siege.[42]

Early in 1593 Kwon Yul led his men farther north in preparation for the anticipated allied attack on Seoul. Incorporating a unit of monk-soldiers under the priest Choyong into his ranks, he set to work strengthening a dilapidated fortress on a hill outside the village of Haengju on the north bank of the Han River ten kilometers west of the capital. It was a highly defensible position, protected at its rear by a steep drop-off down to the Han. If an attack came, it would have to be made uphill and from the north, straight into the Koreans' concentrated fire.

With the retreat of the Ming army, Kwon Yul's fortress at Haengju emerged as the greatest immediate threat to the Japanese in Seoul. On March 14 they decided to do something about it. Some hours before dawn, the west gate of the city was opened and a long line of troops filed out and turned toward Haengju, marching along the north bank of the Han to the accompaniment of drums and horns and gongs. The daimyo on horseback in the lead constituted an all-star cast from the Korean campaign. There was Konishi Yukinaga, leader of the first contingent that had spearheaded the invasion, recently back in Seoul after the retreat from Pyongyang. There were third contingent leader Kuroda Nagamasa, and Kobayakawa Takakage, hero of the Battle of Pyokje. There were Hideyoshi's adopted son Ukita Hideie, the young supreme commander of all Japanese forces in Korea, and the veteran Ishida Mitsunari, one of the overseers sent from Nagoya to help him. Accompanying them were more than half the troops garrisoning Seoul, a total of thirty thousand men.[43]

The twenty-three hundred Korean troops and monk-soldiers within Haengju fortress, crowded together with thousands of civilians who had fled their villages to seek shelter within the walls, watched the noisy approach of this enemy multitude with growing trepidation. When the Japanese arrived at the base of their hill in the soft light of dawn, the Koreans observed that each soldier had a red-and-white banner affixed to his back, and that many wore masks carved with fierce depictions of animals and monsters and ghosts. Panic was now hovering just beneath the surface, held in check by the calm authority of Commander Kwon Yul. As the Japanese busied themselves below with their pre-battle preparations, he ordered his men to have a meal. There would be no telling when they would have a chance to eat again.

The battle began shortly after dawn. The Japanese, so numerous that they could not all rush at the ramparts at once, divided into groups and prepared to take turns in the assault. Their strength must have seemed overwhelming to the Koreans. For once, however, the muskets of the Japanese were of only limited use, for in having to fire uphill they were unable to effectively target the defenders holed up within. Their lead balls simply flew in an arc over the fort and into the Han River beyond. The advantage was with the Koreans, firing down upon the attacking Japanese with arrows and stones and anything else that came to hand. They had a number of gunpowder weapons as well, including several large chongtong cannons and a rank of *hwacha* (fire carts), box-shaped devices built onto wagons that fired up to one hundred gunpowder-propelled arrows in a single devastating barrage. Alongside these more traditional weapons was an oddity that employed a spinning wheel mechanism to hurl a fusillade of stones. It was called the *sucha sokpo*, the "water wheel rock cannon."

Konishi Yukinaga's group led the Japanese assault. Kwon Yul waited until they were within range, then beat his commander's drum three times to signal the attack. Every Korean weapon was fired at once, bows, chongtong, hwacha, and rock cannons, raking Konishi's ranks and driving his men back. Ishida Mitsunari was the next to the attack. His force too was driven back, and Ishida himself was injured. Next up was Kuroda Nagamasa, the Christian commander of the third contingent, otherwise known by his baptismal name Damien. He had been thwarted once before by Koreans fighting behind walls, at the Battle of Yonan the previous year. This time he took a more cautious approach, positioning musketeers atop makeshift towers so that they could fire into the fortress while the rest of his force held back. A fierce exchange of fire ensued; then Kuroda's men too were forced to retreat.

The Japanese had now attacked Haengju three times and had failed even to penetrate the fortress's outer palisade of stakes. Young Ukita Hideie, determined to make a breakthrough in his, the fourth charge, managed to smash a hole in the obstacle and got near the inner wall. Then he was wounded and had to fall back, leaving a trail of casualties behind. The next unit to attack, Kikkawa Hiroie's, poured through the gap Ukita's forces had opened and was soon attacking Haengju's inner wall, the last line of defense between the Japanese and Kwon Yul's troops. The fighting now was at arm's length, with masked warriors attempting to slash their way past the defenders lining the barricades, while the Koreans fought back with everything they had—swords, spears, arrows, stones, boiling water, even handfuls of ashes thrown into the attackers' eyes. As the fighting reached its peak no sound came from Kwon Yul's drum. The Korean commander had abandoned drumstick and tradition in favor of his sword and was now fighting alongside his men. At one point the Japanese heaped dried grass along the base of Haengju's log walls and tried to set them ablaze. The Koreans doused the flames with water before they could take hold. In the seventh attack led by Kobayakawa Takakage, the Japanese knocked down some of the log pilings and opened a hole in the fortress's inner wall. The Koreans managed to hold them back long enough for the logs to be repositioned.

As the afternoon wore on the Korean defenders grew exhausted and their supply of arrows dwindled dangerously low. The women within the fort are said to have gathered stones in their wide skirts to supply the men along the walls. This traditional type of skirt is still known as a *Haengju chima* (Haengju skirt) in remembrance of this day. But stones alone were not enough to repel the Japanese for long. Then, when all seemed lost, Korean naval commander Yi Bun arrived on the Han River at the rear of the fortress with two ships laden with ten thousand arrows. With these the defenders of Haengju were able to continue the fight until sundown, successfully repelling an eighth attack, then a ninth.[44]

Finally, as the sun dipped below the horizon out beyond the Yellow Sea, the fighting petered out and did not resume. The Japanese had suffered too many casualties to continue. Their dead numbered into the many hundreds, and their wounded, including three important commanders, Ukita Hideie, Ishida Mitsunari, and Kikkawa Hiroie, were many times more. They had in fact been dealt a terrible defeat, the most serious loss on land so far at the hands of the Koreans. Throughout the evening the survivors gathered what bodies they could, heaped them into piles, and set them alight. Then they turned around and walked back to Seoul. One Japanese officer in the disheartened assembly would later liken the scene beside the Han River that day to the *sanzu no kawa*, the "river of hell."[45]

When they were gone, Kwon Yul and his men came out and recovered those bodies that the Japanese had been unable to retrieve, cut them into pieces, and hung them from the log palings of their fort. These grisly trophies were an indication of how much had changed for the Koreans since the beginning of the war, of how the previous ten months had transformed them from shell-shocked, indecisive "long sleeves" into bloodthirsty warriors, bent on revenge. The Japanese would not be able to hold their ground for long against such grim determination, not with their dwindling numbers and growing problems with supplies. Hemmed in by a foe of evidently growing strength, willing to endure enormous hardship and loss to drive them out, the withdrawal of the Japanese from Seoul became certain, with or without the intervention of the Ming Chinese.

Sooner or later, Hideyoshi's troops would have to march south.

CHAPTER 18

Seoul Retaken

SPRING—ARGUABLY THE MOST BEAUTIFUL SEASON IN KOREA. After a harsh winter of ice and snow and cold north winds, the warming weather and first green shoots come as a welcome relief. Clusters of cosmos rise up long-stemmed from the earth, painting country lanes across the land in pastel shades of lavender and pink. The forsythia bloom, and the magnolia trees too, their white flowers so smooth and creamy they look good enough to eat. The farmers head back to their fields to begin another cycle of planting and promise, while yangban gentlemen look on with pen in hand from their shaded stoops, trying to encapsulate in a few choice lines the sublimity of it all.

The spring of 1593 was different. Korea was now into its second year of war, and for many of its citizens the world as they knew it had come to an end. Cities and towns lay in ruins from Pusan to Pyongyang. Families were scattered, children abandoned, the weak and the elderly left behind. Refugees, driven either by the loss of their homes or terror of the Japanese, wandered from place to place in search of food. But there was little for them to find, for fields had been abandoned throughout the land, and cultivation had almost ceased. Starvation gripped the peninsula, and soon a full-fledged famine.

The Japanese army was suffering as well. The long, cold winter, so much harsher than anything the men of Kyushu, Shikoku, and western Honshu had experienced before, had taken its toll through exposure, frostbite, and fatigue. Garrisons throughout the country were chronically short of food. Little could be sent from Japan due to the blockade of the Korean navy, while guerrilla activity made it increasingly dangerous for foraging parties to venture into the countryside in search of food. At garrisons from Pusan to Seoul, Japanese soldiers were hungry and disheartened, and wanted to go home.

The situation was nowhere worse than in the capital of Seoul, now the most northerly point on the peninsula occupied by the Japanese, connected to the south by a tenuously held corridor of territory along the main road. No fewer than 53,000 men were encamped there, no fewer than 53,000 mouths to feed. But food was running short. The situation became critical when a small unit of Chinese and Korean commandos launched a covert operation against the large warehouse complex at Yongsan, just south of the city wall on the banks of the Han River, and succeeded in burning it to the ground. The loss of grain suffered in this raid left the Japanese with food for less than a month and little choice but to commandeer grain from local citizens to keep themselves alive.[1]

In addition to the prospect of starvation, the Japanese in Seoul were also faced with a pestilence that was beginning to decimate their already depleted ranks, the spread of which was no doubt encouraged by the bloated corpses of civilians and livestock that had come to litter the streets. The Buddhist monk Zetaku, a member of second contingent daimyo Nabeshima Naoshige's entourage, recorded the following passage in his diary from these desperate days: "Although corpses of men, women, oxen and horses were piled up in the same place, no one bothered to bury them. The odor filled the heaven and the earth. We Japanese were obliged to stay under these circumstances from March to April [i.e., the third and fourth months of the lunar calendar]. The air became stale with the odor as the heat of the weather increased. Consequently, a great number of men came to be attacked by fever and died."[2]

At invasion headquarters at Nagoya, Toyotomi Hideyoshi received news of the stalled offensive with dissatisfaction. Not fully appreciating the difficulties facing his armies, he ascribed the lack of progress to lack of enthusiasm on the part of his commanders, and wrote urging them to shake off their inertia. In any event he himself would soon be crossing over to Korea to "take charge of everything personally, and then make a triumphal return."[3] Since postponing in July of 1592 his planned departure for the mainland, Hideyoshi had consistently spoken of the third month of 1593—April by the Western calendar—as the time when he would set sail, for he had been told that the seas between Kyushu and Pusan would be calm then and safe to cross. In early 1593 he sent two representatives ahead to Seoul to remind his field commanders of this, assuring them that he would soon be on his way with 200,000 reinforcements under such daimyo luminaries as Tokugawa Ieyasu, Asano Nagamasa, Gamo Ujisato, and Maeda Toshiie.

The arrival of Hideyoshi at the head of a 200,000-man army, so eagerly anticipated in the opening weeks of the war, was viewed with apprehension by the Japanese high command in March of 1593. On the twenty-ninth of the month Supreme Commander Ukita Hideie called a meeting of all the daimyo in Seoul to discuss their concerns. It was generally agreed that the dispatch of additional troops to Korea at this time would only exacerbate an already bad situation, for if they were unable to feed the men currently serving there, how could they accommodate an additional 200,000 mouths? A letter to the taiko was accordingly drafted and signed by all the daimyo present, asking him to delay his planned April crossing in light of the critical shortage of supplies. In Seoul, Hideyoshi was informed, troops were subsisting on gruel made from scraps of anything that could be found. They could hold out there at best until the middle of May. Supplies were also short in Pusan, where Hideyoshi proposed to land, and the prospects for obtaining more looked poor until the Korean harvest, such as it was, had ripened and could be commandeered some time later in the year.[4]

The back of the Korean invasion was now well and truly broken. Even Kobayakawa Takakage, one of the most hawkish daimyo in Korea, knew this, and signed his name on the letter to Hideyoshi. Kato Kiyomasa was persuaded to do likewise when he arrived in Seoul a few days later from his retreat out of the north. But what came next? They could not remain in Seoul indefinitely and wait for the situation to change. If they attempted to do so they would starve. There was only one practical course of action: they had to retreat to the south. First contingent commander Konishi Yukinaga accordingly sent a message north to Commander in Chief Li Rusong expressing a desire to negotiate a settlement. Li, who wanted exactly the same thing, replied with the demand that the Japanese evacuate Seoul and move their armies to the south. He would send envoy Shen Weijing down from Pyongyang to meet with them and work out the details.

Ukita, Konishi, Ishida, and the other daimyo in Seoul were forthcoming in their reports to Hideyoshi about the difficulties they were facing. As usual, however, the "facts" were reported in a way that would not upset the taiko. While the bad news of food shortages and stubborn local resistance was not kept from him, the overall situation was made to appear somewhat rosy by placing Ming China's willingness to negotiate at the fore. As Hideyoshi was led to understand it, the Chinese had been dealt a severe blow in the Battle of Pyokje and now were ready to negotiate a settlement and make concessions. But first the Japanese would have to pull their forces back toward Pusan as a show of good faith. Hideyoshi, ever willing to avoid a fight if his ends could be achieved by less costly means, thus gave his written authorization for the withdrawal, while still continuing to believe that some semblance of victory could be achieved in Korea and that China might yet be coerced into bowing to him.

King Sonjo and his Korean government in exile had by this time left Uiju on the Chinese border to begin what would turn out to be a six-month journey back to Seoul. In the middle of May they would arrive at Sukchon, fifty kilometers to the north of Pyongyang. In July they would move farther south to Kangso, a short distance to the west of the city, and in September on to Hwangju and then Haeju, halfway between Pyongyang and Seoul.[5]

Having now been relegated to the role of minor players in their own war, Sonjo and his ministers were kept in the dark by supreme Ming commander Li Rusong as to his true intentions. Most important, they were not informed that Li had decided after the debacle at Pyokje to avoid further battles and spare his troops, and that he was now intent on achieving the withdrawal of the Japanese from Korea through negotiation alone. The Koreans were certainly aware that Pyokje had shaken the Ming commander, and they could not help but notice as he retreated from Seoul all the way back to Pyongyang that he was reticent to meet the enemy in battle. The stakes were too high, however, for the Koreans to give up on this savior sent by the Celestial Throne. During the coming weeks and months they would continue to hope and to expect that Li would rouse himself again to action and lead his Chinese army in a renewed thrust south, dislodging the Japanese first from Seoul, then driving them back to Pusan and into the sea.

In anticipation of this coming rout, King Sonjo dispatched orders south to Cholla Left Navy Commander Yi Sun-sin to "intercept passage of the enemy retreating by sea and annihilate his . . . transports and war vessels."[6] If Yi could ambush and destroy the ships attempting to ferry the retreating Japanese back home from Pusan, the Koreans could still snatch the total victory that they so craved, the total destruction of every hated "robber" and "dwarf" who had had the temerity to set foot on their soil.

Yi Sun-sin received these orders on March 7. He put to sea the very next day, leading his battleships east into the channel between Koje Island and the coast, where he had beaten the Japanese navy in the Battle of Hansan-do in August of the previous year. Here he rendez-voused with the Kyongsang Right Navy under Won Kyun, a man that Yi was coming thoroughly to despise for his incompetence, cowardice, and love of drink. Soon after Yi arrived, Won launched into a tirade against Yi Ok-ki, the absent commander of the Cholla Right Navy. Where was Yi Ok-ki? Won wanted to know. Why was he late for the rendezvous? If he didn't appear soon Won would go ahead and lead his ships east to fight the Japanese by himself. Yi Sun-sin tried to calm his volatile colleague with assurances that Yi Ok-ki had farther to come than either of them, and that he would soon arrive. And sure enough, at noon the next day, the Cholla Right Navy hove into view—although Yi Sun-sin was disappointed to count fewer than forty ships.

For the next two days heavy rains kept the hundred-odd vessels of the combined Korean fleet riding at anchor in the sheltered channel off Koje Island. Then, as the weather cleared on March 12, they continued east to the waters between Kadok Island and the mainland where the Japanese, Kato Yoshiaki and Wakizaka Yasuharu among them, had established defenses and stationed ships to protect the approaches to Pusan. Here, Yi wrote in his dispatch to the throne, "we waited for the evacuation of the Japanese major units before the big drive of the Ming Chinese army."[7] For the next several days he sent small groups of vessels back and forth in full view of the enemy positions overlooking the channel at Ungchon, hoping to lure their ships into open water, near to where the bulk of the Korean navy, including at least two turtle ships, lay waiting. On the twentieth they had some luck: ten Japanese vessels took the bait and charged out of the neck of the inlet to attack, and were soon surrounded by the Korean navy. Yi's men "poured down arrows on the shrieking Japanese, who fell dead in countless numbers and had their heads cut off by the score."[8]

After that the Japanese at Ungchon became more cautious. They kept their ships moored close to shore at the head of the narrow inlet and their men ensconced in fortifications along the beach and in caves in the surrounding hills. Yi Sun-sin therefore decided to replace his traditional "lure into ambush" strategy with something more aggressive: a coordinated attack from both the sea and the land. He first contacted Kim Song-il, now high commissioner for Kyongsang Province, urging him to send government troops against enemy shore positions so that they would be driven onto their boats and out to sea, where Yi and his battleships could destroy them. (Kim, it will be recalled, was the vice-envoy of the Korean mission who came back from Japan in early 1592 assuring everyone that war would never come. He would become infected with plague and die in a little more than a month.) Kim replied that he was unable to oblige; he was too busy preparing for the arrival of the Chinese army and had few troops to spare. He instead offered the services of "Red Coat General" Kwak Jae-u and his small guerrilla army. This did not suit Yi's plans, so he instead went ahead and organized a combined land and sea operation with his own forces, replacing the idea of a land-based assault with an amphibious landing by groups of monk-soldiers and uibyong civilian volunteers under his command.[9]

For the next three days strong winds lashed the southern coast, forcing the Korean navy to shelter in a cove. Then, on the twenty-fourth, Commander Yi led his navy once again to the waters off Ungchon and put his planned operation into effect. Two groups of vessels filled with warrior-monks and civilian volunteers separated from the main fleet, one to the east and the other to the west, to make landings on either side of the Japanese positions. As expected, this threw the Japanese shore defenses into confusion and drew out a number of enemy ships from their inaccessible inlet anchorages to repel the invaders. Soon a large portion of the Japanese fleet lay exposed in open water, presenting Yi with the opportunity he had been waiting for. The order went out to lean to the oars and the Korean navy raced to the attack. While the bulk of Yi's battleships concentrated on the Japanese vessels milling about in the bay, blasting away with cannons and "giving them a terrible beating with wholesale slaughter," fifteen other ships made a run against those enemy vessels still riding at their moorings, burning them where they lay with showers of fire arrows. The land assault, meanwhile, came off without a hitch. "[O]ur valiant monk-soldiers jumped up with brandishing swords and thrusting spears and charged into the enemy positions, shooting guns and arrows from morning till night until the enemy fell back, leaving behind countless war dead and wounded." This land attack resulted in the release of five Korean prisoners of war, who reported that for the past month some sort of contagion had been sweeping through the Japanese camp—one more piece of good news to cap an already successful day.[10]

The day was not without setbacks for the Koreans. At one point two of Yi's battleships, their captains overeager to win honors, broke formation and darted forward to attack only to collide with each other, capsizing one, seriously damaging the other, and causing several deaths. For Yi, accustomed to inflicting heavy enemy losses at little or no cost to himself, the episode was mortifying. The captains of these two ships, Yi wrote in his dispatch to the throne, had forgotten one of the cardinal rules of battle: that too much disdain for the enemy can bring defeat just as surely as too much fear. But the fault, he concluded, was his own; it was due to his own lack of control.[11]

The day also brought yet another example of Kyongsang commander Won Kyun's unwillingness to fight. In his diary Yi wrote that when a Korean battleship came to be surrounded and attacked by Japanese vessels, Won Kyun and his nearby Kyongsang contingent made no attempt to help. "[He] looked the other way as if [he] did not notice the scene." Yi had words with Won after the battle about his "disgusting cowardice," but his colleague seemed to think nothing of it, and "showed no sense of disgrace."[12]

On April 5 Commanders Yi Sun-sin, Yi Ok-ki, and Won Kyun received word from the north that Commander in Chief Li Rusong had retreated back to Pyongyang, and that the southward push by the Chinese army would not be materializing as soon as they had expected.[13] This was disappointing news, for it meant that the Japanese would not take to their boats any time soon and attempt to return to Japan. The hoped-for decisive battle would therefore have to wait.

For the next month naval activity along Korea's southern coast virtually ceased. The Korean navy maintained its vigilance in the waters west of Pusan and ran down the occasional boat that unwittingly crossed its path. But no further attacks were launched against the Japanese holed up on shore and the ships they had secreted in sheltered coves and narrow inlets. To continue to target Japanese craft, Yi decided, would only deprive the enemy of a means of escape when the big Ming push finally came, and the Koreans in turn of the chance to send them all to the bottom of the sea.

On April 23 a small fishing boat was stopped in nearby waters and the two Japanese on board, a twenty-seven-year-old calling himself Sogoro who "could read and write a little," and a forty-four-year-old illiterate named Yosayemon, were arrested on suspicion of being spies. The two were brought before Yi Sun-sin, who interrogated them through an interpreter. This is what they said:

> We are natives of Izumo, Japan. On the 18th of this month [April 19] we put out to sea in a small boat for fishing and were caught while adrift before a storm. We don't know very much about the daily activity or the way of espionage of the Japanese soldiery, but we heard that an order arrived from the homeland for evacuation of the Japanese armed forces from Korea before Third Moon [April] regardless of victory or defeat, because during two years' stay in a foreign land the Japanese army suffered so many casualties. Therefore, the Japanese army here will go home as soon as its friendly battalions from the north will come to join it.

Commander Yi, finding their words "cunning and vague," had them tortured, but no additional information could be extracted. He then ordered their arms and legs torn from their bodies. Finally they were put out of their misery by having their heads chopped off.[14]

These long weeks of campaigning necessarily brought the three commanders of the Korean navy into close and constant contact. Yi Sun-sin welcomed this opportunity to spend time with his respected younger colleague and friend, Cholla Right Commander Yi Ok-ki. The two men met often on ship and shore to talk, eat, play chess, and compete at archery. Being around Kyongsang Right Commander Won Kyun, on the other hand, was for Yi Sun-sin a trial and aggravation. In his war diary he wrote witheringly of Won's incompetence as a commander, of his cowardice in the face of the enemy, of his "viciousness and malice," and of the constant drinking that made everything worse.[15] There was no one that Yi despised more who was not Japanese.

For Won, writhing in insecurity in the shadow of the more competent Yi, the feeling was mutual. The fact that his ranking superior had fewer years of military service than Won himself only heightened his resentment. It appears that he was not shy about venting his frustrations to those around him; this may have been what Yi was referring to in writing of Won's "viciousness and malice." Nor was the Kyongsang commander's pen idle. In his own dispatches to the throne he hinted that Yi was a coward, that he refused to follow orders and did not revere the king. In the factionalized Korean government there were plenty of officials willing to believe these accusations and file them away, for Yi Sun-sin owed his position to his childhood friend Yu Song-nyong, a leader of the ascendant Easterner faction. He was thus himself an Easterner if only by default, and in turn an enemy to every Westerner who walked the halls of power. Yi for the moment was relatively safe, for with a war on, factional strife had been for the most part subsumed by more immediate concerns for national survival. The Japanese, however, were now on the defensive, and it was beginning to look like peace would be restored within the next several months. When that happened the eclipsed Westerners would surely return to the offensive against the Easterners in the never-ending fight for power. They would not attack Yu Song-nyong directly; that would be too dangerous. They would proceed in the tried and true manner of targeting the appointees and supporters of the man at the top, thereby undermining his power—men like Cholla Left Navy Commander Yi Sun-sin.

By the beginning of May Yi Sun-sin and Yi Ok-ki decided that it would be pointless and even dangerous to remain any longer in the waters off Pusan. The anticipated southward push by the Ming army, and in turn the putting to sea of the Japanese fleet, was coming no time soon, so there was little they could accomplish there. Some sort of contagion, possibly typhoid, had also begun to sweep through the ranks and was threatening to carry off the entire Korean navy if the fleet did not soon disperse.

There was also the practical matter of the season to consider. With the time for planting already well upon them, it was imperative that the men of the Korean navy, mostly farmers, be allowed to return to their fields to sow the year's crops. Otherwise there would be no harvest in the fall. The two Yis accordingly agreed to give their men leave in turns, and to put their vacated warships on "maintenance status" until the Chinese resumed their drive to the south and the time finally came for the decisive battle at sea.

On May 3 Yi Sun-sin returned to his home port of Yosu and Yi Ok-ki to Usuyong farther west, and the bulk of the Korean navy headed off to the fields.[16]

On May 7, 159, Commander in Chief Li Rusong arrived back in Kaesong with Shen Weijing. Li was undoubtedly glad he had spared Shen's life earlier in the year, for the negotiator was now going to prove his worth in achieving the removal of the Japanese from Seoul without the loss of a single life. Not everyone supported Li's intention to negotiate a quick settlement so that he and his army could return home. Li's own superior, Song Yingchang, the government official charged with overseeing military operations in Korea from his head-quarters in Liaodong, had reprimanded him for retreating to Pyongyang following the debacle at Pyokje and now urged him to resume the offensive. The Minister of War in Beijing, however, who was in turn Song's superior, supported the idea of a peace settlement. From his perspective on the home front there was simply not enough money left in the imperial treasury to pay for further fighting. Commander Li was thus able to ignore Song's instructions, and proceeded with his plan to bring the war to an end.[17]

The Koreans, meanwhile, were fuming over Li's unwillingness to fight. They were also becoming fed up with his condescending attitude and his obvious desire to keep them in the dark as to his true intentions, telling them whatever he thought they wanted to hear just to keep them quiet. In early May, for example, in response to a plea from National High Commissioner Yu Song-nyong to attack the Japanese in Seoul, Li penned some soothing words about how he too wanted nothing more than to wipe the enemy out, when in fact he was at that very moment preparing to send Shen Weijing south to negotiate a truce.[18]

Tensions inevitably arose within the allied camp. Relations between Ming commander Li Rusong and Yu Song-nyong became particularly strained, so much so that Li at one point ordered the Korean official seized and beaten. Matters came to a head just prior to negotiator Shen's departure for Seoul on May 8. Yu Song-nyong rode ahead into Kwon Yul's camp at Paju, between the Imjin River and Seoul.[19] A unit of Chinese soldiers was already there, with the Wanli emperor's banner prominently displayed. Beside the banner, Yu observed a poster announcing that negotiations would soon be commencing and that Koreans henceforth were not allowed to attack the Japanese. Yu was furious. The Chinese commander on the scene, possibly in response to the Korean official's evident displeasure, ordered him to bow to the emperor's banner to show proper respect. Yu refused. This banner will be carried into Seoul by the negotiators, he said, and I will bow to nothing that the Japanese bow to. The Chinese commander thundered twice more that Yu must bow. Twice more Yu refused. Then he got on his horse and rode away.

By the following morning Yu Song-nyong's temper had cooled enough for him to realize that he would have to go to Li Rusong and apologize. He rode to Kaesong where the Ming commander was residing and presented himself outside the city walls. A guard peered out at him, but would not open the gate—Commander in Chief Li had clearly heard the story of the previous day's disturbance. Yu turned to the official who was accompanying him. "The commander is angry and is testing us," he said. "Let's wait here for a while."

It started to rain lightly. Someone inside came periodically to the gate to peek out and see whether the two Koreans had left. They had not. Finally, after several hours of patient waiting, the gate was opened and a damp Yu Song-nyong was ushered into the presence of Li Rusong. The apology was duly delivered and the tension eased, at least for that day.

It quickly returned. After leaving Kaesong, Yu headed south again, back toward the Korean army's forward camp north of Seoul. He had not gone far when he came upon a unit of Chinese cavalry. One of the horsemen blocked his way with whip in hand. "Are you the National High Commissioner?" he barked. When Yu replied that he was, the officer grabbed his horse by the reins, yanked the animal around, and started lashing it on the flanks and shouting, "Get out of here! Go back to the north!"

There was nothing for the perplexed Yu to do but return to Kaesong. It was only the next day that he learned what had been the cause of this strange episode: one of Li's commanders had accused Yu of removing all the boats from the crossing at the Imjin River to prevent negotiator Shen Weijing from proceeding to Seoul to meet with the Japanese. It was a false charge, but it resulted only hours later in Yu's arrest and his admittance for a second time into the presence of Li Rusong. This time he found Li pacing back and forth in a towering rage. The Ming commander ordered Yu stripped to the waist and tied to a plank to be given forty strokes with the paddle on his bare back.

It was only thanks to the timely arrival of one of Li's officers that Korea's National High Commissioner was spared a serious beating. When Li attempted to confirm Yu's treason with the man by inquiring about the state of the Imjin crossing, he was told that nothing had happened to the boats there and that the river could be crossed with ease. Li, realizing that Yu Song-nyong had been falsely accused, had him immediately released and apologized profusely. The order then went out for the arrest of Yu's accuser. The man was duly arrested for making a false report and flogged into unconsciousness on the plank intended for Yu.[20]

In Seoul, Konishi Yukinaga and his fellow daimyo had just received orders from Hideyoshi to evacuate the capital and pull back toward Pusan. The timing was fortuitous, the order arriving just days before Ming negotiator Shen Weijing. The Japanese could thus use the dire necessity of retreat as a bargaining chip in negotiations with the Ming Chinese.[21]

On May 8 Shen and an entourage of Ming generals proceeded south from Kaesong to Seoul. They stopped along the way at the Korean army camp at Paju. Shen was accosted here by Korea's commander in chief (*dowonsu*), Kim Myong-won, who expressed to him the universal disapproval among the Koreans of any talk of negotiation and compromise. "The Japanese tricked us before at Pyongyang," Kim said, "and we let them slip away. What makes you think they won't do it again?" But of course that was precisely what Shen intended: to talk the Japanese into marching south without a fight.

The next day Shen and the Chinese generals continued on by boat along the Han River to Seoul with the Wanli emperor's imperial banner prominently displayed. They arrived outside the city walls at Yongsan, the site of the recently destroyed food depot, and were met by Konishi Yukinaga, Kato Kiyomasa, and other daimyo. The two sides then sat down to talk. The Chinese by this point had received intelligence that the Japanese within the capital were in desperate straits and anxious to withdraw, so in the parlay Shen was forceful. "China will strike you from every side with an army 400,000 strong," he warned. "Stay here in Seoul and you will be slaughtered. Or release the two Korean princes and all captured officials and retreat with your armies to the south, and you may live. Which do you choose?" Konishi and his compatriots were eager to choose the latter; they were sick of the fight and wanted to go home. Even gung-ho commanders like Kato Kiyomasa, who had captured the two princes during his foray into the northeast, and Kobayakawa Takakage, architect of the win at Pyokje and a self-proclaimed expert at snatching victory from the jaws of defeat, could not help but see the wisdom of falling back to the south before all their troops starved. They knew, however, that the Chinese were also eager to avoid further bloodshed and that there was thus room for negotiation. Konishi accordingly replied that, while they were not unwilling to entertain the notion of withdrawing from the capital and reaching some sort of amicable settlement with the Chinese, they would first have to receive from China proof of the sincerity of its desire for peace. What sort of proof do you need? asked Shen. Bring us an envoy with authority to negotiate directly on your emperor's behalf, Konishi replied. Then we will see what can be worked out.[22]

The Chinese had no such envoy close at hand. But for Li Rusong this posed no problem. When Shen returned with the Japanese demand, the Ming commander simply pulled two officers from his staff, Xu Yihuan and Xie Yongzu, dressed them up in the robes of high officials, and sent them back to Seoul with Shen. The unflappable Shen thus appeared before Konishi Yukinaga for a second time and introduced his two august-looking comrades as imperial envoys from Beijing, empowered to negotiate with Japan directly in the name of the Wanli emperor himself.[23]

Konishi and his colleagues were satisfied and a deal was made. The Japanese agreed to evacuate the capital and march south with their armies in ten days, on May 19. Konishi also said they would release the two Korean princes, Sunhwa and Imhae, once they reached the south. The daimyo's word was shakier here, for the princes were in the custody of Kato Kiyomasa, who was adamant that he would not release them without direct orders from Hideyoshi himself; they were, after all, the only thing Kato had left to show for his campaign in the northeast. As for the Chinese, they would hold their troops at their present positions north of Seoul until the Japanese were safely away. They also agreed to send Shen Weijing and the two "imperial envoys" south in company with the withdrawing Japanese, and from there on to Nagoya to appear before Hideyoshi to discuss terms for a lasting peace.

A good deal more was said at this conference, mostly empty promises that left both sides feeling they had won the upper hand. Shen, for example, spoke of the coming investiture of Hideyoshi as the King of Japan, a move that would place him alongside Korea's King Sonjo as a vassal of the Ming emperor. Konishi knew that Hideyoshi would never accept such a subsidiary position, but he held his tongue and nodded his head. Shen also made grand promises of what the Japanese could expect in return for such a show of allegiance to China. It could be arranged, he said, that they keep a portion of Korea, perhaps the three southernmost provinces of Kyongsang, Cholla, and Chungchong. The Koreans might even be pressed into sending them tribute. Shen surely knew that neither the Koreans nor Beijing would ever agree to such a thing; he was spinning castles in the air to coax the Japanese out of Seoul. It was just the sort of talk, however, that Konishi Yukinaga wanted to hear, for it gave him something positive to report to Hideyoshi, something to further the fiction that the Ming Chinese had been badly mauled, and were now about to concede.[24]

The Koreans, of course, were told nothing of this.

On the morning of May 19, 1593, the ironclad gates of Seoul were swung open and the 53,000 Japanese troops stationed there began filing out. They crossed the Han River on a bridge of boats that had been previously prepared. The boats, we may assume, were then unlashed and destroyed. Near the front of the column were Chinese negotiator Shen Weijing and the two false envoys, who had agreed to accompany the Japanese to Pusan and then on to Nagoya to appear before Hideyoshi. Behind them rode many of the daimyo luminaries of the Korean campaign. There were Konishi Yukinaga and Tsushima daimyo So Yoshitoshi, the two Christian commanders who had spearheaded the invasion and who now stood at the forefront of the movement to bring the war to an end. Nearby was the diehard Kato Kiyomasa, the bearded Buddhist in his trademark tall gold helmet, grim-faced no doubt in the face of retreat. There was young Ukita Hideie, head of the eighth contingent, one year older but ten years wiser after his experience as Hideyoshi's commander in chief. Kobayakawa Takakage, victor of Pyokje and the veteran of many wars, rode at the fore of his sixth contingent, the epitome of the grizzled warrior in his worn samurai armor. And of course there was Kuroda Nagamasa at the head of the third contingent, not as colorful a character in the historical record perhaps, but certainly as battle hardened as any after many hundreds of kilometers of marching and one year of fighting from Pusan to Pyongyang.

The retreat south began like a carnival parade. Beautiful women, dragooned from among the citizens of Seoul, accompanied the soldiers. Musicians played gay tunes and dancers gamboled among the ranks. Were the Japanese so glad to be at last heading home? Or were they putting a good face on retreat? If it was all an act it was very well done, for according to the Koreans the sound of their merrymaking "filled the mountains and the fields as they made their way south."[25]

Li Rusong, meanwhile, made no move to pursue. He was now encamped with the bulk of his army at Tongpa, just south of the Imjin River, a day's march north of Seoul. From here he refused to advance any farther, ignoring entreaties from the Koreans to lead his troops against the Japanese now that he had tricked them into leaving Seoul and made them vulnerable to attack. What was even more galling, however, was that he now prohibited the Koreans from attacking on their own: as Shen Weijing explained to Yu Song-nyong and Commander in Chief Kim Myong-won, negotiations were now in the works to make Japan a vassal of China, and therefore their soldiers must not be captured or killed. Yu and Kim were incensed by this. "If our country had wanted peace," they said, "we would not have waited until now. The Japanese sent a letter to us from Tongnae asking for peace negotiations, another from Sangju, and a third from Pyongyang. We rejected these overtures because we are angry at their disrespectful behavior toward China. Even if it means death for us all, we will not be humiliated by negotiating with them." The argument grew increasingly heated, until finally one of the Chinese generals shouted, "This is the order of the Emperor! How can you dare refuse to obey?"[26]

Throughout the next week Li Rusong continued to brush aside the Koreans' pleas to attack as the Japanese got farther and farther away. He had no reason to do so. The enemy was moving south, away from the Chinese border. As far as Li was concerned, his objective had been achieved. The Koreans, beside themselves with frustration, began to grumble that he must have taken a bribe from the Japanese in exchange for their safe passage. Perhaps they were right, for the Japanese proceeded south at a remarkably leisurely pace—as if they had no fear of being attacked on the way.

It was at about this time that a 5,000-man Ming force crossed the Yalu River and marched south to reinforce the 40,000-odd Chinese troops already in Korea. They were led by a colorful forty-year-old Sichuan general named Liu Ting, nicknamed "Big Sword Liu" for his supposed ability to wield a 120-catty sword while galloping on horseback. General Liu led an unusual collection of men drawn from the furthest reaches of the vast Ming empire. In addition to his own Sichuan troops, there were soldiers from the vassal kingdom of Thailand and from islands in the southeastern sea, possibly Sumatra and Java. These strange apparitions, clad in unusual clothes and armor and speaking unintelligible tongues, must have seemed like men from another planet to the Koreans and the Chinese. Reports circulated that some of them could swim like fish and were able to scuttle enemy vessels from beneath.[27]

(In November 1592 a delegation of Thai envoys on a tribute mission to Beijing presented the Chinese with an offer from their king, Naresvara, to send a fleet of warships in a direct attack on Japan, which would be under-defended with so many of Hideyoshi's troops tied up in Korea. It was both a show of loyalty to the Ming, and was probably also backed by a desire on Naresvara's part to see Japan "dealt with," for it was known even in his distant part of Asia as a source of pirates, adventurers, and troublemakers. The proposal was discussed, and rejected, by the Chinese on February 6, 1593, much to the indignation of Naresvara's envoys. The subsequent appearance of a token number of Thai troops in Korea—had they perhaps been drawn from the entourage of the tribute mission?—may have been a face-saving alternate contribution suggested by the Ming.[28])

"Big Sword" Liu led his army south by the main road, first to Pyongyang, then across the Imjin River and into Commander in Chief Li Rusong's forward camp. With their arrival the Imjin War became a thoroughly international conflict, involving combatants from the length and breadth of Asia.

The Koreans and their Chinese allies entered Seoul on May 20, the day after the Japanese withdrawal. What they saw pierced their hearts: the city was destroyed. The damage had begun on the night King Sonjo had fled in June of the previous year, in the orgy of vandalism wrought by the Koreans themselves, angry over what they felt was the betrayal of their king. During the next ten months the Japanese had done the rest.

"When I entered the capital with the Ming soldiers," recalled National High Commissioner Yu Song-nyong, "I saw that scarcely one in a hundred citizens still remained. Those few people to be seen were all starving. They were gaunt, sick, and exhausted, the color of their faces like that of a ghost. The weather at this time was extremely hot and humid, so the dead bodies and horse carcasses that lay exposed and unattended throughout the city had begun to rot, emitting such a stench that passersby had to plug their nostrils."[29]

Yu wandered within the walls in what must have been a state of shock. Private residences that had survived the flames had been long since abandoned and looted. Government offices and schools were destroyed. The city's three royal palaces were gone. On the sprawling grounds of King Sonjo's former residence of Kyongbok-gung, "the Palace of Shining Happiness," all that remained were blackened stone pillars and a few stinking outbuildings, uninhabitable after many months of use by the Japanese as barracks and stables. By the time Yu reached Chongmyo where the ancestral tablets of the Choson kings were traditionally kept, he could bear no more. Upon sighting the burned-out ruins of this, the most sacred place in the city, he broke down entirely, wailing like an orphaned son.

Yet another outrage discovered by the Koreans was the desecration of the royal tombs at Chongnung, a short distance north of Chongmyo. Three burial mounds here bearing the remains of King Chungjong, who had reigned from 1506 to 1544, together with his father and his wife, had been dug into by the Japanese and the corpses removed and burned. But strangely, one body had been left lying in the open, removed from its grave but otherwise untouched. It was a male, and appeared to have been dead for about fifty years. Was this Chungjong himself? Aged government ministers who had served the former king were brought out to view the remains. An old doctor who had examined the king in life was also found, and provided detailed information on his appearance. Other descriptions were retrieved from history books and diaries. In the end, it was decided that the body was not that of King Chungjong. All the evidence seemed to point to the conclusion that the king's remains had been burned by the Japanese, and this unidentified corpse left behind to fool the Koreans into reinterring and revering a commoner in a sacred tomb meant for a king. The body was thus buried elsewhere— but with all royal honors, just in case.[30]

The first few days after the freeing of Seoul were like a time in hell. Rice was so scarce that a mere three liters of it cost a whole bolt of

cloth, while a good-sized sack went for the price of a horse. Those who
had not yet starved to death were reduced to the lowest form of animal
existence. People hunkered in gutters, picking through garbage for any
scrap of food. Some resorted to cannibalism. It is said that when a
drunken Chinese soldier vomited in the street, starving men crawled to
the spot and fought over the right to eat the steaming mess. Yu Song-
nyong ordered government grain distributed to ease the desperation.
But for many the relief came too late. People continued to die, some
from hunger, others from the typhus epidemic that deprivation had
brought on. When the contagion had run its course, the dead bodies
littering the streets were gathered up and dumped outside the city's
Water Mouth Gate for cremation. The pile reportedly rose three meters
higher than the walls.[31]

After surveying the destruction of the capital, National High
Commissioner Yu Song-nyong rode back north to Tongpa where the
main body of the Ming army was still encamped. In a voice breaking
with emotion, he again urged Li Rusong to pursue the retreating
Japanese, this time to exact revenge for what they had done to Seoul. Li
tried to calm Yu with words of sympathy, claiming that the only thing
holding him back was the fact that the Japanese had removed all the
boats from the Han River, leaving him with no way to get his troops
across. "If you will agree to pursue the Japanese," replied Yu, "I will
see that there are boats at the Han to ferry your men across." The
chagrined Li Rusong could do nothing but agree.

Armed with Li's assurance that the Japanese would at last be
pursued, Yu Song-nyong sent out a public appeal for all available boats
to be brought to the river crossing south of Seoul. By the time he
reached the Han, eighty vessels had been assembled. This heartening
news was rushed back to the Ming commander and, as promised, he
sent ten thousand men marching south under his younger brother, Li
Rubo. They reached the Han the following day and the hastily assembled fleet of small craft began ferrying them across. Then, just as the
vessel bearing Li Rubo himself had reached the midpoint of the river,
the commander suddenly complained that his feet were paining him
and that he would have to return north to recuperate. He would resume
the pursuit, he assured the incredulous Koreans, just as soon as he felt

better. When they saw their commander turning back, the Chinese soldiers who had already reached the Han's south bank recrossed the river and followed him north. Yu Song-nyong was left behind, fuming in anger. The whole thing, he said bitterly, was just another of Li Rusong's tricks to keep the Koreans quiet while he let the Japanese escape.[32]

In the days that followed, Li Rusong moved from his Imjin River camp into what was left of Seoul. He made his headquarters in the Nambyol-gung, the former headquarters of Japanese supreme commander Ukita Hideie, one of the few respectable dwellings still standing and inhabitable. The Koreans continued to appear before him daily, pressing him to pursue the retreating Japanese. Cholla Army Commander Kwon Yul, hero of the Battle of Haengju, was particularly adamant, saying that if Li would not set out after the fleeing enemy, then he, Kwon, would do so with the men under his own command. Li Rusong vetoed this in no uncertain terms and had the boats Yu Song-nyong had assembled at the Han River removed to ensure that his orders were obeyed. The Chinese and Korean armies thus continued to sit idle as the Japanese got farther away.[33]

Finally, at the beginning of June, a full twenty days after the Japanese had withdrawn from the capital, a letter arrived from Li Rusong's civilian superior, Song Yingchang, now headquartered in Pyongyang, ordering him to cease his delaying and get on with the pursuit. The Koreans believed that Song's letter was merely a blind, that he was no more eager than Li to send Ming soldiers into battle and had thus intentionally delayed his orders to advance so that there would be no chance of actually catching the Japanese. This was not necessarily true. Since China's entry into the war, Song had consistently been more hawkish than Li. When one considers the time it took for documents to be conveyed between Seoul and Pyongyang, and the time it would have taken for Song to realize that Li was in fact not going to pursue, but intended to remain idle in Seoul, the twenty days it took for his orders to reach the capital do not seem so suspicious.

In any event Li Rusong did as he was ordered. He gathered his forces, crossed the Han, and proceeded south along the main road. He traveled slowly, stopping here and there for prolonged rests, clearly

making no effort to gain on the retreating Japanese. When he reached
the Sobaek mountain range that cut a diagonal swatch across the peninsula, he received word that the Japanese had left behind forces blocking
Choryong (Bird Pass), and had large contingents amassed farther south
at Taegu. This intelligence brought Li up short. He fell back to Chungju,
sending other units ahead to continue the pursuit in his stead, including
"Big Sword" Liu and his Siamese troops and "ocean imps." This force
bypassed Choryong and proceeded south in a wide arc with the intention of outflanking the Japanese and forcing them back all the way to
the coast. Skirmishes subsequently occurred to the west of Taegu, but no
major engagements. The Japanese, no longer wanting a "decisive
battle" with the Chinese, fell back to Korea's southeastern tip and Li
Rusong called off his pursuit.[34]

The Japanese arrived back on Korea's southern coast in the middle
of June 1593. Their supplies were now gone, and they were living off
the land. They thus could not consolidate their forces into one big camp;
they would have to be spread out to afford each unit an adequate foraging
range. Seventeen forts were accordingly constructed around the original
beachhead at Pusan, stretching from Sosaengpo in the east, where Kato
Kiyomasa made his camp, to Konishi Yukinaga's base at Ungchon in
the west, to the islands of Koje and Kadok offshore. Most were situated
on promontories and hilltops protected on one or more sides by the sea.
Fortifications of stone and earth and wood were built all around, and
moats dug on the landward side for additional protection.[35]

The Chinese, meanwhile, joined by Korean forces under Kwon Yul
and others, established camps at Uiryong and Changnyong a short
distance to the north and waited to see what the Japanese would do.
Hopes were soon dashed that they would sail back to Japan: intelligence was received that enemy soldiers were planting vegetables and
grain at many of the camps, a sign that they intended to stay for at least
the next several months.[36] By the time the Koreans realized this, any
chance of launching an offensive was gone. The Japanese were too
concentrated and too deeply dug in to be dislodged. The two sides thus
settled down to a standoff that would last for the next four years.

CHAPTER 19

Negotiations at Nagoya, Slaughter at Chinju

[A] report has come saying that the envoys who have come from China to apologize have arrived at the harbor of Korea and are waiting for a favorable wind [to sail to Nagoya].... I shall be back [to Osaka] in triumph shortly.[1]

Hideyoshi to his wife O-Ne, early May 1593

AT INVASION HEADQUARTERS AT NAGOYA on the island of Kyushu, Toyotomi Hideyoshi gave every appearance of regarding developments in Korea in a positive light. He does not seem to have considered the retreat of his troops south to the Pusan perimeter as any sort of setback. Nor did he bemoan the loss of what has been estimated as a third of his 158,800-man expeditionary force. On the contrary, in his correspondence Hideyoshi wrote as if his troops in Korea had already achieved their core objective and were now logically withdrawing toward home. No, they had not succeeded in marching to Beijing as he had envisioned in his pre-invasion plans drawn up in early 1592. But they had advanced north almost all the way to the Chinese border and had given the Ming a good shaking up, to say nothing of the devastation they had wrought in China's vassal Korea. They had awakened China to the extent of Hideyoshi's power, so much so that Beijing was now sending two envoys to him to convey China's apologies and receive his demands. Surely this had to be deemed a success.

Did Hideyoshi really believe that he had somehow emerged victorious from the largely disastrous Korean campaign? Was he really so self assured as to think that the Wanli emperor was about to accede to his demands without Japanese troops having set foot on Chinese soil? Probably not. Hideyoshi's true assessment of the situation in Korea was almost certainly closer to reality than he ever publicly acknowledged. His foremost reason for engaging in such dissembling was his concern for the stability of Japan, and more particularly for his own security as its supreme ruler. In order to complete the unification of the country as rapidly as he did, it had been necessary for Hideyoshi throughout the 1580s to seek accommodations with other powerful daimyo, men like Tokugawa Ieyasu, Shimazu Yoshihiro, Mori Terumoto, and Date Masamune, leaving them with sizable landholdings and bases of power. Now, in 1593, he must have known that his control over these former rivals remained tenuous, and was likely to crumble the moment they scented weakness. To acknowledge the failure of his Korean campaign was therefore not an option for Hideyoshi. To maintain the appearance of his own boundless power, the taiko had no choice but to paint defeat in Korea as victory at home.

This is not to say that beneath the bravado, the talk of "accepting China's apologies" and making a "triumphal return" to Osaka, Hideyoshi had an accurate idea of the situation in Korea and in faraway Beijing. He had clearly been misled, by both the Chinese and his own daimyo generals, into overestimating the strength of his position. To bring hostilities to a quick end on the peninsula, Ming commander in chief Li Rusong, through his negotiator Shen Weijing, had encouraged the Japanese to believe that Beijing was prepared to go to great lengths to accommodate Hideyoshi and reach a lasting peace. Toward this end Li had disguised two of his own officers as imperial envoys and sent them south to accept Hideyoshi's terms, all without the knowledge of his superiors in Beijing. Hideyoshi's commanders in the field, meanwhile, notably Konishi Yukinaga, played their own willing part in the charade, softening what they knew to be their master's true thirst for conquest into a mere desire for recognition and trade, for they were just as eager to avoid further bloodshed. Thanks to this two-sided duplicity, the reports that found their way back to Hideyoshi naturally led him to believe that he stood to gain much more from the Korean campaign than was actually the case. The physical conquest of China might be no longer in the cards. But perhaps a readjustment in the balance of power in Asia was, a negotiated readjustment that would officially recognize the might and the importance of Hideyoshi, elevating him to a position of equality with the emperor of the Ming.

In addition to the misleading reports he was receiving from Korea, a second factor serving to cloud Hideyoshi's judgment was his preoccupation with other things. Indeed, one wonders just how much attention the aging taiko was paying to matters overseas. Throughout the first year of the war in Korea, he continued to hone his skills at poetry and linked verse. His teahouses, both the rustic Yamazato and the glorious golden tearoom, remained central fixtures in his life. He also became deeply immersed in the study of noh theater under the tutelage of master Kurematsu Shinkuro of the Konparu school. This alone entailed long hours practicing the elaborate movements and voicings of the art and memorizing pages and pages of dialog. In April of 1593, just as his troops were evacuating Seoul, Hideyoshi wrote to his wife O-Ne that he had already learned ten noh plays and that he had in fact "become very skilled in these numbers and I will try to learn more."

And then there were the taiko's eccentric entertainments, the little diversions he staged for the amusement of himself and the daimyo luminaries residing with him at Nagoya. On one occasion he organized an earthy costume ball in his melon garden where everyone came attired as common folk. Tokugawa Ieyasu, the most powerful man in Japan after Hideyoshi himself, was a reed merchant; the stately Maeda Toshiie came as a monk with a begging bowl; the taiko's nephew Hideyasu was a pickled-melon vendor, and Kyoto governor Maeda Gen'i a nun. As for Hideyoshi, he wandered among his guests as a melon hawker kitted out in black hood, robe, and wide-brimmed hat, calling out, "Melons! Melons! Get your nice fresh melons!"[2]

The poetry, the tea, the noh, the parties. These were preoccupations for the taiko, but it would be too much to say that they signaled in themselves a wholesale loss of interest on his part in events overseas. That would come a little later, on June 21, 1593. On that day Hideyoshi

received news from Osaka Castle that his concubine Yodogimi was
pregnant. Rumors soon started making the rounds that the child was not
Hideyoshi's, but had been fathered by a secret lover of Yodogimi's,
possibly one of the noh actors that the taiko kept around him. There is
no hard evidence to support such claims, only speculation: Hideyoshi
was growing old and weak and his libido was undoubtedly flagging; he
did not have a good track record of fathering children with any of his
numerous concubines, even in the prime of his life; the child in question would grow into a handsome man, with a face completely unlike
the taiko's homely visage.[3] In support of Hideyoshi's paternity, on the
other hand, is the fact that Yodogimi had resided together with him at
Nagoya until early 1593, and so there had been opportunity for her
legitimately to conceive. As for Hideyoshi himself, he never questioned
that he was the father. The aging taiko, now in his late fifties, greeted
the news with untrammeled delight. Here was a second chance to have
a real heir following the death of his first child Tsurumatsu in 1591.
Here was a second chance to build the house of Toyotomi based not on
adoption, but on blood. In his correspondence Hideyoshi feigned
indifference to the momentous event, but only so as not to attract the
capricious attention of the gods: to show the full extent of his happiness
might tempt them into taking the source of that happiness away.[4] But he
was happy. Deliriously happy. The subsequent birth of a son in late
August would carry him away from Nagoya, never to return. In time
the child would become an obsession for Hideyoshi, completely over-
shadowing the situation in Korea.

*   *   *

*As imperial envoys have come from the Great Ming country to bring
an apology, be assured that I shall agree with them about peace
negotiations. After giving orders about the administration of Korea,
I shall be back [to Osaka] in triumph around the 10th month. I shall
try to put on noh [for the envoys], and after sending them back, I am
looking forward to visiting you.... Hachiro [Ukita Hideie] has already reached the bay of Pusan without any trouble, so do not
worry. I am very happy about it.[5]*

Hideyoshi to Ukita Hideie's mother, June 26, 1593

Xie Yongzu and Xu Yihuan, the two Chinese generals sent south by Ming commander in chief Li Rusong disguised as imperial envoys, arrived at Pusan at the beginning of June, in company with negotiator Shen Weijing. Shen remained in Pusan to act as intermediary between the Chinese and Japanese, heading off any difficulties that might imperil the tenuous truce. Xie and Xu, together with Konishi Yukinaga, continued on by ship to Hideyoshi's headquarters at Nagoya. They arrived on June 14, 1593. The two envoys left their vessel at the quay and rode through the streets on white horses, accompanied by a retinue of a hundred and fifty men. Among the solemn procession were a number of musicians playing Chinese instruments to impress upon bystanders the importance of these visitors and the gravity of the occasion. The envoys were taken first to private quarters outside the castle walls, then were moved inside the enclosure to be nearer Hideyoshi.[6]

On June 22 Konishi Yukinaga and a gathering of daimyo formally received Xie Yongzu and Xu Yihuan on Hideyoshi's behalf in a large reception hall at Nagoya Castle. A discussion was then held between the two sides. No interpreter was present, so communication took place in writing using Chinese characters. The Ming envoys immediately got to the point: "Why are there still Japanese troops in the Korean provinces of Kyongsang and Cholla?"

The monk Genso, who was an expert in written Chinese and thus serving as scribe for the Japanese side, replied, "When the tail of our army was passing through those regions the Koreans there stopped us and prevented us from withdrawing completely."

Xie and Xu knew this was untrue, but wrote that they would investigate. "In the meantime, by keeping your troops in the south you are breaking our agreement, so you must withdraw them at once."

The Japanese changed the topic. China, Genso wrote, first had to show that it was sincere in its desire for peace. It could do this by accepting Japan as a tributary vassal. If this was done, Japan in turn would be willing to help Beijing deal with the Jurchen tribes that were known to be such a source of trouble along the empire's eastern frontier. The Ming envoys politely declined the offer, pointing out that the Jurchen had been loyal to the Ming emperor for the past ten years and were no longer a problem. Beijing thus had no need for Japanese aid.

Genso then turned attention to the causes of the war. "Our country initially asked Korea to mediate with China on our behalf," he explained, "and convey Hideyoshi's desire for good relations to the Emperor in Beijing. The King of Korea agreed, and sent envoys to our country. Three years then passed and nothing was done. So finally we gave up on the Koreans and sent a few soldiers across the sea to convey the taiko's wishes directly to the Chinese Emperor. The Koreans responded with violence and blocked us from passing."

The war, then, had been entirely the Koreans' fault. Japan was now upset, Genso continued, because even though "we never had any intention of attacking China, the Ming government listens only to the Koreans' twisted version of the facts and allows us no opportunity to speak to them directly. If these attempts to falsify our true intentions continue, Hideyoshi will lead his army to Liaodong to state his case to the Emperor in person."

This too the Ming envoys knew to be untrue. They had come to Nagoya, however, to clear an impasse, so they let Genso's explanation stand: Hideyoshi's intentions were peaceful and the Koreans to blame for the war. Taking up the brush again, they wrote, "We are now satisfied that what Konishi Yukinaga conveyed to us last year through Shen Weijing was in fact a true reflection of the taiko's wishes. So there is no need for Hideyoshi to visit China to appeal to the Emperor."[7]

Hideyoshi never learned what actually was said in this written conversation. With only a limited knowledge of Chinese characters, his understanding of what had transpired was based solely on the encouraging and entirely misleading reports that Konishi Yukinaga and others fed him. For the month that Xie and Xu remained at Nagoya the taiko therefore continued to believe that they had come to Japan to apologize for China's recent aggression and cater to his demands, and thus he treated them with the utmost generosity to show his satisfaction. He had all the highest-ranking daimyo at Nagoya entertain them lavishly with banquets and drinking and the exchange of gifts. He personally treated them to a tea ceremony in his golden tearoom, and possibly to a performance of noh with himself in the starring role, an experience the Chinese must have found surreal. Hideyoshi also laid on a uniquely taiko-esque entertainment, a waterborne parade in which hundreds of boats were sculled by singing oarsmen past the comfortably seated guests, each boat bearing a daimyo's emblem and giant imperial chrysanthemums, its bows heaped with opulent displays of swords and spears and other weaponry, all inlaid with gold and mother-of-pearl.[8]

Hideyoshi intended these various displays to impress upon the Ming envoys that he and his nation were rich and powerful and civilized and deserving of China's respect. But, as he had in his prewar reception of envoys from Korea, the taiko went too far: in trying to aggrandize himself, he took on an air of superiority that only served to offend. This was nowhere clearer than at one of the banquets he hosted, an account of which was recorded by Che Man-chun, a well-educated Korean naval officer and prisoner of war who was put to work as a clerk in the taiko's entourage before managing to escape. According to Che, the affair took place in a reception hall at the center of Nagoya Castle. In a neighboring courtyard dancers and singers entertained while crowds of onlookers jostled for a peek inside. Hideyoshi himself did not appear in the hall. He sat on a dais in the six-story castle that formed the center-piece of his walled city, overseeing the event but well beyond reach, as befitted his lofty position. His daimyo subordinates and Chinese guests were seated on two facing platforms in the hall below. Significantly, the platform bearing the Japanese was higher, and more richly decorated with red brocade tapestries and gilt-edged folding screens; the Chinese were obliged to sit on a lower floor, with a bamboo screen behind. Such treatment of representatives from the Wanli emperor—even bogus ones—would have been viewed by both the Chinese and the Koreans as the height of incivility, a glaring indication that, behind the strength of arms and riches, the Japanese were still the barbarians that Beijing always took them for.[9]

In order to "look down on the enemy," understand that you should take your stand on the highest ground, even if it is only slightly ele-vated. Indoors, the seat of honor should be regarded as the high ground. [10]

Miyamoto Musashi (1584–1645)
Go-rin no sho (The Book of Five Rings)

*   *   *

While Hideyoshi wined and dined the Ming envoys at Nagoya, his commanders in Korea were preparing once again for battle. Their target: Chinju. This strongly fortified southern city, sixty kilometers to the west of Pusan, had remained a sore spot with the Japanese ever since they had failed to take it in November of the previous year. In that battle a disciplined force of only 3,800 Koreans held out for five days against a 15,000-man army from Mori Terumoto's seventh contingent from Honshu, inflicting such heavy casualties—some accounts put the figure as high as fifty percent—that the Japanese were forced to withdraw. This loss never ceased to rankle the Japanese. It also left an enemy stronghold in uncomfortably close proximity to their defensive perimeter on Korea's southern tip. There were a number of hawks within the Japanese camp, meanwhile, notably Kato Kiyomasa and Kobayakawa Takakage, who felt angry and humiliated at the unexpected setbacks suffered in the war, and who now urged Hideyoshi to allow them the opportunity to inflict one final attack against the incompliant Koreans, a parting blow to remind them and in turn the Chinese that the might of Japan remained undiminished and would have to be appeased.

It was for these three reasons that Hideyoshi, although ostensibly immersed in negotiations with the two Ming envoys, sent the order to Kato in Korea: attack Chinju. Wipe it off the map.

News of the planned assault on Chinju soon reached the ears of Ming negotiator Shen Weijing at Pusan, passed to him by Konishi Yukinaga, who claimed that he had tried without success to dissuade Kato from launching such an attack. Shen in turn warned Commander in Chief Kim Myong-won, explaining that the Japanese were out to avenge themselves upon the Koreans for defeating them at Chinju the previous year, for destroying so many of their ships, and for repeatedly ambushing Japanese soldiers who were out working in the fields. Shen assured Kim that the coming attack would be a single act of face-saving aggression, and not part of any renewed offensive to grab more territory. The Koreans should therefore keep clear of Chinju for a time and let the Japanese have their revenge, for then they would be satisfied and would surely return home.[11]

Some among the Koreans were willing to accept Shen Weijing's advice. Guerrilla leader Kwak Jae-u, the famous "Red Coat General," said that while he was prepared to sacrifice his own life, he was not willing to throw away the lives of his men in what was clearly a lost cause. Others, however, were determined to hold the city at any cost. Government-official-turned-guerrilla-leader Kim Chon-il was one of the first to enter Chinju at the head of three hundred volunteers ("an unruly mob gathered from the streets of Seoul," observed Yu Song-nyong),[12] and immediately tried to assume overall command, much to the aggravation of the city's magistrate, So Ye-won. Others followed: Hwang Jin, army commander of Chungchong Province, with seven hundred men; Kyongsang Army Commander Choi Kyong-hoe with five hundred; Vice-Commander Chang Yun with three hundred; guerilla leader Ko Chong-hu, who had seen his father Ko Kyong-myong slain in the Battle of Kumsan, with four hundred. Yi Chong-in, the magistrate of Kimhae, also arrived and assumed a leadership role.[13]

In Seoul, Li Rusong received the news of the planned Japanese attack with understandable consternation and dispatched orders to his generals in the south to take steps to halt the move. From his camp near Taegu, "Big Sword" Liu Ting sent a message to Kato Kiyomasa at Ulsan reminding him that any aggression against Chinju would be an abrogation of the armistice that existed between their two armies, and would lead to further hostilities. Kato made no reply. Liu also sent an aide to Chinju itself to inspect the city's defenses and offer assurance of Chinese support in the event of an attack.

By the middle of July between 3,000 and 4,000 Korean defenders had gathered within the walls of Chinju,[14] a force roughly equal to the one that had held off 15,000 Japanese attackers in November of the previous year. They were by no means all crack troops, however, and would be facing an army of possibly 93,000, the bulk of Hideyoshi's remaining invasion force plus reinforcements recently sent from Japan.[15] There was no way the Koreans could stand against such over-whelming numbers, the largest single enemy force so far assembled in the war. "Red Coat General" Kwak Jae-u saw this clearly, and urged his friend Hwang Jin not to throw his life away trying to defend the place. Hwang agreed that Chinju was probably doomed. He had already

given his word to Kim Chon-il and others, however, that he would stay
and fight. So stay and fight he must. As Kwak Jae-u rode sadly away,
knowing he would never see Hwang again, the defenders of Chinju
raced to stockpile food and arms in preparation for the coming fight.
Then the gates of the city were closed and barred.[16]

In the second week of July a tidal wave of Japanese troops began
filing out of the chain of forts encircling Pusan and moving west toward
Chinju, looting and burning as they went. Kato Kiyomasa led the operation. This was a bit of appeasement thrown his way by Hideyoshi, in
exchange for the two Korean princes he would soon be required to
release. Kato was keeping these two royal teens, Sunhwa and Imhae, in
comfortable confinement at his fort at Ulsan, and was not eager to give
them up. He would have to, however, if negotiations with China were
to bear any fruit. As a sop to his honor he was given Chinju instead.

By this time several tens of thousands of terrified civilians had
joined the defenders holed up inside Chinju: women and children, the
infirm, the aged, driven to take refuge by the violence of the Japanese
advance. As this tremulous multitude peered out over the walls on the
nineteenth of July, enemy units began arriving and took positions on
three sides of the city: Ukita Hideie's forces on the east, Konishi
Yukinaga's on the west, Kato Kiyomasa's on the north. A fourth unit,
Kikkawa Hiroie's, could be seen on the other side of the Nam River,
cutting off retreat to the south. Still others established an outer perimeter
to guard against counterattack, until Chinju was surrounded "in a hundred
layers" and looked like "a small, lonely boat in the middle of a sea."

The assault began the following day, ashigaru foot soldiers peppering the ramparts with musket fire, keeping the Koreans down while
their comrades filled in portions of the moat that had previously been
dug outside the north wall. With this obstacle overcome, a unit of men
advanced to the wall itself and began prying stones out from the base.
The effort came to an abrupt halt when a cascade of stones fell down on
them, killing some and driving the rest back.

The fighting continued day and night through July 21 and 22, the
Japanese taking turns assaulting the walls and then falling back to rest,
keeping up an unrelenting pressure on the Korean defenses. Then, on
the twenty-third, they began erecting a mound of earth with a blockhouse

on top adjacent to Chinju's west gate, planning to use the elevation to fire their muskets over the wall and into the city. Inside the fortress the Koreans responded by rushing to build an elevated blockhouse of their own. The work was completed in a single night, many of the women within the city working alongside Chungchong Army Commander Hwang Jin in hauling basketfuls of soil and packing it in place. By morning the Japanese and the Koreans faced each other from atop similar elevated platforms, one outside the wall, the other within. In the exchange of fire that ensued, the Koreans managed to destroy the Japanese blockhouse with their cannons and, at least for the moment, put an end to the threat.

On the twenty-fourth the Japanese went to work again on the base of Chinju's fortifications. The men assigned to the task, this time holding stout wood and leather shields over their heads, advanced to the base of the wall and began prying out the lower course of stones. The Koreans responded with a barrage of arrow and musket fire, but could not penetrate the thick roofs under which the Japanese were sheltered. It was only by dropping heavy stones down on the Japanese that they were finally able to kill some and drive the rest away.

At about this time it started to rain in torrents. It began for the Koreans as a welcome relief, for they were able to snatch a little rest when the Japanese, unwilling or unable to use their muskets in the wet, were forced to call off their assault. (By the late sixteenth century the Japanese had invented a cover for their arquebuses that allowed them to fire them in the rain, but it was an imperfect solution for keeping a wick lit and powder dry.) The downpour, however, soon turned into a curse, for the dampness went to work on the glue holding the Koreans' composite bows together, rendering some of them useless, and also began washing away the soil at the damaged portions of the walls, weakening them even further.

During the respite the Japanese sent a message into the beleaguered city demanding its surrender. "The Chinese have already given up," it read. "Why do you dare continue to resist?" Commander Kim Chon-il sent a reply flying back over the walls: "Three hundred thousand Chinese soldiers have been sent to help us. When they arrive you will all be destroyed." The Japanese scoffed at this bravado, hoisting their trouser legs above the knee and miming effeminate Chinese officials running away.[17]

Inside the city everyone was exhausted and spirits were low. In an effort to boost morale, Kim Chon-il climbed to a high lookout and, peering over the wall, announced that he thought he could see fighting going on in the distance, a sign that the reinforcements Ming general "Big Sword" Liu Ting had promised would soon be arriving to save them. This lifted everyone's spirits for a time. But it was a lie. The Chinese were not coming, and Kim Chon-il knew it. Turning to his colleague Choi Kyong-hoe he said, "After I beat this enemy I will chew the flesh of Helan Jinming." Kim, feeling abandoned and betrayed, was likening "Big Sword" Liu to a reviled commander from China's Tang dynasty (618–907) who, in a well-known episode that forever blackened his name, refused to come to the aid of a beleaguered comrade and thereby ensured his defeat.

From his camp outside the city, Kato Kiyomasa was making preparations for a renewed attempt to undermine the walls. This time he had his men fashion four *kame-no-kosha*, or "turtle wagons," heavily built carts with stout wooden roofs. These crude vehicles were wheeled up to the base of the walls, and parties of men went to work with crowbars on the lower courses of stones, prying them out one by one. The Koreans could see what was happening below but were unable to stop it, their arrows and musket balls and stones bouncing harmlessly off the roofs of the wagons. Someone finally had the idea of dropping oil-soaked cotton down onto the contraptions and setting them alight. Kato, calmly perceiving the weakness, promptly ordered more carts built, this time with fire-retardant ox hides nailed to the roof.[18]

While this was going on, Japanese forces were applying pressure at many other places around the city. Five more elevated firing platforms were erected in front of the east and west gates, and a bamboo palisade was constructed along one side, allowing Kato's musketeers to take up positions close to the walls. Inside the city, Hwang Jin, Kim Chon-il, and Kimhae magistrate Yi Chong-in fought desperately to repel these various advances, but their men were growing exhausting. During a lull in the fighting Hwang Jin leaned over the wall to assess the situation. "The trench out there is full of enemy dead," he observed. "There must be more than a thousand. . . ." At that moment a Japanese soldier hiding at the base of the wall aimed his musket straight up at Hwang's exposed head and fired, sending a ball through the Chungchong Army commander's helmet and into his skull. He fell down dead on the spot. Kim Chon-il replaced the fallen commander with Chinju magistrate So Ye-won, but So quickly proved unsuited for the task. The strain of six days of fighting had left the militarily inexperienced civil official unhinged, crying and riding around aimlessly on his horse, his scholar's hat tossed carelessly to one side. Kyongsang Army Commander Choi Kyong-hoe, seeing that So's erratic behavior was adversely effecting morale, intended initially to kill him as an example to the men, but in the press of events merely pushed him aside and replaced him with Vice-Commander Chang Yun. Within hours Chang himself was dead, killed by a musket ball just like Hwang Jin.

On July 27 the repeated forays by the Japanese to pry stones away from Chinju's fortifications finally succeeded in collapsing a portion of the east wall. Kato Kiyomasa's men were the first to enter the city. For the Koreans sheltering inside the end had come. They cried out to Kim Chon-il: "Commander! The enemy has breached the walls! What should we do?" There was nothing that Kim could tell them. He did not have enough men to resist the Japanese troops now pouring into the city; everyone was exhausted after a week of battle, every arrow had been fired, every stone had been thrown. And now there was no way at all to escape. Those who chose to die fighting did so with swords and spears and bamboo staves, no match for the muskets and katana of the Japanese. The rest abandoned their positions and raced from one wall to the other, searching in vain for a way to get out. As the Japanese proceeded to tear the city to pieces, Kim Chon-il and his eldest son Kim Sang-gon, accompanied by army commander Choi Kyong-hoe, guerrilla leader Ko Chong-hu, and a few others, retreated to the Choksongnu pavilion on the south wall of the city overlooking the Nam River. After bowing to the north, toward the capital and their king, the men embraced and, with tears streaming down their faces, bid one another farewell. Then they joined hands and threw themselves into the water below.

Yi Chong-in continued to resist until the bitter end, fighting off the

attacking Japanese in a rearguard action that took him onto the rocks at
the edge of the Nam River. Here he is reported to have seized two
Japanese in his arms and shouted, "Kimhae Magistrate Yi Chong-in is
dying here!" He then cast himself into the water, carrying the two
soldiers down with him.

Chinju magistrate So Ye-won met a less glorious end. Okamoto
Gonojo, a samurai in the service of Kikkawa Hiroie, came upon him
sitting on a tree stump, injured and exhausted, and cut off his head. It
rolled down an embankment and was lost in the grass. Not wanting to
lose the prize, Okamoto sent two men down to retrieve it, and later had
it pickled in salt and sent to Japan for presentation to Hideyoshi.[19]

At least sixty thousand Koreans lost their lives in the Second Battle
of Chinju. Most were killed in the massacre that followed the taking of
the city, an orgy of destruction that has been called the worst atrocity of
the war.[20] The Japanese under Kato, Ukita, and Konishi had no mercy.
They did not leave a cow or dog or chicken alive. In a frenzy of revenge
against a nation that refused to be conquered, they pulled down the
walls and burned all the buildings. They filled the wells with stones.
They cut down every tree. When the destruction was finished Chinju
ceased to exist. Since the beginning of the war, the Korean annals
would later report, no other place had been so thoroughly destroyed,
nor had loyalty and righteousness been so magnificently displayed.[21]

A large number of civilians committed suicide in the wake of the
fall of Chinju, many by drowning themselves in the Nam River. The
most famous instance involved a local female entertainer, or *kisaeng*,
named Non-gae, then no more than twenty years old. Shortly after the
fall of the city, Non-gae went out onto the rocks at the base of the
Choksongnu pavilion, where a group of senior Japanese commanders
were having a banquet to celebrate their success. When the Japanese
saw her beckoning to them seductively, "they gulped down their spit"
but no one dared to approach. Finally one of them, reportedly a samurai
named Keyamura Rokunosuke from Kato Kiyomasa's contingent,
drunkenly climbed down from the pavilion and out onto the rocks,
Non-gae luring him on with an amorous smile. When he reached her
she took him in a passionate embrace, then suddenly jumped into the
river below, dragging them both to their deaths.[22] This act of defiance

and self-sacrifice would become widely celebrated in the decades that followed. In the eighteenth century the Chinese characters *ui-am*, meaning "righteous rock," were carved on the face of the rock from which Non-gae was thought to have leapt. A shrine and commemorative stone would be later erected nearby. Today Non-gae is the symbol of the city of Chinju, and her story known to virtually every Korean.

On July 27, the day that the walls of Chinju were breached and the fate of the city sealed, Toyotomi Hideyoshi prepared a statement for the edification of the Chinese outlining his version of the war and its causes. The document was not addressed directly to the Ming envoys, now in their fifth week of residence at Nagoya. It went instead to Konishi Yukinaga and the three commissioners, Otani Yoshitsugu, Mashita Nagamori, and Ishida Mitsunari, with instructions that they communicate its contents to the Ming Chinese. The document was full of bravado and self-aggrandizement. Beneath the window dressing, however, it is clear that Hideyoshi's understanding of the conflict, and more generally his view of the world, was too far removed from that of the Chinese and the Koreans for there to be any common ground between the two sides. And without common ground, there was no basis for peace.

The document began with the standard recitation of Hideyoshi's predestined greatness: how he was conceived by a ray of sunlight that entered his mother's womb; how his mother was told in a dream that the virtue of her unborn son would in time shine throughout the world. Hideyoshi next cataloged how he had put an end to chaos and unified Japan in just ten years, annihilating anyone who stood in his way and establishing "national prosperity and wealth." Nor had the Japanese people been the only ones to benefit from Hideyoshi's munificence. In stamping out the wako pirates formerly based in western Japan, he had put an end to centuries of raiding and killing that had plagued the Chinese coast. "By reason of this, all your coast provinces and the inhabitants therein are enjoying safety and prosperity. Are these not the things for which you have been striving for generations without success?"

Hideyoshi, in short, had done a great service not only to his own people but to the Chinese as well. It was in fact Beijing's lack of gratitude that had caused the present war. "Perhaps you have ignored our nation," opined Hideyoshi, "believing she is too small to take any action, no matter how she may be dealt with." He therefore decided to send an army to China to demand the appreciation that he was rightfully due. He had been prepared to do so in 1589, but had postponed his plans when the Koreans sent envoys to him requesting that they be allowed to mediate between himself and China and thus avoid a war. At this same time, Hideyoshi added, "Korea pledged to open her kingdom to us, obstructing neither the roads on which our fighting men would advance nor the lines of communication or transportation, when we should be ready to invade Tai-Min [China]." Hideyoshi promised the Koreans to postpone his campaign against China for three years. He patiently waited for this period of time, until 1592. "But Korea made no report to us. She thus deceived our country, and committed a serious international crime, for which she should not remain unpunished."

And so the taiko unleashed his troops. The Koreans now evinced their duplicity yet again, for far from allowing his expeditionary forces free passage through their kingdom, they "made all possible military preparation, building strongholds at strategic points and throwing up extensive works of defense.... [But] every time they clashed with our men, they were routed. Thousands upon thousands of Koreans thus lost their lives. Finally, they set fire to their national capital, reducing it to ashes." The Chinese at this point attempted to intervene and save their vassal state, but their armies too were defeated. Hideyoshi again offered up Korea as a convenient place to lay the blame. Just as their duplicity had led Japan and China into an unnecessary war, so was their "untrustworthiness and trickery" the real cause of Ming defeat.

But now Hideyoshi was willing to bring hostilities to an end. China "has sent two envoys to our military headquarters [who] explained the imperial desire with respect to terms of peace. We have therefore prepared our peace terms as set forth on a separate sheet.... Further detail will be given orally by our four representatives."[23]

The terms of peace that Hideyoshi referred to were set down in writing that same day. Like the preceding document, it was not addressed directly to the Ming envoys, but to Konishi, Otani, Mashita, and Ishida, together with instructions to "explain the contents in detail to the imperial envoys of Great Ming."[24]

Hideyoshi's letter contained seven demands:

1. ... As evidence of sincerity, the imperial families of the two nations [China and Japan] shall enter into marriage relations. The Ming emperor shall send one of his daughters to Japan to be married to the emperor of Japan as his empress.

2. ... Henceforth, trade relations shall be renewed and both the government and the merchant ships of each nation shall be permitted to sail to the country of the other for trade purposes.

3. International friendship and good will shall be permanent, misunderstandings and misinterpretations being eliminated. Duly authorized state ministers of the two nations shall make sworn statements to this effect in written form, and exchange these statements as evidence of good faith and sincerity.

4. ... [I]f all the foregoing terms are accepted by Tai-Min [China], notwithstanding the fact that Korea had been rebellious against our country, we are willing, in order to show our good will to Tai-Min, to divide the eight provinces of Korea into two main divisions, and to return four provinces, including the one in which the national capital is situated, to the King of Korea....

5. When we return the four provinces to Korea, that nation shall send one of her royal princes and one or possibly two of her statesmen of rank of state minister across the sea to Japan and have them remain here as hostages.

6. In 1592, the first division of our troops captured two royal princes of Korea and held them as prisoners of war.... [O]ur four representatives [Konishi, Otani, Ishida, and Mashita] shall arrange with Chin Yugeki [Shen Weijing] with respect to the returning of these two royal princes to their home.

7. The state ministers in power in Korea should make sworn statements in written form to the effect that henceforth Korea shall neither oppose Japan nor overlook her generosity, and shall remain faithful to Japan, generation after generation.... [25]

The two Chinese envoys found these seven demands appallingly presumptuous. Items one and four in particular were so far beyond the realm of possibility that they must have seemed a joke. To give up one of the daughters of the Wanli emperor in marriage to the emperor of Japan signified that Hideyoshi expected a relationship of equality to be established between the two nations, something that from the Chinese perspective could never exist. China, after all, was the Middle Kingdom, the center of the world, the land without peer. If approached with the proper degree of humility, Beijing might condescend to accept Japan as a vassal state on a par with Korea. But it could never, ever, acknowledge Japan as an equal. To do so would be to turn the world on its head. As for the partitioning of Korea—Hideyoshi proposed keeping the provinces of Kyongsang, Cholla, Chungchong, and Kangwon—this too was met with disbelief, for it was asking China to relinquish a portion of its inviolate sphere of influence, one of the very things that made it so great.

Konishi and his colleagues did their best to soothe the irate envoys, pointing out that these seven conditions were not a list of intractable demands, but rather terms to be discussed and negotiated upon. With regard to items one and four, for example, the joining together of the two imperial families in marriage and the partitioning of Korea, they pointed out that Hideyoshi was not insistent on gaining both demands. For China to relent on either one of these points would be regarded as an acceptable basis for peace. And the return of the two captive Korean princes, Konishi hastened to add, was to take place regardless of the outcome of negotiations. It was a gift, a show of sincerity on Hideyoshi's part that the envoys could take back with them to Beijing.[26]

Konishi was probably correct when he told the Ming envoys that Hideyoshi intended the demands as a starting point for negotiations. Just how much the taiko was willing to compromise, however, remains unknown. The demands themselves already represented a great step down from Hideyoshi's initial plan to conquer Korea and China and make them a part of his envisioned empire. Now he was willing to settle for some sort of equal partnership with the Ming, with Korea somewhere underfoot, shouldering the blame for the war so that the two big powers could save face. It might to fair to say, therefore, that he was not prepared to bend very much further.

It is interesting to note that Hideyoshi was dealing with the Wanli emperor much as he had with rival daimyo during his campaign to unify Japan, notably his foremost preunification rival, Tokugawa Ieyasu. Just as Hideyoshi had driven Tokugawa into accepting peace in the 1580s by convincing him of his own willingness to engage in a long and costly war, so the taiko took the fight out of the Ming in 1593, maintaining a chain of camps in southern Korea and laying waste to Chinju to let them know that he meant business. As Hideyoshi had demanded hostages from Tokugawa, he now asked for a daughter from the Wanli emperor, plus a Korean prince and top officials. As he had appeased Tokugawa by allowing him to retain most of his previous land holdings, Hideyoshi now offered to let the Wanli emperor retain suzerainty over the northern half of Korea.[27]

But of course the Wanli emperor was no daimyo, and the Ming empire no mere rival's domain. China was not prepared for a moment to negotiate with Hideyoshi as an equal or to meet him even halfway on the demands he had made. Had Hideyoshi known his adversary better, he would have understood this. But it is evident that he did not. When the truth of Beijing's intractability finally became clear, the taiko's spontaneous display of rage is ample testimony to the fact that he did indeed expect the Wanli emperor to accept him as an equal, and to give in to at least some of his demands.

This realization, however, still lay more than three years away. Until then, mutual misunderstanding would be the order of the day, misunderstanding perpetuated by the representatives of both China and Japan. These intermediaries knew better than their masters just how far apart the two sides were. They also knew, however, that if a light were shone on this gaping void, negotiations would fall to pieces and fighting resume. It seemed to be in everyone's best interests, therefore, to falsify a picture of approaching common ground.

The Koreans were nervous after the fall of Chinju. The question on everyone's mind: was the attack on that city part of a larger Japanese push westward into Cholla Province, which they had failed to subdue during their offensive the previous year? At the beginning of August the worst fears seemed to materialize, as word spread that the Cholla towns of Kwangyang and Sunchon had been attacked and looted by the Japanese.

Ming negotiator Shen Weijing had already been recalled to Seoul by this time to answer for the Japanese attack on Chinju. He was summoned into the presence of Commander in Chief Li Rusong, where he was subjected to a fiery harangue. "You told us the Japanese only wanted to retreat!" began Li. "You told us that there would be no more attacks! How do you account for what has happened at Chinju?"

Shen explained that Chinju was a special case. Ever since failing to take the city in November of the previous year, the Japanese had been thirsting for revenge. But now the thing was done; they had brought the city to its knees. They had exacted their revenge and were satisfied. There thus would be no more offensives anywhere in the south.

"But what of these reports from the Koreans?" Li shot back. "That the Japanese are already advancing into Cholla Province?"

"Those reports are not true," replied Shen. "The Japanese have no intention of attacking that province."[28]

As it turned out Shen was right. At his base at Yosu, Cholla Left Naval Commander Yi Sun-sin looked into the reports that nearby Sunchon and Kwangyang had been taken by the Japanese and found them to be false. The towns had indeed been attacked and looted, but the culprits had been Koreans clad in Japanese clothing. Many were refugees from neighboring Kyongsang Province, driven from their homes by the panic that had spread following the fall of Chinju. As was often the case in such social upheaval, some had turned to lawlessness in order to survive, with Sunchon and Kwangyang, lying directly in the path of retreat west from Chinju, becoming two obvious targets. The brigands, working together with opportunistic locals, broke into government warehouses and looted private homes, relying on their Japanese garb to keep the populace passive with fear.

Yi Sun-sin kept his naval forces on alert for the next several days on the chance that he was wrong and the Japanese were indeed moving into Cholla. But the offensive never came. As Yi finally concluded, "Men's rumors are unreliable."[29]

The two Ming envoys, Xu Yihuan and Xie Yongzu, had in the meantime returned to Korea from Hideyoshi's headquarters at Nagoya. Traveling with them was a middle-aged Christian named Naito

Tadatoshi, otherwise known as Naito Joan, "Joan," the Portuguese version of "John," being the Christian name he had been given at his baptism thirty years before. Naito carried with him Hideyoshi's list of seven demands for delivery to Beijing. This task had been entrusted to him by Konishi Yukinaga in part because he was a trusted member of the latter's household, and also because he could read and write Chinese characters, a necessary prerequisite for communicating directly with the Ming.[30]

There was trouble from the very day Naito and the Chinese landed at Pusan. The envoys, informed by the irate Koreans of the recent sack of Chinju, approached Konishi Yukinaga to demand an explanation. How could Beijing believe that Japan sincerely desired peace when Japanese troops engaged in acts of aggression while negotiations were under way? Konishi did his best to explain the incident away, blaming the hawks within the Japanese camp, in particular Kato Kiyomasa. The Ming envoys, as eager as Konishi to keep negotiations alive, eventually accepted this and made no further protest. Kato's grudging release of the two captive Korean princes at this time undoubtedly helped to ameliorate the situation. In accordance with Hideyoshi's direct order, the two young men were set free from Kato's Sosaengpo camp to be reunited with their father, King Sonjo, then making his way back to Seoul from his place of refuge in the north. At the urging of various government ministers, they would then proceed on to Pyongyang to personally thank Song Yingchang, the top Ming official in Korea, for facilitating their release after more than a year "in the tiger's mouth."[31]

Hideyoshi's seven demands, meanwhile, were heatedly debated on both sides. The Ming envoys, together with every Chinese general and official who learned of the paper, insisted that it be altered before being presented in Beijing, for it would never be accepted in its present condition and would only lead to renewed hostilities. Even Hideyoshi's own commanders could not agree about its contents. They were by and large of one mind as to the need for peace, but could not agree on terms, even those set down by the taiko. Hideyoshi's document, after all, was not addressed directly to the Chinese, but rather to Konishi Yukinaga and Hideyoshi's three other representatives. They—or more precisely Japanese envoy Naito Joan—were to serve as Hideyoshi's intermediary in the coming talks in Beijing. There was thus plenty of room for tinkering with the taiko's demands before they ever reached Beijing. From the moment he set foot on Korean soil, Naito was thus inundated from both sides with urgent suggestions and arguments as to what he should and should not say when he reached China and appeared before the imperial court.

The Koreans for their part were dissatisfied. The Chinese high command had cut them out totally from the prosecution of the war and was now leaving them out of the peace negotiation process as well. King Sonjo and his government were not informed of the details of what had transpired at Nagoya, but they feared that the Chinese were entertaining thoughts of appeasement, something the Koreans did not want at all. What they wanted was revenge.

For many, negotiator Shen Weijing became the particular focus of their growing resentment of the Chinese. He was viewed as unpredictable and untrustworthy, a silk-tongued schemer who would sell the Koreans down the river if it furthered his interests. King Sonjo developed such a hatred for the man that on one occasion he woke up in the middle of the night seething with anger and wanting to kill him.[32]

Further concern was caused by the news that the Ming negotiators had returned from Kyushu with a "Japanese general" in tow, a representative from the enemy who would travel north through the length of their kingdom on his way to Beijing. King Sonjo observed that the Japanese were cunning, and had perhaps dispatched this so-called envoy merely to gather intelligence about Korea's military strength and defenses. There was even talk of blocking Naito Joan's way, but in the end nothing came of it.[33]

After an argument-filled but inconclusive few days in Pusan, Naito and the two Ming envoys proceeded on horseback north to Seoul. For Naito it was the start of what would be a painfully slow trip to Beijing, one that would take nearly a year and a half. The Ming government, suspicious of the continued Japanese presence in southern Korea and the recent attack on Chinju, would not give him permission to travel farther than Seoul, then Anju, and finally Liaodong, unable to satisfy itself that Hideyoshi was sincere in his desire for peace and not merely playing some sort of game. The release of the two Korean princes was an encouraging sign. But if the Japanese truly wanted peace, the Chinese pointed out, why did they keep the bulk of their army in Korea? And why had they established a chain of fortresses in the south? The Japanese responded in kind: if the Chinese truly wanted peace, why were their expeditionary forces still encamped in Korea?

There was only one way to break the impasse: a mutual withdrawal of troops. On the first day of September 1593, Hideyoshi dispatched orders recalling roughly half of his soldiers from Korea, a total of somewhere between forty and fifty thousand men. The subsequent ferrying of troops back to Japan took place without interference from the Korean navy, Yi Sun-sin and his fellow commanders having received orders in August not to attack.[34] The troops that Hideyoshi left in Korea would remain in place for the next three years, until Ming protests finally prompted him to order a more complete withdrawal.

The Chinese at the same time were pulling their forces back toward the north. On September 4 Commander in Chief Li Rusong left Seoul and, with the bulk of his expeditionary force, began the long march to the Yalu River and Liaodong Province beyond. This alarmed the Koreans, for they did not believe that the Japanese were sincere in their expressed desire for peace. In a report in October, the Office of the Inspector-General cautioned that the piecemeal troop withdrawals the Japanese were making were designed to trick the Chinese into pulling their own forces out of Korea. "Once the Japanese know that the Ming army has returned to China and we are left defenseless, they will surely return and attack us again. If they do, how will we stop them?"[35] The Chinese were not interested in hearing about such concerns. With the antiwar faction now ascendant in Beijing, they were committed to getting their troops out of Korea as quickly as they reasonably could. A reserve force of just ten thousand men under "Big Sword" Liu Ting and one other commander was left behind to guard the truce and act as a bodyguard for King Sonjo. They would remain in Korea until the end of 1594, when all Ming troops would be withdrawn.[36]

On his way home to China, Li Rusong stopped to bid farewell to

King Sonjo and members of the Korean government, who were then on a brief layover in the town of Hwangju, en route back to Seoul. During the course of his various farewells he spoke with much pathos of how his seven months on the peninsula had aged him. "For the sake of your country," he told the Koreans, "my beard and mustache have all turned gray." The Koreans acted suitably impressed, and nodded gravely as Li recounted again how his ancestors had originally come from Korea, and how his own father had thus urged him to do his best for their country. In private, however, at least one official groused, "Just because his ancestors came from Isan County doesn't mean he knows anything about Korea."[37]

In the formal audience that followed between Commander Li and King Sonjo, no mention was made of the differences that existed between them on the matter of negotiating with the Japanese. This was a time for formal thanks, first to Li himself, and more important to the august personage who had sent him and whom he now represented on Korean soil, the Wanli emperor himself. "We have our country today because of your efforts on our behalf," said Sonjo humbly. "It is a debt we can never repay." He then got down on his knees and made a formal bow, hands clasped in front of his forehead, his head nearly touching the floor.

Later in the meeting one of the Korean officials asked the commander if he would ever return to Korea. Li assured him that he would, for "how could I stay away so long as the Japanese remain?" He then mounted his horse and, with a pack train bearing the gifts bestowed upon him by his hosts, proceeded north to the Yalu and then west to Beijing. He would never return.[38]

Li Rusong arrived in Beijing to a mixed reception. Officially he was awarded with the customary promotion and increase in stipend in recognition of his service. Unofficially he was denounced in many quarters for the policy of appeasement he had followed in his dealings with the Japanese. It was because of this negative sentiment that he was kept waiting for another posting for the next four years. Finally, in the face of considerable opposition, he was appointed regional commander of Liaodong Province in 1597. Not long after arriving in his new command, Mongol tribes from the north launched raids into Liaodong, providing Li with a chance to redeem himself in battle. His campaign against the marauders began well enough, with a heartening victory. In a subsequent night attack, however, Li stumbled into an ambush and was killed, along with many of his men. He was buried with full honors as a hero of the state. His vacant post was passed to his younger brother, Li Rumei.[39]

On August 29, 1593, a son was born at Osaka Castle to Yodogimi, concubine to Toyotomi Hideyoshi. The taiko received the news in Nagoya with joy and exultation. Here was the heir he had given up on ever having; here was the son who would preserve the name of Toyotomi after he himself was gone. Just days after the arrival of these happy tidings, Hideyoshi packed up his train and left Nagoya, never to return.

Hideyoshi's party must have made an interesting sight as it wended its way out of the castle and onto the main road to the north. European fashions, introduced by the Portuguese, were now all the rage among the nation's elite, with everybody who was anybody making an effort to obtain at least one item of this strange and exciting garb. There were a few among the taiko's retinue who had thrown themselves entirely into the craze, proceeding north in a complete outfit of cape, ruffed shirt, and breeches. Others contented themselves with a decorative crucifix or rosary. As for Hideyoshi, it is hard to imagine that he did not at least dabble in the trend with a ruff or belt or cross. Judging from what we know of his eccentric tastes—it is known, for example, that he liked veal, a dish that revolted most of his daimyo—a little excess in this regard would have been entirely likely.[40]

Prior to setting out on his journey to Osaka, Hideyoshi sent instructions ahead to his wife O-Ne as to how his new son should be named. "Even the lowest servants," he wrote, "should not call him with the honorific 'o'. You should call him plainly Hiroi, Hiroi. I shall make a triumphal return very soon."[41] It was a Japanese custom to give derogatory names to newborn children so as not to attract the attention of the gods, for they were a capricious lot who seemed to delight in taking away those things which mortals cherished most. Thus it was that Hideyoshi had chosen the name Sute, "thrown away," for his first son Tsurumatsu, who had died at the age of two in 1591. For his second son, who would come to be known as Hideyori, Hideyoshi selected the unassuming name Hiroi, "gleaned." It was an apparently fortunate choice of names, for the gods did not direct any unwanted attention on the boy. He would live to become a man—if only a very young one.

CHAPTER 20

Factions, Feuds, and Forgeries

ON OCTOBER 24, 1593, King Sonjo arrived back in the Korean capital of Seoul after an absence of more than a year and a half. Little had been done to restore the city since the evacuation of the Japanese in May. The nation was too spent. With Kyongbok Palace and all the other royal enclosures now in ruins, Sonjo was forced to make his residence in the relatively modest mansion of Prince Wolsan, the grandson of King Sejo, on the grounds of what is today Toksu Palace. The building was renovated to the extent that the nation's depleted treasury would allow, and nearby property confiscated and added on. This temporary royal residence came to be known as the Chongnung Detached Palace. Sonjo was unhappy with the arrangement and spoke of rebuilding at least a portion of his former residence at Kyongbok-gung. But his kingdom was in no condition to undertake such a costly project. He would have to remain at Chongnung Palace until his death in 1608. His successor would eventually renovate and move into Changdok Palace, a smaller and inferior residence to Kyongbok, but one not requiring such an infusion of cash to restore. Kyongbok-gung itself, the Palace of Shining Happiness, would lay in ruins for the next 270 years.[1]

With King Sonjo back in the capital and the Japanese confined to the south, the government of Korea could at last begin the job of rebuilding the nation and returning it to some semblance of normalcy. The task would be undertaken with Yu Song-nyong at the helm. On November 19 he was appointed prime minister of the State Council (*uijongbu*), replacing Choi Hung-won, who was obliged to retire for reasons of ill health.[2] The challenges facing Yu and his ministers were immense, for Korea's economy had been almost destroyed. The upheavals of war had caused food production to fall off so drastically that famine was everywhere, and with it contagious disease. The situation in some areas was so extreme that Yu would later write of children and the aged being abandoned by families who could no longer care for them, and of young men forced into a life of crime. In the most desperate cases husbands turned against wives and sons against fathers, killing and eating their flesh as the only way to survive.[3]

The government's most immediate concern, understandably enough, was with national security. Beginning in mid-1593 and continuing to the end of 1596, the meager resources of the country were thrown into a campaign to strengthen fortifications, particularly in the south, to guard against the possible return of the Japanese. The aim of this building campaign differed from that undertaken prior to the start of the war. At that time the goal had been to surround towns and cities with expansive walls—mostly low earthen ramparts and flimsy wooden stockades—so that the largest number of people could be accommodated inside. The subsequent course events had demonstrated how wrong this strategy was: the kilometers of walls made towns difficult to defend and easy prey for the militarily experienced Japanese. With the building program begun in 1593, the Koreans returned to what they did best: the construction of impregnable mountain fortresses of stone, compact and easy to defend, situated to take advantage of the natural terrain. The location of these forts gives a clear indication of how the Koreans' concept of defense had changed since early 1592. Previously they had expected in the event of an invasion to meet and repel the enemy before he had a chance to advance very far inland, and had thus largely confined their construction efforts to centers lying between the southern coast and the city of Taegu one hundred kilometers inland. The Koreans now knew that the Japanese were too strong to be stopped by such a forward defense. Any renewed aggression would have to be gradually brought to a halt by a defense in depth, a defense based upon a network of fortresses extending a further three hundred kilometers north, from Taegu all the way to Seoul. A string of forts was also built along the westernmost border of Kyongsang Province to meet any

Japanese move against Cholla. Such a defense in depth, Yu Song-nyong observed, would be like "a double door or a double wall. . . . [E]ven though the enemy might be able to penetrate one of the layers, there would always be another one [behind it]."[4] It is a testament to the quality of these fortifications that a number are still standing today, for example Kongsan near Taegu, Toksan in the vicinity of Suwon, and most notably Namhansansong (South Mountain Fortress) south of Seoul.[5]

Beginning in the latter part of 1593 the Korean government also set to work modernizing its army, which the Ming generals frankly told them was behind the times in terms of both weaponry and organization. Prime Minister Yu Song-nyong wholeheartedly agreed, conceding, "Basically [our troops] do not know anything about fighting, and they have no units such as platoons, squads, banners, or companies to which they are attached. They are in confusion and without order, make a big racket and run around in chaos, not knowing what to do with their hands, feet, ears, or eyes." As for weaponry, he continued, "When [our] soldiers are lined up against the enemy ranks, our arrows do not reach the enemy while their musket balls rain down upon us." It was therefore imperative to start manufacturing muskets, and in a wider sense to start borrowing and adapting superior things from other nations.[6]

In response to Yu's urging for adaptation and progress, King Sonjo authorized the adoption of the musket as a standard weapon for the army, and ordered the establishment of a Military Training Agency in Seoul that in the coming months would grow to employ ten thousand men. He also ordered—again upon Yu's recommendation—the printing and distribution of the military training manual *Jixiao xinshu* by the famous Chinese general Qi Jiguang (1528–1588), which detailed how to organize an army and train soldiers in the "three skills": using the musket, the sword, and the bow. General Qi's manual would become the basis for much of the reorganization of the Korean military undertaken between 1594 and 1596 by Prime Minister Yu.

The new Korean army that took shape during this three-year period was an adaptation of General Qi's *chin-gwan* model. The Koreans called it the *sogo* system. The smallest unit was the squad of eleven men. There were three types of these squads: archer squads, musketeer squads, and hand-to-hand "killer" squads armed with sword and spear. Three squads, one of each type, formed a platoon; three platoons formed a company; five companies formed a battalion, and twenty-five battalions formed a division, totaling in theory 12,375 men.

Before this new type of army could be formed, the Korean government first had to find a way to feed it, no small problem considering that the nation's economy was now in ruins. There was only one solution: make the army a militia. Yu Song-nyong and his colleagues found ample justification for this in the Chinese military classics, and accordingly applied the principle to almost every military unit, even to the Military Training Agency in Seoul. Throughout the mid-1590s the ten thousand troops making up this premier force would divide their time between training in the capital and working in the fields on government land. Elsewhere in the country soldiers were assigned to units near their homes and were commanded by local men. This saved the time and expense that would otherwise have been wasted in traveling long distances, and not incidentally made men less likely to try to avoid their duty. These local troops met periodically for training, and less frequently for large-scale exercises involving the entire locally based division. Other than that they were free to work their farms or practice their craft, and in so doing contribute to the nation's rebuilding.[7]

In the Korean navy, meanwhile, a number of fundamental changes had been instituted as well. In September of 1593 Cholla Left Navy Commander Yi Sun-sin, who had given the Japanese fleet so many drubbings during the first year of the war, was promoted to the newly created post of Supreme Navy Commander of the Three Provinces of Kyongsang, Cholla, and Chungchong. He was thus now the ranking superior of his colleagues Cholla Right Navy Commander Yi Ok-ki and Kyongsang Right Navy Commander Won Kyun, and the top naval officer in the south. Yi had previously moved his home port eastward from Yosu to Hansan Island, half the distance to the Japanese stronghold at Pusan, so that he could keep a closer watch on the enemy camped in their line of fortresses encircling the port. Hansan-do would remain the headquarters for the Korean navy in the south until 1597.

Little in the way of naval activity took place throughout the remainder of 1593. As Yi Sun-sin reported to the government in Seoul, the

Japanese refused to come out onto open water and engage his ships in battle.[8] Although Yi remained bellicose in his diary and dispatches, the break in the fighting was probably welcome, for simply maintaining his navy under the conditions then prevailing in Korea was a difficult task. With the kingdom's agricultural base in disarray and tax revenues slowed to a trickle, he could not expect anything from the central government in the way of support. He and his colleagues were obliged to rely on their own resources simply to keep their men fed and their ships afloat. Back in the spring of 1593 Yi had bowed to the inevitable and released half his men to return to their fields to grow the food that the nation so badly needed. Those kept in service were put to work farming and fishing and manufacturing salt and earthenware to sell in the markets for cash. In this way Yi managed not only to keep his command alive, but started to stockpile a reserve of grain in government warehouses in anticipation of the coming counter-offensive to drive the Japanese out of Korea. Won Kyun in neighboring Kyongsang Province appears to have been less successful, complaining in his dispatches to Seoul of dire hardship throughout his command, with some of his men on the point of starvation.[9]

Yi Sun-sin also began unraveling the secrets of the Japanese muskets he had captured in his earlier sea battles, for in his opinion "no other weapons are more effective." During the first half of 1593 he put his ablest men to work examining and testing these captured weapons. By the end of the summer they had developed an effective copy, one "whose shooting force is exactly the same as the Japanese guns, although the fire-kindling apparatus at the breech is somewhat different." Since they were relatively easy to manufacture, Yi commanded that workshops be set up in every town and port under his command to turn out copies. He also sent five samples to Seoul, with the suggestion that officials in every province begin producing weapons of their own.[10]

And so Korea began to get back on its feet after a year and a half of war. The nation had been driven to the very edge of the abyss, but thanks to its stubborn unwillingness to surrender coupled with military aid from China, the crisis had been averted and the nation had been

saved. True, the Japanese were still encamped on the peninsula's southern coast, but it now was hopefully just a matter of time before they
would tire of the game and reboard their ships for home.

It was in this very return to normalcy, however, where trouble lay,
for in government circles in Choson Korea business as usual meant
factional strife. Since the start of the war the overriding concern for
national survival had forced the contending elements within the government to set their differences aside and work together in what
amounted to a coalition government. But now that the worst of the
crisis had seemingly passed, factional lines were quietly redrawn. For
the Westerners this meant looking for ways to chip away at the ascendant Eastern faction, of which Prime Minister Yu Song-nyong was now
the most prominent member. In the political game it was dangerous to
go after Yu Song-nyong himself, for he wielded too much power and
had the ear of the king. Instead they looked for chinks in his armor by
scrutinizing the conduct of the members of his camp.

One member the Westerners were monitoring was Yu's childhood
friend and protégé, Supreme Navy Commander Yi Sun-sin, the recently
promoted head of the Korean navy in the south. Since the beginning of
the war Kyongsang Navy Commander Won Kyun had been providing
interested parties in Seoul with a growing file of criticisms of Yi,
beginning with his failure to rush to Won's aid in May of 1592. With
Yi's promotion in September to the rank of supreme naval commander,
this bitterness of Won's became even stronger, for he resented the fact
that a formerly junior officer with fewer years of service than himself
should outrank him.[11] He was now prepared to say or do almost anything to bring his nemesis down. Yi was acutely aware of this, and in
his diary began making frequent references to Won's growing hostility
and belligerence:

> *June 13, 1593:* Yun Tong-ku brought me his commander's [Won
> Kyun's] war report draft addressed to the King. I found his wording
> in that report to be maliciously deceptive.
> *June 19, 1593:* Won Kyun transmitted dispatches with false reports,
> causing a profound sensation among many navy units. His truculent
> and perverse acts making mischief for his friendly forces with such
> deception cannot be adequately depicted.

August 17, 1593: Commander Won Kyun uttered nothing but extraordinary tricks and wicked designs. Nothing could be accomplished by his words. Joint operation will surely result in immeasurable disaster! His younger brother, Yon, arrived later and begged to take away some rice.

August 27, 1593: After dark, Right Admiral Yi Ok-ki came to my boat and said that . . . Won Kyun talked nonsense as he brought false accusations against me. All that he says is absurd.

August 31, 1593: In the evening Admirals Won Kyun, Yi Ok-ki and Chong Kol came to a staff meeting in my cabin, where Won Kyun jabbered all the time with pointless words. He kept contradicting himself.

September 13, 1593: Won Kyun again uttered many absurdities. His treachery cannot be expressed properly with ordinary words.

September 20, 1593: [Won Kyun] became drunk, bellowing out mad words of a vicious nature. Astounding!

September 22, 1593: Won Kyun came to me and uttered many vicious and deceitful words. What a dangerous man![12]

Won was indeed dangerous. Although he often appears in Yi's diary as an ineffectual, drunken buffoon, he was shrewd and calculating, and knew what was needed to bring a rival down. From early in the war and continuing on to the end of 1594, Won repeatedly sent dispatches to Yi urging him to join him in attacking the Japanese. Yi saw through these messages as mere ploys to make him look bad; Won had no wish to go on the attack. Just how duplicitous these calls to action were became clear in July of 1593 when, after receiving two letters from Won "urging me to go with him and attack the enemy," Yi called his bluff with a return communication ordering a joint attack. The Kyongsang commander "failed to answer [the order]," Yi wrote in his diary, "using the alibi that he was drunk."[13]

Won Kyun continued to play this game throughout 1594, "proving" that Yi Sun-sin was an unfit commander by sending him one frivolous call to action after another. If Yi took the bait and led his ships into action, he would be unable to accomplish much, not with the Japanese holed up on shore and unwilling to fight, and thus would look ineffectual. If he ignored Won's letters, Won could then accuse him of shirking his duty. It was a simple strategy, designed to damage Yi no matter what he did. And it began to have its intended effect. Members of the Western faction in Seoul were the first to take note of Won's accusations, for Yi was a friend and appointee of Prime Minister and Eastern faction leader Yu Song-nyong. Even among the Easterners, however, there were those who came to wonder about Yi. Frustrated by the fact that the Japanese seemed set to negotiate their way out of an unjust war, many within the government were looking to Yi to strike a blow, as he had done so effectively earlier in the war, and now were disappointed to find his ships idle.

In April of 1594 Yi Sun-sin finally had an opportunity to redeem himself: a report arrived at his Hansan-do base that a squadron of enemy ships was probing westward beyond the perimeter of Japanese forts. The movement appears to have been nothing more than a small-scale raiding expedition composed of thirty-one ships; the Japanese in Korea were now desperate for food and had to venture further to get it. They would not get far. On the twenty-third and twenty-fourth, squadrons of warships from Yi's fleet hunted down and destroyed all thirty-one of the Japanese ships just north of Koje Island, eight of them at Chinhae, on the very doorsteps of Konishi Yukinaga's Ungchon camp. Very little actual fighting took place. The Japanese crews ran for shore and fled inland as soon as they spotted the Korean navy arrayed offshore in crane wing formation, leaving their beached vessels behind for Yi's men to pick through and then burn at their leisure. Yi was not entirely satisfied with this outcome. He had tried to arrange a coordinated attack with government army units stationed along the coast so that they would be waiting on shore to cut the Japanese sailors down when they beached their ships and fled. But his call to action went unanswered, and so the Japanese, although they lost their ships, were able to get away.

The operation ended on a sour note on April 25 with the arrival at Yi's flagship of a field order from Ming general Dan Zongren, then visiting Konishi Yukinaga at his camp at Ungchon, commanding him to call off his attack so as not to jeopardize peace negotiations. "Many Japanese commanding officers have become filled with relenting hearts," Dan wrote, "with their weapons packed up and their soldiers given rest to prepare to go home; therefore, your warships are also expected to return to their home bases and not approach the Japanese positions." This angered Yi Sun-sin. He was opposed to any sort of settlement with the Japanese other than their complete and immediate destruction, and replied to General Dan that as "a subject of Korea... I cannot live with these robbers under the same heaven." Yi concluded by saying,

> Where is the evidence of packing their weapons to go home across the sea? You talk of peace, but it is a peace which the Japanese offer with their habitual trick and deception. However, we are not in a position to disobey your instructions, so we are going to forbear for a time while we report it to our King. In the meantime we wish Your Excellency to enlighten the Japanese fellows on the consequences of obedience and disobedience to heaven.[14]

Forbearing was in fact not so very hard for Yi to do; with the thirty-one enemy vessels already destroyed, there was little else for him to attack. He thus returned to his base on Hansan-do—and promptly fell ill with typhoid.[15]

In his official report on the operation, Kyongsang Navy Commander Won Kyun attempted to claim credit for all the enemy ships destroyed. Although desperately ill, when Yi Sun-sin heard of this he forced himself to sit up in bed and composed a harshly worded report of his own berating Won for lying and accusing his men of submitting the heads of Korean civilians as Japanese war dead to inflate their battle honors. Yi then gave a painstaking accounting of every Japanese ship destroyed to set the record straight. At the final tally Won's forces had actually burned or sunk only eleven of the thirty-one vessels; Cholla ships had claimed the rest. Won visited the still very ill Yi a few days later to apologize for the inaccuracies in his account, and beseeched him to soften his own report before sending it on to Seoul. Yi agreed. He then returned to his sick bed and remained indisposed for the next two weeks.[16]

Although Commander Yi survived his encounter with typhoid fever, many of his men did not. During the coming months the disease would decimate the ranks of the unified Korean navy, now largely concentrated into a single camp on Hansan Island. By June, 1,704 sailors had died, 3,759 others were ill, and lack of manpower was becoming a serious worry. Yi wrote to Seoul complaining that local magistrates seemed oblivious to the emergency and were neglecting to send him reinforcements. "Under these circumstances," he noted, "I was obliged to recruit wandering beggars to fill the vacancies . . . , but having been starved for food too long many of them soon died."[17]

Negotiations between Japan and China, meanwhile, were in danger of falling apart. Naito Joan, the envoy sent north by Konishi Yukinaga to deliver Hideyoshi's seven demands to Beijing, had been denied permission by the Ming to proceed any farther than Liaodong Province, and was now waiting on the Chinese frontier. The sticking point was the letter he carried. To Song Yingchang, the Chinese civilian official charged with overseeing military affairs in Korea, Hideyoshi's demands were presumptuous and insulting, the rantings of a barbarian unfamiliar with the ways of the world. They thus did not merit transmission on to the capital, for they would only serve to cause offense and lead in all likelihood to a resumption of war.

Throughout the latter half of 1593 Konishi Yukinaga, working with Ming negotiator Shen Weijing, proceeded to drop Hideyoshi's demands one by one in an attempt to break this impasse. He had little choice. It was Japan, after all, that wanted something from China, not the other way around. China's world was already complete. On his own initiative Konishi pared the taiko's demands down to the very bone, until finally he stated that his master would be satisfied with just one province of Korea, an indemnity payment of twenty thousand taels of silver from the Choson court, and a resumption of trade relations with China.

Song, not surprisingly, refused even this. All he would consent to consider was the revival of tribute trade as it had once existed between the two nations. For that to take place, however, Hideyoshi first would have to receive investiture as King of Japan, just as the Ashikaga shogun had done nearly two centuries before. In other words, he would have to become a vassal of the emperor of China.

This intransigence put Konishi Yukinaga in a difficult spot. He had been able so far to drop most of Hideyoshi's demands on his own, without the taiko's knowledge. To satisfy the Chinese on the point of submission, however, would require a document from Hideyoshi himself, something he clearly would never consent to write. There was only one thing Konishi could do to keep the game alive: forge a letter of submission himself. He did so with the connivance of the ever-resourceful Shen Weijing, who evidently knew how to word such things. The resulting document put some remarkably un-taiko-esque words into Hideyoshi's mouth, and stands today as a testament to the amazing latitude for deception that existed in international diplomacy four hundred years ago.

In Konishi's and Shen's forged letter, dated February 10, 1594, Hideyoshi stated that Japan was "a small and humble country" and "a child of China." He himself stood in "fear and awe" of the Celestial Throne, and earnestly beseeches the Wanli emperor to accept him as a vassal. This had indeed been his sole desire all along. He had sent his army to Korea merely because he wished to seek tributary relations with Beijing. The unreasonable Koreans had refused to grant him right of way and had drawn him into a war that had unfortunately come to involve the Ming. But now, Hideyoshi concluded, "I prostrate myself and I beg Your Majesty to let that light of the sun and moon shine forth with which He irradiates the world, to extend that nourishing capacity of heaven and earth with which He overspreads and sustains all things that there are . . . and to bestow on me the title of an imperially invested vassal king."[18]

The Koreans expressed a good degree of skepticism when they learned of the contents of this spurious document. It did not sound at all like the Hideyoshi they knew, but was clearly a forgery, probably from the pen of the shady Shen Weijing.[19] The Chinese, however, had fewer reservations, for the letter said exactly what they wanted to hear. The impasse in Liaodong would soon be broken.

The negotiations between China and Japan were causing the Koreans a great deal of concern. Was their bitter enemy Hideyoshi going to be appeased instead of punished for his unwarranted aggression? For that would be the upshot if even a single one of his demands was accepted in Beijing. And even worse, was he going to be appeased at Korea's expense? The fact that the Koreans were being cut out of the negotiation process only served to heighten their fears on this score, and led some to voice their dissatisfaction loudly enough for the Ming Chinese to hear.

It was at about this time that Song Yingchang, the Ming official in charge of overseeing affairs in Liaodong and Korea, was forced to resign and return to China, the victim of the factional wrangling that affected the government in Beijing nearly as strongly as its counterpart in Seoul. A growing bone of contention in the Chinese capital was the Korean war itself, a prowar faction on one side urging its aggressive prosecution, an antiwar faction on the other, led by Minister of War Shi Xing, demanding its hasty conclusion so as to spare the treasury any further expense. Song Yingchang's dismissal marked a victory for the doves. His replacement, Ku Yangqian, moved east into Liaodong to take up his new post with a determination to restore peace in Korea through negotiation and thus solve the "Japan problem," and so was anxious to quiet the grumbling emanating from Seoul that the war should be continued in order to punish Hideyoshi. Toward this end he sent an envoy, Hu Ze, south to talk the Koreans into supporting the negotiation process. Upon his arrival in Seoul, Hu lectured Korean government officials at length on what he considered the central issues of gratitude and common sense:

> The Wan-li emperor was angered when the Japanese dwarfs invaded your country, and thus he sent soldiers to drive them back. Now the Japanese have fled back toward the south, your captured princes have been returned, and two thousand li of your kingdom have been restored. China spent a great deal of money to accomplish this for you, and sacrificed the lives of many horses and men. Our emperor and our government have treated you well.
>
> But now we can provide nothing more. The campaign is finished. The Japanese dwarfs have been made afraid of our might, and have asked to surrender and send us tribute. We think it would be appropriate now to accept them as vassals. We are doing this to save your country. Choson now has no food. Your people are killing and eating one other in order to survive. With this being so, how can you ask us to continue the fighting? How can you ask for further aid? If we do not accept Japan as a vassal, they might attack your kingdom again, and this time they might destroy you. Is that what you want?[20]

Hu Ze was particularly anxious while in Seoul to talk King Sonjo into sending a message to Beijing requesting that Hideyoshi be accepted as a vassal. Although Hu did not spell out his reasons for wanting this done, it was clearly to add weight to the arguments of Minister of War Shi Xing's antiwar faction. It was an appeal for help from the Korean king, after all, that had drawn the Chinese into the war in the first place. To get him now to support a peace initiative was thus a perfect way to undermine the prowar camp. King Sonjo, however, refused to comply. "How could I ask such a thing of China," he told Hu Ze, "after requesting military assistance to fight the Japanese at the beginning of the war?" Hu conceded that it might not be judicious to dispatch such a request at the present moment. But it could be done early in the coming year. In your next report to the emperor on the Japanese situation, he suggested, you could discreetly broach the idea that Hideyoshi should be appeased with an offer of tributary relations. Surely that would do no harm to your country. Sonjo again refused. Hu Ze then tried a more aggressive tack. Ku Yangqian, he said, had no more troops to send to Korea, so it would not be possible any time soon to launch a counter-offensive. The only way to get the Japanese out of Korea in the short term was therefore through negotiation. Otherwise they would remain on the peninsula for another ten or twenty years. Sonjo listened politely, but still would not agree.[21]

Hu Ze remained in Seoul for three months, alternately cajoling and haranguing the Koreans to accept negotiations with Japan and the terms of peace that would ensue. By the time he finally returned north, the man who had sent him, Ku Yangqian, had, like Song Yingchang before him, been dismissed as a result of factional strife. Ku's removal and the subsequent appointment of Sun Kuang as civilian overseer of eastern affairs marked a small victory for the hawks in Beijing. No move was made to halt negotiations with Japan, however, and the tug of war between the pro- and antiwar factions continued unabated.[22]

In the south, meanwhile, Konishi Yukinaga was doing some cajoling of his own. In late 1594 he sent an agent named Yojiro to the camp of Kim Ung-so, the Korean army commander of Kyongsang Province, bearing gifts and an invitation to parlay. Kim reported this to his superiors in Seoul and was given permission to go and see what the enemy general had to say. The meeting took place in December, Kim and his officers on one side, Konishi, So Yoshitoshi, and the monk Genso on the other.

Konishi began with the now tired refrain that the war had been entirely the Koreans' fault; their refusal to allow the Japanese to pass through their country on a mission of peace to China had left Hideyoshi no alternative but to attack. Kim Ung-so would have none of it. All your talk of desiring only peace, he said, is nothing but a smokescreen. We know it, and the Ming Chinese know it as well. That is why the emperor sent his great army to stop you. Besides, Kim added, if all you want is peace, then why did you attack Chinju last summer? And why did you plunder Kyongju last fall?

That had nothing to do with me, replied Konishi. Those two acts were entirely the doing of Kato Kiyomasa; they did not reflect the wishes of Toyotomi Hideyoshi at all. All the taiko wanted, he assured Kim, was to become a vassal of the Ming. And all he now asked of the Koreans was that they intercede with Beijing on his behalf.[23]

The Koreans did not trust Konishi. It was obvious to them that the so-called letter of surrender from Hideyoshi was a forgery and that there was thus no real basis for a true and lasting peace. Korean prime minister Yu Song-nyong, who was ill at the time and convalescing outside of the capital, wrote to King Sonjo urging him to communicate directly with Beijing so that the Chinese government would understand that "the Japanese will never be satisfied with becoming a vassal state and paying tribute to China." In the end, however, pressure from the antiwar faction in the Ming capital had its intended effect. Toward the end of 1594 King Sonjo finally caved in and dispatched a letter to the Wanli emperor supporting the idea of negotiating with Hideyoshi, and requesting that toward this end Japanese envoy Naito Joan be allowed to continue his mission to Beijing. It was clearly a letter the king did not want to write. As a vassal of China, however, he found it difficult to ignore the prodding of the representative officials of that great land. Sonjo's letter was to prove an important document, for it undermined the hard-liners within the Ming government who opposed negotiation. If the Koreans themselves, the most aggrieved party in the entire affair, were in favor of treating with the Japanese for terms of peace, then there was little reason not to at least receive Naito and see how little he could be persuaded to accept.

After a journey of nearly a year and a half, most of it spent waiting in Liaodong, the Japanese envoy thus was granted permission to proceed to Beijing.[24]

Although King Sonjo had now given his support to the reception of the envoy Naito Joan, he and his government ministers remained deeply distrustful of the Japanese and of any talk of peace. They had good reason to be. Beginning in the spring of 1595 Kato Kiyomasa, angered by Konishi Yukinaga's twisting of the taiko's demands, embarked on some diplomacy of his own, laying before first the Chinese and then the Koreans the original list of seven conditions for peace that Hideyoshi expected to be met, and in so doing contradicting everything that had been said and promised by Konishi and Shen Weijing.

The first of these meetings took place between Kato and a group of Ming officials in April, at the former's Sosaengpo camp near Ulsan, a day's journey north along the coast from Pusan. Kato began by saying that Konishi and Shen Weijing were conducting negotiations under false pretenses. "What they are doing is all a vicious trick." He then proceeded to outline the actual conditions for peace that Hideyoshi had drawn up back in 1593, from the demand for a Ming princess in marriage and four of Korea's eight provinces to the requirement that a Korean prince be sent as a hostage to Japan. Finally, to make things crystal clear, Kato took up a brush and wrote some of his assertions on a piece of paper that he handed to the Chinese. His characters were poorly written and difficult to read, the Korean chroniclers were careful to note, but the gist was this: "The things Konishi has asked for were not ordered by Hideyoshi. How could anyone presume to think that he would want to become a mere vassal of the Ming? Envoys should be sent again from China to Japan, to hear the truth directly from the taiko himself."[25]

Kato's blunt talk did nothing to sway the Ming Chinese. The officials came away from the meeting suspecting that he wanted to discredit Konishi's and Shen's efforts at diplomacy so that he himself could take the lead in the negotiation process. Undeterred, Kato tried again to make Hideyoshi's true demands known, this time to the

Koreans. In May of 1595, and then again in August, he met with a group of officials and the battle-hardened monk commander Yujong, who had succeeded his aged master Hyujong the year before as supreme commander of Korea's monk-soldiers. On both occasions Kato carefully conveyed Hideyoshi's original demands so that nothing would be misunderstood, and Yujong just as carefully explained why each demand was utterly unacceptable, both to the Koreans and to the Chinese. In the end nothing came of the talks; the two sides were too far apart, and neither was willing to give an inch. Kato's efforts at diplomacy in fact were entirely counterproductive, for in confirming for the Koreans their suspicions that Hideyoshi wanted much more than to become a mere vassal of the Wanli emperor, he firmed their resolve not to negotiate, but to resist the Japanese at every turn.[26]

By this time, however, peace negotiations had advanced too far to be stopped. Naito Joan had reached Beijing.

Kato Kiyomasa was right of course: Toyotomi Hideyoshi entertained no thoughts whatsoever of becoming a vassal of China. Had he known that his representative Konishi Yukinaga had forged a letter stating that this was what he desired, the taiko would probably have ordered him to commit suicide, a common response to acts of disloyalty and deceit. Fortunately for Konishi he never found out.

Just how unrepresentative the forged letter was of Hideyoshi's wishes becomes evident by contrasting it with the orders he dispatched to his army in Korea in early 1594:

1. Although it would be very desirable to renew military activities immediately, yet, acting upon the suggestions of the military leaders in Korea, we have decided to suspend our military activities in that country throughout this year [1594].
2. In the coming year [1595], if the pending international problem has not reached a solution, Kampaku Hidetsugu [Hideyoshi's adopted son and heir] shall be requested to cross the water to Korea at the head of a large army. Therefore, all the strongholds in Korea must be well equipped....
3. As to provisions for the troops, in addition to what we have already sent, we are now sending about 30,000 koku of rice....
4. Because Tai-Min [China] has apologized and expressed regret for

engaging in military activities in Korea, and has sued for peace, a truce in now in force. However, we have reason to question that nation's sincerity. We shall therefore prepare for a permanent military occupation of Korea by strengthening all the military castles and strongholds to the fullest degree. We regard Korea as a part of our domain, the same as Kyushu.[27]

Hideyoshi clearly thought that some of his war objectives could still be achieved. China had apologized for resisting him (or so he thought) and was now suing for peace (or so he thought). And if they did not offer suitable concessions he would launch his forces again. At the very least he expected to come away from the negotiating table with a large piece of Korea, a piece that he already considered "a part of our domain, the same as Kyushu."

In this document Hideyoshi went on to assure his troops in Korea that replacements would soon be arriving and that they would all get a chance to return to Japan for a furlough. There was thus no reason for anyone to "become restless." This reference to restlessness evinces awareness on the taiko's part of dissention among the ranks of his soldiers in Korea, an awareness he addressed directly in the following lines: "All the men at home in Japan . . . are assigned to work of one kind or another in connection with the present campaign. In fact, our fighting men in Korea are doing less work than are the Japanese at home."[28]

Hideyoshi's assertion to the contrary, the Japanese troops stationed in Korea did not consider themselves lucky to be there. Far from it. They were exhausted from the heavy work of building fortifications. They had not seen their friends and relations for a year and more and were desperately homesick. They were hungry, for supplies did not often arrive from Japan, and the land about their forts had been laid waste by the Koreans in an effort to starve them out. Then the cold of winter set in, a piercing, bitter cold unlike anything they had known back home, a cold that their strongly built but poorly heated quarters did little to keep out. And finally, early in 1594, typhoid fever spread from camp to camp, carrying off hundreds, possibly thousands.[29]

Under these conditions desertion became common. Some soldiers attempted to slip back home to Japan. Others offered their services to the Koreans. This latter group came to number in the thousands, and constituted such a significant force that the Koreans formed them into units called *hangwaedae* (surrendered Japanese corps) and incorporated them into their army and navy.[30] These men would never return to Japan. They settled in Korea after the war and became naturalized citizens. It was a relatively easy shift in allegiance to make—certainly easier than it would have been for a Korean—for after two centuries of civil war the average Japanese did not have such a strong sense of "nation." The men of the hangwaedae may have been susceptible to feelings of guilt for having betrayed their families or their village or their former daimyo lord, but the thought of betraying Japan as a whole would have caused them little remorse.[31]

In order to provide comfort to and quell discontent among his largely Christian force, Konishi Yukinaga sent a request to the Jesuit fathers back in Japan for a priest to be sent over to Korea. The Jesuits, who regarded Konishi as their staunchest ally, readily complied, dispatching Father Gregorio de Cespedes of Spain and a Japanese lay brother toward the end of 1593. Father de Cespedes, a forty-three-year-old missionary with sixteen years of service in Japan and a remarkable grasp of the language, would become the first European on record ever to visit the Korean mainland.

Father de Cespedes arrived on Tsushima en route to Korea in early December 1593. Rough seas and adverse winds prevented him from proceeding any farther for the next eighteen days. He spent the time ministering to the island's small Christian community as a guest of Maria, wife of Tsushima daimyo So Yoshitoshi and daughter of Konishi Yukinaga. Finally, "by the help of God," de Cespedes managed to reach Korea's rocky southern shore on December 27, landing near Konishi's fortress at Ungchon. The priest was initially impressed by the impregnability of the complex that had been constructed to resist Korean and Chinese attack. "[G]reat defensive works have been erected there which are admirable," he wrote, "considering the short time in which they were completed. They have built high walls, watch towers, and strong bastions, at the foot of which all the nobles and soldiers of Augustin [Konishi], his subjects and allies, are encamped. For all there are well built and spacious [barracks]. Houses with stone walls are built for the chiefs. . . . For one league around there are various fortresses."

The general conditions de Cespedes saw around him, however, were not good:

> The cold in Korea is very severe and without any comparison with that of Japan. All day long my limbs are half benumbed, and in the morning I can hardly move my hands to say mass, but . . . I am cheerful and don't mind my work and the cold.
>
> All these Christians are very poor, and suffer from hunger, cold, illness and other inconveniences. . . . Although Hideyoshi sends food, so little reaches here that it is impossible to sustain all with them, and moreover the help that comes from Japan is insufficient and comes late. It is now two months since ships have come, and many craft were lost.
>
> An understanding regarding peace is not reached yet, and those who should come to conclude it never arrive. Many suspect that this delay is nothing but a trick in order to keep the Japanese waiting until summer, when ships of the Chinese armada may arrive, and an army by land.[32]

Father de Cespedes remained in Korea until April 1594, ministering to the men under the Christian commanders he knew as Augustin (Konishi Yukinaga), Darius (So Yoshitoshi), Sancho (Omura Yoshiaki), Protius (Arima Harunobu), Damien (Kuroda Nagamasa), and others. He had no opportunity to meet Koreans during this time other than the unfortunate wretches being sent back to Japan as slaves. The father in fact was kept in close confinement in the camps of the Christian daimyo between Pusan and Ungchon, for news of his presence in Korea would have posed some danger to Konishi if it reached the ears of Toyotomi Hideyoshi. Back in 1587 Hideyoshi had issued an edict expelling the Jesuits from Japan in response to their overaggressive proselytizing, which at its height had extended to the destruction of Buddhist temples and shrines.[33] The order was not rigorously enforced; it had been intended more to slap the Christians into line than snuff them out entirely. After a period of lying low the Jesuit fathers were able to resume their work, albeit with more caution, and were soon joined by a second order, the Franciscans of Spain. The taiko's edict, however, was never rescinded, and thus Konishi's harboring of a Jesuit in 1594 remained technically illegal. If Hideyoshi were to find out about this, the repercussions could be severe.

Hideyoshi did find out. He was informed by Kato Kiyomasa, the ardent Buddhist daimyo Father de Cespedes described as Konishi's "arch rival." Upon receiving word that he was now in the taiko's bad graces, Konishi sent de Cespedes back to Japan. Then, in the summer of 1595, he made a hurried trip himself to Kyoto to repair the damage that Kato had done. He succeeded very handily, explaining to Hideyoshi that he had summoned the Jesuit to his camp in Korea to inquire why the annual "Black Ship" from Macao, laden with the foreign trade goods Hideyoshi so desired, had not come to Japan the previous year. Konishi, in short, had merely been looking out for the taiko's interests. Hideyoshi accepted this explanation, and the checkmated Kato, when he found out, knew better than to press the matter further.[34]

With the forged letter of submission from Hideyoshi now in hand, and with King Sonjo of Korea having provided his own written support for negotiations with Japan, the Ming government granted Naito Joan permission to proceed to Beijing. He arrived in the city toward the end of 1594 and was questioned closely by officials there for a month while the Chinese considered how best to proceed. The option of resuming hostilities to punish Hideyoshi for what everyone regarded as his unpardonable conduct had by this point been discarded; the war had already cost about ten million taels of silver, and the dangerously depleted imperial treasury could afford no more. The only matter for debate was thus the terms for peace that would be offered to Naito. Minister of War Shi Xing took a conciliatory approach, suggesting that Hideyoshi be granted both investiture as a vassal king and the right to engage in tribute trade. Others thought this was too generous. It was finally decided to deny the Japanese request for tributary trade relations, and to grant Hideyoshi only investiture as a vassal king—an empty formality that would cost nothing more than a silk robe and a large sheet of paper.

In an audience before the Wanli emperor on December 17, 1594, Naito Joan was presented with the following three conditions for peace:

1. Hideyoshi would receive investiture as a vassal king, but would not be allowed to send tribute [and thus engage in the lucrative practice of tribute trade].

2. All Japanese soldiers still in Korea must return to Japan; they could not remain even on the island of Tsushima in the strait between the two nations.

3. Japan must pledge never to invade Korea again.[35]

Naito accepted these terms and swore an oath to abide by them. He then prepared to leave Beijing for the long trip back to Japan.

The Ming court now set about making preparations for the investiture of Toyotomi Hideyoshi. An edict conferring upon him the title of King of Japan was drawn up and transcribed onto an appropriately elegant piece of paper. A golden seal was forged, royal vestments tailored, and a regal crown crafted and boxed. For the task of transporting these accoutrements to Japan and bestowing them upon Hideyoshi, an imperial mission was formed in February 1595 with Li Zongzheng serving as ambassador and Yang Fangheng as vice-ambassador. Li and Yang, together with an entourage of several hundred people, proceeded east from Beijing and arrived in Korea in May. Here they learned that the Japanese were still encamped on the southern tip of the peninsula, in contravention of the three conditions for peace that Naito Joan had carried on ahead of them. They thus settled down in Seoul and refused to continue any farther.

*   *   *

The Army's Strategic Power *states: "When the army is mobilized and advances into the field, the sole exercise of power lies with the general. If in advancing or withdrawing the court interferes, it will be difficult to attain success."*[36]

Three Strategies of Huang Shih-kung
1st century B.C.

On Korea's southern coast, Japanese naval activity had all but ceased following the loss of thirty-one ships to the Korean navy in April of 1594. There was little on the water for Supreme Naval Commander Yi Sun-sin to attack. Yi remained for the most part at his base on Hansan

Island, fighting regular bouts of fever, practicing his archery, and fretting over his ill son and mother, whom he was unable to visit owing to the duties of his office. He often resorted to fortune-telling to see what the future held. The results were usually propitious. But he could not help but worry.

A particular source of concern continued to be Won Kyun, the resentful Kyongsang naval commander whom Yi now described in his diary as "a monstrous coward.... His evil and refractory acts cannot be expressed fully."[37] Throughout 1594 Won continued to hammer away at Yi's reputation in his dispatches to the court in Seoul, accusing him most damagingly of refusing to attack the Japanese despite Won's own urgings to do so. This was misleading at best, and at worst a lie. So long as the Japanese remained within the safety of their fortified coastal positions and kept their vessels anchored near shore or hidden up inaccessible inlets, there was little any naval commander could do to fight them. The task obviously was better suited for the army. It also bore mentioning that when Yi *had* led his ships to the attack earlier that year, the Chinese commander in the south had promptly ordered him to desist on the grounds that he was upsetting the negotiation process.

Such considerations were lost on many a government minister in Seoul. Official communications started flowing south reprimanding Yi Sun-sin for being idle and for not taking a more aggressive stance against the Japanese. These calls to action from scholars who knew nothing of warfare caused Yi a great deal of aggravation. "Though I swore with other captains of war to avenge our slaughtered countrymen...," he fumed in his diary, "the enemy has taken his positions in deep trenches and high fortresses on steep hills inaccessible to us. It is not wise to proceed frivolously. A wise captain of war should keep to the rule 'Know yourself and know the enemy is the surest way to secure success in a hundred battles.' "[38]

Finally, in November, Yi received an official letter ordering him into action from Kwon Yul, the hero of the Battle of Haengju who in July had replaced Kim Myong-won as commander in chief of Korea's armed forces. Yi suggested that for a sea attack to have any chance of success it should be undertaken in coordination with a landward assault by army units. Kwon Yul would not comply. Yi therefore had to proceed into battle alone, with a fleet of ships to fight an enemy on land. He set sail on the ninth of the month, on what would prove an entirely fruitless campaign:

> *November 11:* Our warships weighed anchor and dashed into . . . Changmunp'o, but the enemy, perched on the steep heights, did not come out to fight. . . .
>
> *November 12:* The enemy with their vessels pulled alongside the shore did not come out to fight. . . .
>
> *November 17:* Early in the morning, ordered advance guard out to the enemy lairs in Changmunp'o, but the Japanese planted a sign in the ground reading "Japan is now talking peace with Ming China, so we need not fight."
>
> *November 19:* Made an early departure and arrived at the enemy base in Changmunp'o, but as previously the enemy did not come out.[39]

The government in Seoul in the meantime was looking into the strained relationship between Yi and Won Kyun. An investigator was sent south to question both men regarding the matter, and the strengths and weaknesses of each were debated and weighed in a series of discussions in court. It was conceded to Yi that Won Kyun did habitually refuse to obey his orders and that he was often belligerent and hostile toward his ranking superior. The general attitude, however, was that such conduct should be forgiven, for Won had formerly been senior to Yi and thus had a right to be resentful now that Yi outranked him. Won's counter-accusations, on the other hand, were accorded considerable weight. Many came to believe that Yi Sun-sin had lost his former fighting spirit and was now reticent to attack the Japanese, even when he received direct orders to do so.

The affair was finally settled in early 1595. Won Kyun, it was decided, was guilty of refusing to obey Yi's orders, but did not deserve to be punished. His enmity toward Yi, however, was too great to leave him in his current post, and so in March he was transferred north to command the army of Chungchong Province. It could scarcely be called a reprimand; the new post in fact carried a higher court rank. Won nevertheless was displeased with the reassignment, and initially refused to perform the bowing-out ceremony relinquishing his naval

command.[40] After much persuasion he complied, and was replaced as
Kyongsang Right Navy commander by Bae Sol, "a haughty man,"
observed Yi Sun-sin's nephew Yi Pun, "who would bend his head to no
one."[41] As for Yi Sun-sin, the Border Defense Council (*bibyonsa*)
concluded that he did deserve punishment for ignoring government
orders to attack the enemy. Since there was no one suitable to replace
him as supreme naval commander, however, Yi was left where he was
for the time being. The threat of punishment hanging over his head, the
bibyonsa observed, "will encourage him to do a better job."[42]

After serving for a year as army commander of Chungchong
Province, Won Kyun was transferred back to the south, this time to the
post of Cholla Province army commander, and so was able to observe
his nemesis at close hand once more, watching for any misstep, real or
imaged, that could be reported to the capital to blacken Yi's name. Yi
himself remained on Hansan Island throughout these months, wracked
by anxiety for his country, his family, and himself, as the government
in Seoul scrutinized his every move. It was at about this time that he
composed his now-famous poem "Hansan Isle," expressing the loneli-
ness and cares of his embattled command:

> By moonlight I sit all alone
> in the lookout on Hansan isle.
> My sword is on my thigh,
> I am submerged in deep despair.
> From somewhere the shrill note of a pipe . . .
> will it sever my heart strings? [43]

Despite the best efforts of Won Kyun and his Western faction supporters, Yi Sun-sin managed to maintain his position, if not his reputation,
throughout 1595 and 1596. Other military leaders were not so lucky.
The fate of Kim Dong-nyong, commander of an army of civilian volunteers in the southern province of Cholla, is a good example of what
could happen to a man in the deadly serious game of personal rivalry
and factional strife.

Kim Dong-nyong was born into an upper-class yangban family in
the southwestern province of Cholla in 1567. At the start of the

Japanese invasion he was living in a mountain hut, undergoing the customary three years of mourning for his deceased mother, wearing rough clothes, not shaving, and eating simple meals. He did not leave his retreat right away, and so the early months of the war passed him by. But then his brother was killed alongside guerrilla leader Cho Hon at the Battle of Kumsan, one of the so-called Seven Hundred Martyrs. With that Kim came off his mountain to look for ways to help the cause.

At the urging of his father, Kim sold his family's home and land and used the money to outfit a private army of five thousand civilian volunteers. He raised this force too late to participate in any of the great battles of 1592 and early 1593. His combat experience was confined to small-scale actions such as the combined land and sea attack against the Japanese camp at Changmunpo, which Kim undertook in November 1594 together with fellow uibyong leader Kwak Jae-u, the "Red Coat General," and Supreme Naval Commander Yi Sun-sin.[44] A tremendous reputation nevertheless started to grow up around the man, sparked, perhaps, by his personal flamboyance and charisma, then fueled by yarning around uibyong campfires. Stories were told of how he could fall off a roof and jump up unhurt; of how he had caught a tiger and sent it into a Japanese camp, instilling such fear among the enemy that they trembled at the mere mention of his name; of how he could ride his horse into a forest and cut down all the trees with his slashing sword. These tales of supernatural power spread throughout the kingdom, and led Crown Prince Kwanghae to bestow upon Kim the title "Flying Tiger General." Others called him "God General."[45]

Kim Dong-nyong's growing reputation led inevitably to feelings of jealousy in others, in particular Korea's cadre of professional army officers, with whom the twenty-seven-year-old civilian commander was in direct competition. Foremost among Kim's detractors were Chungchong Army Commander Yi Si-on and Kyongsang Commander Kim Ung-so. They had their first chance to bring him down in early 1596, when charges were brought against Kim Dong-nyong of cruelty. Kim was arrested and taken to Seoul for trial, but was subsequently cleared and released.[46]

A few months later Yi Si-on spearheaded a second attack. He sent out agents to spread rumors that Kim Dong-nyong was secretly in league with a local rebel who had recently been captured and executed for attempting to spark an uprising in Chungchong Province and over-throw the king. The rumor, as intended, found its way to Seoul, and resulted in Kim's being arrested again, this time on charges of treason. His fate was sealed when two captured rebels were coerced into testi-fying that Kim was indeed a rebel sympathizer and intent on perpetrating a coup. In Kim's trial no one dared speak out in his defense; the charge was too grave. But neither would Kim confess. He was tortured six times over a period of twenty days, until his knees were broken and his face reduced to a bloody pulp, but still he continued to deny the charge. "Even if I die a thousand times," he said, "the only sin I will confess to is my failure to complete the period of mourning for my mother. My anger against the Japanese was so great that I had to take up arms and fight them instead. I may deserve to die for this failure to do my duty. But not for disloyalty to my king."[47]

Kim Dong-nyong died in his cell a few days later. When word of his fate reached the south, guerrilla leaders there became increasingly reticent to step to the fore and head armies of their own, lest they too attract the ire of others and be falsely accused and killed.[48]

CHAPTER 21

Meanwhile, in Manila...

THREE YEARS HAD NOW PASSED since first word of Hideyoshi's plan to conquer Asia had reached the Spanish in Manila. It had arrived in the form of a letter from the taiko demanding the Philippines' capitulation, delivered by a Japanese adventurer named Harada Magoshichiro. Harada, anxious to elicit a favorable response from the Spanish, had tried to soften the belligerent tone of Hideyoshi's letter, and presented the governor with gifts that he purported to be from the taiko, but that he had probably purchased himself. The governor, Gomez Perez Dasmarinas, remained unconvinced. He found Hideyoshi's letter arrogant and threatening, and unacceptable by the standards of international diplomacy as he knew them. He did not want to cause trouble for his young and still vulnerable colony, however, so in his reply the governor maintained a conciliatory tone, expressing his desire for good relations with the taiko, and assuring him that King Philip, "the greatest monarch in the world," in turn would be glad to extend his hand "in true friendship and alliance." As a further sign of goodwill he sent along a few presents in return for the gifts that Hideyoshi's envoy had supposedly brought from Japan.[1]

Governor Perez Dasmarinas placed his return letter and presents in the hands of a Dominican priest named Juan Cobo, with orders to carry them personally to Japan and, while there, to gather as much information as he could about Hideyoshi's true intentions. Father Cobo arrived at Nagoya in the summer of 1592 and subsequently had an audience with Hideyoshi in which he tried to impress upon him the greatness of

King Philip II, pointing out on a globe the many nations and colonies over which he reigned, including his namesake, the Philippines. Father Cobo's discourse was not hyperbole. Philip II's Spain was in fact the greatest European power that had ever existed, possessing an empire that in terms of size and population was even larger than the Roman Empire at its height. It was the western hemisphere's equivalent of China in the East, Europe's own Middle Kingdom. Hideyoshi was interested in Father Cobo's globe, but was unimpressed by his talk of the greatness of Spain, for he had derived the wrong impression from the presents the priest had brought. These were misconstrued to the taiko as tribute from the Philippines, and thus a sign that those islands were bowing to his threats.

The second letter Hideyoshi sent to Governor Perez Dasmarinas was therefore even more aggressive and presumptuous than the first. He began with the standard recitation of how the sun had shone upon him at birth, portending that he would become "lord of all between the rising and the setting sun, and that all kingdoms must render me vassalage and bow down before my door; and unless they do it, I will destroy them with war." Then,

> I have conquered all the kingdom of Xapon [Japan], and that of Coria [Korea], and many of my commanders have asked my permission to go and capture Manila. Learning this, Faranda [Harada] and Funguen told me that ships went there from here, and came back, and so the people there appeared not to be enemies, for which reason I did not send troops. I made war against the Koreans and conquered as far as Meaco, because they failed to keep their word. Afterward my soldiers killed many Chinese and many nobles who came to help the Koreans. In view of this they humbled themselves, and sent an ambassador who . . . said that the Chinese desired eternal friendship with the kingdom of Xapon. I have sent many of our people to Coria to occupy the fortresses and await the embassy. Should they break their word again, I will go in person and make war upon them; and after going to China, Luzon will be within my reach. Let us be friends forever, and write to that effect to the king of Castilla [Philip II]. Do not, because he is far away, let him slight my words. I have never seen those far lands, but from the accounts given I know what is there.[2]

Father Juan Cobo was shipwrecked and died on his return voyage to Manila, and so it was not until April of 1594 that a copy of Hideyoshi's letter was finally delivered to the governor of the Philippines. By this time Gomez Perez Dasmarinas was himself dead as well, killed by the Chinese crew of his galley while on an abortive expedition south from Manila to conquer the clove-producing island kingdom of Ternate in the Moluccas. The new governor was his son, Luis Perez Dasmarinas, appointed temporarily until a suitable replacement could be sent out from Madrid. The younger Perez Dasmarinas was annoyed by the arrogance of Hideyoshi's letter. He was particularly incensed to read that the envoy and presents his slain father had sent to Japan had been interpreted "as tokens of obedience."[3] Don Luis therefore wrote a long letter of reply to the taiko designed to clear away any misunderstanding. He began by pointing out the falseness of Hideyoshi's belief that the sun had portended his greatness at birth. Such a thing, explained Don Luis with renaissance logic, was "in no wise possible or practical," for the sun "has no more life or power than what God gave it, and this does not go to the extent of taking or giving away kingdoms, which can only be done by God himself." Don Luis was informing Hideyoshi of these facts "because it is right that I do so, and in order that your Grandeur be not deceived by what is nothing else than the false flattery of ignorant people."

After deflating the tale of Hideyoshi's miraculous birth, the young governor went on to expound on the greatness of King Philip II of Spain: "My king's power is such, and the kingdoms and countries under his royal and Christian rule are so many, that his power and greatness is beyond compare with that of many kings and lords.... His dominions here [in Asia] are but a corner." In fact, "were it not that our divine and Christian laws prevent us from taking unjustly from any one that which does not belong to us, and if affairs were in accordance with power and strength, my king only would be the one obeyed and acknowledged" as the most powerful sovereign in the world. Fortunately for Japan, King Philip had no desire to assert his authority in such an uncivilized way. He and in turn his representatives in the Philippines wanted only friendship with Hideyoshi, but "with less formality and more frankness than in your royal letters hitherto received."[4]

Don Luis read his letter to Hideyoshi before a council of war convened in Manila on April 22, 1594, adding that he would have written "with more decision and heat," but did not want to provoke Hideyoshi into declaring war and putting the colony in danger. He then asked the gathered officials and dignitaries for their opinions. The lieutenant governor, Pedro de Rojas, observed that the letter "was very prudent and discreet, and that its warmth and spirit were proper" in view of the arrogance of Hideyoshi's own words. The portion pointing out the falsity of the prophesies surrounding Hideyoshi's birth, however, was ill advised. It would be better, de Rojas suggested, "to follow the reserved and dignified style generally used among such personages, and to leave out some words." The rest of the assembly agreed, and the offending passage was accordingly removed. An amended version of Don Luis's letter, "briefer and less likely to provoke and annoy," was read before the council six days later and unanimously approved.

Following the dispatch of Luis Perez Dasmarinas's amended letter, relations between Toyotomi Hideyoshi and the Spanish in Manila entered a two-year lull. The silence would be broken, with ultimately bloody repercussions, with the wreck of the treasure galleon *San Felipe* in the autumn of 1596.

CHAPTER 22

"You, Hideyoshi, are hereby instructed...to cheerfully obey our imperial commands!"

ON FEBRUARY 8, 1595, THE WANLI EMPEROR, acting on the suggestion of Minister of War Shi Xing, appointed Li Zongzheng as imperial envoy with the task of investing Toyotomi Hideyoshi as a vassal of Ming China. Li set out on his long journey to Japan with the onset of spring, accompanied by Vice-Envoy Yang Fangheng and a train of retainers, porters, and horses. In their baggage they carried a patent of investiture declaring Hideyoshi King of Japan, together with a crown, a golden seal, and dozens of courtly robes for the taiko and his inner circle of daimyo lords.

The Ming delegation arrived in Seoul in May only to learn that thousands of Japanese soldiers still remained in a string of camps along Korea's south coast. This was a violation of the three preconditions for investiture that Japanese envoy Naito Joan had agreed to on Hideyoshi's behalf. The second stipulation had clearly stated that all Japanese troops were to be withdrawn not only from Korea, but also from the island of Tsushima in the straits between the two nations. Why, Envoys Li and Yang wanted to know, had this withdrawal not taken place? Refusing to proceed any further with their mission until they were satisfied on this score, the two Ming dignitaries settled down in the Korean capital and began a wait that would last for six months.

When the envoys' message reached the south, Konishi Yukinaga sought to break the impasse by sending a portion of his forces back to Japan from the outlying camps at Ungchon, Changmunpo, Sojinpo, and Koje Island. Those remaining in Korea were concentrated in the vicinity of Pusan. This only partially ameliorated the Ming delegation, and so Vice-Envoy Yang was sent on to Pusan alone while Envoy Li remained in Seoul. Konishi responded by closing two more camps, at Kimhae and Tongnae, drawing the troops stationed there into the garrison at Pusan. That, he said, was as much as he would do. Only when Li Zongzheng himself came south would the Japanese agree to withdraw completely from Korea. Besides, added Konishi disingenuously, if all his soldiers were sent back home, who would welcome Li to Pusan and escort him to Japan?[1]

After a month of wrangling, Envoy Li finally relented and continued to Pusan. Upon his arrival in October of 1595, however, the evacuation of Japanese troops that he and Yang had been led to believe would now take place failed to materialize. The Ming mission thus bogged down again, with Li and Yang demanding complete withdrawal before they would proceed another step. Konishi was now in a bind, for a number of his fellow daimyo commanders were adamantly refusing to quit Korea without first receiving orders to do so from Hideyoshi himself. In February 1596 Konishi accordingly set sail for Japan to confer with the taiko. Shen Weijing accompanied him as far as Nagoya, ostensibly to make arrangements for the welcoming of the Ming dignitaries.

With Konishi away, Kato Kiyomasa now attempted to insert himself once again into the negotiation process. From his camp near Ulsan he sent messages to the Ming delegation quartered at Pusan, stating that Konishi had deceived them into thinking Hideyoshi wanted to submit to China and become a vassal king. To drive the point home, he assured the envoys that if they proceeded with their mission they would only succeed in enraging the taiko and in turn very likely would lose their heads. These threats of death, coupled with the strain of close confinement within a Japanese military camp, went to work on Envoy Li Zongzheng's nerves until finally they broke. In May, some time in the middle of the night, he slipped out of the Pusan camp with just the clothes on his back and began a panicked race north, arriving at the city of Kyongju after several days of hard walking over back routes and mountain trails. When the Japanese assigned to tend Li awoke the next morning to find him gone, they began scouring the countryside to run him down. But the Ming official was too elusive. After arriving bedraggled at Kyongju, he made his way north to Seoul, and eventually on to a prison cell in Beijing.[2]

Konishi was on his way back to Korea when he received word of Li's flight. For the Christian daimyo this was a potential disaster, the calamitous collapse of the delicately balanced house of cards he had carefully constructed over the past three years. He immediately sent a messenger back to Fushimi to inform Hideyoshi of the mess that his rival had caused and succeeded in turning the taiko against Kato Kiyomasa, so much so that a letter was sent to Korea ordering the disgraced daimyo back to Japan. Kato sailed for home in early June and spent the next month in Kyoto, waiting for Hideyoshi to either grant him an audience or order his death. Konishi, meanwhile, continued on to Pusan to see how the situation could be repaired.[3]

As it turned out the damage Kato had done was slight. Vice-Envoy Yang Fangheng took control of the situation and calmed the agitated Japanese by retrieving his superior's abandoned seal of office—Li had fled in such haste that he had left even this behind—and assuming the leadership of the delegation. An imperial order was in time dispatched from Beijing making Yang's appointment official and promoting Ming negotiator and Konishi confidant Shen Weijing to the now-vacant post of vice-envoy. A new patent of investiture for Hideyoshi and replacement royal robes were also sent, the originals by this time having become soiled.[4] Konishi Yukinaga now announced the happy news that Hideyoshi was eagerly awaiting their arrival at Fushimi Castle in Kyoto and that as yet another show of good faith even more troops would be sent back to Japan; only a very small force would be left in Korea to garrison the fortress at the port of Pusan. This at last satisfied the Chinese. On July 10, 1596, Ming envoys Yang and Shen and a delegation of some three hundred Chinese set sail for Japan.

There was just one more thing Konishi had to do to complete his charade of a negotiated peace. Upon returning to Pusan from his visit with the taiko, he insisted that Seoul appoint an envoy of its own to accompany the Ming delegation. His intention was undoubtedly to give Hideyoshi the false impression that the Koreans were joining with the Ming Chinese in submitting to him and apologizing for the war. But Konishi gave no intimation of this when making his request. "If a Korean envoy does not accompany the Chinese embassy to Japan," he explained, "the peace will be only between Japan and China, and Korea will have no part in it. This will lead to grave troubles."[5]

King Sonjo and his ministers had no faith in Hideyoshi's alleged desire for peace, and discounted his earlier letter of submission to Beijing as a forgery, perpetrated by Konishi Yukinaga and Shen Weijing—which of course it was. They were thus strongly opposed to the upcoming Ming mission to Japan and had no desire to join it. The decision, however, was not theirs to make. Shen Weijing, the mission's new vice-envoy, sent his nephew back from Nagoya to urge that a Korean envoy be appointed at once. Envoy Yang concurred. With these two men representing the authority of the Wanli emperor, there was nothing the Koreans could do but comply.

The matter was discussed at length in Seoul. The first thought was to appoint a low-ranking military official as envoy as a sign of Korea's disdain for Japan. Then it was pointed out that a military official, lacking the scholarship and sophistication of a civil official, might do something to embarrass the kingdom. In the end it was decided to appoint a civil official as envoy, someone capable and well educated, but not too highly ranked. The man selected for the job was Hwang Sin, a thirty-six-year-old government inspector from the southwestern province of Cholla. Pak Hong-jang was appointed as his second in command. The two men, bearing a letter from King Sonjo to Hideyoshi that said not a word about submission or apology, set sail for Japan two months after the Ming delegation. They caught up to them at Sakai, the gateway port to Osaka and Kyoto, and from there proceeded on together to the taiko's palace at Fushimi.[6]

It had taken three years of slow and uncertain negotiations for the Chinese and Korean envoys to arrive at this point. Through it all Toyotomi Hideyoshi waited patiently at Osaka Castle and in nearby Kyoto, overseeing construction of his retirement palace at Fushimi.

Since returning to the capital region from his Nagoya invasion head-quarters in September of 1593, the taiko seems to have paid little attention to the war and to subsequent peace negotiations. In his fifty-odd personal letters that have survived from this period, not a single mention is made of these events. Had he lost interest in the project? Or was he simply keeping silent about a costly overseas adventure that had not gone according to plan?

The truth probably lies somewhere in between. For all the misinformation he received from the Korean front, Hideyoshi could not have helped but conclude from the withdrawal of his armies to Pusan that his original grand design could not be achieved and that the war had in fact been lost. This grim realization lay in part behind his patience throughout the long process of negotiation with the Chinese: ambiguity and delay were preferable to accepting defeat.[7] It seems likely, moreover, that Hideyoshi understood throughout these interminable talks that his representative Konishi Yukinaga was taking certain liberties with the demands he had originally laid down in order to coax a face-saving settlement from the Ming, although just how great those liberties were the taiko certainly did not know. Indeed, if Hideyoshi was completely in the dark with regard to his representative's machinations, then why did he recall Kato Kiyomasa in disgrace to Japan when the latter attempted to expose Konishi's presumed disloyalty in altering his master's demands? Although Hideyoshi never openly expressed a willingness to compromise, by 1596 he was clearly ready to settle for some sort of show of submission, even an empty one, from the court in Seoul and the Ming Chinese, something that could be held up to the nation as further proof of the greatness of the name of Toyotomi and as justification for a long and costly war.

While Hideyoshi waited for Konishi to deliver the Ming envoys to him, he found no end of things with which to occupy himself. Enjoying the fruits of being taiko was for him a full-time job. First there was the construction of Fushimi Castle to attend to, located on the side of Momoyama, "Peach Mountain," just outside Kyoto. He had embarked upon the project in September of 1592, initially as an unassuming retirement villa where he could quietly live out his days, puttering about with his poetry and tea. In the following year this modest design was changed. Perhaps Hideyoshi wished to impress the Ming envoys when they eventually arrived with a show of extravagance and grandeur even greater than his castle at Osaka. Or perhaps he was anxious to provide himself and his newborn son Hideyori with a more imposing presence in the capital, something to rival the Jurakutei, the palace occupied by his nephew Hidetsugu, the kampaku of Japan and still his official heir. Whatever the reason, by the end of 1593 the plan for Fushimi had been so greatly expanded that it would take the work of 250,000 laborers to see it complete.

The result would be unlike anything previously built in Japan. While Fushimi contained a nod to defense in its five-story keep, this did not dominate the grounds as did the donjon at Osaka Castle. The sprawling complex was instead centered on an aesthetically engineered park enclosure of gardens, cherry trees, rustic teahouses, noh stages, and moon-viewing pavilions, with a stream meandering throughout for pleasant boat excursions. In Fushimi we thus see Japan's sengoku civil war architecture, the soaring castle keeps and unassailable stones walls that regional warlords needed for defense, give way to a natural aestheticism and refinement that would come to dominate Japanese palace design. Their chief purpose would no longer be to provide a safe haven in time of war, but to encourage the pursuit of culture and refinement in peacetime.[8]

As the taiko oversaw the work at Fushimi, his study of noh theater became something of an obsession, consuming many hours of his day and leaving him often physically exhausted. He had begun his studies while still residing at Nagoya, inviting experts from the various acting schools to his camp to tutor him and favored daimyo within his inner circle. In April of 1593 he wrote to his wife O-Ne that he had so far memorized ten plays, and was determined to learn more.[9] Over the coming months he did. Then, to the forced delight of all, he began staging performances with himself in the lead, and on occasion with such dignitaries as Tokugawa Ieyasu and Maeda Toshiie backing him up. For his first public effort the taiko chose *Yumi Yawata*, a play celebrating the pacification of Japan in ancient times and the legendary conquest of Korea, and thus heavy with parallels to the current situation.[10] Hideyoshi threw himself into this and subsequent performances with gusto and confidence; judging from his letters he appears to have been immune to the nervous tension one might have expected from an eager amateur with just a year's training. Hideyoshi regarded himself as accomplished from the start, and assumed that everyone would be delighted to see him act. As he wrote to his wife a year or two into his tutelage,

> Although you have repeatedly sent me letters, I have sent no reply as I have had no free time because of noh.... My noh technique becomes more and more accomplished; whenever I present the *shimai* [dance portion] of various plays, the whole audience praises it very much. I have already done so for two plays, and after resting a little, I shall act again on the 9th day and show it to all the ladies in Kyoto.... Around the 14th or 15th day, I shall have some free time and will go to Fushimi to hasten the construction work. I shall stay there three to five days, and then visit you quickly so that we can talk together. I shall perform noh at your residence to show [you and others]. Look forward to it.[11]

Hideyoshi's infatuation with noh culminated in early 1594 with the commissioning of a series of "new noh plays" glorifying the key events and achievements in his life. They were written by a Hideyoshi retainer and cheerleader named Omura Yuko and would star, of course, Hideyoshi himself. Omura is said to have composed ten plays for the taiko in all, of which five survive today: *The Pilgrimage to Yoshino, The Pilgrimage to Koya, The Conquest of Akechi, The Conquest of Shibata,* and *The Conquest of Hojo.* Hideyoshi performed the first of these in Osaka in April 1594, as a special treat for Hidetsugu. In time everyone who was anyone, from resident daimyo and their families to Emperor Go-Yozei himself, would be similarly favored. We can imagine the energetic applause that greeted the end of each of these fetes, the shower of compliments from sycophants eager to please, the crooning of court ladies that the taiko's skill was beyond compare. The one sour note on record comes from the Jesuit father Luis Frois, who witnessed a demonstration of Hideyoshi's acting prowess during a visit to Fushimi sometime in the mid-1590s. "[S]ometymes he...intruded and danced amongst the rest," recalled Frois, "but wth suche an evill grace, as well argued an impotent and dotinge old man."[12]

*   *   *

For all the time and energy that Hideyoshi lavished upon his study of noh, and for all the money and labor he threw into his grand conception at Fushimi, these were not his chief obsessions from 1593 until his death. That distinction went to his newborn son Hideyori, delivered by the taiko's concubine Yodogimi in August of that year and given the unpresuming nickname Hiroi, "gleaned." From that moment onward Hideyoshi grew increasingly consumed with love and worry for this, his only surviving child. His concern would come to overshadow everything else, including his war in Korea and dispute with the Ming.

Having lost his first son Tsurumatsu at the age of two, Hideyoshi could not help but fret about Hideyori's health. Whenever he was called away during the first year of the child's life, he pestered Yodogimi with letters filled with advice on how "O-Hiroi" should be cared for, giving strict and at times even threatening orders on what should and should not be done. "Is O-Hiroi increasingly in good health?" reads a typical note. "Does he suck milk?... [P]lease make Hiroi drink enough milk and take great care of him. Please eat enough food [to make] your milk sufficient [for him]." And again, "[P]lease don't use moxa on my honorable Hiroi. It will be a crime if you, Mama, invite someone to apply it to him." And again, "It is important that you spare no effort to prevent Hideyori from catching a chill.... [P]lease give strict orders [to your men] to take care against fire. Every night please send your men to inspect the rooms two or three times. You must not be careless."[13]

When Hideyori was still a toddler, Hideyoshi, his self-styled "daddy taiko," began addressing letters directly to him during his occasional absences, letters filled with pride and love for his growing boy, and expressions of anguish at having to be apart from him even for the shortest time.

[When Hideyori was two years old]
You sent me a letter promptly and I am very happy about it; I intend to have some free time and hurry back. Because you are fond of masks, I have sent someone to find some, even in China, as a present.[14]

[When Hideyori was three]
[B]ecause I love you deeply, I shall be back to kiss your lips.[15]

I am very sorrowful because I left you yesterday without saying goodbye. I think you, too, had the same feeling and I am forever complaining about it here. I am writing this letter because I have such deep affection for you.[16]

[When Hideyori was four]
You have sent me a *katabira* and various *dofuku* for the seasonal festival; I am very happy and I shall wear them, rejoicing and wishing you a long and happy life. On the actual day of the seasonal festival I shall certainly be back and kiss you. How wonderful it will be![17]

I shall be back very soon at the end of the year. Then I shall kiss your lips. Your lips should be kissed by no one else, even a little bit. I can imagine how you are growing finer and finer.[18]

[When Hideyori was five]
I have understood that Kitsu, Kame, Yasu, and Tsushi have acted against your wishes. As this is something extremely inexcusable, ask your Mother, and then bind these four persons with a straw rope and keep them like that until your Father comes to your side. When I arrive, I shall beat them all to death.[19]

In 1595 Hideyori was two years old and in good health, and showed every sign of surviving to adulthood. It was thus time for Hideyoshi to act to secure the child's future. Back in 1592, not long after the death of his first son, Tsurumatsu, the taiko seemingly accepted that he would never father a son of his own, and appointed his sister's twenty-four-year-old son Hidetsugu as kampaku and heir. Hidetsugu proved a less than ideal choice. A frequent criticism leveled against him was that he took an unnatural delight in killing, a predilection that earned the young man the name "murdering regent." He is said to have enjoyed strolling through the countryside with a musket in hand, taking shots at unsuspecting farmers working in the fields. While practicing his archery one day, he summoned a passing traveler and skewered him for target practice. According to the Jesuit Luis Frois, Hidetsugu would also on occasion take on the job of public executioner to hone his skill with a sword. He was even said to have "ripped upp woemen to see their entrailes and place of conception."[20]

Hidetsugu understood from the moment of his stepbrother's birth that his own position as heir was in peril. After several years of evidently faithful service to the taiko, he thus began to plot, secretly soliciting support from among the major daimyo in an attempt to build a power base from which to challenge the baby boy. The effort was doomed from the start. Hideyoshi had never granted Hidetsugu much real power to go along with the title of kampaku, and so few daimyo saw anything to be gained by siding with him. In the end his scheming was betrayed to Hideyoshi. In August of 1595 Hidetsugu was stripped of his title and packed off to the monastery at Mount Koya in the province of Kii, a common place of exile for daimyo and dignitaries. A few days later a letter arrived from Hideyoshi ordering him to kill himself. The former kampaku obeyed without hesitation, slitting open his belly in the suicide ritual known as seppuku. A number of his retainers followed his example. His severed head was then sent to Kyoto for viewing.[21]

Although Hidetsugu was now removed from the scene, Hideyoshi was still not satisfied. To root out any hint of challenge to Hideyori's position as heir, the taiko ordered Hidetsugu's chief vassals to take their own lives as well. Then he had his wives, children, and relations rounded up and killed. Luis Frois witnessed this gruesome spectacle, in which thirty-one women and three children met their end. Of the latter the eldest was only five. They were drawn in carts through all the main streets of Kyoto for everyone to see, presenting such a pitiable sight, Frois observed, that "nothinge was there heard but sighinges, and groanes, able to have mooved not onlie men but stoanes into compassion and mercie, and suche as pearced the verie bowels of the most barbarous beholders." The condemned were then taken to the place of execution. Here they were greeted by the sight of Hidetsugu's head, prominently displayed as a warning to all. The children were removed from the carts first and killed. Then it was time for the ladies. They were led forward one by one in order of rank, they knelt on the ground, and their heads were struck off. When the killings were over the thirty-four corpses were buried together in a pit, and a shrine erected on top bearing the inscription "Tomb of the Traitors."[22]

During the months that followed, Hideyoshi leveled Hidetsugu's former Kyoto palace, the Jurakutai. Some of the buildings were destroyed outright; others were dismantled and moved to Fushimi. He also called upon each of his daimyo to swear an oath of loyalty to his new heir Hideyori. This taking of oaths of loyalty to the child would become something of an obsession with Hideyoshi, a duty he would require his chief vassals to perform again and again over the coming three years.

When Fushimi Castle was still in the planning stages, Hideyoshi stipulated that it was to be made impervious to earthquakes, or as he described it to the writhing of the *numazu*, the giant catfish that bore the earth on its back.[23] He had good reason to be concerned. Earthquakes, a perennial problem in Japan to begin with, had become increasingly frequent in recent years, prompting fears that a gigantic cataclysm might not be far off.

It wasn't. At eight o'clock in the evening of August 30, 1596, the most powerful quake in living memory struck the capital region, heavily damaging much of Osaka and Kyoto. Hundreds of homes were destroyed. The huge Buddha that Hideyoshi had ordered constructed, in part from melted-down weapons collected in his various sword hunts, was shaken to pieces. Huge tsunamis pounded the coast. Ponds hundreds of meters across rose up from the ground. At Fushimi, every structure either collapsed or was so seriously shaken that it would have to be later pulled down. Hideyoshi himself managed to escape with his life, cradling the precious Hideyori in his arms and accompanied by the child's mother, Yodogimi. Four hundred other members of the household lay crushed in the ruins.

It was because of this catastrophe that Kato Kiyomasa was able to win his way back into Hideyoshi's good graces. Kato, it will be recalled, had just weeks before been ordered back from Korea for meddling in peace negotiations with China. He was now waiting in Kyoto for an audience with the taiko or the order to kill himself. As soon as the great quake struck, Kato, thinking of nothing but the safety of his master, rushed to Fushimi and found Hideyoshi, Yodogimi, and little Hideyori sitting stunned on a mat in front of the ruins. Upon seeing Kato, Hideyoshi exclaimed, "Tora! How quickly you have come!" This friendly use of Kato's nickname Tora, "Tiger," was an

indication that all was forgiven. In the heartfelt discussion that followed, Kato was able to convince Hideyoshi that he had never been
anything but scrupulously loyal and that everything he had said and
done had been intended solely to achieve Hideyoshi's desires. The two
men parted on the best of terms, and would remain so to the end.[24]

At the time of the great earthquake of 1596, the Chinese delegation
bearing the patent of investiture declaring Hideyoshi King of Japan
was residing at the port city of Sakai near Osaka, waiting to be received
by the taiko so that they could deliver their document and return home.
The calamity necessitated a further delay, for the impressive Hall of a
Thousand Tatami Mats that had been specially built at Fushimi for
receiving foreign embassies had been almost completely destroyed. A
suitably grand venue thus had to be arranged elsewhere. Osaka Castle,
one wing of which had escaped the earthquake more or less intact, was
the eventual choice. For the next two months repair work proceeded
around the clock. In October all was ready.

Ming envoy Yang Fangheng and vice-envoy Shen Weijing were
granted an audience by Hideyoshi at Osaka Castle on October 22. They
proceeded to the castle in company with the Korean delegation under
Hwang Sin, grudgingly sent by the government in Seoul. When they
arrived outside the fortress's huge gate, a messenger came out to meet
them with word that the Koreans were not to be allowed inside.
Hideyoshi, he said, was upset that the Koreans had not sent the two
royal princes and a top government minister as he had demanded, but
only an official of lowly rank. The undoubtedly distraught Hwang was
thus left waiting outside while the Chinese delegation entered alone.
    Inside the castle the Chinese were ushered into a great reception
hall and brought before a platform set in front of a yellow screen. Yang
stood at the fore. Shen took up a position a step behind, holding up the
patent of investiture and gold seal reverently before him. After a time
the yellow screen opened and a small, wizened old man stepped onto
the platform above the Ming delegation, supporting himself with a
cane, accompanied by two attendants dressed in blue. This was
Toyotomi Hideyoshi, the taiko himself. He nodded to the Chinese

envoys, then turned to the crowd of daimyo present and asked why these visitors did not prostrate themselves before him in the customary way. Konishi Yukinaga quietly explained that these were distinguished envoys from China and could not be expected to do such a thing. The Chinese, meanwhile, were waiting for Hideyoshi to prostrate himself before the imperial edict that Shen Weijing continued to hold aloft. Did this barbarian warlord not understand the sacred nature of the document? Or was he delivering a studied insult? Again one of Hideyoshi's quick-thinking attendants stepped forward to smooth things out. The taiko did not intend any disrespect by not kneeling, he communicated to the Ming. He was simply unable to do so because of a painful boil on his knee. The gross misunderstanding that existed between Hideyoshi and the Chinese was thus papered over for one more day, with each thinking the other was willing to submit. The investiture document was duly handed over, then the gold seal, the crown, and the silk robes, and the Ming delegation retired.[25]

The farce finally came to an abrupt and almost comic end at a banquet Hideyoshi hosted the following day. The taiko appeared resplendent in his new Chinese crown and robes, the garb of a vassal king presented to him by the envoys. Some forty of his daimyo, including Konishi Yukinaga, were arrayed before him in similarly colorful scholarly robes, the large crest on the front of each indicating the court rank Beijing had granted to them. Sitting opposite were the Ming envoys, Yang and Shen, backed by members of their delegation. The Korean envoy, Hwang Sin, was once again barred from the proceedings and forced to wait outside. The affair proceeded amiably enough, with toasts and smiles and entertainments. Hideyoshi then retired to a summer house on the palace grounds and summoned his attending priests, including Saisho Shotai, an expert on written Chinese, to translate the weighty documents from the Wanli emperor into words he could understand.

This was the moment of truth Konishi Yukinaga had for so long feared. He previously had urged Saisho to soften any language in the documents likely to offend the taiko. Whatever Saisho's response may have been to Konishi, when the time came to translate he was scrupulously honest. What followed must surely rank as one of the greatest diplomatic blunders of all time; the thunderous bursting of a bubble of misunderstanding that had been allowed to grow for the past three years.

"You, Toyotomi Hideyoshi," the priest intoned,

> have risen in the island country and have learned how to revere Chung Kuo [China]. You have sent an envoy to the West in order to express your admiration of us and your devotion to us.... Your reverence and obeisance have been sincerely expressed.... With our special grace, we hereby invest you as "King of Japan." The imperial patent of this investiture is hereby conferred upon you. You are now in our imperial favor; our imperial coronet and robes are herewith sent over the sea to you.... You, Hideyoshi, are hereby instructed to comply with our commands and to stand ready to fulfill your obligations to our throne as a loyal subject. You are also instructed reverently to conform with the imperial desire and to maintain your everlasting existence by following the imperial guidance and by cheerfully obeying our imperial commands![26]

The priest then took up the second document, the imperial edict. It began by reprimanding Hideyoshi for his aggression in Korea, "a nation that has strictly adhered to her tributary duties and obligations to our throne." The Ming now understood, however, that Hideyoshi had done so because he wanted to become a vassal of China, and felt that Korea was preventing him from conveying his petition. But "[n]ow that you have realized with regret how serious was your error," the document continued, "you have withdrawn your troops" and have "reverently prepared in written form your former petition and have presented it to our court." Beijing therefore was prepared to grant his request and accept him as a vassal. The honor was granted, however, with limitations. First, Hideyoshi must withdraw the last of his forces from Korea; "not a single Japanese shall be permitted to remain." Second, he must promise never to invade that country again. And third, he and his successors must agree never to seek the trade privileges with China that were normally due a tributary state. If Hideyoshi ignored this final ruling and attempted to send ships uninvited, "our coast guards may fail to differentiate between a jewel and a stone and may mistake tribute-bearing ships from Japan for pirate vessels," and so destroy them. "You shall not deviate from our instructions," the edict concluded, "but you shall reverently obey and adhere to our imperial command."[27]

Almost every line in these two documents was a slap in Hideyoshi's face. He had dispatched his armies overseas not to submit to the Ming, but to conquer them. While this lofty objective had proved beyond his reach, he nevertheless expected to come away from the invasion of Korea with something to show for his efforts, a portion of that peninsula perhaps, a handful of important hostages, a princess from Beijing, something he could use to aggrandize his name and make the war seem worthwhile. But this arrogantly worded patent of investiture and condescending edict—this was nothing but an insult designed to humiliate him, a written assertion that he had lost the war. In a towering rage, he tore off his Chinese robes and threw his crown to the floor. According to Luis Frois, the taiko "flew into such a Passion and Rage, that he was perfectly out of himself. He froth'd and foam'd at the Mouth, he ranted and tore till his Head smoak'd like Fire, and his Body was all over in a dropping Sweat."[28]

Hideyoshi's initial reaction was by all accounts so extreme that for a moment the very lives of the Chinese and Korean envoys were in danger. The monks present at the reading of the investiture documents managed to calm him somewhat by pointing out that China was the fount of the world's civilization and learning and that it had been customary since ancient times for neighboring states to receive investiture from it, just as the taiko had himself now done. Indeed, they said, Hideyoshi had received a great honor with this investiture, for it was an indication that China recognized his greatness and achievements. While these words of flattery succeeded in taking the edge off the taiko's rage, he remained very angry, and sent out word to the foreign emissaries that they were to leave Japan at once, and that he would give them no reply to deliver to Beijing. Ming envoy Yang Fangheng and his Korean counterpart Hwang Sin accordingly gathered up their delegations and immediately departed.

Hideyoshi's wrath next turned on those daimyo he considered responsible for orchestrating the whole embarrassing affair. Konishi Yukinaga was in the greatest peril, for he had been at the forefront of negotiations with the Chinese. It was only thanks to the intercession of members of Hideyoshi's inner circle, including his concubine Yodogimi, that Konishi was not now ordered to take his own life. Hideyoshi was reminded that, although Konishi had assumed the most active role in negotiations, other daimyo bore equal responsibility for the outcome, in particular Otani Yoshitsugu, Mashita Nagamori, and Ishida Mitsunari, the three men appointed together with Konishi as the taiko's personal representatives. If Konishi were to be punished, others therefore would have to be punished as well.[29] The duplicity of the Chinese may also have been pointed to as having unwittingly led Konishi astray. In the end Hideyoshi merely removed Otani, Mashita, and Ishida from their posts and ordered Konishi to return to Korea with his army, where after a few months in the taiko's bad graces he was forgiven and his reputation restored.

It took the Ming envoys a full month to get clear of Japan. First they had to travel hundreds of kilometers back to Nagoya on the island of Kyushu, then they were forced to wait on into November for the weather to turn favorable enough to attempt the sea crossing to Pusan. During this time Hideyoshi, either on his own or due to the persuasion of others, came to accept that there was little to be gained by sending the envoys away in such a brusque manner and resuming his quarrel with China. A messenger was therefore sent after the retreating delegation bearing presents and a note from Hideyoshi stating that he had no argument with Beijing. While he regarded the offer of investiture as an insult, the document read, "I intend to put up with it." What Hideyoshi would not put up with was peace with Korea. For years the Koreans had prevented Japan from establishing good relations with China, he claimed. They were in fact wholly to blame for the war. And now, after Hideyoshi had magnanimously released the two Korean princes, the Seoul government had refused to send them to him to express their thanks as he had requested, but instead insulted him by dispatching a lowly official. This he would not accept. To seek redress from the Koreans for the harm they had done and the insults delivered, Hideyoshi was once again gathering his armies to reinvade their land.[30]

Korean envoy Hwang Sin was by this time in the depths of despair. The threat of a second invasion does not seem to have bothered him as much as his inability to deliver King Sonjo's letter to Hideyoshi and thus complete his mission. At a meeting at their joint camp in Nagoya, Hwang poured out his heart to Ming envoy Yang Fangheng, saying that it would be better for him to die than to return to Seoul with the king's letter still in hand. Yang tried to calm the distraught official, urging him to return to Korea with the Chinese as soon as the weather permitted. "Hideyoshi would not accept your letter," Yang reasoned. "So if you return to your country and give it back to your king, there should be no trouble. It is only natural that you should do this." Hwang replied that this was easy for Yang to say, for he had successfully delivered his documents and thus could not be accused of failing to do his duty. "But I did not receive any sign of submission from Hideyoshi," Yang countered. "So in fact I have been no more successful than you."[31]

In the end Hwang took Yang's advice and returned to Korea with the Ming delegation. As expected, he fell in for a good deal of criticism in Seoul for his failure to deliver the king's letter, and was demoted as punishment. For many, however, both the failure of Hwang's mission and Hideyoshi's rude behavior toward the Chinese and Korean envoys merely confirmed what they knew all along: that Hideyoshi should never have been trusted and that it had been a mistake to try to negotiate with him. It was in fact generally believed by the Koreans that the past three years of negotiation had been merely a ploy by the Japanese to get the Chinese army out of Korea so that they could launch a second attack. It was even suggested that Hideyoshi's insulting treatment of the Chinese envoys was a cunning strategy to anger the Ming emperor into precipitously sending an invasion fleet against Japan that the Japanese could ambush and destroy. King Sonjo himself was of this opinion—he had sent an envoy to Japan only because the Chinese had pressured him to do so—and thus was not surprised or sorry about the failure of Hwang's mission. He summoned the harried envoy to an audience where he was thanked for his efforts and rewarded with gifts.[32]

Envoy Yang Fangheng and Vice-Envoy Shen Weijing attempted to depict their mission as successful upon their return to Beijing. Toyotomi Hideyoshi, they declared, had accepted investiture with appropriate humility and thanks. Their story did not hold up for long. The absence of any sort of official letter from Hideyoshi, only tribute presents that subsequently were proved to have been purchased by the envoys themselves, put their account in serious doubt. Intelligence from sources in Korea, followed by a request from King Sonjo for military support to resist a second Japanese invasion, entirely discredited the two men.

The whole story of the mission when it came out was regarded by all as a national disgrace. Any talk of peace with Japan was now anathema. The barbarian Hideyoshi's unprecedented rejection of the honor of vassalage was considered an affront of such magnitude that the only possible response was to raise a second army and drive him into the sea. This shift in sentiment spelled doom for those who had formerly been most prominently in support of peace. Envoy Yang confessed all and was summarily dismissed from office. Vice-Envoy Shen Weijing continued to assert until the bitter end that the whole botched affair was a misunderstanding and that peace still could be restored. He hurried back to Korea to sort things out, and then allegedly attempted to defect to the Japanese side when events began to turn against him. He would be arrested and sent back to Beijing before he could make good his escape, and was subsequently executed for treason. His wife and children were sold into slavery to further expunge his sin.[33]

As for Minister of War Shi Xing, the most prominent supporter of peace negotiations since 1593 and the man who had entrusted Shen with the task to such disastrous effect, the initial feeling was that he should be sentenced only to exile. At this juncture the Wanli emperor overcame his usual inertia to issue an edict demanding something more severe:

> During the entire period of peace negotiations with the outside barbarian nation Japan, Shi Xing deceived his lord and disgraced his state. You, State Ministers, in the trial of his case, must adhere strictly to your duty and enforce the laws of the nation. In fact, Shi has committed high treason against both the nation and the throne. . . . We should consider it disloyal to the throne if you should have sympathy for your former comrade and friend.[34]

Any thoughts of mercy were thus cast aside, and Shi Xing was sentenced to death. The former minister of war died in prison before the sentence could be carried out, reportedly of starvation. His family and relations were exiled to a distant border province to live out their lives.

On October 20, 1596, the Spanish galleon *San Felipe*, bound from Manila to Acapulco with a cargo of Asian goods officially valued at one and a half million silver pesos but probably worth a good deal more, was driven ashore by foul weather onto the Japanese island of Shikoku. The local authorities were initially friendly, but would not allow the Spaniards to repair their vessel and leave without first receiving permission from the taiko. The Spaniards accordingly sent representatives to Kyoto with gifts to appeal to Hideyoshi for the release of their ship and its cargo. When they arrived in the capital, just days after the Ming envoys had been sent packing, Hideyoshi would not see them. The Franciscan priests previously sent to Kyoto from Manila by Governor Gomez Perez Dasmarinas to smooth relations with Japan also worked strenuously to secure the ship's release, but to no avail.

The reason for Hideyoshi's recalcitrance was that he had decided to keep the *San Felipe*'s valuable cargo, first to reconstruct his earth-quake-shattered castle at Fushimi and second to help fund his planned reinvasion of Korea. He thus sent his representative Mashita Nagamori south to Shikoku to seize the vessel and imprison its passengers and crew. It was a heavy financial blow for the Spanish in Manila, for their livelihood depended on the annual galleon carrying Oriental silks and ceramics and spices to Mexico to be sold for silver coins. And more was to come. On December 8 the Kyoto residence of the Spanish Franciscans was surrounded and six priests and several Japanese converts taken prisoner. One month later they were sentenced to death. "Inasmuch as these men came from the Luzones," read Hideyoshi's edict, "from the island of Manila, in the capacity of ambassadors, and were allowed to remain in the city of Miaco [Kyoto], preaching the Christian religion, which in former years I have strictly forbidden: I order that they be executed together with the Japanese who embraced their religion."[35]

Hideyoshi's reasons for issuing this edict remain a matter for speculation. According to the most straightforward account, when Mashita Nagamori arrived on Shikoku to take possession of the *San*

Felipe, the ship's pilot showed him a map of the far-flung possessions of King Philip II, presumably to impress on him that Spain was a major power and not to be trifled with. How had Spain managed to conquer so many lands? Mashita asked. The pilot's reply was horribly ill-judged. First the priests go in, he said, and convert the people to their religion. Then the soldiers follow and subdue them. This assertion of Christian missionaries serving as a fifth column, preparing foreign lands for conquest from within, confirmed what for the Japanese was a longstanding suspicion and prompted Hideyoshi to act. He initially intended to launch a wholesale pogrom and execute everyone professing the faith, but was eventually persuaded to confine his edict to the newly arrived Franciscans in Kyoto, excluding the Jesuits mainly because they were essential intermediaries in the trade with Macao.

The Jesuits would later claim that the Franciscans brought this trouble on themselves with their strident, impolitic behavior. There seems to be some truth in this. The Jesuits, having been active in Japan since 1549, were more familiar with the country and its ways. They possessed excellent linguistic skills, which allowed them clearer communication and understanding and, thanks to their focus on the upper classes (they reasoned that if they converted the elite the poor would naturally follow), ties with powerful daimyo that they were able to use to their advantage. The Franciscans, on the other hand, were newcomers to Japan. They did not know much about the language and society and, ministering mainly to the lower classes, had few influential Japanese friends. They were not willing to take the advice of the more seasoned Jesuits, however, particularly the suggestion that they be cautious in their work. They insisted on going about in their distinctive Franciscan cassocks and proselytizing in open defiance of Hideyoshi's 1587 anti-Christian edict, and they scoffed at the Jesuits for their circumspection and for disguising themselves in Buddhist robes. It was through this reckless behavior, the Jesuits claimed, that the Franciscans sealed their fate.

The Franciscans for their part would attribute the coming tragedy to a Jesuitical plot to drive them out of Japan. There may be some truth in this as well, for a fierce rivalry existed between the Jesuits and Franciscans, a rivalry that was national as well as sectarian, the Jesuits hailing mainly from Portugal and the Franciscans from Spain. Portugal at this time was a part of the Spanish Empire, but resented its subsidiary role and continued to regard Spain as an overseas trading rival. The Jesuits especially were tied up in this mercantile tug-of-war, serving as intermediaries in the Black Ship trade between Nagasaki and Portuguese Macao, and were not eager to see trade links develop between Japan and Spanish Manila. This, coupled with disagreements over missionary practice and proprietary rights, ensured that relations between the two sects were less than cordial, and may have led the Jesuits to make anti-Franciscan statements to important Japanese friends. The Japanese, meanwhile, were only too glad to fuel the rivalry between the two orders and in turn between Portugal and Spain, for from greater foreign rivalry came better opportunities for trade.[36]

The road to execution for the twenty-six condemned Christians— six Franciscan priests, seventeen local converts, and three Japanese Jesuit lay brothers included by mistake—began with the slitting of their noses and ears, and a ride on oxcarts through the streets of Kyoto, Osaka, and Sakai to expose them to public ridicule. They were then transported southwest to the port of Nagasaki on the island of Kyushu, the main entrepôt for Japanese commerce with the outside world. Here, on February 5, 1597, they were affixed to crosses with iron staples at their throats, wrists, and ankles, and slowly tormented to death. Their bodies were left hanging there for many weeks, until only the bones remained. These were spirited away by local Christians and preserved as holy relics.

News of the crucifixions reached Manila in May, brought by the Spanish passengers and crew of the *San Felipe*, who after being released by Hideyoshi had found their way home aboard trade ships out of Nagasaki with little more than the shirts on their backs. One of the few things they were allowed to take away was a letter of farewell from one of the martyred Franciscan fathers, Martin de Aguirre, addressed to Antonio de Morga, lieutenant governor of Manila. The letter ended with a warning about Hideyoshi:

> This king's greed has been much whetted by what he stole from the "San Felipe." It is said that next year he will go to Luzon, and that he does not go this year because of being busy with the Coreans. In

order to gain his end, he intends to take the islands of Lequois [the Ryukyus] and Hermosa [Formosa, i.e., Taiwan], throw forces from them into Cagayan [on northern Luzon], and thence to fall upon Manila, if God does not first put a stop to his advance.[37]

Spain's new governor of the Philippines, Francisco Tello, responded by sending another ambassador to Japan, this time with a letter expressing his anger at what had happened and requesting that Hideyoshi return the cargo he had seized from the *San Felipe*. He did not neglect to include gifts, however, "for the Japanese are wont to give or receive embassies in no other manner." In addition to cloth, swords, and gold and silver ornaments, an elephant recently received as a present from the king of Thailand was sent along, all done up in silk and accompanied by native keepers clad in matching garb. (It would have annoyed the Thais to have known that their gift had been recycled in this manner, for they were aligned with China and had sent token forces to Korea to fight against Hideyoshi's troops.) Hideyoshi received this mission in an outwardly friendly manner and was clearly delighted with the elephant, the first ever seen in Japan. But he declined to concede anything to the ambassador in turn. The Franciscans, he said, had brought about their own deaths by failing to heed his edict banning Christian activity. If "either religious or secular Japanese proceeded to your kingdoms," the taiko explained in his reply to the Spanish governor, "and preached the law of Shinto therein, disquieting and disturbing the public peace and tranquility thereby, would you, as lord of the soil, be pleased thereat? Certainly not; and therefore by this you can judge what I have done."[38] As for the cargo of the *San Felipe*, Hideyoshi would gladly return it if he could. But this was impossible as everything had been dispersed.

The Spanish were not pleased. According to Antonio de Morga:

Taicosama [Hideyoshi] rejoiced over his answer to the ambassador, for he had practically done nothing of what was asked of him. His reply was more a display of dissembling and compliments than a desire for friendship with the Spaniards. He boasted and published arrogantly, and his favorites said in the same manner, that the Spaniards had sent him that present and embassy through fear, and as an acknowledgment of tribute and seigniory, so that he might not destroy them as he had threatened them at other times in the past, when Gomez Perez Dasmarinas was governor. And even then the Spaniards had sent him a message and a present by Fray Juan Cobo, the Dominican.[39]

While this mission was under way, the Spanish in Manila were taking every precaution to prepare for a rumored Japanese invasion, fears of which had been rekindled with the receipt of Father Aguirre's warning in May of 1597. The threat quickly began to assume greater dimensions with the subsequent arrival of rumors that Harada Magoshichiro, the Japanese adventurer who had brought Hideyoshi's first demand for submission to Manila in 1592, had been given permission by the taiko to mount a Philippine invasion. This alarming intelligence prompted the Spanish to deport the many Japanese then residing in Manila and to allow Japanese merchant ships to remain in port only for as long as it took to transact their business. Then, since it was believed that the Japanese would proceed to Manila by way of Taiwan, the governor sent two ships north to reconnoiter that island and to warn the authorities in the southern Chinese province of Guangdong of what the Japanese were up to.

Nothing ever came of this planned Japanese move against Manila. According to Antonio de Morga, Harada did not possess the means to get the enterprise off the ground on his own and was unable to enlist the help of more powerful men. After several months of fruitless effort, he was obliged to give up the idea upon Hideyoshi's death. Japan's conquest of the Philippines would thus have to wait for another 350 years.

In Japan, meanwhile, Hideyoshi's daimyo commanders were preparing for a second invasion of Korea. The operation would lack the grand scope of the first invasion, the objective of which had been nothing less than the conquest of China and in turn all of Asia. This second invasion would be a simple land grab. To soothe the taiko's wounded pride and to have something to show for the costly first campaign, his commanders would seize the southern half of Korea.

One of the most important lessons the Japanese learned from the first invasion, and which they now strove to apply to the second, was that the Korean navy posed a serious threat. This small but effective force had been instrumental in breaking the back of the campaign of 1592–93 by blocking the Japanese from transporting reinforcements and supplies north via the Yellow Sea. For a second invasion to have any chance of success, the Korean fleet would therefore first have to be destroyed and Japanese naval supremacy established along the south coast. In the months leading up to the second invasion Hideyoshi's daimyo commanders worked to achieve this end on two fronts. First, they placed greater emphasis on their own navy, assembling a stronger fleet than they had had in 1592. And second, they set out to weaken the Korean navy before the first battle was ever fought—by neutralizing its supreme commander, Yi Sun-sin.

CHAPTER 23

The Arrest and Imprisonment of Yi Sun-sin

BY THE SUMMER OF 1596 Korea's supreme naval commander Yi Sun-sin had lost a good deal of support of the government in Seoul. The work of bringing him down had been begun by his rival, Kyongsang Right Navy Commander Won Kyun, at the very start of the war, with a stream of accusations that Yi avoided battle, disobeyed orders, and consistently hogged all the glory for himself. The feud between these two men reached such a clamorous state that in 1594 Yi requested a transfer. It was ultimately Won, however, who was shifted elsewhere, first to the post of Chungchong Army commander, and later to the command of the Cholla Army. Here he continued to pour invective against Yi into any willing ear, repeating the same charges in the hope that sooner or later they would stick enough to bring his nemesis down.[1]

While Won Kyun continued to chip away at Yi Sun-sin's reputation, a new threat to the commander came to be posed by his own inability to strike a blow against the Japanese. Yi's stunning victories early in the war had led the Korean government to expect a great deal from him. But these same victories had also made the Japanese navy cautious. In 1593 it began avoiding engagements with the Korean fleet, keeping its sailors holed up in shore fortifications and its ships hidden in inaccessible inlets. With the enemy no longer willing to fight there was little Commander Yi could do. The government in Seoul, however,

did not appreciate this. They continued to press Yi into battle against an
enemy that was no longer there. And when he failed to produce results,
they began to question his suitability for command. Had the hero of
1592 lost his nerve? Was he resting on his laurels after being promoted
too high? Was Won Kyun perhaps correct in claiming that Yi had never
been so very great, but was merely a self-aggrandizing schemer who
had built a reputation for himself by stealing the victories of others?

In a series of court discussions beginning in July of 1596, leading
members of the Western faction suggested to King Sonjo that it might
be in the best interests of the nation to dismiss Yi Sun-sin and give his
command to Won Kyun. On the twenty-first of that month, Left
Minister and Western faction leader Kim Ung-nam called Yi Sun-sin a
"retiring sort," and observed to the king that "if we want to protect
Korea from the Japanese, it would be best to send Won Kyun south to
lead our navy." Won, Kim asserted, was the only man up to the task.[2]
At this point Sonjo was unwilling to consider replacing Yi Sun-sin with
Won Kyun, the abilities of whom he had reason to doubt. By early
December, however, he was starting to waver. Peace negotiations
between China and Japan had by this time come to a crashing halt, and
the fear of a second Japanese invasion had the Korean government in a
state of apprehension. Following a glowing account by Third Minister
of War Cho In-duk of Won Kyun's prewar career as an army officer
serving along the northern frontier, Sonjo agreed that he did indeed
seem brave.[3] The court discussion on December 25 went even more in
Won's favor, with renewed suggestions that he at least be returned to
naval command, perhaps back to his old post in charge of the Kyongsang navy. Prime Minister Yu Song-nyong, a leader of the Eastern
faction and mentor of Yi Sun-sin, judiciously conceded that Won was
one of those rare commanders skilled in warfare both on land and at
sea. "He has consistently made mistakes, however, and so should not be
reassigned to the navy."

King Sonjo did not agree. It was his opinion that Won's rebellious
behavior while serving under Yi Sun-sin as Kyongsang Right Navy
commander was due primarily to his resentment at Yi's getting more
praise from the government than he himself received, even though he
fought bravely. "I have heard that in one battle," the king added, "Yi

held back and Won did most of the fighting."

"Yes," agreed Minister Yi Dong-yol. "Prior to one of their campaigns Won Kyun had to call Yi to battle fourteen or fifteen times before Yi would consent to join him. They subsequently destroyed about sixty enemy ships between them, but in his report Yi claimed all the credit for himself."

Then Minister of the Right Yi Won-ik spoke up. "Even if Yi Sun-sin didn't sink every enemy vessel by himself," he observed, "he clearly has done more than Won Kyun to kill Japanese." The discussion ended inconclusively with Yi Sun-sin remaining in office, but his ability to gain victory now in serious doubt.[4]

Yi Won-ik, incidentally, would remain the only prominent member of the Western faction to support Yi Sun-in over Won Kyun in this and subsequent debates.[5] This uncharacteristic crossing of factional lines probably stemmed from the fact that he had personally inspected the southern navy and met with both Won Kyun and Yi Sun-sin the year before. During this tour he found Won to be "a rough character," capable only of swearing incoherently when questioned about Yi Sun-sin. Yi Sun-sin, on the other hand, came across as reasoned, well-spoken, and intelligent. "I was not only impressed with the defensive plans established by Admiral Yi," Won-ik would later write, "but was astonished at his deep thought."[6] Yi Won-ik thus returned to Seoul with a high opinion of Yi Sun-sin and little regard for Won Kyun, and to his credit stuck by his assessment throughout the coming months.

While the tide of government opinion was now turning against Yi Sun-sin, his ultimate demotion and imprisonment were still by no means certain. It would take the intervention of the Japanese to topple him completely. In the beginning of 1597, as the vanguard of Hideyoshi's army was preparing to return to Korea, a spy named Yojiro appeared at the camp of Kyongsang Right Army Commander Kim Ung-so. His arrival did not strike Kim and his officers as particularly suspicious, for Yojiro was well known to them as something of a double agent: a native of Tsushima, fluent in both Japanese and Korean, who secretly favored Korea and professed a desire to settle permanently in the kingdom. Kim and his officers thus listened carefully to what he had to say. Yojiro explained that he had come bearing a secret message from

Konishi Yukinaga. Konishi, he said, blamed the meddling of his rival Kato Kiyomasa for the failure of peace negotiations with China and was eager to get rid of him once and for all. Kato was now preparing to return to Korea at the head of a fresh invasion army. He would be passing by a certain island off the coast on his way to Pusan. Yojiro gave the location and the exact time. "If the Korean government will order its navy to ambush Kato at sea on his way to Korea," he concluded, "your country will be able to capture and kill this great general. And you will be doing Konishi a great favor at the same time."[7]

The spy Yojiro did his job well. Kim Ung-so came away from the meeting believing his tale and relayed it immediately to his superior, Commander in Chief Kwon Yul. Kwon too found Yojiro's story plausible. The rivalry between Konishi and Kato was well-known to the Koreans and the desire of the one to betray the other easy to believe. The commander thus endorsed Kim's report and forwarded it to Seoul. After a brief debate the government concluded that the secret communication from Konishi seemed legitimate, and that the opportunity it presented them to eliminate an important enemy commander should be acted on without delay. Orders were accordingly drawn up and sent south to Yi Sun-sin: gather your fleet and ambush Kato Kiyomasa while he is still at sea.

Commander Yi was immediately suspicious of Yojiro's tale. It sounded to him like a trap, and so he delayed putting to sea. Kyongsang Army Commander Kim Ung-so, convinced that the intelligence was correct, was angered by this and informed Seoul of Yi's unwillingness to act. Kwon Yul was also annoyed by the naval commander's foot dragging, and on March 8 went in person to Hansan Island to order Yi into action. Yi replied that leading the entire Korean fleet through rock-infested waters to a rendezvous at a time and place of the enemy's choosing was not just risky, but foolhardy. Even if Yojiro's intelligence was correct, the risk was not worth the reward. Kwon did not agree. Commander Yi was to do as he was told, he said, and put to sea at once.[8]

Yi Sun-sin set out with his fleet soon after that, heading east toward Kadok Island. He had not gone far when the spy Yojiro appeared once again at the camp of Kyongsang Army Commander Kim Ung-so, this time with the news that Kato Kiyomasa had already arrived safely in Korea and that the opportunity to ambush him at sea was consequently lost. This piece of news was true. Kato had landed near Pusan on March 1, one week before Kwon Yul ordered Yi Sun-sin into action. The wily Yojiro, however, knew how to play Commander Kim and in turn the government in Seoul. It was a shame, he said, that Yi Sun-sin had allowed such a great opportunity to slip away. If only he had acted, Kato now would be dead.[9]

The judicious prodding worked. The Korean government did not stop to consider that perhaps Yi had been correct in thinking that the entire episode was a Japanese trick designed to ambush the Korean navy, which it likely was. The perception that an opportunity had been missed to eliminate one of the most hated of the Japanese commanders for the moment seems to have clouded the judgment of everyone concerned. "How could I now expect Yi Sun-sin to bring us Kato's head?" bemoaned a now thoroughly disenchanted King Sonjo upon hearing the news. "It would have been better if he had led his ships into action and lost them all, than to sit on Hansan Island doing nothing."[10] These were words Sonjo certainly would come to regret.

The final court discussion regarding what to do with Yi Sun-sin took place on March 14, 1597. Second Minister Without Portfolio Yun Tu-su opened the session by reiterating the accusations against Yi. "He has been just sitting on Hansan Island these past months," Yun said. "And now he has let Kato Kiyomasa slip past. Something has to be done about this."

"Sun-sin has indeed committed a serious sin," ruminated Third Minister Without Portfolio Chong Tak.

"Lately the Border Defense Council has said that many of our commanders habitually ignore orders," said King Sonjo, "because the government hasn't held them firmly enough in check. This has been a perennial problem in China, generals not doing as they are told, and now it has come to our kingdom. Even if Yi Sun-sin were now to go out and kill Kato Kiyomasa, he cannot be forgiven. Something has to be done."

Prime Minister Yu Song-nyong, who had recommended Yi for high command on the eve of the war, now attempted to explain himself: "I have known Yi since we were children. He always wanted to become a general, and I assumed he would make a good one."

"Is he well educated?" asked the king.

"Yes. And he is strong and decisive. That is why I recommended him to the post of naval commander. But he was promoted to too high a rank following his successes in 1592. I can only assume this made him complacent."

Sonjo was not interested in excuses. "Yi Sun-sin cannot be forgiven," he repeated. "How can we condone a commander who, by not obeying orders, sets himself higher than the government?"

Left Minister Kim Ung-nam then suggested that Won Kyun be returned to naval command, perhaps to his former post as head of the Kyongsang Navy. "There is no one better for the job."

Not everyone favored the idea at first. The king pointed out that Won, while brave, was at times too impetuous. "If we reappoint him to the command of the Kyongsang Navy, who will control him and prevent him from charging at the Japanese without thinking?" Any reservations about Won's suitability for naval command, however, were soon pushed aside in the general rush to see Yi Sun-sin brought down. Even Yi's own mentor Yu Song-nyong said nothing in his defense. He either believed the charges against his protégé, or more likely considered it expedient to avoid a political battle he could not win.

Then Chong Tak spoke up. While Yi Sun-sin certainly deserved to be replaced, he said, it would be unwise to do so at such a critical juncture, with a second Japanese offensive about to begin. It would be better to leave him where he was and to deal with his disobedience later. The wisdom of this was generally agreed. In the end it was decided to appoint Won Kyun to the command of the Kyongsang Navy and to leave Yi Sun-sin for the time being in charge of the fleets of Chungchong and Cholla Provinces.[11]

It is interesting to note that King Sonjo and his ministers, while clearly angry over what they regarded as Yi Sun-sin's failure to obey orders, decided for the sake of stability only to take away a portion of his command. There was no talk at this time of throwing him into prison. The pressure for sterner punishment would come from further down the hierarchy of power. It was here, among ambitious young officials with much to prove and far to climb, that factional fighting typically was most energetically pursued. This was particularly true of the Censorate, the collection of three highly influential government organs tasked with scrutinizing the conduct of the government and military. Many a fledging official had got his start here, using the power of remonstrance to bring down factional opponents and advance his own career.

It was now a protest from one of these organs, the Office of the Inspector-General, that sealed the fate of Yi Sun-sin. On March 21, six days after the court resolved merely to reduce Yi's command, the OIG sent a letter to King Sonjo questioning the decision. Yi Sun-sin, the letter asserted, had failed to do his duty and had disobeyed a direct order, and thus should not be left in command of anything at all. He should be removed from office and thrown into prison.[12] The OIG's protest had its intended effect. Two days later King Sonjo dispatched an official south to Hansan Island to arrest Yi and bring him to Seoul, and at the same time install Won Kyun as commander of Korea's naval forces in the south. The official reached Yi's base on April 12. The transfer of command was made that same day, the supplies, weapons, and gunpowder that Yi had so painstakingly stockpiled over the years being handed over to the man he most despised. Yi was then bound with rope, placed in a cage on the back of a cart, and sent north to the capital to be imprisoned and interrogated regarding the charges brought against him: that he had refused to obey orders; that he had betrayed his country by allowing an enemy to escape; and, in a nod to Won Kyun, that he had claimed credit for victories and services that should rightly have gone to others. These were serious accusations punishable by death.[13]

While Yi Sun-sin awaited his fate in a prison cell in Seoul, a war of words was waged between the Eastern and Western factions over his fate, the former trying to save their man, the latter intent on having him killed. In an attempt to shed more light on the affair, the government sent an investigator south to Hansan Island to look into the matter and examine Yi's conduct. This investigator's sympathies clearly lay with the Westerners. After a brief tour of the south that did not even include a stop at Hansan-do as ordered, he returned to Seoul with a conveniently damning story to further vilify Yi. According to unsubstantiated reports, the investigator said, Kato Kiyomasa's ship had run aground on an island offshore while en route to Pusan, stranding the commander for seven days, an easy target for the Korean navy if Yi Sun-sin had only taken the trouble to attack him. This tale was regarded by some with justifiable suspicion. Government minister Kim Myong-won, former commander in chief of the armed forces and now back in the civil service, remarked to King Sonjo that he considered it "ridiculous" for anyone to suggest that "born sailors" like the Japanese would be stranded like this for seven whole days. Many others, however, were only too willing to believe anything that served to further blacken Yi's name.[14]

In the end it was a personal appeal to King Sonjo from Minister Without Portfolio Chong Tak that saved Yi Sun-sin's life. The seventy-year-old Chong, esteemed by the king for his wisdom and age, eloquently argued that, while the charges against Yi were indeed grave, his service to the nation in 1592–93 merited serious consideration. This advice was eventually accepted, and an almost certain sentence of death was commuted to loss of position alone. After a month of confinement and several harsh interrogations that possibly included torture, Yi was released from prison and sent south under guard to Kyongsang Province to report to his new post. Henceforth the fifty-two-year-old former naval commander would serve as a common soldier of the lowest rank in the army of Commander in Chief Kwon Yul.[15]

*   *   *

First day, fourth moon: Clear. I came out from the prison cell, and entered the house of a servant of Yun Kan's outside the South Gate (Seoul).... Governor Yun Cha-sin came to comfort me, and the Section Chief of the Border Defense Council Yi Sun-ji came to see me. I could not keep back my unhappy feeling. The Governor went out and returned in the evening with wine. (Yun) Ki-hon also came. They comforted me.... Chief State Councilor Yu Song-nyong sent me his servant, Privy Councilor Chong Tak, Minister Sim Hui-su, Left State Councilor Kim Myong-won, Vice Minister Yi Chong-hyong, Chief Censor No Chik, Deputy Councilors Ch'oe Won and Kwak Yong, each sent someone to inquire about my health.[16]

An understandably bitter Yi Sun-sin was released from prison on May 16, 1597. He was immediately surrounded by friends and supporters, plying him with wine to boost his spirits. On the following day he met with his friend and mentor Prime Minister Yu Song-nyong, and in a talk that lasted all through the night heard much of the recent happenings surrounding his case. Then, on May 18, he began his long journey south to Kyongsang Province to enter the service of Kwon Yul as a common soldier.

Yi Sun-sin's journey south was a slow and unhappy affair.[17] He stopped first as his family's home at Asan in Chungchong Province. Here he was greeted by the sight of blackened stumps surrounding his ancestors' graves: a forest fire had recently consumed the site. Then, after a few days spent visiting friends and relations, Yi received word that his eighty-year-old mother had passed away. Earlier in the war she had moved south to Yosu to be near her son. She died while en route by boat back north to Asan.

As so often happened with Yi, the event of his mother's death was preceded by signs. On the morning of May 26 he awoke from a confusing and upsetting dream. He described it to his two sons Tok and Yol, but they could make nothing of it. There was clearly meaning in it, however; to a sixteenth-century Korean virtually every dream had meaning. Then suddenly Yi thought of his mother, "and hot tears rolled down my cheeks." He sent a messenger to the coast to meet the boat and inquire after her health. Two days later the sad news arrived: his mother was dead. "I jumped up in surprise," Yi writes, "then tumbled over. How could the sun in heaven be so dark?" Over the following days Yi accompanied his mother's body to the family home at Asan for burial. "I wept as if my bowels were torn to pieces with grief. How can I express all of the emotions I have had? On reaching home we placed her casket in a room . . . until the funeral day. It rained in torrents. As I was exhausted with grief and the order to present myself at the southern military camp weighed on my mind, I could not but cry aloud. All I could conceive was that I had better die soon."[18]

After the funeral rites were complete, Yi, now clad in the white clothes of mourning, was obliged to resume his journey south. Upon reaching Kyongsang he established himself and his two sons in a modest house in the mountains above Kwon Yul's camp. He would remain there for the rest of the summer, ostensibly serving Kwon as a guard in this remote outpost, but in fact left to his own devices, cared for by a small staff of servants while he waited for the tide of opinion against him to turn.

PART 5

THE
SECOND INVASION

No ruler should put troops into the field
merely to gratify his own spleen;
no general should fight a battle simply out of pique.[1]

Sun Tzu Ping Fa (Master Sun's Art of War)
4th century B.C.

CHAPTER 24

"Water, Thunder, and Great Disaster"

HIDEYOSHI'S OBJECTIVE IN HIS SECOND INVASION of Korea was completely different from the first. In 1592 he had his sights set on China. Korea was merely the highway to the prize, to be traversed as quickly as possible so that the real battle could be joined, the battle for Beijing. By 1597 Hideyoshi had given up this plan. To be sure, he continued to make sporadic references to expanding his empire across the whole world. His orders launching the second invasion, for example, included the following bold words: "First Korea and its eight circuits [provinces], then Great Ming and its more than four hundred provinces, South Barbary, the Kirishitan Country and all beyond, down to the distant islands and as far as the fortunes of war continue, all will be subjugated by the force of Hideyoshi's reputation."[1] But this was only bluster. The taiko now understood that China was too vast and too distant for even a great conqueror like himself to subdue. This time Korea itself was his target, or more precisely the southern half of the peninsula.

And what were Hideyoshi's designs for the southern half of Korea? The answer is clouded by the fact that he and his field commanders did not share the same objectives. The subsequent course of events makes it clear that daimyo like Kato Kiyomasa, Konishi Yukinaga, and Kuroda Nagamasa planned to conquer the southern three provinces of Kyong-sang, Cholla, and Chungchong and transform them into a province of

Japan. This would satisfy Hideyoshi by expanding his empire and glorifying his name, and more important would open up vast new territories for redistribution to those daimyo who had subdued it—the promise of larger, richer fiefdoms in return for risking life and limb. Hideyoshi himself, however, does not seem to have had designs on conquest. At the start of the second invasion he in fact would forbid his commanders from marching on Seoul. They were simply to rampage through southern Korea for a month or two, he ordered, then return to the coast. The purpose of this was to save face after the humiliating outcome of the first campaign and subsequent negotiations with Beijing. If the taiko's armies were to return to Korea and devastate half the kingdom before returning home, it would serve to punish the Koreans for daring to stand against him, and demonstrate to the Chinese that Hideyoshi still had the power and resolve to challenge them any time he wished.

It is likely that Hideyoshi was also intent on bolstering his reputation at home when he sent his armies back to Korea in 1597. The Ming emperor's refusal to treat him as at least an equal, coupled with the Koreans' refusal to send him even a prince as a hostage as he had demanded, marked the first time in the taiko's career that he had been unable to force or otherwise coerce an adversary into a position of his choosing. Hideyoshi could not afford to let such an outcome stand, for it carried with it the taint of weakness, the first sign that the aging dictator, now past sixty and in unmistakable physical decline, was no longer the indomitable force he once had been. Seen in this light, Hideyoshi had little choice but to reinvade Korea. He had to do so to demonstrate to his own people that he remained their master, a benevolent provider when served without question, but a terrible conqueror when resisted or crossed. He needed to remind them of this not just for his own sake, but also for the sake of his heir and only natural son. Hideyori was just four years old in 1597, a long way from being able to defend his right to rule should his father pass away. By reasserting himself in Korea, Hideyoshi thus was sending a message not just to the Chinese and to the Koreans that he was not to be trifled with. He was also sending a message to his own daimyo, the headstrong barons he had so recently brought under his sway: the house of Toyotomi was strong and determined and would brook no challenge. Anyone attempting to resist it would be made to pay a terrible price.

By the time negotiations had fallen apart in the latter part of 1596, Japanese troop withdrawals from Korea to appease the Ming envoys had reduced their forces there to just a few thousand. In the months that followed, this tenuous toehold on the peninsula was strengthened to 20,390, still all clustered in the vicinity of Pusan. Kobayakawa Hideaki, the adopted son of Kobayakawa Takakage, the hero of the Battle of Pyokje who had died of natural causes earlier that year, commanded a garrison of 10,390 men at Pusan itself. Five thousand men under Tachibana Munetora were stationed fifteen kilometers west at the port of Angolpo. One thousand men under Takahashi Saburo were offshore on Kadok Island. Asano Chokei was at Sosaengpo, near the town of Ulsan to the north, with 3,000 men, and Kobayakawa Hidekane, brother of Takakage, was on the island of Chuk-do in the Naktong River delta with 1,000.[2] No offensive movement was undertaken at this time. The job of these various units was to reestablish a beachhead in preparation for the arrival of the main invasion force.

On March 19, 1597, Hideyoshi issued orders mobilizing an additional 121,100 men for his second Korean campaign. Nearly half of this force, 56,700 men, originated from Kyushu. The remainder came from Shikoku (24,400) and western Honshu (40,000).[3] They joined the 20,390 troops already stationed in and around Pusan, bringing the total strength of Hideyoshi's second invasion force to 141,490—not much smaller than the 158,800-man army he had sent to Korea in 1592. They were for the most part first-class troops, virtually all of the samurai commanders and many of the men having experienced combat and hardship during the first invasion. They were stronger for it. But they were also warier. They returned to Korea with little of the optimism of 1592, the assumption that the trek to China would be a romp. This time they knew they would be facing an implacable foe, the Koreans weak but bitter and hating, the Chinese army large and strong. This time they knew that the war they were entering would be a deadly conflict, one that would see many of them killed before an end was reached, whatever that end might be.

In overall command was Kobayakawa Hideaki, a fifteen-year-old nephew of Hideyoshi's on his wife O-Ne's side. Young Hideaki had as a child been adopted first by the taiko with the name Hashiba Hidetoshi, and later by first invasion veteran Kobayakawa Takakage, who had no sons of his own. It is doubtful that this lad would have wielded much real power. He was more a figurehead, a representative in the field of his uncle Hideyoshi. Under Hideaki came twenty-three-year-old Ukita Hideie, supreme commander of the first invasion army, and beside him eighteen-year-old Mori Hidemoto, replacing his cousin Terumoto, who had served in Korea in 1592–93. Kuroda Yoshitaka, the father to Kuroda Nagamasa and a Christian like his son (his baptismal name was Simeon), served them as a sort of chief of staff. This fifty-year-old veteran likely did much to guide the hands of these younger men who ostensibly outranked him.

It is remarkable that men so young as Kobayakawa Hideaki, Mori Hidemoto, and to a lesser extent Ukita Hideie should have been entrusted with such lofty positions of command. One reason for this may have been that they would have been a more compliant conduit for Hideyoshi's orders and thus more useful to him in such positions than older, more ambitious men. It should be borne in mind, moreover, that they were not "generals" or "commanders in chief" in the sense that existed in China and Korea, and indeed in modern armies today. Hideyoshi's second invasion force was still very much controlled by the daimyo commanders of its individual units. Each was in effect an independent army, coming together in loose collaboration to achieve a common goal. This fact had resulted in a good deal of in-fighting and working at cross-purposes in the first heady months of war in 1592, as some of Hideyoshi's more headstrong commanders competed for personal honors in what they initially assumed would be an easy war. There would be less of this in the second invasion. The daimyo that returned to Korea in 1597 were better disciplined and more willing to work together. It has been suggested that this was because they were placed under tighter discipline.[4] With a fifteen-year-old and an eighteen-year-old in command, this is questionable. A more plausible explanation is that Hideyoshi's commanders knew better this time what they were up against and thus disciplined themselves. They returned to Korea with a better sense of the strength of the enemy, of their own vulnerability, and thus of the need to work together if they were to succeed.

The Japanese started returning to Korea at the beginning of March 1597. On the first day of the month Kato Kiyomasa, at the head of ten thousand men aboard two hundred ships, landed at Chuk Island at the mouth of the Naktong River, where a small body of troops was already garrisoned. They encountered no resistance. Kato dispatched a message to Seoul from his master Hideyoshi, presumably threatening Choson with destruction and demanding compliance.[5] Then he sent a ship first east to Pusan and then north to Sosaengpo to post the following announcement to the citizens of Kyongsang: "The Japanese army of Kato Kiyomasa, having received the command of his Excellency the Taiko, has crossed the sea again and returned to this place. A representative has already been sent to Seoul. While awaiting his report, the people of Kyongsang Province shall not doubt the validity of this announcement, nor shall they attempt to run away in fear."[6]

On March 2 Konishi Yukinaga arrived at Pusan with his seven thousand troops. He then sailed fifteen kilometers west to Angolpo, where he proceeded to collect timber to repair and strengthen the fortress he had evacuated the year before. In the coming campaign Konishi would serve initially as something of an overseer to the navy, an assignment that Hideyoshi perhaps hoped would make his fleet more cohesive and effective following its disappointing performance in 1592–93. Over the next several months Konishi would be joined at Angolpo by naval commanders Todo Takatora, Kato Yoshiaki, and Kurushima Michifusa, all from the sixth contingent, and by Wakizaka Yasuharu from the seventh, making this port to the west of Pusan the invasion force's main naval base.[7]

From early March until the middle of August additional forces continued to arrive on Korea's south coast. Shimazu Yoshihiro reinforced Kadok Island with ten thousand men. Kuroda Nagamasa, Mori Yoshimasa, and others settled at the port of Anpo. Nabeshima Naoshige and his seventeen-year-old son Katsushige made for the island of Chuk-do with twelve thousand men, while Mori Hidemoto's gargantuan thirty thousand-man force and the ten thousand men under Ukita Hideie joined young Kobayakawa Hideaki at Pusan.

This buildup of forces was a slow and methodical affair. There was no intention this time as in 1592 of making a lightning thrust northward and slashing a route to Seoul. Hideyoshi's commanders instead spent several months massing their forces and strengthening their defenses in a string of camps on the peninsula's southeastern tip, establishing a beachhead from which they could extend their reach west into Cholla Province and north into Kyongsang. They had returned to Korea to seize and hold territory, not merely to pass through.

In addition to the time it took to transport men, horses, and supplies from Japan, another possibly more important factor behind the ponderous start to Hideyoshi's reinvasion may have been the problem of obtaining food. Feeding more than 140,000 men over a period of many months would take a tremendous amount of rice, more than the Japanese could ship to Korea from home. Attempting to supply troops with rice from Japan would also put a heavy strain on the nation's peasantry and tie up a portion of the navy with onerous transportation duties. It was for this reason that Hideyoshi decided to put his expeditionary forces on a more self-sufficient footing than had been the case in 1592. For the second invasion of Korea his armies were expected to seize rice from the Koreans and live off the land. This may account for the long delay between the return to Korea of the Japanese beginning in March and the launching of their land offensive in September: they were waiting for Korea's rice harvest to ripen so that they could commandeer it. It almost certainly was also the reason why their land offensive would begin with a thrust into Cholla Province: Cholla, the kingdom's most fertile region, was the breadbasket of Korea. It contained all the rice the Japanese would need.[8]

The return of Japanese troops to their kingdom in 1597—called *chongyu jaeran* in Korea, "the reinvasion of the year *chongyu* (fire-rooster)"—was of course not unexpected by the Koreans. They had been making efforts to strengthen the nation's defenses throughout the relatively peaceful years since the end of the first invasion. Mountain fortresses and the walls of key cities had been rebuilt at numerous locations throughout the south. Muskets had been approved for adoption by the army and were now in limited use in many units, although still far below the numbers employed by the Japanese. New cannons, which had proved their worth in the first invasion, were cast to replace those destroyed in battle and captured by the Japanese. *Hwacha* (fire wagons), which shot up to one hundred gunpowder-propelled arrows in a single volley, were turned out as well. Efforts were also made to refine new weapons such as the rock-throwing *sucha sokpo* (water wheel rock cannon), which had been used to good effect at the Battle of Haengju in early 1593.[9]

The Koreans therefore were not idle during the long break in the war. Their defensive preparations, however, came nowhere near what would be required to repel Hideyoshi's second campaign. There was a good reason for this: the first invasion had devastated the southern half of the kingdom and effectively ruined the economy. With the population facing famine and starvation, the government in Seoul had had no choice but to focus its efforts on getting farmers back into the fields growing grain to feed the nation. Keeping the people fed and the kingdom alive was such an all-consuming task that there was little manpower or resources left over for making any sort of substantial military preparations. It was for this reason that the government had given up the idea of maintaining a large standing army. Apart from a few thousand professional soldiers stationed in and around the capital, Korea's army was now composed of local militias, farmer soldiers who would be summoned from their fields only when it came time to fight. The navy, meanwhile, had of necessity gravitated toward a similar form of self-sufficiency. Soon after the cessation of hostilities in 1594, Supreme Naval Commander Yi Sun-sin had sent his sailors back to their homes on an alternating basis to work their fields and thus keep their families fed. The Korean fleet therefore contracted by half during the interwar years. That any sort of fleet existed at all in the south in early 1597 was a testament to the resourcefulness and determination of Yi Sun-sin himself. From 1593 until the end of 1596 Yi operated farms to grow food for his men and raised money through the production of salt to pay for the maintenance of his fleet, all with only the most meager government support.

Indeed, the government was able to undertake some of its most significant defensive work, the construction and strengthening of fortresses in the south, only because it cost the nation so little. A good deal of this work was completed by monks, criticized from the earliest days of the Choson dynasty as being leeches on society, and persecuted so vigorously that they were no longer even officially recognized as monks. The government was able to put several thousand members of this underclass to work on projects throughout the kingdom by dangling the prospect of rewards and honors for their leaders, official recognition of its two main sects, and certification of monkhood to any monk volunteering for one year of service in the construction brigades. These concessions cost Seoul almost nothing. The government was for the most part offering to return to the Buddhists some of the things it had taken away from them over the previous two hundred years. As it turned out, moreover, the monks received even less than that. When settling its accounts in the wake of the war, the government was stingy in the rewards and honors it bestowed, and imposed so many restrictions on certification of monkhood that few could make the grade.[10]

The devastation Korea had suffered during Hideyoshi's first invasion was undoubtedly the most significant reason why it was unable to do more to strengthen its defenses. But it was not the only reason. When the Korean government asked for and received military aid from China at the beginning of the war, it gave up some of its independence and in turn some of its ability to defend itself, if only in its own mind. Now, on the eve of Hideyoshi's second campaign, the option of calling for Ming intervention had come to replace national preparedness as the main plank in Korea's defense policy. Seoul now regarded the Chinese army as its ultimate weapon of deterrence. For King Sonjo and his ministers, the guarded confidence they felt in being able once again to summon this force overshadowed any defense preparations they may have been able to make on their own. While they certainly did make an effort to build walls, organize militias, and strengthen mountain fortresses, therefore, had they not possessed this China option they probably could have done more. Indeed, when it became clear toward the end of 1596 that the Japanese intended to resume their offensive, one of the first things the Korean government did was to send a succession of representatives to Beijing with memorials requesting military aid.

*   *   *

It took a week for reports of the return to Korea of large numbers of Japanese troops to reach Seoul. Among the communications was the letter from Hideyoshi that Kato Kiyomasa had dispatched to the capital from the peninsula's south shore. The Border Defense Council (*bibyonsa*) refused to receive it; they did not wish to appear to be negotiating with the enemy without prior approval from Beijing.[11] Fearing that the enemy would again make a lightning advance toward the capital as they had in 1592, Kwon Yul, hero of the Battle of Haengju and now commander in chief of Korea's armed forces, proceeded to Choryong (Bird Pass) in the Sobaek mountains, the most defensible point on the central road to Seoul. In 1592 this gap had been left unguarded. The Koreans did not wish to see this mistake made again. Kwon had the fortifications along the pass strengthened and stationed a sizable body of men there to guard them. It was a wise move, but unfortunately futile: Choryong Pass, so important in 1592, would play no significant part in the battles to come.

In Seoul, meanwhile, another memorial requesting military aid was hastily drawn up and dispatched to Beijing, together with reports on the latest developments in the south. The Ming government received it in a much different mood than it had King Sonjo's first pleas for help back in 1592. To begin with, it was already angry at Hideyoshi for his unprecedented rejection of their offer of vassalage and his rude treatment of their envoys. The sentiment in Beijing was therefore overwhelmingly hawkish. The government had anticipated a renewal of Japanese aggression in Korea, moreover, and so preparations were already under way to dispatch a second expeditionary army eastward when King Sonjo's latest memorial arrived. Xing Jie had been appointed to the position of general oversight of military affairs in the eastern regions, under which Korea was included. A strictly civilian official as was the custom, he would make his headquarters, "Army Gate," initially in Liaodong Province. Yang Hao, a man with both military and civil experience, was appointed to serve beneath Xing as *Jingli Chaoxian junwu*, overall regulator of military affairs in Korea. In the coming campaign he would be the de facto supreme commander of all Ming forces sent to stop the Japanese. Beneath Yang Hao would come Ma Gui, the actual commander in chief of the Chinese expeditionary force, the same position held previously by Li Rusong. Finally, beneath Ma were the generals in charge of each of the army's main divisions: Yang Yuan, Dong Yiyuan, and Liu Ting—the same "Big Sword" Liu who had seen action in Korea back in 1593.[12]

Appointing generals for service in Korea was easy for Beijing. Finding soldiers for them to command was not. The first Korean campaign had put a severe strain on the treasury, leaving the empire with little cash to fund a large army, in particular the salaries that had to be paid to the mercenaries that it had come to rely so heavily on. The financial situation was so acute that the Wanli emperor momentarily had to suspend his usual hibernation from administrative duties to approve a request for a number of silver mines to be opened to replenish state coffers. When this endeavor failed to yield enough wealth, he gave his stamp to a series of increasingly onerous special taxes that soon had the provinces in an uproar.[13] Nor was Korea Beijing's only concern. It had other problems to deal with that necessitated a military presence elsewhere. Most important of these was the growing threat on the northeastern frontier, where a charismatic chief named Nurhaci had over the previous twenty years united all the Jurchen tribes of the region and amassed a highly disciplined army of between thirty and forty thousand cavalrymen and forty and fifty thousand infantry.[14] No fighting was currently taking place on this front. That would come later. The necessity of guarding Liaodong Province's eastern border from Nurhaci's looming menace, however, made it impossible to do the most convenient thing and simply transfer the bulk of the Liaodong Army to Korea, it being the nearest army to that theater. The best that China could do was to dispatch immediately a token force from Liaodong and then mobilize additional troops from elsewhere in the empire, including regions as distant as Guangdong and Fujian Provinces on the south coast and Sichuan in the far west. It would therefore take several months for the Chinese to return in force to Korea. Yang Yuan, commanding the initial brigade from nearby Liaodong, would be the first to arrive in July of 1597; "Big Sword" Liu, stationed two thousand kilometers away in Sichuan, would be the last. (The Ming navy would also be ordered to Korea for the first time in the war, but it would not arrive until later in the year.)

Despite the difficulties it faced in raising troops to send to Korea, the Ming government managed to scrape together a significantly larger force than it had in 1593. It did not approach the 100,000-man army Ming official Xing Jie had envisioned prior to the start of the campaign. But it came close. Accordingly to the Chinese historical record, initial mobilizations of army units yielded 38,000 troops. They would be joined over the coming months by approximately 16,000 additional troops from outlying regions of the empire. The naval units that eventually found their way to Korea added another 21,000 men. At the height of the second Korean campaign, therefore, Ming army and navy forces totaled approximately 75,000 men.[15]

General Yang Yuan, the first Ming commander to respond to Korea's call for help, crossed the Yalu River in late June at the head of three thousand Liaodong soldiers and immediately proceeded to Seoul. This was Yang's second tour of duty in Korea; he had served as Left Division commander under Li Rusong in 1593. After a few days' rest in the capital he was then seen off by the Koreans on his continuing journey to the south. King Sonjo himself presided over the pomp and ceremony, urging wine upon the general and presenting him with a gift as a sign of his kingdom's gratitude. As they parted outside Seoul's Great South Gate, Yang assured Sonjo that he was not afraid of the enemy. "If they come," he said, "I will fight."[16]

With advance Ming forces now on their way to the front and others soon to arrive, the Korean government began to feel surer of itself in the face of the Japanese threat. This confidence is evident in a scolding letter that Seoul now dispatched to Hideyoshi, just four days after General Yang left the capital. The Emperor of China, Hideyoshi was informed, was angry at his incomprehensible desire to engage in renewed aggression. Army and navy forces were thus being raised to strike him down. Japan could not hope to resist this force, for "compared to China your tiny country is like one small island among sixty-six. You have already been made a vassal king of China, so what you are now doing is unacceptable, and will be duly punished by the order of heaven. The earthquake that devastated your country last year was a sign of this celestial disapproval. Yet even though you were given such a clear sign, you still refuse to cease your aggression and lead a peaceful life. You are already sixty years old. How many more years do you think you have left ?"[17]

As this letter was being carried by messenger to Pusan, General Yang Yuan proceeded with his three thousand men to the town of Namwon in southern Cholla Province, sixty kilometers from the coast. Namwon, overlooking the string of forts that the Japanese had maintained on Korea's southeastern tip after retreating south in 1593, had served as a forward base for Chinese troops until their withdrawal in 1595. Now, with the Japanese reestablishing themselves in the south, it was to Namwon that Ming troops returned. If the Japanese attempted to advance toward the north, it would be here that the Chinese would block them.

General Yang reached Namwon toward the end of July and set up camp inside the town's fortifications. Its walls and towers were strongly built and in good repair, and so he determined it to be a suitable base from which to take on the Japanese. This caused local officials and commanders some concern. In line with the new Korean commitment to defending mountain strongholds rather than trying to hold cities and towns, they urged Yang to move his forces to the unassailable fortress on nearby Mt. Kyoryong. Yang brushed this advice aside. Instead he set his men to work strengthening the defenses of Namwon itself. He had the walls of the fortress heightened and a deep trench excavated all around the outside, at the bottom of which were laid felled trees with sharpened branches intact to make it more difficult to cross.[18]

Shortly after Yang Yuan reached Namwon, "Attacking General" Chen Yuzhong led an additional two thousand Ming troops south from Seoul to the city of Chonju, fifty kilometers to the north of Yang's advance base. Should the Japanese take or bypass Namwon, it would be Chen's job to present them with a second line of resistance. He was to be aided in this by a Korean force camped nearby at Unbong under Kyongsang Army Commander Kim Ung-so.[19]

While General Yang dug himself in at Namwon and General Chen at Chonju, the Japanese were making preparations of their own. One of their foremost concerns was the Korean navy. This force had been instrumental in scuttling their first invasion by blocking the sea route north via the Yellow Sea, preventing the ferrying of men and supplies to the increasingly distant front. Hideyoshi's commanders did not intend to let this happen again. For their land offensive to be successful, the Korean navy first would have to be destroyed.

The Japanese had already taken steps to achieve this end. Earlier in the year Konishi Yukinaga had sent his spy Yojiro to the Koreans with information regarding the movements of his rival Kato Kiyomasa, urging them to do both him and themselves a favor by ordering the navy out to meet and kill him. When naval commander Yi Sun-sin refused to do so for fear of sailing into a trap, Yojiro returned to report on the golden opportunity that had been missed. This clever nudge, delivered when it was, helped to turn the government in Seoul, already wracked with doubts about Yi, entirely against him. Korea's supreme naval commander, the man who had led the Korean navy so success-fully at the start of the war, was dismissed from office on charges of refusing to obey orders and submitting false reports claiming too much glory. After suffering the ignominy of imprisonment and torture, Yi now resided in a mountain hut near the south coast, ostensibly serving as a common soldier in the army of Commander in Chief Kwon Yul, but in reality left to himself while he awaited exoneration.

It would not be long in coming. Won Kyun, Yi Sun-sin's replace-ment as supreme naval commander, proved every bit as incompetent as Yi had claimed all along. Upon assuming office on Hansan Island, Won took up residence with his concubine in the Council Hall where Yi had formerly met with his officers and men, and then proceeded to neglect his command. As the threat of a second Japanese offensive loomed, Won whiled away the hours getting drunk, meting out punishments, and venting his anger on all who ventured near, particularly those officers whom he regarded as resentful of his leadership and still loyal to Yi. Such behavior soon resulted in a breakdown of discipline within the Korean navy. It started to be whispered among the men that Commander Won did not have what it would take to defeat the Japanese and that their only chance of surviving any coming battle would be to run away. Officers began to ignore Won's orders and laugh at him behind his back. Others grew frustrated and either left their posts in protest or were driven away. By the middle of the summer Yi Sun-sin's formerly formidable navy was rapidly losing its fighting spirit and increasingly in danger of falling apart.[20]

Yi Sun-sin remained well apprised of the situation at his place of exile in southwestern Kyongsang Province. Several of his former officers visited him there throughout July and August to report what was happening, in some instances delivering the news with tears in their eyes. Yi, already sick with grief over the recent death of his mother, sank deeper into depression as he recorded in his diary "the evil deeds of the rascal Won Kyun."

> Yi Kyong-sin, arriving from Hansan, talked a lot about the wicked Won (Kyun), saying that after having ordered out one of his clerks ... to the mainland to purchase food grains, he attempted to seduce the wife, but instead of submitting herself to his desire, the woman jumped out of his embraces with wild shrieks. Won employs all means to entrap me. This also is one of my ill-fortunes. The cargoes of his bribes in transit continue their procession on the roads leading to Seoul. In this way he has been pulling me down to the abyss deeper and deeper as in the days gone by. [21]

During these months Yi continued to search for signs of what the future held, both for the nation and himself. On June 22 he had a dream in which "I killed a ferocious tiger by striking it with my fist, then skinned it and waved it in the air."[22] Did this slaying of a tiger possibly symbolize Yi's wish to strike at the Japanese who had returned to Korea? Or was it perhaps an embodiment of a desire to destroy Won Kyun, the man he considered most responsible for his troubles? It is tempting to lean toward the latter interpretation, for judging from Yi's diary Won Kyun was in his thoughts more often during this period than were the Japanese.

Four days later, on June 26, Yi summoned an aide to read Won's fortune by consulting the Book of Divination. "The first sign," Yi recorded later that day, "came out as 'water, thunder, and great disaster.' This means that the Heavenly wind will corrupt and destroy the original body. It is a very bad omen."[23]

*   *   *

As the Korean navy was falling into disarray, the Japanese fleet gathering at Pusan had been made stronger than anything the Koreans had faced back in 1592. It was composed of roughly the same number of ships as in the first invasion fleet, a force of some one thousand vessels all told, and was led by many of the same commanders, among them Kato Yoshiaki, Todo Takatora, and Wakizaka Yasuharu. This time, however, a number of heavy war galleys armed with cannons had been added to what was otherwise a mass of lightly built and lightly armed transports. These were still not as formidable as the Koreans' panokson (board-roofed ships) and kobukson (turtle ships), but they nevertheless represented an improvement. Also improved were discipline and leadership. The rivalries and attendant lack of coordination among Japanese naval commanders—many of whom hailed from wako pirate stock—had been a liability in the first invasion made glaringly apparent by Yi Sun-sin's own highly coordinated and disciplined fleet. In 1597 the Japanese navy was less prone to such counterproductive behavior. Hideyoshi, realizing the importance of a strong, unified navy, had for the second invasion appointed Konishi Yukinaga to high naval command, where his forceful leadership would serve to better galvanize former pirate barons like Todo and Wakizaka into a more effective fighting force.[24] The commanders themselves also undoubtedly began the campaign with a greater willingness to work together, for they knew this time the challenge they faced. The Japanese navy in 1597 was therefore somewhat stronger, better led, and better disciplined than it had been in 1592, all qualities that would stand it in good stead in the great sea battle to come.

The Japanese did not make a move in force against the Korean navy at Hansan-do. Instead they sought to lure it to Pusan. On July 19 the Japanese spy Yojiro appeared once again at the camp of Kyongsang Army Commander Kim Ung-so. He informed Kim that the Japanese were planning to begin their offensive into Cholla Province in six weeks' time, on the first day of the eighth month (September 11). Konishi's forces would enter the province via Uiryong and Chonju; Kato's group would follow a route farther to the north, through either Kyongju or Miryang and Taegu. Yojiro wanted the Koreans to know this, he said, so that they could block the advance and quickly bring the war to an end. Otherwise the fighting could drag on for another ten years. Yojiro then inquired about the state of the Korean navy. He wondered because 150,000 more Japanese troops were soon expected to arrive from Tsushima to reinforce the 30,000 to 40,000 soldiers already on Korean soil. If the Korean navy was in good shape and ready to fight, and if it was ordered to sail east toward Pusan, it could attack and destroy this main force when it attempted to land and thus halt the second invasion before it could even begin.[25]

In his report of this meeting, Kim Ung-so stated that Yojiro could have been sent by the Japanese to plant false information and that he perhaps should not be believed. On the other hand, Kim added, a good deal of the information made sense. It therefore should not be ignored.

It wasn't. Yojiro's intelligence was accepted with credulity by many within the Korean government, particularly by Commander in Chief Kwon Yul. Kwon felt that an opportunity had been handed to them to deal the Japanese a blow that would halt their invasion in its tracks. He thus issued a directive to newly appointed Supreme Naval Commander Won Kyun: lead your fleet east to patrol the waters off Pusan, and attack the Japanese navy when it attempts to land.[26]

Won, comfortable with his wine and his concubine on Hansan Island, now found himself in the same position his predecessor Yi Sun-sin had been in four and a half months before. If he obeyed the order to attack, he risked sailing into a trap and seeing his fleet destroyed. If he did not, he could be accused of timidity and refusing a command, the same accusations Won himself had leveled at Yi. At first Won delayed for as long as he could. He responded to Kwon Yul's orders by suggesting that it would make more sense for the army to attack Angolpo first, the main enemy coastal fortification on the way to Pusan, and for the navy then to move in once the Japanese defenses were in disarray. Kwon Yul angrily brushed the suggestion aside. He felt that Won Kyun had made it only as an excuse to do nothing. The Border Defense Council (*bibyonsa*) in Seoul agreed. Since Angolpo was located on a peninsula, the bibyonsa observed, a land assault there would put the army in danger of being cut off by Japanese units stationed in neighboring camps. No, Kwon felt, the only reasonable course of action was for the

Korean navy to attack first. Apparently moderating his objectives, the commander in chief ordered Won to patrol the waters off Kadok-do, half the distance to Pusan, cutting off the enemy forces stationed on that island and preventing the Japanese from advancing farther west.[27]

There is no Korean commander from the Imjin War who has come to be more reviled than Won Kyun. It is thus easy to think the worst of him, and to accept without question Kwon Yul's accusation that Won was delaying attacking the Japanese simply because he did not want to fight. There is probably a good deal of truth in this. In Won's defense, however, it should be pointed out that a coordinated attack by land and sea forces such as he suggested was something that Yi Sun-sin himself had frequently recommended, but had rarely been able to carry out for want of cooperation from the army. Won's recommendation of it, therefore, may not have been entirely a ruse. It is also worth noting that the Koreans had come to expect a great deal more of their navy than of their army since Yi Sun-sin's victories in the early days of the war, a tendency that Kwon Yul was now perpetuating by placing the entire responsibility of resisting the Japanese on Won Kyun's shoulders alone. It is thus easy to imagine that Won felt unreasonably put upon, so much so that he ignored orders from above. Kwon, after all, was directing him to accomplish something that Kwon himself was unwilling—or more likely unable—to do.

By the end of July Won Kyun's questionable conduct as supreme naval commander, and specifically his unwillingness to move against the Japanese, had cost him a good deal of support from both the government and the army. On July 4 Overseer of Military Affairs (*dochechalsa*) Yi Won-ik met with Yi Sun-sin at the latter's mountain hut and spoke of his longstanding concerns about Won. He also intimated that King Sonjo had come to regret replacing Yi with Won. ("However," commented a still-bitter Sun-sin in his diary, "the heart of his majesty is doubtful!") In his own meeting with Yi Sun-sin at the end of the month, Commander in Chief Kwon Yul spoke even more strongly against Won. Won's repeated assurances that he would soon sail out to fight the Japanese, Kwon said, were nothing but bluster. All he did was idle his days away in the Council Hall on Hansan Island, ignoring the advice of his captains and commanders, the disaffection of his men, and the disarray around him. "It is clear," said Kwon, "that he will ruin our naval forces."[28]

On July 31 Won Kyun bowed to the mounting pressure to act from his superior Kwon Yul and made a cautious foray east from his Hansan Island base. He never made it past neighboring Koje-do. While cautiously advancing along the coast of that island, the fleet ran into a small squadron of Japanese ships probing west from Pusan. After a brief and inconclusive skirmish, Won ordered his ships about and promptly returned to Hansan-do.[29]

Kwon Yul was unsatisfied by this half-hearted and short-lived campaign. He continued to press Won to go boldly into action to destroy the Japanese fleet. Won finally caved in on August 17. Gathering the entire Korean fleet in the south, a force of more than two hundred ships, the reluctant naval commander sailed eastward again, with Pusan as his goal.

Japanese spies stationed in the hills overlooking Hansan Island watched his ships depart. The enemy fleet anchored in the vicinity of Pusan thus had warning that the Korean navy was on its way. They let it come. Won Kyun in the meantime led his fleet around Koje Island and north along the coast past Angolpo. Here they surprised and destroyed a small group of Japanese ships, then continued on toward Cholyong-do, an uninhabited island in the waters off Pusan.[30]

It was now August 20, 1597. As the Koreans neared Cholyong-do, they ran into the main of the Japanese fleet, an estimated five hundred to one thousand ships arrayed in a vast battle line.[31] Conditions did not favor the Koreans. They were tired, hungry, and thirsty after a long day at sea, and were further crippled by a serious lack of confidence in their commander. The wind had picked up and was blowing with alarming force, whipping the water into high waves and forcing the Koreans' formation to drift apart. The day was also almost done, confronting Won's men with the prospect of fighting in the dark and further adding to their sense of foreboding. Won Kyun now displayed more of the erratic behavior that Yi Sun-sin and certain members of the government had earlier expressed concern about.[32] Ignoring the daunting odds against him, and more significantly the fact that the time and place of battle was not of his choosing, Won gave the command for a general attack, an ill-coordinated charge into the heart of the enemy armada. The Japanese responded with a display of tactical savvy worthy of Yi Sun-sin himself. Instead of meeting the Koreans head on, they fell back, forcing Won's ships to pursue. After a brief retreat, they then turned and drove them back. A series of further retreats and advances followed, the Japanese commanders using the freshness of their own men to wear down the already fatigued Koreans until they scarcely had the strength to row.

Finally, when Won's men were thoroughly exhausted, the Japanese fleet turned one last time and attacked in earnest. In the ferocious charge that followed, thirty Korean ships were boarded and burned or otherwise lost. Those vessels surviving the assault were soon scattered across the water in a disorganized rout, their terrified crews sculling through the darkness on adrenaline alone.

For the Koreans the disaster was only beginning to unfold. Upon reaching Kadok Island, Won's captains put in to allow their parched crews to run ashore and fetch water. The Koreans knew that a large Japanese garrison was on this island. Won's men evidently assumed they could drink and get away before the enemy had time to respond. They were mistaken. They leaped off their ships and rushed ashore in search of water, and ran straight into an attack by three thousand of Shimazu Yoshihiro's men. An additional four hundred of Won's men were killed in this engagement and several more vessels destroyed.

From Kadok-do the by now demoralized remnants of the Korean navy continued to retreat west, around the north end of Koje Island and south into Chilchonnyang, the strait between Koje and the small island of Chilchon. It was not a safe place to stop. The channel was too narrow to allow the heavy Korean battleships room to maneuver should the Japanese attack. Commander Won nevertheless would remain immobile here with his fleet for an entire week, incapacitated by feelings of depression and rage. Upon reaching Koje-do, Won received a severe dressing-down from his superior Kwon Yul, who had come out to meet him from his nearby headquarters at Kosong. The commander in chief was so livid over news of the defeat and losses Won had suffered at Pusan and Kadok-do that at one point in the encounter he struck the commander—common enough in the Korean military when reprimanding a soldier, but a rare insult when inflicted upon an officer of Won's high rank. Won was so incensed by the blow that he retired to his flagship, took out his bottle, and refused to see anyone, even his own captains. The Korean navy thus sat idle in Chilchon Strait until August 27, deprived of its leader, waiting for the end.

The Japanese navy, meanwhile, was not resting on its laurels. Shortly after the first clash in the waters off Pusan, squadrons of Japanese ships began moving west in pursuit of the Koreans. These units, under naval commanders Todo Takatora, Wakizaka Yasuharu, Shimazu Toyohisa, Kato Yoshiaki, and Konishi Yukinaga, met on August 22 at the port of Angolpo to plan joint action against the remainder of the Korean fleet, which they had ascertained was now holed up in Chilchon Strait fifteen kilometers southwest. At the same time Shimazu Yoshihiro was ferrying two thousand of his men from their base on Kadok-do to the neighboring island of Koje. Once ashore he marched them across the neck of the island and arrayed them along the northwest coast, overlooking the Korean navy at anchor in the channel below. The Koreans would now be hemmed in when the final attack came, by Japanese ships before them and a Japanese army behind.

In the strait of Chilchonnyang Won Kyun and his commanders knew nothing of this. Won, his confidence shaken by the Japanese and his pride deeply wounded by the blow from Kwon Yul, remained in seclusion aboard his flagship, lost in a stupor of anger and drink. As the days passed he made little attempt to draw up a plan or rally his men. He also neglected to gather intelligence on enemy movements from the farmers and fishermen residing along the coast. As the hours ticked by the Korean navy sat placidly at anchor, paralyzed, leaderless, blind to the gathering storm.

That storm broke in the early hours of August 28. The Japanese fleet at Angolpo under Konishi, Todo, Wakizaka, Kato Yoshiaki, and Shimazu Toyohisa, numbering as many as five hundred ships, sculled under a full moon the short distance to the north end of Chilchonnyang where the Korean navy lay. Shortly after midnight three guns were fired to signal the attack. With that the lead ships of the armada moved into the strait. The Koreans, unaccustomed to night warfare and badly demoralized from their earlier mauling, were soon overwhelmed. One ship after another was closed with and boarded, the terrified men aboard being shot with muskets and arrows or cut down by sword and the vessel set alight. Those ships that escaped destruction by beaching on Koje Island were similarly destroyed by the Japanese troops lying in ambush there, as were the hundreds of survivors who managed to leap into the water and swim to shore. Only a few vessels made it to the south end of the strait and the open water beyond, but even these were soon chased down and destroyed. Nabeshima Naoshige's son Katsu-shige would later describe the sight of all these burning Korean ships as even finer than the view of cherry blossoms at Yoshino.[33]

By dawn almost the entire Korean fleet had been burned or sunk, and Commander Won Kyun was dead. After a desperate struggle, he retreated south down Chilchon Strait and then west toward the mainland with the Japanese in pursuit. When they reached land Won's crew beached his flagship and raced into the hills to save their lives. According to one of his men who survived to make a report, Won was too old to keep up to the rest of his fleeing crew and soon sat down to rest under a pine tree, sword in hand. When this witness last looked back, five or six Japanese soldiers were nearing the commander, their swords drawn. It is assumed that Won Kyun's head was cut off— although his body was never recovered so just how he was killed remains unknown. Also killed in action was Cholla Right Navy Com-mander Yi Ok-ki, Yi Sun-sin's stalwart right hand from the first days of the war. He had hung on in Chilchon Strait to the bitter end. Then, with the annihilation of the fleet certain, he is said to have jumped into the sea and drowned himself rather than allow the Japanese to take his head. Chungchong Naval Commander Choi Ho met a similar end. [34]

The only senior officer to escape the battle was Kyongsang Right Navy Commander Bae Sol. During the week of idleness leading up to the end, Bae had approached his superior Won Kyun and urged him to move the fleet to a safer location. When Won refused, Bae quietly shifted the twelve ships under his command to a secluded inlet farther down the strait, and when the Japanese attacked he fled.[35] This act of cowardice would earn Bae the enmity of many, including Yi Sun-sin. It would also serve as a counterpoint in subsequent appraisals of Won Kyun, it being pointed out by at least one chronicler that while Won was of course responsible for the defeat at Chilchonnyang, he at least had died in battle, unlike others who ran away.[36]

After fleeing Chilchonnyang, Bae Sol raced south to the Korean navy's home port on Hansan Island to burn the camps, destroy weapons and supplies, and move everyone left there off the island before the Japanese arrived. He then shepherded his small squadron of vessels further west to safety. This tiny force, a total of just twelve ships, was nearly all that was left of the Korean navy—all that was left to block the Japanese armada from entering the Yellow Sea.

News of the destruction of the Korean navy was greeted with enthusiasm back in Japan. In the letters of congratulation he wrote to the commanders involved, Toyotomi Hideyoshi thanked them for "doing the nation a great service."[37] Todo Takatoro was singled out as deserving particular praise, his squadron having reportedly destroyed some sixty enemy vessels. Shimazu Toyohisa claimed to have bagged an additional one hundred and sixty smaller craft, a figure he probably achieved by including small civilian junks and fishing boats that had been rounded up and burned.[38]

The news was received with dismay in Seoul. Just hours after the first reports of the disaster arrived on September 3, King Sonjo summoned his ministers and representatives from the Border Defense Council to discuss the situation and decide how best to respond. Sonjo began by expressing his dissatisfaction with the course of action the navy had pursued. "We should have concentrated only on protecting our naval base at Hansan-do," he said. "This disaster occurred because Won Kyun was pushed to attack too soon." At first Sonjo was careful not to mention from where this pressure to attack had come, but eventually his true feelings came out: "This happened because the commander in chief [Kwon Yul] put so much pressure on Won to attack."

But recriminations were useless now, as Sonjo himself acknowledged. "This is in the past," he said. "Now we have to select a new supreme naval commander and collect whatever ships are still left in the area. And we have to report this to China." The representatives of the Border Defense Council remained silent, evidently unwilling to confront this central issue of whom to choose to replace Won Kyun. Finally Minister of Punishments Kim Myong-won and Minister of War Yi Hang-bok said what everyone else knew must be done. They recommended that Yi Sun-sin be rehabilitated and returned to his former command. King Sonjo readily complied. The order reappointing Yi Sun-sin supreme naval commander was drawn up that same day and dispatched immediately to the south.[39]

Yi Sun-sin, counting the days in his mountain hut at Chogye near the southwestern coast of Kyongsang Province, received first word of the fate of the Korean navy as night was falling on August 28. The news was brought to him by an exhausted sailor, naked and bleeding, who told of "a thousand Japanese vessels" in the waters off Pusan and of the subsequent scattering and retreat of Won Kyun's navy. Subsequent reports revealed that the battle had been a rout. According to one, "Won Kyun hardly saw the enemy before he ran away to land first, followed by other commanders and chief officers, deserting their ships and crews."[40]

Water. Thunder. Great disaster. The signs in the Book of Divination had been correct.

On August 30 Commander in Chief Kwon Yul rode up from his nearby headquarters to visit Yi and discuss possible courses of action. With the limited information they had, they were unable to reach any decision as to how best to meet the Japanese thrust into Cholla that they both knew now was coming. Finally Yi proposed that he embark westward on an unofficial inspection tour along the coast to determine the state of the region's defenses and in turn how best to proceed. Kwon agreed. Yi gathered his small entourage of loyal followers and set off that same day on a journey that would cover more than seven hundred kilometers and last thirty days.[41]

Two weeks later, during a stop on the border between Kyongsang and Cholla, Yi Sun-sin had a dream. In it he saw portents that an august command would soon arrive from the king. He was thus not surprised when an emissary arrived from Seoul the next day, bearing a royal order reappointing him to the post of supreme naval commander of the three provinces of Kyongsang, Cholla, and Chungchong. "I prostrated myself before the written royal orders," Yi wrote in his diary, "and presented . . . my sealed and waxed acknowledgement of their receipt.

"I then started on my journey without delay, taking the road to Tuch'i."[42]

CHAPTER 25

The Japanese Advance Inland

IT WAS NOW SEPTEMBER 1597. The Korean navy under Won Kyun had been destroyed the previous month, leaving the sea route clear around Korea's southwestern tip and into the Yellow Sea. The rice fields of southern Korea were also ready to harvest, offering the prospect of plenty of food. It was therefore time for Hideyoshi's army to begin its land offensive, the big push north from Pusan.

Hideyoshi planned this second offensive in a very different manner from the first. In 1592 he had envisioned co-opting the Koreans into his empire with as little violence as possible, and so ordered his commanders to treat the locals with as much kindness as circumstances allowed. Hideyoshi harbored no such illusions in 1597. The Koreans, he now knew, were too stubbornly independent to be eased into his polity with a restrained approach. The only way to deal with them was with an iron fist. His orders this time were to "mow down everyone universally, without discriminating between young and old, men and women, the clergy and the laity—high-ranking soldiers on the battlefield, that goes without saying, but also the hill folk, down to the poorest and meanest—and send the heads to Japan."[1]

This request for heads, the usual trophies of war, was not meant to be taken literally. They were much too bulky to be shipped to Japan considering the numbers and the distance involved. But Hideyoshi did want evidence of the accomplishments of his army, proof that it was doing what he had told it to do. His troops were accordingly ordered to cut off the noses of the people they killed and to submit them at one of the designated collection points that would be set up. Here they were to be counted by specially appointed inspectors, then salted and packed in casks and shipped to Japan.

The land offensive of 1597 thus was to be undertaken with a degree of ruthlessness that went beyond anything seen in 1592. As a prelude, the commanders of Hideyoshi's armies issued proclamations to the Koreans in the regions they were about to invade stating that farmers who did not return to their fields would be hunted down and killed. Public officials would be executed as a matter of course, together with their wives and children, and their houses would be burned. Rewards were promised to anyone betraying an official attempting to hide. The common people, then, were to be allowed to live only if they did exactly as told. Everyone else was to be "wiped out."[2] It would be a campaign of terror and extermination similar to that launched by the Nazis in occupied Europe in 1939. The armies of both Hitler and Hideyoshi, observes historian Jurgis Elisonas, "suffered under the delusion that they could keep a resistance movement from forming by terrorizing the populace into collaboration."[3]

The plan was to move inland in two main thrusts meeting in northern Cholla Province, one veering toward the right, the second to the left. Two great armies were organized for the purpose: a 65,300-man Right Army under the overall command of Mori Hidemoto and a 49,600-man Left Army under Ukita Hideie—a combined invasion force of 114,900 men.

Ukita's Left Army was the first to embark. Its objective: Namwon, held by allied Chinese and Korean forces. Troop movements began on September 11, Ukita marching west from Pusan as far as the Cholla border, then northwest toward the city. Other units followed by ship from camps at Pusan, Angolpo, Kadok Island, and points between, among them forces under Konishi Yukinaga, So Yoshitoshi, Shimazu Yoshihiro, and Hachizuka Iemasa. They made their way to Koje Island, then proceeded farther west into previously Korean-held territory, past Namhae Island and into Kwangyang Bay and finally up the Somjin River as far as their ships could go. When these forces stepped ashore the men were still fresh and only ten kilometers from Namwon. The one concern was the horses. The close confinement aboard the ships

JAPANESE INVASION FORCES, SEPTEMBER 1597 [4]

RIGHT ARMY	
COMMANDER	**MEN**
Kato Kiyomasa	10,000
Kuroda Nagamasa	5,000
Nabeshima Naoshige & Katsushige	12,000
Ikeda Hideshi	2,800
Nakagawa Hidenari	2,500
Chosokabe Motochika	3,000
Mori Hidemoto *	30,000
TOTAL	65,300

LEFT ARMY	
COMMANDER	**MEN**
Konishi Yukinaga	7,000
So Yoshitoshi	1,000
Matsuura Shigenobu	3,000
Arima Harunobu	2,000
Omura Yoshiaki	1,000
Goto Genga	700
Hachizuka Iemasa	7,200
Mori Yoshinari	2,000
Ikoma Kazumasa	2,700
Shimazu Yoshihiro	10,000
Shimazu Tadatoyo	800
Akizuki Tanenaga	300
Takahashi Mototane	600
Ito Yuhei	500
Sagara Yorifusa	800
Ukita Hideie *	10,000
TOTAL	49,600

*Commander in Chief

had left a large number of mounts unfit for immediate use. Konishi and his fellow commanders pastured the animals in nearby fields and camped beside the river to wait for them to recover their strength.

Not long into this period of convalescence, a report was received from a local priest that twenty thousand enemy troops were garrisoned inside Namwon, with twenty thousand reinforcements on the way. Konishi and his comrades held a meeting to consider their options in light of this information and decided that they should attack Namwon immediately, before these supposed reinforcements arrived, even though a number of their horses remained lame and unfit.[5] They broke camp and marched the short distance to the city on September 23, where they joined Ukita Hideie in surrounding the fortress.

Fifty thousand Japanese soldiers now stood poised to attack Namwon. They were not faced by twenty thousand defenders as the priest had claimed. Gathered inside the fortress were only three thousand Ming troops led by General Yang Yuan, a thousand Koreans under Cholla Army Commander Yi Bok-nam, plus a number of civilians. The fortifications that the allied Chinese and Korean forces defended nevertheless demanded respect. The first obstacle the Japanese had to face was a deep trench encircling the fort. The bottom of the trench was lined with spiky-limbed tree trunks, making it doubly difficult to cross. Then there were the defenses of the fort itself, stout stone walls nowhere less than four meters high interspersed with towered gates rising higher still. To overcome these obstacles and take Namwon would require skill and guile in addition to force. Otherwise casualties would be unacceptably high.

The tentative opening moves of the battle were made that same day, September 23. A small force of one hundred Japanese soldiers were the first to approach the fortress. They spread out in a wide arc and began peppering the walls with musket balls, drawing fire from the defenders within so that the daimyo commanders observing from the rear could determine the enemy's positioning and strength.

The Japanese began to attack in earnest the following day. The first obstacle to clear was the trench. Working under heavy cannon and arrow and musket fire from the fortress, units of Japanese began filling in the trench at several locations with straw and earth. When these crossing points were complete, large numbers of troops began streaming

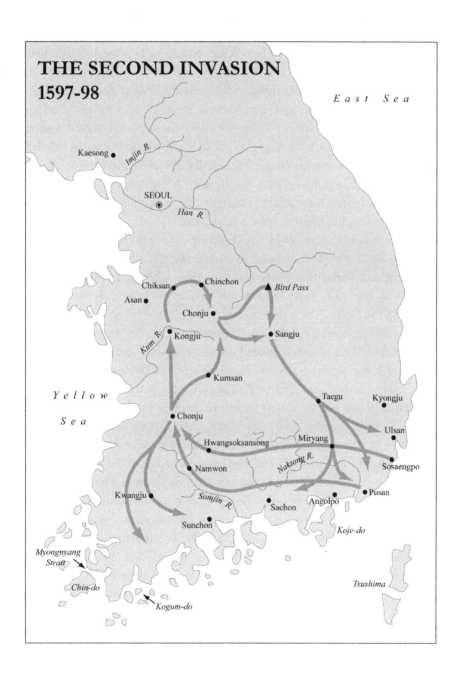

THE SECOND INVASION
1597-98

East Sea

Kaesong ●

Imjin R.

SEOUL ◉

Han R.

Chiksan ● ● Chinchon ▲ *Bird Pass*

Asan ●

Chonju ●

Kum R. Kongju ● ● Sangju

Kumsan ●

Yellow Taegu ● ● Kyongju

Sea Chonju ●

Hwangsoksansong ● Miryang ● Ulsan →

Namwon ● *Naktong R.* Sosaengpo ●

Kwangju ● *Somjin R.* Pusan ●

Sachon ● Angolpo ●

Sunchon ●

Koje-do

Myongnyang
Strait →

Chin-do *Tsushima*

→ Kogum-do

across to take cover among the remains of the houses clustered outside
the fortress itself. General Yang Yuan had previously ordered these
structures burned, but the smoking ruins still provided adequate
protection.

A lull occurred in the fighting the next day, September 25, the day
of the lunar equinox and the harvest festival of Chusok. Perhaps
seeking to take advantage of the occasion, the Japanese raised a shout
that they wished to talk. Yang Yuan sent out a man to see what they
wanted. He returned, as Yang undoubtedly had expected he would, with
a letter demanding the fortress's surrender. Yang refused. With that the
Japanese resumed their attack, stronger this time than before, and continuing on into the night despite a heavy rain.

Throughout these days of fighting the Japanese commanders
outside the fortress continued to scrutinize the walls and assess the
strength and disposition of the forces within. Chinese troops were positioned at the east, west, and south of the enclosure; Korean forces
guarded the north. They were growing exhausted by now, their arrows
were running low, and the determination of some was beginning to
wear thin. Ukita, Konishi, and their comrades correctly surmised that
General Yang would expect an attack to come at those places where the
walls were lowest and that he had accordingly stationed his men most
thickly at these points. It was therefore decided to attack the wall at its
highest point, by the fortress's south gate, where few soldiers were
likely to be. To prepare for this assault, the Japanese commanders sent
their men into the nearby fields to cut and bundle up the rice stalks that
were still green and wet from the previous day's rain. The allies within
Namwon noted these bundles being stockpiled outside but could not
fathom what they were for. They found out the next day. When darkness had fallen on September 26, and before the moon was up, the
Japanese unleashed a two-hour barrage of musket and cannon fire
against Namwon, forcing the defenders to keep their heads down and
deafening them with the noise. Under cover of this distraction, parties
of men stole up to the wall and quietly began to erect a massive pile of
straw, heaping it up against the stones until a spongy ramp led straight
to the top. When the barrage finally stopped and the Chinese and
Koreans were able to peek out, the ramp was complete and Japanese

troops were storming over the walls, samurai Matsuura Shigenobu reportedly leading the way. The allies fought back as best they could, but were unable to drive the Japanese back or set fire to the pile of moist rice stalks they were using as a ladder. Soon the fortress was filled with thousands of Japanese attackers, samurai warriors at the lead, eager for the glory of hand-to-hand combat.[6]

Okochi Hidemoto, author of the *Chosen ki,* was among them. After cutting off the heads of two men, he recalled that this was "the day dedicated to his tutelary kami (Hachiman) dai Bosatsu, [so] he put down his bloodstained blade and, pressing together his crimson-stained palms, bowed in veneration toward far-off Japan. He cut off the noses and placed them inside a paper handkerchief which he put into his armour." Shortly thereafter Okochi brought down a third enemy warrior on a horse, this one with a thrust of his blade to the groin. The man fell off the far side of his mount into a group of nearby samurai, who promptly began to hack at his neck. Okochi instantly intervened, explaining his groin thrust and claiming the head for himself.[7]

By this time Ming commander Yang Yuan was gone. When he saw that Namwon was about to fall, he led three hundred men in a retreat out the fortress's west gate. They had to fight their way out through strong Japanese resistance. Yang himself was wounded twice by musket fire, and only one hundred of his men survived. Placing their commander on a stretcher, this small band managed to get clear of the battle and raced north. They reached Chonju to find it deserted. The Ming general assigned to hold the city, Chen Yuzhong, had not only ignored the call for help that Yang had sent him on the eve of the battle, he had fled north upon hearing of the fall of Namwon. Yang and his party thus continued on to Seoul. They arrived in the capital the following week.

Back at Namwon almost everyone was dead, including Cholla Army Commander Yi Bok-nam and his men, every civilian who had remained in the city, and numerous others who had been cut down outside. The priest Keinen, serving with the Japanese army as a chaplain and physician, recorded in his diary that "the only people to be seen were those lying dead on the ground. When I looked around the fortress at dawn the next day I saw bodies beyond number heaped up along the roadside."[8] He would later encapsulate the trauma of the scene in a poem:

> Whoever sees this
> Out of all his days
> Today has become the rest of his life. [9]

After the battle the Japanese set to work cutting off the nose of every corpse. According to Okochi's firsthand account, 3,726 noses were collected at Namwon. Konishi Yukinaga's men accounted for 879 of them, Ukita Hideie's contingent placed second with 622, Hachizuka Iemasa's third with 468, and Shimazu Yoshihiro's fourth with 421.[10] These were submitted by samurai to their daimyo commanders, then were passed on to the designated "nose collection officer" for salting, packing, and shipment home to Japan.

While Konishi and his Left Army colleagues were attacking Namwon, Kato Kiyomasa and forward units of the Right Army were busy else-where. Leaving his coastal fort at Sosaengpo in the middle of September, Kato led his ten thousand-man force inland along a westerly route, intent on beating the Left Army to Namwon and attacking the fortress there first.[11] He was accompanied by the veteran Nabeshima Naoshige at the head of twelve thousand men, and by Kuroda Nagamasa with five thousand. They had advanced about sixty kilometers when they came upon the mountain fortress of Hwawangsansong, defended by a force of Korean volunteers under the famous "Red Coat General" Kwak Jae-u, recently returned to active military service as regional commander of Kyongsang Right Province. Judging the walls of the fort to be impregnable and the men inside dangerously determined, Kato, Nabeshima, and Kuroda decided to bypass this knot of resistance and continue on their way.[12]

They felt differently about the next mountain fortress they came to, named Hwangsoksansong after the thousand-meter-high Mt. Hwangsok on the slopes of which it stood. This fortress guarded the strategically important mountain pass leading from Kyongsang Province to Cholla. It therefore had to be taken.

Hwangsoksansong was one of several mountain strongholds in southern Korea that had been either built or repaired in the years leading up to the second invasion. Weapons and supplies were stock-piled inside, and local magistrates were instructed to lead civilians there for safety in the event of a renewed attack. When the Japanese began to move inland, Kwak Jun, the forty-seven-year-old magistrate of the surrounding county of Anum, was placed in charge of Hwangsoksansong. He entered the fortress with two of his sons, a son-in-law, and a force of several hundred militiamen. They were joined by Cho Chong-do, the elderly magistrate of neighboring Hanam County, together with his wife and children, and by Kimhae governor Baek Sa-rim, who had been sent by Inspector General Yi Won-ik to provide military expertise.

Baek was the only one among these three officials with a military background. As the Japanese neared the fortress it was thus to him that everyone inside looked for leadership. They were sorely disappointed. When Baek saw the odds arrayed against them, 27,000 Japanese warriors against no more than a few thousand Koreans, many of them civilians, he led his family to a secluded part of the fortress, lowered them on a rope over the wall, and stole away into the trees. When his disappearance was discovered any determination to hold Hwangsoksansong quickly drained away. As the Japanese surrounded the fortress, Nabeshima on the west, Kuroda on the east, Kato on the south, the people inside ran to Kwak Jun in a panic, pleading with him to lead them in an escape. Kwak refused. Although he knew they could not withstand the coming onslaught, he would not accept the ignominy of flight. This, he said, is the place I will die.

The Japanese attacked Hwangsoksansong on September 26. They took it that same day. Most of the civilians jumped over the walls and attempted to flee when the fighting began, leaving Kwak and his few hundred militiamen to defend the fortress alone. Kwak died trying to stave off the final assault. His two sons were cut down as they cradled his body and wept. The Japanese then flooded into the fortress, killed almost everyone and started collecting noses. The final tally was 353 Korean soldiers killed within the fortress itself, plus several thousand civilians in the valley below.[13] Among the dead were Cho Chong-do and his entire family, and the son-in-law of Kwak Jun. When Kwak's daughter heard of her husband's death, she grew despondent and hanged herself.[14]

Shortly after they captured Hwangsoksansong, word reached the Japanese that the Left Army had already taken Namwon. With this objective no longer available to them, Kato, Nabeshima, and Kuroda set out instead for Chonju, fifty kilometers farther north. By the time they arrived the city had been deserted by both civilians and troops: upon receiving news of the fall of Namwon, Chinese general Chen Yuzhong had withdrawn with his two thousand men and retreated north toward Seoul. Kato and his compatriots thus marched into Chonju on September 30 without a fight, where they were soon joined by a portion of the army that had taken Namwon. After garrisoning the city, this forward army fanned out west toward the coast and northeast toward Kumsan to subdue the northern half of Cholla Province. Nabeshima Naoshige led his forces farther north to take Kongju, the main city in Chungchong Province. Kato Kiyomasa's contingent headed northeast to occupy the town of Chongju. Kuroda Nagamasa, finally, ventured farthest north into Kyonggi-do, the province bordering Seoul.

By the beginning of October the Japanese army therefore seemed well on its way to achieving its objective of seizing the southern half of Korea as Hideyoshi's consolation prize. They had been in much the same position five years before, however, only to see their initial gains slip away due in part to unremitting Korean resistance. Breaking this resistance was now a prime concern of the daimyo commanders. They intended to do so by terrorizing the local population. A good example of this is seen in the proclamation Ukita Hideie issued to the people of Cholla Province in September, reiterating the hard-line policy on resistance that the Japanese army had first announced upon returning to Korea earlier in the year. It was a standard announcement that was being made by all commanders throughout the south:

- Farmers will return to their villages and concentrate on farming.

- Officials and their families will be killed, and their homes burned.

- A reward will be paid to anyone providing information on the whereabouts of officials in hiding.

- Henceforth farmers [who heed this proclamation] will be spared. Those who remain in hiding in the mountains will be killed and their homes burned.

- Report any instances of Japanese troops killing or mistreating [law-abiding] Korean farmers.[15]

Ukita and his fellow daimyo were deadly serious in their demand for compliance. From the start of the offensive their campaign to pacify the provinces of Kyongsang, Cholla, and Chungchong was accompanied by the most horrific atrocities perpetrated against the region's civilian population. People were killed almost daily well outside the time frame of any significant battle, and their noses hacked off by the hundreds, even the thousands. We know this because the units responsible, ever mindful of recording the proof of their valor, kept meticulous records and receipts, some of which have survived to this day:

To: Kuroda Nagamasa
Noses from 23 enemy dead slain in battle taken and duly recorded.
    1597, 8th month, 16th day
    Kumagai Naomori, Kakimi Kasunao, Hayakawa Nagamasa

To: Nabeshima Katsushige
Noses taken yesterday and today in lieu of heads verified as 90.
    1597, 8th month, 21st day
    Kumagai Naomori, Kakimi Kasunao, Hayakawa Nagamasa

To: Nabeshima Katsushige
Noses taken today verified as 7.
    1597, 8th month, 22nd day
    Kakimi Kasunao, Kumagai Naomori, Hayakawa Nagamasa

To: Nabeshima Katsushige
Noses taken today in lieu of heads verified as 264.
    1597, 8th month, 25th day
    Kumagai Naomori, Kakimi Kasunao, Hayakawa Nagamasa

To: Todo Takatora
346 noses taken.
    1597, 8th month, 26th day
    Oda Kazuyoshi

To: Kikkawa Hiroie
Total number of noses taken verified as 480.
    Hayakawa Nagamasa
    1597, 9th month, 1st day

To: Kikkawa Hiroie
Total number of noses taken verified as 792.
    Hayakawa Nagamasa
    1597, 9th month, 4th day

To: Kuroda Nagamasa
Total number of noses taken verified as 3,000.
    1597, 9th month, 5th day
    Hayakawa Nagamasa[16]

With the Japanese now rapidly advancing toward Seoul, panic seized the populace. Citizens packed their possessions and prepared to flee into the countryside, and the Korean government began discussing plans for its own evacuation. It was immediately decided that Crown Prince Kwanghae and the queen should be sent northwest into the rugged province of Hamgyong, to safeguard the future of the monarchy and rally the people there once again to resist the Japanese. Government ministers then sat down with King Sonjo to consider options for his own safety. No mention was made of his remaining in Seoul. Although Sonjo bemoaned the fact that he had been considered a coward ever since fleeing the capital the first time in 1592, flight once again seemed the only reasonable alternative. The only questions were whether to travel by land or by sea, and what town to head to in the far north.[17]

The Ming forces that had abandoned the south were no more resolute. General Yang Yuan, badly wounded and borne on a stretcher, arrived in the capital on October 4 with the tattered remnants of his army, a total of scarcely one hundred men. He was greeted outside Seoul's South Gate by King Sonjo, who wept at the sight of the general's wounds. After receiving Sonjo's thanks for having suffered so much trying to defend Korea—the heartfelt exchange reduced everyone including Yang to tears—the general and his men resumed their journey north toward the Yalu River and China beyond.[18] Yang would later be tried and beheaded for his failure at Namwon. As for General Chen Yuzhong, he received one hundred strokes of the rod as punishment for abandoning Chonju and retreating north without a fight, and was sent back home in disgrace.[19]

Commander in Chief Ma Gui had in the meantime also developed cold feet. Arriving in Seoul with a thousand crack troops in the middle of August, he had initially planned to march his forces south to Kongju to meet the Japanese advance. He changed his mind after learning of the decimation of Yang Yuan's army. Concluding that the Japanese could not be stopped with the limited forces at his disposal, Ma dispatched a message north to his superiors recommending that Korea be abandoned and all Ming forces amassed along the north bank of the Yalu River to defend China's own territory should it come under attack.[20]

Ma's superior Yang Hao did not agree. Upon hearing of the defeat at Namwon, the supreme Ming commander of military affairs in Korea journeyed south to Seoul from his headquarters at Pyongyang to take charge of the situation and quash any talk of retreat. After criticizing Ma and his fellow commanders for their lack of determination, Yang gathered all the Chinese troops on the scene, those who had abandoned the south plus reinforcements recently arrived, a total of eight thousand men, and sent them south under Ma into the hills of Kyonggi Province to ambush the Japanese when they drew near Seoul. This was all done in secret. Yang told the Koreans nothing of his plans, presumably to prevent word of the ambush from leaking to the Japanese.[21]

This Ming army, a combination of foot soldiers and mounted troops, took up positions along the main road seventy kilometers south of the capital, just past the garrison town of Chiksan, near what is today Pyongtaek City. Selecting a place where the passage between the mountains was narrow and rough, the Chinese divided into three sections, one remaining by the road and the other two branching to the left and right. They then hid themselves well and sat down to wait.

Luckily for Ma and his men, the Japanese force approaching from the direction of Chonju was not particularly large. It was the vanguard of Kuroda Nagamasa's five thousand-man force,[22] pressing into Kyonggi Province to establish the northernmost edge of Japan's new holdings in Korea while their colleagues secured the territory to the south. The two sides met on the morning of October 16. Korean accounts state that Kuroda's force was caught off guard; the first indication they had that something was amiss was the clang of cymbals issuing from the trees signaling the Chinese attack. According to the

Japanese, Kuroda's men saw the assembled Ming troops from some distance away and charged at them despite being badly outnumbered, intent on holding them on the low ground until their comrades arrived. Things went badly for the Japanese at first. But, as they had hoped, Kuroda's main force soon raced to the scene, drawn by the sound of gunfire. With the balance of forces now even, the fighting continued without resolution until the end of the day, with heavy casualties on both sides. The rival forces then drew apart, gathered their dead and wounded, and made camp for the night. Sometime in the evening the Ming commander summoned his officers and said, "Judging from the determination the Japanese showed today, they will probably fight to the death tomorrow. So we must do the same."

The Japanese tried to take the upper hand at dawn, advancing against the Chinese in crane-wing formation, attempting to crush them within two enveloping wings. They failed. The Chinese, although hard pressed by musket fire, eventually drove Kuroda's men back with arrows and light cannons and muskets of their own, then charged and sent them scattering in retreat back toward the south. An additional force of two thousand cavalrymen sent from Seoul by Yang Hao arrived on the scene just in time to swing the balance and join in the chase. While Ma's exhausted men sat down to rest, these fresh cavalry-men galloped down the road after the retreating Japanese, adding a few more enemy heads to the tally before finally turning back. When it was all over the total number of Japanese dead was estimated at between five and six hundred. Chinese casualties likely ran into the hundreds as well.[23]

The Battle of Chiksan had not been a crushing defeat for the Japanese. They lost no more than six hundred men and inflicted significant casualties in return upon the Ming Chinese. The battle nevertheless marked the turning point in Hideyoshi's second invasion of Korea, the point of his army's farthest northern advance before turning back toward the south. It was not a rout, but rather a carefully considered strategic retreat. The Japanese fell back at their own pace, taking time as they went to inflict still more death and destruction on the Korean people as neither the Choson nor the Ming army made a serious attempt to pursue. They were prompted to turn back mainly by the now-certain knowledge that a large Ming army was assembling in the north and would soon be moving their way. To take on this expeditionary force in their present situation, the Japanese knew, would be foolhardy, spread out as they were in towns and cities all across the provinces of Kyongsang, Cholla, and Chungchong. There was also the approaching Korean winter to consider and the attendant difficulty of obtaining supplies, a difficulty that would be further exacerbated by the Korean navy under a reinstated Yi Sun-sin, which was about to deny Japanese ships access to the supply route north through the Yellow Sea. Taking these considerations together, there was only one sensible course of action for the Japanese army to take: they had to fall back toward the south.

CHAPTER 26

"Seek death and you will live; seek life and you will die"

YI SUN-SIN WAS HALFWAY THROUGH his tour of inspection of Korea's southern coastal defenses when the messenger from Seoul caught up with him, bearing the royal order reappointing him supreme naval commander of Kyongsang, Cholla, and Chungchong Provinces. The date was September 13, 1597. At the time of Yi's removal from office, Korea's navy had consisted of at least two hundred warships manned by disciplined crews. In the course of his inspection tour Yi now found that nothing of this force remained. Thanks mainly to the poor leadership of his replacement, Won Kyun, almost the entire navy had been destroyed in the Battle of Chilchon Strait on August 28, leaving the sea route west entirely unguarded.

Yi could easily have given up at this point without too much loss of face. After all, with no fleet to command or men to lead what good could he possibly do? A great deal, as it turned out. The next six weeks would be in fact the finest hour in this Korean naval hero's already illustrious career. Equipped with just thirteen ships and armed with little more than a fierce reputation and unshakable courage, Yi Sun-sin would take on a Japanese armada of two hundred ships, and stop it in its tracks.

When Yi Sun-sin arrived in southern Cholla Province from Kyongsang he found the region in panic and turmoil. The roads were filled with refugees. When they saw Yi passing they greeted him like a savoir, crying out, "Our Admiral is come again! Now we can be safe!" Local officials everywhere were in hiding or had fled into the hills, desperate to escape what the Japanese proclamations promised would be certain death for them. Near Sunchon Yi found three officials cowering in a warehouse. Sunchon itself was completely deserted. The local army commander there had run off as well, leaving behind an unguarded armory full of weapons. Yi hastily organized a squad of monk-soldiers to bury the weapons. Elsewhere Yi was angered to find that fleeing officers and officials had burnt armories, food stores, and government offices—the latter presumably to prevent any evidence of who they were from falling into enemy hands—and was particularly astonished to hear of an army garrison that had knocked down the walls of its own mountain fortress rather than risk inflaming the ire of the advancing Japanese.[1]

As he made his circuitous way west, Yi attempted to restore order by posting guards at armories and warehouses that had not already been destroyed, reprimanding officials for cowardice, flogging officers and men guilty of dereliction of duty, and punishing civilians for any crime. One staff officer received eighty blows for failing to obey an order to ship weapons west to safety from the naval port of Yosu; a provisions inspector was beaten for stealing the grain in his care; two abalone divers had their heads cut off and publicly displayed for attempting to make off with some cattle by first creating a panic with shouts of, "The Japanese thieves have come! The Japanese thieves have come!"[2] In this way Yi Sun-sin reestablished what classical Chinese military doctrine termed his "awesomeness," that combination of fear and respect that a leader needed to instill in his people if he were to effectively govern or command. "If by executing one man the entire army will quake, kill him," advised the fourth-century B.C. treatise *T'ai Kung's Six Secret Teachings*. "If by rewarding one man the masses will be pleased, reward him. . . . When punishments reach the pinnacle and rewards penetrate to the lowest, then your awesomeness has been effected."[3]

It was the conduct of Kyongsang Navy Commander Bae Sol that Yi Sun-sin found most reprehensible and deserving of punishment. Bae, it will be remembered, had fled at the start of the Battle of Chilchonnyang when the Korean navy had been destroyed, thus saving himself and the twelve ships under his command. "Being told of the terror-stricken flight of Bae Sol," Yi wrote in his dairy on September 22, "I was thoroughly indignant and disgusted. Having flattered the clique in power he was promoted...beyond his capacity, thus gravely threatening the national defense. Yet the Royal Court does not look into the matter. What a mistake!"[4]

On September 28 Yi Sun-sin arrived at the port of Hoeryongpo on the southwestern corner of Korea, where he had previously arranged to meet Bae Sol and resume command of the fleet. Bae was late to the rendezvous, and then behaved badly when he finally arrived, absenting himself from the ceremony where the royal decree restoring Yi Sun-sin to command was displayed for all the captains to bow to, formally acknowledging his authority. Outraged by this impertinence, but unable to punish the Kyongsang commander directly because of his lofty rank, Yi resorted to the customary practice of indirect punishment: one of Bae's officers was tied down and beaten in his place, receiving a total of twenty strokes. This set the tone for future relations between Yi and Bae. Two weeks later the disgraced Kyongsang commander sent a message to Yi stating that he was ill and requesting that he be excused from office to recuperate on land. After receiving Yi's approval, Bae left the fleet and ran away. He would not serve in the navy again.[5]

The Korean fleet of which Yi Sun-sin resumed command was a sorry force indeed. Bae Sol brought just ten ships to Hoeryongpo; he had escaped the Chilchonnyang battle with twelve ships, but two of these had somehow gone astray by the time he joined up with Yi. Two more vessels, both of them in poor condition and undermanned, arrived a week later under newly appointed Cholla Right Navy Commander Kim Ok-chu, then a third was produced from some other quarter, giving Yi a total of just thirteen warships with which to hold back the Japanese.[6] As for manpower, Yi started the month of October with some one hundred and twenty men, most of them demoralized after their recent defeat and apt to flee at the first sight of the Japanese. To make the most of this modest force, Yi is said to have ordered that all his vessels be fitted out like turtle ships, with stout timber sides and spiked roofs to protect the crews within. Considering the limited time and resources available, this construction work must have left his ships looking like rough-hewn floating forts. Yi also set to work bolstering the courage of his shaken men. He knew that the only way to withstand the coming Japanese onslaught would be for each man to fight like a cornered tiger—and the only way to get a man to fight like that was first to talk him out of his fear. "We are under orders of the King," Yi said in one of many stirring talks to his men. "Since the situation has reached this extremity we must resolve to die together. Why should we hesitate to repay the royal bounty with our glorious deaths? There is only one choice for us now to make: victory or death!" After stirring up the fighting spirit of his men, Yi led them in swearing a solemn oath: they would meet and defeat the Japanese or die in the attempt.[7]

Shortly after arriving at Hoeryongpo, Yi decided that the harbor there was too confined and thus led his tiny fleet forty kilometers farther west to the port of Oranpo. Here he received word that Japanese ships had already advanced into the waters off Cholla Province and would soon be drawing near. On October 8 an advance party of eight enemy vessels appeared at Oranpo and very nearly spooked the Koreans into a panicked retreat. Yi aboard his flagship did not move as the enemy approached. Then, when they had drawn near, he gave the order to attack and plunged straight at them. This display of courage and bravado threw the Japanese into a headlong retreat back toward the east, carrying news to the main fleet that the Korean navy was not yet completely destroyed. It also restored in Yi's own captains some of that confidence that they had known when they had served under him before.[8]

Twenty kilometers to the west of Oranpo was the island of Chin-do. Just past Chin-do lay the Yellow Sea. On October 8 the Japanese fleet was thus on the verge of achieving its objective of securing a sea route north, and the Koreans were backed up almost as far as they could go. With it now clear that a decisive battle would soon be fought, Yi Sun-sin fell back with his little squadron into the channel between Chin-do and the mainland, establishing a temporary base here on Korea's extreme southwestern tip while he scouted the terrain and made plans for the fight. He did not have long. On October 17 a report arrived that Japanese ships had returned to Oranpo, just a few hours away from the new Korean base on Chin-do. Thirteen of their ships were already anchored there. A week later enemy strength at Oranpo had risen to fifty-five ships. A few days after that it stood at two hundred, possibly more.[9]

The Japanese armada that was now advancing west had accomplished a great deal during the previous two months. After decimating the Korean navy at Chilchon Strait, it had helped ferry troops along the coast and up the Somjin River to Namwon in preparation for the assault on the Chinese and Korean forces there, thus playing a part in another significant victory. With this task complete it then turned its attention to establishing a safe and reliable sea route from Pusan to the Yellow Sea. By the end of September this naval force of several hundred ships had secured the entire coastal region of Kyongsang Province and islands offshore, including the former Korean naval base on Hansan-do, and was poised to enter Cholla Province. It was under the command of Todo Takatora, Kato Yoshiaki, and Wakizaka Yasuharu, the same men who had engineered the destruction of the Korean navy the month before. They were joined by Kurushima Michifusa, whose brother Michiyuki had been killed by Yi Sun-sin's forces at the Battle of Tangpo in 1592. From their base on the Kyongsang-Cholla border, Todo and his fellow commanders first sent small scouting parties westward to map the route to the Yellow Sea and identify any points of resistance. It was one of these units that was met and chased off by Yi Sun-sin at Oranpo on October 8. It hurried back east to report the engagement, the first indication since the Battle of Chilchon Strait that the Korean navy had some fight left in it still. Only a handful of vessels had been sighted, however—nothing the Japanese could not handle with their vast preponderance of ships. The main body of the Japanese navy thus continued its cautious advance west, anticipating one final encounter with the remnants of the Choson navy, one more chance to destroy the few ships the Koreans had left.

An advance squadron of thirteen Japanese ships was once again off Oranpo on October 17. This time they encountered no resistance and took possession of the harbor. They then continued west toward the island of Chin-do in search of the retreating Korean navy. Yi Sun-sin had received warning of the approach of this enemy force and thus had his fleet on alert and in battle formation when the Japanese ships appeared at their Chin-do base at four o'clock that afternoon. This time the Koreans had no difficulty in repelling the attack, but high winds and the strong tidal flow through the channel made it impossible for them to give chase. Instead they returned to their base and prepared for a second attack. Yi suspected that the Japanese would launch a surprise assault after dark, much as they had done so successfully at the Battle of Chilchon-nyang. He thus ordered his captains to remain alert, adding that anyone failing to do his duty in the coming fight would be harshly punished.

Yi Sun-sin was right. At ten o'clock that evening the thirteen Japanese vessels crept up to the Koreans and opened fire with the cannons that their ships were now equipped with. The Koreans, unnerved at the prospect of fighting in the dark, wavered for a time before Yi was able to prod them into moving to attack. Finally, after a running battle that lasted two hours, the Japanese once again were driven back toward Oranpo. This time they did not return.[10]

Things remained quiet for the next several days as the Japanese built up their forces at Oranpo in preparation for a final assault. Yi spent the time continuing his careful observations of the surrounding waters and of the time and speed of the tides. He was particularly interested in Myongnyang Channel, the narrow passage between Chin Island and the mainland, just 250 meters across at its narrowest point, through which the Japanese would have to pass to gain access to the Yellow Sea. To Yi's experienced eye this stretch of water presented distinct tactical possibilities. To begin with, the gap was so narrow that the Japanese would not be able to pass through in battle formation. They would have to break their fleet into smaller squadrons in order to advance. Myongnyang's immensely strong tidal flow also caught Yi's attention. The current here was among the fastest in Korea, ripping through the strait "like a cataract" at a top speed of 9.5 knots, as fast or faster than a Japanese warship could travel, even over short distances.[11] If Yi were to meet the Japanese fleet as it was passing through the neck of Myongnyang, therefore, he would reduce the odds against him, for only a portion of the enemy force would be able to take him on while the remainder lay trapped to the rear. By timing his attack with the flow of the tide, moreover, he could meet the enemy with more

than just his handful of ships. He would have on his side the full force
of the sea.

On October 24 Yi received intelligence that two hundred Japanese
ships were at or nearing Oranpo. It was time to prepare to fight. The
next day he fell back with his fleet further to the west, passing all the
way through Myongnyang Channel and into the open water beyond.
His plan was to attack the Japanese at the mouth of the channel as they
attempted to clear the narrow passage and its formidable tidal flow. Yi
anchored his fleet in a little bay just beyond the mouth of the channel,
out of sight of the Japanese. In the open water beyond he arrayed a long
line of fishing boats, filled with refugees who had been drawn to Yi's
base over the past few weeks in the hope that the Korean navy would
keep them safe. By arranging these small unarmed craft in something
approximating a battle line, but too distant to be clearly seen, Yi hoped
the Japanese would mistake them for a large Korean fleet and assume
his own thirteen battleships to be only a vanguard squadron.

The Koreans were now backed up into the Yellow Sea itself. There
was nowhere left for them to retreat. They either had to stop the
Japanese at this very point or die in the attempt. Later that night Yi
Sun-sin summoned his captains to issue orders for what he knew would
be the decisive clash the following day. "According to the principles of
strategy," he said, " ' He who seeks his death shall live, he who seeks
his life shall die.' Again, the strategy says, 'If one defender stands on
watch at a strong gateway he may drive terror deep into the heart of the
enemy coming by the ten thousand.' These are golden sayings for us.
You captains are expected to strictly obey my orders. If you do not,
even the least error shall not be pardoned, but shall be severely
punished by martial law."[12]

Yi was quoting to his men from the ancient Chinese military
classics, possibly the fourth-century B.C. treatise *Wu Tzu Ping Fa*
(Master Wu's Art of War). In a series of discussions with his lord on
how to govern his kingdom and conduct his wars, the renowned
military commander turned scholar Wu Qi observed, "If the soldiers are
committed to fight to the death they will live, whereas if they seek to
stay alive they will die."[13] The idea was that by casting off all fear of
death, a soldier would transcend the normal limits of courage and fight

with an almost inhuman degree of ferocity, taking five, ten, twenty of
the enemy with him before he himself was killed. The Chinese called a
force of such men a "death army" and considered it a fearsome thing.[14]
With regard to fighting an enemy whose numbers are great when yours
are few, Master Wu advised, "Avoid them on easy terrain, attack them
in narrow quarters. Thus it is said, for one to attack ten, nothing is
better than a narrow defile. For ten to attack one hundred, nothing is
better than a deep ravine. For one thousand to attack ten thousand,
nothing is better than a dangerous pass."[15]

Yi Sun-sin had chosen Myongnyang Channel as his "dangerous
pass." And to make the most of his few hundred men, he intended to
transform them into a "death army." By forcing them into a situation
where they believed there was no chance of survival, Yi hoped they
would acquire the necessary courage and ferocity to take on the enemy's
vastly superior numbers, and maybe even win.

The main body of the Japanese fleet arrived at the southern end of
Myongnyang Channel the next morning, October 26, from the direction
of Oranpo. In his diary Yi Sun-sin states that these enemy forces
numbered approximately two hundred ships. Yi's nephew gives a higher
estimate in his own account of the battle, stating that refugees with a
better view of the situation atop nearby hills counted three hundred
Japanese ships, "then lost count of those sailing behind, because there
were so many of them that they filled the sea."[16] In either case the odds
were appalling against the Koreans' own thirteen ships. As Yi had
foreseen, however, the vast Japanese fleet was unable to advance
through Myongnyang in a mass. Dividing into four or five groups, the
first squadron ventured tentatively into the channel, moving easily with
the current, followed by a second, then a third. They had not yet seen
Yi Sun-sin's battleships waiting in ambush just beyond the channel's
mouth, only a long line of vessels in the far distance, well beyond
Myongnyang. Was their intelligence mistaken? Did the Koreans still
have a sizable fleet?

When the first of the Japanese ships reached the end of the channel
and entered the calmer waters beyond, Yi Sun-sin ordered his fleet to
move to the attack from the shelter of their hidden bay. Yi himself led
the way in his flagship. "Have no fear!" he cried to his terrified crew.

"Even if the enemy has one thousand warships, they will not dare come near us!" With that Yi's turtle ship dashed ahead, blasting away with cannons and fire arrows at the startled Japanese. The other ships in the Korean fleet initially followed his lead, but then began to lag behind as their captains and crews caught sight of the enemy armada crowding Myongnyang Channel, heading their way. When Yi glanced back and saw this, he was tempted to turn around and cut off the head of one of the captains to hang from the mast as a warning to all. But he was already in the thick of the battle and could scarcely turn back now. Instead he waved a signal flag at the laggards and sounded a shell trumpet, ordering them to join the fight. When the first of these ships drew near, the vessel captained by Koje Island magistrate An Wi, Yi roared across the water: "An Wi! Do you want to die by court martial! Do you think you'll survive if you run away!" With that An Wi and the other captains charged ahead and were soon enveloped like Yi by one hundred and thirty-odd Japanese ships.

The battle that ensured was unlike anything the Korean navy had experienced before. They had faced frightening odds in 1592, but nothing so frightening as this, thirteen against one hundred and thirty, with still more Japanese warships waiting to the rear. Never before had Yi placed them in such a desperate situation. They responded, however, as Yi had hoped. On that fall morning, with their backs to the Yellow Sea, Yi Sun-sin's diminutive force conquered their fear and became a "death army." They charged at the Japanese fleet with wild abandon, ramming their stout prows into the enemy's weaker hulls, blasting at them with cannons from point-blank range, setting them alight with fire arrows, flailing with clubs and spears and stones when parties of enemy warriors as thick as "black ants" attempted to climb aboard.

The Japanese flagship, identifiable by its soaring superstructure and profusion of banners and flags, was singled out by the Koreans for particularly heavy fire, and was soon in flames and sinking. Shortly thereafter a surrendered Japanese who had previously defected to the Korean side and who was now serving aboard Yi's flagship caught sight of a familiar figure bobbing in the water, clad in a red brocade uniform such as would be worn by a high-ranking Japanese commander. "Is that Matashi," he cried out, "the Japanese commander from Angolpo?" Yi

Sun-sin had the corpse hooked and dragged on deck. The Japanese soldier examined the body closely and confirmed his earlier identification. "I am positive. It is he—Matashi!" According to the Koreans this "Matashi" was none other than Japanese naval commander Kurushima Michifusa. He had been sent to Korea to lead the naval forces previously commanded by his brother Michiyuki, who had been killed in the Tangpo battle in 1592. Now it was Michifusa's turn to meet a glorious end. Upon learning that he had an important enemy commander on board, Yi Sun-sin ordered the body cut into pieces and hung from the mast for the enemy to see.[17]

The Japanese made repeated attempts that morning to force the Koreans from the mouth of Myongnyang Channel. Each time they were driven back. Eventually the waters were awash with the wreckage of their warships and the bodies of their dead. And still the Koreans stood firm, Yi's flagship steady "like a castle in the middle of the sea." Thirteen stood against one hundred and thirty, and stopped them in their tracks.

Then the tide began to turn, and with it the second phase of Yi Sun-sin's plan began to unfold. Backed up by the attacking Koreans into the mouth of Myongnyang Channel, the Japanese were unable to withstand the strength of the reversing current and were forced back in the direction from which they had come. The Koreans, inspired by their initial success and moving easily now with the tide, attacked with renewed vigor, inflicting further damage as the battle continued back down the neck of the strait. By the time the Japanese reached open water and the exhausted Koreans gave up their pursuit, thirty-one ships of Hideyoshi's navy had been destroyed, while Yi's fleet remained intact. With that the Japanese navy began to fall back toward the border of Kyongsang Province, then farther still toward Angolpo and Pusan. It would give up all thought of gaining access to the Yellow Sea, and would not venture west again.[18]

Most Korean accounts of the Battle of Myongnyang assert that Yi Sun-sin had suspended a chain or cable across the channel prior to the battle, one end secured to the mainland, the other to a point on Chin Island. This chain, the story goes, was left slack while the Japanese fleet advanced up the channel, allowing them to pass over it without notice. Then the tide turned, forcing the Japanese back. As they neared the spot where the cable lay, it was winched taut by men stationed at either end, thus capsizing several Japanese ships and blocking the others from retreat while Yi's ships continued to pick them apart. There is little evidence to support this account. Yi Sun-sin himself makes no reference to a chain in his war diary, and it is hard to believe he would have neglected to do so had he in fact used one, for it surly would have been a noteworthy thing. Yi's nephew Yi Pun does not mention it either in his biography of his famous uncle, written not long after the war by someone who knew the commander well. Nor does Yi's friend and mentor Yu Song-nyong in his account of the war. It is likely that the story of the chain was an embellishment or misinterpretation of the facts that entered into the oral tradition of the Imjin War sometime in the seventeenth century, and from there came to be accepted as fact.[19]

Yi Sun-sin's success in the Battle of Myongnyang, with or without a chain, is perhaps the finest example of his tactical brilliance, the point where his leadership during seven years of war rose from the extraordinary to the sublime and from there entered into legend. In modern times Western writers have been effusive in their praise of him, comparing Yi to such great men as his English contemporary Sir Francis Drake, and to Lord Horatio Nelson, who defeated Napoleon's navy at the Battle of Trafalgar in 1805. But ironically, it was among Yi's former adversaries that some of his greatest admirers arose. During the Meiji era officers in Japan's newly minted modern navy came to regard the Korean commander as the epitome of the spirit of *bushido*, "the way of the warrior," as practiced at sea. Prior to doing battle with Russia's Baltic fleet in the Russo-Japanese war in 1905, for example, Lieutenant Commander Kawada Isao recalled in his memoirs that "naturally we could not help but remind ourselves of Korea's Yi Sun-sin, the world's first sea commander, whose superlative personality, strategy, invention, commanding ability, intelligence, and courage were all worthy of our admiration."[20] Following the battle, which was a tremendous victory for the Japanese, Admiral Togo Heihachiro himself took up this praise of Yi. At a party that was held in his honor, Togo took exception to one eulogy comparing him to Lord Nelson and Yi Sun-sin. "It may be proper to compare me with Nelson," said the admiral, "but not with Korea's Yi Sun-sin. He is too great to be compared to anyone."[21]

*　　*　　*

On November 22, 1597, one month after the Battle of Myongnyang, Yi Sun-sin awoke at dawn with a curious dream still clear in his mind. He had been riding across a hillock when his horse stumbled and threw him into a stream. His youngest son, Myon, then somehow appeared, picked him up, and embraced him tightly. Yi, ever a firm believer in the portents in dreams, could not determine what this one meant. Later that same day he found out. Toward evening he received a letter from his family home in Asan, which he had just learned had been burned to the ground by the Japanese during their march of destruction back toward the south. At the very sight of it, Yi wrote in his diary, "my bones and flesh shuddered and my head became dizzy." He tore open the envelope to find a letter inside from his second son, Yol, with the characters "With Weeping" brushed on the front. The admiral knew at once that Myon was dead, struck down by the Japanese when he attempted to defend his home. Pouring his broken heart into his diary late into the night, he wrote these words to his departed son: "I should die and you should live. That is the natural order! Now you are dead and I am alive! . . . My son, where have you gone, leaving me behind? . . . I wish to follow you to the grave, to stay and weep together, but if I do, your brothers and sisters and your mother will have no one to support them. Thus I endure, with live body but a dead soul."[22]

Yi fell into a deep depression after that. His health also began to suffer, dragged down no doubt by his emotional state and the meager diet he imposed upon himself for the duration of his mourning. Some time later he had a dream in which Myon beseeched him in tears to avenge his death. "Father," Myon cried, "kill the Japanese who killed me!" Upon waking, Yi asked his staff officers what the dream might mean. Someone suggested that the spirit of his son was perhaps disturbed by a recently captured Japanese soldier who was in custody aboard Yi's own ship. Yi ordered the man interrogated under torture, and not surprisingly extracted a confession that he was the very one who had killed his son, some three hundred kilometers to the north.[23]

It is written in the Chinese military classics: "If you flog a person's back, brand his ribs, or compress his fingers in order to question him about the nature of his offense, even a state hero could not withstand this cruelty and would falsely implicate himself."[24] If Yi Sun-sin was not specifically aware of this passage, his common sense surly told him as much. The fact that he went ahead and acted as he did is an apt reminder that, despite his many achievements, Korea's supreme naval commander was not an infallible superhero, but a flesh-and-blood man. Succumbing to his need to find someone to punish for his son's death to ease his troubled mind, Yi accepted as true the confession that had been forcibly extracted from the Japanese prisoner, even though it was unlikely he was guilty of the offense.

The man was executed by having his flesh peeled off his body.

CHAPTER 27

Starvation and Death in a "Buddha-less World"

OCTOBER 1597 HAD NOT BEEN A GOOD MONTH for the Japanese army in Korea. On the sixteenth its northern advance had been blunted by a small Ming force at Chiksan, seventy kilometers south of Seoul. Ten days later its fleet was blocked by the Korean navy from entering the Yellow Sea. Despite these setbacks, however, Japanese losses remained fairly light: a hundred or so men killed in the assault on Namwon, another six hundred in the Battle of Chiksan, and thirty-one ships lost to Yi Sun-sin at Myongnyang. In fact, considering that several thousand Chinese and Korean soldiers had been killed so far, plus civilians numbering in the tens of thousands, it has to be concluded that Hideyoshi's army was a long way from being beaten.

Why then did the Japanese decide to withdraw and return south to their forts? First, Hideyoshi ordered them to do so. There is evidence to suggest that he never intended his armies to retain control of the territory they marched through. According to two separate reports from Japanese soldiers captured and interrogated at or shortly after the Battle of Chiksan, the taiko instructed his commanders at the start of the offensive to rampage through the southern part of Korea, killing everyone in their path, then fall back to the south.[1] These reports support the supposition that Hideyoshi never had designs on conquest in his second invasion of Korea, but only a desire to punish the Koreans, impress the Chinese, and in so doing vent his spleen and save some face.

If Hideyoshi did not wish to conquer the southern part of Korea, many of his commanders certainly did. They had no intention of risking life and limb for the sake of their master's wounded pride. They wanted something tangible, like conquered lands and larger fiefs, to show for their effort. In November of 1597, however, Hideyoshi's order to withdraw coincided with their own strategic interests. It was now evident that the Chinese were again committed to providing military aid to Korea. The presence of Ming troops at Namwon and Chiksan was concrete evidence of this, and intelligence reports indicated that these were but advance units of a much larger force being amassed somewhere to the north, a force said to number 100,000 men or more. If the Japanese were to attempt to hang on to all the territory they had seized in Kyongsang, Cholla, and Chungchong Provinces with this huge army bearing down upon them, particularly with winter coming on and with it the promise of scant supplies, their widely distributed garrisons would be easy targets to be picked off one by one. There was only one sensible course of action to meet this looming threat: fall back and consolidate in the string of forts around Pusan.

As the Japanese proceeded with their withdrawal to the south they continued to inflict still more cruelty upon Korea's civilian population. Noses hacked off the faces of the massacred were submitted by the thousands at the nose collection stations set up on the way, where they were carefully counted, recorded, salted, and packed.

> To: Kikkawa Hiroie
> Number of noses taken verified as 437.
>> 1597, 9th month, 11th day
>> Hayakawa Nagamasa

> To: Nabeshima Katsushige
> Number of noses taken verified as 1,551.
>> 1597, 9th month, 13th day
>> Hayakawa Nagamasa

> To: Kuroda Nagamasa
> 300 noses taken.
>> At Kaeryong, 1597, 9th month, 19th day
>> Takenaga Gensuke

To: Kikkawa Hiroie
10,040 noses from the dead were taken by units at Chinwon and Yanggwang.
    1597, 9th month, 26th day
        Kakimi Kasunao, Kumagai Naomori, Hayakawa Nagamasa

To: Akana Hisauji
A total of 365 noses were delivered to the Nose Collection Officer.
    1597, 10th month, 2nd day
        Kikkawa Hiroie[2]

In addition to collecting noses from the slain, the retreating Japanese took captives. The priest Keinen traveling with Kato Kiyomasa's contingent recorded the following description of the horrors he witnessed as civilians who survived the massacres were rounded up and marched south. "Among the many kinds of merchants who have come over from Japan," he wrote, "are traders in human beings, who follow in the train of the troops and buy up men and women, young and old alike. Having tied these people together with ropes about the neck, they drive them along before them; those who can no longer walk are made to run with prods or blows of the stick from behind. The sight of the fiends and man-devouring demons who torment sinners in hell must be like this, I thought."[3] Some of these unfortunates would be put to work building fortifications along the south coast in preparation for the anticipated Ming advance. A good number of them would be worked to death, or have their heads cut off when they became too exhausted to be of any more use. Others, 50,000 Koreans or more,[4] were transported back to Japan. After spending a few days or weeks in prison camps on Kyushu and Shikoku,[5] many were put to work as farmers, laborers, or artisans in the fief of their daimyo owners, where they were left in relative freedom to rebuild their lives as best they could. Others were sold to other daimyo and resettled elsewhere. Few would ever see Korea again. After what was undoubtedly a period of severe bitterness and heartache, these unwilling immigrants had no choice but to accept their fate and be gradually absorbed into Japanese society.

Of all the Korean prisoners taken to Japan, none would have a more visible impact on that nation's culture than artisans skilled in the manufacture of ceramics. Prior to the war Korean methods of ceramic production were more advanced than those employed in Japan, and Korean pottery in great demand. One of the few benefits that the Japanese derived from Hideyoshi's invasion of Korea was the acquisition of this technology by capturing Korean potters and sending them back to Japan—evidently on such a large scale that Korea's own ceramic industry was thrown into a severe postwar decline.[6] Shimazu Yoshihiro, for example, sent at least seventeen potters to his fief in Satsuma on the island of Kyushu. Mori Hidemoto similarly resettled potters in the area around Yamaguchi on the western tip of Honshu. The house of Hosokawa had not sent a contingent of its own to Korea, but nevertheless managed to acquire Korean potters to staff kilns in Tango Province just west of Kyoto. Despite their evident unwillingness to be in Japan—the Korean head of the Hosokawa production line attempted to escape more than a dozen times—the techniques these Koreans brought with them revolutionized the Japanese ceramic industry, leading to the development of such ceramic types as Satsuma ware, Karatsu ware, Agano ware, Hagi ware, and Arita ware. It is for this reason that Hideyoshi's Korean campaign is sometimes referred to by Japanese historians as *yakimono senso*, "the pottery war." [7]

The vast majority of Koreans taken captive during the second invasion were uneducated and illiterate, and thus unable to leave behind a written record of what they experienced as prisoners in Japan. But there were a few exceptions. No In was a well-educated, upper-class Korean who was wounded and captured at the Battle of Namwon in September 1597. He was kept in Korea for a time, then shipped to the island of Shikoku in Japan, where he discovered Koreans were being bought and sold as slaves. Although he heard many tales of misery from other Korean captives, No himself was treated quite well by the Japanese because of his status and education. He even became something of a celebrity, with samurai and monks paying him to write poems and calligraphy in Chinese characters and to critique their own efforts at classical composition. No nevertheless remained desperately unhappy; concern over the fate of his parents troubled him particularly. In February 1599 he therefore tried to escape. The attempt failed, but it resulted in his fortuitous transfer to the port of Sakai near Kyoto, where he met travelers from China who agreed to take him home with them. Thanks to these Chinese seafarers, and to the considerable degree of freedom the Japanese seem to have accorded him, No eventually reached the Chinese mainland and from there made his way back to Korea. He arrived only to learn that his parents had died two years before.[8]

Chong Hui-duk had much the same experience during his own time in captivity. He and his family were chased down by Japanese naval forces on November 6, 1597, as they were attempting to sail westward to safety. With capture imminent, Chong's mother, wife, sister, and sister-in-law all jumped into the water and drowned themselves rather than risk the dishonor of being raped. The rest of the family was taken alive. Chong's sick father and his children were released three days later. Chong Hui-duk and his brother were sent together with about one hundred other prisoners to Shikoku, where they spent a miserable winter in close confinement, exposed to the weather and wracked by hunger and fever. As an example of the brutal treatment captives often received, Chong wrote of witnessing the Japanese hacking at the corpse of a dead Korean to test the sharpness of their swords. Once Chong was identified by his captors as an educated man, however, his life greatly improved. He was given more freedom than most other captives and was allowed to earn money copying books and working as a ghost-writer. Finally, in mid-1599, he was given permission to return to Korea. He arrived home during the harvest season to find his entire village burned to the ground.[9]

The third and final scholar to leave behind an account of his captivity in Japan is also the most famous. His name was Kang Hang. Kang, born into a distinguished family in the southern province of Cholla, was raised to a life of scholarship and passed the civil service examination at the young age of twenty-one. During the first invasion of 1592–93 he remained in Cholla-do, working to supply the nation's army. He served in various government posts in Seoul after that, then returned home to Cholla in 1596 to begin what he thought would be a quiet life of teaching and study.

With the second Japanese invasion in 1597, Kang, now thirty years of age, once again went to work supplying food and weapons, this time to the allied forces garrisoning Namwon. It was not long after the fall of that city that Kang Hang and his family were captured by the Japanese. On November 2, 1597, forces under Todo Takatora stumbled upon the vessel that Kang had procured to carry himself and his family west to safety with Yi Sun-sin's fleet. After abandoning his youngest son and daughter on the shore to die, the Japanese sent Kang and the remnants of his family eastward on a journey first to Tsushima, then on to Todo's fiefdom of Ozu on the island of Shikoku. One of Kang's nephews fell ill on the way and was thrown overboard; another nephew and a niece died from disease two months later. Kang himself, being a well-educated man, was at first given clerical duties in the household of the Ozu daimyo, then was transferred to Hideyoshi's own Fushimi Castle as the extent of his knowledge came to be better appreciated. Here he was solicited by scholars, monks, and the better educated among the daimyo for advice on poetry and classical composition, and also instruction in the principles of Neo-Confucianism, which was not yet well understood in Japan. Kang Hang has indeed been identified by some Korean scholars as the main conduit for the transmission of Neo-Confucianism to Japan, an abridged and "Japanized" form of which would come to have a profound influence on that nation in the centuries to come.[10] Although this is an overstatement—the transmission of Neo-Confucianism to Japan occurred over the course of a century or more—it must be admitted that Kang Hang played a significant role in the process.

Kang Hang, like other well-educated Koreans taken forcibly to Japan, was treated remarkably well during his period of captivity, certainly better than prisoners from the lower ranks of society. This did not prevent him, however, from thinking constantly of escape. He made two attempts to purchase a boat with his earnings and sail to Korea with his family. Both failed. Then he realized that the best way he could serve his country would be to gather intelligence about the Japanese to aid the Korean government in dealing with them in the future. The report that Kang eventually produced, completed during his journey back to Korea as part of a postwar prisoner repatriation, was initially entitled *Kongorok* (Record of a Criminal), a name chosen by Kang to express the shame he felt at having lived as a captive in an enemy's land. In later years his disciples would rename it *Kanyangnok* (Record of a Shepherd), a reference to a Chinese officer named Su Wu whose loyalty to his king never wavered during nineteen years of captivity among the Huns in the first century B.C. As will be discussed later, this work would do much to shape Korea's policy toward Japan in the decades and indeed the centuries following the conclusion of the Imjin War.[11]

Not all the Koreans taken captive during the second invasion were resettled in the islands of Japan. An unknown number were sold to Portuguese and Italian traders at the slave market in Nagasaki and were transported to such far-flung places as the colony of Macao in southern China, to Goa on India's western coast, and even to Europe on the other side of the world.

In his early-seventeenth-century account of his journey around the world, the Florentine merchant Francesco Carletti mentions visiting a slave market in Nagasaki and seeing "an infinite number of [Korean] men and women, boys and girls, of every age, and they all were sold as slaves at the very lowest prices." Carletti bought five of them "for little more than twelve scudos," the equivalent of roughly 440 grams of silver. He had them baptized, and took them with him on his continuing journey west. He set four free in Goa on the west coast of India. The fifth continued on with Carletti to Europe and subsequently settled in Rome, where he went by the name of either "Antonio" or "Antonio Corea," depending on which edition of Carletti's account one consults.[12]

There is a family with the surname "Corea" living today in the Calabrian village of Albi on Italy's southern tip who believe they are descended from this Imjin War captive Carletti took to Europe. One of them, named Antonio Corea like his supposed ancestor, wrote to the president of Korea in 1986 to learn more about his roots, and then visited the country in 1992 at the invitation of the Seoul government to take part in events commemorating the four hundredth anniversary of the start of the Imjin War.[13] Subsequent DNA testing failed to find evidence of Asian ancestry in the genes of Antonio Corea and his Albi clan.[14]

Back in Korea, Hideyoshi's forces had completed their withdrawal to the south and were now busy repairing and strengthening existing fortifications and erecting new ones. The defensive perimeter that

began to take shape in November 1597 was once again centered on the
port of Pusan, as had been the enclave established in 1593. This time,
however, it was significantly longer, extending from Ulsan in the east
all the way to Sunchon in the west, a total of fourteen fortresses spread
over more than 250 kilometers.

Konishi Yukinaga and the men of the second contingent anchored
the western end of this fortress chain at the town of Sunchon on the
coast of Cholla Province. Tsushima daimyo So Yoshitoshi and the
thousand men under his command stationed themselves on the island of
Namhae, inside the border of Kyongsang Province thirty kilometers to
the east. Next came Sachon, a fortified town just south of Chinju. Fifth
contingent leader Shimazu Yoshihiro and his son Tadatsune initially set
up camp in the town's existing castle, then erected a new fortress on
more defensible ground a little farther to the south, on a tongue of land
extending into Chinju Bay. Continuing farther east, Tachibana Muneshige held Kosong, the former headquarters of Commander in Chief
Kwon Yul; Yanagawa Tsunanobu was encamped with one thousand
men on the northern end of Koje Island; Nabeshima Naoshige's twelve
thousand-man contingent was divided between the fortress town of
Changwon and the nearby island of Chuk-do; the crucially important
harbor at Pusan was garrisoned by the eighth and ninth contingents
from western Honshu, a massive force of forty thousand men commanded respectively by Mori Hidemoto and Ukita Hideie; Kuroda
Nagamasa's third contingent was positioned north along the coast in the
fort at Sosaengpo.

Anchoring the eastern end of the fortress chain at Ulsan, finally,
was Kato Kiyomasa. After leading his forces back south the previous
month—stopping to burn the city of Kyongju and nearby Pulguk
Temple en route—Kato set his lieutenant Asano Yukinaga[15] to work
erecting a fortress on a hill named Tosan just east of the town, situated
in a fork in the Taehwa River with convenient access to Ulsan Bay and
the open sea beyond. Time, they knew, was short. With the allied
Chinese-Korean army on its ponderous way south, it would take all the
energy the Japanese could beat out of their workers to prepare the walls
and defenses necessary to make an effective stand.

Work proceeded without halt at Tosan from early in the morning until late at night. "From all around," wrote the priest Keinen, "comes the sound of the hammers and the blacksmiths and the workmen, and the swish and scraping of the adze. With the dawn it grows more and more terrible, but if it means we will not be defeated I can put up with the banging I am being subjected to even in the middle of the night."[16] Korean slaves and conscripted peasants shipped over from Japan were sent into the nearby mountains under heavy guard to fell trees and prepare the thousands of meters of lumber needed to build the fort. Others were put to work hauling stones and digging trenches and moats. Anyone deemed to be careless immediately had his head cut off, Korean and Japanese alike. When supplies ran short Asano's captains cut the laborers' rations, then drove some of them, including their own countrymen, into the mountains to starve.[17]

The fortress that began to take shape in the bitter cold of the Korean winter consisted of an outer earthen rampart around an inner enclosure, which in turn had a citadel tucked up in the back with stone walls ten to fifteen meters high. Tosan, then, was a fortress within a fortress, affording Asano and his men a fallback position should the outer walls be breached. If they could complete construction before the Chinese and Koreans attacked, they would make them pay a terrible price.[18]

Seven hundred kilometers to the east in Kyoto, casks containing the salted noses of the slain in Korea were beginning to pile up. Hideyoshi received them gratefully, dispatching congratulatory letters to his commanders in the field acknowledging receipt of the evidence of their martial valor and thanking them for their service. He then ordered the relics entombed in a shrine on the grounds of Hokoji Temple, and set Buddhist priests to work praying for the repose of the souls of the hundreds of thousands of Koreans from whose bodies they had come— an act that chief priest Saisho Jotai in a fit of toadyism would hail as a sign of the taiko's great mercy and compassion.[19] The shrine initially was known as the *hanazuka*, "Mound of Noses." Several decades later this would come to be regarded as too cruel-sounding a name, and would be changed to the more euphonious but inaccurate *mimizuka*, "Mound of Ears," the misnomer by which it is known to this day.[20]

Apart from the sporadic orders and letters of congratulations issued in his name to his commanders in Korea, Hideyoshi by this point seems to have lost interest in his second Korean campaign. Prior to the invasion he had indicated that he might return to the headquarters he had built at Nagoya on Kyushu to personally oversee operations in Korea. But he never undertook the journey. He remained in and around Kyoto and Osaka throughout the autumn of 1597 and into the spring of 1598, overseeing repair work on Fushimi Castle, touring about the capital, relaxing with his beloved tea ceremony, and spending time with his young son Hideyori, whose security as heir was now his foremost concern. To set the vulnerable little boy up to rule after he himself was gone, Hideyoshi required his daimyo repeatedly to swear oaths of loyalty to him. He also made sure that Hideyori was equipped with all the trappings of manhood. His coming-of-age ceremony was performed in October 1597, an official title with junior fourth rank, lower grade, was bestowed upon him in the same month, and then in the following May he was promoted to a higher office with junior second rank. All this occurred before Hideyori was five years old.[21]

It is clear from this almost frantic concern for his son's future that Hideyoshi knew his remaining time on earth was short. He was in fact now entering his final year of life. His appetite was poor, and his face, never full at the best of times, had become alarming gaunt. His strength was ebbing as well, making it increasingly difficult for him to travel any great distance; a trip to Kyushu to oversee the Korean campaign, even if he had wanted to make it, was now more than he could do. The taiko's mind, however, was still sharp and active, and the nation he had united still very much in his grasp. Even in his final decline he would brook no opposition—not against himself, and certainly not against his son. In a letter to Hideyori in the summer of 1598 he wrote, "I have understood that Kitsu, Kame, Yasu, and Tsushi have acted against your wishes. As this is something extremely inexcusable, ask your Mother, and then bind these four persons with a straw rope and keep them like that until your Father comes to your side. When I arrive, I shall beat them all to death." Hideyoshi then gave the five-year-old lad some advice for holding on to power: "Should anyone try to thwart the will of Lord Chunagon [Hideyori], he must beat and beat such a man to death, and then nobody will be against him."[22]

*   *   *

In Seoul, meanwhile, Chinese forces were steadily be amassed under Regulator of Korean Affairs Yang Hao, as forward units began moving cautiously toward the south. Commander in Chief Ma Gui, spearheading the southward advance, arrived at Chonju on November 23 to find the city free of Japanese, then proceeded farther on to Namwon. Both cities lay in ruins, Namwon from the battle two months before that had seen Ma's colleague Yang Yuan so badly defeated, Chonju razed by the Japanese prior to pulling out. "Dead bodies are piled up like mountains," Ma reported back to Seoul, "and not a house is left standing."[23]

Ma Gui's southward advance ground to a halt as soon as he reached Namwon. He was now in close proximity to the Japanese forces encamped on the coast, this time large concentrations of them, not the relatively small unit he had faced at Chiksan. To lead his modest vanguard army any farther, he sensibly concluded, therefore would be foolhardy. There was also the problem of food and supplies to consider, which were proving increasingly difficult to obtain the further he advanced, particularly now that winter was approaching. After combining forces with other small Ming units in the area, Ma pulled back north twenty kilometers toward Chonju, established a camp, and sat down to wait for reinforcements and supplies.

They would not be long in coming. By early December forty thousand Ming troops had arrived in Seoul from China's Liaodong Province and regions farther west, bringing the total number of Chinese soldiers in Korea to the neighborhood of sixty thousand.[24] Xing Jie, the Ming official in overall charge of military affairs in Korea and the eastern regions of the empire, arrived soon after. He would remain in the capital for the next several months, overseeing operations from his headquarters, known as Army Gate, and meeting frequently with King Sonjo to discuss the course of the campaign.

The great Ming army that had been assembled in Seoul finally began to march south in the middle of December, much to the satisfaction of the Koreans, who felt the Chinese had already taken far too long to get their offensive under way. Yang Hao led the way in overall command. Beneath him were Left Army Commander Li Rumei with 12,600 men, Right Army Commander Li Fangchun with 11,630 men, and Gao Ze with his Central Army of 11,690 men.[25] At Yang Hao's invitation King Sonjo accompanied them on horseback for the first few kilometers. The procession began in a suitably stately manner with Sonjo riding alongside Yang Hao. Then, upon exiting Seoul's South Gate, Yang spurred his horse into a gallop, forcing the Korean king to do likewise in order to keep up. Although not a skilled horseman, Sonjo managed to race along behind the Ming commander as far as the Han River and survived Yang's demonstration with his dignity intact.[26] What had Yang intended to prove by this? It is possible that he was annoyed at the grumbling the Koreans had been doing about the amount of time that he had taken to prepare for his advance. By challenging Sonjo to a race, Yang was perhaps driving home the point that the king and his ministers were scholars, not warriors, and thus should leave the conduct of the war to experts like him.

After this rather unseemly beginning, Yang Hao's army crossed the Han and began its long, cold trek toward the Japanese in the south. Upon receiving word that this force was on its way, Ma Gui's army left its camp north of Namwon and began moving east. The two forces met at Kyongju on January 26, 1598, to form a combined Ming army of forty thousand men. They were then joined by ten thousand Korean soldiers under Commander in Chief Kwon Yul, bringing the total to fifty thousand. This enormous force then proceeded on toward Ulsan, the easternmost link in the Japanese fortress chain and, it was hoped, an easy target for Yang Hao's vastly superior numbers.

The fighting commenced three days later, on January 29, as forward Chinese units neared the town of Ulsan. A feigned retreat drew the town's Japanese garrison charging out in pursuit, straight into a larger Chinese force that was waiting to the rear in crane wing battle formation. As many as five hundred Japanese were killed in the engagement. The rest retreated to the fortress at Tosan where the bulk of the Japanese force lay, one kilometer east. After gathering the heads of the slain, the Chinese marched into Ulsan and took possession of the town, then followed the fleeing Japanese on toward Tosan and set up camp outside the walls. Throughout the rest of the day additional Ming and Korean units continued to arrive on the scene, cutting off the fortress completely on the landward side. By the following morning the situation for the Japanese at Tosan had become extremely grave. Peering over the wall in the early light of dawn, the priest Keinen, attached to the Japanese contingent as a scholar and medical practitioner, observed that "the castle was surrounded by countless troops, who were deployed in any number of rings that encircled us. There were so many of them covering the terrain that one could no longer tell apart the plain and the hillsides."[27]

Kato Kiyomasa by this time had resumed command inside the fort. He had arrived from Sosaengpo by boat during the night, summoned by an urgent call for help from twenty-one-year-old Asano Yukinaga, who he had left in charge at Tosan. Kato managed to slip up the Taehwa River and into the fortress from the south before the Chinese and Koreans could seal off that side. The defensive situation inside the fortress, he soon discovered, was less than ideal, for construction was not yet complete. The enemy had arrived too soon. Of greatest immediate concern were the three gates that pierced the outer wall. At least one of these was unfinished and off its hinges, leaving a hole in the fortress's defenses. It was a weakness the allies quickly discovered and exploited when they began their attack on the following day. After a deafening dawn cannon barrage that started many fires within Tosan, Ming and Korean troops charged at the gap in the wall and began flooding into the fortress, forcing Kato and his men to fall back into the inner enclosure, abandoning their outer camp and a good deal of their supplies. The loss of much of their food, which had been scanty to begin with, would prove a severe hardship for the Japanese. For the moment, however, it bought them enough time to close and bar the gates of the inner fortress and array men along the walls, while the enemy troops outside paused to lay claim to the loot.

After this lull in the battle, the Chinese turned their attention to Tosan's more formidable inner citadel. They rushed at the walls in such numbers that, despite heavy losses, it seemed certain that they would clear the parapets and flood inside, using the bodies of their fallen comrades as a ramp. At one point, a Japanese account tells us, Ming forces managed to secure a large hook to the top of the wall, "and fifty or even a hundred men [took] hold of the attached rope to pull the wall down.

When this happened we fired on them from the side, but out of fifty men five or ten still hung on and pulled to the end. It has to be said that they are extremely brave warriors." Cannon fire, meanwhile, raked the top of the walls. A ball hit one of Kato's bodyguards, cutting him in two at the waist, leaving only his legs behind.[28] Somewhere inside, the priest Keinen huddled together with one of his companions, struggling to prepare himself for what seemed imminent death. "[C]lusters of Chinamen were clinging to the walls," he wrote in his diary, "climbing up them and into the fortress. As they burst inside, [my companion, the priest] Ryoshin said to me: 'Today is the Saint's Memorial Day. How happy we should be! We shall surely go to paradise on this blessed day.' He laughed in his joyful prayer, and his words gave me strength. . . . But my time had apparently not come yet; or was it that Japan's fate had not yet been sealed? The Chinamen withdrew."[29]

With Chinese and Korean losses approaching alarming proportions, the assault on the inner fortress was eventually called off and cannons dragged forward to batter down the walls. It was soon discovered, however, that even the largest guns could not touch the place. Since the citadel was built on high ground, the best the Chinese could do from their position lower down the hill was to level head-on shots straight into the impenetrable stone foundation or glancing blows off the more vulnerable upper walls, neither of which had any significant effect. After a steady barrage that lasted throughout the rest of the day, the effort was abandoned, and the two opposing armies settled down for the night.

All the fighting up to this point took place before Yang Hao and Ma Gui arrived on the scene. They were still in the rear, working together with Prime Minister Yu Song-nyong and Left Minister Yi Dok-hyong to secure supplies for their huge expeditionary force. When they finally arrived outside Tosan on or about February 1, they decided to place the fortress under siege rather than expend any more men in repeated frontal assaults. If they could keep their troops fed and their lines strong, the Japanese would starve and weaken and eventually submit. Ming commander Gao Ze was accordingly ordered to spread his Central Army along the east side of the fortress, and Li Fangchun and his Right Army were sent to the hold the west. The Left Army under Li Rumei moved to the south of Tosan to the banks of the Taehwa River to block reinforcements from arriving by sea. General Po Gui, finally, guarded the road from Pusan, which the Japanese garrisons farther south would have to use in any attempted counterattack by land.[30]

It was a sensible plan, this besieging of Tosan, for the Japanese inside the fortress were already desperately short of food. No longer able to receive supplies from outside, Kato and his men were forced to kill and eat their horses. When this source of nourishment was gone they probed the soil for roots and picked through old cooking fires for burnt grains of rice. Then they stripped the mud off the walls and ate it. Some are said to have even resorted to cannibalism. Water was also in very short supply. Whatever there was on hand at the start of the siege was issued mainly to the musketeers, who would be most needed to repel any coming attack. The rest were left to fend for themselves. According to Japanese commander Okochi Hidemoto's account of the siege, an enterprising water seller, evidently aware of the growing desperation of the Japanese inside the fortress, approached the wall one day offering water at the astronomical price of fifteen silver coins per cup. Those few men with any money bought as much water as they could afford. The others drank the urine that these lucky few later passed.[31]

And then there was the cold. On February 3 a stiff wind blew up and the temperature fell. The Japanese defenders, already weakened by starvation and thirst, now began to freeze. With little fuel on hand to use for fires, the men suffered terribly from frostbite, their hands and feet blackening and swelling to such a size that the flesh burst open and fluid leaked out. Many would lose fingers and toes before the ordeal was over. Some froze to death where they sat.

As the siege progressed, the allied troops stationed outside Tosan began to kill or capture a growing number of Japanese soldiers who were driven in their desperation to steal out of the fortress at night in search of water and food. Some were cut down as they picked through the possessions of the dead that lay unburied outside the walls. Others were ambushed at neighboring streams and wells. Commander Kim Ung-so reportedly rounded up as many as one hundred enemy soldiers a night at the well he was ordered to guard. All of these men were thin and weak and unable to fight, and most only too glad to surrender.[32]

By the fourth of February the siege of Tosan seemed well on the way to achieving success. According to Japanese soldiers who were captured or surrendered, the defenders inside the fortress were now so weakened by hunger and disease that of the original ten thousand-man force only a thousand were in any condition to fight.[33] Kato Kiyomasa and his first contingent, it seemed, were now beyond being able to help themselves. Their only hope lay with their comrades to the south.

Since the beginning of the siege the other garrisons in the Japanese fortress chain had in fact been attempting to come to the aid of the defenders at Tosan. The most aggressive approaches were made from seaward by squadrons of Japanese ships that ventured up the Taehwa River to the south side of the fort. The forays were small at first, just twenty or so ships from nearby Sosaengpo that Li Rumei and his Left Army were able to drive off with cannon fire. As the days passed, however, more ships began to arrive from other Japanese strongholds further along the coast, notably a fleet with two thousand fighting men aboard sent by Konishi Yukinaga all the way from Sunchon. They advanced up the Taehwa River daily with the tide, putting increasing strain on Li Rumei and his men and raising concerns that an amphibious counterattack might not be far off. Army units from other strongholds in the Japanese fortress belt, meanwhile, were marching north to apply pressure from inland. Kuroda Nagamasa sent a force up from his fortress at Yangsan. So did Hachizuka Iemasa, Ukita Hideie, and Mori Hidemoto from their own respective camps. These gathering reinforcements did not attack the numerically superior Chinese-Korean army surrounding Tosan, but instead made a great show of their presence by planting banners and flags on nearby hilltops in the hope that the allies would grow nervous and lift their siege.

This application of pressure eventually had its intended effect. Yang Hao began to fear that if the Japanese forces advancing on Ulsan launched a coordinated counterattack from both the land and the sea, his own forces would at the very least suffer heavy losses before fighting them off, and might even be defeated. Yang had not come to Ulsan for that. He had come expecting to win a relatively easy victory with minimal loss, after which they would move on down the enemy's fortress belt to claim a second prize. The prospects for maintaining the siege, moreover, were now looking grim. To begin with, his own men were suffering from the bitter cold almost as badly as were the Japanese. Feeding the fifty thousand Chinese and Korean soldiers camped outside the fortress was also proving difficult, particularly in the depths of winter with nothing growing in the fields. Obtaining fodder for his horses was yet another concern. During just the first week of the siege a thousand of the animals collapsed and died.

With the threat of a Japanese counterattack now looming large, and with it becoming increasingly difficult to maintain his own army in the field, Yang Hao decided that action rather than waiting was the most prudent course. He either had to take Tosan at once or lift his seige and fall back to Kyongju. He accordingly launched one final, all-out assault on February 19, beginning at dawn. Inside the fortress most of the defenders who were not yet dead huddled together in a collective stupor, too weakened by starvation and thirst and disease to pick up their arms and move to the walls. The one exception was the corps of musketeers. At the start of the siege Kato Kiyomasa had ordered that these crucially important soldiers be allotted most of the available food and water, a brutal but prescient decision that would now save the garrison from annihilation. When the Ming soldiers outside began their charge these musketeers still had the energy to put up a strong defense, driving back wave after wave with a withering hail of lead. Yang kept up the attack for three hours, until five hundred of his men lay dead or dying in heaps at the base of the wall.

By midmorning the desire to fight had drained out of Yang Hao. Discouraged by his inability to take the fort and increasingly worried by the Japanese reinforcements approaching up the Taehwa River to the front and massing in the hills behind, the Ming commander ordered his men to lift the siege and pull back. The withdrawal did not go well. As the Ming troops began breaking camp, word spread that Japanese troops were storming ashore from ships at the south of the fort. Fears of a Japanese counterattack sent men running north toward Kyongju in an undisciplined retreat.

The Korean troops at Tosan had been told nothing of Yang's order to withdraw. They were left to deduce the state of affairs from the commotion they could observe in the Chinese camps, the cavalry units riding off, the smoke rising from piles of burning supplies, the cries of the wounded being left behind. The Japanese units camped on the nearby hills saw what was happening as well. Sensing that the advantage was turning their way, they charged after the retreating allied troops, cutting down large numbers of stragglers, particularly among the Koreans, and sending the rest into flight.[34]

It was a beaten and demoralized allied army that straggled north into Kyongju. Subsequent estimates of the number of Chinese and Korean soldiers killed during the three-week siege would range from eighteen hundred to ten thousand, the lower figure being suggested by those officials eager to support Yang Hao, the higher by those just as eager to bring him down. The truth probably lies somewhere between, in the range of several thousand killed and at least as many injured.[35] Whatever the number, the setback left Yang Hao thinking only of retreat. He had lost too many men; maintaining his army in the field in winter was too difficult; the Japanese were too tenacious; and—a favorite excuse among the Chinese—the Korean troops were too unreliable. After holding discussions with his generals, the supreme Ming commander decided to return to Seoul for the time being and resume the offensive some time later in the year. He set out for the capital toward the end of February, leaving behind a garrison of Ming troops under Ma Gui and Koreans under Kwon Yul at Kyongju to ensure that the Japanese remained on the coast. He would not return.

Back at Tosan the Japanese were emerging from the shock of their terrible ordeal. Their losses had been horrific. According to one estimate, fewer than a thousand men survived from the original garrison of ten thousand. Many had been killed in the fighting; still more had been carried away by hunger, thirst, exposure, and disease. Still, the siege for them had been a triumph. The fact that Tosan's half-starved defenders could fight off an army many times its size demonstrated once again, and this time in a most unequivocal manner, the fighting spirit of the Japanese warrior and the superiority of the Japanese musket.

Just days after the battle, Asano Yukinaga sent a letter to his father in Japan saying, "When troops come [to Korea] from the province of Kai, have them bring as many guns as possible, for no other equipment is needed. Give strict orders that all men, even the *samurai*, carry guns."[36] This was a remarkable suggestion, that samurai warriors carry guns. Since the introduction of the musket into Japanese warfare fifty years before, its use had been relegated to the ranks of the ashigaru, the foot soldiers. The higher-ranking samurai class, while not questioning for a moment the value of the weapon, rarely condescended to use it personally, preferring instead the sword and lance and bow. Any country bumpkin, after all, could be taught to fire a musket in just a few days, whereas it took years to master the more traditional weapons of war. A samurai's skill in the use of these weapons was a great point of pride, which is why in normal circumstances he declined to wield a gun. But of course the siege of Tosan had been anything but normal. It was the most desperate struggle the Japanese had endured in Korea since the start of the war. That Asano, writing just days after the battle, was urging that samurai now be armed with muskets is an indication of the key role that weapon had played in the victory—and in turn of what a very close thing the siege had been.

The victory at Tosan had in fact been such a close thing for the Japanese that it came to be regarded by some as a miracle. In his account of the battle, Commander Okochi Hidemoto wrote that the ability of himself and his comrades to hold out against such appalling odds "certainly was not something achieved by mere humans." Rather it was a "divine mystery" aided by "Japan's ninety-eight thousand gods of war," and in turn a sign that what they were doing in Korea was part of a "sacred destiny" that Hideyoshi was leading them toward.[37]

But of course the survival of the garrison at Tosan was no divine mystery. It was an example of what desperate men could do when adequately armed and fighting for their lives. For the average foot soldier the engagement had been nothing more than a horrifying time in hell, a journey through what the priest Keinen described as a "Buddha-less world."[38] As they watched the besieging army retreat, then welcomed their own comrades into the fortress and accepted their offers of food, many of the defenders who were still ambulatory suddenly found themselves unable to stand. With the weeks of unremitting strain and privation finally at an end, the remaining wisps of strength holding them together gave way entirely and they collapsed to the ground. Many of these traumatized survivors would eventually be restored to health and return to Japan. The memory of Tosan, however, would remain with them always. For years afterward veterans of the siege would be plagued by nightmares of what they had endured, fighting for their lives again and again whenever they lay down to sleep.[39]

CHAPTER 28

"Even Osaka Castle
is only a dream"

SUPREME MING COMMANDER YANG HAO was not unduly discouraged by the rout of his army at Tosan. Although he had failed to take the fortress, the Japanese inside had been made to suffer terribly, and by all accounts had lost a lot of men. The prospects for ultimate victory, moreover, seemed almost certain, for Yang's own forces were steadily increasing while the strength of the Japanese was slowly being whittled away. Fresh Ming forces were at that very moment moving across China's eastern frontier to the Yalu River, which marked the border between the Middle Kingdom and Korea. Among them was a contingent of Sichuan troops under "Big Sword" Liu Ting and reinforcements from China's northeastern province of Liaodong under General Dong Yiyuan. Naval units under Admirals Chen Lin and Deng Zilong, meanwhile, were making their way along the Chinese coast from the southern province of Guangdong and the eastern province Zhejiang. They would cross the Yellow Sea and reach Korea in early May.[1]

Yang Hao thus returned north to Seoul in late February 1598 in an upbeat mood. The retreat from Tosan had been only a temporary setback. He had every intention, after resting his men and incorporating the newly arrived reinforcements into his command, of launching a second, more powerful offensive, probably sometime in June when the weather would be warmer and supplies easier to obtain. Yang's civilian superior, Xing Jie, agreed with his assessment, and sent a report to

Beijing highly supportive of Yang's prosecution of the war. The Korean government also supported Yang. It had been thanks to his leadership, after all, that the second Japanese invasion had been blunted and the "bandits" confined to their forts in the south. Unlike his predecessor Li Rusong, moreover, Yang now seemed intent on finishing the job of driving Hideyoshi's army entirely out of Korea. Despite their disappointment over the retreat from Tosan and the reservations they had over some of the decisions he had made, the Koreans therefore continued to think highly of Yang Hao and continued to regard him as the best man for the job. All that he needed was a little more time.

Unfortunately for Yang, Xing, and the Koreans, the setback at Tosan was not so quickly forgotten in Beijing. Too many men had been killed to overlook. A relatively low-ranking official from the Board of War named Ding Yingtai was accordingly dispatched to Seoul to investigate the situation and draw up a report.

Yang Hao sensed danger. Ding was known to belong to the faction that opposed China's military involvement in Korea, and so it was certain that he would use his report to attack Yang and in turn those officials who were supportive of the war. To protect himself from this anticipated assault, Yang sent a letter of resignation to Beijing citing the usual excuse of poor health. Xing Jie came to his support, dispatching a second report to the emperor praising Yang for his hard work and courage. After reading Xing's assessment of China's supreme commander in Korea, the Wanli emperor reaffirmed his confidence in Yang and refused to accept his resignation.[2]

Ding Yingtai in the meantime had finished his investigation in Seoul and was on his way home to Beijing. The report he carried with him would soon cause a storm.

The Japanese in their chain of forts along the south coast of Korea were not feeling overly confident in the wake of the siege of Tosan. While it was heartening that the fortress had held out and the massive Chinese and Korean army been driven back, the victory had been costly, and the entire engagement a very close thing that could easily have turned into disaster. Judging from reports of additional Ming reinforcements massing in the north, it also seemed only a matter of time before a second, even larger offensive was launched against them. On March 3, 1598, three weeks after the fight for Tosan, a number of Hideyoshi's daimyo commanders thus sent a letter back to Japan requesting permission to abandon some of their more vulnerable fortresses so that they could consolidate their forces at a few key points.[3]

Hideyoshi initially refused. He had launched his second invasion of Korea to punish the Koreans for not acceding to his demands, and to show the Chinese that he was a force to be reckoned with, a force fully equal to the Wanli emperor on his Celestial Throne. Hideyoshi's purpose, in short, was to demonstrate his power. That is why he denied the request from his commanders to close some of their forts and consolidate their troops, for this would send his enemies entirely the wrong message: that he was vulnerable and weak rather than indomitable and strong.

On the other hand, the taiko had already achieved the basic objective of his second invasion. The very act of sending his armies back to Korea had shown Beijing that he remained as strong and as determined as ever and could march through their tributary state any time he wished. As for punishing the Koreans, the gruesome Mound of Noses in Kyoto was ample proof of this. So what was the point of prolonging the campaign?

In fact there was none. With his demonstration of power already made, it was now mainly a question of how best to bring the affair to a close in a suitably face-saving way. Hideyoshi clearly felt that the closure of fortresses so soon after the end of the Ming winter offensive would undermine his message of strength and resolve, and so he would not approve it. Leaving his troops as they were in Korea, however, was proving increasingly untenable. First, there was the problem of supplies. With Korea's southern regions now devastated and depopulated after two invasions and six years of war, it was impossible for the Japanese forces stationed there to adhere to the taiko's directive to live off the land. Much of the food they needed had to be shipped from Japan, a tremendous logistical burden considering the number of men to be fed. Hideyoshi also was undoubtedly sensitive to the risk he was running in keeping his army in Korea. Even if his troops managed to beat off a second Ming offensive, they would probably suffer heavy casualties and add little to the demonstration of power that had already been made. If they were defeated, conversely, untold damage would be done to Hideyoshi's and in turn Japan's reputation.

Considering these two factors—the difficulties of maintaining an army in Korea and the balance of risk and reward—it was only a matter of time before the taiko accepted his commanders' advice that a change had to be made in the deployment of his troops. On June 26, four months after the end of the Ming offensive and so ostensibly not precipitated by it, Hideyoshi dispatched orders to Korea recalling roughly half his troops to Japan, including the contingents led by Ukita Hideie, Mori Hidemoto, and Hachizuka Iemasa. Supreme Commander Kobayakawa Hideaki was also withdrawn. Forces remaining in Korea were encamped at Ulsan (10,000 men under Kato Kiyomasa); Sosaengpo (5,000 under Kuroda Nagamasa); Pusan (5,000 under Mori Yoshinari); Kimhae and Changwon (12,000 under Nabeshima Naoshige and Nabeshima Katsushige); Koje Island (1,000 under Yanagawa Tsunanobu); Kosong (7,000 under Tachibana Munetora); Sachon (10,000 under Shimazu Yoshihiro); Namhae Island (1,000 under So Yoshitoshi); and Sunchon (13,700 under Konishi Yukinaga)—a total of 64,700 men.[4]

Japan's war in Korea still had half a year to go. These troop withdrawals in June, however, marked the beginning of the end. From this point on Hideyoshi's main concern would be extracting himself from the peninsula with his dignity intact.

Eight months had now passed since Yi Sun-sin and the remnants of the Korean navy had stopped the Japanese fleet in the Battle of Myongnyang. It had been an important victory, for not only had Yi's thirteen vessels prevailed over an enemy squadron of two hundred ships and more, they discouraged the Japanese from making any further attempt to advance westward along the coast. Upon receiving word of the Myongnyang engagement at his headquarters in Seoul, supreme Ming commander Yang Hao observed that "There has never been such a great victory in recent years," and ordered that a roll of red brocade and some silver be presented to Yi Sun-sin as a reward for his service. The Korean government meanwhile started mulling over the possibility of promoting Yi to junior first rank, the second-highest court rank in the land and normally reserved for the loftiest civil officials. Yi's supporters pushed for the promotion, and rumors drifted south into Yi's camp that the reward would soon be his. Not everyone, however, was eager to see him promoted. Certain government ministers claimed that Yi's rank was already high enough, and that to raise him any higher would leave the government with nothing to confer on him when the war was finally won. Although they did not say so, these ministers may also have been reticent to see Yi placed on too high a pedestal, as this would further highlight their own mistake in throwing him in prison in early 1597 and dooming the Korean navy by turning it over to Won Kyun. Whatever the reason, Yi's promotion was ultimately blocked. When the reward list was delivered to his base on December 24, most of Yi's officers were on it, including An Wui, one of the captains who had lagged behind in the Battle of Myongnyang. Yi's own name was not there. All he received was a commendation from the king and the presents from Yang Hao. Yi gives no hint of disappointment in his diary, but surely he must have felt slighted.[5]

After the Battle of Myongnyang, Yi Sun-sin led his diminutive naval forces thirty kilometers north from the scene of the engagement to establish a temporary base on the island of Pohwa, off what is today the city of Mokpo. An Wui, now promoted to command of the Cholla Right Navy, was sent forward to his new station off the southern coast of Cholla to guard against a possible second Japanese advance toward the Yellow Sea. Not long after this, An for some reason abandoned his assigned position and fell back with his few ships to Yi's base on Pohwa-do. Yi Sun-sin was annoyed by this, for An Wui "has left the sea lanes entirely open to the Japanese." In his report to Seoul Yi clearly tied his decision to move his own base forward to this failure on the part of An to hold his assigned position in the front.[6]

On May 23, 1598, Yi Sun-sin led his ships east to establish a new base on the island of Kogum-do, fifty kilometers closer to the Japanese fortress belt but still well clear of their westernmost stronghold at Sunchon. Yang Hao in Seoul was of the opinion that Yi should keep advancing and reclaim the Korean navy's former base on Hansan Island, now in the heart of the Japanese perimeter and therefore a convenient launching point for strikes against their forts.[7] Yi did not agree. Dire circumstances had forced him to expose himself and his men to extreme peril in the Battle of Myongnyang. With the Japanese confined to their chain of forts, there was no need to take such risks again by moving ahead to Hansan. Yi's main concern now was to rebuild his navy in a place of safety. Kogum-do, he believed, was the ideal spot for this. The island was an even better base than Hansan-do, Yi observed, first for its strategic location in the waters off Cholla Province, second for its mountainous and thus easily defensible terrain, and third for the excellent views in every direction that the tops of those mountains afforded.[8]

Yi's most pressing task upon arriving at Kogum-do was to secure food for the eight thousand men that had already flocked to serve under him in the wake of the victory at Myongnyang. The ample population and farmland on the neighboring islands of Chi-do and Choyak-do held the promise of future supplies. To meet his more immediate needs, Yi instituted a system of passes for the hundreds of refugee boats traversing the sea lanes around Kogum-do, many of them on their way home after fleeing the Japanese naval advance. Large vessels were required to pay a levy of three *sok* of rice (a *sok* is equal to about five bushels); medium-sized ships two sok, and small ships one. Most were glad to pay, for the presence of the Korean navy in the area meant safety. In this manner Yi Sun-sin collected ten thousand sok of rice in the space of just ten days, enough to feed his men for the next several months.[9]

Yi now had men willing to fight and food enough to feed them. What he still did not have was ships. He had managed to stop the Japanese advance with just thirteen vessels, but to go on the offensive would require many more. Yi had set men to work building new warships and scraping together copper and iron to forge new cannons not long after the Battle of Myongnyang, when hope began to return that the Korean navy might survive.[10] Ming commander Yang Hao in Seoul aided the effort by dispatching emergency orders and presumably funds to shipyards nationwide, orders that by March of 1598 were already starting to be filled. By the twenty-eighth of the month the shipyard at Cholsan in the northwestern province of Pyongan had completed eight of an expected twenty ships; Changsangot in Hwanghae Province had churned out forty vessels and had just ten to go; Anmingot in Chungchong Province was only beginning work, but was expected to turn out ten; Byonsan in Cholla Province had refurbished thirteen vessels it had on hand and thus had just seven more ships to build from scratch to meet its quota of twenty. Shortly after Yi Sun-sin's move to Kogum-do, therefore, sixty-one warships were finished and ready for delivery, and another thirty-nine were being built. The Korean navy was on the verge of returning to respectable strength.[11]

In April of 1598 news of a rebellion in Liaodong Province on China's eastern frontier necessitated the postponement of the second Ming offensive, initially planned to begin in June. "Army Gate" Xing Jie hastened north from Seoul to take charge of the situation, and the troops then still on their way to Korea were diverted to the trouble spot until order was restored. Most of the Ming troops that had participated in the assault on Tosan were in the meantime sent south again following a month of recuperation in Seoul to establish camps in towns across central and northern Kyongsang Province. General Ma Gui himself returned south in April and made his headquarters at Sangju, halfway between the capital and the Japanese fortress chain. He and his men would spend the next several months waiting—waiting for reinforcements to arrive so that the second offensive could begin.[12]

Ming naval forces in the meantime were amassing along Korea's eastern coast. It had taken the Chinese government a long time to arrange for these squadrons to be sent across the Yellow Sea; throughout the first several months of the second invasion it was considered necessary to keep all naval forces on alert in home waters to protect China from a possible direct Japanese attack. Beijing, after all, was only two hundred kilometers from the coast, a distance the Japanese had shown they could traverse in ten days or less. The first fleet movements therefore did not take place until the fall of 1597, and even then were intended solely to protect China's own eastern coastline rather than its embattled vassal across the Yellow Sea. One hundred and fifty ships from Zhejiang Province were initially sent north to the port of Lushun (Port Arthur) on the tip of the Liaoning Peninsula. They were later reinforced by two thousand men from the Nanjing fleet and then by an additional two thousand men aboard eighty-two ships from the Wusung fleet. Few if any of these vessels were proper warships.

China's provincial authorities, as fearful as their counterparts in Beijing of a Japanese attack, were unwilling to compromise home defense by releasing the strongest vessels in their fleets. The squadrons assembled at Lushun were thus composed of lightly built galleys, useful for ferrying troops and supplies but not really suitable for naval warfare.[13]

Chinese fears of a Japanese attack against their own coastline began to abate with the news of Yi Sun-sin's victory in the Battle of Myongnyang in October 1597. When it became clear that the Japanese would not be entering the Yellow Sea, Beijing issued orders for its naval forces at Lushun to move south and take up positions along Korea's east coast. Most of these ships would remain here for the rest of the war, a forward buffer to guard against any future Japanese advance by sea, but still well clear of the front.

Admiral Chen Lin was the man selected to command those Ming naval forces that would eventually join Yi Sun-sin at his Kogum Island base. Chen was a grizzled old campaigner who had served in both the Ming army and navy going all the way back into the early 1560s. He had seen plenty of action in his time against rebellious frontier tribesmen and raiders, was reportedly an expert in the use of artillery,[14] and had won special honors for his success in combating the pirates who had for so many years plagued China's long and vulnerable coast. Like most Ming commanders, however, his career was not unblemished. Zealous government censors had seen to that. In 1583 a mutiny by some of Chen's troops, precipitated by his attempt to restore discipline which had grow lax during several years of peace, led to his being severely criticized and charged with treating his men too harshly. The charges were later dropped, but with his reputation tarnished Chen found it necessary to resign. He was not reappointed until after the start of the war in Korea in 1592. His return to command lasted for just one year. In 1593 he was dismissed on charges of trying to buy favor by giving an expensive gift to the Minister of War. This second period in the wilderness lasted until 1596. In that year Chen's supporters in Beijing managed to get him restored to command to put down a tribal rebellion in Guangxi Province on the border with Vietnam. Chen took the post but declined the regular troops that came with it. Instead he summoned trusted soldiers from his former command and outfitted and supplied them with his own money. Chen's subsequent success in quelling the rebellion, coupled with his willingness to nearly bankrupt himself to do so, proved an effective antidote to the charges that he was unprincipled and greedy, and led to a loftier appointment as naval command of the Guangdong fleet, guarding the coast near what would one day be Hong Kong.[15]

Chen Lin arrived at Tongjak at the mouth of the Han River in May of 1598. King Sonjo, accompanied by a retinue of officials and soldiers, made the journey out from Seoul to receive him, and expressed satisfaction as he reviewed 3,400 fighting men standing in formation under the admiral's command. Compared to them, the king observed with proper self-deprecation, the Korean army looked like "children playing." Then, feeling obliged to reciprocate with a show of his kingdom's homegrown martial talent, Sonjo ordered some of the Korean soldiers in attendance to give a demonstration of swordsmanship. Chen Lin was clearly unimpressed. As he watched the display, he deeply embarrassed the Koreans by laughing and being openly scornful of what he regarded as a sorry lack of skill. With that the affair came to an end and King Sonjo and his ministers returned to Seoul, shaking their heads at the quality of man that Beijing had sent to their aid. Word soon spread to watch out for Chen Lin—that the Ming admiral was arrogant, rude, and likely avaricious.[16]

Chen Lin left Tongjak and headed south in July to join forces with the Korean navy under Yi Sun-sin. Korean sources say that he set off with five hundred ships. If this number is correct then many of them were probably small galleys and transports. Chen's contribution to the coming campaign in fact would be more in terms of manpower than ships. Five thousand men from the Guangdong squadron would accompany him south aboard six warships and an indeterminate number of lighter craft.[17] In the battles to come Chen would place most of his men aboard Yi Sun-sin's heavy warships to fight alongside Korean crews, an indication that most of the ships he had brought from China were probably unsuitable for combat and thus held in the rear.

In April rumors began to circulate in Korea that Toyotomi Hideyoshi had died at Fushimi Castle in Japan. The news had been picked up by a spy from one of the Japanese fortresses and was duly relayed to Seoul. The Korean government discounted the report as an unsubstantiated rumor. So did supreme Ming commander Yang Hao.[18]

They were right. Hideyoshi was still alive—although far from in good health. He was in fact slipping fast. In a short note to an acquaintance dated July 20, 1598, the taiko expressed anguish at his rapidly deteriorating health. "As I am ill and feel lonely," he wrote, "I have taken up the brush. I have not eaten for fifteen days and I am in distress. Since I went out for amusement yesterday to a place where some construction work is going on, my illness has become worse and worse, and I feel I am gradually weakening. . . . [T]his one single letter is worth ten thousand letters written in normal circumstances."[19] It was one of the last letters the taiko would have the strength to write.

In July and again in August Hideyoshi's wife O-Ne arranged for the imperial court to hold a sacred *kagura* dance to pray for her husband's recovery. Emperor Go-Yozei sent orders to temples and shrines in and around Kyoto for prayers to be offered to restore the taiko to health. But nothing seemed to help. Hideyoshi was dying.[20]

As his final days wound down, Hideyoshi's thoughts focused increasingly on his son. Hideyori was still not quite five, and thus at the mercy of those men entrusted to protect him and his interests once Hideyoshi himself was gone. As he had done in 1595 and in 1596, the taiko now called upon his senior daimyo to again renew their oaths to serve his heir Hideyori just as they had served him. The first of these was signed on August 17, 1598:

> Item: I will serve Hideyori. [My] service [to him], just like [my service to] the taiko, shall be without negligence. Addendum: I will know no duplicity or other thoughts at all.
>
> Item: As for the laws and [Hideyoshi's] orders as they have been declared up to the present time, I will not violate them in the slightest.
>
> Item: Inasmuch as I understand it to be for the sake of public affairs, I will discard personal enmities toward my peers and will not act on my own interests.
>
> Item: I will not establish factions among [my] associates. Even if

there are lawsuits, quarrels, or disputes and [they involve] parents and children, brothers, or complainants whom I know, I resolve, knowing no partiality, [to act] in conformity with the law.

Item: I will not return willfully to my fief without asking leave.[21]

Would these men really serve young Hideyori once the taiko was dead? Hideyoshi's repeated demand for loyalty oaths indicates he feared they would not. Japan in 1598 was a loose federation of powerful men, each possessing large armies, enormous holdings of land, and loyal only to Toyotomi Hideyoshi. Allowing them this degree of personal wealth and power had been one of the key factors behind Hideyoshi's success in unifying Japan, for it had made serving him an acceptable proposition—better than fighting bitter and costly wars at the risk of losing all. There was one glaring weakness in this system, however: it all depended on Hideyoshi's existence at the center. It was his commanding presence that kept rival daimyo in check and the unity of Japan intact. Remove Hideyoshi from the picture, and what was left? On the one hand a crowd of ambitious and independent-minded daimyo. And on the other a boy scarcely five years old.

In the month of July a report reached Seoul that a huge swarm of insects had descended from the north to blanket all the fields in Yonchon near the Imjin River north of Seoul. The same thing had happened back in 1592, the year imjin, just prior to the start of the first Japanese invasion and six years of war. Many considered the reappearance of these insects a sign that another calamity was about to occur.[22]

Chinese Board of War official Ding Yingtai was now back in Beijing to deliver his report on his investigation into the Battle of Tosan. This document, which Ding presented to the Celestial Throne on July 6, was an all-out attack not just against Yang Hao, but against the entire pro-war faction in Beijing, all the way up to Grand Secretaries Zhang Wei and Shen Yiguan, the highest-ranking officials in the land. Yang, Ding charged, had tried to cover up the magnitude of the casualties he had suffered at Tosan; Zhang and Shen had participated in the cover-up, so they were guilty too. Yang had fled the battle, and was thus a coward;

Zhang and Shen had hidden the truth of his flight from the emperor, submitting only those reports that made the commander look good. Yang had written false reports; Zhang and Shen had willingly accepted them. Yang had secured his appointment in the first place through bribes; Zhang's were the palms he had greased. The list went on and on, a total of twenty-eight charges in all for which Ding felt Yang should be tried, plus ten other errors for which the commander should feel "ashamed."

Ding's attack was so inflammatory and so wide reaching that there was no way for the Ming government now to lay the matter aside. Yang Hao first of all had to be dismissed. A messenger was dispatched to Seoul to relieve him of command and order him back to China to await the verdict in his case. Ding Yingtai, the new poster boy for the antiwar and in turn anti-Zhang and -Shen faction, was then sent back to Korea to conduct a more thorough investigation, not just into the Battle of Tosan but into the prosecution of the war as a whole. This time Grand Secretaries Zhang and Shen made sure that the dangerous Ding did not go alone. Xu Guanlan, a Board of War official like Ding but from the opposing prowar faction which supported Zhang and Shen, was sent along to conduct a parallel investigation of his own.

Ten days later, on July 16, a copy of Ding's report reached Seoul. On the twentieth a member of Yang Hao's staff met with Korean officials to fill them in on the political struggle that was taking place in Beijing. On one side, he explained, was the prowar faction led by Grand Secretary Zhang Wei. It considered the threat posed by Japan to be real and China's loyal vassal Korea well worth saving, and was thus intent on seeing the war through to the end. On the other side was the antiwar faction led by Board of War Minister Shi Xing and Grand Secretary Zhao Zhigao. They contended that Hideyoshi had never planned to move against China. This was just a Korean exaggeration designed to draw Beijing into a regional struggle that was really none of its concern. The Ming government therefore should stop sending military aid to Korea and end its involvement in the war.

All this was devastating news for the government in Seoul. Ding Yingtai, it seemed, was their mortal enemy, a "malicious specter" as King Sonjo called him, out to ruin the war effort when the struggle was on the verge of being won. It was also considered a grievous insult that Ding and the antiwar faction he spoke for should besmirch the integrity and loyalty of Korea with baseless charges that it had lied about the threat posed by Japan. This stung like a slap in the face. After long discussion, it was decided that the situation was so critical that some sort of counter-memorial had to be drawn up and sent to Beijing protesting Ding's attack. After this was done, a public demonstration was organized in the streets of Seoul to show support for Yang Hao, and a petition was presented to the Army Gate headquarters of Xing Jie protesting Yang's dismissal, all in the knowledge that everything would be promptly reported to Beijing. All this was done, of course, to counter Ding's attack more than to protect Yang Hao. Yang was now little more than a pawn in a bigger game of political intrigue.[23]

Although the antiwar faction in Beijing was now on the offensive, it was still a long way from overturning China's policy of prosecuting the war. Nothing therefore was preventing those Ming units previously dispatched to Korea from continuing on their way to reinforce the troops already near the front. These units had been diverted north into Liaodong Province while en route to Korea in April to help quell a rebellion that had unexpectedly arisen on the Manchurian frontier. By June order had been restored in Liaodong, and the Korea-bound troops were released and ordered to proceed to Seoul.

It was therefore not until July of 1598, many months after setting out from his base in western China, that "Big Sword" Liu Ting arrived in Seoul with the twenty thousand soldiers under his command, mainly troops from the province of Sichuan and tribal fighters from the regions bordering Burma and Thailand. This was Liu's second visit to Korea. He had served in the kingdom for two years during the first half of the war, impressing the Koreans with his upright and gentlemanly conduct, his ability to discipline his men, and his staunch refusal to accept any gift—a wise precaution considering that he had already been denied promotion twice during his career after being censored for taking bribes.[24] Liu's relations with the Koreans would not be quite so cordial upon his return to Seoul. The general himself was undoubtedly feeling a good deal of strain, for with the increasing strength of the antiwar

faction in Beijing he could ill afford to make even the slightest mistake
or suffer anything that could be perceived as defeat. The Koreans on
their side were feeling some understandable resentment toward the
Chinese in the wake of the Ding Yingtai attack and the realization that
elements in Beijing questioned the loyalty of their kingdom. It was thus
perhaps inevitable that friction should arise between "Big Sword" Liu
and his Korean hosts.

Shortly after arriving in Seoul Liu submitted a request to the Korean
government that Crown Prince Kwanghae and a number of top government ministers accompany him south to the front. The Koreans
made no reply. That made Liu angry. Why, he wanted to know, don't
representatives from the Korean government come and consult with me
so that we can make plans for winning this war? This brought out a
reluctant band of officials led by Yi Dok-hyong, now Minister of the
Right. Liu explained that the outcome of the coming offensive would
hinge on the availability of supplies. His army obviously needed food
to fight; without it they would be useless. If he proceeded south on his
own, the local people and officials would be reluctant to provide him
with the supplies he needed. If the crown prince and top ministers
accompanied him, on the other hand, and took on the task of requisi-
tioning supplies, the respect that the locals felt for them would ensure
that Liu's troops were adequately provided for.

Yi Dok-hyong and his colleagues hemmed and hawed. Yes, they
conceded, food was indeed short in the south, and so we need to put a
great deal of effort into obtaining it. But the crown prince's health is
not good, so it would be imprudent to send him. Nor would it be wise to
send the top ministers, for that would remove the head from the government and bring affairs to a standstill in Seoul.

Liu erupted. "In any other country," he roared, "the king himself
would go to the front! But you Koreans, you won't even send your
crown prince!"

The Koreans refused to budge on the matter and eventually Liu
calmed down. "Here is the situation," he said at last. "If you give me
enough supplies, I can do my job. If you don't, I cannot. I presently
have 20,000 men with me here. Add to this the troops already in the
south and the total is 25,000. Even if we forget about their food

requirements for next month, if the Korean government can come up with enough supplies to keep my men going for just three months, from September through November, we can succeed. That is all I ask."[25]

Liu was evidently unsatisfied with the assurances he received, for in a meeting with King Sonjo five days later he reiterated his demand that the crown prince and officials accompany him south. Sonjo politely declined. Liu said that the crown prince could come alone, without any of the ministers. Sonjo again declined. Liu then said that having even just one of the three top government ministers along would do. Sonjo seemed more amenable to this idea, so Liu went on to consider the options. Prime Minister Yu Song-nyong, he said, is the head of the government, so he should remain in Seoul. Nor can Minister of the Left Yi Won-ik be spared, for he is responsible for liaison with Xing Jie at "Army Gate." Minister of the Right Yi Dok-hyong, on the other hand, is responsible for liaison with Yang Hao's office, and Yang has now been dismissed. So surely Dok-hyong can be spared.[26]

In the present climate of tension the Koreans were feeling less inclined to concede to every Ming demand. Liu's almost rude assertiveness left them in an even less obliging mood. His forceful request was nevertheless neither unreasonable nor unexpected. Since early in the war top government ministers had frequently accompanied Ming armies for the specific purpose of arranging supplies. Prime Minister Yu Song-nyong himself had served in this capacity on numerous occasions, most recently accompanying Yang Hao's army south in January of 1598 in their failed attempt to dislodge the Japanese at Tosan. So while Sonjo would say no more to Liu's request than he would "think about it," the Korean government ultimately had little choice but to agree. When "Big Sword" Liu Ting set out for the south in early August, Minister of the Right Yi Dok-hyong went with him.

Admiral Chen Lin arrived on Korea's south coast on August 17 to join forces with Supreme Naval Commander Yi Sun-sin at Yi's base on the island of Kogum-do. Both Yi and his superiors in Seoul were apprehensive about how effective this joining of forces would be, for the Koreans had developed a generally unfavorable impression of Chen's character and ability. From their initial encounters with the man the

Korean government found him to be arrogant, temperamental, and overly quick to punish. General Liu Ting additionally informed them that Chen appeared to have little grasp of strategy and as such was not much of a leader. "When I talked to the admiral earlier," Liu said, "he only boasted about capturing a handful of Japanese pirates, and tried to talk it up into a big victory."[27] There was thus concern in Seoul that Chen's presence in the south, far from helping the Korean cause, might actually prove a hindrance, particularly if the admiral tried to assert his authority over the more capable Yi Sun-sin.[28]

The Korean naval commander, having been forewarned by Seoul to treat Chen Lin with care, prepared a banquet to honor the Ming fleet's arrival, then led his ships out to meet Chen at sea and conduct him personally into port. This respectful hospitality went over well with Chen. By the end of the evening he and his men were stuffed with food and happily drunk, and cordial feelings reigned between the two camps.

Two days later a report was received that more than a hundred Japanese vessels were probing west along the coast and nearing Kogum Island. The Ming admiral and Yi Sun-sin immediately set out together at the head of their respective fleets. The report was quickly proved false; only two enemy ships were sighted, both of which managed to get away unscathed. Yi and Chen spent one night in the area then returned to base, leaving behind a squadron of Korean ships under Song Yo-chong plus thirty Ming vessels to ambush any Japanese craft that might later appear.

The hundred-ship Japanese fleet never did materialize. A handful of ships did stumble into the area a few days later, however, possibly searching the coast for food and booty. In the skirmish that followed, the Koreans under Song did all the fighting, capturing or destroying every Japanese vessel and taking numerous heads. The Ming forces assigned to aid them just looked on, unable to enter the fray, they said, because of "unfavorable winds." When Chen Lin heard of this—he was drinking wine with Yi Sun-sin at the time in the new Council Hall that Yi had built—he was so embarrassed by the poor showing of his men that he smashed his cup to the floor and flew into a rage. Yi moved quickly to calm him. Since you have come so far to help us, he said, it would only be fitting that any victories achieved by us should be considered as your own. Yi then promised to hand over to Chen forty of the seventy heads that had been taken in the skirmish so that he could present them to Beijing as evidence of his valor. Another five heads went to one of Chen's subcommanders, who sent a servant by later with a demand for a share for himself.[29]

In his official report to Seoul Yi Sun-sin did as he promised and credited Chen and his Ming forces with taking forty-five enemy heads. But he also sent a second, unofficial report detailing the truth of what had transpired, namely that the Koreans had done the fighting while the Chinese hogged the glory. King Sonjo was pleased. The affair confirmed the low character of the Ming admiral and in turn the moral fiber of Yi Sun-sin, who was willing to sacrifice his own battle honors for the greater good of the nation. The affair nevertheless very nearly led to disaster when rumors of the two conflicting reports began circulating throughout the south—one can imagine how Yi's proud men would have repeated the tale—and came to the attention of a Chinese official touring the area. Upon arriving back in Seoul, the official demanded to see Yi's dispatch so that he could report on the matter to Beijing. The Koreans, realizing that to hand over a copy of Yi's second, true report would cause trouble for Chen Lin, sent only Yi's first, fabricated account, and the matter was eventually dropped.[30]

Toyotomi Hideyoshi, now on his deathbed in Fushimi Castle, continued to be plagued with worry for his son Hideyori right up to the end. Two weeks before his death he sent the following letter to the Five Regents (*go-tairo*), the five senior daimyo responsible for safeguarding Toyotomi rule, literally begging them this time to look out for his heir:

> To: [Tokugawa] Ieyasu
> Chikuzen [Maeda Toshiie]
> [Mori] Terumoto
> [Uesugi] Kagekatsu
> [Ukita] Hideie

> Until Hideyori reaches adulthood, I am asking for the help of the people whose names are listed in this document. This is the only request I want to make.

I repeat: concerning the business of Hideyori, I am begging and begging you five. The details have been conveyed to the five men [the "Five Commissioners" who ranked just below the "Five Regents" to whom this letter was addressed]. I am loath to part. I end here.[31]

As they did every time Hideyoshi requested it, his senior daimyo pledged their loyalty to Hideyori and the house of Toyotomi. But still Hideyoshi could not rest in peace, for he knew from personal experience the nature of ambitious men. Sixteen years before, in 1582, he had himself sworn loyally to serve the heir of his own master Oda Nobunaga, only to renege on his word and seize power for himself. Did Hideyoshi now feel any guilt? Or was he more likely aware simply of the futility of it all, the futility of extracting oaths from men who in the end would pursue their own interests regardless of what they had sworn? As he had betrayed the heir of Nobunaga, what would prevent Tokugawa, Maeda, and the other daimyo from betraying Hideyori after Hideyoshi was gone?

As he lay on his deathbed, reflecting on his life and the prospects of his son, Hideyoshi summoned the energy to compose a traditional poem of farewell:

> I am as
> The dew which falls,
> The dew which disappears.
> Even Osaka Castle
> Is only a dream.[32]

After one of the most remarkable rises to power the world had ever seen, from peasant boy in Nakamura village to lord of Japan and would-be conqueror of Asia, all was now about to disappear—like dew at the first touch of the sun.

Toyotomi Hideyoshi died on September 18, 1598. He was approximately sixty-two years old. One of his final commands was for the war in Korea to be brought to a close, and for all his men to return home.

CHAPTER 29

The Last Act

YANG HAO, THE DISMISSED SUPREME COMMANDER of Chinese forces in Korea, left Seoul on August 12, 1598, for the long journey back to Beijing to face the charges leveled against him by antiwar hatchet man Ding Yingtai. A visibly moved King Sonjo saw him off at Hongje, a reception area just outside the city walls on the main road to the north. A gathering of elderly government officials was also present to express the nation's sorrow. They shed bitter tears as Yang seated himself in his sedan chair, then repeatedly blocked the road in the traditional manner to show their reluctance to see him go.[1]

The man sent to replace Yang was Wan Shide. Previously Wan had served as governor of Tianjin, a temporary post the Ming government had created in 1597 for the purpose of overseeing coastal defense and the shipment of supplies to the expeditionary forces in Korea. He would not arrive in Seoul until the end of the year, and consequently would not be on hand for the coming campaign.[2]

At Fushimi Castle in Kyoto the demise of Toyotomi Hideyoshi on September 18 was being kept a secret. The Five Regents Hideyoshi had appointed to protect his son Hideyori's interests, foremost among them Tokugawa Ieyasu and Maeda Toshiie, together with the Five Commissioners responsible for the day-to-day running of the government,[3] continued to issue reports for a week or more stating that the taiko was still alive. Keeping the death of a ruler secret for a time like this is not unusual in a totalitarian state. When so much power is concentrated in the hands of one man, the death of that man is invariably regarded by those around him as a time of instability and danger, and a common reaction is to keep the death secret until the transition of power is complete. General fears of instability probably lay in part behind the desire of the Five Regents and the Five Commissioners to withhold the news that the taiko had died. But there was more. Hideyoshi had reportedly given his consent to end the war in Korea and bring the troops home just days before his death. Tokugawa Ieyasu and his colleagues were eager to see this done. For them the second invasion had been an ill-advised adventure that was costing too much. The timing, however, was problematic. If news of Hideyoshi's death arrived in Korea together with orders calling off the war and withdrawing the troops, the daimyo commanders in the field might suspect that the instructions came from Tokugawa and company, and did not actually reflect the dying wishes of the taiko. After having already invested so much blood in the campaign, some of them might then feel honor bound to ignore the withdrawal order and carry on the fight.

Withholding news of the taiko's passing was an obvious way around this snag. On September 25 the Five Commissioners wrote to Nabeshima Naoshige in Korea with the good news that "the Taiko is at length recovering from his illness." He was now sending two emissaries to inspect the situation at the front and deliver his instructions, and to consult with Nabeshima and his fellow commanders on the best way to end the war. Similar reassurances regarding Hideyoshi's health were sent to Shimazu Yoshihiro at his fortress at Sachon, together with the information that "some time ago he issued instructions for peace," the details of which were being conveyed to Korea in the hands of two emissaries, Tokunaga Toshimasa and Miyagi Toyomori. Hideyoshi's own seal was applied to one of these letters addressed to Shimazu— obviously by someone else, for the taiko had been dead for a week.[4]

The instructions that Tokunaga and Miyagi carried to Pusan left no doubt that the Five Regents and Five Commissioners in Kyoto were anxious to bring the war to a quick and certain end. The daimyo commanders were ordered to negotiate a face-saving withdrawal with the Chinese and the Koreans as had been attempted back in 1593, but this time on cut-rate terms. There would be no demand for a daughter from the Ming emperor, for open trade with China, for the ceding to Japan of the southern half of Korea. The Japanese were now willing to abandon all their fortresses in Korea if the Koreans would hand over just one of their princes as a hostage. If the Koreans refused even this, then the Japanese would settle for some rice, honey, and tiger and leopard skins.[5]

As things turned out, they would not get even this.

On September 18, seven months after the retreat from Tosan and the very day Hideyoshi died, a new allied army of Ming and Korean troops set out again to attack the Japanese in the south. As in the previous campaign the force was divided into three columns. This time, however, it would not converge on just one point in the Japanese chain of forts. The plan was to fan out and attack the chain at three separate points.

General Ma Gui, the highest-ranking Ming field commander and the second-highest-ranking Ming representative in Korea after "Army Gate" Xing Jie, headed southeast to attack Kato Kiyomasa's Tosan fortress just outside Ulsan. Ma had been with Yang Hao during the first unsuccessful attempt to break this stronghold on the easternmost end of the Japanese fortress chain. Now he was tasked with completing the job. He had with him a combined force of 29,500 men: 24,000 Ming troops, both cavalry and foot soldiers, reinforced by 5,500 Koreans under General Kim Ung-so. Recently arrived general Dong Yiyuan made for Shimazu Yoshihiro's fortress at Sachon at roughly the center of the chain. He had a total of 26,800 Ming troops under his command, plus 2,300 Koreans led by Kyongsang Right Army Commander Chong Ki-ryong, making for a combined force of 29,100 men. Heading for Konishi Yukinaga's fortress at Sunchon on the western end of the chain, finally, was General "Big Sword" Liu Ting. Liu commanded an army of 26,000 Ming troops, the bulk of them cavalry units and contingents of ethnic fighters from Burma and other exotic locales along the periphery of the Middle Kingdom. He took only about half this army south with him, however, some 13,600 men; perhaps he felt that supplies would not be adequate to feed his entire force. The general would be joined in the south by 10,000 Koreans under Commander in Chief Kwon Yul, giving him a combined field army of 23,600 men.[6]

As the summer of 1598 drew to a close, 68,400 Chinese and Korean troops were thus converging on the Japanese perimeter, as 30,000 reserve troops waited to the rear in Seoul. Nor was this all. After months of delay, Ming naval forces under Chen Lin had at last arrived to reinforce the Korean fleet under Yi Sun-sin. Chen reached Yi's base on the island of Kogum-do in August with 5,000 men aboard a handful of service-able battleships and a host of smaller craft, adding significant manpower to the 16,000 troops that had by this time flocked to Yi's command.[7] Still more weight was added with the arrival of a Zhejiang squadron under Deng Zilong, an old Ming veteran who, like Chen, had commanded troops and fought battles all across the empire, from the Burmese border in the southwest to Fujian Province on the coast facing Taiwan. Also like Chen, Deng was just returning to service from a prolonged period in official disfavor: he had been criticized and dis-missed for some perceived misstep he had taken in the border war with Burma in 1592, and had been forced to remain in retirement for the next six years.[8]

The total allied force gathering to strike the Japanese from both land and sea therefore totaled nearly 100,000 men.

Ding Yingtai, the antiwar Ming official who had caused such an uproar with his recent attack on Yang Hao and the war effort in Korea, was now making his way back to Seoul to widen his investigation. He evidently felt himself in some danger while passing through Liaoyang, an army town on the Chinese frontier filled with Yang supporters, for he remained indoors during his stopover and was wary of what he ate in case it might be poisoned.[9] By the time he reached northern Korea, however, Ding's confidence was high—so much so that word preceded him to Seoul that he had added "Army Gate" Xing Jie, the highest-ranking Ming official in Korea, to his list of guilty parties.[10]

When Ding arrived outside the walls of Seoul on October 3, King Sonjo was not there to greet him. It was customary for the king to come out of the city to welcome all Ming officials, even ones of Ding's low rank, so his failure to do so was an obvious snub. Sonjo saved his welcome instead for Xu Guanlan, the official sent by the prowar faction in Beijing to conduct an investigation of his own. The display was more to underscore the king's loathing for Ding than to demonstrate any special respect for Xu. Throughout the coming months the Koreans would remain suspicious of him and uncomfortable with his presence, for it soon became evident that Xu was concerned only with facts and numbers and had no regard for the bigger issues involved. Most important, he did not seem to appreciate the need to clear King Sonjo and his ministers of Ding's outrageous charge that they had lied to Beijing about the scope of the Japanese threat to involve China in the war.

The first thing Ding and Xu set out to do upon their arrival was to determine the true extent of Yang Hao's losses at Tosan. Both men gathered detailed reports from Korean officials and from the commanders who had been on the scene, then conducted head counts of Ming troops to find out how many men were missing. From this information Xu Guanlan drafted a report concluding that casualties at Tosan had been in the neighborhood of two thousand. Ding Yingtai was not satisfied with this figure and continued to dig. He had various individuals arrested and interrogated, including the female companion of one of Yang Hao's close friends; the homes of officials and officers were ransacked in search of damning evidence; army clerks were rounded up and beaten en masse on charges of falsifying the casualty numbers. It was Ding's contention that ten thousand men had been lost at Tosan, and he was determined to prove it.[11]

His investigation into the Battle of Tosan and the conduct of Yang Hao was of course only the starting point in Ding Yingtai's antiwar campaign. He had already gone on to accuse Grand Secretaries Zhang Wei and Shen Yiguan, "Army Gate" Xing Jie, and numerous other prowar Ming officials of a variety of misdeeds. Everyone working for the war effort was in fact under Ding's close scrutiny and vulnerable to a career-destroying charge. But even this was not enough. It was not enough merely to weed out the bad elements within the Ming government who were supporting the war at such a heavy cost in men and wealth. Ding wanted to get to the root of the problem. He wanted to expose the culprits responsible for dragging China into the whole debacle back in 1592.

The answer Ding came up with was that the Koreans were to blame. He laid bare what he regarded as their perfidy in a report entitled "Plot of the Tributary Buffer to Wickedly Make Common Cause with the

Outlaws." He submitted the document just days after his arrival in Seoul—a fact that would seem to indicate he had come to Korea with his "findings" already in hand. The Koreans, Ding charged, were not the innocent victims of unprovoked aggression that they had tried to paint themselves as. On the contrary, they had actually invited the Japanese to invade their country in 1592 as a prelude to a move against China, for they hoped that in the ensuing Sino-Japanese struggle they would be able to seize for themselves fertile land north of the Yalu River presently under Ming control. King Sonjo, his government, and indeed his entire nation were thus guilty of disloyalty to the Celestial Throne, a charge amounting to nothing less than treason.[12]

Ding Yingtai had no real evidence to support these claims. The charge that the Koreans wished to seize Chinese territory north of the Yalu was based on the fact that, more than a thousand years before, the ancient Korean kingdom of Koguryo had regarded that land as part of its territory. If the kings of Koguryo considered it their land, Ding evidently reasoned, the kings of Choson Korea must necessarily want to reclaim it. As for the charge that the Koreans had invited Hideyoshi to invade the mainland, Ding cited as proof the long history of "good relations" that had existed between Korea and Japan as recorded in the history books, in particular the various political missions that had been exchanged, the trade that had taken place, and the Japanese trading colonies that the Koreans previously allowed to exist along the southeast coast. "This proves," Ding concluded, "that the story that the Japanese were in fact invited here is not just empty talk!"

And there was more. "The current king of Korea, Yi —," Ding continued, referring to King Sonjo, "is a tyrant to his subjects and wallows in debauchery. He impudently lured the Japanese to invade our empire and scoff at Heaven's Court, and has formed a gang with Yang Hao to deceive the Son of Heaven." Sonjo and his government also dated their documents using Japanese year titles in big characters while consigning the proper Chinese year title to small print underneath. This was completely untrue, but Ding nevertheless cited it as an example of how the Koreans "esteem Japan while keeping China in the distance." Ding additionally claimed—again falsely—that the honorific titles used by the Koreans to refer to their king indicated that they regarded him as an equal to the emperor in Beijing. This showed that their claims of having served China loyally and obediently for two hundred years really didn't amount to much. "If your Majesty were to rebuke Korea with regard to these matters," Ding sneered, "what words will King Sonjo and his ministers use to explain themselves?"[13]

The Koreans were astounded by these reckless accusations. The two hundred years of loyalty to China of which they proudly spoke, dating back to the beginning of the Choson dynasty in 1392, had been entirely sincere and not a sham as Ding Yingtai now claimed. Any dealings Korea had had with Japan during this time had been undertaken for the purpose of controlling what Seoul and in turn Beijing regarded as a barbarian nation beyond the pale of the civilized world. This was what Korea's longstanding policy of sadae-kyorin diplomacy was all about: on the one hand "serving the great" (sadae) in its relationship with China, and on the other hand cultivating "neighborly relations" (kyorin) with potentially hostile outside groups to prevent them from causing trouble and to keep them in their place. Korea had therefore permitted limited trade with Japan through the island of Tsushima for many years, because this served to co-opt the rulers of that island so that they could then be used to control the threat of wako pirates based in Japan. Korea had also exchanged envoys with Hideyoshi prior to 1592 because it had hoped this would quell his warlike intentions and teach him his place in a Beijing-centered world. At no time in its dealings with Hideyoshi had Korea ever betrayed China and "made common cause with the outlaws" as Ding asserted. On the contrary, in attempting to cultivate neighborly relations with Japan, Korea had been doing the very thing that Ding said it had not: it had been faithfully serving China as a "tributary buffer," a buffer between the civilized center and the barbarian outside world.

The Imjin War obviously marked a failure on the Koreans' part to keep the barbarian world at bay. It was a failure for which they had paid a terrible price. They had lost more people in the war than could ever be counted. Cities had been destroyed, the economy shattered, entire regions laid waste. They were grateful that China had come to their aid, and they had repeatedly thanked Beijing for having sacrificed so much. But they also knew that if Korea had not resisted Hideyoshi's invasion and absorbed its full destructive impact, his armies would have marched on to Beijing to wreak havoc there. The Koreans could have spared themselves much of this hardship simply by allowing the Japanese army to march through their kingdom as the taiko had demanded. But they never considered this for a moment. They resisted Hideyoshi's force as best they could, bringing upon themselves the ruination that he had planned to unleash on China. They had therefore served the Middle Kingdom very well indeed.

Ding Yingtai's anti-Yang Hao, antiwar, and now anti-Korea accusations thus did more than just cause the Koreans anxiety that China might withdraw from the war, leaving them vulnerable to a renewed Japanese offensive. It wounded them at a much deeper level. King Sonjo felt this hurt most keenly, for all Ding's wild talk of disloyalty and betrayal amounted to a personal charge of treason—treason against the emperor in Beijing, the Son of Heaven, who had granted him the authority to rule. In the Confucian worldview, loyalty to one's lord was the most sacred duty of all, and betrayal of one's lord in turn the most heinous crime. It was therefore a charge that Sonjo could not bear. On October 20, the same day that Ding's report was leaked to the Koreans, the king issued the following memorandum:

> I am the vassal on China's eastern frontier. When the Japanese warlord Hideyoshi first began to threaten us, I adhered to my duty and did what was right, and broke off all contact with him. For this my country was smashed and my house destroyed, and I was forced to drift about like a refugee. Through it all, however, I have firmly guarded my integrity as a vassal, just as a river twists and turns a hundred times but always finds its way east to the sea. Even if I die ten thousand times, I will have nothing to regret.
>
> Yet despite this I have been charged with what amounts to nothing less than a crime. I have personally witnessed how this deceitful fellow [Ding Yingtai] has recklessly slandered those who have been loyal and honest, seemingly intent on upsetting the grand design of the universe. It is for this reason that I am declaring the truth with all my strength, so that our Emperor might see clearly into the innermost heart of this malicious specter.

In the meantime, since he considered himself under indictment, awaiting either punishment or exoneration, King Sonjo could not continue to occupy the throne and perform his kingly duties. "Henceforth," his memorandum concluded, "all matters previously handled by myself are to be referred to and decided by the Crown Prince.... Inform the senior officials of this."[14]

With that Sonjo retired from office and went into seclusion. He would remain locked in his apartments for a week, the wound on his psyche manifesting itself in a host of physical ailments: his appetite was gone; he could not sleep; he felt tired and listless; his chest pained him; his eyesight was dim and his ears blocked up; his legs were lame with rheumatism.

Deprived of their king and head of state, the Korean government was thrown into turmoil. Unlike the Ming government in Beijing, which had long since learned to manage without the participation of the Wanli emperor, who had withdrawn from most of his state duties many years before, the Korean king was an integral part of the government; his oversight and approval were required in all sorts of state matters both great and small. Without King Sonjo's presence the government therefore could not function. Day after day ministers and top officials submitted memorials urging him to return to his office. The first came from Prime Minister Yu Song-nyong, written on behalf of all the officials in the government. The king's actions, Yu pointed out, were only making matters worse, for Ding Yingtai could now accuse him of refusing to perform his duties. In any case, Yu continued, how can a physician treat you if you do not come out from your rooms? King Sonjo would not relent. A physician, he replied, could do him no good. His illness had been brought on by the unfounded charges of the bestial Ding, and thus the only cure was exoneration from the Celestial Throne.[15] Elder statesman Yun Tu-su next urged Sonjo to consider the critical stage that the war effort was at. For the sake of the nation he must rise above his personal hurt and resume his essential duties of directing the armed forces and arranging supplies. Again Sonjo refused. The principle involved was too great to be superseded by earthly concerns.[16]

King Sonjo maintained his stand for a week, rejecting all pleas to come out of his apartments and return to the throne. He finally relented on October 27. The pressure of the dozens of memorials sent to him had been too much. He undoubtedly was also somewhat heartened by reports that opposition was mounting against Ding Yingtai. Every major Ming official in Seoul, including "Army Gate" Xing Jie, had by this time denounced Ding, and according to reports just in from Beijing anti-Ding sentiment was mounting there as well. Xing Jie also informed King Sonjo that Xu Guanlan, who had been dispatched to Korea to conduct an investigation of his own, had submitted a report recommending that King Sonjo and his nation be completely cleared of all Ding's groundless charges. It was an encouraging start to what would eventually become a major turning of the tide against Ding Yingtai.[17]

Although King Sonjo was back on the throne, he and in turn his ministers had neither forgotten nor forgiven the charges of disloyalty that Ding had leveled against them. The matter would remain a sore point in relations between Seoul and Beijing for the next several months, until Ding's eventual dismissal and recall to China and the subsequent receipt of an edict from the Wanli emperor exonerating Sonjo and recognizing him as a good and loyal king.[18]

Ming General Ma Gui arrived at Ulsan on Korea's southeast coast in the latter part of October, just as King Sonjo was going into seclusion in Seoul. Ma had with him the 24,000 Chinese troops of his Eastern Route Army, plus 5,500 Koreans under Kyongsang Army Commander Kim Ung-so. A survey of the Japanese fortifications on the neighboring hill called Tosan revealed an even more impregnable stronghold than the allied forces had attacked earlier in the year. In their assault in January against the still unfinished fortress, troops under Ma, Yang Hao, and Korean commander in chief Kwon Yul had breached the stronghold's outer defenses in just a day of fighting through a gaping hole in the wall where a gate had yet to be hung. Ma now observed that the outer gates were in place and all work on the place complete. A moat had also been dug around the fortress and filled with water diverted from the nearby Taehwa River. The 10,000-plus defenders inside under Kato Kiyomasa were evidently ready for a fight.[19]

As they had done at the first battle of Tosan, the allied Chinese and Korean troops surrounded and laid siege to Kato's fortress. Once this was accomplished, however, Ma Gui made no move to press ahead with an attack. The only action that took place were minor skirmishes fought by allied units roaming the surrounding countryside to mop up isolated squads of Japanese troops. Ma already had firsthand experience from January of how difficult it was to storm Tosan and was not eager to risk the many thousands of casualties—not to mention his career—in making a second attempt. In any case what was the point? The Japanese were now hemmed in along the coast and seemed to be preparing for a general withdrawal. Why, then, waste troops to drive them out of Korea, when they would probably leave of their own accord if the allies would simply be patient?

Ma Gui was willing to be patient. His colleague Dong Yiyuan, commanding general of the Central Route Army, was not. Dong reached Korea's southern coast at a point 150 kilometers to the west of Ma in the final week of October. He took possession of the remains of Chinju without a fight, then proceeded to Sachon, where he scored a second victory when the town's five hundred-odd Japanese defenders, ordered to evacuate, abandoned the old fort and began to fall back. Eighty of them were caught and killed by Dong's troops. The rest managed to rejoin the main Japanese force in the newly built fortress a few kilometers south, on a headland extending into Chinju Bay.[20]

There were now 8,000 Japanese troops holed up inside this fortress south of Sachon, under the command of sixty-three-year-old Shimazu Yoshihiro and his twenty-year-old son Tadatsune. They were outnumbered more than three to one by the 29,100-man army gathering outside the walls, 26,800 Chinese soldiers under Dong and 2,300 Koreans under Kyongsang Right Army Commander Chong Ki-ryong.[21] Shimazu, however, was a wily old campaigner with decades of combat experience in Japan's wars of unification. He also knew something of fighting the Chinese, having been a major participant in the Battle of Namwon in September of the previous year. He stood calmly in a tower bordering his castle's east gate, watching the enemy take Sachon and then his forward outposts, holding his son back from making a precipitous frontal attack. It would be wiser, he knew, to let the Chinese first expend some of their strength against the stout walls of his fort.

General Dong Yiyuan, unlike his colleague Ma Gui, had not previously faced the Japanese and consequently went into the battle with his confidence high, impatient for a win. He launched his assault on October 30, 1598. Cannons were first brought forward and a barrage directed at the walls. An unusual siege engine was also used, a "wooden lever," one Japanese chronicler called it, equipped in some manner with "gunpowder jars."[22] Positioned against the fortress's main gate, it was ignited, and blasted the thick timbers to pieces. With that the order to attack was given and the allied forces charged at the smoking hole. Shimazu, having held his men back up to this point, now ordered his musketeers to fire into the mass of bodies at the base of the wall. Chinese and Korean casualties quickly mounted, but still they continued to press forward.

Just then a tremendous explosion erupted in the very center of the attacking Ming troops. Fire had gotten into the "gunpowder jars" of the siege engine that had blown open the gate. The thunderous explosion sent bodies flying, and sent a wave of confusion through the ranks of the attackers. Then they turned and began to retreat.

Shimazu lost no time in taking advantage of the situation, ordering companies of men out from the eastern and western gates of the fortress to chase after the retreating Chinese and Koreans. The momentum of the battle now swung to the Japanese. Their charge sent the allied forces into retreat, the disciplined Japanese close on their heels, cutting down whole units as they went. By the end of the day a trail of dead bodies extended from the walls of Shimazu's fortress all the way north to Chinju.[23]

Shimazu Yoshihiro would later claim that his men slaughtered 38,700 enemy troops that day[24]—typical hyperbole for the Japanese but nowhere near the truth. The Battle of Sachon was nevertheless a resounding victory for the daimyo commander's outnumbered men. According to more reliable Korean sources, between seven and eight thousand mainly Chinese troops were killed, most of them slaughtered as they attempted to flee, and vast amounts of supplies were lost.[25] Ming general Dong Yiyuan tried to downplay the disaster in his reports by painting it as a stalemate. Losses had been heavy on both sides, he claimed, and the setback only temporary. "After my army rests, we will attack again." The Koreans did not believe him. Neither would Dong's superiors in Beijing.[26]

*   *   *

"Big Sword" Liu Ting in the meantime was moving south toward the western end of the Japanese fortress chain with the 13,600 Chinese troops of his Western Route Army, 10,000 Koreans under Commander in Chief Kwon Yul, and Minister of the Right Yi Dok-hyong to help arrange supplies. The fortress they were making for was under the command of Konishi Yukinaga. It was on the south coast of Cholla Province, a few kilometers past the town of Sunchon, and was known to the Koreans as *waegyo*, "Japanese bridge," after the bridge spanning the seawater-filled moat that had been excavated on the fortress's landward side. It was by all accounts a formidable affair, in effect a fortified island perched on the edge of Kwangyang Bay, surrounded by stone and earthen walls, all carefully constructed to afford the 15,000 defenders within a clear field of fire at any attacking force.

In Yi Dok-hyong's opinion, Liu Ting was reluctant to attack Waegyo, for when they got into southern Cholla Province he seemed to purposefully slow his advance. The Ming general insisted on a lengthy stop in the town of Chonju to offer sacrifices and to hold oath-taking ceremonies for his men. A special ceremony was also held for the benefit of the Koreans accompanying Liu, including Kwon Yul and Yi Dok-hyong, in which they were required to sign an oath to obey without question all orders from Chinese commanders and to provide the Ming forces with all necessary food and supplies. The oath was then sealed with a drink of chicken blood mixed with wine.[27]

When this large allied force finally neared Waegyo, Konishi sent a letter out to Liu asking to meet with him for peace negotiations. Liu was delighted. The pretext of a meeting, he explained to Yi Dok-hyong, would draw Konishi out of his fortress so that he could be captured. Liu accordingly dispatched a favorable reply into the Japanese camp.[28]

Contact by this time had been established between Liu Ting and the naval forces under Korean commander Yi Sun-sin and Chinese admiral Chen Lin. The plan was to launch a concerted attack against Konishi's fortress, Liu from the land and Chen and Yi from the sea. The assault began on October 19, the day when Liu and Konishi were appointed to meet. Liu disguised one of his officers as himself and sent him forward toward the Japanese fortress as the bulk of the allied army waited in the rear. The ruse seemed to be working. The gates of the fortress opened and a figure presumed to be Konishi emerged, evidently expecting to sit down for a parlay. Unfortunately for Liu, allied artillery units, either his own or from the ships advancing with the tide from seaward, opened fire on the fortress at that moment, sending Konishi and his men racing back through the gates before they could be seized.[29]

For the next three days the allied navy continued to bombard the Japanese fortress with cannonballs, arrows, and spitting fire, advancing with the morning tide then withdrawing in the evening as the tide was going out. It was a dangerous game. Using naval forces to attack entrenched enemy positions on land often entailed more risk than it was worth, for it meant operating close to shore in perilously shallow water, exposed to whatever massed firepower the enemy might possess. Yi Sun-sin knew this from his experiences earlier in the war. The only sensible way to employ battleships against shore fortifications, he knew, was in coordination with a land attack by army units, so that the enemy was placed under pressure from two sides. This was indeed now the plan. Unfortunately for Chen and Yi, it did not work. Each time they drew near the Japanese fortress they found themselves exposed to the full force of Konishi's firepower, for General Liu Ting was not applying pressure to the fortress on the opposite, landward side. He was busy building war machines for an attack he planned to launch at some unspecified future date. After October 21 the allied navy thus gave up its one-sided campaign and pulled back to wait for Liu to begin his attack.[30]

For the next week construction work continued within "Big Sword" Liu's camp on a variety of siege engines, stoutly built wheeled enclosures that could be used to move cannons and men up close to the fortress walls. Finally, on October 30, everything was ready. Chen Lin went ashore that day to arrange with Liu a coordinated attack, one he hoped Liu would participate in this time. It was set to begin at dawn the following day, October 31.

The allied navy advanced with the tide at six o'clock that morning, to within range of Konishi Yukinaga's fortress to commence their attack. Confidence was high among the ranks of the Koreans and Chinese, for they had been joined two days before by an additional hundred Ming ships recently arrived from the north. They kept up their assault for the next six hours in the face of stiff musket fire, inflicting significant losses on the Japanese defenders, according to Yi Sun-sin, but at a cost of quite a few casualties of their own. Yi himself lost a relative in the engagement, a cousin of his wife's who was serving under him as captain. The allied fleet was finally forced to pull back with the ebbing tide in the early afternoon.

On the other side of the fortress, Liu Ting's forces were having all sorts of problems. The first units to charge at the walls had been unable to make it beyond the wooden fence that Konishi had erected around the front of his fort. They were stopped here by a screen of musket fire, then were driven back by a Japanese force that came charging out from one of the gates. A second wave of men was sent forward, but it too was driven back, as was a third led by Liu Ting himself. The musket fire issuing from within the Japanese fortress was simply too heavy for his troops to get through. The wheeled siege engines that Liu had spent so many days building were in the meantime proving useless. They were heavy and difficult to move, and when finally maneuvered into position served only as a magnet for concentrated Japanese fire—so much so that the Ming troops fighting from within could do nothing more than hunker down and try not to be hit. The first day of all-out fighting at Waegyo thus ended with the combined allied sea and land attack blunted and Konishi's men secure.

On the following day Chen Lin and Yi Sun-sin, urged on by a message from Liu Ting to continue with their attacks, advanced yet again on the Japanese fortress, this time with the evening tide. In the enveloping darkness they were able to proceed very close to shore to bombard the enemy's positions and presumably sink any ships that were anchored nearby. (The hundreds of ships Konishi needed to ferry his men back to Japan apparently were not anchored in the waters off Waegyo, an easy target for allied cannons. It is possible that these vessels were hidden up narrow inlets nearby, a precaution the Japanese commonly took after the Korean navy emerged as a serious threat in 1592.) Finally, at around midnight, Commander Yi observed that the tide was turning, and led his ships into deeper water before they ran aground. Admiral Chen made no move to follow. Yi dispatched a message to his flagship advising him to pull his forces back while there was still time. Chen either did not want to listen or failed to act in time. Soon thirty-nine of his ships were trapped in the shallows, unable to retreat. The Japanese, mistaking these accidental groundings for some sort of amphibious landing, stormed out the back of the fortress to attack the ships where they lay. Desperate hand-to-hand fighting ensued. Yi Sun-sin sent some of his own ships forward to drive off the attacking forces with their cannons, thereby saving 140 of the trapped Ming troops. All of the grounded vessels, however, were either burned or captured. Two were later sent back to Japan and moored alongside the Korai Bridge in Osaka, where they became a popular attraction.[31]

Fighting on the other side of the fortress had by this time long since ceased. Liu Ting had received word earlier in the day of the disastrous defeat of his colleague Dong Yiyuan's army at Sachon to the east, and was now anxious to avoid a similar debacle. The Korean commanders and officials on the scene became aware of the change in Liu when a Korean who had been captured and hauled inside the Japanese fortress earlier in the battle began shouting over the wall, "All the Japanese are fighting at the other side of the fortress! There are no soldiers defending this side! Attack the walls here and you'll be able to break in!" Yi Dok-hyong, Kwon Yul, and others went to "Big Sword" Liu and urged him to launch an attack at the point the captive had indicated. Liu refused. He would make no more attacks against Konishi's fortress. He had already made up his mind to retreat.[32]

The Battle of Sunchon ended the next day, November 2, with one final assault by the Korean navy led by Yi Sun-sin. Admiral Chen Lin, badly shaken by the losses he had suffered the previous day, took little or no part in the attack. Neither did Liu Ting. After several hours of fighting, Yi withdrew his ships. Two days later he received word that Liu Ting's army was breaking camp and falling back north to the town of Sunchon. The Ming general withdrew from Waegyo without burning his supplies, leaving them behind for the Japanese to claim. This was particularly aggravating to Yi Dok-hyong, for the Korean government minister had accompanied Liu south at the general's behest specifically to ensure a sufficiency of supplies. With Liu unwilling to launch a coordinated assault on Konishi's fortress from the land, it was pointless for the allied navy to continue putting its own forces at risk in one-sided attacks from the sea. Yi Sun-sin and Chen Lin accordingly pulled their ships back in disgust.[33]

At the opposite end of the Japanese fortress chain, Commander in Chief Ma Gui had already broken off his siege of Kato Kiyomasa's Tosan stronghold. He did so on November 2, upon receiving word of the defeat suffered by the Central Route Army in the Battle of Sachon. Fearing the possibility of counterattack from the direction of his now-exposed flank, Ma gathered up the forces he had arrayed around Tosan and led them forty kilometers north to Kyongju. After garrisoning his cavalry units in this ancient capital of the Silla kingdom, the Ming commander proceeded a short distance to the west and established his headquarters at a place called Sinwon. He would remain here for the next six weeks, keeping a close eye on Kato's garrison at Tosan, watching for any sign that they were preparing to leave.[34]

The Ming forces sent to Korea to deal with the second Japanese invasion were huge by any standard. The resources of the Middle Kingdom had been strained to the limit to send them, and the imperial treasury, already in bad shape, had been seriously depleted. China, in short, had done nearly all it could do. News of the defeats at Sachon and Sunchon thus caused a great deal of consternation in Beijing. Upon receiving word of these events, the Wanli emperor issued an edict castigating Dong Yiyuan, Liu Ting, Ma Gui, and all their subcommanders in the very harshest terms, some for being "self-conceited" and for having "disregarded the fighting strength and skill of the enemy," others for "being cowardly and effeminate." "[T]he military divisions of our army," the emperor continued, "were not distributed or handled in accordance with military laws and regulations. Military commands and orders were neither enforced nor obeyed. Consequently, when a division of our army was forced to retreat, all the other divisions hastily followed, thus bringing great military disaster to our entire army. Our military men have thus disgraced and dishonored our nation and have lowered our military prestige and standing." The brunt of the punishments that were subsequently meted out fell upon Dong Yiyuan's

Central Route Army, which had suffered by far the greatest losses in the Battle of Sachon. Two of Dong's subcommanders were ordered beheaded. A third received a temporarily suspended death sentence, to be lifted should he redeem himself with future distinguished service. Dong himself was demoted one rank.[35]

News of Hideyoshi's death, initially suppressed by the inner circle of senior daimyo now wielding power in Kyoto, had by this time reached his commanders in Korea, together with the taiko's dying wish that the war be ended and his armies brought home.[36] Commissioners Asano Nagamasa and Ishida Mitsunari were on their way to invasion head-quarters at Nagoya on the island of Kyushu to oversee the withdrawal. Tokunaga Toshimasa and Miyagi Toyomori, the two representatives sent across to Korea to help arrange a peace settlement, were on the scene at Pusan. The instructions they brought with them were essentially this: withdraw all Japanese forces from Korea quickly and completely, and with as much dignity as it was possible to maintain. Konishi Yukinaga had already taken steps in this direction. Now, with clear orders from home in hand, some of his fellow commanders began to follow suit, opening communications with their Ming counterparts so that an armistice could be arranged and their troops evacuated without a fight. Others, notably Kato Kiyomasa and Nabeshima Naoshige, would continue to resist; they had no desire to give up their toehold in Korea after having so recently blunted the allied offensive. Such hawkish sentiment, however, would quickly be overcome by the course of events. When it became clear that many of their colleagues were preparing to withdraw, and with them the bulk of the army in Korea, Kato and like-minded commanders would be left with no choice but to pull out as well.[37]

The overtures of peace that the Japanese now made came as no surprise to the generals commanding the three Ming armies in the south. Ma Gui, Liu Ting, and Dong Yiyuan had suspected for some time that the Japanese were planning to leave. The first signs of this had appeared earlier that year in June, when the enemy retreat to the coast had been followed by the evacuation of fully half of Hideyoshi's second invasion force. Then there were the messages that Konishi

Yukinaga had sent to "Big Sword" Liu prior to the latter's attack on Sunchon, requesting to meet so that a negotiated settlement could be reached. The allies were also now receiving reliable intelligence that Hideyoshi, the war's architect, had indeed died earlier in the year, on September 18 to be exact, and that the political situation in Japan was quite tense. Clearly the Japanese wanted to evacuate Korea. It was just a question of when and how. Judging from their fierce resistance in the battles at Sachon and Sunchon, however, it was also clear that they would not be forced into a headlong retreat. The wisest course of action as the Ming generals saw it was to cease all attacks, take up defensive positions, and wait for the Japanese to pack up and leave.

A month and a half of tenuous truce ensued, smoothed by a series of messages passed between the Ming and Japanese camps. Communication not surprisingly was lightest at the eastern end of the Japanese perimeter, Kato Kiyomasa's fortress at Tosan, for Kato was under the least amount of pressure. The Ming forces opposing him, the East Route Army under General Ma Gui, were encamped well to the north in the vicinity of Kyongju, and were giving no indications of a desire to attack. The allied navy, meanwhile, was based more than two hundred kilometers to the west, leaving the sea route open for the passage of his ships. Throughout the month of November and into December Kato was thus able to send horses and excess supplies back to Japan, together with some of his men, all without fear of enemy interference.[38] The situation was very different for Kato's colleagues at the opposite end of the fortress chain. At his Waegyo fortress, Konishi Yukinaga was hemmed in from landward by Liu Ting's West Route Army, encamped at the town of Sunchon a few kilometers north, and from seaward by the allied navy under Yi Sun-sin and Chen Lin. It was thus imperative for Konishi to reach some sort of understanding with the enemy before making any attempt to board his ships and leave. This was easily done with Liu Ting. Liu, anxious to avoid further bloodshed now that the war in his opinion was won,[39] proved receptive to the messages and gifts that Konishi dispatched to his camp. He would make no move against Waegyo until after the Japanese had completed their withdrawal.

The Koreans of course were not happy about this. They wanted more than to see the Japanese quietly leave their country and the war

brought to an end. They were after revenge—revenge for the unprovoked aggression that had devastated their nation after nearly seven
years of war. Their army, however, was not powerful enough for the
task; without the aid of General Liu's ground troops there was little
they could do. What the Koreans did have, however, was a powerful
navy under Yi Sun-sin, the one native force that had proved itself
capable of taking on and defeating the otherwise unbeatable Japanese.
Commander Yi had no intention of allowing the Japanese to leave the
peninsula without a fight, and for the moment at least, Admiral Chen
Lin seemed to agree.

Upon receiving news on December 5 that Konishi Yukinaga would
soon be evacuating his fortress and attempting to return to Japan, Yi
Sun-sin and Chen Lin once again led their combined fleet north toward
Waegyo, anchoring in the lee of a small island a few kilometers
offshore and laying a blockade across the neck of Kwangyang Bay. If
Konishi's men attempted to board their ships and leave, two hundred or
more Korean and Chinese warships would be there to attack them
before they ever reached the open sea. Konishi was concerned, and also
a little confused. Had this enemy flotilla arrived simply to observe his
departure? Or would it attack when he put out to sea? The Japanese
commander got his answer two days later, on December 10, when a
squadron of ten ships that he presumably sent out to test the intentions
of the allies was promptly attacked and driven back.[40]

This aggressive response led Konishi to believe that General Liu
Ting had broken his word that he would allow the Japanese to evacuate
in peace. He accordingly took two of the hostages Liu had sent him as
evidence of his good faith, cut off their hands, and sent them back to
the general's Sunchon camp as a sign of his displeasure. Liu replied
that any agreement existing between them applied only to his ground
forces; he had no control over what was happening at sea.[41] Konishi
therefore found it necessary to approach Chen Lin with overtures of
peace. The very next day he sent one of his captains to Chen's camp
under a flag of truce with presents of swords, two hogs, and two barrels
of wine, together with a request that a way be opened so his forces
could leave. More meetings took place on December 12 and again on
the thirteenth, each accompanied by still more gifts.

Konishi's diplomacy had its intended affect; by December 13 Chen Lin had expressed a willingness to comply. Winning over Chen, however, solved only part of the problem. There was also Yi Sun-sin to consider. Chen himself first tried to talk Yi into allowing the Japanese to withdraw without a fight. The Korean commander refused. "I cannot talk peace," he said, "nor can I let a single enemy seed go home in peace." When word of this reached Konishi, he sent a representative directly to Yi with the same gifts and entreaties he had given to Chen Lin—possibly on the assumption that the Korean commander resented being ordered about by Chen and would be more amenable if approached directly. If so he was mistaken. Yi sent the man packing.

Chen Lin now stepped in and attempted to resolve the situation by taking action of his own. He informed Yi that he was going to pull his ships out of the blockade and move east to Namhae Island, to clear away the last remnants of enemy forces he said were still there. For Yi this was the last straw. Already angered by Chen's truckling with Konishi, he now made it clear that he expected the Ming admiral to do his part in maintaining the blockade. Besides, Yi pointed out, the bulk of the Japanese garrison had already left Namhae. Most of the people still there were Koreans who had been taken prisoner and forced to work for the Japanese. Chen brushed this aside. They collaborated with the enemy, he said, and as such should be regarded as enemies themselves. He therefore would go to Namhae and cut off their heads.

Yi, angry now: "Your emperor commanded you to annihilate the enemy in order to save the lives of our countrymen. Now you intend to kill them instead of rescuing them. That is not the august wish of the emperor!"

"The emperor gave me a long sword!" Chen roared back, reaching for his weapon in a threatening way.[42]

Yi refused to budge, and Chen did not press the matter further. The blockade of Waegyo remained in place, at least for one more day.

Konishi Yukinaga sent a final representative to Chen Lin on December 14, this time to request that a single boat be allowed to pass to carry a message to the Japanese garrisons to the east that they should go ahead with their plans to withdraw. Chen agreed. The vessel was allowed through the blockade—and promptly made its way to Shimazu

Yoshihiro's neighboring fortress at Sachon to summon help for
Konishi's beleaguered men. When Yi Sun-sin learned of the boat's
passage later that day, he rightly suspected that enemy reinforcements
would not be long in coming. When they arrive, he explained to his
subcommanders, our ships will be vulnerable to a pincers attack, a
combined assault by Konishi's fleet from the north and enemy reinforcements from the east. Considering this risk, the best course of
action would be to lift the blockade and move east across Kwangyang
Bay to meet the approaching enemy fleet before it could join forces
with Konishi.

Korean sources say that Chen Lin felt guilty when he realized what
he had done in letting that one boat pass through the blockade. But it is
likely that the cagey admiral knew exactly what he was doing. He had
wanted Yi Sun-sin to lift his blockade of Waegyo. And now it was
being lifted.

The men of the allied Korean-Ming navy were served a hearty meal
before setting out from Waegyo on December 14. With a battle in the
offing it might be the last hot food they would see for days. The fleet
then raised anchor and moved east under the cover of darkness to
Noryang Strait, a narrow passage between the island of Namhae and the
mainland at the east end of Kwangyang Bay. If reinforcements were
coming to aid Konishi, they would have to pass this way.[43]

On the evening of December 15, some three hundred Japanese ships
began congregating at Noryang, just as Yi Sun-sin had suspected they
would. Most were from Shimazu Yoshihiro's fortress at Sachon, which
lay beyond the strait and across Chinju Bay twenty-five kilometers to
the east.[44] Tsushima daimyo So Yoshitoshi is also reported to have been
present with a force of his own. They intended to join forces with
Konishi's besieged troops at Waegyo to drive off the allied navy, then
put to sea together for the return voyage to Japan. It would not work out
that way. Shortly after midnight the combined allied navy appeared at
the far end of the strait, blocking the entrance into Kwangyang Bay.

The Japanese passed through Noryang Strait shortly before dawn
the next morning to find the allied navy waiting for them in the open
water beyond. The bulk of the fleet comprised eighty-five heavy
Korean vessels, board-roofed warships with presumably a few turtle

ships as well. Interspersed between these were two types of Chinese craft: six large war junks equipped with sails and oars, and fifty-seven smaller oar-propelled galleys, both well-armed with a variety of cannons, the heaviest of them weighing nearly three hundred kilograms and firing two-kilogram iron balls. The entire force was divided into three squadrons, Yi Sun-sin in command on the right (with 2,600 Ming fighters on board his ships to fight alongside his own men), Chen Lin at the center, and Ming commander Deng Zilong on the left.[45] Shimazu Yoshihiro for his part commanded a larger fleet, but a significant portion of his vessels were lightly built transports—good for ferrying men back to Japan, but no match for a cannon or the ramming prow of a Korean battleship. He was therefore in for a serious fight.[46]

Chen Lin at the center of the formation was one of the first to engage. Soon his flagship was surrounded by Japanese vessels pouring out of the strait, and the old Ming admiral, who had been willing at Waegyo to let the Japanese go in peace, was forced to fight for his life in the decisive battle Yi Sun-sin had wanted all along. The musket fire grew so intense that Chen's men were forced to take cover, giving the Japanese the opportunity to close with his vessel and send boarding parties scrambling onto the deck. In the hand-to-hand fighting that ensued Chen's own son was injured when he blocked a sword thrust directed at his father. One of Chen's commanders managed to skewer the attacker with a trident and cast him overboard before he could finish the young man off.

Seeing that Chen's flagship was surrounded and in trouble, left wing commander Deng Zilong and two hundred of his Zhejiang fighters transferred to a Korean warship so that they could go to his aid. One of the other vessels in the allied fleet, mistaking the commander and his men for an enemy boarding party, came up behind them and opened fire, causing many casualties and disabling the ship. The stricken vessel was soon set upon by the Japanese and Deng and all his men were killed.[47]

Yi Sun-sin's squadron had in the meantime raced in from the right and was now rampaging through the enemy ranks, leveling mortar broadsides into their hulls and spewing flames across the decks with hwapo fire cannons. Much of the fighting occurred at such close range that the Koreans are said to have been able to hurl burning pieces of wood across the way and onto the Japanese ships.[48] Yi's heavily built turtle ships and board-roofed ships were as usual largely impervious to the musket fire that the Japanese threw back, the light balls unable to penetrate the thick wooden hulls and roofing. Yi's own warship reportedly destroyed a total of ten enemy vessels, including what appeared to be a flagship, judging from the high platform with red awning erected on its deck. Yi personally fired the arrow that felled one of the commanders seated there. The sight of this attack forced the Japanese vessels surrounding Chen Lin's command ship to break off their attack and rush to protect their leader, thereby easing the pressure on the Ming admiral. Yi's men managed to fight off the assault, and destroyed the Japanese flagship with hojunpo mortars and fire.

The combined strength of the Korean and Chinese navy eventually proved too much for Shimazu Yoshihiro's larger but less powerful fleet. One by one his ships were set on fire and sunk, clogging the icy water at the entrance of Noryang Strait with blazing wreckage, abandoned armor and weapons, and burned men struggling to stay afloat. It is said that Shimazu's own flagship capsized when it ran onto a rock, and the daimyo commander himself nearly gaffed and hauled aboard by allied sailors before being saved by Japanese ships that rushed to his aid.[49] The Japanese nevertheless had a good deal of fight left in them still. Desperate now to break through the enemy fleet and get away home to Japan, they continued to fire back with their muskets with considerable effect, filling the air with a curtain of lead that caused many casualties aboard the Korean and Chinese ships. At one point Korean captain Song Hui-rip, a close friend of Yi Sun-sin, was struck in the helmet by a musket ball and fell unconscious to the deck. He eventually came to his senses, bound up his head and continued to fight.[50] Others were not so lucky. The list of Korean dead would include many rank-and-file fighting men, several captains, and even top commanders.

With the battle now going against them, the Japanese began fighting a rearguard action south along the coast of Namhae Island and toward the open sea. Yi Sun-sin remained in close pursuit, determined not to let a single "enemy seed" escape. He stood at the bow of his ship, shouting encouragement to his men and beating on the war drum to urge on the other vessels in the fleet. At his side stood his eldest son, Yi Hoe, and his nephew, Yi Wan, son of an elder brother who had died many years before.

Suddenly the Korean commander clutched his chest and slumped to the deck. A stray bullet had struck him high on the left side, near the armpit, entering his chest and possibly piercing his heart. It was at least the third time Yi had been wounded during his twenty-two years of military service. This time the wound was fatal. Knowing that the sight of their fallen leader would adversely affect the morale of his men, Yi gasped out to Hoe and Wan, "Don't let the men know. . . ." And then he died. Struggling to maintain their composure, the two men carried the commander's body into his cabin before the calamity could be noticed. For the remainder of the battle Yi Sun-sin's personal banner was kept flying from the topmast as Yi Wan continued to beat the war drum, sending reassurance to the squadron that his uncle was still in the fight and victory therefore assured. It would only be later, after the battle was won, that word of the commander's death was allowed to spread through the fleet. Chen Lin himself is said to have been greatly shocked by the news, slumping down and beating his chest in grief as cries of mourning arose from the Korean ships gathered nearby.[51]

By the time the smoke had cleared toward the end of the day, the Japanese fleet was gone. It had been a clear victory for the allies. According to the report on the battle that government minister Yi Dok-hyong sent to Seoul, about two hundred of Shimazu's ships had been destroyed and an "uncountable number" of his men either killed or drowned.[52] Chen Lin would put the numbers at two hundred Japanese ships destroyed, one hundred ships captured, and five hundred heads taken, adding that "we don't know how many of their men drowned as their bodies have not yet risen to the surface."[53]

While the Battle of Noryang was being waged at the eastern end of Kwangyang Bay, Konishi Yukinaga's forces were evacuating their fortress at Waegyo to the west and boarding their ships to return to Japan. No allied vessels were in the vicinity to stop them. When he received intelligence of this, General Liu Ting advanced from his headquarters at Sunchon and took possession of Waegyo without a fight. General Dong

Yiyuan did the same at the abandoned Japanese stronghold at Sachon. Konishi's fleet in the meantime made its way east to Pusan, the hundred surviving ships of Shimazu Yoshihiro following behind. They reached Pusan on December 21 and immediately began organizing the final evacuation.[54]

At the opposite end of the Japanese fortress chain, Kato Kiyomasa was calmly evacuating his Tosan fortress, free from any pressure from nearby armies or enemy fleets. He set fire to his camps and the last of his stores on December 15, on the eve of the Battle of Noryang, then boarded his ships and put out to sea. When General Ma Gui received word of this, he raced down from his headquarters near Kyongju to pick off any stragglers and take possession of the fort. All he found was a message left behind by Kato. The Koreans and Chinese, it said, should not think that he had evacuated his fortress out of weakness; if Kato had chosen to do so he could have stayed and held Tosan for as long as he liked. Nor should they assume that Japan had been weakened by the death of Hideyoshi. The government remained stable, and the nation remained strong. Japan could in fact return and attack Korea any time it wished. It would therefore be in Korea's best interests to approach Japan to arrange a lasting peace. Kato, consistently one of the most loyal and unrelenting of Hideyoshi's daimyo commanders, thus left Korea conceding nothing to the allies. Japan remained an indomitable force, he in effect warned. Make an effort to appease us, or you might suffer more of the same.[55]

With the Japanese now gone from Waegyo, Sachon, and Tosan, there was talk among the Chinese of marching on the exposed heart of the enemy perimeter at Pusan. By the time any serious movement was made in this direction, however, the Japanese there had evacuated as well. The last of their ships set sail for home on December 24, 1598, bringing to an end the Imjin War.[56]

For the rest of December Chen Lin and Yi Si-on, former Chungchong Army commander and now Yi Sun-sin's replacement as head of the Korean fleet, roamed the waters off the southeast coast of Korea, running down the odd Japanese ship that had been left behind, routing stragglers out of caves, and laying claim to abandoned stores. Chen would return to China to receive the highest military honors to be bestowed on any Ming commander who served in the Korean campaign. He died in June of 1607.[57]

The body of Yi Sun-sin, meanwhile, was transported back to the Korean navy's base on Kogum Island, then carried in procession to the Yi family home at Asan to be buried on a hill near the tomb of the commander's father, Yi Chong. As the coffin slowly proceeded along the icy roads on its journey north, weeping people gathered along the route to bow their heads and walk behind. The Korean government, which had remained suspicious of Yi until the very end, only now became generous with its recognition and rewards, bestowing on him the posthumous rank of Minister of the Right and ordering a shrine built at his former base at Yosu on the south coast, with sacrifices to be offered to the commander's spirit in the spring and autumn of every year. Additional honors would follow as the years passed and Yi's reputation grew, notably the bestowal in 1643 of the title *Chungmugong*, "Minister of Loyal Valor," an honorific that is now commonly used by Koreans to refer to the revered commander. Numerous other shrines and monuments would also be erected at places like Hansan-do, Kogum-do, Koje-do, and Asan, mostly by local authorities and grateful citizens who felt that Yi Sun-sin had saved their land.[58]

Prime Minister Yu Song-nyong in the meantime was out of a job, the victim of the factional strife that came to be waged with renewed intensity as the war was winding down. The contending factions had been on the scene all along. The Japanese invasion had simply forced them to paper over their rifts and set aside their grudges while they dealt with the bigger issue of national survival. At the start of the war Yu's Eastern faction held the preponderance of power. The opposing Westerners bided their time for the next six years, working with the Easterners for the good of the nation as they quietly secured for themselves the lofty posts of Minister of the Left (Yi Won-ik) and Minister of the Right (Yi Dok-hyong).[59] Finally, in November of 1598, with the Japanese on the verge of withdrawing from Korea, they made a move to unseat Yu Song-nyong. After a barrage of criticisms leveled at the elder statesman by anti-Eastern censors, an attack that King Sonjo tried to fend off, Yu was dismissed from office, and Yi Won-ik took his place.[60]

It was during his retirement that Yu Song-nyong penned his important work *Chingbirok*, "A Record of Reprimands and Admonitions," an account of the war coupled with a warning to future generations of what had gone wrong. In the preface he used a quote from the *Shih-ching*, the Chinese "Book of Odes," to explain his reason for writing the book: "I have been chastised, and I will guard against future calamities."[61] Yu lived in quiet retirement until his death in 1607 at the age of sixty-five.

Antiwar investigator Ding Yingtai, who had caused King Sonjo and his government such anguish with his charges of disloyalty to the Son of Heaven, remained in Korea throughout the winter of 1598–99, roaming about in search of improprieties to support his sagging case. He was a spent force, with no supporters in either Seoul or Beijing now that the war was won. He was finally recalled to China on March 16, 1599 to face charges of fabricating lies to attack innocent people. According to one Korean account, evidently based more on wishful thinking than fact, he was subsequently executed by having his body cut in two at the waist.[62] Chinese sources state merely that Ding was ordered to return to his hometown in central China, where he spent the rest of his life in obscurity, working as a teacher.[63]

Two months after Ding's departure, the long-awaited edict from the Wanli emperor arrived in Seoul, exonerating King Sonjo of the despised official's charges. The weight of false accusation that had so oppressed Sonjo for more than a year was thus finally removed, and his relationship with Beijing restored to its former cordial balance. Sonjo would remain on the throne until his death in 1608.

Ming general "Big Sword" Liu Ting returned to China in early 1599 to resume his command in Sichuan Province, keeping the tribes there under control and the western borders of the empire safe. In the bestowal of military honors later that year he received second honors after Admiral Chen Lin for his service in Korea. Liu continued to serve his country into his late sixties. He died in combat fighting the Manchus in 1619. The details of his death remain obscure. Chinese sources recorded that Liu was killed in action, the Manchus claimed that he was captured and put to death, while the Koreans asserted that he committed suicide by blowing himself up with a charge of gunpowder.[64]

Supreme Commander Yang Hao, who had been sacked for the controversial losses he had suffered at Tosan, remained in retirement for a decade before being restored to official favor and recognized for his service in Korea. His return to command lasted until 1619, when he led his army into an even greater defeat in the campaign to deal with the Manchu threat. The official estimate put Yang's losses at a staggering 45,890 men. This time he was arrested and thrown in prison. Nine years later he was put to death.[65]

In 1599, the year following his death, Toyotomi Hideyoshi was enshrined as a *kami*, a native deity, to be worshiped according to the rituals of Japan's ancient Shinto religion. It was common practice in Japan for local communities to worship their own *ujigami*, or group deity, that watched over them. The great clans had personal ujigami as well. The formerly powerful Ashikaga and Genji houses, for example, worshiped the kami Hachiman. The house of Toyotomi, conversely, had none; it had only recently been established and thus lacked any sort of pedigree and the kami that came with it. Hideyoshi therefore decided to become a kami himself after his death, a deity with the power to protect his vulnerable son and family group and influence events in their favor. The instructions he left behind were followed to the letter, and he was accordingly enshrined as the deity Toyokuni daimyojin.[66] He is still worshiped in Kyoto to this day, at Toyokuni Shrine, next to the National Museum. During the festival that is held here every year on September 18, the anniversary of the taiko's death, a tea ceremony is performed, and a cup is offered to his spirit.

The gate standing in front of Toyokuni Shrine, moved here in 1880 when the site was restored, is one of the few original structures from Hideyoshi's once magnificent Fushimi Castle that can still be seen today. (The buildings on the site where Fushimi once stood just outside Kyoto are reconstructions dating from 1964.) Another surviving remnant are the floorboards from the castle's main hall. On September 8, 1600, as Fushimi was about to fall to rival forces during the struggle for power that followed Hideyoshi's death, 380 samurai loyal to Tokugawa Ieyasu committed mass suicide inside this building, covering the floor with their blood. When Tokugawa subsequently ordered Fushimi razed, these stained boards were carefully preserved, and were later distributed for use in seven Kyoto-area temples. The best place to see them today is at Genkoan Temple just north of the city center. If you look up you can see the stains on the boards of the ceiling, darkened with age but still clear after more than four hundred years. Here and there hand- and footprints can be discerned in the blood.

PART 6

AFTERMATH

COMING HOME AFTER A WAR
I couldn't bear the home-sickness,
So I sped my donkey a thousand leagues.
Spring is in its prime as of old,
But I find no man in the streets.
The storm has swept over the whole land,
Even the sun and moon are eclipsed.
All the prosperity that grew here is gone:
It is a chaos as at the world's dawn.[1]

Chang Hyon-gwang (1554–1637)

CHAPTER 30

What Came Next

HIDEYOSHI'S ARMIES RETURNED TO JAPAN at the end of 1598 with little to show for their nearly seven years of war. True, they had taken many Korean slaves who were subsequently put to work in the fields back home or sold for cash in the markets. They had captured Korean potters with advanced skills who would enrich Japan's own ceramics industry. They had brought back a large supply of hand-crafted movable type, invented by the Koreans two centuries before, a prerequisite for the brief efflorescence in Japan's own publishing industry that would follow.[1] Thousands of valuable books were looted and hauled back to Japan, and with them all the knowledge they contained; many would be incorporated into a library founded by Tokugawa Ieyasu. Paintings, scrolls, and religious artifacts were also taken, even stone pagodas and unusual trees. It was in reference to these captured items that the Japanese would subsequently come up with such names for Hideyoshi's invasion of the mainland as the War of Abduction, the Pottery War, and the War of Celadon and Metal Type.[2] All these cultural enrichments, however, were poor compensation for the tens of thousands of Japanese troops who lost their lives in the conflict (a reasonable estimate is seventy to eighty thousand men, some killed in the fighting, most the victims of hardship and disease), and the untold wealth and resources that had been sucked out of Japan's economy to support the entire affair. Nothing less than the conquering of vast new lands could have justified such a tremendous expense, and that Hideyoshi's armies had failed to do. So it was that the Japanese came up with yet another epitaph for

Hideyoshi's ambitious war to seize all of Asia: *ryoto-jabi*, the "Dragon-head Snake-tail Campaign," the war that began with grand designs that petered out to nothing.[3]

For Korea the Imjin War had been a great deal more. It remains to this day the worst calamity that has ever befallen the nation, to be rivaled only by the Korean War of 1950–53 for devastation and loss of life. The number of Koreans killed outright in Hideyoshi's invasion of 1592–98, the soldiers who lost their lives in battle and the civilians who were slaughtered, easily ran into the hundreds of thousands. When one adds to this the people driven from their homes who subsequently died of starvation and disease, plus those taken as slaves to Japan never to return, the figure rises possibly as high as two million—approximately twenty percent of the kingdom's population.[4]

The scorched-earth policy pursued by the Japanese in the latter part of the war, coupled with the flight of farmers from their fields, additionally dealt a serious blow to Korea's economy, a blow that fell most heavily on the breadbasket provinces of Kyongsang and Cholla in the south. In the survey of 1601, the first conducted in the wake of the war, it was found that only 300,000 kyol of cultivated, tax-paying land remained in the kingdom, down from the 1.5–1.7 million kyol assessed just prior to the war in 1592.[5] This loss of four-fifth's of Korea's farm-land meant not only a tremendous drop in the amount of food being produced, but also a huge reduction in the amount of taxes the government could collect, taxes that were now desperately needed to fund the nation's rebuilding. It was a blow from which Choson Korea would never fully recover. One hundred years after the war, the amount of land under cultivation still had not returned to prewar levels. Two hundred and fifty years after the war, Kyongbok Palace in Seoul, the residence of the king and thus the center of the kingdom, still remained a burned-out shell. The government lacked the funds to rebuild it.[6]

In addition to all this death and destruction, the Imjin War plunged Korea into a period of profound social and political upheaval. To begin with, a significant portion of Korea's slave population—according to census data a third of all Koreans were slaves at this time[7]—was able to assume commoner status, for with numerous slave registers having been destroyed during the course of the war, either by the Japanese or by opportunistic slaves, slave ownership was consequently impossible to prove. This did not result, however, in any significant decline in the size of Korea's slave population; that would not occur for another hundred years, culminating with the abolition of slavery in 1894. What likely occurred was that the slaves who escaped to commoner status during the confusion of the war either slipped back into slavery at a later date, or were replaced by commoners who became slaves themselves. This latter group would have done so of their own volition as a way to escape starvation and an inability to pay the heavy taxes that the government was forced to impose, signing away their freedom and the freedom of their descendants to the most influential local family that would take them. For a typical peasant this entailed entering into a sharecropping arrangement, scratching out a meager livelihood on a small patch of ground on which he paid a fixed rent.[8]

Changes were also taking place at the opposite end of the social scale. The government, its tax revenues down to a mere fraction of prewar levels, was forced to sell upper-class yangban status and official titles to the highest bidder to raise desperately needed funds. The number of yangban in Korea accordingly increased, and with it the number of individuals eligible to serve as public officials. This in turn intensified the factional fighting that resumed once peace was restored, for there were now more men competing for a fixed number of government posts. The same political infighting that had so divided the Korean government prior to the Japanese invasion would thus reach a peak of intensity in the years 1600–1650 and would continue until the closing days of the Choson dynasty, leaving the government embroiled in an endless series of obscure political wranglings, blind to the changes taking place in the outside world.

While Hideyoshi's invasion of Korea and attempt to conquer China failed to achieve even one of its objectives, it contributed to the downfall of the Ming dynasty in ways the taiko never could have foreseen. In sending armies to Korea to block Hideyoshi's advance, Ming China, which had been in poor financial shape to begin with, was forced to expend more manpower and wealth than it could possibly afford, ultimately weakening itself to the point where it would be unable to respond effectively to threats arising elsewhere. It has been estimated that ten million taels—368,550 kilograms—of silver were spent to send the first expeditionary army to Korea in 1593–95, and another ten million in the second campaign of 1597–98, a total of 737,100 kilograms of the precious coin.[9] Another estimate puts the total cost of the war for the Ming at twenty-six million taels, just under a thousand metric tons of silver.[10] Such a tremendous outflow of wealth had drained the imperial treasury by the end of the war, a fact that would have a profound impact on China's ability to defend itself, for by the late sixteenth century its armies were composed largely of mercenary soldiers, men who served only when they received payment every month. No silver, therefore, meant no national defense.

The situation was exacerbated by the generally weak state of the Chinese empire at the start of the war, a weakness manifested notably in its inability to maintain an army large enough to meet its considerable needs. With a limited number of troops available, the only way Beijing could respond to Korea's call for help was to strip forces from other parts of the empire, weakening its defenses in one place to build them up in another. This shifting about of China's armed forces would have the greatest impact on the northeast frontier, where the Middle Kingdom ran into Manchuria. It had traditionally been a trouble spot that required careful guarding, for mounted Jurchen tribesmen—they would later call themselves "Manchus"—were in the habit of launching raids across the border wherever counterbalancing forces were not stationed to hold them back. By the last decade of the sixteenth century these scattered tribes had become a serious threat, for they were now united under a chieftain named Nurhaci who was intent on creating a state of his own. Beijing saw this threat emerging. With its armed forces tied up in Korea, however, there was little it could do but try to co-opt Nurhaci with court titles and opportunities for tribute trade. The Jurchen warrior remained obliging for a time, consolidating his position and building up his strength as the Chinese looked helplessly on, knowing what was coming but lacking the resources to stop it.

The inevitable finally happened in 1616: Nurhaci broke with Beijing and established an independent empire of his own, one that covered all of Manchuria right up to China's northeast border. He called his new state Chin, "Gold," after the regime that had ruled that area in the twelfth and thirteenth centuries before succumbing to the Mongols of Kublai Khan. Then he began to spread his reach, sending his armies into Chinese territory to seize cities near the border, forcing Beijing to respond. Straining its resources to the limit, the Ming government scraped together an expeditionary force of 90,000 men, which it sent north in 1619 under reinstated Commander in Chief Yang Hao in the hopes of crushing Nurhaci and reasserting its control. As a tributary state, Korea was expected to contribute to the enterprise. Seoul obliged with a 10,000-man army, but it did so with reservations, for it was clear that the Ming dynasty now was weak and might not emerge the victor. The two Korean commanders appointed to lead the force (one of them was Kim Ung-so, who had figured prominently in the war with Japan) were accordingly ordered to hold their men back when the fighting began, and to surrender if things went badly—which they did. The final confrontation in April of 1619 was a disaster for the Chinese. As the Koreans delayed their advance as per orders from Seoul, Nurhaci's massed cavalry took on the four separate Ming columns one by one, killing a total of 46,000 Chinese troops and two commanding generals, including "Big Sword" Liu Ting. A third general who escaped the initial carnage died in a later engagement. The fourth general, Li Rubo—the same Li who had served in Korea back in 1593 in the expeditionary force commanded by his elder brother Li Rusong—committed suicide when charges were subsequently leveled against him. Commander in Chief Yang Hao, who was held responsible for the debacle, languished in prison for nine years before being put to death.

With the Ming now in peril, Korea's king Kwanghae, who had succeeded his deceased father Sonjo in 1608, together with the support of an Eastern splinter faction called the Great Northerners, tried to shift the government from its traditional pro-Ming stance to one of non-alignment, balancing his kingdom between the sinking Ming and the rising Chin. The effort would prove Kwanghae's undoing. The Western faction, which had been biding its time in the political wilderness, seized on the issue and used it to oust Kwanghae from the throne in 1623, to be replaced by his nephew, crowned King Injo, and a return to unwavering Ming support. Behind the self-serving political motives involved, the move was a testament to the loyalty the Koreans felt toward the Ming. Many of the men in power sincerely believed that Korea owed Beijing an undying debt for the aid it had provided in the war with Japan. Unfortunately for them, it also gave the state of Chin, now ruled by Nurhaci's son Abuhai, a reason to invade the peninsula, first in 1627 and then again in 1636 when the Koreans continued to resist. When King Injo finally surrendered and the Manchu troops went home, they left behind a large stone tablet on the banks of the Han River, an inscription carved in Manchu on one side and Chinese characters on the other: "God gives frost as well as dew; behold his severity as well as his loving kindness."[11] As a sign of their supplication, the Koreans were required to send two of their princes as captives to the Manchu court, make regular tribute payments, and provide troops for the ongoing campaign to conquer the Ming, which by that time was almost complete.

One of the last acts of the dying Ming dynasty was to send a request for military aid to—of all countries—Japan. In 1649 Ming loyalists, driven out of Beijing in 1644 by the Manchus and sheltering on islands offshore from what is now Shanghai, mingling with pirates with Japanese connections, sent an envoy to Nagasaki bearing a copy of the Buddhist Tripitaka as a gift to elicit soldiers from Japan. The mission was a failure. The authorities at Nagasaki were interested in the Buddhist scriptures and offered to buy them for a substantial amount of silver. They refused, however, to receive the Ming envoy as a representative of a superior court, nor did they have any interest in talk of military aid. After a discouraging week in the port, the Ming envoy concluded that it would be "inappropriate to sell the court's imperial possession like a peddler," and so re-boarded his vessel and sailed back to China with his priceless cargo intact. The Tripitaka was returned to its monastery, and the Ming dynasty disappeared.[12]

The fall of the Ming dynasty and the rise of the Qing (Pure) was not as traumatic as many previous dynastic changes. It has even been called "the least disruptive transition from one major dynasty to another in the whole of Chinese history."[13] It was so because in the end the Ming were weakened to the point where a power vacuum effectively existed in the region around Beijing, one that the Manchus simply had to march into and fill. Once in power, moreover, the Manchus left things largely as they were, for they admired Ming culture and society and had no desire to change things (beyond requiring that everyone wear Manchu dress and that males shave the top of their heads and braid their hair in back into a long Manchu-style queue). Indeed, the Manchus portrayed themselves as protectors of a great tradition that the enfeebled Ming were no longer able to preserve. Other than the initial resentment caused by the imposition of the queue, the Qing dynasty thus would not be regarded by the Chinese so much as a time of "suffering under barbarian domination," as had been the case during the Yuan dynasty, when China was ruled by the Mongol descendants of Genghis Khan. Many Chinese in fact welcomed the stability that the Manchus brought.

Nostalgia for Ming times nevertheless remained an enduring theme in China for centuries to come, and in Korea men continued to speak with emotion of the brotherly relationship that had formally existed between their two nations, and of the undying debt that Koreans owed to the Ming for their help in the Imjin War. "Our Emperor Shen-tsung [the Wanli emperor]," wrote one Korean scholar in 1865, "mobilized the troops of his empire and exhausted the material of his empire in driving out the wicked invaders and restoring the rivers and mountains of our ruined country of 3,000 li. Not one blade of grass, not one hair did the Emperor spare.... People of olden times have never been able to forget [the need] to repay this debt.... As long as it takes mulberry fields to be changed into the sea, the obligation will never be forgotten."[14]

A state of wary peace descended upon Japan for more than a year after the end of the Korean campaign. Toyotomi Hideyori, the taiko's five-year-old son and heir, remained with his mother Yodogimi in seclusion at Osaka Castle, under the protection of the Five Regents and Five Commissioners, foremost among them Tokugawa Ieyasu and Maeda Toshiie, the senior daimyo Hideyoshi had appointed to run the country and safeguard the lad's inheritance until he came of age. Signs soon began to appear, however, of instability behind the scenes. First the governmental structure that Hideyoshi had set in place began to fall apart as individual regents and commissioners and numerous other daimyo left the capital region to take care of affairs in their own domains during this time of potential upheaval. Then, in 1599, Maeda Toshiie died. Maeda was the only senior daimyo with experience and power enough to rival Tokugawa Ieyasu. His stature was further raised by the fact that he made his residence alongside Hideyori at Osaka Castle and was thus the regent most directly responsible for the well-being of the helpless young heir. Maeda's passing left Tokugawa the single most powerful daimyo in Japan, a position he used in early 1600 to move from Fushimi Castle near Kyoto into Osaka Castle to take Hideyori under his domineering wing. During the following months the fifty-eight-year-old regent continued to profess in words his loyalty to Hideyoshi and in turn Hideyori, but his actions made it increasingly clear that, after thirteen years of patient allegiance to the house of Toyotomi, he was out to seize power for himself.

The battle lines for a civil war now began to be drawn. On the one side was Tokugawa Ieyasu, backed by a growing number of daimyo who saw him as the most powerful force in post-Hideyoshi Japan and thus the most advantageous camp to join. Most of these men were based in eastern Japan where Tokugawa's own domain was located. Joining them were such Korean war veteran commanders as Kuroda Nagamasa, Nabeshima Naoshige, So Yoshitoshi, and Hideyoshi stalwart Kato Kiyomasa to name but a few. (Kato's siding with Tokugawa is a good example of how daimyo loyalty was directed toward Hideyoshi's person, and thus quickly evaporated following his death.) Standing opposed to this pro-Tokugawa faction was a loose federation of daimyo, mainly from western Japan, centered on Ishida Mitsunari, one of the Five Commissioners. Ishida, like Tokugawa, claimed that his sole concern was safeguarding the legacy of Hideyoshi, but in fact he had ambitions of his own for seizing the reins of power. He was joined by Korean war notables Ukita Hideie, one of the titular heads of both the first and second invasion and since his return to Japan one of the Five Regents sworn to protect Hideyori; Mori Terumoto, another of the regents, formerly a naval commander who had fought against Yi Sun-sin; Konishi Yukinaga, the Christian daimyo from Kyushu who had spearheaded both invasions and guided much of the diplomatic maneuvering between; Shimazu Yoshihiro, victor of the Battle of Sachon where so many noses had been taken; and Kobayakawa Hideaki, the adopted heir of Kobayakawa Takakage, the Kyushu warrior who had bested the Ming army at Pyokje in 1593. Old Takakage had died child-less in 1597 at the age of sixty-five.

On October 21, 1600, after half a dozen preliminary engagements, the combined armies of the two contending factions, one from eastern Japan and the other from the west, met in a narrow valley near a village called Sekigahara, a hundred kilometers northeast of Kyoto, to deter-mine the course of the history of Japan. It was an enormous battle involving a reported 150,000 men: a disciplined 70,000-man army of easterners under Tokugawa Ieyasu against a tenuous coalition of 80,000 westerners led by Ishida Mitsunari. Ishida met Tokugawa's army with the main body of his force at eight o'clock in the morning as a heavy fog began to lift. He left Kobayakawa Hideaki's contingent in reserve on a nearby hill, with the intention of summoning it to attack when the time was right. Several hours of pitched battle ensued without result. Finally Ishida lit the signal fire calling Kobayakawa Hideaki's forces to attack. Kobayakawa did not respond. Unbeknownst to Ishida, the twenty-three-year-old daimyo had secretly switched sides, wooed some-time earlier to the Tokugawa cause by Kuroda Nagamasa. He hesitated for a time, then led his men in an attack against Ishida's own force. This last-minute defection turned the tide of the battle in Tokugawa's favor, breaking the western army and sending it into retreat.

What has been called "the greatest transfer of landholding in Japanese history" took place in the wake of the Battle of Sekigahara, when the fiefs of eighty-seven daimyo who had fought against Tokugawa were confiscated and handed over to men more fortunate in their choice of sides.[15] Many of these dispossessed daimyo, including western army leader Ishida Mitsunari, were either killed or committed suicide in the approved manner by slitting open their bellies. Konishi Yukinaga, a Christian who viewed suicide as a mortal sin, declined this way out and was beheaded. It is said that it took his executioner three blows of the sword to completely sever his head. Others who had opposed Toku-gawa but now displayed a willingness to submit were in most cases stripped of their lands but allowed to live. Ukita Hideie, for example, was dispossessed and banished to the tiny island of Hachijojima, where he would live, forgotten, until the age of ninety. Shikoku daimyo Chosokabe Morichika, son of Korean invasion commander Chosokabe Motochika who had died the previous year, similarly lost everything. So did Tachibana Muneshige. Mori Terumoto was one of only three anti-Tokugawa daimyo who were allowed to keep some land, retaining a third of his formerly huge holdings in the vicinity of present-day Hiroshima. Those daimyo who had actively sided with Tokugawa, meanwhile, received correspondingly handsome rewards, in some cases doubling the size of their domains. Benefiting most was Kuroda Nagamasa. In recognition of the crucial service he had performed in winning Kobayakawa Hideaki over to the Tokugawa side, thereby tipping the scales in the Battle of Sekigahara, the thirty-two-year-old daimyo was moved to a new fief centered on Fukuoka Castle, a domain more than four times as large as the one he had previously held. Kato Kiyomasa, who had shared Higo Province on Kyushu with Konishi Yukinaga, was given his rival's domain and thus made master of the entire province. Maeda Toshinaga, the eldest son of recently deceased regent Maeda Toshiie, received the confiscated lands of his brother Toshimasa, who had broken with Toshinaga and sided with Ishida. Others who had sworn allegiance to Tokugawa without participating in any of the fighting were merely confirmed in possession of their present fiefs. So Yoshitoshi, brother-in-law of the now dead Konishi Yukinaga, was among this group. His domain on Tsushima Island, the stepping-stone that Hideyoshi's expeditionary forces had used to invade Korea, would remain under So family control for two and a half centuries to come.

During the course of this unprecedented upheaval, Toyotomi Hideyoshi's son Hideyori was left untouched. He retained control of the formidable Osaka Castle, plus a surrounding domain valued at 650,000 koku—only a third of the land his father had left him but still one of the largest fiefs in the country. Tokugawa Ieyasu understood that the time was not yet ripe to move against the boy—not with the imposing memory of Hideyoshi still gripping the psyche of Japan. To attempt to crush the house of Toyotomi now, just two years after the taiko's death, would put the still-tenuous allegiances that Tokugawa had recently won to a severe test, one that would almost certainly drive some of his allies to rebel and side with Hideyori. After winning the Battle of Sekigahara and establishing himself as military dictator or *shogun*, Tokugawa thus patiently waited for the next fourteen years.

In the meantime, Tokugawa began making attempts to restore diplomatic relations with Korea as a means of legitimizing his new regime. Tsushima daimyo So Yoshitoshi welcomed the order to reestablish contact, for his agriculturally poor island traditionally derived much of its livelihood from the special trade privileges granted to it by the Koreans, and was suffering now with those links cut. The first few envoys sent to Korea from Tsushima were either taken captive or sent packing the moment they arrived at Pusan—not surprising, considering the enmity the Koreans felt toward the Japanese; in the immediate aftermath of the war there was even talk in Seoul of sending a punitive expedition against Tsushima to punish it for what was seen as its recent betrayal. This closed-door policy, however, did not last long. In 1601 a fourth Tsushima envoy succeeded in getting his message delivered to Seoul and returned home with a reply. If Japan really wanted peace, the letter from the Choson government said, then it must return the Korean citizens it had taken captive in the war. This opening of communications led to the dispatch of a Korean envoy to Tsushima in 1602 to investigate the sincerity of Japan's desire for peace, and of a second mission in 1605 that traveled all the way to Kyoto for an audience with Tokugawa Ieyasu. As a result of this mission, led by the venerated monk Yujong, who had commanded an army of warrior-monks during the war with Japan, more than five thousand Korean captives were repatriated—scarcely a tenth of the total number taken, but enough to appease the Koreans and keep the diplomatic game alive.[16]

A vast conceptual gulf still existed between the two nations. First there was the gulf between how each side viewed the war: a Japanese defeat in the eyes of the Koreans, a victory of sorts to the Japanese because they had "punished" Korea and in turn demonstrated their power to the Ming. There was also a serious difference between how each side regarded the diplomatic exchanges currently taking place and, most important, how they viewed their respective positions in the world. The So family of Tsushima, through whose hands all diplomatic correspondence passed, worked energetically to remove as many of these conceptual impediments as they could by amending some documents and forging others outright. In 1606, for example, they sent a forged letter to Seoul in which Tokugawa Ieyasu referred to himself as "King of Japan," thereby acknowledging to the satisfaction of the Koreans the primacy of the Ming emperor and in turn Japan's secondary status in a China-centered world. More commonplace changes undertaken by the So included converting dates on Japanese documents to the Chinese system so as not to offend the Koreans. To satisfy Edo in turn, the So similarly doctored Korean documents to give them the sort of subservient spin that the Tokugawa shogunate desired. Both sides were aware that some sort of diplomatic sleight of hand was taking place on Tsushima, but both chose to overlook it for the sake of furthering relations. The more outrageous lies, however, would never have been condoned; the Koreans had no intention of appearing even the slightest bit subservient, while the Tokugawa shoguns regarded themselves as above the Chinese, not below. The ruse finally ended in the early 1630s when a power struggle within the So house brought the whole affair into the open, obliging Edo to intervene. Starting in 1635, Zen priests well versed in written Chinese, the language of Asian diplomacy, were dispatched to Tsushima to oversee all correspondence and contact with Korea. In the same year the problem of finding a diplomatically inoffensive name for the shogun that would be acceptable both to the Koreans and the Japanese was solved with the creation of the title *Nihonkoku taikun*, "Sovereign Lord of Japan," from which the English word "tycoon" is derived.[17]

It is clear why the Tokugawa shoguns wanted to restore diplomatic relations with Korea: it served to legitimate their recently established regime. But why were the Koreans willing to resume relations so soon after the war? The policies then being formulated in Seoul were influenced in part by a report entitled *Kanyangnok* (Record of a Shepherd), written by Imjin War captive Kang Hang and presented to the government upon his repatriation in 1600. In *Kanyangnok* Kang Hang made no secret of his feelings toward the Japanese. He loathed them. They were, he wrote, "a horrid people," "a mortal enemy" to the Koreans, and Japan itself "a lair of dogs and pigs." But they were also too dangerous to be ignored. This, Kang pointed out, was where Korea had made its greatest mistake. Throughout the sixteenth century the government had blithely adhered to its traditional policy of guarding its northern borders more assiduously than the south, failing to recognize that Japan's increasing militarism coupled with its expertise in the use of firearms had made it a greater threat than Manchuria's Jurchen tribes. Henceforth, Kang advised, "the defense on the [southern] border must be increased one hundred times." Kang Hang also recommended establishing relations with whatever regime was in power in postwar Japan. Failure to do this, he suggested, might lead to renewed Japanese aggression within the space of several decades. But "as the Japanese nature puts emphasis on an alliance, if we ally [with Japan] perhaps we will keep [about] one hundred years' peace." To forge such an alliance Kang urged a return to the prewar expedient of funneling all contact between the two nations through the island of Tsushima and its lord So Yoshitoshi. The duplicitous So, however, should henceforth be kept on a much shorter leash, for it was now clear that he had used his prewar role as intermediary to manipulate affairs to his own advantage and ultimately betray Korea. He and his descendants should be appeased with strictly supervised opportunities to trade to make them dependent upon and loyal to Korea, as was commonly done to pacify border tribes. In being granted access to Korea, however, they should be confined to a single trading station on the south coast. This would serve to deny the Japanese any opportunity to gather intelligence on Korea's road networks and inland defenses, which they had put to such good use in planning their invasion in 1592. "To handle the Japanese," Kang concluded, "is firstly to handle Tsushima, and to handle Tsushima there is no other means than this."[18]

These recommendations would form the basis for Korea's postwar policy toward Japan. Contact between the two countries was confined to the limited trade access granted to the daimyo of Tsushima and to congratulatory missions dispatched in either direction to commemorate the ascension of each Korean king and each shogun in Japan. The Tokugawa shogunate welcomed the arrival in Edo of these occasional goodwill embassies—indeed, they requested them—for they could be portrayed to the public as tribute missions from a subservient Korea and in turn of the long reach of the shogun's arm. The Koreans were likewise glad of the chance to travel to Japan, for it gave them an opportunity to gather intelligence about the country and ascertain whether it was preparing for war. The Japanese for their part, however, never sent formal missions in turn to Korea; the Koreans would not have received them if they had. All diplomatic correspondence from Edo arrived in Korea in the hands of envoys from Tsushima, the only Japanese the Koreans would allow to set foot on their soil. Once in Korea, moreover, every Tsushima delegate was confined to the immediate vicinity of Japan House, a walled compound just outside Pusan, and kept under constant surveillance. No one was allowed to travel north to Seoul.[19] The Japanese would occasionally complain of these restrictions, and certain daimyo lords, eager to join the So family in trading with Korea, would assert that Seoul should open itself more to commerce with Japan. But nothing ever came of it. The situation remained unchanged until the early nineteenth century when, after more than two centuries of stability and peace, the two countries allowed their infrequent diplomatic exchanges to cease altogether and their trade links through Tsushima to sink to new lows.

At the onset of winter in 1614, Tokugawa Ieyasu led an army of 194,000 men against Osaka Castle to finish off Toyotomi Hideyoshi's son and heir Hideyori, now a young man of twenty-one. The task proved more difficult than Ieyasu had foreseen, for Hideyori commanded a force of some 90,000 men, most of them *ronin* (masterless samurai, literally "men of the waves") led by dispossessed former daimyo, the vanquished detritus of Sekigahara who had gravitated to Osaka during the intervening years. After attacking the castle for one month and laying siege to it for a second, Tokugawa determined that the edifice would not fall to brute force, so he approached Hideyori and concluded a truce. Tokugawa promised to lift his siege and leave, while Hideyori agreed in part to allow some of the outer fortifications of his castle to be leveled as a sign of his desire for peace. With that the conflict seemingly came to an end, and Tokugawa's army made a grand show of marching away.

But not everyone left. A contingent of Tokugawa's men remained behind and set to work making the alterations to the outer defenses of Osaka Castle, ostensibly as stipulated in the truce. It quickly became evident that their work was far exceeding anything Hideyori had agreed to. By the time his protestations reached Tokugawa and demolition work was halted, the outer and inner moats had been filled in and many key walls knocked down, severely weakening the once impregnable castle—just as Tokugawa had planned. Five months later, in May 1615, the wily old warrior returned to Hideyori's now vulnerable stronghold with a second great army, and this time succeeded in destroying the place. Hideyori and his mother, Yodogimi, committed suicide in the flames. Hideyori's eight-year-old son was subsequently beheaded to end his line.

With the destruction of Osaka Castle and with it the house of Toyotomi, Japan fell completely under the sway of Tokugawa Ieyasu. Ieyasu himself, now in his seventy-fourth year and anxious to ensure a smooth succession, had already passed on the title of shogun to his son Hidetada and begun to work behind the scenes formulating the policies that would make the Tokugawa shogunate "the most enduring regime in Japanese history."[20] It would be enduring because Ieyasu, unlike his predecessors Hideyoshi and Oda Nobunaga, established the post of shogun rather than his own person at the center of the web of political allegiances binding the nation together. These allegiances, and in turn the peace they ensured, would therefore remain in place long after Ieyasu was gone.

The Tokugawa shogunate under Ieyasu's son Hidetada and his successors became increasingly conservative in its drive for stability and peace. One of their first concerns was to keep the nation's formerly restive daimyo obedient and in place. The confiscation and redistribution of fiefdoms that took place after Sekigahara and the fall of Osaka Castle—a process known as "smashing the daimyo"—had already done much to achieve this. The promulgation of new laws completed the task. Henceforth, for example, daimyo lords were prohibited from constructing new castles; even repair work on existing defenses had first to be reported and approved. Ieyasu's heirs also had to come up with something for Japan's samurai warrior class to do other than wage war. The answer was found in the Neo-Confucian ideas that had been filtering into the country for the past few centuries from the Asian mainland, most recently in the person of Kang Hang, the Korean scholar official taken captive during the Korean campaign. Over the following decades Japan's samurai gradually came to be "civilized" into a political and intellectual elite similar to the scholar-official upper class of China and Korea. The nation's social order meanwhile was frozen into an unchangeable hierarchy, farmers and merchants at the bottom lorded over by the privileged samurai class, with the shogunate at the top wielding absolute control. Had Hideyoshi been born into this Tokugawa world, he would have remained an unknown farmer from the cradle to the grave.

The growing conservatism of the Tokugawa shogunate also manifested itself in policies designed to regulate Japan's contacts with the outside world, in particular with the West. Moves were taken starting in 1614 to stamp out Christianity, now viewed as subversive and a danger to the state. In 1635 foreign travel was prohibited on pain of death. Four years later the Portuguese were expelled and all contacts severed with the Catholic nations of Europe. Next to be prohibited was the ownership of oceangoing vessels. Henceforth the shogunate would pursue a policy of *sakoku*, or "seclusion," a policy that would see foreign commerce rigorously controlled, and infrequent diplomatic relations maintained with just the neighboring kingdoms of Korea and the Ryukyu Islands.

With its emphasis on stability, peace, and seclusion, it was perhaps inevitable that the musket, the Western innovation that had played such an important role in the wars to unify Japan and the subsequent invasion of Korea, would come to be rejected. It did not disappear from the scene as completely as is sometimes stated; there were an estimated 200,000 firearms in Japan at the start of the Tokugawa period and roughly the same number at the end.[21] With no wars left to fight, the musket was simply placed in the closet, so to speak, copied and refined by generations of gunsmiths but not fundamentally changed—an instrument of technological interest and artistic achievement akin, perhaps, to the costly daimyo clocks that were then finding their way into the homes of the elite. The samurai, who had rarely carried muskets into battle to begin with, relegating them instead to lower-class foot soldiers, came once again to focus on the sword, bow, and spear, the preferred weapons of the past, when combat was a affair of honor fought by men standing face to face.

In an interesting footnote, when the American survey ship *Vincennes* landed in 1855 on Tanegashima, the island off the south coast of Kyushu where Portuguese traders first introduced the musket into Japan back in 1543, the vessel's captain noted in his report to Washington that "These people seemed scarcely to know the use of firearms."[22]

The Tokugawa period was a time of rapid urbanization, economic growth, and prosperity for Japan. No longer burdened with supplying manpower and wealth for wars of national unification and continental conquest, farmers were left to their farming and merchants to their trade. The amount of land under cultivation doubled. Cities expanded, none more so than the shogunate's capital at Edo, which exploded from an insignificant fishing village into a sprawling metropolis that would later be renamed Tokyo. Living standards improved, the population soared, and the nation as a whole grew increasingly rich, thanks to the shogunate's emphasis on stability and peace.

Its policy of seclusion, however, would eventually prove its undoing. By the early nineteenth century ships from Europe and the United States were beginning to appear in Asian waters in increasing numbers—trade ships and whalers and survey vessels mapping the coasts. With all this sea traffic now in the area, ships inevitably began landing on Japan's shores in search of water and fuel. The shogunate, alarmed by these incursions, issued orders in 1825 to all daimyo with coastal domains to drive away any foreign ship that approached the shore and to arrest and execute any foreign seamen who attempted to land. The incidents of hostility that followed angered the nations of the West, where offering aid to sailors in need was regarded as a fundamental duty expected of all nations and a basic law of the sea. Japan's unwillingness to open itself to international trade was also considered unacceptable in the atmosphere of expansion that was then so pervasive in the West. In the end it was the Americans who came to kick down the door. In 1853 Commodore Matthew Perry arrived with a fleet of "Black Ships" in Edo Bay to demand that Japan open to trade and navigation. The Tokugawa shogunate, knowing that it could not resist the technologically advanced West with its own withered armed forces and sixteenth-century guns, had no choice but to sign a treaty with the Americans when Perry returned for an answer the following year.

The Tokugawa shogunate's inability to stand up to American gunboat diplomacy, its first sign of weakness in more than 250 years, caused nationwide humiliation, discontent, and agitation. Cries went up for change on two fronts: first the expulsion of all foreigners from Japan, and second the restoration of the emperor, since the twelfth century little more than a figurehead controlled by a succession of strongmen like Nobunaga, Hideyoshi, and now the Tokugawa shoguns. The movement eventually became a groundswell that brought the shogunate to an end and ushered in the Meiji era (1868–1912), named after the emperor who occupied the throne. It would be a time of reform and modernization under such slogans as "independence and self-respect."[23] Western education was promoted. Industries were set up and train lines built. Western fashions were adopted. Modern buildings were constructed. And modern armies and navies were established, equipped with the latest guns and ships.

From the beginning of the Meiji era the thoughts of powerful men began to turn to conquest overseas. This was something new for Japan. Apart from the invasion of Korea in 1592–98, which was itself an aberration, the result of Hideyoshi's personal agenda rather than a national desire to expand, Japan's leaders had always been content to remain within the confines of their island domain. Why, then, the change? First, the Western powers that Meiji Japan was now striving to emulate were then in the midst of a period of colonial expansion of their own, one that would see a quarter of all dry land on the face of the earth seized and divided up between the late 1870s and the start of World War I. As part of its drive to become a great power, Japan became eager to claim territory for itself. The Japanese were also motivated by a desire to restore national self-confidence and prestige after their humiliating inability to resist the gunboat diplomacy of the United States. To assuage their pride, they needed to prove themselves equal to the West. That meant they had to modernize. They had to build up their strength. And they had to acquire colonial possessions, just like every other major power.

In 1869, after Tokyo's first approaches to Seoul to initiate modern diplomatic and trade relations had been curtly rebuffed—it was still Korean policy to funnel all Japanese contact through Tsushima—leading Meiji statesman Kido Takayoshi wrote in his diary that Japan "should determine without delay the course our nation is to take, then dispatch an envoy to Korea to question officials of that land about their discourtesy to us. If they do not acknowledge their fault, let us proclaim it publicly and launch an attack on their territory to extend the influence of our Divine Land."[24] Kido was not alone in his views. A punitive expedition against Korea was considered by many to offer several advantages. It would occupy Japan's rebellious former samurai, who had lost their status with the demise of the Tokugawa shogunate; it would secure for Japan a foothold on the peninsula before the Western powers beat them to it; it would establish Japan as a leading Asian power; and it would avenge the failure of Hideyoshi's invasion of Korea nearly three centuries before.

Nothing came of this initial expansionist talk. In 1871 fifty top Meiji government officials, including Kido Takayoshi, were sent on a two-year "learning mission" to the United States and Europe, bringing back with them a deeper understanding of where Western power came from and how empire building worked. With these newly returned statesmen back at the helm, talk of invading Korea was deemed premature, a move that would set Japan against China and Russia before it had the industrial and military might to take them on. For its first expansionary step Japan instead opted for a less confrontational "formalizing of its border," annexing the Kuril Islands in 1875 and the Ryukyu Islands in 1879, officially claiming those regions traditionally considered in Tokyo to be culturally, if not politically, Japanese. Renewed approaches were also made to Korea, but in a more sophisticated way. After the Koreans obligingly attacked a Japanese survey ship that approached Kanghwa Island in 1875—the vessel had been provocatively accompanied by gunboats—Tokyo sent an emissary to Beijing to request that it pressure its tributary state to accept the inevitable of opening to the outside world. China, which had itself been open to the West since its defeat by the British in the Opium Wars of 1839–42, was anxious to avoid any sort of international conflict and duly instructed

Korea to enter into negotiations with Japan. The result was the Treaty of Kanghwa in 1876 establishing modern diplomatic and trade relations between Tokyo and Seoul—all carefully weighted to the advantage of Japan.

The Korean government at this time was as divided as ever by factional strife, each camp more concerned with besting its political rivals than in forming a coherent foreign policy to replace Seoul's now-defunct reliance on isolation. There were three nodes of power on the scene: King Kojong, who came to the throne in 1864 by way of adoption into the royal house; the young man's birth father, the Taewongun, who had served as regent until Kojong's recent coming of age; and Kojong's wife, Queen Min, backed by her influential family. At first the Taewongun and his group took a reactionary, antiforeign stance, pulling King Kojong in one direction while Queen Min's pro-modernization, pro-Japan camp pulled him in another. This lasted until the reactionaries attacked the Japanese legation in Seoul, giving the Japanese an excuse to send troops to Korea to protect their citizens, and in turn forcing China to remove the Taewongun before his followers provided Tokyo with any further cause to intervene. By the time the Taewongun was allowed to return to Seoul in 1885, he had reversed himself to support Japan, and Queen Min had in turn become anti-Japanese, a move that would lead to her murder ten years later in a Japanese-incited palace attack. King Kojong, meanwhile, remained caught in the middle, turning alternately to the Russians, the British, and the Americans for advice.

In 1894 the Tonghak peasant uprising gave both the Japanese and the Chinese cause to send additional forces to Korea, the Japanese to safeguard their growing interests, the Chinese in response to a call for help from Seoul. After a quarter century of modernization, Japan was now feeling confident of its position on the peninsula and of its ability to challenge Qing China, which was by this time sinking into a morass of corruption, mismanagement, and weakness. The Sino-Japanese War of 1894–95 was the result. Mobilizing just eight thousand ground troops and twenty-one small but modern warships, the Japanese efficiently crushed Qing army units at Pyongyang, sank several Chinese ships in the northern reaches of the Yellow Sea, and went on to seize the Liaodong Peninsula on China's eastern border. In the treaty that ended the war in April 1895, China relinquished its age-old influence over Korea by declaring the nation independent, handed over to Japan the island of Taiwan, and agreed to pay a huge indemnity, a promise that it would have to borrow heavily from the West to fulfill.

The Sino-Japanese War placed the Qing dynasty on its final slide to oblivion. In the aftermath of the conflict, Britain, Russia, and Germany, awakened to the true extent of China's weakness, began demanding trade concessions and territorial leases that Beijing was powerless to refuse, "cutting up the Chinese melon" into semi-colonial spheres of influence. The Qing dynasty, the last dynasty to govern China after more than two millennia of imperial rule, eventually collapsed in 1912, replaced first by a shaky republic, then by a prolonged period of civil war.

Japan, meanwhile, emerged from the war with a tremendous surge of self-confidence and pride. It had successfully taken its first real step toward colonial expansion with the acquisition of Taiwan and had established itself as the leading state in East Asia—and in turn a rising challenge to Russia. The tsar's empire, which during Hideyoshi's time did not extend much beyond the Ural Mountains, now stretched all the way to the Pacific Ocean, bringing Russia's colonial ambitions into conflict with Japan. Tokyo initially sought to avoid a conflict with its giant neighbor by acquiescing to Moscow's demand that it return the Liaodong Peninsula to China, ostensibly for the sake of preserving peace in the region. In fact Russia wanted the peninsula for itself; it needed an ice-free port on its Pacific side, and the Liaodong Peninsula had two. The issue was finally settled in the Russo-Japanese War of 1904–05 from which Japan once again emerged the unexpected victor, thereby establishing itself as a bona fide great power.

By this time Japan had won the admiration and respect of many in the West. It was seen as a model of Asian modernization and good government, with all the qualities necessary to lead its less developed Asian neighbors to "enlightenment" through benevolent colonial rule. In a 1904 report to Washington, American minister to Korea Horace Allen observed that "These people [the Koreans] cannot govern themselves. They must have an overlord as they have had for all time.... Let Japan have Korea outright if she can get it.... I am no pro-Japanese enthusiast, as you know, but neither am I opposed to any civilized race taking over the management of these kindly Asiatics for the good of the people and the suppression of oppressive officials, the establishment of order and the development of commerce."[25] In the following year American journalist George Kennan added his two cents: "There is now in progress in the Far East a social and political experiment which, in point of interest and importance, is not surpassed, I think, by anything of the kind recorded in history. For the first time in the annals of the East, one Asiatic nation is making a serious and determined effort to transform and civilize another.... It is a gigantic experiment, and it may or may not succeed; but we, who are trying a similar experiment in the Philippines, must regard it with the deepest interest and sympathy."[26]

In 1905 Korea was made a protectorate of Japan to the general acquiescence or approval of the great Western powers. The Koreans, like the Taiwanese ten years before, tried to resist, even forming "righteous armies" as they had during the Imjin War. All such efforts were brutally suppressed by the Japanese at a cost of nearly twelve thousand Korean lives. In 1910 Tokyo annexed the peninsula outright.

By siding with the allies in World War I, Japan was able to add a few more bits and pieces to its empire by seizing former German possessions in the Far East, the treaty port of Qingdao on China's eastern coast, plus a number of Pacific islands. This marked the end of Japan's first expansionist phase, when it built an empire during the age of imperialism by following the example and abiding by the rules of the West. Tokyo's thirst for territory, however, remained unquenched. With the government coming increasing under military control, Japan went on to seize Manchuria and a large portion of eastern China in 1931–32. Then, beginning on December 7, 1941, it made a grab for the Western world's Asian colonial possessions, bringing it first and foremost into conflict with the United States. It was a contest Japan could not, and would not, win.

At its point of greatest wartime expansion in 1942, Japan's empire extended across Korea, Manchuria, eastern China, Indochina, Southeast Asia, and much of the South Pacific. It was the same territory Toyotomi Hideyoshi had set out to conquer back in 1592.

*   *   *

After a period of estrangement following World War II, a myriad of economic, diplomatic, cultural, and educational ties began to develop between Korea and Japan, binding the two nations together in a relationship that is today closer than at any time in the past. Tensions, however, have not disappeared. The largest source of contention remains Japan's occupation of the peninsula from 1905 to 1945 and its actions in World War II, when Korean men were conscripted as slave labor for wartime industries and women were forced into prostitution as "comfort women" for the empire's troops. The Koreans want apologies and compensation, more than the Japanese are willing to give. Conflicts also regularly arise over how each nation views their shared history. Beginning in 1982, the way history was being taught to Japanese students came under harsh criticism by both the Koreans and Chinese, they charging that new textbooks introduced into the schools attempted to rationalize and sugarcoat Japan's militaristic past, primarily its conduct in World War II, but also during Hideyoshi's invasion of the mainland four hundred years before. Tokyo has ordered limited changes to the controversial textbooks over the years and has tried to appear more sensitive in the eyes of the world. But it has not done enough as far as the Koreans are concerned. They continue to urge the Japanese to acknowledge their "past wrongdoings" and to teach history "objectively through balanced descriptions which take into account the views of their neighbors."[27] Some Japanese are sympathetic to these concerns. Others counter that Seoul is merely using the textbook issue for diplomatic and economic gain, or that the whole thing is a bugbear that Korea's opposition leaders like to throw into the political arena to put pressure on the party in power.[28]

Yet another source of disagreement between Korea and Japan is the mimizuka in Kyoto, the misnamed "ear tomb" where the tens of thousands of noses that Hideyoshi's troops cut off during the Imjin War were subsequently interred. In 1990 a Korean Buddhist monk named Pak Sam-jung traveled to Kyoto and, with the support of a private local organization, conducted a ceremony in front of the tomb to comfort the spirits residing there and guide them home to Korea. Over the next six years the Japanese organization that hosted this event spearheaded a drive to get the mimizuka itself sent home, submitting a petition bearing twenty thousand signatures to Kyoto city officials, and pledging to bear the cost of excavating the contents of the tomb and shipping them to Korea, together with the nine-meter-high earthen mound and the stone pagoda on top. When Pak Sam-jung returned to Kyoto in 1996, the tomb's return seemed imminent. "These noses were cut off as trophies of war for Toyotomi Hideyoshi," he announced upon leaving Seoul. "They have been there in Kyoto for four hundred years. It is now our duty to see them returned to Korea to assuage the grief of the 126,000 people whose remains are buried there."[29]

In the end the necessary permission to move the mimizuka was not forthcoming from the Japanese government. It was decided that, as an officially designated national cultural asset, the tomb should stay where it was. It remains in Kyoto to this day, little known and not often visited, and not well marked for tourists. It is just west of Kyoto National Museum and Toyokuni Jinja, the Shinto shrine dedicated to Toyotomi Hideyoshi, who was deified as a kami after his death. Funding from the government is insufficient to care for the site, so the work is done by local residents, who volunteer to cut the grass and tidy up the grounds.[30]

NOTES

PART 1: THE THREE KINGDOMS
1. William Henthorn, *A History of Korea* (New York: Free Press, 1971), 148.

CHAPTER 1: *Japan: From Civil War to World Power*
1. From Nampo Bunshi's early-17th-century account in *Teppo-ki* (Story of the Gun), in *Sources of Japanese Tradition*, vol. 1, ed. Ryusaku Tsunoda, William Theodore de Bary, and Donald Keene (New York: Columbia University Press, 1964), 308–312; C. R. Boxer, *The Christian Century in Japan, 1549–1650* (Berkeley: University of California Press, 1951), chap. 1.
2. Stephen Turnbull, *The Samurai Sourcebook* (London: Cassell, 1998), 128–134.
3. Delmer Brown, "The Impact of Firearms on Japanese Warfare, 1543–98," *Far Eastern Quarterly* 7, no. 3 (May 1948): 238.
4. The weight of the bullet fired by these early Japanese guns varied from 10 to 110 grams (ibid., 238, n. 9).
5. Stephen Turnbull, *Samurai Warfare* (London: Arms and Armour Press, 1996), 74–75.
6. Gwynne Dyer, *War* (Toronto: Stoddart, 1985), 30.
7. Ibid., 73–76; Peter Newark, *Firefight! The History of Personal Firepower* (Devon: David & Charles, 1989), 15–17.
8. Asao Naohiro, "The Sixteenth-Century Unification," in *The Cambridge History of Japan*, vol. 4, *Early Modern Japan*, ed. John Whitney Hall (Cambridge: Cambridge University Press, 1991), 43–44.
9. This account from the *Ehon Taikoki* (1797–1802) appears in George Elison, "Hideyoshi, the Bountiful Minister," in *Warlords, Artists, and Commoners: Japan in the Sixteenth Century,* ed. George Elison and Bardwell Smith (Honolulu: University of Hawai'i Press, 1981), 223. Some sources give more precise birth dates for Hideyoshi. In his *Life of Toyotomi Hideyoshi,* for example, Walter Dening specifies January 1, 1536. Such dates were likely invented by contemporary and Edo-period biographers. No one knows for certain when Hideyoshi was born. It is possible he did not know himself.

10. That Hideyoshi was regarded as small even by his countrymen, who were themselves considered small by the first European visitors to Japan, would suggest that by modern standards he was very small indeed.

11. Elison, "Hideyoshi," 224; Mary Elizabeth Berry, *Hideyoshi* (Cambridge, Mass.: Harvard University Press, 1982), 9 and 57.

12. Walter Dening, *The Life of Toyotomi Hideyoshi*, 3rd ed. (Kobe: J. L. Thompson, 1930), 176.

13. Hideyoshi to Date Masamune, circa 1590, in C. Meriwether, "A Sketch of the Life of Date Masamune and an Account of His Embassy to Rome," *Transactions of the Asiatic Society of Japan* 21 (1893): 17.

14. A koku was equal to five bushels, or 40 gallons, or 182 liters. In 1598 small fiefdoms in Hideyoshi's Japan consisted of 10,000–30,000 koku. Tokugawa Ieyasu, Hideyoshi's richest vassal, controlled a domain valued at 2,557,000 koku. George Sansom, *A History of Japan, 1334–1615* (Stanford, Calif.: Stanford University Press, 1961), 413–414.

15. Hideyoshi to Gosa, 13/4/Tensho 18 (May 16, 1590), in *101 Letters of Hideyoshi*, trans. and ed. Adriana Boscaro (Tokyo: Sophia University, 1975), 37–38.

16. Elison, "Hideyoshi"; H. Paul Varley and George Elison, "The Culture of Tea"; Donald Keene, "Joha, a Sixteenth-Century Poet of Linked Verse"; all in Elison and Smith, *Warlords*.

17. Hur Nam-lin, "The International Context of Toyotomi Hideyoshi's Invasion of Korea in 1592," *Korea Observer* 28, no. 4 (Winter 1997): 691.

18. James Murdoch, *A History of Japan during the Century of Early Foreign Intercourse (1542–1651)* (Kobe: Printed at the office of the "Chronicle," 1903), 305; Berry, 207–208.

19. Jurgis Elisonas, "The Inseparable Trinity: Japan's Relations with China and Korea," in *The Cambridge History of Japan,* vol. 4, *Early Modern Japan*, ed. John Whitney Hall (Cambridge: Cambridge University Press, 1991), 267.

20. Berry, 91.

21. "Wu-tzu," in *The Seven Military Classics of Ancient China*, trans. Ralph Sawyer (Boulder, Colo.: Woodview Press, 1993), 208.

22. Hideyoshi to the King of Korea, Tensho 17 (1589), in Homer Hulbert, *Hulbert's History of Korea*, vol. 1 (New York: Hillary House, 1962), 347.

23. "The first modern army that could not have been defeated by the army of Alexander the Great [330 B.C.] was probably the army of Gustavus Adolphus [A.D. 1620]." Col. T. N. Dupuy, U.S. Army, ret'd., quoted in Dyer, 29. It was King Adolphus of Sweden, driven by a need to raise an effective army from a population of less than a million and a half, who first made firearms the dominant weapon in his army. The devastating impact of his rapid volley fire prompted other nations to quickly follow suit (Dyer, 61–62).

24. Bert Hall, *Weapons and Warfare in Renaissance Europe* (Baltimore: Johns

Hopkins University Press, 1997), 207 and 209. Spain had the largest army in Europe at this time. Throughout the latter part of the sixteenth century it averaged 60,000–65,000 men, briefly peaking at 86,000 men in March of 1574. The largest army the French could muster in the late sixteenth century was about 50,000 men; the English army in Elizabethan times hovered around 20,000–30,000, while the Dutch had some 20,000 men under arms.

CHAPTER 2: *China: The Ming Dynasty in Decline*

1. Chu Hsi and Lu Tsu-ch'ien, *Reflections of Things at Hand*, trans. Wing-tsit Chan (New York: Columbia University Press, 1967), 69.
2. Confucius, *The Analects (Lun yu)*, trans. D. C. Lau (London: Penguin Books, 1979), 155 (book 19:13).
3. John Fairbank, *China. A New History* (Cambridge, Mass.: Harvard University Press, 1992), 130.
4. Louise Levathes, *When China Ruled the Seas: The Treasure Fleet of the Dragon Throne, 1405–1433* (New York: Simon & Schuster, 1994).
5. Ray Huang, *1587. A Year of No Significance: The Ming Dynasty in Decline* (New Haven, Conn.: Yale University Press, 1981), 89–90.
6. Edward L. Dreyer, *Early Ming China. A Political History, 1355–1435* (Stanford, Calif.: Stanford University Press, 1982), 76–79. By 1393 at least 326 wei had been formed.
7. From 1480 until approximately 1590 the annual cost of maintaining China's border garrisons increased by almost nine times, from 559,000 ounces of silver to 4.94 million ounces. (Albert Chan, *The Glory and Fall of the Ming Dynasty* (Norman: University of Oklahoma Press, 1982), 197–198.)
8. Huang, *1587*, 160.
9. Chan, 51.
10. Minister of War Chang Shih-ch'e in 1562, in Elisonas, "Trinity," 252–253.
11. Chan, 201.
12. Ibid., 205–207.
13. *Ming Shih*, chap. 322, quoted in Kwan-wai So, *Japanese Piracy in Ming China during the 16th Century* (East Lansing: Michigan State University Press, 1975), 181.
14. Charles Hucker, "Hu Tsung-hsien's Campaign against Hsu Hai, 1556," in *Chinese Ways in Warfare*, ed. Frank Kierman Jr. and John Fairbank (Cambridge, Mass.: Harvard University Press, 1974), 274–282; So, 144–156.
15. Ray Huang, "The Lung-ch'ing and Wan-li Reigns, 1567–1620," in *The Cambridge History of China*, vol. 7, *The Ming Dynasty, 1368–1644, Part 1*, ed. Denis Twitchett and John Fairbank (Cambridge: Cambridge University Press, 1988), 557.
16. Francisco de Sande, Governor of the Philippines, "Relation of the Filipinas

Islands," June 7, 1576, in *The Philippine Islands, 1493–1898*, vol. 4, trans. and ed. Emma Blair and James Robertson (Cleveland, Ohio: A. H. Clark, 1903), 58–59.

17. "Memorandum of the Various Points Presented by the General Junta of Manila," in Blair and Robertson, vol. 6, 197–229. (The meeting was held on April 20, 1586; the memorandum was prepared and signed on July 26.)
18. Huang, *1587*, 42.
19. Qi Jiguang, *Lien-ping Shih-chi* (1571), ibid., 172–173.
20. Ibid., 156–188; L. Carrington Goodrich, ed., *Dictionary of Ming Biography*, vol. 1 (New York: Columbia University Press, 1976), 220–224.
21. General Qi was even dragged into the picture and accused of procuring a young plaything for Chang at great personal expense (Huang, *1587*, 184–185).
22. Charles Hucker, *The Censorial System in Ming China* (Stanford, Calif.: Stanford University Press, 1966), 43.
23. Wang Yi-t'ung, *Official Relations between China and Japan, 1368–1549* (Cambridge, Mass.: Harvard University Press, 1953).

CHAPTER 3: *A Son Called* Sute: *"Thrown Away"*

1. Hideyoshi to Koya, no date (1589), in Boscaro, *Letters*, 34. Although Hideyoshi addressed this letter to Koya, one of his wife O-Ne's ladies-in-waiting, he undoubtedly intended it to be read to O-Ne herself.
2. Hideyoshi to Lady O-Mandokoro, 1/5/Tensho 18 (June 2, 1590), ibid., 39.
3. Hideyoshi to Koya, no date (1589), ibid., 34.
4. Hideyoshi to Chunagon, 24/10/no year (1585–91?), ibid., 25. (Chunagon was one of O-Ne's ladies-in-waiting.)
5. Hideyoshi to Lady Gomoji (Go-Hime), undated, ibid., 9.
6. Hideyoshi to Tomoji, 4/9/no year (1585–91?), ibid., 22.
7. Hideyoshi to O-Chacha (Yodogimi), no date (1590), ibid., 43. "Denka" was Hideyoshi's title as kampaku.

CHAPTER 4: *Korea: Highway to the Prize*

1. This view of the origins of the name Nippon was first suggested by William Aston in his translation of the *Nihongi (Chronicles of Japan)*, and is reiterated in Bruce Cumings, *Korea's Place in the Sun* (New York: W. W. Norton, 1997), 38.
2. Ilyon, *Samguk yusa*, trans. Ha Tae-hung and Grafton Mintz (Seoul: Yonsei University Press, 1972), 32–33.
3. Masuid, *Meadows of Gold and Mines of Precious Stone*, quoted in Cumings, 37.
4. David Pollack, *The Fracture of Meaning* (Princeton, N.J.: Princeton University Press, 1986), 12, 15–23, and chaps. 1 and 2 passim.
5. Wang, 17–18.
6. J. S. Gale, "The Influence of China upon Korea," *Transactions of the*

Korea Branch of the Royal Asiatic Society 1 (1900): 24.

7. At the start of the Choson dynasty in 1392, this grading of foreign nations was made quite clear by the government ranking accorded to visiting envoys to the court in Seoul. On a scale from the lowest rank of 9B to the highest of 1A, the Jurchen envoy, for example, was pegged at 4B—more to appease these troublesome people than out of any high regard the Koreans had for them—while the Ryukyu Islands fared more poorly at 5B. Etsuko Hae-jin Kang, *Diplomacy and Ideology in Japanese-Korean Relations* (New York: St. Martin's Press, 1997), 50–51.

8. Ibid., 66.

9. Between 1392 and 1422, for example, Korea sent some 45,000 horses to the Ming court (Henthorn, *History*, 154). China reciprocated with shipments of things like cotton cloth and silk.

10. Donald Clark, "Sino-Korean Tributary Relations under the Ming," in *The Cambridge History of China*, vol. 8, *The Ming Dynasty, 1368–1644, Part 2*, ed. Denis Twitchett and Frederick Mote (Cambridge: Cambridge University Press, 1998), 273 and 279; Dreyer, 115.

11. Gale, "Influence of China," 11.

12. The words of a Chinese envoy to the Korean court in 1487, in J. S. Gale, "Han-yang (Seoul)," *Transactions of the Korea Branch of the Royal Asiatic Society* 2 (1902): 38.

13. Clark, "Tributary Relations," 280 and 283. The number of embassies the Koreans sent to China increased markedly during times of crisis or uncertainty, whereas during periods of quiet they tended to be less frequent.

14. Etsuko Hae-jin Kang, 55.

15. Korean envoy Kang Kwon-son on a visit to Iki Island in 1444, in Elisonas, "Trinity," 243.

16. Letter from Korean king Taejong to Tsushima daimyo So Sadamori, 7th month, 1419, in Etsuko Hae-jin Kang, 59.

17. Sin Ch'ojung, "On the Deceitfulness of Buddhism," and Yun Hoe, "On the Harmfulness of Buddhism," in a memorial submitted to King Sejong in 1424, quoted in Peter Lee, ed., *Sourcebook of Korean Civilization*, vol. 1 (New York: Columbia University Press, 1993), 551–552.

18. Edward Wagner, *The Literati Purges: Political Conflict in Early Yi Korea* (Cambridge, Mass.: Harvard University Press, 1974).

19. Hanguk chongsin munhwa yonguwon, *Hangukin mul daesajon*, vol. 2 (Seoul: Chungang ilbo, 1999), 2056–2057; Peter Lee, trans. and ed., *Pine River and Lone Peak: An Anthology of Three Choson Dynasty Poets* (Honolulu: University of Hawai'i Press, 1991), 11–20 and 43–44. (Chong Chol's pen name was Songgang, "Pine River.")

20. Richard Rutt, trans. and ed., *The Bamboo Grove: An Introduction to Sijo* (Berkeley: University of California Press, 1971), poem 13.

21. Ha Tae-hung, *Behind the Scenes of Royal Palaces in Korea* (Seoul: Yonsei University Press, 1983), 162.

22. Hulbert, vol. 1, 338–340.

23. Cho Kwang-jo, "On the Superior Man and the Inferior Man," in Peter Lee, *Sourcebook*, vol. 1, 505.

PART 2: PRELUDE TO WAR
1. Elisonas, "Trinity," 271.
2. Ha Tae-hung, *Behind the Scenes,* 166.

CHAPTER 5: *"By fast ships I have dispatched orders to Korea . . . "*
1. Adrian Forsyth, *A Natural History of Sex* (New York: Charles Scribner's Sons, 1986), 40.
2. Berry, 91.
3. A typical Japanese *nagae-yari* (long-shafted spear) of the later sengoku period was 3 *ken* (4.8 meters) long, making it more of a pike than a spear. This was the length favored by Hideyoshi, Tokugawa Ieyasu, and several other prominent daimyo. Oda Nobunaga outdid them all by equipping his spear corps with 3½ *ken* (5.6 meter) weapons, the longest spears known to have been used in Japan (Turnbull, *Samurai Warfare*, 71–73).
4. Wilbur Bacon, "Record of Reprimands and Admonitions (Chingbirok)," *Transactions of the Korea Branch of the Royal Asiatic Society* 48 (1972): 11–12.
5. Ibid., 11.
6. *Sonjo sillok*, vol. 4 (Seoul: Minjok munhwa chujin hee, 1987–89), 268 (20/10/Sonjo 20; Dec. 8, 1587).
7. *Sonjo sujong sillok*, vol. 3 (Seoul: Minjok munhwa chujin hee, 1989), 51–52 (9/Sonjo 20; Oct. 1587).
8. Yu Song-nyong, *Chingbirok* (Seoul: Myongmundang, 1987), 13; *Sonjo sujong sillok*, vol. 3, 85–86 (12/Sonjo 21; Feb. 1589).
9. Hideyoshi to the King of Korea, Tensho 17 (1589), in Hulbert, vol. 1, 347.
10. Yu Song-nyong, 13–14; *Sonjo sujong sillok*, vol. 3, 105–106 (7/Sonjo 22; Sept. 1589).
11. *Sonjo sillok*, vol. 5, 124 (18/11/Sonjo 22; Dec. 25, 1589) and 155 (6/3/Sonjo 23; April 9, 1590); Etsuko Hae-jin Kang, 93.
12. "[W]hether one was allowed to ride it [a palanquin] up to, or beyond, and then how far beyond, the castle gates, were carefully graded to rank and status" (Ronald Toby, *State and Diplomacy in Early Modern Japan* [Princeton, N.J.: Princeton University Press, 1984], 193, n. 62). In the Koreans' estimation Yoshitoshi's rank did not give him the privilege to ride his sedan chair into the temple grounds.
13. Yu Song-nyong, 14; Etsuko Hae-jin Kang, 89.
14. The other major urban centers in Japan at this time—Osaka, Kamakura, Sakai, Nara, and Hakata—were much smaller, with populations ranging downwards from 10,000 (Berry, 275, n. 53).

15. Ibid., 202.
16. A Chinese account of what might be regarded as a typical Korean reception of a Ming ambassador in Seoul can be found in Richard Rutt, "Ch'ao-hsien fu," *Transactions of the Korea Branch of the Royal Asiatic Society* 48 (1973): 47–48.
17. King Sonjo to Hideyoshi, "King of Japan," 3/Wanli 18 (April 1590), in Yoshi Kuno, *Japanese Expansion on the Asiatic Continent*, vol. 1 (Berkeley: University of California Press, 1937), 301.
18. Yu Song-nyong, 15–16.
19. Dening, 283.
20. Hideoyshi to the King of Korea, winter, Tensho 18 (1590), in Kuno, vol. 1, 302–303; *Sonjo sillok*, vol. 5, 172–173 (13/1/Sonjo 24; Feb. 6, 1591).
21. *Sonjo sujong sillok*, vol. 3, 186–189 (2/Sonjo 24; March 1591).
22. Ibid., 208 (3/Sonjo 24; April 1591).
23. King Sonjo to Hideyoshi, "King of Japan," spring, Wanli 19 (1591), in Kuno, vol. 1, 303–304.
24. *Sonjo sujong sillok*, vol. 3, 221 (6/Sonjo 24; July 1591).
25. King Shonei to Hideyoshi, 17/5/Tensho 17 (June 29, 1589), in Kuno, vol. 1, 305–306.
26. Hideyoshi to King Shonei, 18/2/Tensho 18 (March 23, 1590), ibid., 306.
27. Although the crowns of Portugal and Spain were united in 1580 under Philip II, rivalry continued to exist between the two in the Far East: rivalry over empire, trade, and religious monopolies. It was therefore in keeping with the times that a Portuguese trader would try to turn Hideyoshi against a Spanish possession.
28. Hideyoshi to the Philippines, 15/9/Tensho 19 (Nov. 1, 1591), translated from the original Japanese in Kuno, vol. 1, 308–309, and from the Spanish translation received by the Governor of the Philippines in Blair and Robertson, vol. 8, 260–261.
29. Gomez Perez Dasmarinas to Hideyoshi, June 11, 1592, translated from the Spanish original in Blair and Robertson, vol. 8, 263–267, and from the Japanese translation in Kuno, vol. 1, 310–311.
30. Testimony of Antonio Lopez before Governor Dasmarinas, June 1, 1593, in Blair and Robertson, vol. 9, 45. (Lopez was a Chinese Christian who accompanied Father Cobo to Japan. The father died on the return journey to Manila.)
31. Hideyoshi to the Portuguese Viceroy of India at Goa, 25/7/Tensho 19 (Sept. 12, 1591), in Kuno, vol. 1, 313–314.

CHAPTER 6: *Preparations for War*

1. The present-day city of Nagoya on central Honshu did not exist in the sixteenth century. It was then the site of the village of Nakamura, the birthplace of both Hideyoshi and his general Kato Kiyomasa.
2. "This witness saw with his own eyes that the city of Nangoya is a city of

one hundred thousand or more inhabitants. This city was built and settled in five months. It is three leguas long, and nine leguas in circumference" (testimony of Captain Joan de Solis before Gomez Perez Dasmarinas, Spanish governor of the Philippines, May 24, 1593, in Blair and Robertson, vol. 9, 35).

3. Bernard Susser, "The Toyotomi Regime and the Daimyo," in *The Bakufu in Japanese History*, ed. Jeffrey Mass and William Hauser (Stanford, Calif.: Stanford University Press, 1985), 137.

4. There was only one instance of a daimyo openly resisting Hideyoshi's demand for troops. Umekita Kunikane, a vassal of the Shimazu clan on Kyushu, refused to participate in the Korean invasion and set out to attack Hideyoshi at his Nagoya headquarters in 1592. He was met and killed before he ever reached Nagoya (Berry, 278, n. 21).

5. Bert Hall, 208.

6. Katano Tsugio, *Yi Sun-sin gwa Hideyoshi*, trans. Yun Bong-sok (Seoul: Wooseok, 1997), 245; George Heber Jones, "The Japanese Invasion, " *The Korean Repository* 1 (1892): 116.

7. Yi Hyong-sok, *Imjin Chollan-sa*, vol. 2 (Seoul: Imjin Chollan-sa Kan-haeng hoe, 1967), 1714–1715; Sansom, 318–19.

8. Hulbert, vol. 1, 350.

9. Hideyoshi to Shimazu, Tensho 19 (1591), in *The Documents of the Iriki,* trans. and ed. Asakawa Kanichi (Tokyo: Japan Society for the Promotion of Science, 1955), 333. According to Hideyoshi's orders Shimazu was to contribute 15,000 men to the invasion force, but according to Asakawa his actual contribution was no more than 10,000 and possibly less.

10. The muster rolls of the various companies assembled at Nagoya "suggest that no more than half of those on the strength of a contingent drafted for service in Korea were fighting men; the rest did construction and transport duties" (Elisonas, "Trinity," 272).

11. G. A. Ballard, *The Influence of the Sea on the Political History of Japan* (New York: E. P. Dutton, 1921), 51; Kuno, vol. 1, 152–153.

12. Asao, 54; Samson, 288 and 309; Berry, 254, n. 46. With regard to Nobunaga's iron ships, samurai historian Stephen Turnbull writes that they were "reinforced in some way with iron. It is unlikely that they were covered with iron sheets, which would have made them 'ironclad battleships,' though a certain priest saw the ships as they put to sea, and describes these magnificent vessels as 'iron–ships' " (*Samurai Warfare*, 38).

13. Boxer, *Christian Century,* 140–142.

14. Katano, 88; Yi Hyong-sok, vol. 2, 1720.

15. According to Hulbert, vol. 1, 350, Hideyoshi's fleet "consisted of between three and four thousand boats. This gives us an idea as to the capacity of the boats used in those days. According to this enumeration each boat carried sixty men. They were probably undecked, or at most but partially decked, boats of about forty or fifty feet in length by ten in breadth."

Hulbert's description of the average transport as being fairly small is probably accurate, but the total number of 3,000 to 4,000 he cites is too high, having been based on the assumption that each vessel made just one crossing to Korea carrying a single load of soldiers. The entire force of 158,800 in fact did not cross to Korea all at once; it did so over the course of several weeks. It is likely, therefore, that many if not most of the transports ferried more than one load of troops across from Tsushima and Kyushu, a journey that in good weather could be done in a day.

16. The three top posts in the Korean government during the Choson dynasty were Prime Minister (*yong-uijong*), Minister of the Left (*chwa-uijong*), and Minister of the Right (*u-uijong*).

17. Bacon, "Chingbirok," 16.

18. Ibid., 16–17; Etsuko Hae-jin Kang, 92–93; Hur, 705–706.

19. *Sonjo sillok*, vol. 5, 196–197 (24/10/Sonjo 24; Dec. 9, 1591) and 197 (2/11/Sonjo 24; Dec. 17, 1591); *Sonjo sujong sillok*, vol. 3, 224–225 (10/Sonjo 24; Nov.–Dec. 1591). The subsequent official embassy to Beijing, led by Han Ung-in, left Seoul on December 9, 1591.

20. William Henthorn, "Some Notes of Koryo Military Units," *Transactions of the Korea Branch of the Royal Asiatic Society* 35 (1959): 67.

21. Samuel Dukhae Kim, "The Korean Monk-Soldiers in the Imjin Wars: An Analysis of Buddhist Resistance to the Hideyoshi Invasion, 1592–1598" (Ph.D. dissertation, Columbia University, 1978), 20.

22. The designations "Left" and "Right" army and navy are somewhat confusing as they were applied to the southern provinces of Kyongsang-do and Cholla-do, for when viewed on a map the "Left" regions lay to the east and the "Right" regions to the west. This was due to the fact that the designations were assigned from the perspective of the capital of Seoul. Looking south from there, the eastern halves of Kyongsang and Cholla Provinces are indeed on the left and the western halves on the right.

23. See the chapter on "Military Command of the Choson Dynasty" in Yi Sun-sin, *Nanjung ilgi: War Diary of Admiral Yi Sun-sin*, trans. Ha Tae-hung and ed. Sohn Pow-key (Seoul: Yonsei University Press, 1977), xiii–xv.

24. Yu Song-nyong, 18.

25. Wagner, 18.

26. Park Yune-hee, *Admiral Yi Sun-shin and his Turtleboat Armada* (Seoul: Hanjin Publishing Company, 1978), 67; Samuel Dukhae Kim, 21.

27. *Sonjo sujong sillok*, vol. 3, 223–224 (7/Sonjo 24; Aug. 9, 1591); Yu Song-nyong, 17–18; Samuel Dukhae Kim, 18.

28. Jho Sung-do, *Yi Sun-Shin: A National Hero of Korea* (Ch'ungmu-kong Society, Naval Academy, Korea, 1970), 54.

29. John Boots, "Korean Weapons and Armor," *Transactions of the Korea Branch of the Royal Asiatic Society* 23, part 2 (Dec. 1934): 3–18.

30. Boots, 20, gives this interesting translation from an old Korean source of how to make gunpowder: "Take one pound of saltpeter, one *yang* of sulphur

and 5 *yang* of the ash of the willow; grind it together into flour, making it into one mixture. Put it into a big wooden bowl with one rice bowl of water, and with a wooden tamper strike it ten thousand times. . . . When it becomes about half dry, take it out and dry it in the sun. Then pound it some more until it becomes like a small bean. . . . After that, take it out and with good water take out the strength of the saltpeter. Dip it into water about 20 times, then weigh out one *tone* of it and, placing it in the palm of a man's hand, set fire to it. When it burns, if it is not necessary to pull the hand away, it can be used in a gun" (1 *tone* = 3.8 grams; 1 *yang* = 10 *tone*).

31. Yang Jae-suk, *Dashi ssunun imjin daejonchaeng*, vol. 1 (Seoul: Koryo-won, 1994), 178–184; Park Yune-hee, 75–76.
32. Yang Jae-suk, *Dashi ssunun*, vol. 1, 187–197; Boots, 22–23.
33. Yang Tai-zin, "On the System of Beacons in Korea," *Korea Journal* 11, no. 7 (July 1971): 34–35. The problems plaguing Korea's beacon fire system were not overcome until the military took it over in the mid-18th century and began handing out the task of beacon tending to retired soldiers, who "were often glad to get the post, which carried with it land enough to support a family, rights to woods or sometimes to fisheries." The system remained in effect until 1894, when the establishment of the telegraph rendered it obsolete.
34. Yu Song-nyong, 19–20.
35. Ibid., 49; *Sonjo sujong sillok*, vol. 3, 227–228 (11/Sonjo 24; Dec. 1591) and 231 (3/Sonjo 25; April 1592).
36. Park Yune-hee, 125–140; Jho Sung-do, 17–48; Yi Pun, "Biography of Yi Sun-sin," in *Imjin changch'o: Admiral Yi Sun-sin's Memorials to Court*, trans. Ha Tae-hung and ed. Lee Chong-young (Seoul: Yonsei University Press, 1981), 199–210. (Yi Pun was the nephew of Yi Sun-sin, and served under him during the later years of the Imjin War.)
37. Yu Song-nyong, 18–19; *Sonjo sillok*, vol. 5, 178 (13/2/Sonjo 24; Mar. 8, 1591); *Sonjo sujong sillok*, vol. 3, 228 (11/Sonjo 24; Dec. 1591).
38. Diary entry for 5/3/Imjin (April 16, 1592), Yi Sun-sin, *Imjin changch'o: Admiral Yi Sun-sin's Memorials to Court*, trans. Ha Tae-hung and ed. Lee Chong-young (Seoul: Yonsei University Press, 1981), 11. (The Korean title of Yu Song-nyong's military treatise is *Chungson chonsu bangryak*.)
39. "The Book of Lord Shang," in *The Art of War in World History*, ed. Gerard Chaliand (Berkeley: University of California Press, 1994), 244.

CHAPTER 7: *The Final Days*

1. The Jesuit Luis Frois of Portugal witnessed the occasion. Elison, "Hideyoshi," 332, n. 16.
2. Park Yune-hee, 95–96.
3. H. Paul Varley and George Elison, "The Culture of Tea: From Its Origins to Sen no Rikyu," in *Warlords, Artists, and Commoners*, ed. George Elison and Bardwell Smith (Honolulu: University of Hawai'i Press, 1981), 217–219.

Hideyoshi's flashy Kigane stood in glaring contrast to the "way of tea" as practiced by his own tea master, Sen no Rikyu, who for obscure reasons Hideyoshi ordered to commit suicide in 1591, which he soon came to regret. The rustic Yamazato, on the other hand, was the epitome of Rikyu's style, and in turn of chado as it is practiced in Japan today. For a concise overview of chado, see Sen Soshitsu XV, "Chado: The Way of Tea," *Japan Quarterly* 30, no. 4 (Oct.-Dec. 1983): 388–394. (Sen Soshitsu is a descendant of Sen no Rikyu.)

4. Yu Song-nyong, 21.
5. Diary entries for 16/1/Imjin and 25/2/Imjin (Feb. 27 and April 7, 1592), Yi Sun-sin, *Imjin changch'o*, 4 and 10.
6. Diary entry for 12/4/Imjin (May 22, 1592), ibid., 16.
7. Katano, 97–98.
8. "The Precepts of Kato Kiyomasa," in *Ideals of the Samurai: Writings of Japanese Warriors*, trans. William Scott Wilson (Burbank, Calif.: Ohara Publications, 1982), 127–132.
9. Several older English-language accounts of Hideyoshi's invasion of Korea, for example in Hulbert, vol. 1, 351, and Jones, 119, describe Kato as an "old warrior" who resented "the boy" Konishi. This is not correct. Konishi was in fact the older of the two, having been born around 1556, and Kato in 1562.
10. Kuroda Nagamasa, "Notes on Regulations," in Wilson, 133–141.

PART 3: IMJIN

1. Lionel Giles, trans., *Sun Tzu on the Art of War* (Taipei: Ch'eng Wen Publishing Company, 1971), 32.

CHAPTER 8: *North to Seoul*

1. The ten heavenly stems were hard wood, soft wood, sun fire, kitchen fire, mountain earth, sand earth, rough metal, refined metal, seawater, and rainwater.
2. Yu Song-nyong, 50; *Sonjo sillok*, vol. 5, 201–202 (13/4/Sonjo 25; May 23, 1592); dispatch of 15/4/Wanli 20 (May 25, 1592), Yi Sun-sin, *Imjin changch'o*, 19–20.
3. Sansom, 355.
4. Ibid., 354.
5. In response to a list of questions regarding the Japanese invasion that Beijing subsequently submitted to the government of Korea, it was reported that four hundred Japanese ships anchored at Pusan in the initial invasion, and that this number then rose to between seven and eight hundred. *Sonjo sillok*, vol. 6, 253 (11/11/Sonjo 25; Dec. 14, 1592).
6. Giuliana Stramigioli, "Hideyoshi's Expansionist Policy on the Asiatic Mainland," *Transactions of the Asiatic Society of Japan*, third series, 3

(Dec. 1954): 94.

7.   Katano, 102–103.

8.   Konishi here was following Hideyoshi's lead in eschewing the traditional brocade banner in favor of something more prosaic. Early in his career Hideyoshi had stuck a gourd on the end of a pole and made it his banner. He later added an additional gourd for each of his subsequent victories, until his "gourd-banner" was heavy with evidence of his success. William Griffis, *Corea: The Hermit Nation* (New York: Charles Scribner's Sons, 1894), 97.

9.   Ibid., 96.

10. Katano, 100–102.

11. Min Jong-jung, "Nobong-chip," in *Saryoro bonun imjin waeran. Ssawo chuggi-nun swiwo-do kil-ul bilryo jugi-nun oryop-da*, compiled by Chinju National Museum (Seoul: Hyean, 1999), 39–40; Hulbert, vol. 1, 351–352.

12. *Yoshino Jingozaemon oboegaki*, quoted in Stephen Turnbull, *Samurai Invasion* (London: Cassell, 2002), 51.

13. *Sonjo sujong sillok*, vol. 3, 233, 4/Sonjo 25 (May 1592).

14. Min Jong-jung, "Nobong-chip," in *Saryoro bonun*, 41–44; *Sonjo sujong sillok*, vol. 3, 232 (4/Sonjo 25; May 1592).

15. Yu Song-nyong, 72; *Sonjo sujong sillok*, vol. 3, 252 (5/Sonjo 25; June 1592); Jho Sung-do, 70. This traditional account of how Won Kyun lost his fleet has been challenged by Yi Jae-bom in *Won Kyun-ul wihan byon-myong* (Seoul: Hakmin-sa, 1994), 34. Yi hypothesizes that the Japanese navy did not venture much west of Pusan until twenty days after the start of their invasion because Won was putting up an effective defense from his base on Koje Island. I disagree. For the first two weeks of the invasion the Japanese navy was busy ferrying troops to Pusan from Nagoya and Tsushima, and thus was not free to begin probing west along the Korean coast. It was only after this job was done, sometime in early June, well after Won's fleet had disappeared, that Japanese ships began advancing toward the Yellow Sea.

16. This third alternative is suggested by Turnbull, *Samurai Invasion*, 54.

17. Lee Hyoun-jong, "Military Aid of the Ryukyus and Other Southern Asian Nations to Korea during the Hideyoshi Invasion," *Journal of Social Sciences and Humanities* 46 (Dec. 1977): 17.

18. Report by Yun Kwan on military setbacks suffered against the Jurchen, in Henthorn, *History*, 118.

19. Diary entries for 15–18/4/Imjin (May 25–28, 1592), Yi Sun-sin, *Imjin changch'o*, 16–17.

20. "Ssu-ma Fa" (The Marshal's Art of War), in Sawyer, 139.

21. Diary entries for 18–22/4/Imjin (May 28–June 1, 1592), Yi Sun-sin, *Imjin changch'o*, 17–18, and for 1–3/5/Imjin (June 10–12, 1592), Yi Sun-sin, *Nanjung ilgi*, 3–4; dispatch of 30/4/Wanli 20 (June 9, 1592), Yi Sun-sin, *Imjin changch'o*, 28; Park Yune-hee, 144–145; Roger Tennant, *A History*

of Korea (London: Kegan Paul, 1996), 166–167.

22. Choi Byong-hyon, trans., *The Book of Corrections* (Berkeley: Institute of East Asian Studies, University of California, 2002), 55–56 and 27, footnote 11.

23. *Sonjo sujong sillok*, vol. 3, 233 (4/Sonjo 25; May 1592).

24. James Palais, *Confucian Statecraft and Korean Institutions: Yu Hyongwon and the Late Choson Dynasty* (Seattle: University of Washington Press, 1996), 79.

25. *Sonjo sillok*, vol. 5, 202 (17/4/Sonjo 25; May 27, 1592).

26. Stephen Turnbull, *The Samurai: A Military History* (London: Osprey Publishing, 1977), 204–206; Turnbull, *Samurai Sourcebook*, 48–49; Griffis, *Corea*, 97.

27. Turnbull, *Military History*, 205.

28. Yu Song-nyong, 62–64; *Sonjo sujong sillok*, vol. 3, 234–235 (4/Sonjo 25; May/June 1592). According to Yu Song-nyong, Yi Il had "800 to 900" men at Sangju, while the *sillok* says he had "no more than 6,000." Yu's lower figure is the one usually quoted in Korean accounts of the battle and is the one I have given in the text.

29. *Sonjo sujong sillok*, vol. 3, 238–239 (4/Sonjo 25; May 1592).

30. Burton Watson, trans., *Records of the Grand Historian of China: Translated from the Shih chi of Ssu-ma chien*, vol. 1 (New York: Columbia University Press, 1961), 217. ("Grand Historian" Ssu-ma ch'ien [c. 145–90 B.C.] was the first major Chinese historian whose work has survived until today.)

31. *Taikoki*, quoted in Turnbull, *Samurai Invasion*, 59.

32. Murdoch, 323. There are discrepancies in the literature regarding when Kato's and Konishi's forces joined up. Murdoch's account, based upon information Konishi himself provided the Jesuits, seems the most authoritative.

33. *Sonjo sujong sillok*, vol. 3, 238–239 (4/Sonjo 25; May/June 1592).

34. This was not the first time that the validity of "fighting with a river to one's back" had been undermined by technological change. In 1575 Hideyoshi himself, then a general in Oda Nobunaga's army, was a witness to this fact in a battle against Takeda Katsuyori. Takeda, considering his situation desperate, resorted to the borrowed Chinese strategy known in Japanese as *haisui-no-jin* (arranging troops with water to the rear), and positioned his traditionally armed force of fifteen thousand with their backs to the Takinosawa River. In the ensuing battle, the hand-to-hand fighting that Takeda expected his desperate men would excel at never occurred. Hideyoshi's army simply stood back and mowed them down with musket fire (Dening, 157–158).

35. *Sonjo sillok*, vol. 5, 202 (27/4/Sonjo 25; June 6, 1592).

36. Katano, 123–126; Murdoch, 324; Jones, 149.

37. Hulbert, vol. 1, 359–360; *Sonjo sillok*, vol. 5, 203 (28/4/Sonjo 25; June 7, 1592).

38. *Sonjo sillok*, vol. 5, 203–204 (28/4/Sonjo 25; June 7, 1592).

39. *Sonjo sillok*, vol. 5, 206 (29/4/Sonjo 25; June 8, 1592); *Sonjo sujong sillok*, vol. 3, 240–241 (4/Sonjo 25; May/June 1592).

40. *Sonjo sillok*, vol. 5, 206–207 (30/4/Sonjo 25; June 9, 1592); *Sonjo sujong sillok*, vol. 3, 244–245 (5/Sonjo 25; June 1592).

41. Hulbert, vol. 1, 366.

42. Jones, 149.

43. Yang Jae-suk, *Imjin waeran-un uri-ga igin chonjaeng iottda* (Seoul: Garam, 2001), 103–109.

44. *Taikoki*, quoted in Turnbull, *Samurai Invasion*, 63–64.

45. For example, Park Yune-hee, 107.

46. *Sonjo sillok*, vol. 5, 216–217 (3/5/Sonjo 25; June 12, 1592); Jones, 151–152.

47. *Sonjo sujong sillok*, vol. 3, 248 (5/Sonjo 25; June 1592); Alan Clark and Donald Clark, *Seoul: Past and Present* (Seoul: Hollym, 1969), 99–102. The Japanese also established a military camp at what is today Seoul's Itaewon district (ibid., 152–153).

48. Order issued by Hideyoshi on 1/Bunroku 1 (Feb. 1592), in Cho Chung-hwa, *Paro chapun imjin waeran-sa* (Seoul: Salmgwa-ggum, 1998), 40.

CHAPTER 9: *Hideyoshi Jubilant*

1. Hideyoshi to Saisho (a lady-in-waiting to his mother Lady O-Mandokoro), 6/5/Bunroku 1 (June 15, 1592), in Boscaro, *Letters*, 45–46. The festival Hideyoshi refers to is the Chrysanthemum Festival, which falls on the ninth day of the ninth month.

2. Hideyoshi to O-Ne, 6/5/Bunroku 1 (June 15, 1592), ibid., 46.

3. Hideyoshi to Kato Kiyomasa and Nabeshima Naoshige, 3/6/Bunroku 1 (July 11, 1592), in Kuno, vol. 1, 324–325.

4. Yamakichi (Hideyoshi's private secretary) to Ladies Higashi and Kyakushin (ladies-in-waiting to Hideyoshi's wife), 18/5/Bunroku 1 (June 27, 1592), ibid, 318.

5. Some of these articles are quoted in Turnbull, *Military History*, 210.

6. Articles 1–4 and 17–22 are from Ryusaku Tsunoda and others, *Sources*, vol. 2, 318–319 (articles 17–22 are numbered in this source as 18–23). Articles 16, 23, and 24 are from Kuno, vol. 1, 316–317.

7. Yamakichi to Ladies Higashi and Kyakushin, 18/5/Bunroku 1 (June 27, 1592), in Kuno, vol. 1, 320.

8. Ibid., 320.

9. According to Berry, 276–277, n. 2, "After 1587 Hideyoshi's constant inquiries into the health of his intimates are combined with comments upon his own health, particularly his failing appetite.... His eye problems, which caused him to postpone departure for Nagoya and supervision of the Korean campaign in 1592, caused him the greatest difficulty, although we know little about them in detail." One of the earliest references Hideyoshi made to his deteriorating health was in a letter to his mother in 1585: "I am becoming dark in complexion and thin in body, and the trouble with

my eyes is worse. I would like to write a reply to Gomoji, but my eyes are getting bad, so please understand my condition." Hideyoshi to Iwa (a lady-in-waiting to his mother), 11/8/Tensho 13 (Oct. 4, 1585), in Boscaro, *Letters*, 22.

10. Hideyoshi to Saisho (a lady-in-waiting to his mother), 6/5/Bunroku 1 (June 15, 1592), in Boscaro, *Letters*, 45–46.
11. Emperor Go-Yozei to Hideyoshi, summer 1592, in Kuno, vol. 1, 323.
12. Ibid., 324.
13. Dening, 254–255.
14. Asakawa, 393.
15. Berry, 278, n. 21.
16. Dening, 254.
17. Hideyoshi to Koya (a lady-in-waiting to his wife), 20/6/Bunroku 1 (July 28, 1592), in Boscaro, *Letters*, 47.

CHAPTER 10: *The Korean Navy Strikes Back*
1. Dispatch of 30/4/Wanli 20 (June 9, 1592), Yi Sun-sin, *Imjin changch'o*, 27.
2. Diary entry for 3/5/Imjin (June 12, 1592), Yi Sun-sin, *Nanjung ilgi*, 4.
3. Park Yune-hee, 122–123.
4. Dispatch of 10/5/Wanli 20 (June 19, 1592), Yi Sun-sin, *Imjin changch'o*, 31–32; *Sonjo sillok*, vol. 5, 303 (21/6/Sonjo 25; July 29, 1592).
5. Dispatch of 10/5/Wanli 20 (June 19, 1592), Yi Sun-sin, *Imjin changch'o*, 34–35.
6. Ibid., 36–37.
7. Dispatch of 30/4/Wanli 20 (June 9, 1592), ibid., 28.
8. Dispatch of 10/5/Wanli 20 (June 19, 1592), ibid., 38.
9. For example, Katano, 190.
10. Park Yune-hee, 150, makes this suggestion, based upon the claim that Todo Takatora had not yet arrived in Korea.
11. Ibid., 141–142.
12. *Taejong kongjong daewang sillok* (Seoul: Sejong daewang kinyom saophwe, no date), vol. 5, 304 (5/2/Taejong 13; Mar. 7, 1413). The passage reads: "While passing by Imjin Island, the king viewed a kobukson and a Japanese ship fighting against each other." Two years later an official named Tak Sin sent a memorial to King Taejong recommending the further development of kobukson. *Taejong sillok*, vol. 7, 11–12 (16/7/Taejong 15; Aug. 20, 1415).
13. Dispatch of 14/6/Wanli 20 (July 22, 1592), Yi Sun-sin, *Imjin changch'o*, 40–41.
14. Yi Pun, 210.
15. *Sonjo sujong sillok*, vol. 3, 253 (5/Sonjo 25; June 1592).
16. Nam Chon-u, *Yi Sun-sin* (Seoul: Yoksa bipyongsa, 1994), 68–81; Yang Jae-suk, *Dashi ssunun*, vol. 1, 212–213; Horace H. Underwood, *Korean Boats and Ships* (Seoul: Yonsei University Press, 1979), 76–77; Jho Sung-do,

57–63; Park Yune-hee, 71–74.

17. Choi Byong-hyon, 122.

18. There is, however, an enigmatic reference in Japanese sources. At the Battle of Angolpo in August 1592, the *Korai Funa Senki* records that "Among the large [Korean] ships were three mekura-bune [blind ships, i.e., turtle ships], covered in iron, firing cannons, fire arrows, large (wooden) arrows and so on" (Turnbull, *Samurai Invasion*, 106). This reference to the ships being "covered in iron" does not necessarily mean they were covered with iron plates. It could refer to the iron spikes on their roofs.

19. Bak Hae-ill, "A Short Note on the Iron-clad Turtle-boats of Admiral Yi Sun-sin," *Korea Journal* 17, no. 1 (Jan. 1977): 34–39.

20. Diary entry for 13/2/Imjin (March 26, 1592), Yi Sun-sin, *Imjin changch'o*, 8.

21. Underwood (80) made this point back in 1933: "It was not necessary for him [Yi Sun-sin] to make his ship iron-clad for he needed protection only against musket-balls and arrows. This he had in 4 inch timbers."

22. Murdoch, 336, n. 17.

23. Hulbert, vol. 1, 377.

24. Jones, 187.

25. Griffis, *Corea*, 134.

26. Hulbert, vol. 1, 376–377.

27. Choi Du-hwan, ed., *Chungmugong Yi Sun-sin chonjip* (Seoul: Wooseok Publishing Co., 1999), 81 and 83; Cho Song-do, *Chungmugong Yi Sun-sin* (Seoul: Yongyong munhwa-sa, 2001), 80; Underwood, 78. With regard to the iron-plating controversy, the illustration of the *tongjeyong* turtle ship depicts what appear to be wooden planks covering the roof of the vessel. They look exactly like the planks of the hull. The roof of the *Cholla chwasuyong* turtle ship is covered with some sort of hexagonal pattern that is today often assumed to indicate iron plates.

28. Yi Pun, 212.

29. Mekura-bune, "blind ships," were vessels with covered decks and no openings through which enemy boarders could enter.

30. *Taiko-ki*, quoted in A. L. Sadler, "The Naval Campaign in the Korean War of Hideyoshi (1592–1598)," *The Transactions of the Asiatic Society of Japan*, second series, 14 (1937): 188.

31. This embellishment first appeared in Yi Pun's biography of his uncle, written at the beginning of the seventeenth century. (Yi Pun was not present at the battle.) It has been repeated in more recent works, for example in Park Yune-hee's biography of Yi (153), which states that after the engagement the admiral "dug the bullet out of the wound, several inches deep, with his sword."

32. Dispatch of 14/6/Wanli 20 (July 22, 1592), Yi Sun-sin, *Imjin changch'o*, 42; diary entry for 29/5/Imjin (July 8, 1592), Yi Sun-sin, *Nanjung ilgi*, 5.

33. Japanese accounts of the Battle of Tangpo state that Kurushima, upon seeing the destruction of his men and ships, landed on a nearby island and

committed seppuku, the ritual act of suicide (Murdoch, 336).

34. Dispatch of 14/6/Wanli 20 (July 22, 1592), Yi Sun-sin, *Imjin changch'o*, 43.
35. Ibid., 44.
36. Park Yune-hee, 158; Sadler, "Naval Campaign," 192; George Kerr, *Okinawa: The History of an Island People* (Tokyo: Charles E. Tuttle, 1958), 151–152 and 155.
37. The names of Yi Sun-sin, commander of the Cholla Left Navy, and Lee Sun-sin, captain of the Pangtap port under the senior Yi's command, are composed of different Chinese characters but pronounced the same, and thus are easily confused. To distinguish between them I have used the respective surnames "Yi" and "Lee," which are both common English renderings of the Korean surname 이.
38. Dispatch of 14/6/Wanli 20 (July 22, 1592), Yi Sun-sin, *Imjin changch'o*, 48; *Sonjo sillok*, vol. 5, 304 (21/6/Sonjo 25; July 29, 1592).
39. "Three Strategies of Huang Shih-kung," in Sawyer, 297. (The "Three Strategies" dates from the end of the first century B.C.)
40. Yi Sun-sin, *Imjin changch'o*, 56; *Sonjo sujong sillok*, vol. 3, 257 (6/Sonjo 25; July 1592).
41. *Sonjo sillok*, vol. 6, 124 (1/9/Sonjo 25; Oct. 5, 1592).
42. Alexander Kiralfy, "Japanese Naval Strategy," in *Makers of Modern Strategy: Military Thought from Machiavelli to Hitler*, ed. Edward Mead Earle (Princeton, N.J.: Princeton University Press, 1943), 464–465; Ballard, 51; Turnbull, *Military History*, 213.

CHAPTER 11: *On to Pyongyang*

1. *Sonjo sillok*, vol. 5, 210 (2/5/Sonjo 25; June 11, 1592); *Sonjo sujong sillok*, vol. 3, 245 (5/Sonjo 25; June 1592). The top three posts in Korea's *uijongbu*, or State Council, were *yonguijong, chwauijong*, and *u-uijong*, which I have translated respectively as Prime Minister, Minister of the Left, and Minister of the Right. These titles are also sometimes rendered as Chief State Councilor, Second State Councilor, and Third State Councilor.
2. *Sonjo sillok*, vol. 5, 216–217 and 221 (3/5/Sonjo 25; June 12, 1592); *Sonjo sujong sillok*, vol. 3, 245–246 (5/Sonjo 25; June 1592).
3. Yu Song-nyong, 78–79.
4. *Sonjo sillok*, vol. 6, 308 (4/12/Sonjo 25; Jan. 6, 1593); *Sonjo sujong sillok*, vol. 4, 41 (11/Sonjo 26; Nov.–Dec. 1593).
5. Han Myong-ki, *Imjin waeran hanchung kwangye* (Seoul: Yuksa bibyongsa, 1999), 430.
6. Samuel Dukhae Kim, 24–25.
7. W. G. Aston, *Hideyoshi's Invasion of Korea* (Tokyo: Ryubun-kwan, 1907), 21; Gari Ledyard, "Confucianism and War: The Korean Security Crisis of 1598," *The Journal of Korean Studies* 6 (1988–89): 84–85.
8. Ray Huang, "Lung ch'ing," 566–567; Goodrich, vol. 1, 830–832.
9. Letter dated 16/5 (June 25), 1592, in Park Yune-hee, 112–113.

10. Aston, 14–15.
11. "Wei Liao-tzu," in Sawyer, 258.
12. Yu Song-nyong, 86–87; *Sonjo sujong sillok*, vol. 3, 247–248 (5/Sonjo 25; June 1592).
13. Hulbert, vol. 1, 372–373; Jones, 182–183.
14. Giles, 77.
15. Ibid., 6–7.
16. "The Methods of Ssu-ma," in Sawyer, 142.
17. Yu Song-nyong, 88–90; *Sonjo sujong sillok*, vol. 3, 247 (5/Sonjo 25; June 1592); Hulbert, vol. 1, 379–382; Murdoch, 326–329.
18. Kato Kiyomasa to Hideyoshi, 1/6/Bunroku 1 (July 9, 1592), in Park Yune-hee, 118–119.
19. *Sonjo sillok*, vol. 5, 270–272 (2/6/Sonjo 25; July 10, 1592). Chong Chol accompanied King Sonjo north to Uiju following his return from exile, and in 1593 was sent on a mission to China to convey Korea's thanks for its military assistance in the war. Later that year he was forced to resign from office again by renewed Easterner pressure. He spent his last days in quiet retirement on Kanghwa Island, where he died on February 7, 1594.
20. Turnbull, *Samurai Invasion*, 137.
21. "The Methods of Ssu-ma," in Sawyer, 139.
22. Yu Song-nyong, 98–100.
23. *Sonjo sillok*, vol. 5, 276–277 (9/6/Sonjo 25; July 17, 1592); Yu Song-nyong, 102–103; Pak Dong-ryang, "Kigae sacho," in *Saryoro bonun*, 68–69.
24. The Chinese military classic *Wei Liao-tzu* lists the following rule for holding a city wall: "The rule for defending a city wall is that for every *chang* [ten feet], you should employ ten men to defend it, artisans and cooks not being included. Those who go out [to fight] do not defend the city; those who defend the city do not go out [to fight]" (Sawyer, 253).
25. Yu Song-nyong, 111–112; *Sonjo sillok*, vol. 5, 294 (15/6/Sonjo 25; July 23, 1592); Aston, 20–21; Hulbert, vol. 1, 386–387.
26. *Sonjo sillok*, vol. 5, 301 (19/6/Sonjo 25; July 27, 1592).
27. Yu Song-nyong, 112–113; Park Yune-hee, 117–118. One hundred thousand *sok* of rice equals approximately 7,200 metric tons.
28. Yu Song-nyong, 114–118; Hulbert, vol. 1, 388.
29. *Sonjo sillok*, vol. 5, 284–287 (13/6/Sonjo 25; July 21, 1592).
30. Ibid., 299 (18/6/Sonjo 25; July 26, 1592); *Sonjo sujong sillok*, vol. 3, 267 (6/Sonjo 25; July 1592).
31. *Sonjo sillok*, vol. 5, 306 (22/6/Sonjo 25; July 30, 1592).
32. Ha Tae-hung, *Behind the Scenes*, 170.

CHAPTER 12: *The Battle for the Yellow Sea*
1. Hideyoshi to Wakizaka Yasuharu, 23/6/Bunroku 1 (July 31, 1592), in Park Yune-hee, 159.
2. Yu Song-nyong, 129.

3. Yi Sun-sin does not give a precise number in his battle report. According to the Japanese chronicle *Korai funa senki*, however, at the coming Battle of Angolpo, "Among the large [Korean] ships were three mekura-bune [blind ships, i.e., turtle ships]" (Turnbull, *Samurai Invasion*, 106).

4. Dispatch of 15/7/Wanli 20 (August 21, 1592), Yi Sun-sin, *Imjin changch'o*, 59. The enemy commander Yi refers to may have been Wakizaka Sabei or Watanabe Shichiemon, who served under fleet commander Wakizaka Yasuharu and are known to have been killed in the battle.

5. Ibid., 56–60; *Sonjo sujong sillok*, vol. 3, 279 (7/Sonjo 25; Aug. 1592).

6. *Wakizaka ki*, in Turnbull, *Samurai Invasion*, 104.

7. Yi Sun-sin, *Imjin changch'o*, 56, footnote; Park Yune-hee, 165.

8. Dispatch of 15/7/Wanli 20 (Aug. 21, 1592), Yi Sun-sin, *Imjin changch'o*, 62–63.

9. Ibid., 61; *Sonjo sujong sillok*, vol. 3, 279 (7/Sonjo 25; Aug. 1592).

10. Dispatch of 10/9/Wanli 20 (Oct. 14, 1592), Yi Sun-sin, *Imjin changch'o*, 76.

11. Yi Pun, 215.

12. Hideyoshi to Todo Sado no Kami (Todo Takatora), 16/7/Tensho 20 (Aug. 23, 1592), in Elisonas, "Trinity," 279, n. 66; Turnbull, *Samurai Invasion*, 107.

13. Yu Song-nyong, 129.

14. For example: "So ended, we may well believe, one of the greatest naval battles of the world. . . . It signed the death-warrant of the invasion. It frustrated the great motive of the invasion, the humbling of China" (Hulbert, vol. 1, 400). Also: "[I]t was a naval battle that really decided the campaign and saved Korea, even when a hostile force of close to two hundred thousand of the finest soldiers of the age were encamped upon her soil" (Murdoch, 337).

CHAPTER 13: *"To me the Japanese robber army will be but a swarm of ants and wasps"*

1. "Wei Liao-tzu," in Sawyer, 243.

2. Yu Song-nyong, 125; Kuno, vol. 1, 156; Hulbert, vol. 1, 400.

3. *Sonjo sillok*, vol. 6, 35 (20/7/Sonjo 25; Aug. 26, 1592); Yu Song-nyong, 124–126; Turnbull, *Samurai Invasion*, 135–136.

4. Yu Song-nyong, 124–126; Ryusaku Tsunoda, trans. and L. Carrington Goodrich, ed., *Japan in the Chinese Dynastic Histories: Later Han through Ming Dynasties* (South Pasadena, Calif.: P. D. and Ione Perkins, 1951), 142; Hulbert, vol. 1, 401.

5. Yu Song-nyong, 135.

6. Turnbull, *Samurai Invasion*, 136.

7. Kuno, vol. 1, 156.

8. Ibid., 157.

9. Lee Hyoun-jong, 13–24.

10. Kuno, vol. 1, 159.
11. Dispatch of 17/9/Wanli 20 (Oct. 21, 1592), Yi Sun-sin, *Imjin changch'o*, 72.
12. Ibid., 69–75; *Sonjo sujong sillok*, vol. 3, 287 (8/Sonjo 25; Sept. 1592).
13. The Koreans also were not eager to accept help from Nurhaci. Yu Song-nyong in particular sent a petition to King Sonjo in October urging him to reject the offer.
14. Tsunoda and Goodrich, 142; Goodrich, vol. 1, 730–731.
15. *Sonjo sillok*, vol. 6, 106–108 (17–18/8/Sonjo 25; Sept. 22–23, 1592).
16. Aston, 25.
17. Ibid., 24–25; *Sonjo sillok*, vol. 6, 137–138 (8/9/Sonjo 25; Oct. 12, 1592); Yu Song-nyong, 135–136.
18. *Sonjo sillok*, vol. 6, 132 (4/9/Sonjo 25; Oct. 8, 1592).
19. Goodrich, vol. 1, 830–832.
20. Ibid., 830–832.
21. Stramigioli, 99–103.

CHAPTER 14: *A Castle at Fushimi*
1. Sansom, 363.
2. Hideyoshi to Koya, no date (1589), in Boscaro, *Letters*, 34. Koya was a lady-in-waiting to Hideyoshi's wife, O-Ne, who in turn took responsibility for the care of Hideyoshi's mother.
3. Hideyoshi to Lady O-Mandokoro, 1/5/Tensho 18 (June 2, 1590), ibid., 38–39.
4. Sansom, 363.
5. Yamakichi (Yamanaka Kichinai) to Ladies Higashi and Kiyakushin (ladies-in-waiting to Hideyoshi's wife), 18/5/Bunroku 1 (June 27, 1592), in Kuno, vol. 1, 319–320.
6. Hideyoshi to Maeda Gen'i, 11/12/Bunroku 1 (Jan. 13, 1593), in Boscaro, *Letters*, 48.
7. Sen Soshitsu XV, 392.
8. Hideyoshi to Maa (his youngest concubine), 26/12/Bunroku 1 (Jan. 28, 1593), in Boscaro, *Letters*, 49.

CHAPTER 15: *Suppression and Resistance*
1. Letter dated 26/5/Bunroku 1 (July 5, 1592), in Park Yune-hee, 112.
2. Elisonas, "Trinity," 275.
3. Imperial Japanese Commission, *History of the Empire of Japan* (Tokyo: Dai Nippon Tosho Kabushiki Kwaisha, 1893), 281–282.
4. Kato Kiyomasa to Hideyoshi, 1/6/Bunroku 1 (July 9, 1592), in Park Yune-hee, 118.
5. Yu Song-nyong, 91.
6. Ibid., 92; Hulbert, vol. 1, 389–390.
7. Elisonas, "Trinity," 275.
8. Yi Sik, "Yasa chobon," in *Saryoro bonun*, 126–128; Yu Song-nyong, 92–93;

Sonjo sujong sillok, vol. 3, 281–283 (7/Sonjo 25; Aug. 1592).

9. Shimokawa Heidayu, "Kiyomasa Korai no jin oboegaki," in Turnbull, *Samurai Invasion*, 79.

10. Kato Kiyomasa to Ki(noshita) Hanasuke, 20/9/Bunroku 1 (Oct. 25, 1592), in Elisonas, "Trinity," 275–276.

11. Palais, *Confucian Statecraft*, 82.

12. Ha Tae-hung, *Behind the Scenes*, 173.

13. Yun Hyong-gi, "Choya chomjae," in *Saryoro bonun*, 106.

14. Pak Dong-ryang, "Kijae sacho," in *Saryoro bonun*, 108; Yu Song-nyong, 145–146.

15. Ha Tae-hung, *Behind the Scenes*, 173–174; Hulbert, vol. 1, 392.

16. *Sonjo sillok*, vol. 6, 76 (7/8/Sonjo 25; Sept. 12, 1592); Hulbert, vol. 1, 393.

17. Yun Hyong-gi, "Choya chomjae," in *Saryoro bonun*, 106; "Somyo chunghung-gi," ibid., 106–107; Hanguk chongsin, vol. 1, 111–112.

18. "Sonmyo bugam," in *Saryoro bonun*, 120.

19. *Sonjo sujong sillok*, vol. 3, 283–285 (7/Sonjo 25; Aug. 1592); "Sonmyo bugam," in *Saryoro bonun*, 121–122; Yi Myong-han, "Baekju-chip," ibid., 123–125; Yi Hyong-sok, vol. 1, 402.

20. *Sonjo sujong sillok*, vol. 4, 32–33 (6/Sonjo 26; July 1593); Hulbert, vol. 1, 394.

21. Hankuk chongsin, vol. 1, 485–486; Yu Song-nyong, 145; *Sonjo sujong sillok*, vol. 3, 276 (6/Sonjo 25; July 1592) and 286 (7/Sonjo 25; Aug. 1592); Hulbert, vol. 1, 395–396; Jones, 188.

22. Yi Su-kwang, "Chibongyusol," in *Saryoro bonun*, 110; Mun Yol-kong, "Cho Hon shindobi," ibid., 111.

23. Samuel Dukhae Kim, 25–26.

24. Ibid., 26–28.

25. Ibid., 81–82.

26. "Chungbong Choson saenghaengjang," in *Saryoro bonun*, 113–114; Samuel Dukhae Kim, 80–84; *Sonjo sujong sillok*, vol. 3, 288 (8/Sonjo 25; Sept. 1592); Yi Hyong-sok, vol. 1, 455.

27. Samuel Dukhae Kim, 86–89; *Sonjo sujong sillok*, vol. 3, 294–295 (8/Sonjo 25; Sept. 1592).

28. Samuel Dukhae Kim, 86–90.

29. Sin Kyong, "Chaejo bonbangji," in *Saryoro bonun*, 132–134; *Sonjo sujong sillok*, vol. 3, 307 (9/Sonjo 25; Oct. 1592); Jones, 187–188.

30. William Griffis, quoted in Boots, 36–37.

31. Yu Song-nyong, 143; Yi Hyong-sok, vol. 1, 514.

32. Hulbert, vol. 1, 407.

33. Quoted in Yang Jae-suk, *Dashi ssunun*, vol. 1, 193.

34. *Sonjo sujong sillok*, vol. 3, 305–306 (9/Sonjo 25; Oct. 1592).

35. Yang Jae-suk, *Dashi ssunun*, vol. 1, 192–193; Yu Song-nyong, 143–144; Turnbull, *Samurai Invasion*, 125; Hulbert, vol. 1, 407–408; Joseph Longford, *The Story of Korea* (London: T. Fisher Unwin, 1911), 164–165. Korean

historian Choi Du-hwan successfully test fired a reconstructed pigyok chinchollae from a daewangu mortar for a program broadact on Korea's KBS TV on January 12, 2002. The delayed fuse worked perfectly. The only problem was that the sphere, which was made from heavy cast iron based on archaeological finds, did not blow apart when the gunpowder ignited. The lid sealing the top of the device where the fuse was inserted simply blew off and the shrapnel packed inside blasted out of the hole. (The lid on the test-fired device was held in place by metal wedges tapped into the gaps around the edge.)

36. Hanguk chongsin, vol. 1, 344; Palais, *Confucian Statecraft*, 84–85.
37. Turnbull, *Samurai Invasion*, 129. The Japanese *naginata*, comparable to the European glaive, was a polearm with a knife-like blade on the end. The Korean version featured a wider and heavier blade than the Japanese, and would have been a fearsome thing to have thrust in one's face.
38. Heung Yang-ho, "Haedong myongjangchon," in *Saryoro bonun*, 144–147; *Sonjo sujong sillok*, vol. 3, 310–311 (10/Sonjo 25; Nov. 1592); Yi Hyong-sok, vol. 1, 556; Hulbert, vol. 1, 406–407; Turnbull, *Samurai Invasion*, 129–130.

CHAPTER 16: *Saving History*
1. *Sonjo sillok*, vol. 6, 146–147 (13/9/Sonjo 25; Oct. 17, 1592); *Sonjo sujong sillok*, vol. 3, 278 (7/Sonjo 25; Aug. 1592); Yu Song-nyong, 133.
2. *Munhon pigo*, quoted in G. M. McCune, "The Yi Dynasty Annals of Korea," *Transactions of the Korea Branch of the Royal Asiatic Society* 29 (1939): 63, n. 7.
3. *Kukcho pogam*, ibid., 58.
4. McCune, 74–76; *Sonjo sujong sillok*, vol. 3, 278 (7/Sonjo 25; Aug. 1592).

PART 4: STALEMATE
1. "Wu-tzu," in Sawyer, 208.

CHAPTER 17: *The Retreat from Pyongyang to the "River of Hell"*
1. Hints of a general lack of enthusiasm for the Korean campaign were now beginning to appear in letters sent home from the front (Sansom, 357). In letters home dated August 17 and 20, 1593, Date Masamune attributes the deaths of many Japanese troops to the fact that "the water in this country is different." They were likely contracting cholera or typhus. Date also spoke of an outbreak of beriberi in which eight of ten sufferers died (Turnbull, *Samurai Invasion*, 155).
2. Ibid., 151. Turnbull concludes that by April 1593 the Japanese had 53,000 men left from their original 158,800-man invasion force. This loss, representing an overall decline of nearly sixty-seven percent, appears too high, for it exceeds the sixty-five percent loss sustained by Konishi's first

contingent, which Turnbull states "suffered the most." (The figure of 53,000 more likely represents the number of troops in Seoul at that time.) A more accurate loss figure is provided by the Jesuit father Luis Frois, who was close to Konishi Yukinaga. Frois wrote that of the 150,000 Japanese soldiers and laborers who crossed to Korea in 1592, one-third died, mostly the victims of disease, hunger, exhaustion, and cold (Luis Frois, *Historia de Japan*, ed. Josef Wicki (Lisbon: Bilioteca Nacional de Lisboa, 1976–1982), vol. 5, 599).

3. Elisonas, "Trinity," 276.
4. Goodrich, vol. 1, 832; Huang, "Lung-ch'ing," 568.
5. Huang, *1587*, 179–180; Chan, 55.
6. Chan, 205–207.
7. Stamigioli, 103; *Sonjo sillok*, vol. 6, 295–297 (30/11/Sonjo 25; Jan. 2, 1593) and 304 (3/12/Sonjo 25; Jan. 5, 1593).
8. *Sonjo sillok*, vol. 6, 305 (3/12/Sonjo 25; Jan. 5, 1593). Yun Gun-su was at this time Minister of the Board of Rites.
9. Kuno, vol. 1, 162.
10. *Sonjo sillok*, vol. 6, 368–369 (25/12/Sonjo 25; Jan. 27, 1593).
11. *Sonjo sujong sillok*, vol. 3, 322 (12/Sonjo 25; Jan. 1593).
12. Samuel Dukhae Kim, 90 and 92.
13. Yi Hyong-sok, vol. 1, 650–651. In a meeting with King Sonjo, Yi Dok-hyong estimated that between 12,000 and 20,000 Japanese troops were stationed at Pyongyang (*Sonjo sillok*, vol. 6, 371 [27/12/Sonjo 25; Jan. 29, 1593]).
14. Yu Song-nyong, 155.
15. Ibid.
16. *Sonjo sillok*, vol. 7, 26 (11/1/Sonjo 26; Feb. 11, 1593).
17. Turnbull, *Samurai Invasion*, 140.
18. *Sonjo sillok*, vol. 6, 368–369 (25/12/Sonjo 25; Jan. 27. 1593).
19. Ibid., vol. 7, 26 (11/1/Sonjo 26; Feb. 11, 1593).
20. Samuel Dukhae Kim, 92–93; Turnbull, *Samurai Invasion*, 139.
21. *Sonjo sillok*, vol. 7, 25–28 (11/1/Sonjo 26; Feb. 11, 1593); Yu Song-nyong, 156–157.
22. *Sonjo sillok*, vol. 7, 28 (11/1/Sonjo 26; Feb. 11, 1593); Sin Kyong, "Chaejo bonbangji," in *Saryoro bonun*, 161; J. S. Gale, *James Scarth Gale and His History of the Korean People*, ed. Richard Rutt (Seoul: Royal Asiatic Society, 1972), 262–263.
23. *Yoshino Jingozaemon oboegaki*, in Turnbull, *Samurai Invasion*, 141.
24. Hulbert, vol. 2, 7.
25. Goodrich, vol. 1, 833.
26. Ibid.
27. *Sonjo sillok*, vol. 7, 28 (11/1/Sonjo 26; Feb. 11, 1593).
28. *Yoshino Jingozaemon oboegaki*, in Turnbull, *Samurai Invasion*, 142.
29. Yu Song-nyong, 161–162.

30. The Imjin River at this time of year was said to have posed a considerable obstacle, for with the warming of the weather the ice had broken into a welter of grinding blocks, making it difficult to take a boat across. The Koreans solved this problem by throwing a rope bridge made from arrowroot vines across the river, a feat that has been hailed as the world's first suspension bridge (Hulbert, vol. 2, 8–9). With the ice preventing supporting piles from being driven into the riverbed at midstream, two thick cables were stretched across the river, suspended from a framework of heavy timbers on either bank, and were twisted and thus tightened until they were well clear of the water and ice. Willow branches were then laid between them and dirt packed on top to make a walkway. With this structure in place, the allied troops were able to cross the river in safety (*Sonjo sujong sillok*, vol. 4, 8–9 [1/Sonjo 26; Feb. 1593]).
31. Griffis, *Corea*, 113–114; Turnbull, *Samurai Invasion*, 143.
32. Murdoch, 345.
33. According to Turnbull, the Japanese chose not to make their stand at the Imjin River because it "would provide but a small obstacle to the Korean army who were familiar with its layout" (*Samurai Invasion*, 145).
34. *Sonjo sillok*, vol. 7, 113 (5/2/Sonjo 26; March 7, 1593).
35. Yi Hyong-sok, vol. 1, 674 and 677–678.
36. Yu Song-nyong, 163–164; *Sonjo sillok*, vol. 7, 113–114 (5/2/Sonjo 26; Mar. 7, 1593); *Sonjo sujong sillok*, vol. 4, 8–9 (1/Sonjo 26; Feb. 1593); Goodrich, vol. 1, 833–834; Murdoch, 345; Elisonas, "Trinity," 280–281; Turnbull, *Samurai Invasion*, 143–148.
37. Yu Song-nyong, 164; Goodrich, vol. 1, 834.
38. *Sonjo sujong sillok*, vol. 4, 9 (1/Sonjo 26; Feb. 1593); Turnbull, *Samurai Invasion*, 143.
39. *Sonjo sujong sillok*, vol. 4, 13 (2/Sonjo 26; Mar. 1593).
40. Samuel Dukhae Kim, 94.
41. Yu Song-nyong, 170.
42. Hanguk chongsin, vol. 1, 160; Wilbur D. Bacon, "Fortresses of Kyonggi-do," *Transactions of the Korea Branch of the Royal Asiatic Society* 37 (1961): 16.
43. Yi Hyong-sok, vol. 1, 697 and 699.
44. *Sonjo sujong sillok*, vol. 4, 14 (2/Sonjo 26; March 1593); Sin Kyong, "Chaejo bonbangji," in *Saryoro bonun*, 170–171; Kang Song-mun, "Haengju daechop-eso-ui Kwon Yul chonnyak-gwa chonsul," in *Imjin waeran-gwa Kwon Yul changgun*, ed. Chang Chong-dok and Pak Jae-gwang (Seoul: Chonjaeng kinyomgwan, 1999), 110–113.
45. Sansom, 358.

CHAPTER 18: *Seoul Retaken*
1. Elisonas, "Trinity," 281; Goodrich, vol. 1, 834.
2. Park Yune-hee, 182.

3. Hideyoshi to Maa, 26/12/Bunroku 1 (Jan. 28, 1593), in Boscaro, 49. (Maa, the twenty-one-year-old daughter of Maeda Toshiie, was one of Hideyoshi's concubines.)

4. Mashita Nagamori, Ishida Mitsunari, Otani Yoshitsugu, Kato Mitsuyasu, Maeno Nagayasu, Kuroda Nagamasa, Konishi Yukinaga, Mori Yoshinari, Kato Kiyomasa, Nabeshima Naoshige, Fukushima Masanori, Ikoma Chikamasa, Hachizuka Iemasa, Otomo Yoshimune, Yoshikawa Hiroie, Kobayakawa Takakage, and Ukita Hideie to Hideyoshi, 3/3/Bunroku 2 (April 4, 1593), in Katano, 243–244.

5. *Sonjo sillok*, vols. 8–9, passim (4–9/Sonjo 26; May–Oct. 1593).

6. Dispatch of 6/4/Wanli 21 (May 6, 1593), Yi Sun-sin, *Imjin changch'o*, 88.

7. Ibid.

8. Diary entry for 18/2/Kyesa (Mar. 20, 1593), Yi Sun-sin, *Nanjung ilgi*, 16.

9. Dispatch of 17/2/Wanli 21 (Mar. 19, 1593), Yi Sun-sin, *Imjin changch'o*, 87–88.

10. Dispatch 6/4/Wanli 21 (May 6, 1593), ibid., 90–91.

11. Ibid., 94.

12. Diary entry for 22/2/Kyesa (Mar. 24, 1593), Yi Sun-sin, *Nanjung ilgi*, 18.

13. Diary entry for 4/3/Kyesa (April 5, 1593), ibid., 20.

14. Dispatch of 6/4/Wanli 21 (May 6, 1593), Yi Sun-sin, *Imjin changch'o*, 92.

15. Diary entries for 8/2/Kyesa–20/3/Kyesa (Mar. 10–April 21, 1593), Yi Sun-sin, *Nanjung ilgi*, 13–23.

16. Dispatch of 6/4/Wanli 21 (May 6, 1593), Yi Sun-sin, *Imjin changch'o*, 93.

17. *Sonjo sujong sillok*, vol. 4, 17 (4/Sonjo 26; May 1593); Goodrich, vol. 1, 834; Ledyard, "Confucianism," 85.

18. Yu Song-nyong, 178.

19. Cholla Province Army Commander Kwon Yul moved his base to Paju shortly after his victory in the Battle of Haengju in the middle of March.

20. Yu Song-nyong, 178–180.

21. Stramigioli, 104–105.

22. *Sonjo sujong sillok*, vol. 4, 17–18 (4/Sonjo 26; May 1593).

23. Ibid., 18; Kuno, vol. 1, 164–165.

24. Murdoch, 345–346; Kuno, vol. 1, 165–166; Aston, 32–33.

25. Cho Kyong-nam, "Nanjung chapnok," in *Saryoro bonun*, 176; *Sonjo sujong sillok*, vol. 4, 18–19 (4/Sonjo 26; May 1593).

26. *Sonjo sillok*, vol. 8, 64–65 (24/4/Sonjo 26; May 24, 1593) and 81–82 (28/4/Sonjo 26; May 28, 1593).

27. Ibid., 8 (3/4/Sonjo 26; May 3, 1593); Goodrich, vol. 1, 964–965; Hulbert, vol. 2, 14.

28. O. W. Wolters, "Ayudhya and the Rearward Part of the World," *Journal of the Royal Asiatic Society of Great Britain and Ireland* (1968): 166–172; Geoff Wade, "The *Ming shi-lu* as a Source for Thai History—Fourteenth to Seventeenth Centuries," *Journal of Southeast Asian Studies* 31, no. 2 (Sept. 2000): 293.

29. Yu Song-nyong, 183–184; *Sonjo sujong sillok*, vol. 4, 18–19 (4/Sonjo 26; May 1593).

30. *Sonjo sujong sillok*, vol. 4, 21–22 (5/Sonjo 26; June 1593).

31. Hulbert, vol. 2, 11–12.

32. Yu Song–nyong, 184–185; *Sonjo sujong sillok*, vol. 4, 18–19 (4/Sonjo 26; May 1593).

33. Cho Kyong-nam, "Nanjung chapnok," in *Saryoro bonun*, 176; Hulbert, vol. 2, 12.

34. Yu Song-nyong, 185; *Sonjo sujong sillok*, vol. 4, 20 (5/Sonjo 26; June 1593); Goodrich, vol. 1, 965.

35. Yi Hyong-sok, vol. 2, 1721, identifies the seventeen camps as follows: two at Sosaengpo (Kato Kiyomasa and others); Ilgwangpo (Ito Yuhei, Shimazu Tadatoyo and others); Kijang (Kuroda Nagamasa); Tongnae (Kikkawa Hiroie); two at Pusan (Mori Terumoto); two at Kimhae (Nabeshima Naoshige); Kadok Island (Kobayakawa Takakage, Tachibana Munetora and others); Angolpo (Wakizaka Yasuharu); three at Ungchon (Konishi Yukinaga, So Yoshitoshi, Matsuura Shigenobu and others); and three on Koje Island (Shimazu Yoshihiro and others). According to *Sonjo sujong sillok*, vol. 4, 20–21 (5/Sonjo 26; June 1593), there were only sixteen camps.

36. *Sonjo sillok*, vol. 8, 125–126 (21/5/Sonjo 26; June 19, 1593).

CHAPTER 19: *Negotiations at Nagoya, Slaughter at Chinju*

1. Hideyoshi to O-Ne, no date (context suggests early May 1593), in Boscaro, *Letters*, 53.

2. A. D. Sadler, *The Maker of Modern Japan: The Life of Tokugawa Ieyasu* (London: George Allen & Unwin, 1937), 179.

3. Cho Chung-hwa, *Paro chapun*, 69–71. Among the candidates rumored to have been Yodogimi's lover were Hideyoshi intimate Ono Harunaga, the actor Nagoya Sansu, and Ishida Mitsunari. Ishida can be ruled out, for he was in Korea when Yodogimi conceived in late November or early December 1592. Cho Chung-hwa suggests that the rumors concerning Ishida may have been started by Kato Kiyomasa and Fukushima Masanori to damage his reputation.

4. Sansom, 365.

5. Hideyoshi to Fuku (Ukita Hideie's mother), 27/5/Bunroku 2 (July 26, 1593), in Boscaro, *Letters*, 57.

6. Michael Cooper, *Rodrigues the Interpreter* (New York: Weatherhill, 1974), 99; *Sonjo sujong sillok*, vol. 4, 23 (6/Sonjo 26; July 1593).

7. Katano, 252–257.

8. Griffis, *Corea*, 124.

9. After his escape from Nagoya and return to Korea in September of 1593, Che Man-chun was interrogated by Yi Sun-sin and his report forwarded to the Korean court at Hwangju (Dispatch of 8/Wanli 21 [Aug. 1593], Yi

Sun-sin, *Imjin changch'o*, 116–117).

10. Miyamoto Musashi, *The Book of Five Rings*, trans. Thomas Cleary (Boston: Shambhala, 1993), 34.

11. *Sonjo sujong sillok*, vol. 4, 24–25 (6/Sonjo 26; July 1593).

12. Yu Song-nyong, 189.

13. *Sonjo sillok*, vol. 9, 61 (16/7/Sonjo 26; Aug. 12, 1593). According to Yi Hyong-sok, vol. 1, 723, Kim Chon-il had five hundred men, and Choi Kyong-hoe had six hundred.

14. According to Choi Hyo-sik, there were 8,000 Korean defenders present at the Second Battle of Chinju: a local garrison of 2,400, plus 3,000 reinforcements under Kim Chon-il, Hwang Jin, and Choi Kyong-hoe, plus units of uibyong and monk-soldiers (*Imjin waera-gi Yongnam uibyong yongu* [Seoul: Kukhakjaryowon, 2003], 92–93). According to Yi Hyong-sok, vol. 1, 723, reinforcements under Kim, Hwang, and Choi totaled only 1,800.

15. This figure of 93,000, which is commonly quoted in accounts of the battle, is taken from Japanese sources, and may be too high. According to *Sonjo sujong sillok*, vol. 4, 24 (6/Sonjo 26; July 1593), the attacking Japanese army totaled only 30,000. Che Man-chun, a Korean naval officer captured by the Japanese and pressed into service as a clerk at Nagoya, also stated that 30,000 Japanese troops were present at the Second Battle of Chinju (Dispatch of 8/Wanli 21 [Aug. 1593], Yi Sun-sin, *Imjin changch'o*, 118).

16. Sin Kyong, "Chaejo bonbangji," in *Saryoro bonun*, 179.

17. *Sonjo sujong sillok*, vol. 4, 26–27 (6/Sonjo 26; July 1593).

18. Griffis, *Corea*, 125; Aston, 36; Turnbull, *Samurai Invasion*, 158–159.

19. Kuroda Kafu, in Turnbull, *Samurai Invasion*, 159.

20. Palais, *Confucian Statecraft*, 83.

21. This account of the Second Battle of Chinju is based on *Sonjo sujong sillok*, vol. 4, 26–29 (6/Sonjo 26; July 1593); *Sonjo sillok*, vol. 9, 61–64 (16/7/Sonjo 26; Aug. 12, 1593); Yu Song-nyong, 187–190; Sin Kyong, "Chaejo bonbangji," in *Saryoro bonun*, 177–180; Hong Yang-ho, "Hae-dongmyong jangjin," ibid., 186–187. According to the Japanese account in the *Taikoki*, 25,000 Koreans were killed in the battle. Most of these "fell from the cliffs and were drowned" (Turnbull, *Samurai Invasion*, 160).

22. Yu Mong-in, *Ou yadam*, quoted in Chong Dong-ju, *Non-gae* (Seoul: Hangilsa, 1998), 152–153. *Ou yadam*, written in 1621, contains the earliest known account of the Non-gae story.

23. Kuno, vol. 1, 329–332.

24. Elisonas, "Trinity," 282.

25. Kuno, vol. 1, 328–329. An alternate translation appears in Berry, 214.

26. Stramigioli, 106–107.

27. Berry, 215.

28. *Sonjo sillok*, vol. 9, 74 (18/7/Sonjo 26; Aug. 14, 1593).

29. Diary entries for 7–11/7/Kyesa (Aug. 3–7, 1593), Yi Sun-sin, *Nanjung*

ilgi, 45–48.

30. M. Streichen, *The Christian Daimyo: A Century of Religious and Political History in Japan (1549–1650)* (Tokyo: Rikkyo Gakuin Press, c. 1900), 196. It was common practice in Japan at this time for a vassal to assume the surname of his master. In his dealings with the Chinese, Naito Joan thus referred to himself as "Konishi Joan." Similarly, in their initial meetings with Shen Weijing in the fall of 1592, Konishi Yukinaga and So Yoshitoshi introduced themselves as "Toyotomi Yukinaga" and "Toyotomi Yoshitoshi."

31. *Sonjo sillok*, vol. 9, 196 (5/8/Sonjo 26; Aug. 30, 1593) and 214 (23/8/Sonjo 26; Sept. 17, 1593).

32. Ibid., 15 (6/7/Sonjo 26; Aug. 2, 1593).

33. Ibid., 11–12 (5/7/Sonjo 26; Aug. 1, 1593).

34. Dispatch of 10/8/Wanli 21 (Sept. 4, 1593), Yi Sun-sin, *Imjin changch'o*, 104.

35. *Sonjo sillok*, vol. 9, 297 (16/9/Sonjo 26; Oct. 10, 1593).

36. *Sonjo sujong sillok*, vol. 4, 37–38 (8/Sonjo 26; Sept. 1593). According to Huang ("Lung-ch'ing," 570), 16,000 Ming troops were left in Korea.

37. *Sonjo sujong sillok*, vol. 4, 39 (8/Sonjo 26; Sept. 1593).

38. *Sonjo sillok*, vol. 9, 189–193 (14/8/Sonjo 26; Sept. 8, 1593).

39. Goodrich, vol. 1, 834–835.

40. Cooper, *Rodrigues*, 104.

41. Hideyoshi to O-Ne, 9/8/Bunroku 2 (Sept. 4, 1593), in Boscaro, *Letters*, 59.

CHAPTER 20: *Factions, Feuds, and Forgeries*

1. *Sonjo sujong sillok*, vol. 4, 40 (10/Sonjo 26; Oct.–Nov. 1593); Clark and Clark, 75, 87–88, 103, and 105; Hong Soon-min, "Transformation of the Choson Dynasty Palaces and the Kyonghui Palace," *Seoul Journal of Korean Studies* 10 (1997): 128.

2. *Sonjo sillok*, vol. 10, 51 (27/10/Sonjo 26; Nov. 19, 1593); *Sonjo sujong sillok*, vol. 4, 41 (11/Sonjo 26; Nov.–Dec. 1593). Ming envoy Si Xian, then in Seoul, recommended Yu Song-nyong for the post of prime minister and suggested that he be given overall control of state and military affairs. This was not just a reflection of the favorable impression Si had of Yu, but also of growing irritation over what was regarded in Beijing as King Sonjo's overreliance on Chinese assistance. Envoy Si in fact brought with him to Seoul a proposal that Sonjo relinquish the throne. Yu and other officials persuaded him to withdraw it. (Information provided to the author by the So-ae Memorial Foundation, Seoul.)

3. Yu Song-nyong, 192.

4. Palais, *Confucian Statecraft*, 87.

5. Samuel Dukhae Kim, 95–102.

6. Palais, *Confucian Statecraft*, 515–516 and 519.

7. Ibid., 88–90.

8. *Sonjo sillok*, vol. 8, 167 (29/5/Sonjo 26; June 27, 1593).
9. Ibid., vol. 9, 48 (15/7/Sonjo 26; Aug. 11, 1593).
10. Dispatch of 8/Wanli 21 (Sept. 1593), Yi Sun-sin, *Imjin changch'o*, 110.
11. *Sonjo sujong sillok*, vol. 4, 37 (8/Sonjo 26; Sept. 1593).
12. Diary entries for 15/5/Kyesa (June 13, 1593) to 28/8/Kyesa (Sept. 22, 1593), Yi Sun-sin, *Nanjung ilgi*, 28–57.
13. Diary entries for 5, 10, and 11/6/Kyesa (July 3, 8, and 9, 1593), ibid., 36–38.
14. Yi Sun-sin's letter to Dan Zongren, quoted in Yi's dispatch of 10/3/Wanli 22 (April 29, 1594), *Imjin changch'o*, 161–162, and in Yi Pun, 219.
15. Diary entries for 3–6/3/Kabo (April 22–25, 1594), Yi Sun-sin, *Nanjung ilgi*, 78–80; dispatch of 10/3/Wanli 22 (April 29, 1594), *Imjin changch'o*, 164–170.
16. Diary entries for 7 and 13/3/Kabo (April 26 and May 2, 1594), *Nanjung ilgi*, 80–81.
17. Dispatch of 20/4/Wanli 22 (June 8, 1594), *Imjin changch'o*, 180–182.
18. Forged letter from Hideyoshi to the Wanli emperor, 21/12/Wanli 21 (Feb. 10, 1594), in Elisonas, "Trinity," 283, and Stramigioli, 108. The complete text of the forged letter is given in Cho Kyong-nam, "Nanjung chapnok," in *Saryoro bonun*, 195–196.
19. *Sonjo sillok*, vol. 12, 124 (24/5/Sonjo 27; July 11, 1594).
20. Yu Song-nyong, 192–193. For an alternate translation see Aston, 39–40.
21. *Sonjo sillok*, vol. 12, 88–90 (11/5/Sonjo 27; June 28, 1594).
22. Yu Song-nyong, 194; *Sonjo sujong sillok*, vol. 4, 42 (11[intercalary]/Sonjo 26; Dec. 1593–Jan. 1594), 67 (5/Sonjo 27; June-July 1594), and 76–77 (8/Sonjo 27; Sept.-Oct. 1594).
23. *Sonjo sujong sillok*, vol. 4, 82 (11/Sonjo 27; Dec. 1594).
24. Ibid., 79 (9/Sonjo 27; Oct. 1594).
25. Ibid., 89–90 (3/Sonjo 28; April 1595).
26. Yujong, "Bunchungseonan-nok," in *Saryoro bonun*, 197–201.
27. Hideyoshi to his troops in Korea, 16/1/Bunroku 3 (Mar. 7, 1594), in Kuno, vol. 1, 332–333.
28. Ibid., 333.
29. In his dispatch to Seoul of 10/3/Wanli 22 (April 29, 1594), Yi Sun-sin reported that a Korean prisoner who had escaped from the Japanese camp at Ungchon stated that "Many of [the Japanese] have died of illnesses or fled home while undergoing hardships in building houses and city walls" (*Imjin changch'o*, 163).
30. In his war diary Yi Sun-sin referred frequently from late 1594 onward to "surrendered Japanese" being allocated to serve in his ranks. Yi questioned some of these men as to why they had surrendered and was told that "their commanding officer was a cruel fellow, driving them hard, so they ran away" (8/1/Pyongsin (Feb. 5, 1596), *Nanjung ilgi*, 193). Yi appointed one of them, a man named Minami Uyemon, as unit leader, and employed them mainly as laborers. By Yi's own account these surrendered

Japanese were treated reasonably well while serving in the Korean navy. They were given a feast and gifts of wine and were allowed a good deal of freedom in governing and disciplining themselves.

On a sultry evening in August, 1596, Yi Sun-sin wrote of the Japanese under his command putting on "a drama with the make-up of actors and actresses . . . to entertain themselves with their native farce for enjoyment of the day"—a rudimentary form of kabuki, one assumes, performed in the midst of a Korean naval camp (diary entry for 13/7/Pyongsin [Aug. 6, 1596], ibid., 233). It must have been a surreal sight, akin, perhaps, to turncoat Nazi soldiers singing German beer songs on a British army base during WWII.

31. Kenneth Lee, *Korea and East Asia* (Westport, Conn.: Praeger, 1997), 105.
32. The two letters Father de Cespedes sent home from Korea appear in full in Ralph Cory, "Some Notes on Father Gregorio de Cespedes, Korea's First European Visitor," *Transactions of the Korea Branch of the Royal Asiatic Society* 27 (1937): 38–45.
33. Hideyoshi's 1587 edict appears in David J. Lu, *Japan: A Documentary History* (Armonk, N.Y.: M. E. Sharpe, 1997), 197.
34. Streichen, 192; Luis de Guzman, *Historia de las Missiones* (Alcalca, por la biuda de Ian Gracian, 1601), vol. 12, chap. 37.
35. *Sonjo sujong sillok*, vol. 4, 79 (9/Sonjo 27; Oct. 1594); Yu Song-nyong, 194; Stramigioli, 110.
36. "Three Strategies of Huang Shih-kung," in Sawyer, 300.
37. Diary entry for 17/10/Kabo (Nov. 28, 1594), Yi Sun-sin, *Nanjung ilgi*, 126–127.
38. Diary entry for 3/9/Kabo (Oct. 16, 1594), ibid., 117.
39. Diary entries for 29/9/Kabo and 1 and 3/10/Kabo (Nov. 11, 12, and 14, 1594), ibid., 123–125.
40. Diary entry for 27/2/Ulmi (April 6, 1595), ibid., 142.
41. Yi Pun, 220.
42. *Sonjo sillok*, vol. 14, 75–76 (1/12/Sonjo 27; Jan. 10, 1595); *Sonjo sujong sillok*, vol. 4, 85 (12/Sonjo 27; Jan. 1595).
43. Rutt, *Bamboo Grove*, poem 9.
44. Diary entry for 4/10/Kabo (Nov. 15, 1594), Yi Sun-sin, *Nanjung ilgi*, 124.
45. *Sonjo sujong sillok*, vol. 4, 45 (12/Sonjo 26; Jan. 1594); Yi Si-yang, "Chahae pildam," in *Saryoro bonun*, 207–208; Hong Yang-ho, "Haedongmyong changjon," ibid., 207.
46. *Sonjo sujong sillok*, vol. 4, 100 (2/Sonjo 29; Mar. 1596).
47. "Sodae kinyon," in *Saryoro bonun*, 210.
48. *Sonjo sujong sillok*, vol. 4, 109–111 (8/Sonjo 29; Sept. 1596). The rebel with whom Kim Dong-nyong was accused of being in league was Yi Mong-hak. The antigovernment movement Yi Mong-hak led in Chungchong Province was the most serious uprising to occur during the war.

CHAPTER 21: *Meanwhile, in Manila...*

1. Gomez Perez Dasmarinas to Hideyoshi, June 11, 1592, in Blair and Robertson, vol. 8, 266–267.
2. Hideyoshi to Gomez Perez Dasmarinas, no date, ibid., vol. 9, 123–124.
3. Comment made by Don Luis Perez Dasmarinas before a council of war in Manila on April 22, 1594, ibid., vol. 9, 125.
4. Don Luis Perez Dasmarinas to Hideyoshi, no date (the letter would have been written around April 20 or 21, 1594), ibid., vol. 9, 126–130.

CHAPTER 22: *"You, Hideyoshi, are hereby instructed... to cheerfully obey our imperial commands!"*

1. Yu Song-nyong, 195; *Sonjo sujong sillok*, vol. 4, 94–95 (8/Sonjo 28; Sept. 1595).
2. *Sonjo sujong sillok*, vol. 4, 98 and 102 (1 and 4/Sonjo 29; Feb. and May 1596); Aston, 41–42.
3. Streichen, 199–200.
4. Huang, "Lung-ch'ing," 571.
5. Hulbert, vol. 2, 26.
6. Yu Song-nyong, 196–197; Han Chi-yun, "Haedong yoksa," in *Saryoro bonun*, 211.
7. This follows Berry, 216.
8. Ibid., 228–229.
9. Hideyoshi to O-Ne, 5/3/Bunroku 2 (April 6, 1593), in Boscaro, *Letters*, 51.
10. Elison, "Hideyoshi," 337–338, n. 75.
11. Hideyoshi to O-Ne, no date (1594–95?), in Boscaro, *Letters*, 67.
12. Elison, "Hideyoshi," 244.
13. Hideyoshi to Yodogimi, 25/?/? (Nov. or Dec. 1593); no date (1594?); and 8/12/Keicho 2 (Jan. 15, 1598), in Boscaro, *Letters*, 62, 69, and 72.
14. "Daddy" (Hideyoshi) to Lord Hiroi (Hideyori), 7/?/? (1594–95?), ibid., 70.
15. Hideyoshi to Lord O-Hiroi, 2/1/Keicho 1 (Jan. 31, 1596), ibid., 70.
16. "Daddy" to Lord O-Hiroi, 17/?/? (1595–96?), ibid., 70–71.
17. "Daddy Taiko" to Hideyori, 3/5/Keicho 2 (June 17, 1597), ibid., 71.
18. "Daddy" to Hideyori, 2/12/Keicho 2 (Jan. 9, 1598), ibid., 72.
19. Hideyoshi to Lord Chunagon (a title granted to Hideyori in 1598), 20/?/Keicho 3 (summer 1598), ibid., 73.
20. Luis Frois, "The Second Epistle of the deathe of the Quabacondono," in Berry, 221.
21. Streichen, 179–180.
22. Frois, "Second Epistle," in Berry, 219.
23. Hideyoshi to Kyoto Governor Maeda Gen'i, 11/12/Bunroku 1 (Jan. 14, 1593): "Because the problem of *numazu* is so important for the construction of Fushimi, I would like to have the castle constructed in such a way that it will be hard to attack from the *numazu*" (Boscaro, *Letters*, 48).
24. Dening, 263–264; Sansom, 363.

25. Han Chi-yun, "Haedong yoksa," in *Saryoro bonun*, 211–212; Yu Song-nyong, 197; Elisonas, "Trinity," 284–285.
26. Imperial patent of investiture from the Wanli emperor to Hideyoshi, in Kuno, vol. 1, 335–336.
27. Imperial edict from the Wanli emperor to Hideyoshi, ibid., 336–339.
28. An early 18th-century English translation of Luis Frois' account, in Cooper, *Rodrigues*, 116.
29. Streichen, 202.
30. *Ryocho Heijo Roku: Chosen Seibatsu-ki; Razan Hideyoshi-ju*, in Stramigioli, 114–115; *Sonjo sujong sillok*, vol. 4, 112–113, 9/Sonjo 29 (Oct. 1596); Han Chi-yun, "Haedong yoksa," in *Saryoro bonun*, 211–212.
31. Sin Kyong, "Chaejo bonbangji," in *Saryoro bonun*, 213–215.
32. *Sonjo sujong sillok*, vol. 4, 114–115 (12/Sonjo 29; Jan.–Feb. 1597).
33. Aston, 52–53; *Sonjo sujong sillok*, vol. 4, 120 (2/Sonjo 30; March-April 1597).
34. Imperial edict of the Wanli emperor, in Kuno, vol. 1, 169–170.
35. Edict by Hideyoshi, 20/11/Keicho 1 (Jan. 8, 1597), in Antonio de Morga, *Sucesos de las Islas Filipinas* (Mexico, 1609), in Blair and Robertson, vol. 15, 122–123.
36. George Elison, *Deus Destroyed* (Cambridge, Mass.: Harvard University Press, 1973), 135–139; Boxer, *Christian Century*, 237–239.
37. Father Martin de Aguirre to Antonio de Morga, Lieutenant Governor of Manila, Jan. 28, 1597, in Morga, *Sucesos*, in Blair and Robertson, vol. 15, 124–125.
38. Hideyoshi to Francisco Tello, Governor of the Philippines, in Boxer, *Christian Century*, 169.
39. Morga, *Sucesos*, in Blair and Robertson, vol. 15, 128.

CHAPTER 23: *The Arrest and Imprisonment of Yi Sun-sin*

1. *Sonjo sujong sillok*, vol. 4, 85 (12/Sonjo 27; Jan. 1595); *Sonjo sillok*, vol. 14, 75–76 (1/12/Sonjo 27; Jan. 10, 1595).
2. *Sonjo sillok*, vol. 18, 160–161 (26/6/Sonjo 29; July 21, 1596).
3. Ibid., vol. 19, 153 (21/10/Sonjo 29; Dec. 10, 1596).
4. Ibid., 205–207 (7/11/Sonjo 29; Dec. 25, 1596).
5. Yi Hyong-sok, vol. 2, 992.
6. Yi Won-ik, *Ori-jip*, quoted in Yi Pun, 221–222. Yi Sun-sin writes of Yi Won-ik's visit in his diary, 19–29/8/Ulmi (Sept. 22–Oct. 2, 1595), in *Nanjung Ilgi*, 172–174.
7. Yu Song-nyong, 201; Cho Kyong-nam, "Nanjung chapnok," in *Saryoro bonun*, 230.
8. *Sonjo sujong sillok*, vol. 4, 119–120 (2/Sonjo 30; Mar. 1597).
9. Yu Song-nyong, 202.
10. *Sonjo sillok*, vol. 20, 108–109 (23/1/Sonjo 30; Mar. 10, 1597).
11. Ibid., 127–130 (27/1/Sonjo 30; Mar. 14, 1597).

12. Ibid., 154–155 (4/2/Sonjo 30; Mar. 21, 1597); Yi Jae-bom, 120–121.
13. *Sonjo sillok*, vol. 20, 240 (4/3/Sonjo 30; April 19, 1597); Yi Pun, 222–224.
14. Yi Pun, 224; Yu Song-nyong, 201–202.
15. The most complete English-language accounts of Yi Sun-sin's downfall can be found in Jho Sung-do, 178–186, and Park Yune-hee, 189–195.
16. Diary entry for 1/4/Chongyu (May 16, 1597), Yi Sun-sin, *Nanjung ilgi*, 257.
17. Choi Du-hwan gives a day-by-day breakdown of Yi's journey south in *"Chukgoja hamyon sallira": Chungmugong Yi Sun-sin gyore-rul kuhan myonoh 88 kaji* (Seoul: Hakminsa, 1998), 220.
18. Diary entry for 16/4/Chongyu (May 31, 1597), Yi Sun-sin, *Nanjung ilgi*, 261.

PART 5: THE SECOND INVASION

1. Giles, 158.

CHAPTER 24: *"Water, Thunder, and Great Disaster"*

1. The seventh and concluding item in Hideyoshi's orders launching the second Korean invasion, recorded in the *Chosen ki* (Korean Record) of samurai Okochi Hidemoto, in George Elison, "The Priest Keinen and His Account of the Campaign in Korea, 1597–1598: An Introduction," in *Nihon kyoikushi ronso: Motoyama Yukihiko Kyoju taikan kinen rombunshu* (Kyoto: Shinbunkaku, 1988), 28.
2. Yi Hyong-sok, vol. 2, 1725.
3. Ibid., 1723.
4. Dening, 253.
5. The bibyonsa refused to accept the letter when it arrived in Seoul (*Sonjo sillok*, vol. 20, 154 [1/2/Sonjo 30; Mar. 18, 1597]).
6. Han Chi-yun, "Haedong yoksa," in *Saryoro bonun*, 224; *Sonjo sillok*, vol. 20, 99 (21/1/Sonjo 30; Mar. 8, 1597).
7. Park Yune-hee, 197.
8. According to Murdoch, 355, Hideyoshi's "commanders had asked for supplies from Japan, and had pointed out that if these were not forwarded they would have to wait till the grain ripened in Korea; but Hideyoshi, in consistent adherence to the maxim of subsisting the war in the enemy's country, had ordered his generals to wait till harvest-time."
9. Palais, *Confucian Statecraft*, 85.
10. Samuel Dukhae Kim, 99–102 and 116.
11. *Sonjo sillok*, vol. 20, 154 (1/2/Sonjo 30; Mar. 18, 1597).
12. Yu Song-nyong, 204.
13. Goodrich, vol. 1, 331. Yang Jae-suk quotes the figure of 80,000 Ming troops mobilized for Korea by the end of 1597 (*Imjin waeran*, 312).
14. Huang, "Lung-ch'ing," 576; Kuno, vol. 1, 170–171.
15. Huang, "Lung-ch'ing," 572.
16. *Sonjo sillok*, vol. 21, 163–164 (21/5/Sonjo 30; July 5, 1597).

17. Ibid., 172–173 (25/5/Sonjo 30; July 9, 1597).
18. Yu Song-nyong, 204; *Sonjo sujong sillok*, vol. 4, 125 (5/Sonjo 30; June/July 1597).
19. *Sonjo sujong sillok*, vol. 4, 120 (2/Sonjo 30; Mar./April, 1597); Han Chi-yun, "Haedong yoksa," in *Saryoro bonun*, 226.
20. Yu Song-nyong, 205; Sin Kyong, "Chaejobongbangji," in *Saryoro bonun*, 233.
21. Diary entry for 8/5/Chongyu (June 22, 1597), Yi Sun-sin, *Nanjung ilgi*, 267–268.
22. Ibid., 267.
23. Diary entry for 12/5/Chongyu (June 26, 1597), ibid., 269.
24. Sansom, 360–361.
25. *Sonjo sillok*, vol. 21, 250–253 (14/6/Sonjo 30; July 27, 1597).
26. Yu Song-nyong, 206; *Sonjo sillok*, vol. 21, 237 (11/6/Sonjo 30; July 24, 1597).
27. *Sonjo sillok*, vol. 21, 298–299 (28/6/Sonjo 30; Aug. 10, 1597).
28. Diary entry for 17/6/Chongyu (July 30, 1597), Yi Sun-sin, *Nanjung ilgi*, 280.
29. *Sonjo sujong sillok*, vol. 4, 125 (6/Sonjo 30; July/Aug., 1597).
30. Yu Song-nyong, 206; Cho Kyong-nam, *Nanjung chapnok*, quoted in Yi Jae-bom, 154.
31. Park Yune-hee, 198.
32. In the court discussions preceding Won's reappointment to naval commander in March of 1597, King Sonjo observed that "Won Kyun is brave, but he doesn't think much. It we reappoint him to Kyongsang naval command, who will control him and prevent him from charging at the Japanese precipitously?" (*Sonjo sillok*, vol. 20, 129 [27/1/Sonjo 30; Mar. 14, 1597]).
33. Sadler, "Naval Campaign," 202.
34. This account of the Battle of Chilchonnyang is based on accounts in *Sonjo sillok*, vol. 22, 26–27 (22/7/Sonjo 30; Sept. 3, 1597); *Sonjo sujong sillok*, vol. 4, 126 (7/Sonjo 30; Aug./Sept., 1597); Yu Song-nyong, 205–207; Park Yune-hee, 198–200; Jho Sung-do, 190–191; Aston, 55–56.
35. Yu Song-nyong, 207.
36. Cho Kyong-nam, "Nanjung chapnok," in *Saryoro bonun*, 237.
37. Hideyoshi to Kato Yoshiaki, Todo Takatoro, and others, 13/9/Keicho 2 (Oct. 23, 1597), in Cho Chung-hwa, *Dashi ssunun imjin waeran-sa* (Seoul: Hakmin-sa, 1996), 133–137.
38. Sadler, "Naval Campaign," 202.
39. *Sonjo sillok*, vol. 22, 27–31 and 33 (22/7/Sonjo 30; Sept. 3, 1597); *Sonjo sujong sillok*, vol. 4, 126 (7/Sonjo 30; Aug./Sept., 1597).
40. Diary entries for 16 and 21/7/Chongyu (Aug. 28 and Sept. 2, 1597), Yi Sun-sin, *Nanjung ilgi*, 290–291 and 293.
41. Diary entry for 18/7/Chongyu (Aug. 30, 1597), ibid., 292. A map of Yi's journey listing dates, distances, and every stop along the way appears in Choi Du-hwan, *Chukgoja*, 235.

42. Diary entries for 2–3/8/Chongyu (Sept. 12~13, 1597), Yi Sun-sin, *Nan-jung ilgi*, 295–296.

CHAPTER 25: *The Japanese Advance Inland*
1. The seventh and concluding item in Hideyoshi's orders to his com-manders, recorded in the *Chosen ki* (Korean Record) of samurai Okochi Hidemoto, in Elison, "Keinen," 28.
2. Hideyoshi's instructions to Inspector General Ota Kazuyoshi, ibid., 28.
3. Elisonas, "Trinity," 290–291.
4. Yi Hyong-sok, vol. 2, 1728.
5. Griffis, *Corea*, 130.
6. This account of the Battle of Namwon is based on Yu Song-nyong, 212–215 (Yu's account is based on eyewitness testimony from Kim Hyo-ui, one of the few survivors of the battle.); Sin Kyong, "Chaejobonbangji," in *Saryoro bonun*, 238–241; *Sonjo sujong sillok*, vol. 4, 127–128 (9/Sonjo 30; Oct. 1597); Yang Jae-suk, *Imjin waeran*, 321–325; Aston, 56–57; Hulbert, vol. 2, 32–33.
7. Okochi Hidemoto, *Chosen ki*, in Turnbull, *Samurai Invasion*, 194.
8. Keinen, *Chosen nichinichi ki*, in Yang jae-suk, *Imjin waeran*, 324–325.
9. Turnbull, *Samuari Invasion*, 196.
10. Okochi Hidemoto, *Chosen ki*, in Cho Chung-hwa, *Paro chapun*, 111. According to a Japanese soldier captured on November 3, about one hundred Japanese were killed in the Battle of Namwon (*Sonjo sillok*, vol. 22, 198 [2/10/Sonjo 30; Nov. 10, 1597]).
11. According to information from a Japanese officer captured by the Koreans some weeks later, Kato set out from Sosaengpo intent on beating Konishi to Namwon, but failed to do so because of the circuitous route he took (*Sonjo sillok*, vol. 22, 207 [3/10/Sonjo 30; Nov. 11, 1597]).
12. Yu Song-nyong, 209–210.
13. Hideyoshi to Nabeshima Naoshige, Kato Kiyomasa, Kuroda Nagamasa, and others, 22/9/Keicho 2 (Nov. 1, 1597): "I have noted with satisfaction that the head of the governor of Kimhae was cut off by Kuroda Nagamasa, and that 353 Choson soldiers inside the fortress were killed, along with several thousand civilians in the valley below" (Cho Chung-hwa, *Dashi ssunun*, 108–109). The Japanese evidently mistook someone else's head for that of Kimhae governor Baek Sa-rim, for Baek is known to have fled Hwangsoksansong before the battle.
14. Yu Song-nyong, 209–211; *Sonjo sujong sillok*, vol. 4, 126–127 (8/Sonjo 30; Sept.–Oct. 1597); Yi Hyong-sok, vol. 2, 1002–1003.
15. Ukita's proclamation is reproduced in Cho Chung-hwa, *Paro chapun*, 145.
16. These and other "nose receipts" are reproduced, together with Korean translations, in Cho Chung-hwa, *Dashi ssunun*, 116–125.
17. *Sonjo sillok*, vol. 22, 93–96 (18/8/Sonjo 30; Sept. 28, 1597).
18. Ibid., 104 (24/8/Sonjo 30; Oct. 4, 1597).

19. Yu Song-nyong, 215; *Sonjo sujong sillok*, vol. 4, 128 (9/Sonjo 30; Oct.–Nov. 1597); Sin Kyong, "Chaejobonbangji," in *Saryoro bonun*, 241.
20. Han Chi-yun, *Haedong yoksa*, in *Saryoro bonun*, 227.
21. *Sonjo sujong sillok*, vol. 4, 128 (9/Sonjo 30; Oct.–Nov. 1597).
22. Yi Hyong-sok, vol. 2, 1021–1022. Other sources, including Elisonas, "Trinity," 287, name Kato Kiyomasa's contingent as being the Japanese force involved in the Battle of Chiksan.
23. *Sonjo sillok*, vol. 22, 131 and 133 (8–9/9/Sonjo 30; Oct. 18–19, 1597); *Sonjo sujong sillok*, vol. 4, 128 (9/Sonjo 30; Oct.-Nov. 1597); Cho Kyong-nam, "Nanjung chapnok," in *Saryoro bonun*, 242–243; Turnbull, *Samurai Invasion*, 199–200.

CHAPTER 26: *"Seek death and you will live; seek life and you will die"*

1. Diary entries for 4–13/8/Chongyu (Sept. 14–23, 1597), Yi Sun-sin, *Nanjung ilgi*, 296–301.
2. Diary entries for 13, 17, 25/8/Chongyu (Sept. 23 and 27 and Oct. 5, 1597), ibid., 301, 302, and 304–305.
3. "T'ai Kung's Six Secret Teachings," in Sawyer, 65–66.
4. Diary entry for 12/8/Chongyu (Sept. 22, 1597), Yi Sun-sin, *Nanjung ilgi*, 300.
5. Diary entries for 19/8/Chongyu and 2/9/Chongyu (Sept. 29 and Oct. 12, 1597), ibid., 303 and 307.
6. Yi Sun-sin does not clearly state in his war diary the size of his fleet on the eve of the Battle of Myongnyang. The most authoritative source on this is Yi's report to Commander in Chief Ma Gui, which was subsequently relayed to Seoul: "I joined with Kim Ok-chu and others and collected thirteen warships and thirty-two *chotam-son* [smaller scouting boats] and blocked the sea route in Haenam [southwestern Korea]" *Sonjo sillok*, vol. 23, 27 [10/11/Sonjo 30; Dec. 18, 1597]).
7. Yi Pun, 226.
8. Diary entry for 28/8/Chongyu (Oct. 8, 1597), Yi Sun-sin, *Nanjung ilgi*, 305–306.
9. Diary entry for 7 and 10/9/Chongyu (Oct. 17 and 20, 1597), ibid., 307 and 310.
10. Diary entry for 7/9/Chongyu (Oct. 17, 1597), ibid., 307–308.
11. Park Yune-hee, 211.
12. Diary entry for 15/9/Chongyu (Oct. 25, 1597), Yi Sun-sin, *Nanjung ilgi*, 311.
13. "Wu Tzu," in Sawyer, 215.
14. Joseph Needham and Robin Yates, *Science and Civilization in China,* vol. 5, part 4, *Military Technology: Missiles and Sieges* (Cambridge: Cambridge University Press, 1994), 42–43. The authors make the interesting point that "Whereas in the West expectation of death could lead to a loss of drive, in East Asia the same situation often led to just the opposite, a feeling of fury."
15. "Wu Tzu," in Sawyer, 220.
16. Yi Pun, 228.

17. Japanese accounts agree that Kurushima Michifusa was killed this day in the Battle of Myongnyang, but assert that the body cut up by Yi Sun-sin was not his, but rather that of a *ronin* (masterless samurai) named Hata Shinji (Park Yune-hee, 213).

18. Diary entry of 16/9/Chongyu (Oct. 26, 1597), Yi Sun-sin, *Nanjung ilgi*, 312–315; Yi Pun, 227–29; *Sonjo sillok*, vol. 23, 27 (10/11/Sonjo 30; Dec. 18, 1597); *Sonjo sujong sillok*, vol. 4, 128 (9/Sonjo 30; Oct.–Nov. 1597); Park Yune-hee, 211–213; Jho Sung-do, 196–201.

19. Cho Chung-hwa states that no historical evidence exists to support this story of the chain, but that many people nevertheless still firmly believe it (*Paro chapun*, 150–151).

20. Kim Tae-chun, "Yi Sun-sin's Fame in Japan," *Journal of Social Sciences and Humanities* 47 (June 1978): 94.

21. Ibid., 95; Park Yune-hee, 18.

22. Diary entry for 14/10/Chongyu (Nov. 22, 1597), Yi Sun-sin, *Nanjung ilgi*, 322.

23. Yi Pun, 231.

24. "Wei Liao-tzu," in Sawyer, 258. (Wei Liao-tzu, "The Book of Master Wei Liao," was written in the latter half of the fourth century B.C.)

CHAPTER 27: *Starvation and Death in a "Buddha-less World"*

1. Report of an interrogation of a soldier from Mori's contingent, captured on November 3, in *Sonjo sillok*, vol. 22, 198 (2/10/Sonjo 30; Nov. 10, 1597); report of an interrogation of a Japanese officer serving under Kato Kiyomasa, in *Sonjo sillok*, vol. 22, 207–208 (3/10/Sonjo 30; Nov. 11, 1597). According to the latter report, Kato and Konishi had initially intended to take Seoul, but Hideyoshi forbade it. He ordered them instead to march through the southern part of Korea in the ninth month, killing everyone along the way, then return south to their coastal fortresses in the tenth month.

2. These "nose receipts" are reproduced in Cho Chung-hwa, *Dashi ssunun*, 116–119 and 125–131.

3. Elison, "Keinen," 33.

4. Elisonas, "Trinity," 293.

5. In the city of Fukuoka today there is a subway station called Tojinmachi, "Chinaman Town," a reference to a prison camp located here during the latter part of the war. Few if any Chinese prisoners were ever kept here. The apparent misnomer stems from the fact that the Japanese tended to lump Koreans together with Chinese as *tojin*, "Chinamen."

6. Etsuko Hae-jin Kang, 108.

7. Jon Carter Covell and Alan Covell, *Korean Impact on Japanese Culture: Japan's Hidden History* (Elizabeth, N.J.: Hollym, 1984), 106–109.

8. Peter Lee, *The Record of the Black Dragon Year* (Seoul: Institute of Korean Culture, Korea University, 2000), 38–40. No In's account of his experiences is titled *Kumgye ilgi* (Diary of Kumgye). "Kumgye" was

No's pen name.

9. Ibid., 41–42. Chong Hui-duk wrote of his captivity in *Wolbong haesang nok* (Record of Wolbong's Sea Voyage). "Wolbong" was Chong's pen name.

10. See, for example, Kim Ha-tai, "The Transmission of Neo-Confucianism to Japan by Kang Hang, a Prisoner of War," *Transactions of the Korea Branch of the Royal Asiatic Society* 37 (1961): 83–103.

11. Lee, *Black Dragon Year*, 40–41 and 53–54; Etsuko Hae-jin Kang, 111–125.

12. Francesco Carletti, *My Voyage around the World*, trans. Herbert Weinstock (New York: Pantheon, 1964), 115. Weinstock's translation, which refers to the Korean simply as Antonio, is based on a manuscript copy of Carletti's account that Italian scholars now believe is "closer to the lost original than the 1701 [published] edition or the later versions derived from it" (xiv). The 1701 and 1878 editions refer to the Korean as Antonio Corea (Francesco Carletti, *Ragionamenti di Francesco Carletti* [Firenze: Nella Stamperia di Giuseppe Manni, 1701], Second Account, 40; Francesco Carletti, *Viaggi di Francesco Carletti da lui raccontati in dodici ragionamenti* [Firenze: G. Barbera, 1878], 198).

13. "I 'Korea chipsongchon' hu-e Antonio-si moguk pangmun," *Pusan maeil shinmun*, Nov. 30, 1992.

14. Cho Chung-hwa, *Dashi ssunun*, 197. A second piece of evidence sometimes cited of Korean Imjin War captives in Europe is a charcoal drawing by the Flemish artist Peter Paul Rubens (1577–1640) depicting a young man clad in distinctive Korean garb from the mid-Choson dynasty. It currently hangs in the J. Paul Getty Museum in Malibu, California, above the title "Korean Man." It has been suggested that the man in the drawing may even be Antonio Corea himself, who could have conceivably crossed paths with Rubens during the artist's eight-year stay in Italy from 1600 to 1608. This is unlikely, as Rubens is believed to have done the drawing in Antwerp in 1617. A more plausible explanation is that the man in the drawing is not Korean at all, but rather a Jesuit missionary, or perhaps one of Rubens's assistants, modeling the costume of a foreign land in which the Society of Jesus had hopes of proselytizing. This interpretation is supported by the following facts. First, the outfit worn by the man in the drawing appears to be a *chollik*, a long coat worn by yangban noblemen during the Choson dynasty—definitely not a garment for the lower classes who comprised the vast majority of Imjin War captives. (In any case the garment would have been worn out by 1617.) Second, the Jesuits are known to have taken examples back to Europe of the native garb of those countries where they worked or hoped to work. In 1617 Rubens made a drawing of the priest Nicolas Trigault clad in one such costume, a Chinese robe and what appears to be a Korean hat ("Portrait of Nicolas Trigault S.J. in Chinese Costume," Metropolitan Museum of Art, New York). The artist drew his "Korean Man" at roughly the same time, possibly using an outfit provided by Trigault, as a study for an Asian figure in his later

painting "The Miracles of St. Francis Xavier" (Kunsthistorisches Museum, Vienna).

15. Also known as Asano Nagayoshi.

16. Keinen, *Chosen nichinichi ki*, in Turnbull, *Samurai Invasion*, 205.

17. Ibid., 206–207; Keinen, "Chosen nichinichi ki," in *Saryoro bonun*, 254; Griffis, *Corea*, 137. Keinen notes that the abandonment of Japanese peasants was a violation of Hideyoshi's order that no laborers should be left behind in Korea.

18. Yang Jae-suk, *Imjin waeran*, 351; Griffis, *Corea*, 137.

19. Elisonas, "Trinity," 292.

20. According to Cho Chung-hwa, *Dashi ssunun*, 121–122, this name change was made by the government-sponsored scholar Hayashi Rasan (1583–1657) in the early years of the Tokugawa era.

21. Berry, 233.

22. Hideyoshi to Chunagon-sama (Hideyori), 20/(4–8)/Keicho 3 (sometime between May and Sept., 1598), in Boscaro, *Letters*, 73.

23. *Sonjo sillok*, vol. 22, 261 (21/10/Sonjo 30; Nov. 29, 1597).

24. Ibid., vol. 23, 52 (4/12/Sonjo 30; Jan. 10, 1598).

25. Yi Hyong-sok, vol. 2, 1043.

26. *Sonjo sujong sillok*, vol. 4, 130 (11/Sonjo 30; Dec. 1597).

27. Elison, "Keinen," 35.

28. *Matsui monogatari* and *Kiyomasa Korai no jin oboegaki*, in Turnbull, *Samurai Invasion*, 213.

29. Elison, "Keinen," 35–36.

30. *Sonjo sillok*, vol. 23, 116–117 (3/1/Sonjo 31; Feb. 8, 1598).

31. Okochi Hidemoto, "Chosen ki," in *Saryoro bonun*, 260–261.

32. Yu Song-nyong, 223.

33. *Sonjo sillok*, vol. 23, 135–136 (14/1/Sonjo 31; Feb. 19, 1598).

34. This account of the Battle of Tosan is derived from *Sonjo sillok*, vol. 23, 100–138 passim (28/12/Sonjo 30 to 16/1/Sonjo 31; Feb. 3–21, 1598); *Sonjo sujong sillok*, vol. 4, 130–131 (12/Sonjo 30; Jan. 1598); Yu Song-nyong, 222–224; Yang Jae-suk, *Imjin waeran*, 350–353; Yi Hyong-sok, vol. 2, 1045–1046; Griffis, *Corea*, 137–144; Hulbert, vol. 2, 35–37; Goodrich, vol. 1, 170.

35. Ledyard, "Confucianism," 93, n. 29.

36. Asano Yukinaga (also called Yoshinaga) to Asano Nagamasa, 11/1/Keicho 3 (Feb. 16, 1598), in Brown, 241.

37. Elison, "Keinen," 26–27.

38. Ibid., 38.

39. Griffis, *Corea*, 143.

CHAPTER 28: *"Even Osaka Castle is only a dream"*

1. *Sonjo sujong sillok*, vol. 4, 133 (2/Sonjo 31; Mar. 1598); Goodrich, vol. 1, 170.

2. Ledyard, "Confucianism," 86–87.

3. Letter from Ukita Hideie and twelve other daimyo to Hideyoshi's representatives Ishida Mitsunari, Natsuka Masaie, Mashita Uemon, and Maeda Gen'i, 26/1/Keicho 3 (Mar. 3, 1598), in Elisonas, "Trinity," 287, footnote 75.

4. Yi Hyong-sok, vol. 2, 1726 (Yi also lists a secondary thousand-man unit at Pusan under Terazawa Masanori); Turnbull, *Samurai Invasion*, 217; Berry, 233; Murdoch, 357.

5. Yi Pun, 230; *Sonjo sillok*, vol. 22, 254 (20/10/Sonjo 30; Nov. 28, 1597); Diary entry for 16/11/Chongyu (Dec. 24, 1597), Yi Sun-sin, *Nanjung ilgi*, 330.

6. *Sonjo sillok*, vol. 23, 279–280 (18/3/Sonjo 31; April 23, 1598).

7. Ibid., vol. 24, 5–6 (3/4/Sonjo 31; May 7, 1598).

8. Yi Sun-sin's report to Seoul, ibid., vol. 23, 279–280 (18/3/Sonjo 31; April 23, 1598).

9. Yu Song-nyong, 217–218.

10. Yi gives little information in his war diary of what shipbuilding activity was going on under his command, but it is clear that work was taking place, for in his entry on 10/12/Chongyu (Jan. 16, 1598) he mentions that "I went to the shipbuilding yard," and on 2/1/Musul (Feb. 7, 1598) that "At dawn a new warship was completed" (Yi Sun-sin, *Nanjung ilgi*, 333 and 337).

11. *Sonjo sillok*, vol. 23, 235 (22/2/Sonjo 31; Mar. 28, 1598).

12. Ibid., 305 (29/3/Sonjo 31; May 4, 1598); *Sonjo sujong sillok*, vol. 4, 133 (3/Sonjo 31; April-May, 1598).

13. Goodrich, vol. 1, 169–170.

14. Huang, "Lung-ch'ing," 573.

15. Goodrich, vol. 1, 167–169.

16. *Sonjo sillok*, vol. 24, 7–9 (5–6/4/Sonjo 31; May 9–10, 1598); *Sonjo sujong sillok*, vol. 4, 136 (6/Sonjo 31; July, 1598).

17. Yi Pun, 232; Yang Jae-suk, *Imjin waeran*, 357.

18. *Sonjo sillok*, vol. 23, 303–304 (27 and 29/3/Sonjo 31; May 2 and 4, 1598).

19. Hideyoshi to Gomoji, 17/6/Keicho 3 (July 20, 1598), in Boscaro, *Letters*, 76.

20. Berry, 234.

21. Oath of loyalty dated 15/7/Keicho 3 (Aug. 16, 1598), ibid., 234–235.

22. *Sonjo sujong sillok*, vol. 4, 136 (6/Sonjo 31; July 1598).

23. Ledyard, "Confucianism," 87–90; Huang, "Lung-ch'ing," 573; Hulbert, vol. 2, 39.

24. Goodrich, vol. 2, 964–965.

25. *Sonjo sillok*, vol. 24, 209–210 (28/6/Sonjo 31; July 30, 1598).

26. Ibid., 222–223 (3/7/Sonjo 31; Aug. 4, 1598).

27. Ibid., 210 (28/6/Sonjo 31; July 30, 1598).

28. Yu Song-nyong, 218.

29. Yi Pun, 232–233; *Sonjo sillok*, vol. 24, 314 (13/8/Sonjo 31; Sept. 13, 1598).

30. Yi Pun, 233–234; *Sonjo sillok*, vol. 25, 103 (5/10/Sonjo 31; Nov. 3, 1598);

Jho Sung-do, 208–210; Park Yune-hee, 228–230.

31. Hideyoshi to Ieyasu, Chikuzen, Terumoto, Kagekatsu, and Hideie, 5/8/Keicho 3 (Sept. 5, 1598), in Boscaro, *Letters*, 77.

32. Ibid., 77–78. An alternate translation in Berry, 235, reads, "My life / Came like dew / Disappears like dew. / All of Naniwa / Is dream after dream."

CHAPTER 29: *The Last Act*

1. *Sonjo sillok*, vol. 24, 248–249 (11/7/Sonjo 31; Aug. 12, 1598); *Sonjo sujong sillok*, vol. 4, 140 (7/Sonjo 31; Aug. 1598).

2. Goodrich, vol. 2, 1451–1452; *Sonjo sujong sillok*, vol. 4, 158 (10/Sonjo 31; Nov. 1598); *Sonjo sillok*, vol. 25, 182 (25/11/Sonjo 31; Dec. 22, 1598).

3. The Five Regents (*go-tairo*) were Tokugawa Ieyasu, Maeda Toshiie, Mori Terumoto, Uesugi Kagekatsu, and Ukita Hideie. The Five Commissioners (*go-bugyo*) ranked just below them were Ishida Mitsunari, Natsuka Masaie, Mashita Nagamori, Asano Nagamasa, and Maeda Gen'i.

4. Letter from the Five Commissioners to Nabeshima Naoshige, 25/8/Keicho 3 (Sept. 25, 1598); letter from Mashita Nagamori (one of the Five Commissioners) to Shimazu Yoshihiro, same date, in Elisonas, "Trinity," 288.

5. Ibid., 288–289.

6. *Sonjo sillok*, vol. 25, 120–121 (12/10/Sonjo 31; Nov. 10, 1598); Yang Jae-suk, *Dashi ssunun*, vol. 2, 242–243; Goodrich, vol. 1, 171, and vol. 2, 966; Yang Jae-suk, *Imjin waeran*, 356.

7. Yang Jae-suk, *Imjin waeran*, 357.

8. Goodrich, vol. 1, 170.

9. *Sonjo sillok*, vol. 24, 305 (9/8/Sonjo 31; Sept. 9, 1598).

10. Ibid., 329 (24/8/Sonjo 31; Sept. 24, 1598).

11. Ledyard, "Confucianism," 87 and 91–93.

12. Ibid., 94.

13. *Sonjo sillok*, vol. 25, 32 (21/9/Sonjo 31; Oct. 20, 1598).

14. Ibid., 33–35 (21/9/Sonjo 31; Oct. 20, 1598).

15. Ibid., 39 (22/9/Sonjo 31; Oct. 21, 1598).

16. Ibid., 60 (25/9/Sonjo 31; Oct. 24, 1598); Ledyard, "Confucianism," 100–101.

17. Ledyard, "Confucianism," 103–104.

18. Ibid., 112–114.

19. *Sonjo sillok*, vol. 25, 73 (27/9/Sonjo 31; Oct. 26, 1598) and 89 (30/9/Sonjo 31; Oct. 29, 1598); Yi Hyong-sok, vol. 2, 1086.

20. *Sonjo sillok*, vol. 25, 95 (2/10/Sonjo 31; Oct. 31, 1598) and 103 (4/10/Sonjo 31; Nov. 2, 1598).

21. Ibid., 120 (12/10/Sonjo 31; Nov. 10, 1598).

22. *Seikan roku*, in Turnbull, *Samurai Invasion*, 220.

23. *Sonjo sillok*, vol. 25, 125 (16/10/Sonjo 31; Nov. 14, 1598); Murdoch, 358; Hulbert, vol. 2, 46; Turnbull, *Samurai Sourcebook*, 249–250.

24. This figure of 38,700 is referred to in a letter of appreciation sent from the

Five Regents (Tokugawa Ieyasu and others) to Shimazu Yoshihiro, 9/1/Keicho 4 (Feb. 4, 1599), in Cho Chung-hwa, *Paro chapun*, 164.

25. *Sonjo sillok*, vol. 25, 114 (8/10/Sonjo 31; Nov. 6, 1598) and 116 (10/10/Sonjo 31; Nov. 8, 1598).

26. Ibid., 125 (16/10/Sonjo 31; Nov. 14, 1598).

27. Sin Heum, "Sangchonjip," in *Saryoro bonun*, 265.

28. *Sonjo sillok*, vol. 25, 13 (7/9/Sonjo 31; Oct. 6, 1598).

29. Ibid., 69 (26/9/Sonjo 31; Oct. 25, 1598); Hulbert, vol. 2, 47.

30. Diary entries for 20–22/9/Musul (Oct. 19–21, 1598), Yi Sun-sin, *Nanjung ilgi*, 338–339.

31. Diary entry for 3/10/Musul (Nov. 1, 1598), ibid., 340–341; Report from Commander in Chief Kwon Yul in *Sonjo sillok*, vol. 25, 116 (10/10/Sonjo 31; Nov. 8, 1598); report from Yi Sun-sin in *Sonjo sillok*, vol. 25, 122 (13/10/Sonjo 31; Nov. 11, 1598); Sin Heum, "Sangchonjip," in *Saryoro bonun*, 268; Jho Sung-do, 215–216; Goodrich, vol. 1, 171; Turnbull, *Samurai Invasion*, 224–225.

32. Report from Yi Dok-hyong in *Sonjo sillok*, vol. 25, 119–120 (12/10/Sonjo 31; Nov. 10, 1598); Sim Heum, "Sangchonjip," in *Saryoro bonun*, 268–269.

33. *Sonjo sillok*, vol. 25, 120 (12/10/Sonjo 31; Nov. 10, 1598); diary entry for 6/10/Musul (Nov. 4, 1598), Yi Sun-sin, *Nanjung ilgi*, 341.

34. *Sonjo sillok*, vol. 25, 96 (2/10/Sonjo 31; Oct. 31, 1598) and 128 (20/10/Sonjo 31; Nov. 18, 1598); Goodrich, vol. 1, 171.

35. The Wanli emperor's imperial edict, in Kuno, vol. 1, 172–173.

36. According to Aston, 61, news of Hideyoshi's death on September 18, 1598, reached his commanders in Korea a week after the Battle of Sachon, in other words in early November.

37. Sansom, 389.

38. Goodrich, vol. 1, 171.

39. Ibid., vol. 2, 968.

40. Diary entries for 8–13/11/Musul (Dec. 5–10, 1598), Yi Sun-sin, *Nanjung ilgi*, 342.

41. Jho Sung-do, 218–219.

42. Yi Pun, 235–236; Park Yune-hee, 238–240; Jho Sung-do, 219–221.

43. Ahn Bang-jun, "Noryang kisa," in *Saryoro bonun*, 272–273.

44. The figure of three hundred Japanese ships is given by Korean government minister Yi Dok-hyong, who was at Sunchon with General Liu Ting at the time and thus near the scene of the battle, in the report he sent to Seoul just days after the event (*Sonjo sillok*, vol. 25, 187–188 [27/11/Sonjo 31; Dec. 24, 1598]). Yi Hyong-sok, vol. 2, 1117–1118, gives the higher figure of five hundred ships, manned by twelve thousand troops.

45. Yang Jae-suk, *Dashi ssunun*, vol. 2, 256 and 259–260; Goodrich, vol. 1, 173–174.

46. Dividing the number of men in Shimazu's fleet (twelve thousand) by the

number of his ships (three hundred) gives an average of forty men per ship, suggesting that many of the Japanese vessels in the Noryang battle must have been quite small.

47. Sin Kyong, "Chaejobonbangji," in *Saryoro bonun*, 273–274; Goodrich, vol. 1, 172.
48. Jho Sung-do, 224.
49. Cho Chung-hwa, *Paro chapun*, 174.
50. Ahn Bang-jun, "Noryang kisa," in *Saryoro bonun*, 275–276.
51. Yi Pun, 237–238; Yu Song-nyong, 225; *Sonjo sujong sillok*, vol. 4, 159–160 (11/Sonjo 31; Dec. 1598); *Sonjo sillok*, vol. 25, 187–188 (27/11/Sonjo 31; Dec. 24, 1598); Park Yune-hee, 243–246; Jho Sung-do, 224–228; Yang Jae-suk, *Dashi ssunun*, vol. 2, 259–262.
52. *Sonjo sillok*, vol. 25, 187–188 (27/11/Sonjo 31; Dec. 24, 1598).
53. Ibid., 182 (24/11/Sonjo 31; Dec. 21, 1598).
54. Ibid., 178–179 (21/11/Sonjo 31; Dec. 18, 1598); Turnbull, *Samurai Invasion*, 227.
55. *Sonjo sillok*, vol. 25, 184 (25/11/Sonjo 31; Dec. 22, 1598) and 189 (28/11/Sonjo 31; Dec. 25, 1598).
56. Elisonas, "Trinity," 290.
57. Goodrich, vol. 1, 172.
58. Yi Pun, 238–241; Yu Song-nyong, 226; Jho Sung-do, 230–232.
59. *Sonjo sillok*, vol. 24, 57 (22/4/Sonjo 31; May 26, 1598).
60. Ibid., vol. 25, 112–114 (7–8/10/Sonjo 31; Nov. 5–6, 1598).
61. Bacon, "Chingbirok," 9.
62. Hulbert, vol. 2, 45.
63. Ledyard, "Confucianism," 114.
64. Goodrich, vol. 1, 172, and vol. 2, 967–968; Huang, "Lung-ch'ing," 583.
65. Arthur Hummel, ed., *Eminent Chinese of the Ch'ing Period* (Washington D.C.: U.S. Government Printing Office, 1943), 885–886; Ledyard, "Confucianism," 112–113.
66. Bito Masahide, "Thought and Religion, 1550–1700," in *The Cambridge History of Japan*, vol. 4, *Early Modern Japan*, ed. John Whitney Hall (Cambridge: Cambridge University Press, 1991), 393–395.

PART 6: AFTERMATH
1. Kim Jong-gil, *Slow Chrysanthemums: Classical Korean Poems in Chinese* (London: Anvil Press Poetry, 1987), 79.

CHAPTER 30: *What Came Next*
1. Movable type from Korea would remain in widespread use in Japan only until about 1625. Thereafter, as the Japanese publishing industry became increasingly commercial, publishers returned to the cheaper method of printing from carved wood blocks. According to modern research, eighty

percent of the books published between 1593 and 1625 were printed with movable type. This figure fell to twenty percent between 1625 and 1650, and thereafter to nearly zero (Donald Shively, "Popular Culture," in *The Cambridge History of Japan,* vol. 4, *Early Modern Japan,* ed. John Whitney Hall [Cambridge: Cambridge University Press, 1991], 726–727).

2. Etsuko Hae-jin Kang, 107–108; Tennant, 176.

3. Kuno, vol. 1, 173–174.

4. Tony Michell, "Fact and Hypothesis in Yi Dynasty Economic History: The Demographic Dimension," *Korean Studies Forum* 6 (Winter-Spring 1979/1980): 77–79; Palais, *Confucian Statecraft,* 366. By way of comparison, some one million Korean civilians died as a result of the Korean War of 1950–53.

5. Palais, *Confucian Statecraft,* 104. "In the mid-fifteenth century households held parcels of land measured in *kyol,* not really a measure of land area but a constant measure of crop yield produced by an area that varied from 2.25 to 9.0 acres, depending on the fertility of the land" (ibid., 105–106).

6. Reconstruction of Kyongbok Palace would not begin until 1865. Until then the kings of Choson Korea resided at the smaller subsidiary palace of Changdok (Clark and Clark, 75).

7. James Palais, "A Search for Korean Uniqueness," *Harvard Journal of Asiatic Studies* 55, no. 2 (Dec. 1995): 415.

8. Peter Lee, *Sourcebook,* vol. 1, 179.

9. Edwin Reischauer and John Fairbank, *East Asia: The Great Tradition* (Boston: Houghton Mifflin, 1960), 332–333. (1 *tael* = 1.3 ounces, or 36.855 grams.)

10. Jacques Gernet, *A History of Chinese Civilization,* trans. J. R. Foster (Cambridge: Cambridge University Press, 1982), 431.

11. Gale, *History,* 275–276.

12. "Fengshi Riben jilue (Brief Account of an Ambassadorial Mission to Japan)," in *Voices from the Ming-Qing Cataclysm,* trans. and ed. Lynn Struve (New Haven, Conn.: Yale University Press, 1993), 114–121.

13. Charles Hucker, *China's Imperial Past* (Stanford, Calif.: Stanford University Press, 1975), 295.

14. Yi Pyong-gyu, *Ilsongnok,* quoted in James Palais, *Politics and Policy in Tra-ditional Korea* (Cambridge, Mass.: Harvard University Press, 1975), 229–230.

15. John Whitney Hall, "The Bakuhan System," in *The Cambridge History of Japan,* vol. 4, *Early Modern Japan,* ed. John Whitney Hall (Cambridge: Cambridge University Press, 1991), 144.

16. Toby, 25–35.

17. Elisonas, "Trinity," 294–299.

18. Etsuko Hae-jin Kang, 115, 124, 119, and 121.

19. Tsuruta Kei, "The Establishment and Characteristics of the 'Tsushima Gate,'" *Acta Asiatica* 67 (1994): 39.

20. S. N. Eisenstadt, *Japanese Civilization: A Comparative View* (Chicago: University of Chicago Press, 1996), 185.
21. Turnbull, *Samurai Warfare*, 78–79.
22. Report by Commander John Rodgers, USN, to the Secretary of the Navy, in Noel Perrin, *Giving Up the Gun: Japan's Reversion to the Sword, 1543–1879* (Boston: David R. Godine, 1979), 3–4.
23. Tsunoda and others, *Sources,* vol. 2, 592.
24. Marius Jansen, *The Making of Modern Japan* (Cambridge, Mass.: Belknap, 2000), 362.
25. Horace Allen to William Rockhill, Jan. 4, 1904, quoted in Peter Duus, *The Abacus and the Sword: The Japanese Penetration of Korea, 1895–1910* (Berkeley: University of California Press, 1995), 189.
26. George Kennan writing in *Outlook* magazine, quoted in Marius Jansen, *Japan and China: From War to Peace, 1894–1972* (Chicago: Rand McNally, 1975), 124.
27. Son Key-young, "Seoul Criticizes Tokyo for Authorizing 'Distorted' Textbooks," *The Korea Times*, April 3, 2001; "Seoul's Fury Stems from History," *The Korea Times*, July 9, 2001.
28. Kanako Takahara, "Lawmakers' Views of Past Still Plague Relations," *The Japan Times*, Feb. 14, 2002.
29. Pak Chu-yong, "Imran gui-mudom kot tora-onda . . . Pak Sam-jung sunim chujinjung," *Choson Ilbo*, Jan. 16, 1996; "Gui-mudom silche hwan-kukumjikim bongyokhwa," *Choson Ilbo*, Jan. 16, 1996.
30. Nicholas D. Kristof, "Japan, Korea and 1597: A Year That Lives in Infamy," *The New York Times*, Sept. 14, 1997, section 1.

BIBLIOGRAPHY

Asao Naohiro. "The Sixteenth Century Unification." In *The Cambridge History of Japan.* Vol. 4, *Early Modern Japan,* edited by John Whitney Hall. Cambridge: Cambridge University Press, 1991, 40–95.

Asakawa Kanichi, trans. and ed. *The Documents of the Iriki.* Tokyo: Japan Society for the Promotion of Science, 1955.

Aston, W. G. "Hideyoshi's Invasion of Korea." *Transactions of the Asiatic Society of Japan* 6 (1878): 227–245; 9 (1881): 87–93 and 213–222; 11 (1883): 117–125.

———. *Hideyoshi's Invation [sic] of Korea.* Tokyo: Ryubun-kwan, 1907. (A compilation of Aston's articles in the *Transactions of the Asiatic Society of Japan.*)

Austin, Audrey. "Admiral Yi Sun-sin: National Hero." *Korean Culture* 9, no. 2 (Summer 1988): 4–15.

Bacon, Wilbur D. "Fortresses of Kyonggi-do." *Transactions of the Korea Branch of the Royal Asiatic Society* 37 (1961): 1–63.

———. "Record of Reprimands and Admonitions (Chingbirok)." *Transactions of the Korea Branch of the Royal Asiatic Society* 47 (1972): 9–24.

Bak Hae-ill. "A Short Note on the Iron-clad Turtle-boats of Admiral Yi Sun-sin." *Korea Journal* 17, no. 1 (Jan. 1977): 34–39.

Ballard, George A. *The Influence of the Sea on the Political History of Japan.* New York: E. P. Dutton, 1921.

Berry, Mary Elizabeth. *Hideyoshi.* Cambridge, Mass.: Harvard University Press, 1982.

Bito, Masahide. "Thought and Religion, 1550–1700." In *The Cambridge History of Japan.* Vol. 4, *Early Modern Japan,* edited by John Whitney Hall. Cambridge: Cambridge University Press, 1991, 373–424.

Blair, Emma H., and James A. Robertson, trans. and ed. *The Philippine Islands, 1493–1898.* 55 volumes. Cleveland: A. H. Clark, 1903–1909.

Bonar, H. A. C. "On Maritime Enterprise in Japan." *Transactions of the Asiatic Society of Japan* 15 (1887): 103–125.

Boots, John L. "Korean Weapons and Armor." *Transactions of the Korea Branch of the Royal Asiatic Society* 23, part 2 (Dec. 1934): 1–37.

Boscaro, Adriana. "An Introduction to the Private Correspondence of Toyotomi Hideyoshi." *Monumenta Nipponica* 27, no. 4 (Winter 1972): 415–421.

———, trans. and ed. *101 Letters of Hideyoshi. The Private Correspondence of Toyotomi Hideyoshi.* Tokyo: Sophia University, 1975.

Boxer, C. R. *The Christian Century in Japan, 1549–1650.* Berkeley: University of California Press, 1951.

———. "Notes of Early European Military Influence in Japan (1543–1853)." *Transactions of the Asiatic Society of Japan*, second series, 8 (Dec. 1931): 67–93.

Brinkley, Captain F. *Japan: Its History and Literature.* Vol, 2. Boston & Tokyo: J. B. Millet Company, 1901–02.

Brown, Delmer M. "The Impact of Firearms on Japanese Warfare, 1543–98." *The Far Eastern Quarterly* 7, no. 3 (May 1948): 236–253.

Carletti, Francesco. *My Voyage Around the World.* Translated by Herbert Weinstock. New York: Pantheon Books, 1964.

———. *Ragionamenti di Francesco Carletti.* Firenze: Nella Stamperia di Giuseppe Manni, 1701.

———. *Viaggi di Francesco Carletti da lui raccontati in dodici ragionamenti.* Firenze: G. Barbera, 1878.

Chaliand, Gerard. *The Art of War in World History.* Berkeley: University of California Press, 1994.

Chan, Albert. *The Glory and Fall of the Ming Dynasty.* Norman: University of Oklahoma Press, 1982.

Chinju National Museum. *Bakmulgwan iyagi: imjin waeran* (Museum Story: The Imjin War). Chinju: Chinju National Museum, 2000.

Cho Chung-hwa. *Dashi ssunun imjin waeran-sa* (A Reevaluation of the History of the Imjin War). Seoul: Hakmin-sa, 1996.

———. *Paro chapun imjin waeran-sa* (Corrected History of the Imjin War). Seoul: Salmgwakkum, 1998.

Cho Song-do. *Chungmugong Yi Sun-sin* (Minister of Loyal Valor Yi Sun-sin). Seoul: Yongyong munhwa-sa, 2001.

Choi Byonghyon, trans. *The Book of Corrections: Reflections on the National Crisis during the Japanese Invasion of Korea, 1592–1598.* Berkeley: Institute of East Asian Studies, University of California, 2002.

Choi Du-hwan. *"Chukgoja hamyon sallira": Chungmugong Yi Sun-sin gyore-rul kuhan myono 88 kaji* ("If You Seek Death You Will Live": Chungmugong Yi Sun-sin's 88 Nation-Saving Quotations). Seoul: Hakmin-sa, 1998.

———, ed. *Chungmugong Yi Sun-sin chonjip* (The Complete Works of Chungmugong Yi Sun-sin). Seoul: Wooseok Publishing Co., 1999.

Choi Hyo-sik. *Imjin waeran-gi Yongnam uibyong yongu* (The Righteous Armies of Southeast Korea in the Imjin War). 5 volumes. Seoul: Kukhakjaryowon, 2003.

Choi Sok-nam. *Yi Sun-sin.* 2 volumes. Seoul: Kyo-haksa, 1992.

Chong Dong-ju. *Non-gae.* Seoul: Hangilsa, 1998.

Chu Hsi and Lu Tsu-Ch'ien. *Reflections on Things at Hand.* Translated by Wing-tsit Chan. New York: Columbia University Press, 1967.

Clark, Alan, and Donald Clark. *Seoul: Past and Present.* Seoul: Hollym, 1969.

Clark, Donald N. "The Ming Connection: Notes on Korea's Experience in the Chinese Tributary System." *Transactions of the Korea Branch of the Royal Asiatic Society* 58 (1983): 77–89.

———. "Sino-Korean Tributary Relations under the Ming." In *The Cambridge History of China.* Vol. 4, *The Ming Dynasty, 1368–1644, Part 2,* edited by Denis Twitchett and Frederick W. Mote. Cambridge: Cambridge University Press, 1998, 272–300.

Confucius. *The Analects (Lun yu).* Translated by D. C. Lau. London: Penguin Books, 1979.

Cooper, Michael. *Rodrigues the Interpreter: An Early Jesuit in Japan and China.* New York: Weatherhill, 1974.

———. *They Came to Japan: An Anthology of European Reports on Japan, 1543–1640.* Berkeley: University of California Press, 1965.

Cory, Ralph. "Some Notes on Father Gregorio de Cespedes, Korea's First European Visitor." *Transactions of the Korea Branch of the Royal Asiatic Society* 27 (1937): 1–55.

Covell, Jon Carter, and Alan Covell. *Korean Impact on Japanese Culture: Japan's Hidden History.* Elizabeth, N.J.: Hollym, 1984.

Cumings, Bruce. *Korea's Place in the Sun: A Modern History.* New York: W. W. Norton, 1997.

Dening, Walter. *The Life of Toyotomi Hideyoshi.* 3rd ed. Kobe, Japan: J. L. Thompson, 1930. (First edition published in 1888; second edition in 1904.)

Dreyer, Edward L. *Early Ming China: A Political History, 1355–1435.* Stanford, Calif.: Stanford University Press, 1982.

Duus, Peter. *The Abacus and the Sword: The Japanese Penetration of Korea, 1895–1910.* Berkeley: University of California Press, 1995.

Dyer, Gwynne. *War.* Toronto: Stoddart, 1985.

Eikenberry, Karl W. "The Imjin War." *Military Review* 68, no. 2 (Feb. 1988): 74–82.

Eisenstadt, S. N. *Japanese Civilization: A Comparative View.* Chicago: University of Chicago Press, 1996.

Elison, George. *Deus Destroyed: The Image of Christianity in Early Modern Japan.* Cambridge, Mass.: Harvard University Press, 1988.

———. "Hideyoshi, the Bountiful Minister." In *Warlords, Artists, and Commoners: Japan in the Sixteenth Century,* edited by George Elison and Bardwell Smith. Honolulu: University of Hawai'i Press, 1981, 223–244.

———. "The Priest Keinen and His Account of the Campaign in Korea, 1597–1598: An Introduction." In *Nihon kyoikushi ronso: Motoyama Yukihiko Kyoju taikan kinen rombunshu,* edited by Motoyama Yukihiko Kyoju taikan kinen rombunshu henshu iinkai. Kyoto: Shinbunkaku, 1988, 25–41.

———, and Bardwell L. Smith, eds. *Warlords, Artists, and Commoners: Japan in the Sixteenth Century.* Honolulu: The University of Hawai'i Press, 1981.

Elisonas, Jurgis [Elison, George]. "The Inseparable Trinity: Japan's Relations with China and Korea." In *The Cambridge History of Japan.* Vol. 4, *Early Modern Japan,* edited by John Whitney Hall. Cambridge: Cambridge University Press, 1991, 235–300.

Elliott, J. H. *Spain and Its World, 1500–1700.* New Haven, Conn.; and London: Yale University Press, 1989.

Fairbank, John King. *China: A New History.* Cambridge, Mass.: Harvard University Press, 1992.

Gale, J. S. "Han-yang (Seoul)." *Transactions of the Korea Branch of the Royal Asiatic Society* 2 (1902): 1–43.

————. "The Influence of China upon Korea." *Transactions of the Korea Branch of the Royal Asiatic Society* 1 (1900): 1–24.

————. *James Scarth Gale and His History of the Korean People.* Edited by Richard Rutt. Seoul: Royal Asiatic Society, Korea Branch, 1972. (Gale's *History* was first published serially between 1924 and 1927.)

Garbutt, Matt. "Japanese Armour from the Inside." *Transactions and Proceedings of the Japan Society, London* 11 (1912–13): 134–185.

Gernet, Jacques. *A History of Chinese Civilization.* Translated by J. R. Foster. Cambridge: Cambridge University Press, 1982.

Giles, Lionel, trans. *Sun Tzu on the Art of War.* Taipei: Ch'eng Wen Publishing Co., 1971. (Originally written in the fourth century B.C.; this translation first published in 1910.)

Goodrich, L. Carrington, ed. *Dictionary of Ming Biography.* 2 volumes. New York and London: Columbia University Press, 1976.

Griffis, William Elliot. *Corea: The Hermit Nation.* New York: Charles Scribner's Sons, 1894.

————. *The Mikado's Empire.* New York: Harper & Brothers, 1883.

Ha Tae-hung. *Behind the Scenes of the Royal Palaces in Korea (Yi Dynasty).* Seoul: Yonsei University Press, 1983.

Hall, Bert S. *Weapons and Warfare in Renaissance Europe.* Baltimore: Johns Hopkins University Press, 1997.

Hall, John Whitney, ed. *The Cambridge History of Japan.* Vol. 4, *Early Modern Japan.* Cambridge: Cambridge University Press, 1991.

————, Keiji Nagahara, and Kozo Yamamura, eds. *Japan before Tokugawa: Political Consolidation and Economic Growth, 1500 to 1650.* Princeton, N.J.: Princeton University Press, 1981.

Han Myong-ki. *Imjin waeran gwa hanchung kwangye* (Study on the Relations between Korea and China from Japanese Invasion of Korea in 1592 to Manchu Invasion of Korea in 1636). Seoul: Yuksa Bibyongsa, 1999.

Hanguk chongsin munhwa yonguwon. *Hanguk inmul daesajon* (Who's Who in Korea). Seoul: Chungang ilbo, 1999.

Hatada Takashi. *A History of Korea.* Translated and edited by Warren W. Smith Jr. and Benjamin H. Hazard. Santa Barbara, Calif.: Clio Press, 1969.

Hazard, Benjamin H. "The Creation of the Korean Navy during the Koryo Period." *Transactions of the Korea Branch of the Royal Asiatic Society* 48 (1973): 10–28.

Hazelton, Keith. *A Synchronic Chinese-Western Daily Calendar 1341–1661 A.D.* Minneapolis: University of Minnesota, 1985.

Henthorn, William E. *A History of Korea.* New York: Free Press, 1971.

―――. "Some Notes of Koryo Military Units." *Transactions of the Korea Branch of the Royal Asiatic Society* 35 (1959): 67–75.

Hsü, Immanuel C. Y. *The Rise of Modern China.* New York: Oxford University Press, 2000.

Huang, Ray. *1587, A Year of No Significance: The Ming Dynasty in Decline.* New Haven, Conn.; and London: Yale University Press, 1981.

―――. "The Lung-ch'ing and Wan-li Reigns, 1567–1620." In *The Cambridge History of China.* Vol. 7, *The Ming Dynasty, 1368–1644, Part 1,* edited by Denis Twitchett and John Fairbank. Cambridge: Cambridge University Press, 1988, 511–584.

Hucker, Charles O. *The Censorial System of Ming China.* Stanford, Calif.: Stanford University Press, 1966.

―――. *China's Imperial Past: An Introduction to Chinese History and Culture.* Stanford, Calif.: Stanford University Press, 1975.

―――. "Hu Tsung-hsien's Campaign against Hsu Hai, 1556." In *Chinese Ways in Warfare,* edited by Frank A. Kierman Jr. and John Fairbank. Cambridge, Mass.: Harvard University Press, 1974, 274–282.

Hulbert, Homer B. *Hulbert's History of Korea.* 2 volumes. New York: Hillary House Publishers, 1962. (First published in 1905.)

Hummel, Arthur W., ed. *Eminent Chinese of the Ch'ing Period.* Washington, D.C.: United States Government Printing Office, 1943. (Reprinted in Taipei in 1972.)

Hur Nam-lin. "The International Context of Toyotomi Hideyoshi's Invasion of Korea in 1592: A Clash between Chinese Culturalism and Japanese Militarism." *Korea Observer* 28, no. 4 (Winter 1997): 687–707.

Hwang Won-gu. "Korean World View through Relations with China." *Korea Journal* 13, no. 10 (Oct. 1973): 10–17.

Ilyon. *Samguk yusa.* Translated by Ha Tae-hung and Grafton Mintz. Seoul: Yonsei University Press, 1972.

Iwao Seiichi, ed., and Burton Watson, trans. *Biographical Dictionary of Japanese History*. Tokyo: Kodansha International Ltd., 1978.

Jansen, Marius B. *Japan and China: From War to Peace, 1894–1972*. Chicago: Rand McNally, 1975.

―――. *The Making of Modern Japan*. Cambridge, Mass.: Belknap Press of Harvard University Press, 2000.

―――. "Tosa in the Sixteenth Century: The 100 Article Code of Chosokabe Motochika." In *Studies in the Institutional History of Early Modern Japan*, edited by John W. Hall and Marius B. Jansen. Princeton, N. J.: Princeton University Press, 1968, 89–114.

Jho Sung-do. *Yi Sun-Shin: A National Hero of Korea*. Ch'ungmu-kong Society, Naval Academy, Korea, 1970.

Jones, George Heber. "The Japanese Invasion." *The Korean Repository* 1 (1892): 10–16, 46–50, 116–121, 147–152, 182–188, 217–222, and 308–311.

Kang, Etsuko Hae-jin. *Diplomacy and Ideology in Japanese-Korean Relations: From the Fifteenth to the Eighteenth Century*. New York: St. Martin's Press, 1997.

Kang Song-mun. "Haengju daechop-eso-ui Kwon Yul-ui chonnyak-gwa chonsul" (Kwon Yul's Strategy and Tactics in the Battle of Haengju). In *Imjin waeran-gwa Kwon Yul changgun* (The Imjin War and General Kwon Yul), edited by Chang Chong-dok and Pak Jae-gwang. Seoul: Chonjaeng kinyomgwan, 1999, 103–154.

Katano Tsugio. *Yi Sun-sin gwa Hideyoshi* (Yi Sun-sin and Hideyoshi). Translated by Yun Bong-sok. Seoul: Wooseok, 1997.

Kerr, George. *Okinawa: The History of an Island People*. Tokyo: Charles E. Tuttle, 1958.

Kim Ha-tai. "The Transmission of Neo-Confucianism to Japan by Kang Hang, a Prisoner of War." *Transactions of the Korea Branch of the Royal Asiatic Society* 37 (1961): 83–103.

Kim Jong-gil. *Slow Chrysanthemums: Classical Korean Poems in Chinese*. London: Anvil Press Poetry, 1987.

Kim, Samuel Dukhae. "The Korean Monk-Soldiers in the Imjin Wars: An Analysis of Buddhist Resistance to the Hideyoshi Invasion, 1592–1598." Ph.D. dissertation, Columbia University, 1978.

Kim Tae-chun. "Yi Sun-sin's Fame in Japan." *Journal of Social Sciences and Humanities* 47 (June 1978): 93–107.

Kim Zae-geun. "An Outline of Korean Shipbuilding History." *Korea Journal* 29, no. 10 (Oct. 1989): 4–17.

Kiralfy, Alexander. "Japanese Naval Strategy." In *Makers of Modern Military Thought from Machiavelli to Hitler*, edited by Edward Mead Earle. Princeton, N.J.: Princeton University Press, 1943, 457–484.

Kuno, Yoshi S. *Japanese Expansion on the Asiatic Continent.* Vol. 1. Berkeley: University of California Press, 1937.

Langlois, John D., Jr. "The Hung-wu Reign, 1368–1398." In *The Cambridge History of China.* Vol. 7, *The Ming Dynasty, 1368–1644, Part 1*, edited by Denis Twitchett and John Fairbank. Cambridge: Cambridge University Press, 1988, 107–181.

Ledyard, Gari. "Confucianism and War: The Korean Security Crisis of 1598." *The Journal of Korean Studies* 6 (1988–89): 81–119.

———. "Yin and Yang in the China-Manchuria-Korea Triangle." In *China Among Equals: The Middle Kingdom and Its Neighbors, 10th–14th Centuries*, edited by Morris Rossabi. Berkeley: University of California Press, 1983, 313–353.

Lee, Hyoun-jong. "Military Aid of the Ryukyus and Other Southern Asian Nations to Korea during the Hideyoshi Invasion." *Journal of Social Sciences and Humanities* 46 (Dec. 1977): 13–24.

Lee, Kenneth B. *Korea and East Asia.* Westport, Conn.: Praeger, 1997.

Lee, Ki-baik. *A New History of Korea.* Translated by Edward W. Wagner with Edward J. Shultz. Seoul: Ilchokak Publishers, 1984.

Lee, Peter H. *Pine River and Lone Peak: An Anthology of Three Choson Dynasty Poets.* Honolulu: University of Hawai'i Press, 1991.

———. *The Record of the Black Dragon Year.* Seoul: Institute of Korean Culture, Korea University, 2000.

———, ed. *Sourcebook of Korean Civilization.* 2 volumes. New York: Columbia University Press, 1993.

Levathes, Louise. *When China Ruled the Seas: The Treasure Fleet of the Dragon Throne, 1405–1433.* New York: Simon & Schuster, 1994.

Lo, Jung-pang. "The Emergence of China as a Sea Power during the Late Sung and Early Yuan Periods." *Far Eastern Quarterly* 14, no. 4 (August 1955): 489–503.

Longford, Joseph H. *The Story of Korea.* London: T. Fisher Unwin, 1911.

Lu, David J. *Japan: A Documentary History.* Armonk, N.Y.: M. E. Sharpe, 1997.

Maske, Andrew. "The Continental Origins of Takatori Ware: The Introduction of Korean Potters and Technology to Japan through the Invasions of 1592–1598." *Transactions of the Asiatic Society of Japan*, fourth series, 9 (1994): 43–61.

Mayers, W. F. "On the Introduction and Use of Gunpowder and Firearms among the Chinese." *Journal of the North-China Branch of the Royal Asiatic Society*, new series, 6 (1869–70): 73–104.

McCune, G. M. "The Yi Dynasty Annals of Korea." *Transactions of the Korea Branch of the Royal Asiatic Society* 29 (1939): 57–82.

Meriwether, C. "A Sketch of the Life of Date Masamune and an Account of His Embassy to Rome." *Transactions of the Asiatic Society of Japan* 21 (1893): 1–105.

Michell, Tony. "Fact and Hypothesis in Yi Dynasty Economic History: The Demographic Dimension." *Korean Studies Forum* 6 (Winter–Spring 1979/1980): 65–93.

Miyamoto, Musashi. *The Book of Five Rings*. Translated by Thomas Cleary. Boston and London: Shambhala, 1993. (Miyamoto wrote *Go-rin no sho*, "The Book of Five Rings," in 1645.)

Moran, J. F. *The Japanese and the Jesuits: Alessandro Valignano in Sixteenth-Century Japan*. London: Routledge, 1993.

Morga, Antonio de. *Sucesos de las Islas Filipinas*. In *The Philippine Islands, 1493–1898*, edited by Emma H. Blair and James A. Robertson. Cleveland, Ohio: A. H. Clark, 1903–1909, volumes 15 and 16. (First published in Mexico in 1609.)

Murdoch, James. *A History of Japan during the Century of Early Foreign Intercourse (1542–1651)*. Kobe: Printed at the office of the "Chronicle," 1903.

Nam Chon-u. *Yi Sun-sin*. Seoul: Yoksa bipyongsa, 1994.

Needham, Joseph. *Science and Civilization in China*. Vol. 5, part 7, *Military Technology: The Gunpowder Epic*. Cambridge: Cambridge University Press, 1986.

———, and Yates, Robin D. S. *Science and Civilization in China*. Vol. 5, part 6, *Military Technology: Missiles and Sieges*. Cambridge: Cambridge University Press, 1994.

Nelson, M. Frederick. *Korea and the Old Orders in Eastern Asia*. New York: Russell & Russell, 1967. (First published in 1945.)

Newark, Peter. *Firefight! The History of Personal Firepower.* Devon: David & Charles Publishers, 1989.

O'Neill, P. G. *Japanese Names: A Comprehensive Index by Characters and Readings.* New York and Tokyo: John Weatherhill, 1972.

Palais, James B. *Confucian Statecraft and Korean Institutions: Yu Hyongwon and the Late Choson Dynasty.* Seattle: University of Washington Press, 1996.

————. *Politics and Policy in Traditional Korea.* Cambridge, Mass.: Harvard University Press, 1975.

————. "A Search for Korean Uniqueness." *Harvard Journal of Asiatic Studies* 55, no. 2 (Dec. 1995): 409–425.

Park, Choong-seok. "Concept of International Order in the History of Korea." *Korea Journal* 18, no. 7 (July 1978): 15–21.

Park, Yune-hee. *Admiral Yi Sun-shin and His Turtleboat Armada.* Seoul: Hanjin Publishing Company, 1978.

Perrin, Noel. *Giving Up the Gun: Japan's Reversion to the Sword, 1543–1879.* Boston: David R. Godine, 1979.

Pollack, David. *The Fracture of Meaning: Japan's Synthesis of China from the Eighth through the Eighteenth Centuries.* Princeton, N.J.: Princeton University Press, 1986.

Porter, Robert P. *Japan: The Rise of a Modern Power.* Oxford: Oxford University Press, 1919.

Reischauer, Edwin O., and John K. Fairbank. *East Asia: The Great Tradition.* Boston: Houghton Mifflin, 1960.

Robinson, Kenneth R. "From Raiders to Traders: Border Security and Border Control in Early Choson, 1392–1450." *Korean Studies* 16 (1992): 94–115.

————. "The Tsushima Governor and Regulation of Japanese Access to Choson in the Fifteenth and Sixteenth Centuries." *Korean Studies* 20 (1996): 23–50.

Rodrigues, Joao. *This Island Japon.* Translated and edited by Michael Cooper. Tokyo: Kodansha, 1973.

Rutt, Richard. *The Bamboo Grove: An Introduction to Sijo.* Berkeley: University of California Press, 1971.

————, trans. "Ch'ao-hsien fu by Tung Yüeh." *Transactions of the Korea Branch of the Royal Asiatic Society* 48 (1973): 29–73.

Sadler, A. L. *The Maker of Modern Japan: The Life of Tokugawa Ieyasu.* London: George Allen & Unwin, 1937.

————. "The Naval Campaign in the Korean War of Hideyoshi (1592–1598)." *Transactions of the Asiatic Society of Japan,* second series, 14 (1937): 177–208.

Sansom, George. *A History of Japan, 1334–1615.* Stanford, Calif.: Stanford University Press, 1961.

Saryoro bonun imjin waeran. Ssawo chuggi-nun swiwo-do kil-ul bilryo jugi-nun oryop-da (The Imjin War Through Historical Documents. "Dying in Battle is Easy, But Letting You Pass is Difficult"). Compiled by Chinju National Museum. Seoul: Hyean, 1999.

Sawyer, Ralph D., trans. *The Seven Military Classics of Ancient China.* Boulder, Colo.: Westview Press, 1993.

Sen Soshitsu XV. "Chado: The Way of Tea." *Japan Quarterly* 30, no. 4 (Oct.–Dec. 1983): 388–394.

Shively, Donald. "Popular Culture." In *The Cambridge History of Japan.* Vol. 4, *Early Modern Japan,* ed. John Whitney Hall. Cambridge: Cambridge University Press, 1991, 706–770.

Skubinna, Stephen A. "Hermit Kingdom's Naval Genius: Korean Admiral Yi's Turtle Ships Were the First Ironclads." *Military History* 4, no. 10 (April 1988): 58–59.

So, Kwan-wai. *Japanese Piracy in Ming China during the 16th Century.* East Lansing: Michigan State University Press, 1975.

Sonjo sillok (Authentic Records of King Sonjo). 42 volumes. Seoul: Minjok munhwa chujin hee, 1987–89. (Originally compiled by Ki Cha-hon and others, 1609–1616.)

Sonjo sujong sillok (Authentic Records of King Sonjo, Revised). 4 volumes. Seoul: Minjok munhwa chujin hee, 1989. (Originally compiled by Yi Sik and others, 1643–1657.)

Stramigioli, Giuliana. "Hideyoshi's Expansionist Policy on the Asiatic Mainland." *Transactions of the Asiatic Society of Japan,* third series, 3 (Dec. 1954): 74–116.

Streichen, M. *The Christian Daimyo: A Century of Religious and Political History in Japan (1549–1650).* Tokyo: Rikkyo Gakuin Press, c. 1900.

Struve, Lynn A., trans. and ed. *Voices from the Ming-Qing Cataclysm: China in Tigers' Jaws.* New Haven, Conn.: Yale University Press, 1993.

Susser, Bernard. "The Toyotomi Regime and the Daimyo." In *The Bakufu in Japanese History*, edited by Jeffrey P. Mass and William B. Hauser. Stanford, Calif.: Stanford University Press, 1985, 129–152.

Tennant, Roger. *A History of Korea*. London: Kegan Paul, 1996.

Toby, Ronald. *State and Diplomacy in Early Modern Japan*. Princeton, N.J.: Princeton University Press, 1984.

Tsuchihashi, Paul Y. *Japanese Chronological Tables from 601 to 1872*. Tokyo: Sophia University, 1952.

Tsunoda, Ryusaku, trans., and L. Carrington Goodrich, ed. *Japan in the Chinese Dynastic Histories: Later Han through Ming Dynasties*. South Pasadena, Calif.: P. D. and Ione Perkins, 1951.

————, William Theodore de Bary, and Donald Keene, eds. *Sources of Japanese Tradition*. 2 volumes. New York: Columbia University Press, 1964.

Tsuruta, Kei. "The Establishment and Characteristics of the 'Tsushima Gate.' " *Acta Asiatica* 67 (1994): 30–48.

Turnbull, Stephen. *The Samurai: A Military History*. London: Osprey Publishing, 1977.

————. *Samurai Invasion*. London: Cassell & Co., 2002.

————. *The Samurai Sourcebook*. London: Cassell & Co., 1998.

————. *Samurai Warfare*. London: Arms and Armour Press, 1996.

————. *Samurai Warlords: The Book of the Daimyo*. London: Blandford Press, 1989.

Underwood, Horace H. *Korean Boats and Ships*. Seoul: Yonsei University Press, 1979. (Reprint of *Transactions of the Korea Branch of the Royal Asiatic Society* 23 [1934].)

Varley, H. Paul, and George Elison. "The Culture of Tea: From Its Origins to Sen no Rikyu." In *Warlords, Artists, and Commoners*, edited by George Elison and Bardwell Smith. Honolulu: University of Hawai'i Press, 1981, 187–222.

Wade, Geoff. "The *Ming shi-lu* as a Source for Thai History—Fourteenth to Seventeenth Centuries." *Journal of Southeast Asian Studies* 31, no. 2 (Sept. 2000): 249–294.

Wagner, Edward Willett. *The Literati Purges: Political Conflict in Early Yi Korea*. Cambridge, Mass.: Harvard University Press, 1974.

Wakita, Osamu. "The Social and Economic Consequences of Unification." In *The Cambridge History of Japan.* Vol. 4, *Early Modern Japan,* edited by John Whitney Hall. Cambridge: Cambridge University Press, 1991, 96–127.

Waldron, Arthur. "Chinese Strategy from the Fourteenth to the Seventeenth Centuries." In *The Making of Strategy: Rulers, States, and War,* edited by Williamson Murray and others. Cambridge: Cambridge University Press, 1994, 85–114.

Wang Yi-t'ung. *Official Relations between China and Japan, 1368–1549.* Cambridge, Mass.: Harvard University Press, 1953.

Waterhouse, D. B. "Fire-Arms in Japanese History: With Notes on a Japanese Wall Gun." *The British Museum Quarterly* 27 (1963–64): 94–97.

Watson, Burton, trans. *Records of the Grand Historian of China: Translated from the* Shih chi of Ssu-ma ch'ien. 2 volumes. New York: Columbia University Press, 1961.

Werner, E. T. C. *Chinese Weapons.* Shanghai: Royal Asiatic Society, North China Branch, 1932.

Wilson, William Scott. *Ideals of the Samurai: Writings of Japanese Warriors.* Burbank, Calif.: Ohara Publications, 1982.

Wolters, O. W. "Ayudhya and the Rearward Part of the World." *Journal of the Royal Asiatic Society of Great Britain and Ireland* (1968): 166–178.

Yamagata, I. "Japanese-Korean Relations after the Japanese Invasion of Korea in the XVIth Century." *Transactions of the Korea Branch of the Royal Asiatic Society* 4, part 2 (1913): 1–11.

Yang Jae-suk. *Dashi ssunun imjin daechonjaeng* (A Reevaluation of the Imjin War). 2 volumes. Seoul: Koryo won, 1994.

———. *Imjin waeran-un uri-ga igin chonjaeng iottda* (We Won the Imjin War). Seoul: Garam kihwoek, 2001.

Yang Tai-zin. "On the System of Beacons in Korea." *Korea Journal* 11, no. 7 (July 1971): 34–35.

Yi Hyong-sok. *Imjin chollan-sa* (History of the Imjin War). 2 volumes. Seoul: Imjin Chollan-sa kanhaeng hoe, 1967.

Yi Jae-bom. *Won Kyun-ul wihan byonmyong* (In Defense of Won Kyun). Seoul: Hakmin-sa, 1996.

Yi Pun. "Biography of Admiral Yi Sun-sin." In *Imjin changch'o: Admiral Yi Sun-sin's Memorials to Court.* Translated by Ha Tae-hung. Edited by Lee Chong-young. Seoul: Yonsei University Press, 1981, 199–241.

Yi Sun-sin. *Imjin changch'o: Admiral Yi Sun-sin's Memorials to Court.* Translated by Ha Tae-hung. Edited by Lee Chong-young. Seoul: Yonsei University Press, 1981.

―――. *Nanjung ilgi: War Diary of Admiral Yi Sun-sin.* Translated by Ha Tae-hung. Edited by Sohn Pow-key. Seoul: Yonsei University Press, 1977.

Yu Song-nyong. *Chingbirok* (Record of Reprimands and Admonitions). Seoul: Myongmundang, 1987. (Originally written circa 1604–1607.)

INDEX

Made in the USA
Las Vegas, NV
17 May 2023

72189344R00374